Including Students
with Special Needs

Including Students with Special Needs

A PRACTICAL GUIDE FOR CLASSROOM TEACHERS

Third Edition

Marilyn Friend
University of North Carolina–Greensboro

William D. Bursuck
Northern Illinois University

Allyn and Bacon
Boston • London • Toronto • Sydney • Tokyo • Singapore

Vice President and Editor in Chief: Paul A. Smith
Executive Editor, Special Education and Counseling: Virginia Lanigan
Developmental Editor: Alicia Reilly
Editorial Assistant: Erin Liedel
Senior Marketing Manager: Brad Parkins
Editorial-Production Service: Omegatype Typography, Inc.
Composition and Prepress Buyer: Linda Cox
Manufacturing Buyer: Megan Cochran
Cover Administrator: Linda Knowles
Cover Designer: Studio Nine
Interior Designer: Carol Somberg
Photo Researcher: PoYee Oster, Photoquick Research
Illustrations: Omegatype Typography, Inc.
Electronic Composition: Omegatype Typography, Inc.

Between the time Website information is gathered and then published, it is not
unusual for some sites to have closed. Also, the transcription of URLs can result
in unintended typographical errors. The publisher would appreciate notification
where these occur so that they may be corrected in subsequent editions.

Library of Congress Cataloging-in-Publication Data

Friend, Marilyn Penovich
    Including students with special needs : a practical guide for classroom teachers / Marilyn
  Friend, William D. Bursuck. — 3rd ed.
      p.   cm.
    Includes bibliographical references and index.
    ISBN 0-205-33192-0 (alk. paper)
    1. Inclusive education—United States.   2. Mainstreaming in education—United States.
  3. Special education—United States.   4. Handicapped children—Education—United States.
  I. Bursuck, William D.

LC1201.F75   2002
371.9'046—dc21

                           2001022112

Printed in the United States of America
10 9 8 7 6 5 4 3 2 1   RRD-OH   06 05 04 03 02 01

Contents

chapter **1**

The Foundation for Educating Students with Special Needs   *xxviii*

chapter 2

chapter 3

chapter **4**

Planning Instruction by Analyzing Classroom and Student Needs 110

chapter 5

Students with Low-Incidence Disabilities   *152*

chapter **6**

Students with High-Incidence Disabilities   196

chapter **9**

Instructional Adaptations 308

chapter **10**

Strategies for Independent Learning   *354*

chapter **13**

Approaches for Building Social Relationships 466

Features

Case in Practice

Professional Edge

Special Emphasis On . . .

Technology Notes

Preface

With the full implementation of the regulations of IDEA 97, the trend toward educating students with special needs in inclusive settings has continued to accelerate. It is now commonplace for students with learning and behavior problems to spend most or all of their school days in general education classrooms. Further, students who typically attended special classes or schools, including those with autism, those with significant cognitive disabilities, and those with multiple disabilities, now attend school with their peers without disabilities, often in the same classrooms with support from special education staff provided there. And, as any school professional knows, the number of students with special needs that are not disabilities—students who are English learners, those with attentional problems, and those who are otherwise at risk for school failure—continues to grow. All these trends indicate that expectations for general education teachers are growing: They not only have to respond to the increasingly rigorous academic standards being set in states and local districts, they also have to help a broader range of students than ever before meet such standards.

The third edition of *Including Students with Special Needs: A Practical Guide for Classroom Teachers* reflects our continued strong commitment to inclusive practices, a commitment tempered by our knowledge and experience of the realities of day-to-day teaching. We know that inclusive practices are most likely to succeed with strong and sustained administrative support, extensive professional preparation for classroom teachers as well as special education staff, and a significant dollop of professional common sense regarding the necessity of tailoring educational programs to meet students' needs, not to assign them indiscriminately to a single physical location. We have brought to the project our own backgrounds as teachers in the field and as teacher educators, researchers, and staff developers. We also bring our own diversity: Marilyn with expertise in elementary education, especially in urban settings, and in collaboration and co-teaching; Bill with expertise in secondary education, especially in suburban and rural settings, and in instructional strategies, assessment, and grading practices.

The organization of the book and the amount of space devoted to various topics and subtopics reflect our priorities for preparing general education teachers to instruct effectively the students they will encounter. Our priorities are based on our own experiences in teaching undergraduate and graduate educators, our conversations with our colleagues across the country, and our analysis of the professional literature

Including Students with Special Needs

A PRACTICAL GUIDE FOR CLASSROOM TEACHERS

Third Edition

Marilyn Friend
University of North Carolina–Greensboro

William D. Bursuck
Northern Illinois University

Allyn and Bacon
Boston • London • Toronto • Sydney • Tokyo • Singapore

on preservice and inservice teacher preparation on inclusive practices. We also have listened carefully to the many teachers we meet who are facing the challenges of 21st-century classrooms. We hope that the results of all our discussions, our interactions with others, and our individual struggles to "get it right" have resulted in a book that is reader friendly, yet informative, and research based, yet readable. We hope that this text presents information and suggestions that are effective for teaching students with diverse needs and feasible for today's classroom teacher. Above all, we hope this third edition is responsive to the many issues confronting teachers as they attempt to help all their students succeed.

Organization of the Book

The textbook is divided into three main sections. The **first section** provides fundamental background knowledge of the field of special education as well as current information on how students with disabilities are served within inclusive school environments. Chapter 1 presents a brief history of services to students with disabilities, culminating in the description of key federal legislation that provides the legal basis for serving students with disabilities in public schools. Information on the most recent federal special education legislation—the Individuals with Disabilities Education Act 1997 and its regulations—is included in this chapter.

Chapter 2 introduces the people who specialize in working with students with disabilities. Readers learn about their role in working with other professionals and parents to determine student eligibility for special education, in carrying out educational programs, and in monitoring learning. Not surprisingly, inclusive practices are more easily implemented when school professionals, other staff members, and parents and families work as a team. Chapter 3 discusses the principles of collaboration and the school situations in which professionals are most likely to collaborate to meet the needs of students with disabilities. The special partnerships that are formed when teachers work with paraprofessionals and parents are also considered.

The **second section** of the book provides a framework for thinking about instructional accommodations as an introduction for considering the characteristics of students with disabilities and other special needs. Chapter 4 introduces a step-by-step strategy for adapting instruction, called INCLUDE, that helps teachers accommodate students with special needs in a more deliberate way. This chapter also addresses the dimensions along which accommodations can occur. Chapters 5, 6, and 7 address student characteristics and needs. Although the various federal categories of exceptionality are addressed and related vocabulary introduced, the approach taken in the text is noncategorical; the emphasis is on major physical, psychological, learning, and behavior characteristics and the implications of these characteristics for instruction.

In Chapter 5, readers learn about the characteristics and educational needs of students with low-incidence disabilities, that is, moderate, severe, or multiple disabilities; sensory impairments; physical or health disabilities; and autism. Chapter 6 describes the characteristics and needs of students with high-incidence disabilities,

Professional Edge boxes highlight practical teaching ideas and applications of recent research.

that is, learning disabilities, speech or language disabilities, emotional disturbance, and mild cognitive disabilities. Chapter 7 introduces readers to students who are not necessarily eligible for special education but who have special needs and often benefit from strategies similar to the ones that assist students with disabilities. The students addressed in this chapter are those protected by Section 504, including those with attention deficit–hyperactivity disorder; those who are gifted and talented; those whose native language is not English and whose cultures significantly differ from those of most of their classmates; and students who are at risk because of special situations, including poverty, child abuse, and drug abuse.

The material in the **third section** of the text represents the crux of any course on inclusive practices: instructional approaches that emphasize teaching students effectively both in academic and in social and behavior areas, regardless of disability or special need. Chapter 8 explores both formal and informal assessment strategies that help teachers contribute to the decision-making process for students with disabilities. Chapter 9 provides strategies for adapting curriculum materials, teacher instruction, and student practice activities for both basic-skills and content-area instruction. The emphasis is on adaptations that are relatively easy to make and that may also be helpful for students not identified as having disabilities. Chapter 10 focuses on ways to help students with and without special needs become more independent learners. Specific strategies are described, such as encouraging student self-awareness and self-advocacy skills, developing and teaching learning strategies directly in class, and instructing students how to use these strategies on their own.

One of a teacher's major jobs is to evaluate students' educational progress, through traditional testing and grading as well as through performance-based assessments and portfolios. Teachers may need to adapt all these evaluation practices for students with special needs. Chapter 11 provides options for adapting classroom evaluations for diverse learners to ensure that the information gathered is accurate and helpful in guiding instruction. In Chapter 12, readers learn procedures for group behavior management and strategies for responding to individual student behaviors. They also learn to relate behavior interventions to the current requirement for functional behavior assessment and the development of behavior intervention plans. Together, these techniques and procedures provide teachers with a foundation for classroom management that can positively influence the learning of students with and without disabilities. Finally, inclusive practices are most successful when students with special needs are carefully integrated into the classroom, socially as well as academically. Chapter 13 explores several approaches for building positive relations among students with and without special needs, including cooperative learning, peer tutoring, and social skills training.

Features in the Book

Many of the features from the first and second editions have been retained and enhanced in this third edition. These features have been designed to help readers learn more effectively:

- *Vignettes* serve as introductory cases to help readers think about how the content of chapters relates to teachers and students.

Technology Notes features in each chapter highlight innovations in assistive technology and technology for teaching practice.

- *Key terms* throughout the text are highlighted with boldface type and explained with easy-to-understand definitions provided both in context and in a glossary at the back of the book.
- *Chapter summaries* review key information covered in the chapter.
- *Application activities* at the end of each chapter are designed to encourage students to apply the content in the text to real-life classroom situations.
- *Marginal annotations* are designed to stimulate higher-level thinking.
- *Case in Practice* features clarify key course principles by providing brief case studies of course content in action and teaching scripts as models.
- *Professional Edge* features provide many practical teaching ideas.
- *Technology Notes* features illustrate the impact of the current technology explosion on key aspects of special and general education programming.

New Features of the Third Edition

Based on our use of the textbook and feedback from other users, we have added some new features and enhanced coverage of some topics for this edition. We have added the following:

- A Key Terms and Concepts list at the beginning of each chapter provides a preview of information contained in the chapter as well as an organizer and a teaching and learning tool.
- A *Special Emphasis On . . .* feature has been added to each chapter to highlight topics and issues particularly related to students with special needs in secondary schools. These features outline strategies of particular interest to middle school and high school teachers; stress subject areas often ignored in textbooks (for example, the fine arts); or present information on areas of interest to secondary teachers, such as inclusion in high schools.

In addition to these features, we have increased our attention to the contributions that parents and families make to the education of their children. Consistent with our belief that this topic is integral to the entire textbook and not one that should be isolated in a single chapter, many chapters contain sections or features on working with parents. A second area worthy of note in the third edition is technology. Given the explosion of Internet sites for teachers and the wealth of valuable information available worldwide, every chapter includes marginal notes with pertinent URLs, and many chapters contain separate features that summarize some of the best Internet sites we could locate. We continue to be aware of the importance to teachers of basing their practices on valid research, and, toward that end, we have added research information throughout the text, both in the chapter material itself as well as in features such as Professional Edge. Finally, we strengthened our emphasis on the multicultural framework of understanding others' perspectives, of respecting those perspectives, and of working with families in partnership to create instructional success for pupils.

Overall, we have worked to improve this third edition by retaining many worthwhile components, refining others, and providing new material. We have made additions we think are important, have deleted information that could be sacrificed, and have, at the same time, still offered many opportunities for application and practice. We hope you find our efforts successful.

Supplements to Accompany the Third Edition

The third edition of *Including Students with Special Needs* comes with a rich array of print and media-based supplements for instructors and students using the text in their courses.

Special Emphasis features highlight topics often ignored in inclusion textbooks: issues relevant to middle and secondary school students; and teaching non-academic subject areas.

Instructor's Resource Manual

The Instructor's Resource Manual contains, for each chapter in the text, an overview, outline, activities, discussion questions, transparency and handout masters, and test items. The *updated test item file*, which is also available in *computerized format for IBM and Macintosh*, includes multiple-choice items, true-false items, performance-based items (new to this edition), and case-based application items. Answer feedback and guidelines are provided.

NEW! Companion Website with Online Practice Tests

The Companion Website for *Including Students with Special Needs*, Third Edition, [www.ablongman.com/friend3e] features chapter learning objectives, activities, weblinks, cases, and practice tests for students, plus numerous teaching resources for the instructor, including downloadable PowerPoint presentations to enhance classroom lectures.

NEW! PowerPoint Slide Package

The PowerPoint package is easily accessed from the home page of the Companion Website. More than 100 slides, organized by chapter, are ideal for use as lecture presentations and/or handouts for students. Those instructors who already use PowerPoint as a lecture presentation tool will find this new supplement provides a convenient way to incorporate new slides into their existing slide packages. Those instructors who have *not* used PowerPoint (and perhaps have no intention of doing so!) and/or do not have the PowerPoint program on their computers can rest assured these slides can be easily downloaded onto their hard drives and printed out for use as traditional overhead transparencies and handouts.

Professionals in Action Videotape: Teaching Students with Special Needs

This *Professionals in Action* video (© 2000, 120 minutes in length) consists of five 15- to 30-minute modules presenting viewpoints and approaches to teaching students with various disabilities in general education classrooms, separate education settings, and various combinations of the two. Each module explores its topic using actual classroom footage and interviews with general and special education teachers, parents, and students themselves. The four modules are:

1. Working Together: The Individualized Education Program (IEP)
2. Working Together: The Collaborative Process
3. Instruction and Behavior Management
4. Technology for Inclusion
5. Working with Parents and Families

The "Snapshots" Video Series for Special Education

Snapshots: Inclusion Video (© 1995, 22 minutes in length) profiles three students of differing age levels and with various levels of disability in inclusive class settings. In each case, parents, classroom teachers, special education teachers, and school administrators talk about the steps they have taken to help Josh, Eric, and Tonya succeed in inclusive settings.

Snapshots 2: Video for Special Education (© 1995, 20–25 minutes in length) is a two-video set composed of six segments designed specifically for use in the college classroom. Each segment profiles three individuals, their families, teachers, and experiences. Instructors will find these programs to be of high interest to their students. Instructors who have used the tapes in their courses have found that they help in disabusing students of stereotypical viewpoints and put a "human face" on course material. The topics explored are:

- behavior disorders*
- learning disabilities*
- mental retardation*
- traumatic brain injury
- hearing impairment
- visual impairment

*This segment available with closed captioning for the hearing impaired

The Allyn & Bacon Special Education Transparency Package

The Transparency Package (© 2002) has been revised and expanded to include approximately 100 acetates, over half of which are full color.

The Allyn & Bacon Digital
Media Archive (DMA) for Special Education

The Digital Media Archive electronically provides charts, graphs, tables, figures, weblinks, and video clips on one cross-platform CD-ROM.

Acknowledgments

We are grateful to the many people who helped us during the preparation of the third edition of *Including Students with Special Needs*, for without their assistance and encouragement the project would have undoubtedly stalled. First and most important, we would like to express our gratitude to our families. They have listened to us worry about how to meet our deadlines, agonize over where to find the best sources of new material, and obsess about the knowledge and skills that classroom teachers must have to work with students with disabilities in this age of high standards and teacher accountability. They helped us sort through the conundrums, offered suggestions with the perspective of outsiders who deeply cared, and tolerated our need to hide in our offices as we wrote and rewrote. We cannot possibly say "thank you" in enough ways for their support.

We would also like to thank the individuals who helped us with all the details that are part and parcel to writing a textbook. Graduate assistants Mary Satterfield, Kazuko Matsuda, Meredith Miller, and Kelly Bolas did valiant work locating materials at the library and on the Internet, proofreading, and checking references. Joan Mueller-Cochrane gave us consistently high-quality work and displayed infinite patience in typing the manuscript. Jing Yu took on the daunting responsibility of helping us obtain permission to reproduce various tables and figures found throughout the book, and the results of her persistence are apparent in the materials reproduced herein.

The professionals at Allyn and Bacon have also supported this effort with both words and actions. Executive editor Virginia Lanigan has steered this third edition through the many steps of its creation, offering guidance and encouragement with greatly appreciated patience and good humor. Developmental editor Alicia Reilly offered suggestions for keeping the book clear and focused and helped ensure that we avoided adding too many pages to the final count. Erin Leidel, editorial assistant, assisted both Virginia and Alicia in managing the details of communication and manuscript handling.

We would also like to acknowledge the careful and insightful comments and feedback provided by our reviewers: Mary Banbury, University of New Orleans; Joanne Berryman, University of Kentucky; Rachelle Bruno, Northern Kentucky University; Patricia M. Carlson, Iowa State University; Sandra Cohen, University of Virginia; Harry Dangel, Georgia State University; Patricia Edwards, University of Akron; Rebecca B. Evers, Winthrop University; Jean C. Faieta, Edinboro University of Pennsylvania; Pamela Fernstrom, University of North Alabama; Raymond Glass, University of Maine at Farmington; Deborah Peters Goessling, University of Maine at Orono; James A. Jacobs, Indiana State University–Terre Haute; Julie Jochum, Bemidji State University; Marie C. Keel, Georgia State University; Susan Klein, Indiana University–Bloomington; Earle Knowlton, University of Kansas; Elizabeth B. Kozleski, University of Colorado at Denver; Suzanne Lamorey, University of Missouri; Robert Lauson, Idaho State University; Barbara Mallette, SUNY Freedonia; James K. McAfee, Pennsylvania State University; Catherine McCartney, Bemidji State University; Barbara Niemeyer, Morehead State University; Janice Philpot, Lesley College; Debra P. Price, Sam Houston State University; Robert Reid, University of Nebraska; Diane Rivera, University of Texas; Sam Rust, Seattle University; Sandra K. Squires, University of Nebraska–Omaha; Kate Steffans, Bemidji State University; Carol Chase Thomas, University of North Carolina–Wilmington; Keith Wade Whinnery, University of West Florida; and Ellen Williams, Western Kentucky University. We were often impressed with the care with which they reviewed the manuscript and the insightful suggestions they made. We freely admit that we sometimes questioned their opinions, but we know that they definitely helped us create a better text.

Finally, we continue to be grateful to all of our colleagues and students who influence our thinking about educating students with special needs in general education classrooms. Their comments on the first edition, their questions about best practices, their challenges to our thinking, and their suggestions for better communicating our message have been invaluable. We especially are grateful to the people who take the time to write or phone us to share their impressions of the book, their concerns, and their ideas on what we might do the next time to improve our outcomes. We hope they see their influences in the current edition, and they can know with certainty that we continue to welcome their input.

Including Students with Special Needs

chapter 1

The Foundation for Educating Students with Special Needs

■ Tonya is a first grader who loves school, has a wide circle of friends, and sometimes displays a stubborn streak. She also has many special needs: She uses a wheelchair, and she can use her arms, hands, and fingers only for very simple tasks. She has a significant cognitive disability, and she does not communicate with words, but usually can make her preferences known with her facial expressions. A teaching assistant is almost always available in Tonya's classroom to assist her as she uses the computer and to facilitate Tonya's interactions with her classmates, but the assistant also supports the teacher in routine classroom tasks and helps other students in the classroom as needed. Tonya's parents are actively involved in her education, and they work closely with the teacher and specialists to set goals and monitor progress in reaching them. Tonya's teacher recently made the comment, "I know Tonya is learning more than she can tell us. I can tell by the twinkle in her eye." How likely are you to teach a student like Tonya? What is a cognitive disability? What has led to students like Tonya being in typical classrooms instead of special education classrooms?

■ Aaron has a learning disability that was identified when he was in second grade. Now in eleventh grade, Aaron continues to learn how to compensate for the academic difficulties he experiences. Although he is a bright and personable young man, he reads at about a seventh-grade level. His writing is much like that of a student in second grade. He doesn't like to talk about his learning disabilities (LD); he doesn't want other students to make fun of him or treat him differently because he's "LD." In his U.S. history class, he is most successful on tests when he answers questions orally; he understands the concepts even if he sometimes cannot write his thoughts. Because he doesn't like to be singled out, however, he sometimes refuses to take tests or to get additional assistance during study period, so his grades are lower than they could be. Aaron is an excellent athlete, and on the basketball court he feels equal to his friends. However, his parents are concerned that his interest in sports is distracting him from schoolwork. How often will you meet students like Aaron? What is a learning disability? What types of supports and services do students like Aaron need to succeed in school?

1

Students like Tonya and Aaron are not unusual. They are among the 5.4 million school-age students in the United States who have disabilities that make them eligible for special education (U.S. Department of Education, 1999). But their disabilities do not tell you who they are: They are children or young adults and students first. Like all students, they have positive characteristics and negative ones, they have great days and some that are not so great, and they have likes and dislikes about school and learning.

As a teacher, you probably will instruct students like Tonya and Aaron along with other students with disabilities or other special needs. The purpose of this book is to help you understand students with disabilities and other special needs and learn strategies for addressing those needs. You might be the teacher who makes a profound positive difference in a student's life. With the knowledge and skills you learn for teaching exceptional learners, you will be prepared for both the challenges and rewards of helping them achieve their potential.

What Key Terms and Concepts Define Special Education?

Check Your Learning

What kinds of school services do students with disabilities receive?

When professionals talk about students like Tonya and Aaron, they may use several key terms. For example, when teachers refer to students with **disabilities,** they mean students who are eligible to receive special education services according to federal and state guidelines. **Special education** is the specially designed instruction provided by the school district or other local education agency that meets the unique needs of students identified as disabled. Special education may include instruction in a general education or special education classroom, education in the community for students who need to learn life skills, and specialized assistance in physical education, speech/language, or vocational preparation. In addition, students with disabilities may receive **related services,** that is, assistance required to enable a student to benefit from special education. Examples of related services include transportation to and from school in a specialized van or school bus and physical therapy. All special education and related services are provided to students by public schools at no cost to parents.

Least Restrictive Environment

The basis for educating students with disabilities in general education classrooms is the concept of **least restrictive environment (LRE),** a provision in the federal laws that have governed special education for nearly 3 decades. LRE is a student's right to be educated in the setting most like the educational setting for nondisabled peers in which the student can be successful, with appropriate supports provided (Etscheidt & Bartlett, 1999; Hardman, McDonnell, & Welch, 1997). For many students, the least restrictive environment is full-time or nearly full-time participation in a general education classroom. This is true for both Tonya and Aaron introduced at the beginning of this chapter. Tonya leaves her classroom once a week for physical therapy only, one support best offered in a large space with specialized equipment. Aaron, who can succeed in social studies class when he gives test answers aloud, may leave his classroom for that purpose only. His LRE is a general education classroom; the test procedure is an appropriate support. In 1996–1997, ap-

Connections

Making decisions about placing students in special education programs is discussed in Chapter 2.

proximately 45.7 percent of all school-age students with disabilities received at least 79 percent of their education in general education classrooms (U.S. Department of Education, 1999).

For some students—for example, those who have emotional or behavioral disabilities—being in a general education classroom nearly all day may be too academically and emotionally stressful. For these students, the LRE may be a general education classroom for part of the day and a special education classroom, sometimes called a resource room, for the remainder of the day. Appropriate supports for students with emotional disabilities might include a highly structured behavior management plan implemented by both special education and general education teachers. Identifying an LRE other than a general education setting is a serious decision usually made only after intensive supports are provided in the general education classroom without success. Such supports can include alternative materials or curriculum, assistance from a paraprofessional or special education teacher, adaptive equipment such as a computer, or consultative assistance from a psychologist or counselor. During 1996–1997, approximately 28.5 percent of all students with disabilities were educated in a combination of general education and resource room placements, receiving special education for 21–60 percent of the day. In the same time period, 21.4 percent of students with disabilities spent more than 60 percent of the school day in a separate setting (U.S. Department of Education, 1999).

For a few students, attending a typical school is not in their best interest and does not constitute the least restrictive setting. For example, a student with multiple disabilities who requires intensive medical care may receive education in a hospital setting. Clearly, this setting is very restrictive and used only in extraordinary circumstances. Two other settings that might be the least restrictive for some students are a special school attended only by students with disabilities and a residential facility where students with extraordinary needs attend school and live. A student with severe emotional problems who is clearly a danger to self or others might be educated in one of these settings. In 1996–1997, a total of 4.3 percent of students with disabilities were educated in separate schools, home or hospital settings, or residential settings (U.S. Department of Education, 1999). Chapter 2 presents more about the range of LRE settings considered for students with disabilities.

Mainstreaming

When the LRE concept became part of special education laws during the 1970s, the LRE for most students with disabilities was a part-time or full-time special education class. When such students were permitted to participate in general education, it was called mainstreaming. **Mainstreaming** is the term for placing students with disabilities in general education settings only when they can meet traditional academic expectations with minimal assistance, or when those expectations are not relevant (for example, participation in recess or school assemblies for opportunities for social interactions). Originally, many authors' definitions of mainstreaming (for example, Corman & Gottlieb, 1978; Kaufman, Gottlieb, Agard, & Kukic, 1975) emphasized the importance of involving students with disabilities meaningfully in classroom activities. However, the implementation of mainstreaming now varies widely from place to place. In some schools, students are considered mainstreamed when they participate only in lunch and physical education with other students. In

WWW Resources

The National Information Center for Children and Youth with Disabilities (whose acronym NICHCY, is a holdover from the organization's previous name) provides extensive information on disabilities and disability-related issues for families, teachers, and others. The website includes fact sheets and research briefs on specific disabilities as well as special education law. Most pages are available in Spanish as well as English. NICHCY's website is http://www.nichcy.org.

other schools, students are considered mainstreamed when they receive special education assistance for as little as 30 minutes a day. In both cases, placement depends on the kinds, amount, and intensity of special education services students need, with an assumption that special services can best be offered in a special class.

Inclusion

Over the past 2 decades, the entire structure of special education services has been undergoing significant change. Although the federal law permits the range of least restrictive settings previously described, many educators now seriously question the assumption that students who need more intensive services should routinely receive them in a restrictive setting such as a special education room (for example, Salend & Duhaney, 1999; Stanovich, 1999; Waldron & McLeskey, 1998). They stress that in the past many students with disabilities were only temporary guests in general education classrooms and that few efforts were made to provide assistance so they could be successfully educated with their nondisabled peers. These educators contend that all or most supports for students with disabilities can be provided effectively in general education classrooms when teachers are prepared to work with such students and related concerns are addressed (Hunt & Goetz, 1997; Pearman, Huang, & Mellblom, 1997). They further maintain that if students cannot meet traditional academic expectations, those expectations should be changed, not the setting. They reject the mainstreaming assumption that settings dictate the type and intensity of services and propose instead the concept of inclusion. **Inclusion** represents the belief or philosophy that students with disabilities should be fully integrated into general education classrooms and schools and that their instruction should be based on their abilities, not their disabilities. Inclusion comprises *physical integration*, placing students in the same classroom as nondisabled peers; *social integration*, nurturing student relationships with peers and adults; and *instructional integration*, teaching students based on their needs and not on a predetermined set of curricular standards (Ryan & Paterna, 1997; Villa, Thousand, Meyers, & Nevin, 1996; Wilson, 1999).

Advocates of inclusion believe that students should not be removed routinely from general education classrooms to receive assistance because doing so highlights their disabilities, disrupts their education, and teaches them to be dependent. Further, they maintain that specialized services often can be delivered in general education classrooms. For students with mild disabilities—such as learning disabilities—who typically can succeed in the general education curriculum, this might mean that a special education teacher or a paraprofessional assists them during instruction. It also might mean that adaptations such as simplified materials or alternative assignments are provided for the students.

In some cases, it might be necessary for students to leave the classroom for particular instruction, but this occurs only when classroom supports are insufficient and only for a limited period of time. For students with moderate or severe cognitive disabilities, inclusion might mean the provision of a paraprofessional in the general education classroom for a significant part of the day. It also might involve special education teachers preparing alternative activities for the students, or improvising ways in which the materials for instruction (e.g, foil and wire for a science experiment) can be used by students with disabilities for a related but much simpler task. As for students with milder disabilities, inclusion does not mean that it is wrong to provide any instruction in a separate setting. Occasionally this is necessary, but that decision should be made carefully and reevaluated regularly.

Throughout this text, the term *inclusion* will refer to students' participation in general education settings as full members of the classroom learning community, with their special needs met in this setting the majority of the time. We generally agree that inclusion maximizes the potential of most students, ensures their rights, and is the preferred option whenever possible. Later in this chapter, we address this topic in more detail and from various perspectives.

Check Your
Learning

How do mainstreaming
and inclusion differ?

Because services for students with disabilities and other exceptional learners continue to evolve, teachers in your school might use the words *inclusion* and *mainstreaming* interchangeably, and they might have yet different terms to describe special education services. For example, teachers sometimes say *inclusion* only when referring to students with physical or cognitive disabilities and say *mainstreaming* for students with learning disabilities. To assist you with the vocabulary used in special education programs and instructional approaches, a glossary is provided at the back of this textbook. Although learning the terms used in special education is important, your most essential tasks are to learn about special education services in your school and to define your role in teaching students with disabilities.

How Did Special Education Services Come to Exist?

Special education as it exists today has been influenced by a number of different factors. Although people with disabilities have been identified and treated for centuries (Smith, 1998; Winzer, 1998), special education evolved rapidly only in the 20th century. As special education has grown, it has been shaped by federal law, the civil rights movement and related court cases, and changing social and political beliefs. Figure 1.1 illustrates some factors that have influenced the development of special education.

The Development of Education for Students with Disabilities

When compulsory public education began near the turn of the 20th century, almost no school programs existed for students with disabilities (Scheerenberger, 1983; Yell, Rogers, & Rogers, 1998). Students with disabilities that were relatively mild, that is, learning or behavior problems or minor physical impairments, were educated along with other students because their needs were not considered extraordinary. Many children with significant cognitive or physical disabilities did not attend school at all, whereas others were educated by private agencies and some lived in institutions. In fact, for the first half of the past century, many states explicitly legislated permission for school districts to prohibit some students with disabilities from attending (Yell et al., 1998).

Special classes in public schools began as compulsory education became widespread. Schools were expected to be like efficient assembly lines, with each class of students moving from grade to grade and eventually graduating from high school as

Figure 1.1 Influences on Current Special Education Practices

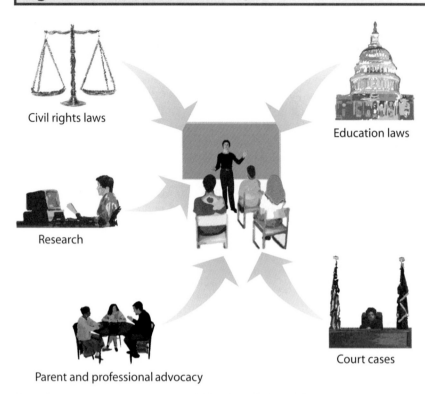

Civil rights laws

Education laws

Research

Court cases

Parent and professional advocacy

FYI

The Council for Exceptional Children (CEC), founded in 1922 by Elizabeth Farrell, is a professional organization for teachers, administrators, parents, and other advocates for the rights of students with disabilities.

productive citizens prepared to enter the workforce (Patton, Payne, & Beirne-Smith, 1986; Scheerenberger, 1983). Special classes were developed as a place for students who could not keep up with their classmates. Because many students with disabilities were still not in school, most of the students sent to special classes probably had mild or moderate learning or cognitive disabilities. Educators at the time believed that such students would learn better in a protected setting and that the efficiency of the overall educational system would be preserved (Bennett, 1932; Pertsch, 1936).

By the 1950s, special education programs were available in many school districts, but some undesirable outcomes were becoming apparent. For example, students in special classes were often considered incapable of learning academic skills. They spent their school time practicing "manual skills" such as weaving and bead stringing. Researchers began questioning this practice and conducted studies to explore the efficacy of special education. When they compared students with disabilities in special education classes to similar students who had remained in general education, they found the latter group often had learned more than the former (Blatt, 1958; Goldstein, Moss, & Jordan, 1965). Parents at this time also became active advocates for better educational opportunities for their children (Blatt, 1987). By the late 1960s, many authorities in the field agreed that segregated special classes were not the most appropriate educational setting for many students with disabilities (Blatt, 1958; Christopolos & Renz, 1969; Dunn, 1968; Hobbs, 1975; Lilly, 1971).

The Impact of the Civil Rights Movement on Special Education

During the 1950s and 1960s, another force began contributing to the development of new approaches to special education. The civil rights movement, although initially addressing the rights of African Americans, expanded and began to influence thinking about people with disabilities (Chaffin, 1975; Rothstein, 1995). In the *Brown v. Board of Education* decision in 1954, the U.S. Supreme Court ruled that it was unlawful under the Fourteenth Amendment to discriminate arbitrarily against any group of people. The Court then applied this concept to the education of children, ruling that the state-mandated separate education for African American students could not be an equal education. This court decision introduced the concept of **integration** into public education, the notion that the only way in which students' constitutional rights to equal opportunity could be protected was when diverse student groups learned together. Soon, people with disabilities were recognized as another group whose rights often had been violated because of arbitrary discrimination. For children, the discrimination occurred when they were denied access to schools because of their disabilities. Beginning in the late 1960s and continuing through today, parents and others have used the court system to ensure that the civil and educational rights of children with disabilities are preserved. Figure 1.2 summarizes several of the court cases that have helped shape special education as it exists today.

Section 504. One of the outcomes of the civil rights movement has been legislation designed to prevent discrimination against individuals with disabilities, whether they are children in schools or adults in the workforce. **Section 504** of the Vocational Rehabilitation Act of 1973 is a civil rights law that prevents discrimination against all individuals with disabilities in programs that receive federal funds, as do all public schools. For children of school age, Section 504 ensures equal opportunity for participation in the full range of school activities (National Information Center for Children and Youth with Disabilities, 1996; Rosenfeld, 1999). Through Section 504, some students not eligible for services through special education may be entitled to receive specific types of assistance to help them succeed in school.

For example, Sondra is a student with a severe attention problem. She cannot follow a lesson for more than a few minutes at a time; she is distracted by every noise in the hallway and every car that goes by her classroom window. Her teacher describes her as a student who acts first and thinks later. Sondra does not have a disability as established in special education law, but she does need extra assistance and is disabled according to Section 504 because her significant learning problem negatively affects her ability to function in school. The professionals at her school are required to create and carry out a plan to help Sondra *access* education. Special education teachers may assist because they know techniques that will help Sondra, but Sondra is not a special education student, nor is she the responsibility of the special educators. Other students who might receive assistance through Section 504 include those with health problems, such as asthma or extreme allergies.

Americans with Disabilities Act. In July 1990, President Bush signed into law the **Americans with Disabilities Act (ADA)** (National Information Center for Children and Youth with Disabilities, 1996). This civil rights law is based on the Vocational Rehabilitation Act of 1973, but it further extends the rights of individuals

> **Cultural Awareness**
>
> Issues related to race and culture continue to exist in special education. Even after more than 30 years of study, litigation, and other attention, students from some minority groups are still overrepresented in special education programs.

Figure 1.2 Court Cases Influencing Special Education

Matters relating to students with disabilities are addressed in federal and state laws. Issues concerning the interpretation of those laws often must be resolved through the courts. Since 1954, hundreds of legal decisions have clarified the rights of students with disabilities and the responsibilities of schools for educating them. In fact, in many instances court decisions have cleared the way for the passage of related legislation. As you review the landmark decisions listed here, you may recognize how each influenced P.L. 94-142, IDEA-97, and related legislation, which we discuss later in this chapter.

Brown v. Board of Education (1954).
This case established the principle that school segregation denies some students equal educational opportunity. Although the decision referred primarily to racial segregation, it has since become the cornerstone for ensuring equal rights for students with disabilities.

Pennsylvania Association for Retarded Children v. Commonwealth of Pennsylvania (1972).
In this suit, the court ruled that schools may not exclude students with mental retardation. The court ordered that a free public education was to be provided to all such students.

Board of Education of Hendrick Hudson School District v. Rowley (1982).
The court ruled that special education services must provide an appropriate education, but that students with disabilities may not be entitled to optimum services. The parents of a student with a hearing impairment were denied the services of an interpreter for their child in school because the child was achieving at grade level.

Daniel R. R. v. State Board of Education (1989).
This court decision established that two factors must be considered in determining the appropriate placement for a student with disabilities. The first factor is whether a student can be satisfactorily educated in the general education setting with supplementary supports provided. The second factor is whether, in cases in which the general education setting is not successful, the student is mainstreamed to the maximum extent appropriate. For Daniel, a student with Down syndrome, the court ruled that the school district had not violated his rights when he was moved from general education after an unsuccessful attempt to include him.

Oberti v. Board of Education of Clementon School District (1993).
In this case concerning a student with Down syndrome, the district court ruled and the court of appeals upheld the ruling that school districts must make available a full range of supports and services in the general education setting to accommodate the needs of students with disabilities. The court further stipulated that just because a student learns differently from other students does not necessarily warrant exclusion from general education. This case is considered crucial in establishing the principles of inclusive practices.

Doe v. Withers (1993).
As Douglas Doe's history teacher, Michael Withers was responsible for making the oral testing accommodations needed by this student with learning disabilities. Although he was also a state legislator, Mr. Withers refused to provide the oral testing and Douglas failed this class, thus becoming athletically ineligible. The court awarded the family $5,000 in compensatory damages and $30,000 in punitive damages. Although this case has limited applicability to other situations, it is widely cited as an example of the extent of general education teachers' responsibility to make good-faith efforts to provide required accommodations for students with disabilities.

Cedar Rapids Community School District v. Garret F. (1999).
In this case, a 12-year-old with significant physical disabilities and above-average cognitive ability required nursing assistance primarily because of the possibility that his ventilator might cease functioning at school. The parents requested that the school provide this service at a cost estimated to be more than $20,000 per year. The school district refused this request. The Supreme Court eventually ruled that the services needed should be provided by the school, acknowledging the financial concern, but noting that the law was intended to ensure that students like Garrett could attend school.

S O U R C E : Adapted from "Medical Services: The Disrupted Related Service," by L. Bartlett, 2000, *Journal of Special Education, 33,* pp. 215–223; *Legal Issues in Special Educations,* by A. G. Osborne, 1996, Boston: Allyn & Bacon; *Special Education Law* (2nd ed.), by L. L. F. Rothstein, 1995, New York: Longman; "Wrights-law Law Library: Caselaw," by P. Wright & P. Wright, 2000. Retrieved June 2000 from the World Wide Web: http://www.wrightlaw.com/main_lawlibrary.htm; "The Least Restrictive Environment Mandate and the Courts: Judicial Activism or Judicial Restraint?" by M. L. Yell, 1995, *Exceptional Children, 61,* pp. 578–581; and "De Jure: Costly Lack of Accommodations," by P. A. Zirkel, 1994, *Phi Delta Kappan, 75,* pp. 652–653.

with disabilities. This law is the most significant disability legislation ever passed (Job Accommodation Network, 2000; Rothstein, 1995). It protects all individuals with disabilities from discrimination, and it requires most employers to make reasonable accommodations for them. Although ADA does not deal directly with the education of students with disabilities, it does clarify the civil rights of all individuals with disabilities and thus has an impact on special education. This law also ensures that buildings, transportation, and other public places are accessible to people with disabilities. As a teacher with a disability, you yourself might be influenced by ADA. For example, if your school is not accessible to wheelchairs and undergoes renovation, ramps, elevators, or wide entries with automatic doors might have to be installed. If you have a disability, this law also protects you from discrimination when you look for a teaching position.

> **Check Your Learning**
>
> Why are Section 504 and the ADA called *civil rights* laws instead of *education* laws? What impact do they have on students, teachers, and schools?

The Legislative Basis for Least Restrictive Environment

Influenced by researchers' growing doubts about the effectiveness of special education classes and by civil rights court cases, by the early 1970s many states had begun to address special education issues by passing laws to guarantee that students with disabilities would receive an appropriate education. In 1975, Congress passed **P.L. 94-142,** the **Education for the Handicapped Act (EHA),** thereby setting federal guidelines for special education services. This law outlined the foundation on which current special education practice rests. It took into account many of the early court decisions that established the civil rights of students with disabilities, and it mandated the concept of least restrictive environment (LRE). For example, this law specifically described categories of disabilities that make students eligible to receive special education. It clarified the related services to which students might be entitled. It also set out procedures for identifying a student as needing special education and outlined the rights of parents who disagree with the educational services offered to their children. The major provisions of P.L. 94-142 are outlined in Figure 1.3.

Public Law 101-476.   Passed in 1990, **P.L. 101-476** reauthorized P.L. 94-142. It also changed the name of P.L. 94-142 to the **Individuals with Disabilities Education Act**

> ## Figure 1.3 Key Provisions of P.L. 94-142, Free Appropriate Public Education
>
> Students with disabilities are entitled to attend public schools and to receive the educational services they need. This education is provided at no cost to parents.
>
> **Least Restrictive Environment**
> Students with disabilities must be educated in the least restrictive environment in which they can succeed with support. For most students, this environment is the general education classroom.
>
> **Individualized Education**
> The instructional services and other assistance for students with disabilities must be tailored to meet their needs. This plan is accomplished by preparing an individualized education program (IEP) annually. The IEP includes a statement of the student's current level of functioning, a set of goals and short-term objectives for reaching those goals, and clear specification of who is responsible for delivering the student's services, how long they will last, where they will be provided, and how progress will be evaluated.
>
> **Nondiscriminatory Evaluation**
> Students should be assessed using instruments that do not discriminate on the basis of race, culture, or disability. In considering eligibility for special education services, students must be assessed by a multidisciplinary team in their native language using tests that are relevant to the area of concern. Eligibility cannot be decided on the basis of only one test.
>
> **Due Process**
> Students with disabilities and their parents are protected in all special education matters through due process procedures; that is, if a disagreement occurs concerning a student's eligibility for special education placement or services, no changes can be made until the issue has been resolved by an impartial hearing and, if necessary, the appropriate court. Likewise, if schools disagree with parents' requests for services for their children, they may also use due process procedures to resolve the dispute.
>
> **Zero Reject/Child Find**
> No student may be excluded from public education because of a disability. Further, each state must take action to locate children who may be entitled to special education services.

(**IDEA**) to reflect more contemporary "person-first" language. In addition, the term *handicapped* was removed from the law and the preferred term *disability* was substituted. This law continued to uphold the major provisions of P.L. 94-142, and it also added significantly to the provisions for very young children with disabilities and for students preparing to leave secondary school (Ysseldyke, Algozzine, & Thurlow, 1992). One other important change was the addition of two new categories of disability: autism and traumatic brain injury. Highlights of the additions P.L. 101-476 brought to special education law are included in Figure 1.4.

Connections

The regulations and procedures for P.L. 105-17 are clarified further in Chapter 2.

Public Law 105-17. In 1997, President Clinton signed into law the **Individuals with Disabilities Education Act Amendments of 1997, P.L. 105-17.** This law reauthorized P.L. 101-476 and added a number of new provisions. Perhaps most importantly for classroom teachers, this law recognized that most students with dis-

Figure 1.4 Additions to P.L. 94-142 Mandated in P.L. 101-476 (IDEA)

Transition Services
Individualized education programs for students who are 16 years of age or older (and those as young as age 14 if appropriate) must include a description of transition services. This provision was designed to ensure that students receive assistance when preparing to leave school upon graduation, whether to find a job, attend a vocational school, or enter a university or college. The transition plan often includes connecting with professionals from other service agencies, including social services and vocational centers.

Early Childhood Education
This law provides funding for projects to improve services to infants, toddlers, and young children with disabilities. Areas of concern are the linkage between medical and early intervention services, assistive technology, parent education, and early identification of children with disabilities.

Severe Disabilities
For students with severe disabilities, this law funds projects that emphasize education in inclusive settings. The intent is to promote programs that include students with severe disabilities in general education settings.

Emotional Disturbance
The law supports projects aimed at improving services for students with severe emotional disturbance. Topics of concern include coordination with mental health services, reduction of student placement in residential treatment facilities away from the students' home communities, collaboration among professionals, and the needs of minority group children.

New Categories of Disability
Two new groups of students were specifically identified in this law as having disabilities that may entitle them to special education services: students who have traumatic brain injury and students who have autism.

SOURCE: Adapted from *Critical Issues in Special Education* (2nd ed., pp. 30–64), by J. E. Ysseldyke, B. Algozzine, and M. L. Thurlow, 1992, Boston: Houghton Mifflin.

---

abilities spend all or most of their school time in general education settings and so it included a provision that a classroom teacher become a member of the team that writes each student's Individualized Education Program. Another important change occurred regarding assessment. Acknowledging that students with disabilities were often excluded from local or state assessments, the law added a requirement that all students with disabilities be assessed like other students, using either the same assessment instruments employed with typical learners, or some type of alternative instrument. Additional details on the provisions of P.L. 105-17 are summarized in Figure 1.5, and they are discussed further in Chapter 2.

Public Law 99-457. In 1986, prior to the passage of P.L. 101-476, Congress enacted **P.L. 99-457.** This act extended the provisions of special education law to very young children, from birth through 5 years of age. The focus for services is on the entire family (Comer & Fraser, 1998; Mahoney et al., 1999). For example, the education plan written for a very young child is called an **Individualized Family Service**

FYI

P.L. 99-457, which amended P.L. 94-142, established Part H, which deals with programs and services for infants and toddlers with special needs and their families. This part of the law was revised again in 1997, and it is now included in IDEA-97 as Part C.

Figure 1.5   Changes to P.L. 101-476 Mandated in P.L. 105-17 (IDEA-97)

General Education Teacher Roles and Responsibilities

At least one general education teacher must participate as a member of the team that writes a student's Individualized Education Program (IEP). In addition, the IEP must directly address student participation in general education and must justify placements that are not in general education.

Parent Participation

The law now clarifies the extent of parent participation in decision making about their children's education. Specifically, IDEA-97 spells out that parents are part of the decision-making team for determining eligibility for special education services as well as for determining the appropriate educational placement for the student. Further, schools must now report to parents on the progress of their children with disabilities at least as often as progress is reported for students without disabilities.

Evaluation and Eligibility

IDEA-97 has several changes related to special education assessment. First, the law clarifies that when parents consent to have their child evaluated, they are not consenting to a possible, future special education placement. Second, students are not eligible for special education because of poor math or reading instruction, or because of language differences. Third, for some students the former requirement that a complete reassessment be completed every 3 years can be modified. That is, already existing information can be used in lieu of repeatedly administering standardized tests.

Assessment of Students

States are required to measure the academic progress of students who have IEPs, either by including them in the standardized assessments other students take, or by using an alternative assessment process. Students are entitled to appropriate adaptations (for example, extended time, large print) during assessment.

Transition

Transition service needs must be addressed in IEPs for students beginning at age 14. These needs must be updated annually, and they must become increasingly detailed as students reach age 16 and beyond, even clarifying services the student will access outside of school (e.g., a community vocational service).

Discipline

As needed, strategies for addressing student behavior must be included as part of the IEP. If a student is suspended or placed in an alternative interim placement, a behavior plan must be developed. In some cases (e.g., when students bring weapons or drugs to school), schools may place students with disabilities in alternative interim placements for up to 45 days. They must continue to receive special education services during this time.

Paraprofessionals

Paraprofessionals, teaching assistants, and other similar personnel must be trained for their jobs and appropriately supervised.

Mediation

States must make mediation available to parents as an early and informal strategy for resolving disagreements about the identification of, placement of, or services for students with disabilities. The cost of mediation is borne by the state. Parents are not obligated to mediate, and mediation may not delay a possible hearing.

SOURCE: Adapted from "The New IDEA," by the American School Board Association, 1997, *American School Board Journal, 184*(12), p. 20; "Changes in IEP Requirements Based on the Reauthorization of IDEA," B. Johns, 1997. *CCBD Newsletter, 11*(2), pp. 1, 4; "Individuals with Disabilities Education Act Amendments of 1997," by P. Marchand. Retrieved June 9, 2000 from http://TheArc.org/ga/qa.html; "The IDEA Amendments of 1997," by the National Information Center for Children and Youth with Disabilities, 1998, *NICHCY News Digest, 26,* pp. 1–41; and "The IDEA Amendments of 1997: Implications for Special and General Education Teachers, Administrators, and Teacher Trainers," by M. L. Yell and J. G. Shriner, 1997, *Focus on Exceptional Children, 30*(1), pp. 1–19.

Plan (IFSP) and may spell out assistance for parents. Parents typically have primary responsibility for teaching their babies and young children because they, not teachers, can take advantage of natural learning opportunities, such as teaching a child to grasp by holding a spoon at lunch. During 1997–1998, approximately 197,300 children from birth through age 2 and 571,000 children from 3 through 5 years old received special education through this program (U.S. Department of Education,

1999). For infants and toddlers, the discretionary services are often provided through home visits by early intervention specialists; for preschoolers, services may occur in special education classes in regular schools or in special schools. Consistent with increasing inclusion for students of school age, a growing trend is to provide education to preschoolers in private preschools and day-care centers that also serve children without disabilities.

As you can see, special education has evolved on the basis of many factors. When special education services began, essentially none of them was offered in public schools; today, comprehensive services in a wide variety of settings are supplied, and both very young children and young adults, as well as students in elementary and secondary schools, benefit from them. As the rights and needs of students with disabilities have been better understood, classroom teachers have become increasingly involved in the education of students with disabilities, a trend that surely will continue.

Check Your Learning

How do P.L. 94-142, P.L. 99-457, P.L. 101-476, and P.L. 105-17 relate to one another?

What Are the Issues Related to Inclusion?

Particularly with the passage of IDEA-97, conversations about inclusive practices have shifted largely from questions about whether inclusion should occur to discussions about how to create effective schools based on this philosophy. No doubt, trying to objectively examine inclusive practices is tremendously difficult because they are influenced not only by the characteristics and needs of students with disabilities but also by teacher knowledge, skill, and receptivity; parent/family commitment and involvement; school policies and procedures; and myriad other factors.

Inclusion and Students

If students in inclusive settings do not make adequate progress, then inclusion is not in their best interest. Over the past several years, a number of researchers have examined outcomes for students who participate fully in general education classes, and although the results are sometimes positive, sometimes they are not. For example, Waldron and McLeskey (1998) studied the achievement of 144 elementary students with mild and severe learning disabilities in two types of programs: (a) inclusive and (b) pullout to a resource room. They found that students with LD who were included made significantly more progress in reading and math than students with LD receiving pullout services. Further, for students with mild LD, more students in the inclusive program made progress comparable to peers without disabilities than did students in the pullout program. For students with severe LD, the amount of progress was comparable regardless of setting. In reviewing the literature on inclusion, others have concluded that the placement of students without special needs into classrooms with peers with disabilities has no adverse effect on their learning (e.g., Salend & Duhaney, 1999).

Other professionals see a more complex picture of inclusion and students. For example, Manset and Semmel (1997) compared eight inclusive models for elementary students, and academic outcomes were one component of their investigation. They found that inclusion can be an effective educational approach for some student but not all, and that the impact of inclusion is mediated by teachers' willing-

How have services for students with disabilities changed over the past 3 decades? What has led to these changes? How do these changes affect you as a professional educator?

ness to change their instructional practices so that they are more individualized, by the ratio of students to staff, and by the availability at some time for intensive one-to-one instruction for students with disabilities. Salend and Duhaney (1999), reviewing empirical literature on inclusive practices, found that students with disabilities in general education settings generally performed better academically than did peers who received services in pullout settings. These results spanned elementary, middle, and high school, where one study found that secondary students in inclusive programs were more likely than peers in other programs to attend postsecondary education, to obtain employment at a high salary, and to be socially integrated into their communities. However, these results pertained primarily to students with physical disabilities and could possibly be attributed to these students' social skills, not the placement.

When Salend and Duhaney examined social outcomes, however, they found varying results. Students with severe disabilities were found to have more social interactions with nondisabled peers when placed in inclusive settings, and they formed more friendships. For students with learning disabilities, however, the results were not as positive: They were less accepted as time went by and had lower academic self-concepts than were typical of peers. In another study, however, students with learning disabilities in classrooms with peers had positive outcomes on measures of friendship quality and peer acceptance (Vaughn, Elbaum, Schumm, & Hughes, 1998).

Many questions still exist regarding inclusive practices and students, and some professionals have grave concerns about the rapid growth of inclusive practices (e.g., Hallahan, 1998). What about students who need the high structure and small-group arrangements that characterize special education settings? For students needing instruction in a separate setting, how much is appropriate and how often should it occur? What are the differences in outcomes for students with learning and behavior disabilities as compared to students with other disabilities? How can students be expected to pass district assessments, particularly at the high school level, if they receive core coursework from special educators who do not have the needed content expertise to teach advanced courses? Is it more or less stigmatizing for students to be in a classroom with peers when they obviously are not learning the same concepts and skills as others?

Part of the answer to these questions about the impact of inclusive practices on students lies in the ability of teachers to teach in a way that is responsive to a wide range of student needs. As you will learn later in this text, much is known about instructional practices that lead to success for students with disabilities, and many of those practices help other students to learn as well (Vaughn, Gersten, & Chard, 2000). As researchers continue to study inclusion, the most effective ways to design programs will become clearer, but it is just as likely that other questions will be raised as well.

Parents and Inclusion

Although parents have expressed some concerns about the range of services available in inclusive programs, they generally have been positive about the impact of such programs on their children. For example, Palmer and her colleagues (Palmer, Borthwick-Duffy, & Widaman, 1998) surveyed 460 parents of students with severe disabilities who attended separate schools. This group of parents and guardians was positive toward inclusion regarding social benefits, but apprehensive toward inclusion regarding educational services. Parents of children in a junior high program felt positive about the program's impact on their children's self-esteem and the amount of individual attention their children received in the general education classroom, and they attributed program success to teacher commitment (Gibb et al., 1997). What seems particularly clear about parents and families and the topic of inclusion is that parents should be actively involved in the decision-making process concerning how their child will receive educational services (Grove & Fisher, 1999; Hunt & Goetz, 1997).

General Education Teachers and Inclusion

The perceptions of teachers regarding inclusion are as complex as the information on inclusion and students. Some teachers are strongly supportive of inclusive practices, and they perceive that it has positive outcomes for students and themselves. For example, Soodak, Podell, and Lehman (1998) found that teachers with a high sense of self-efficacy, that is, a strong belief that their actions can directly affect student outcomes, were more positive about their inclusive programs. Another research team (Helmstetter et al., 1998) found that even for students with severe disabilities, general education teachers provided more instruction than occurred in a special education setting and that the amount of one-to-one attention was equivalent between the two settings.

Most authors have found that teachers' support of inclusive practices is mixed, often contingent on the presence of a variety of supports and conditions. For example, Prom (1999), in a focus group study with an art teacher and a consumer education teacher in a middle school, found that the teachers were positive about making progress toward helping students accomplish their IEP goals and objectives. They were quite concerned about student participation, asserting that without the special

Research Note

In a study of 150 Latino mothers of young children with disabilities, researchers found that they described themselves as good mothers and viewed their child with mental retardation as having a positive impact on their lives (Skinner, Bailey, Correa, & Rodriguez, 1999).

Cultural Awareness

In considering students and their families from diverse backgrounds, it is as important to keep in mind that beliefs and values related to disabilities vary widely within cultures as it is to understand that beliefs and values differ across cultures. Educators' responsibility is to be sensitive to cultural differences, but not to stereotype based on culture.

education teacher's presence in the classroom, the students would not have participated at all. This author as well as others (e.g., Soodak et al., 1998) reported that at least some teachers become more negative about inclusive practices as time passes.

Teacher preparation for inclusion is one issue of high concern to general educators. For example, what are the strategies and practices you anticipate learning from this textbook to help you effectively teach students with special needs? When kindergarten teachers were asked about practices such as making physical adjustments in the room, planning activities to foster social skill development, meeting with others, using technology, learning about children's cultural background, and others, they reported that the strategies would probably be helpful but doubted that it was feasible to implement them (Vaughn, Reiss, Rothlein, & Hughes, 1999). These same teachers expressed concern that they were not prepared to make the accommodations necessary to support students with disabilities. Other teachers have generally expressed reservations about the entire concept of inclusion: When teachers across all school levels who were about to participate in inclusion were asked their opinion, they expressed concern about their lack of coursework or staff development (Vaughn, Schumm, Jallad, Slusher, & Saumel, 1996). One high school teacher even asserted that all teachers who worked in inclusive schools were going to need double majors, one in their content area and one in special education.

One other aspect of teachers' responses to inclusion concerns the critical topic of instructional assistance. Unless teachers are willing and prepared to change their instructional practices, students with disabilities are placed at a disadvantage (Tomlinson et al., 1997). Scott, Vitale, and Masten (1998) did an extensive review of studies examining teachers' use of various tactics to assist students. They found that teachers are generally positive about the need for and desirability of making instructional changes for students with disabilities in their classrooms. However, when those teachers are faced with implementation, many of them do not alter their traditional,

What particular challenges do students with "invisible disabilities"—such as learning and behavior disabilities—face in school? What can you as a teacher do to help them succeed?

whole-group instructional approaches, nor do they incorporate specific changes for students with special needs. Teachers' responses seemed to be unaffected by the amount of experience they had, but their attitude toward inclusion, their knowledge of a range of adaptations, and their perception of the level of support available did influence their thinking on making instructional changes to support students.

Administrators and Inclusion

For a school to be highly inclusive, it is essential that the principal be a strong leader who keeps the vision focused and fosters among staff an understanding of inclusion and the skills and practices needed to implement it. However, only limited empirical information is available regarding principals' perceptions of inclusive programs. Generally, principals report positive attitudes toward inclusive practices (Barnett & Monda-Amaya, 1998; Villa, Thousand, Meyers, & Nevin, 1996), and their attitudes are more positive than those of special education teachers (e.g., Cook, Semmel, & Gerber, 1999). Not surprisingly, principals express concern that general education teachers may not have the skills to instruct students with disabilities in their classrooms (Cook et al., 1999). At least some principals appear to take a wait-and-see approach to inclusive schooling, not actively leading their staff toward such practices (Barnett & Monda-Amaya, 1998).

Putting the Pieces Together

A decade ago, a major concern related to inclusion was the lack of empirical information to support or refute it. Today, the issue is rapidly becoming one of trying to make sense of the many, many studies that are being reported, particularly because some results continue to be contradictory. As you read about inclusive practices, you should keep in mind that the results researchers obtain are influenced by many variables, including the abilities and disabilities, ages, and cultural backgrounds of students; the attitudes, knowledge, and skills of general and special education teachers; the commitment and participation by parents; the degree of support for inclusion from administrators, school policies, and school procedures; the type of outcomes measured; and even the predisposition of researchers to have particular opinions about inclusion. Your responsibility is to continue to learn about this significant dimension of your role as a classroom teacher and to assess critically the quality of the information you read related to this topic. Of course, given the mixed results of this research, it is also important to teach each student based on his/her individual needs and situation—not according to the dictates of any particular philosophy.

Who Receives Special Education and Other Special Services?

Throughout this chapter, we have used the phrase *students with disabilities*. At this point, we will introduce you to the specific types of disabilities that may entitle students to receive special education services, as well as other special needs that may require specialized assistance.

WWW Resources

The Consortium on Inclusive Schooling Practices strives to help states and local school districts to better serve students with and without disabilities. This organization emphasizes creating policies that foster inclusive practices, and its website address is http://www.asri.edu/cfsp/brochure/abtcons.htm.

Check Your Learning

What impact have federal and state laws had on special education? How has teaching students with disabilities changed over the years?

Special Emphasis On . . .

Inclusion in High Schools

Although inclusion is challenging at every grade level, it can be especially complex in high schools because of the density of academic content to be taught and learned, the increased accountability and accompanying high stakes testing, resulting teacher expectations for student achievement, and relatively inflexible schedules. In addition, traditional high school culture often is not conducive to inclusive practices.

For faculty and staff in your high school who grapple with issues related to inclusion, the following resources might be helpful.

NASSP Bulletin. (1998). 82(594).
The special issue of the journal of the National Association of Secondary School Principals (NASSP) is devoted entirely to the topic of special education in secondary schools. It includes a discussion of the importance of all students reaching high standards, overviews the requirements of IDEA-97 and legal issues related to students with disabilities, describes what inclusion should

be, addresses scheduling issues, and examines behavior alternatives for students with conduct disorders.

Jorgensen, C. M. (Ed.). (1998). *Restructuring high schools for all students: Taking inclusion to the next level.* Baltimore: Paul H. Brookes.
This book is designed especially to address achieving inclusion in high schools. It includes fundamental information about inclusive practices and raises many questions about the current priorities and structures of U.S. high schools. The book includes lessons that accommodate all students, and it emphasizes the need to teach self-advocacy skills to students with learning disabilities. The book is praised for its realistic look at the challenges of creating inclusive high schools.

Yanoff, J. C. (2000). *The classroom teacher's inclusion handbook.* Chicago: Arthur Coyle Press.
Written by a former Chicago high school teacher, this straightforward book describes the characteristics and

Categories of Disability in Federal Law

When we say that students have disabilities, we are referring to the specific categories of exceptionality prescribed by federal law. Each state has additional laws that clarify special education practices and procedures; the terms used to refer to disabilities in these state laws may differ from those found in federal law. Check with your instructor for the terms used in your state. According to P.L. 105-17, students with one or more of the following disabilities that negatively affects their educational performance are eligible for special education services.

Learning disabilities (LD).   Students with **learning disabilities (LD)** have dysfunctions in processing information typically found in language-based activities. They have average or above-average intelligence, but they often encounter significant problems learning how to read, write, and compute. They may not see letters and words in the way others do; they may not be able to pick out important features in a picture they are looking at; and they may take longer to process a question or comment directed to them. They may also have difficulty following directions, at-

needs of students with various types of disabilities and special needs. It also includes suggestions for problem solving when students are experiencing difficulties in the classroom.

Stainback, S., & Stainback, W. (Ed.). (1996). *Inclusion: A guide for educators.* **Baltimore: Paul H. Brookes.**
Although not written just for high school teachers, this comprehensive guide for creating inclusive classrooms contains important chapters on the history and rationale for inclusion, strategies for making all students part of a learning community, and approaches for fostering collaboration. A specific chapter addresses issues pertinent to high school teachers, including designing lessons that meet the needs of a diversity of students. The book also tackles the common problem of disruptive student behavior in high schools.

Center for Effective Collaboration and Practice
This federally funded organization is concerned primarily with improving interventions and outcomes for students with emotional and behavioral disabilities. The Center's website addresses many topics of particular interest to high school teachers, including issues related to students transitioning from the world of school to the world of work or college, aggression and violence, the juvenile justice system, and social and mental health services. The site has articles on these topics and also links to other resources related to them. The Center's website address is http://www.air.org/cecp/whatsnew.htm.

Thousand, J. (1997). The evolution of secondary inclusion. *Remedial and Special Education, 18,* **270–285.**
This article offers an alternative way of conceptualizing how secondary schools can be more responsive to inclusion, based on Native American culture. Four critical outcomes are: belonging, mastery, independence, and generosity. It presents a way of tracking students' IEP goals and objectives across courses as well as a form for noting adaptations and modifications students need.

---

tending to tasks, organizing assignments, and managing time. Sometimes these students appear to be unmotivated or lazy when, in fact, they are trying to the best of their ability. Aaron, described at the beginning of this chapter, has a learning disability, but many types of learning disabilities exist, and no single description characterizes students who have one. Learning disabilities are by far the most common special need: Approximately 51 percent of all students receiving special education services in public schools in 1997–1998 had LD (U.S. Department of Education, 1999).

Speech or language impairments.   When a student has extraordinary difficulties in communicating with others for reasons other than maturation, a **speech or language impairment** is involved. Students with this disability may have trouble with **articulation,** or the production of speech sounds. They may omit words or mispronounce common words when they speak. They may also experience difficulty in fluency, as with a significant stuttering problem. Some students have far-reaching speech and language disorders in which they have significant problems receiving and producing language. They may communicate through pictures or sign language. Some students' primary disability is a speech or language disorder, and they

Connections

More complete descriptions of the characteristics and needs of students with disabilities and other special needs are found in Chapters 5, 6, and 7.

may receive services for this. For other students with disabilities, speech/language services supplement their educational services. For example, a student with a learning disability might also receive speech/language services, as might a student with autism or traumatic brain injury.

Mental retardation.   Students with **mental retardation** have significant limitations in cognitive ability and adaptive behaviors. They learn at a far slower pace than do other students, and they may reach a point at which their learning levels off. Although federal listing of disability categories does not distinguish between students with mild mental retardation and those with moderate and severe mental retardation, many state listings do. Despite the degree of mental retardation, most individuals with this disability can lead independent or semi-independent lives as adults and can hold an appropriate job. The term **cognitive disability** is sometimes used instead of mental retardation. In this text, we use the two terms interchangeably.

F Y I

Depression is more common among children than previously thought. More information on this serious disorder can be found in Chapter 6.

Emotional disturbance.   When a student has significant difficulty in the social/emotional domain, serious enough to interfere with the student's learning, an **emotional disturbance (ED)** exists. Students with this disability may have difficulty with interpersonal relationships and may respond inappropriately in emotional situations; that is, they may have trouble making and keeping friends, and they may get extremely angry when a peer teases or plays a joke on them, or show little or no emotion when the family pet dies. Some students with ED are depressed; others are aggressive. Students with ED display these impairments over a long period of time, across different settings, and to a degree significantly different from their peers. A student with an emotional disability is not just a student who is difficult to manage in a classroom; students with this disability have chronic and extremely serious emotional problems.

Autism.   Students with **autism** usually lack appropriate social responsiveness from a very early age. They generally avoid physical contact (e.g., cuddling and holding), and they may not make eye contact. Problems with social interactions persist as these children grow; they appear unaware of others' feelings and may not seek interactions with peers or adults. They may have unusual language patterns, including spoken language without intonation; echolalia, or repetition of others' speech; or little or no language. They may display repetitive body movements, such as rocking, and may need highly routinized behavior, such as a formalized procedure for putting on their clothes or eating their meals, to feel comfortable. Some students with autism have above-average intelligence; others have mental retardation. The causes of autism are not well understood, and the best approaches for working with students with autism are still under considerable debate.

F Y I

Hearing and visual impairments are referred to as *sensory* impairments. Students with these special needs are discussed in Chapter 5.

Hearing impairments.   Disabilities that concern the inability or limited ability to receive auditory signals are called **hearing impairments.** When students are **hard of hearing,** they have a significant hearing loss but are able to capitalize on residual hearing by using hearing aids and other amplifying systems. Students who are **deaf** have little or no residual hearing and therefore do not benefit from traditional devices to aid hearing; however, they may be assisted through the use of advanced

CASE IN PRACTICE

Problem Solving in Inclusive Schools: The Classroom Teacher's Role

At Highland Elementary School, staff members are meeting to discuss David, a third grader with autism. Ms. Dowley is David's teacher; Ms. Jackson is the special educator who provides needed support. Ms. Janes, the school psychologist, is also present.

Ms. Dowley: David is really a puzzle and a challenge. He is behaving so much better in class than he was at the beginning of the year, but he still disrupts the entire class when he has a bad day. One of the parents called yesterday to complain about David taking time away from her daughter and the rest of the class. I'm starting to feel the same way. I hope we can come up with some ideas to improve the whole situation.

Ms. Jackson: What kinds of things seem to trigger the problems?

Ms. Dowley: That's part of my concerns. I'm still pretty new at teaching, and I have my hands full with the whole class. I don't even have time to think carefully about what's happening with David. I just deal with him when he does something inappropriate—bothering another student, refusing to come with the group—without really thinking about how it happened or how to avoid it, if that's possible.

Ms. Janes: You've mentioned problem behavior as one issue. Before we start addressing that, are there any other issues we should be discussing, too?

Ms. Dowley: No. Right now, it's the behavior—and I want to be clear that I really can see all the other gains David has made. I *want* this to work for David and I know his parents do, too. They've been very helpful and always carry through with their part. I know David can be successful in my class—but it'll be much less stressful for all of us if we can work on his behavior.

Ms. Janes: It seems as though we need more information. One question I have is this: What happens with you and the other students when David does something inappropriate—talking in a loud voice, pushing books off the desk?

Ms. Dowley: Well, I try to ignore him, but that usually makes it worse. A few of the other students laugh, and that's not helping either.

Ms. Jackson: Maybe we should focus for a minute or two on when David doesn't have difficulty in class. What are the times of the day or the activities that David does without having behavior problems?

Ms. Dowley: Let's see. . . . He's usually fine and makes a good contribution when we're talking about science concepts. He loves science. When math is activity based, he's fine there, too.

Ms. Janes: Our meeting time is nearly up. I'd be happy to make time in my schedule to observe David, and perhaps Ms. Jackson could, too. I know you need answers right away, but I hope we can get a clearer sense of the pattern of David's behavior so we can find the right strategy for addressing it. If we can get in to observe this week, could we meet next Tuesday to try to generate some strategies?

Ms. Dowley: Sure. That would be great. Let's just work out the details on observing.

REFLECTIONS

Why was this meeting a positive example of teachers addressing a student problem in an inclusive school? What did they do that has set them up for success? If you were trying to understand David better, what other questions would you ask about him? What would you like others to observe in the classroom in relation to him? In relation to you as the teacher? What do you think will happen at the next meeting? On the basis of this case, how would you describe the role of classroom teachers in addressing the challenges of inclusion?

[Technology Notes]

Using Computers

Computers are one of the most readily available and helpful tools you will have for meeting the needs of students with disabilities in your classroom. Here are a few of the ways they can assist you.

1. **Computers as instructional assistants.** With the vast and ever-increasing array of computer software available for students of all ages, individualizing in classrooms and labs has become straightforward. You can provide a simpler math program to students not ready for your lesson on adding fractions; you can offer problem-solving practice at various levels. Computers can also enrich talented students' education and assist all students in maximizing their interests.

2. **Computers as a motivational tool.** For some students, opportunities to work on a computer can be tremendously rewarding. Students who have difficulty completing assignments might earn computer time as part of their instructional program.

3. **Computers as a means for adaptive communication.** Computers can help students communicate their ideas. Voice synthesizers can read to students with vision impairments, and specialized

Advances in computer technology can make a huge difference in the lives and learning of students with disabilities.

printers can translate braille into print or print into braille. For students with disabilities that prevent them from speaking, the computer offers a means to reach others. Computers fitted with picture boards help students with severe cognitive disabilities state their preferences and make their needs known.

4. **Computers as a data collection tool.** Using software that tracks the user's progress within the program, you can monitor student learning. For

technology such as cochlear implants. Depending on the extent of the disability, students with hearing impairments may use sign language, speech reading, and other ways to help them communicate.

Visual impairments. Disabilities that concern the inability or limited ability to receive information visually are called **visual impairments.** Some students are **partially sighted** and can learn successfully using magnification devices or other adaptive materials; students who are **blind** do not use vision as a means of learning and instead rely primarily on touch and hearing. Depending on need, students with visual impairments may use braille, specialized computers, and other aids to assist in learning. Some students need specialized training to help them learn to move around successfully in their environment.

example, most computer writing programs can easily count the number of words written at different intervals, which can provide you with a rough measure of student writing fluency. Likewise, many programs can track the number of math problems completed and the problem-solving level reached, which can give you a general sense of students' strengths and trouble spots.

5. **Computers for teacher record keeping.** Spending 5 or 10 minutes at the end of the school day entering attendance, permission forms returned, student scores, and student behavior data is a systematic and efficient way to keep professional records. Grading software can help you track student progress, as can spreadsheets. Simple files maintained with word processing are appropriate for anecdotal records on students you are concerned about.

6. **Computers for teacher communication.** Teachers can also use computers to manage their many communication responsibilities. For example, you can prepare the class newsletter more easily on a computer than by hand. Letters sent to parents, schedules for and notes on meetings, and your news can all be stored on the computer for future reference. By keeping such files, you can maintain a chronology of your correspondence, and you can also create certain types of letters and notes just once and then copy them for future use.

Many, many websites can assist you in thinking about using computers to work effectively with students with disabilities. The following websites might be especially helpful:

• The Office of Learning Technologies (OLT) within Human Resources Development Canada (HRDC) (http://olt-bta.hrdc-drhc.gc.ca/publicat/bibldise.html#tools) includes on its site a bibliographic listing of articles related to using learning technologies with students with learning disabilities.

• The Rehabilitation Engineering and Assistive Technology Society of North America (http://www.resna.org) is an organization of individuals concerned about technology and disabilities. The site includes a link to resources on making education accessible to individuals with disabilities.

• The Disability Resource Directory (DRD) (http://www.kansas.net/~cbaslock/index.html) has as its goal maintaining a directory of resources for individuals with disabilities. It includes a list of hardware and software for people with disabilities.

• The Center for Applied Special Technology (http://www.cast.org) is dedicated to making education accessible to all students. The website includes links to a wide variety of computer tools that can help students learn as well as other resources related to technology for special education.

Deaf-blindness.   Students who have both significant vision and hearing impairments are sometimes eligible for services as deaf-blind. These students are categorized separately because of the unique learning needs they have, particularly in the domain of communication, and the highly specialized services they require. The degree of the vision or hearing loss may vary from moderate to severe and may be accompanied by other disabilities. Students in this category are likely to receive special education services beginning at birth or very soon thereafter.

Orthopedic impairments.   Students with **orthopedic impairments** have physical conditions that seriously impair their ability to move about or to complete motor activities. Students who have cerebral palsy are included in this group, as are those with other diseases that affect the skeleton or muscles. Students with physical limitations

WWW Resources

Much information is available on the Internet about individuals with disabilities. One helpful source is the Internet Resources for Special Children (IRSC) website. It can be reached at http://www.irsc.org.

FYI

A *primary disability* is one that most significantly influences the student's education. A *secondary disability* is an additional disability that affects education, but to a lesser degree.

Cultural Awareness

Some families consider mental retardation, physical limitations, and sensory deficits disabilities, but they describe their children with learning disabilities as "a little slow" or "needing more help" (Linan-Thompson & Jean, 1997).

Check Your Learning

What are the high-incidence disabilities? What are the low-incidence disabilities? Why are these terms sometimes used instead of federal disability categories?

Connections

Additional information on specific disabilities is included in Chapters 5 and 6.

Research Note

Some teachers express concern about the time needed to work with students with disabilities in general education classrooms. Hollowood, Salisbury, Rainforth, and Palombaro (1995) found no evidence of this in their study of students with severe disabilities.

resulting from accidents may also be called orthopedically impaired. Some students with physical disabilities are unable to move about without a wheelchair and may need special transportation to get to school and a ramp to enter the school building. Others may lack the fine motor skills needed to write and require extra time or adapted equipment to complete assignments.

Traumatic brain injury (TBI).   Students with **traumatic brain injury (TBI)** have a wide range of characteristics and special needs, including limited strength or alertness, developmental delays, short-term memory problems, hearing or vision losses that may be temporary, irritability, and sudden mood swings. Their characteristics and needs depend on the specific injury they experienced, and their needs often change over time. Because TBI is a medical condition that affects education, diagnosis by a physician is required along with assessment of learning and adaptive behavior. Students who experience serious head trauma from automobile accidents, falls, and sports injuries are among those who might be eligible for services as TBI.

Other health impairments.   Some students have a disease or disorder so significant that it affects their ability to learn in school; the category of disability addressing these needs is called **other health impairments.** Students with severe asthma who require an adapted physical education program might be eligible for special education in this category, as might those who have chronic heart conditions necessitating frequent and prolonged absences from school. Students with diseases such as AIDS, sickle-cell anemia, and diabetes may be categorized as other health impaired, depending on the impact of their illness on learning. Also, some students with severe attention deficit–hyperactivity disorder (ADHD) receive special education services in this category.

Multiple disabilities.   The category used when students have two or more disabilities is **multiple disabilities.** Students in this group often have mental retardation as well as a physical disability, but this category may be used to describe any student with two or more disability types. However, this classification is used only when the student's disabilities are so serious and so interrelated that none can be identified as a primary disability.

Developmental disabilities.   Prior to 1997, the category **developmental disabilities** pertained only to children from 3 to 5 years old. However, when P.L. 105-17 was passed, this category was made an option that states could use for children from ages 3 through 9. This category includes youngsters who have significant delays in physical, cognitive, communication, social/emotional, or adaptive development. In 1997–1998, only six states used this category, and most of the children included in it were 6 years old. Only two states reported using this category for students at age 9.

Cross-Categorical Approaches to Special Education

Federal and state education agencies and local school districts use the categories of disabilities just described for counting the number of students in special education and for allocating money to educate them. When you prepare to teach a student, however, you will probably find that the specific category of disability often does not

Professional Edge

New Teachers and Responding to Diversity

Even though most new teachers are learning to expect diversity in their classrooms and express commitment to teaching heterogeneous groups, once in schools they sometimes encounter difficulty implementing their goals. Why does this happen?

Using the Research

Tomlinson and her colleagues (1997) studied elementary, middle school, and high school general education student teachers who had attended a workshop on teaching to diversity. Through observations, field notes, and interviews, the researchers identified the following themes that may interfere with novice teachers' use of strategies to meet student needs:

1. Novices enter a school culture that has implicit rules and procedures not necessarily conducive to inclusive practice.

2. School curricula are "covered"; that is, all students are expected to "get" the same information. The teacher's goal often is to get through the prescribed material.

3. All students get the same amount of time to complete all tasks.

4. The assessment of students generally is standardized, and if reteaching is indicated, it is done for all. Portfolios are considered interesting, but only as a supplement to traditional assessment.

5. Grades usually are a reflection of how much the student "got" in the fixed time allocated for particular lesson content.

6. Students who excel often are kept occupied with extra work and are viewed as somewhat problematic. The goal often becomes keeping them occupied while other students receive needed instruction.

7. Struggling learners are perceived as problems because they often do not master the content in the prescribed amount of time.

8. Classroom management in schools is often done from the front of the room, using whole-group strategies and uniform assignments. For many novice teachers, having multiple activities going on is daunting.

9. Differentiation of instruction is viewed as extraordinary and difficult to implement. Teachers often accept that some students will miss the lesson.

10. Often overwhelmed by being new to teaching, novices tend to succumb to the already-established practices of standardization.

This sobering study has many implications for classroom teachers. To what extent do the findings of these researchers match your experiences thus far in schools? Of the 10 themes, which 3 seem particularly important for you to understand? Either individually or as a group, what strategies could you undertake to ensure that your own commitment to differentiating instruction for students with disabilities and other special needs can be translated from a noble concept into day-to-day practice?

SOURCE: Adapted from "Becoming Architects of Communities of Learning: Addressing Academic Diversity in Contemporary Classrooms," by C. A. Tomlinson, C. M. Callahan, E. M. Tomchin, N. Eiss, M. Imbeau, & M. Landrum, 1997, *Exceptional Children, 63*, pp. 269–282.

---

guide you in discovering student strengths and in devising appropriate teaching strategies. In some states, some of the categories are combined to permit more flexibility for planning educational services. Also, students in different categories often benefit from the same instructional adaptations. Throughout this book, students are sometimes discussed in terms of only two categories. **High-incidence disabilities** are those that are most common, including learning disabilities, speech or language

WWW Resources

An additional website de-
voted to individuals with
disabilities is Special Education Resources on the
Internet (SERI). Topics to
explore on the site include
legal resources, parent resources, medical resources,
and specific disability categories. The website address
is http://www.hood.edu/
seri.

impairments, mild mental retardation, and emotional disturbance. Together, these
disabilities account for more than 80 percent of the disabilities reported in
1997–1998 (U.S. Department of Education, 1999). **Low-incidence disabilities** are
those that are less common and include all the other categories: moderate to severe
mental retardation, multiple disabilities, hearing impairments, orthopedic impairments, other health impairments, visual impairments, deaf-blindness, autism, traumatic brain injury, and developmental delays.

Consistent with a **cross-categorical approach,** characteristics of students with
disabilities are discussed in more detail in Chapters 5 and 6, where more attention
is paid to students' learning needs than to their labels. In addition, although some
strategies specific to categorical groups (e.g., the use of large-print books for students with vision impairments) are outlined in those chapters, most of the strategies
presented throughout the text can be adapted for most students. If you adopt a
cross-categorical approach in your own thinking about teaching students with disabilities, you will see that many options are available for helping students succeed.

Other Students with Special Needs

Not all students who have special learning and behavior needs are addressed in special education laws. Many of these other students, described in the following sections, benefit from the ideas presented throughout this book.

Students who are gifted or talented.   Students who demonstrate ability far above
average in one or several areas, including overall intellectual ability, leadership, specific academic subjects, creativity, athletics, or the visual or performing arts, are considered **gifted or talented.** Erin is included in this group; she seems to learn
without effort, and she is also eager to learn about almost everything. Evan is also
talented; still in elementary school, he has participated in state and national piano
recitals, and his parents have requested that he have access to the music room during recess so he can practice. Students who are gifted or talented are not addressed
in federal special education law. In the majority of states, separate laws exist that
provide guidelines for identifying and educating students with special talents. Funds
are not always provided to implement these laws, however, and so the availability
and scope of services for students with particular talents vary across the country and
even within a particular state.

Students protected by Section 504.   Some students not eligible to receive special
education services nonetheless will be entitled to protection through Section 504
and will receive specialized assistance because of their functional disabilities, as
described previously in this chapter. Among those likely to be included in this group
are students with **attention deficit–hyperactivity disorder (ADHD).** Students
with ADHD have a medical problem often characterized by an inability to attend to
complex tasks for long periods of time, excessive motor activity, and impulsivity.
The impact of this disorder on students' schoolwork can be significant. Identification of ADHD usually requires input from a physician. Students with ADHD may
take medication, such as Ritalin, that helps them focus their attention. The many
students with learning disabilities or emotional disturbance who also have ADHD
are, of course, already receiving assistance through IDEA-97.

Connections

Students with special
needs who are not neces-
sarily eligible for special
education are discussed in
more detail in Chapter 7.

What kinds of support do students with disabilities need in their general education classrooms? How can these supports be offered without disrupting the flow of instruction?

Students at risk. Often, the general term **at risk** refers to students who have characteristics, live in an environment, or have experiences that make them more likely than others to fail in school. Students whose primary language is not English are sometimes considered at risk, and they may need assistance in school learning. They may attend bilingual education programs or classes for English as a second language (ESL) for opportunities to learn English while also learning the standard curriculum. However, some students in this group may also have disabilities.

A second group of at-risk students includes **slow learners,** whose educational progress is below average but who do not have a learning disability or mental retardation. These students are learning to the best of their ability, but they often cannot keep pace with the instruction in most general education classrooms without assistance. They are sometimes described as "falling between the cracks" of the educational system because most professionals agree they need special assistance, but they are not eligible for special education. They sometimes, however, receive assistance in remedial reading or tutorial programs.

Other students who might be considered at risk include those who are homeless or live in poverty, who are born to mothers abusing drugs or alcohol, who are drug or alcohol abusers themselves, or who are abused. Students in these groups are at risk for school failure because of the environments or circumstances in which they live.

You may find that students with special needs who do not have disabilities according to special education laws are particularly puzzling because no single group of professionals is responsible for educating them. As students with disabilities spend increasing amounts of time in general education classes, special education teachers and other special services providers often informally assist teachers in planning and adapting educational activities for these students. Thus, other students with special needs often benefit from the trend toward inclusive education for students with disabilities.

Cultural Awareness

Students whose language at home is not English are sometimes inappropriately assigned to special education because of academic difficulties actually caused by lack of proficiency in English.

Summary

Special education refers to the specialized instruction received by the millions of students in the United States who have disabilities and is based on the concept of the least restrictive environment (LRE). Current special education practices have evolved from a combination of factors, including the inception of compulsory public education early in the 20th century, research questioning instructional practices for students with disabilities, the civil rights movement and related court cases, and a series of federal civil rights and education laws.

The present trend in special education is toward inclusive practices, but understanding inclusion and implementing instructional practices to support it is complex. Teachers' perceptions of inclusion and their knowledge and skills for teaching in diverse classrooms affect the quality of many programs. Parents generally react favorably to inclusion in terms of social outcomes for their children, but they have concerns related to academic and functional outcomes. Data suggest that many students with high-incidence or low-incidence disabilities can succeed in inclusive classrooms, but not all. Essential for inclusion is attention to systemic issues such as administrative leadership, personnel, time allocation, and cost.

Federal law identifies 12 categories of disabilities that may entitle students to special education services: learning disabilities, speech or language impairments, mental retardation, emotional disturbance, autism, hearing impairments, visual impairments, deaf-blindness, orthopedic impairments, traumatic brain injury, other health impairments, and multiple disabilities. However, many other students with special needs also need assistance, including those who are gifted or talented; who have attention deficits; who are at risk, including non-native English speakers and slow learners. Classroom teachers are often responsible for instructing students with disabilities and other special needs.

Applications in Teaching Practice

Understanding Contemporary Special Education Practices

It is a new school year—your first as a teacher in the Danville School District. You learn that you will be responsible for the following students:

- Cassie is a bright young woman who has a visual impairment. To read, she uses a computer that greatly magnifies her materials. She also needs to work in bright light, and she gets fatigued from the effort required to use what little vision she has.

- Ramon is a young man identified as having a learning disability. His reading ability is at an early first-grade level. He also seems disorganized. He often forgets to bring materials and assignments to class, and he even forgets to return permission forms for field trips he wants to participate in.

- Tory lives in a foster home. He was removed from his mother's home because of several incidents of abuse. Tory is an angry child. He often refuses to work; he sometimes loses his temper and throws a book or crumples a paper; and he misses school frequently.

Questions

1. What are the possible strengths that Cassie, Ramon, and Tory might bring to your classroom? How could their possible strengths be emphasized instead of their problems? What is the rationale for assigning these students to a general education classroom? What might be the goals you as a classroom teacher could accomplish with them?
2. If you spoke with a supporter of inclusive practices, what would that person say about the opportunities created by having these students in class? What positive outcomes might that person mention? How would that person discuss your responsibility to make accommodations that help these students succeed?
3. If you spoke with an opponent of inclusive practices, what would that person say about the legitimate concerns you should have about your role in educating Cassie, Ramon, and Tory? What might this person say about student outcomes and systemic supports for inclusion?
4. If you spoke with a parent of Cassie, Ramon, and Tory, what might you expect each to say? What could you do to encourage parent participation for your students?
5. When you think about your responsibilities for educating students with disabilities and other special needs in your classroom—whether in kindergarten or in a senior-level, content-area class—what are your concerns and questions? In what ways do you think you can make a contribution to your students' education? What types of supports might you need? If you write your responses to these questions, keep them with your text and use them as a basis for discussion as you learn more in later chapters.

Special Education Procedures and Services

After you read this chapter, you will be
able to

1. Explain the roles and responsibilities of
   the members of instructional teams for
   students with disabilities.

2. Describe the process through which a
   student may become eligible to receive
   special education services.

3. Name the components of individualized education programs (IEP) and
   provide examples of them.

4. Describe the types of services that students with disabilities may receive and
   the settings in which they may receive
   them.

5. Discuss how parents participate in special education decision making and
   what occurs when parents and school
   district representatives disagree.

6. Outline the role of the general education teacher in the procedures and services of special education.

Key Terms and Concepts

Annual review (p. 55)

Due process (p. 58)

**Individualized education program (IEP)
(p. 34)**

Instructional assistance team (p. 48)

Mediation (p. 59)

Multidisciplinary team (MDT) (p. 51)

Three-year reevaluation (p. 57)

Transition plan (p. 63)

■ Mr. Vazquez is concerned. He teaches third grade,
and one of his students, Marcus, is having increasing difficulty in the curriculum. Marcus reads at a beginning first-
grade level, has learned just a few of the basic addition math
facts, and increasingly is refusing to do any work at all. The
other children are teasing him, and he reacts by using profanity and threatening to "get" them. Mr. Vazquez isn't sure
what to do next; the strategies he has used in the past have
not had an impact, and the difficulties Marcus is encounter-
ing are far beyond typical variations in learning rate and
style. Mr. Vazquez has met with Marcus's mother and step-
father. They report they are having more and more difficulty
getting Marcus to mind them. Marcus's parents are concerned that he doesn't seem to care about school and that he
is spending much of his time hanging out with older boys.
They are worried about gangs and drugs. What steps should
Mr. Vazquez take next? Whom might Mr. Vazquez contact
to help him decide whether Marcus's difficulties are serious
enough to consider assessing him for special education?

■ Ms. Lee, a high school English teacher, has just
pulled from her mailbox something titled "Helping Your
Students with Special Needs Succeed." As she glances
through it, she realizes that it is a summary of the Individualized Education Program (IEP) for Jennifer, one of her students. The summary includes a list of test accommodations
Jennifer should receive, and it mentions steps being taken to
help Jennifer prepare for a vocational program she'll attend
after high school. Ms. Lee notes that the speech/language
therapist, the transition specialist, and the social worker are
mentioned, but the special education teacher is listed as the
person to contact to answer questions. What roles do classroom teachers play in writing and implementing IEP goals
and objectives? What is their responsibility for ensuring that
IEP accommodations are available in the classroom? Who
are the other service providers teachers may work with as
they educate students with disabilities?

■ Ms. Turner teaches science to seventh graders. She
just received a note in her box asking her to attend the annual review for Changyi, a sixth grader who has a severe
physical disability. Ms. Turner gathers her grade book and a
sample of Changyi's work in class as dictated to her personal
assistant. She then jots a few notes to herself to prepare for

the meeting. She knows that the teachers on her middle school team take turns attending students' annual reviews to ensure that a general education point of view is represented. Ms. Turner also knows that Mr. Prather, the assistant principal, and Mr. Tsai, the special education teacher on her team, will attend the meeting, along with Changyi's mother. What is an annual review? What is Ms. Turner's responsibility for participating in the annual review?

FYI

General education teachers' roles in relation to special education are especially critical given the changes occurring throughout education as part of school reform. Many professionals hope that we will soon have one integrated education system (Telzrow, 1999), not a special education system distinct and separate from general education.

As a teacher, you will encounter students who are struggling. Some may appear to be doing everything they can *not* to learn. Others try their best but are still not successful. You might even have students whom you suspect have a vision or hearing problem so serious that it prevents them from learning. You may find yourself wondering whether some of these students should be receiving special education services and who will provide them. This chapter introduces you to people who specialize in working with students with disabilities and procedures for deciding whether a student is eligible for special education services. You will also learn how students' individualized instructional programs are designed and monitored, and which services students with disabilities use. You will discover that parents play a crucial role in special education procedures, and when they or students disagree with school professionals about special services, procedures exist to help them resolve these problems. Most important, you will learn about your role in working with other professionals and parents to determine student eligibility for special education, carrying out students' educational programs, and monitoring student learning.

Who Are the Professionals in Special Education?

Students with disabilities are entitled to a wide range of services. Not surprisingly, many different individuals, sometimes collectively referred to as special services staff, can be involved in the delivery of these services. You will probably interact with some of the professionals, such as special education teachers, almost every day. Others you might work with only occasionally. Some of these professionals serve students indirectly, or they work only with the few students who have the most challenging disabilities. Together, however, these educators create, implement, and evaluate the special education that students with disabilities receive.

General Education Teachers

You, the **general education teacher,** are the first professional discussed in this section because for many students with suspected or documented disabilities, you are the person who has the most detailed knowledge of the students' day-to-day needs in your classroom. Your responsibilities span several areas. You are the person most likely to bring to the attention of other professionals a student whom you suspect may have a disability; that is, you may encounter a student who is reading signifi-

Who are the professionals who support students with disabilities and their classroom teachers? What is the classroom teacher's role in identifying students with disabilities and providing their instruction?

cantly and persistently below grade level, a student whose behavior is so different from other students' that you suspect an emotional disorder, or a student who has extraordinary difficulty focusing on learning. When you suspect a disability, you will document the student's characteristics and behaviors that led to your concern by gathering samples of the student's work, compiling descriptions of the student's behavior, and keeping notes of how you have addressed the student's problem (Safran & Safran, 1996). You will work with special education colleagues to attempt accommodations in your classroom to clarify whether the student's problems need further exploration (Kovaleski, Gickling, Morrow, & Swank, 1999). If the student is referred for assessment for special education, you can contribute information about the student's academic and social functioning in your classroom, and you can help identify the student's strengths, needs, and educational program components. For example, you might help others understand the curricular expectations in your classroom and the types of adaptations that may be necessary for the student to succeed there. If special education services are deemed necessary, you will participate in deciding appropriate goals and objectives. You might also assist special services staff in updating parents on their child's quarterly and yearly progress. Most important, you will be expected to work with special services staff to provide appropriate instruction within your classroom (Bennett, DeLuca, & Bruns, 1997; DeBettencourt, 1999; Salend & Duhaney, 1999; Soodak, Podell, & Lehman, 1998; Stainback, Stainback, & Stefanich, 1996). The responsibilities of a general education teacher are summarized in Figure 2.1.

When all your responsibilities are listed, your role in planning and providing special services to students may seem overwhelming. However, studies of general education teachers' perceptions of their roles in working with students with disabilities generally indicate that teachers are able and willing to contribute to students' education as long as some conditions are met. The most important conditions seem to be administrative leadership, staff preparation, time for teacher planning,

Figure 2.1 General Education Teacher Responsibilities in Special Education

Member of prereferral or intervention assistance team

Provider of day-to-day instruction

Identifier of students with possible special needs

Communication link with colleagues

Member of multidisciplinary team that writes the IEP

Liaison to parents

and adequate funding and other resources for program support (Fox & Ysseldyke, 1997; Taylor, Richards, Goldstein, & Schilit, 1997).

Special Education Teachers

Check Your Learning

What are the typical responsibilities of special education teachers? Why do they have different job titles?

The professionals with whom you are most likely to have ongoing contact in teaching students with disabilities are **special education teachers.** They are responsible for managing and coordinating the services a student receives, including writing and implementing a student's **Individualized Education Program (IEP).** They also typically provide direct instruction to students on their caseloads (Wood, 1998). In addition, they may consult with you regarding a student suspected of having a disability and work with you to determine whether a referral for assessment for possible special education is warranted.

Depending on the state in which you teach and the students in your classroom, you may work with different types of special education teachers. Sometimes, special education teachers are assigned to work with any of the students with disabilities in your class. For example, a special education teacher may support your student with learning disabilities, but also work with a student with a moderate cognitive disability or a communication disorder. That professional works indirectly with other special education professionals to ensure that each student's educational plan is being implemented and monitored. In some locales, special education teachers work with a specific category of students. For example, your school may have a teacher for students with learning disabilities or emotional disabilities. Likewise, a teacher for students with vision or hearing impairments may be available if needed. In states that do not use categorical labels for students, some teachers teach students with high-incidence disabilities or low-incidence disabilities, or they may work with *any* student who has an IEP.

In yet other situations, special education teachers may be designated by the type of services they provide. For example, for some students with high-incidence disabilities in your class, you may work with a **consulting teacher** (Friend & Cook, 2000). This professional might meet with you regularly to monitor student progress and address your concerns about the students but might not directly teach them. You might also work with a **resource teacher** (Evans, Harris, Adeigbola, Houston, & Argott, 1993), who might divide time between directly instructing students and working with teachers.

A third type of special education teacher designated by type of services is an **inclusion specialist** or **support facilitator** (Janney, Snell, Beers, & Raynes, 1995). In inclusive schools, inclusion specialists are responsible for providing some student instruction, for problem solving with teachers, and for coordinating the services the student receives. Often, they focus on ensuring that the needs of students with moderate, severe, or multiple disabilities are being met.

If you work in a school district where each school has only a few students with disabilities, the special educator you interact with might be an **itinerant teacher.** Itinerant teachers often have roles like the professionals just described, but they travel between two or more school sites to provide services to students. Teachers for students with vision or hearing disabilities are sometimes itinerant. However, teachers who specialize in working with students with high-incidence disabilities may also deliver services this way, especially in districts with small enrollments.

One other type of special education teacher is a **transition specialist.** This professional typically works in a high school setting and helps prepare students to leave school for vocational training, employment, or postsecondary education (Brody-Hasazi, Furney, & DeStefano, 1999). No matter what you teach, you might work very closely with a transition specialist, especially in business education, consumer sciences, industrial or other vocational arts, or similar areas. However, this professional also spends time working directly with students to assess their skills and interests, arranges for them to explore vocational and educational opportunities, and assists them in finding and keeping jobs or locating an appropriate college or trade school. A transition specialist also works with community businesses to arrange student job sites and to resolve problems related to student workers (Cronin, 1996). He or she may also serve as a **job coach,** accompanying a student to a job site and helping the student master the skills needed to do the job successfully.

As the nature of special education services changes, so do job responsibilities and titles of special educators. For example, you might find that the professionals in your school who used to be called special education teachers are now referred to as *special services teachers (SSTs).* This change in title represents an effort to delabel teachers and parallels efforts to deemphasize students' labels. As schools work to become more inclusive, the vocabulary related to teachers who work with students

Research Note

Wood (1998) studied teachers' perceptions of their roles in schools that include students with severe disabilities. She found that when inclusion was new, special education and general education kept clear role boundaries. As they worked together, however, those boundaries blurred.

Check Your Learning

Based on the grade and subject area you plan to teach, with which special educators are you most likely to work?

with special needs continues to evolve. More importantly, regardless of the type of special education teachers you work with, you will find that they are important instructional partners, no longer relegated to teaching just in a special education classroom. They support students by creating adapted materials, teaching with you in the general education classroom, working directly and separately with students who have disabilities, and often serving as a coordinator for all the services any single student may receive.

Other Specialists and Related Service Providers

In addition to working with special education teachers, you will have contact with a variety of other service providers. They, too, play important roles in educating students with disabilities.

School psychologists.   These professionals offer at least two types of expertise related to educating students with disabilities. First, **school psychologists** often have a major responsibility for determining a student's cognitive, academic, social, emotional, and/or behavioral functioning. They typically contribute a detailed written analysis of the student's strengths and areas of need; in many school districts, this document is referred to as a "psych. report," that is, a psychological report. In a related role, school psychologists sometimes chair the multidisciplinary team that meets to decide whether a student has a disability and, if so, what types of services are needed.

A second major task for school psychologists is designing strategies to address students' academic and social behavior problems (Rosenfield & Gravois, 1996). Sometimes, school psychologists serve as behavior consultants. Occasionally, they assist a teacher by working with an entire class group on social skills. They might also provide individual assistance to students with emotional or behavioral problems who are not eligible for special education. Unfortunately, many school districts can employ only enough school psychologists to complete required assessment duties; when this occurs, school psychologists are seldom available to assist students or teachers directly (Giangreco, Prelock, Reid, Dennis, & Edelman, 2000).

Counselors.   Although **counselors** most often advise high school students, they also work at other school levels and contribute to the education of students with disabilities (Scarborough & Deck, 1998). For example, counselors in some school districts assess students' social and emotional functioning, including such areas as self-concept; motivation; attitude toward school, peers, and teachers; and social skills. Counselors also can provide services to both teachers and students. For teachers, they might suggest ways to draw out a student who is excessively shy, to build into the curriculum activities designed to enhance students' self-concept, and to create an emotionally safe classroom environment. For students, counselors might arrange group sessions with students from several classes who share specific needs, or they might work with an entire class on how to interact with a peer who has a disability.

Speech/language therapists.   Many students with disabilities have communication needs. Some have mild problems in pronouncing words or speaking clearly. Others have extremely limited vocabulary. Yet others can make only a few sounds and rely on alternative means of communication, such as communication boards. The professionals who specialize in meeting students' communication needs are **speech/language therapists.** They have a tremendously diverse range of school responsibilities. At the primary level, they might work with entire classes on language development or with individual students on pronouncing sounds. At the intermediate level, they might work on vocabulary with a group of students, but might also help a student with a moderate cognitive disability to pronounce some word more clearly or to combine words into sentences. At the high school level, they often focus on functional vocabulary and work mostly with students with low-incidence disabilities. For example, they might help a student with a cognitive disability learn to read common signs and complete tasks such as ordering in a restaurant or asking for assistance.

Social workers. Social workers' expertise is similar to that of counselors in terms of being able to help teachers and students address social and emotional issues. Thus, they may serve as consultants to teachers and also may provide individual or group assistance to students. However, **social workers** have additional expertise. They often are the liaison between the school and the family. For example, they can create a family history by interviewing parents and visiting a student's home; this information may be critical in determining whether a student needs special education services. Similarly, they may help other school professionals work with families on matters such as gaining access to community health services. The school social worker often follows up on teacher reports about the suspected abuse or neglect of students. In some school districts, both counselors and social workers are available to meet student needs. In others, only one of these professional groups is employed.

Physical therapists and occupational therapists. For some students to benefit from education, they require assistance for problems with gross and fine motor skills. Physical and occupational therapists are the professionals who have expertise in these areas.

   Physical therapists assess students' needs and provide interventions related to gross motor skills. They might participate on a multidisciplinary team by assessing such areas as the obviously awkward gait of a student suspected of having a disability. They also interpret information about a student's physical needs that has been provided by a physician. For students with identified disabilities, physical therapists might provide direct training in large muscle movement and control. They also might monitor student needs related to how they should be positioned, whether in a wheelchair, standing with assistance, or on the floor; how their physical needs are affecting their educational needs; and how classroom settings can be adapted to accommodate their needs.

   Occupational therapists are concerned with fine motor skills; they often have the responsibility of assessing students' use of their hands and fingers and developing and implementing plans for improving related motor skills. For example, an occupational therapist may assess whether a student with a severe learning disability can appropriately grip and use a pencil. This professional might help younger students or those with more severe disabilities learn skills for feeding or dressing themselves. Occupational therapists are working increasingly with teachers to incorporate fine motor skills training into classroom routines.

Adaptive physical educators. When students have significant gross or fine motor problems, typical physical education programs in schools may not be able to address their needs directly. **Adaptive physical educators** assess students' motor needs and work with teachers, physical educators, and others to meet them, or they work directly with students. These professionals are experts in adapting traditional physical education activities for students with disabilities. For example, they might create a simplified form of a basketball drill so that a student who has difficulty running can participate in the activity. They also might create activities that help students develop such skills as balancing, skipping, running, or throwing.

Nurses. A link between students' medical and educational needs is provided by **nurses.** They develop student medical histories as needed, and they may screen students for vision and hearing problems. They also provide the team with information about specific medical conditions a student might have and the impact a student's medication might have on educational performance. Further, nurses assist other professionals in deciding whether a student's learning or behavior problem could have a medical basis and discussing such matters with parents. Nurses most often are responsible for ensuring day to day that students with disabilities take required medication and for providing first aid or other emergency treatment. They also work with teachers and families to monitor student medical needs (for example, whether a change in medication is causing drowsiness or hyperactivity).

Administrators. The school principal, assistant principal, and sometimes a special education department chairperson or team leader are the **administrators** most likely to participate actively in the education of students with disabilities. Their role is to offer knowledge about the entire school community and provide perspective on school district policies regarding special education. Administrators assist the multidisciplinary team in determining students' eligibility for services and exploring strategies for meeting their needs. They also play an important role in addressing parent concerns. Every team that determines whether a student is eligible for special education must have administrative representation. For example, in one school, the mother of Marisha, a student with severe language delays, requested that her daughter receive speech/language therapy for 40 minutes daily. School professionals were in agreement that this amount of therapy was not appropriate. Dr. Wade, the principal, worked with the team and the parent to negotiate the amount of speech therapy needed to accomplish Marisha's goals.

In some locales, especially in large urban and suburban districts where it is difficult to ensure that all required special education procedures are followed, a **special services coordinator** is part of the district's administration. Special services coordinators specialize in special education procedural information. They help alleviate the pressure on school administrators for accurately interpreting and following guidelines. They also explain services and options to parents, problem solve with teachers when issues arise, and assist in monitoring to ensure that students with disabilities receive needed supports.

Paraprofessionals. Individuals who assist teachers and others in the provision of services to students with disabilities are called **paraprofessionals** (French, 1999a). Although paraprofessionals, also sometimes referred to as *paraeducators* or *teaching assistants*, may be certified teachers, they are considered noncertified staff according to the terms of their employment; that is, their responsibilities for decision making about students are limited. Paraprofessionals also might be called *instructional assistants*, *aides*, or other titles, depending on local practices.

Research Note

Although many educators see paraprofessionals as essential for inclusion, a risk is that they could have too much responsibility for student learning, in essence, functioning as a child's teacher instead of a support. Marks, Schrader, and Levine (1999), in interviewing paraeducators of students in grades K–8, found this to be the case.

School districts use paraprofessionals in many different ways (French, 1999b; Marks, Schrader, & Levine, 1999). Two of the most common are these: First, some paraprofessionals are assigned to a specific student who needs ongoing individual assistance. For example, students with no ability to move their arms may have a paraprofessional who takes notes for them and completes other tasks such as feeding. A few students have medical conditions requiring that a specially trained paraprofessional be present to monitor their status. Paraprofessionals in this role may be referred to as **personal assistants.** They may also be called **one-to-one assistants.**

Second, and more common, is a paraprofessional who assists in the delivery of special services for many students. These paraprofessionals often work in both inclusive classrooms and special education classrooms as well as on the playground, at assemblies, and during bus duty. They have primary responsibility for working with students with disabilities, but they sometimes also help other students and the teacher as the need arises and time permits. The Professional Edge on pages 40–41 contains more information about working with paraprofessionals.

Other specialists. Depending on student needs and state and local practice, other professionals also may participate in the education of students with disabilities. For example, in some states a **psychometrist** completes much of the individual assessment of students potentially eligible for special education services and of those already receiving services. Sometimes, school districts have **consultants** who are used only when a need exists in their specific area of expertise (for example, significant behavior problems, autism, traumatic brain injury). If you work in a school district in which many students are non-native English speakers, you may also work with **bilingual teachers** or **bilingual special education teachers.** Bilingual teachers are not special educators, but they sometimes help in decision making related to students with disabilities who have limited English skills. Bilingual special education teachers are professionally trained both in special education and in bilingual education (Salend, Dorney, & Mazo, 1997).

Two other types of specialists may provide services to your students with disabilities. One is a **mobility specialist** whose job is to help students with vision impairments learn how to become familiar with their environments and how to travel from place to place safely. They consult with classroom teachers regarding students with vision impairments. The other type of service provider is a **sign language interpreter.** Interpreters are the communication link for students with significant hearing impairments (Jones, Clark, & Soltz, 1997). Interpreters listen to the instruction in a classroom and relay it to students with hearing impairments using sign language. Interpreters might accompany a student all day or might be needed only in academic subjects such as language arts.

Professionals from agencies outside the school are also part of the specialist group. If a student has been receiving services through a hospital or residential program, a physician, nurse, social worker, or other representative from there may work with school personnel to ensure that the student has a smooth transition back to school. Individuals from the medical community also might be involved when students are being assessed for attentional problems or when they have been injured or ill. Professionals from agencies also might be included when a student is receiving assistance from a community service organization or has contact with the juvenile justice system. In these instances, caseworkers may serve as liaisons to the school. Students who are transitioning from school to adult services may need services from a professional in vocational rehabilitation. Finally, parents who wish may obtain an

Connections

Additional information about working with paraprofessionals is included in the Professional Edge on pages 40–41 and also in Chapter 3.

Cultural Awareness

In schools with many students whose native language is not English, bilingual translators could be provided to assist in communication with students and parents.

Professional Edge

Working with Paraprofessionals

No matter what grade level you teach nor the type of school district you teach in, it is likely at some point that you will work closely with a paraprofessional, also called a paraeducator. These individuals are employed by school districts to provide support to students with disabilities, either by working with a particular student one-to-one, or by working in general or special education classrooms with several students.

Although paraprofessionals have been a part of special education services and supports for many years, only recently has much attention been paid to their preparation for their roles. IDEA-97 specifically addresses this issue; it states that paraprofessionals should receive training in the skills needed to do their jobs effectively. Another area of concern for paraprofessionals is the scope of their responsibilities. Paraprofessionals do not have sole responsibility for any aspect of a student's educational program. Rather, they share responsibilities with teachers and other multidisciplinary team members. The following is a list of those shared responsibilities:

- Locate, arrange, or construct instructional materials.
- Assist students with eating, dressing, personal care, and bathroom use.

- Instruct the special education student individually, in small or large groups, and with peers as specified in the IEP or by professionals on the service delivery team.
- Collect student data to contribute to professional team members regarding student progress toward goals.
- Score tests and certain papers using a key.
- Maintain files or records about students.
- Supervise playgrounds, halls, lunchrooms, busses, and loading zones.
- Provide specific health needs (for example, suction tracheotomy tubes, as delegated and trained by school nurse).
- Assist and facilitate appropriate peer interactions.
- Assist students using adaptive equipment or devices.
- Support student behavior and social needs according to plans.
- Participate positively in evaluative or feedback sessions for the improvement of skills.
- Participate in training and coaching sessions to improve skills associated with all duties and tasks assigned.

expert opinion from a specialist not associated with the school, and those individuals can attend team meetings or submit written reports for team consideration.

Connections

Additional information on parent roles in working with teachers and other school professionals is included in Chapter 3.

Parents, students, and advocates. Whenever decisions are being made concerning a student with a suspected or documented disability, the best interests of the student and his or her family must be represented. Parents have the right to participate in virtually all aspects of their child's educational program (National Information Center for Children and Youth with Disabilities, 1998; Osborne, 1996; Rothstein, 1995). Parent involvement spans the following areas:

1. Requesting assessment for special services
2. Providing input on their child's strengths and needs
3. Bringing to the team independent professionals' opinions about their child's needs

- Communicate with professionals about their work and students' progress on assigned tasks.
- Move students from one place to another, assisting students with mobility.
- Contribute to the effectiveness of the team by using appropriate communication, problem-solving, and conflict management strategies.

From the Research

As the list suggests, paraprofessionals offer many valuable services to students and to teachers in support of students. However, particularly when paraprofessionals are assigned to function as personal assistants to students with severe disabilities, problems can occur. Giangreco, Edelman, Luiselli, and MacFarland (1997) noticed the tendency of some assistants to hover around their charges in inclusive settings, and they decided to explore this topic systematically. Based on interview and observational data collected in 16 classrooms in 11 school districts with students ranging in age from 4 through 20 who were served by a total of 134 team members, the researchers found the following problems were caused by paraprofessionals' ongoing proximity to students:

- Interference with ownership and responsibility by general educators

- Separation of students from classmates
- Student dependence on adults
- Negative impact on interactions of students with typical peers
- Limitations on students receiving competent instruction
- Loss of student personal control
- Loss of student gender identity (especially with bathroom use for males with female assistants)
- Interference with the instruction of typical learners

This research strongly suggests that paraprofessionals need clear instruction regarding their functioning in general education classrooms. It also indicates how important it is that you understand not just how paraprofessionals can assist students, but how their actions can unintentionally interfere with students' education, too.

SOURCE: Adapted from "Paraeducators and Teachers: Shifting Roles," by N. French, 1999, *Teaching Exceptional Children, 32*(2), 69–73; and "Helping or Hovering? Effects of Instructional Assistant Proximity on Students with Disabilities," by M. F. Giangreco, S. W. Edelman, T. E. Luiselli, and S. Z. C. MacFarland, 1997, *Exceptional Children, 64*, pp. 7–18.

4. Helping to decide whether their child has a disability and whether the child will receive special services
5. Assisting in writing goals and objectives for their child's educational program
6. Participating in delivering instruction to their child
7. Monitoring their child's progress
8. Seeking assistance in resolving disagreements with school professionals

Often, parents are strong allies for general education teachers. They can assist teachers by reviewing at home what is taught in school, rewarding their child for school accomplishments, and working with school professionals to resolve behavior and academic problems.

Whenever appropriate, students with disabilities can also be active participants in decision making about their own education. Increasingly, educators are involving students so they can directly state their needs and goals and can learn to advocate for

What is the role of parents in their child's learning? How do parents contribute on teams that decide whether a student needs special education services?

Connections

The topics of student self-advocacy and student self-evaluation are addressed in depth in Chapter 10.

WWW Resources

The National Information Center for Children and Youth with Disabilities makes available to parents and others many publications related to special education. Your Child's Evaluation, available at http://nichy.org/pubs/basicpar/bp1text.htm, outlines the entire process of obtaining special education services.

themselves. The extent of student participation on the team depends on the age of the student and the type and impact of the disability. The older the student and the greater his or her cognitive functioning, the greater the participation. Thus, first-grade students with disabilities will not be expected to participate in very many decisions about their education. However, high school students with disabilities are quite likely to attend and participate in team meetings for them and request adaptations to help them learn. These students also might monitor their learning and behavior and assess their progress toward their educational goals. They often have strong opinions about the types of supports that are most helpful to them (Lovitt, Plavins, & Cushing, 1999).

A final team member is an **advocate.** Sometimes, parents sense that they are not knowledgeable enough about the policies and procedures that govern special education to represent themselves. In other instances, they are not sure school district personnel are acting in the best interests of their children. In yet other situations, parents may be uncomfortable interacting with school personnel because of language or cultural differences, or for other reasons. Parents have the right to bring an advocate to team and other school meetings concerning their children. This person serves as their advisor and sometimes their spokesperson. Although advocates often do not have a direct role in implementing the education program for a student with a disability, they might assume responsibilities for the parent. Advocates are sometimes professionals who are compensated by parents for their services. Or they may be volunteers provided through a professional organization or parent support group, or friends or relatives.

How Can You Decide Whether a Student Need Might Be a Disability?

You will play a key role in deciding whether a student in your class should be evaluated for the presence of a disability. Although students with obvious cognitive, sensory, or physical impairments probably have been identified before reaching school age, learning, language, attention, and behavior disabilities often are not diagnosed until children start school. Because you are the professional in daily contact with the student, you are the person most likely to notice an unmet need. It is your judgment that often initiates a special education decision making process.

Analyze Unmet Needs

As you teach, you will sometimes discover that you have a nagging concern about a student. This concern might begin early in the school year, or it might take several months to emerge. When you review student records and your own impressions of the student and your concern, you decide that the student's achievement is not within your classroom's typical range, given the standards of your school district and community expectations. Should you ask other professionals to assess the student for eligibility for special education? Perhaps. But first, you need to ask yourself some questions. These questions are summarized in Figure 2.2.

What are specific examples of unmet needs? Having a nebulous concern about a student is far different than specifically stating what your concerns are. For example, sensing that a student is unmotivated is not a clear concern. What does the student do that leads you to conclude that motivation is a problem? Is it that the student doesn't make eye contact when speaking to you, or that the rewards and consequences that affect other students seem to have no effect—positive or negative—on this student? Vague concerns and hunches should be supported by specific information. Phrases such as "slow learning," "poor attitude toward school," "doesn't pay attention," and "never gets work completed" might have very different meanings to different professionals. To prepare to share your concern with others, then, your first step is to ask yourself, "When I say the student . . . , what are examples that clarify what I mean?"

Is there a chronic pattern negatively affecting learning? Nearly all students go through periods in which they struggle to learn, behave inappropriately, or otherwise cause you concern. Sometimes, a situation outside of school affects students. For example, parents divorcing, families being evicted from their apartments, elderly grandparents moving in with the family, or a family member being injured or arrested might all negatively affect student learning or behavior. However, the impact of these traumatic events should not be permanent, and the student should gradually return to previous levels of functioning.

Students with disabilities may also be affected by specific situations or events, but their learning and behavior needs form a chronic pattern. They struggle over a long period of time regardless of the circumstances. For example, Betsy, who has a learning disability, has difficulty learning sight words no matter what level or how

FYI

The National Resource Center on Family Based Services at the University of Iowa conducts research, provides technical assistance and training, and distributes information on family-centered approaches to serving students with exceptionalities.

Figure 2.2　Teacher Concerns about Student Needs

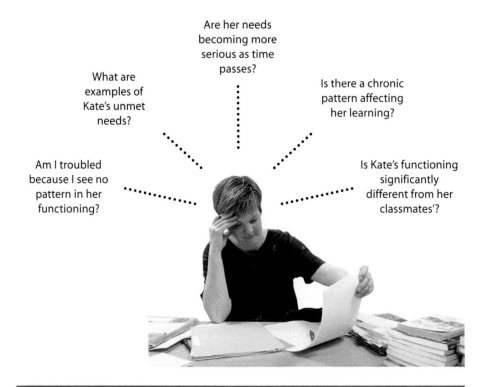

Are her needs becoming more serious as time passes?

What are examples of Kate's unmet needs?

Is there a chronic pattern affecting her learning?

Am I troubled because I see no pattern in her functioning?

Is Kate's functioning significantly different from her classmates'?

creatively they are introduced. Jared, a high school student with an emotional disability, is withdrawn whether sitting in a large class or interacting in a small group. Julianna, an eighth grader who had a severe head injury last year, usually seems to grasp abstract concepts as they are taught, but she struggles to describe or apply them after instruction.

Is the unmet need becoming more serious as time passes?　Sometimes, a student's needs appear to become greater across time. For example, Ben, who seemed to see well at the beginning of the school year, now holds books closer and closer to his face, squints when he tries to read, and complains about headaches. Karen, who began the school year fairly close in achievement to her peers, is significantly behind by November. Indications that needs are increasing are a signal to ask for input from others.

Is the student's functioning significantly different from that of classmates?　As you think about your concerns about a student, you should ask yourself how the student compares to other students. For example, it has been demonstrated in urban settings that students at risk for special education referral are less involved in the classroom and receive less verbal feedback from their teachers (Bay & Bryan, 1992). If you have six students who are all struggling, the reason might be that the informa-

Connections

Chapter 8 contains more about learning how to evaluate student needs using curriculum-based assessment.

tion or skills are beyond the reach of the entire group or that your teaching approach is not accomplishing what you had planned. Even though self-reflection is sometimes difficult, when many students are experiencing problems it is important to analyze how the curriculum or teaching might be contributing to the situation. In such instances, you should make changes in those two areas before seeking other assistance.

However, perhaps you are an elementary teacher who can't seem to find enough books at the right level for one student in your fourth-grade class who is almost a nonreader. Perhaps you are an eighth-grade industrial arts teacher who is worried about letting a student who gets extremely angry use equipment that could be dangerous, and this is the only student about whom you have this level of concern. Many students have needs that do not signal the presence of disabilities. Students with disabilities have needs that are significantly different from those of most other students.

Do you discover that you cannot find a pattern? In some instances, the absence of a pattern to student needs is as much an indicator that you should request assistance as is a distinct pattern. Perhaps Curtis has tremendous mood swings, and you arrive at school each day wondering whether it'll be a good day or a bad day for him. However, you can't find a way to predict which it will be. Or consider Becka, who learns science with ease but cannot seem to master even basic reading skills. You are not sure why her learning is so different in the two subjects. In a third example, in physical education, Tyrone some days seems to have average motor skills but on other days frequently stumbles and cannot participate fully in the learning stations you have created.

Communicate Your Observations and Try Your Own Interventions

Your analysis of your students' unmet needs is the basis for further action. Although you may decide to seek assistance from special education professionals for one of your students, part of your responsibility in attempting to help the student is gathering other information and trying to resolve the problem first.

Contact parents. One of your first strategies should be to contact the family (Dyson, 1996; Turnbull & Turnbull, 1997). Parents or other family members often can inform you about changes in the student's life that could be affecting school performance. Family members can also help you understand how students' activities outside of school might influence their schoolwork, including clubs, gang involvement, employment, and responsibilities at home. Further, by contacting the family, you might learn that what you perceive as a problem is mostly a reflection of a cultural difference. For example, a student whose family emigrated from Thailand is extremely quiet because silence signals respect in her native culture, not because she is unable to participate.

Parents are also your partners in working to resolve some student learning problems. They can assist you in monitoring whether homework is completed and returned to school, whether behavior problems are occurring on the walk home, or whether a physician is concerned about a child's medical condition. If you work with students whose homes do not have telephones and whose parents do not have transportation to come to school, your social worker or principal can help you make needed contact.

Check Your Learning

What questions should you explore to determine whether your concern about a student warrants referral for possible special education services?

Special Emphasis On . . .

The Arts

If you are an art, music, dance, or drama teacher, you might wonder as you listen to discussions of students with disabilities what role you play in their education. In fact, in many school districts you are the professional who is most likely to work with most, if not all, the students with disabilities attending your school. In many cases, these students come to your class along with nondisabled peers. In a few cases, a separate class will have been arranged for them. Teachers in the arts often express the concern that little attention is paid to the support needs of students with disabilities in their classes, and few materials are available to prepare teachers in the arts for working with students with disabilities.

One website that you will find particularly helpful is VSA Arts (formerly Very Special Arts) at http://vsarts.org. Founded in 1974 by Jean Kennedy Smith, VSA Arts is an international organization that creates learning opportunities through the arts for children and adults with dis-

abilities. The organization has affiliates in 41 states and 83 other countries.

VSA Arts includes an online gallery of works by individuals with disabilities, a link to frequently asked questions, a chronicle of the difference that the arts have made in the lives of individuals with disabilities and the programs serving them, and other information about the organization and its work. Educators can link to a VSA Arts site to search for information and websites on topics related to their teaching.

One particularly interesting product available from VSA Arts is Express Diversity!, a set of five modules with art activities designed for fifth graders but adaptable for students in grades 1 through 7. The intent of the modules is to demonstrate that students with a wide range of abilities and disabilities share in the joy of art. The modules include one simulation activity (with cautions about its shortcomings), a creative writing exercise, an art mural activity, a performance art activity, and a visual arts ac-

Contact colleagues. Especially as a new teacher, you will want to discuss your concerns with other professionals to gain an additional perspective on the student's needs. In most schools, a special education teacher arranges to observe the student in your class and then to discuss the observation. If your school psychologist is available, you might ask for consultation assistance. In schools where grade-level teams or other types of teams meet, you can raise your concerns in that context. One hallmark of today's schools is an array of professionals who have expertise in many areas. With a little exploration, you are likely to find that your school has an in-house resource you can access to check your perceptions against a broader perspective.

Try interventions. Part of your responsibility as a teacher is to create a classroom where students can succeed. To cultivate such a setting, you can make adaptations as part of your attempts to address students' unmet needs. For example, have you tried moving the student's seat? Have you removed distracting bulletin board items from the student's line of sight? Have you switched from writing tests by hand to typing them on a computer to make them more legible? Do you give some students only part of their assignment at one time because they become overwhelmed otherwise? Have you observed the student closely to determine whether helping her work one problem is enough to get her to work on the rest? These are just a few alterations that many teachers make without even thinking of them as

tivity. The package of materials also includes letters (Spanish as well as English) that can be sent home to explain the program to parents, bulletin board items, video biography cards about people with disabilities, and other support materials.

S O U R C E : Adapted from VSA Arts, June 2000. Retrieved June 25, 2000 from the World Wide Web: http://www.vsarts.org. Express Diversity! was developed by VSA Arts under a grant from the U.S. Department of Education. However, the contents do not necessarily represent the policy of the U.S. Department of Education, and you should not assume endorsement by the Federal Government.

adaptations; many others are presented throughout this textbook. Sometimes, these small accommodations are sufficient to help a student learn. In any case, you should try common interventions before deciding a student might need special education.

Document the unmet need.   If you anticipate requesting assistance for a student, you need to demonstrate the seriousness of your concern and your systemic attempts to help meet the student's needs. If you have implemented a behavior contract with the student, you can keep a record of how effective it has been. If you have contacted parents several times, you can keep a log of your conversations. If you have tried to decrease the number of times the student misses your first-hour class, you can summarize your attendance data. Strategies to document student needs serve two main purposes. First, they help you do a reality check on whether the problem is as serious as you think it is. If you gather data from other students as a comparison, you can judge whether the unmet needs of one student are significantly different from those of typical students. Second, the information you collect helps you communicate with other professionals. Special service providers cannot possibly meet every need in every classroom. Their work is reserved in large part for extraordinary student needs, and your documentation helps in the decision about providing the assistance you seek.

W W W   R e s o u r c e s

An Internet source of information about a wide variety of special education issues is the Federal Resource Center for Special Education, at http://www.dssc.org/frc. At this website you can learn about a federal project that provides supports to state and local education agencies on many matters related to providing services to individuals with disabilities.

How Do Students Obtain Special Services?

The majority of students who receive special education have high-incidence disabilities that you may be the first to recognize. If you teach at the elementary level, you will probably have students every year whom you refer for possible special services. If you teach in middle school, junior high, or high school, you will find that many students with disabilities have already been identified before they reach your class. However, there are exceptions; students may be found eligible for special education at any time during their school careers. As a teacher, you always have the option of asking a team of professionals to decide whether special education is needed.

Having a serious and documented concern about a student is only the first step in considering whether a disability may be present. Your concern brings the student to the attention of other school professionals so that further information can be gathered and decisions made. The specific and formal procedures that must be followed to determine student eligibility for special education services are designed to ensure that only students who truly need these services receive them. These procedures are described in the following sections and summarized in Figure 2.3, which illustrates the flow of the procedures from beginning to end.

Initial Consideration of Student Problems

FYI

Teams that meet to problem solve about students before consideration of special education might be called teacher assistance teams, intervention assistance teams, instructional support teams, student–teacher assistance teams, or mainstream assistance teams. What are such teams called in your school district?

General education teachers, principals, special services personnel, parents, physicians, and social service agency personnel all may initiate the process of obtaining special education for a student. Most often, however, a student's classroom teacher notices a pattern of academic underachievement, inconsistent learning, serious behavior problems, difficulties in social skills, or a persistent physical or sensory problem. When such problems occur, the teacher brings the student to the attention of others who help decide whether special education is warranted.

Prereferral or instructional assistance teams.   A common way to begin the process of helping a student suspected of having a disability is to bring the problem to the attention of a team (Bahr, Whitten, Dieker, Kocarek, & Manson, 1999; Friend & Cook, 1997). This **prereferral** or **instructional assistance team** often includes general education teachers, special services personnel, and an administrator. Teachers wishing to "bring a student to the team" complete a referral form on which they describe the student's strengths and problems and describe efforts they have made to assist the student. The teacher then meets with the team to discuss the written information, consider alternative strategies for assisting the student, and determine whether the student should have a detailed assessment for potential special education services (Kovaleski et al., 1999; Rankin & Aksamit, 1994). The unifying characteristic of this type of team is an emphasis on problem solving among all members. The Case in Practice on page 50 illustrates how this type of team operates.

Screening.   Not all schools have teams to help make decisions about the need for assessment for special education. In some schools, the school psychologist, counselor, principal, or other professional has the responsibility of **screening** the referral—meeting informally with a general education teacher about a student. This

Figure 2.3 The Decision-Making Process for Special Education

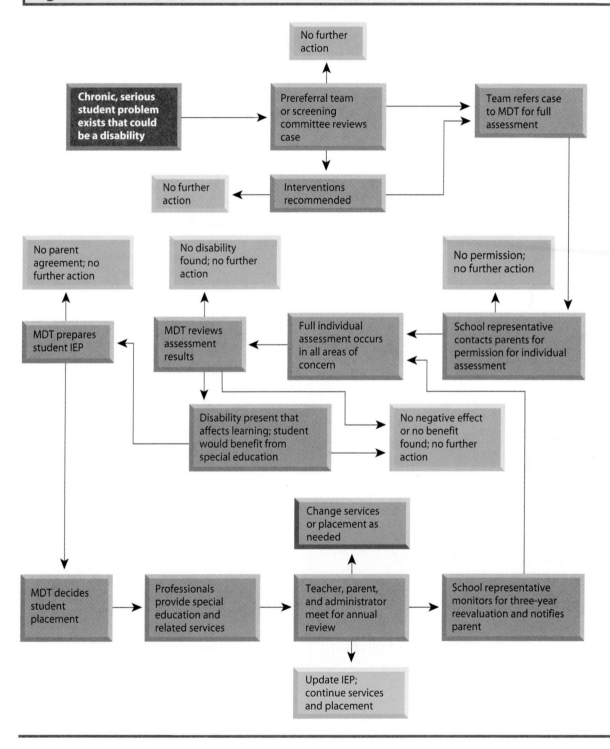

C A S E   I N   P R A C T I C E

Participating in a Team Meeting

It is 3:15 P.M. and Ms. Jacob's students have just left. She gathers a stack of information from her desk and heads toward the conference room for an intervention assistance team meeting. Ms. Jacobs is the fifth-grade representative on the team this year. Along with two other classroom teachers (it just happens to be first and fourth grade this year), a special education teacher, and the assistant principal, Ms. Jacobs meets weekly to problem solve about students and to consider whether any of their needs are so great that a referral for individual assessment should be made.

The first student to be discussed today is third grader Toby. Reviewing her information sheets, Ms. Jacobs sees that Toby is chronically late to school, has what his teacher describes as a sullen attitude, is failing in math and language arts, and has a D in science. Toby's teacher, Mr. Petrovich, is worried that Toby is headed toward failure, especially as he faces the more intense reading load in the intermediate grades. According to Mr. Petrovich, reward systems have not been successful; Toby's dad seems cooperative but tends to forget to follow through on homework monitoring and other requests; and other teachers, including the art teacher and the music teacher, have expressed concern about Toby's future.

As the meeting begins and preliminaries are completed, Ms. Ja-

cobs asks Mr. Petrovich several questions.

Ms. Jacobs: Mr. Petrovich, you've spent a great deal of extra time working with Toby this year. If you were to summarize your greatest concern for him, what would it be?

Mr. Petrovich: Probably his "I don't care and you can't make me" attitude. It seems to be getting worse as the year goes by. Toby is really a good kid; I don't know what's causing his problems—unless it's peer pressure—and I really want to get to the bottom of this.

Ms. Jacobs: Of all the things you've tried with Toby, what seems to have the biggest positive impact on him?

Mr. Petrovich: Right now, what's keeping him going is his interest in art and the computer lab. But Ms. Yancy says that if he doesn't improve his behavior and attitude during art, she feels she is going to have to take away some of his privileges there.

Ms. Jacobs: If you think about Toby's strengths, what might we start with to try to come up with some ideas for him?

Mr. Petrovich: I'd really like to see us work on something that takes advantage of Toby's computer skills. I know he likes art, but it seems like the computer area is one where we could tie in his academic needs. He'd work on the computer all day if I let him, and he's very skilled at finding information and creating art on it. He seems to like the structure and logic of the computer and the fact that it doesn't "get in his face."

Ms. Jacobs: It sounds as though you have an idea in mind.

Mr. Petrovich: I do. I'm hoping all of you can work with me to design some kind of very structured program that combines getting work done and getting to use computer equipment as a privilege. I think we have all the necessary components, we just need to put them together . . . and I think that's a concrete area to work in. I don't think a direct confrontation on attitude is going to have any effect.

The meeting continues with all the team members contributing. After 30 minutes, Mr. Petrovich leaves with a structured work-for-computer-privileges plan and an agreement to review its effectiveness in 3 weeks. Ms. Jacobs stays as the team discusses another student and recommends an individual assessment for this student.

R E F L E C T I O N S

What was it that made this team meeting constructive and productive? What purpose is served by including several general education teachers on the team? How did Mr. Petrovich help make the meeting a success? What other strategies might the team try in addition to the work-for-computer-privileges idea? What might happen when the team reviews the intervention they planned? Given what you have learned about students with exceptionalities, do you think Toby is the type of student who might be referred for an individual assessment?

individual asks about the strategies the teacher has tried to assist the student and may make additional recommendations. If efforts remain unsuccessful and the presence of a disability is suspected, referral for a more comprehensive assessment follows. According to the provisions of IDEA-97, any initial special education referral procedure, whether through a teaming or another screening process, must include the review of existing data about the student (National Information Center for Children and Youth with Disabilities, 1998). By using already-gathered data, school records, and other information, a more informed decision can be made concerning the need for a full assessment.

Diagnostic teaching is sometimes part of screening. A special education teacher or other special services professional may carry out sample lessons with the student, teaching different skills, using different teaching methods, and trying various ways of rewarding the student. By keeping detailed notes of what techniques were effective, this professional can make specific suggestions to teachers or recommend specific types of additional assessment.

When a team initially discusses or screens a student, a parent is not legally required to be involved in the process. However, educators should notify parents of their concerns and enlist parental assistance in trying to solve the problem. In some schools, parents are invited to team meetings. Remember, parents should never be surprised that the possibility of special education is raised—they should have known for quite some time of the existence of any serious problem.

Connections

Chapter 3 discusses professional collaboration, including how teams can work effectively.

The Special Education Referral and Assessment Process

If the decision as a result of team intervention or screening is that a full assessment for possible special education placement should occur, the parents are contacted. Their written permission for assessment must be obtained prior to any individual assessment (Rothstein, 1995). At this point, a **multidisciplinary team (MDT)** assumes responsibility for determining how to assess the student and for deciding whether the student has a disability and is eligible for special education services.

Components of assessment. Assessment involves gathering information about the student's strengths and needs in all areas of concern. Typically, if the student has not had a vision and hearing screening and you have reason to suspect a sensory impairment, these tests precede other assessments. If sensory screening raises concerns, parents are notified of the need for a more complete assessment by a physician or appropriate specialist.

Assessments completed by school professionals may address any aspect of a student's educational functioning (Huefner, 2000). Often, for example, students' cognitive ability is assessed. An individual intelligence test is administered and scored by a school psychologist or another qualified school professional. Academic achievement often is assessed, too. Students complete an individual achievement test administered by a psychologist, special education teacher, psychometrist, educational diagnostician, or other professional. A third area often evaluated is social/behavioral skills. This evaluation might involve a checklist that you and parents complete concerning student behavior, tests given by the school psychologist, or a series of questions asked of the student.

Another domain for assessment is the student's social and developmental history. Often, the social worker meets with the parents to learn about the student's

W W W   R e s o u r c e s

At http://www.wrightslaw.
com/advoc/articles/
iep_guidance.html, you
can view a comprehensive
guide for parents on IEPs,
including general information, related case law, links
to related sites, and examples of appropriate and inappropriate IEP goals and
objectives.

family life and major events in the student's development that could be affecting education. For example, parents might be asked about their child's friends in the
neighborhood and favorite out-of-school activities, their expectations for their child
as an adult, and their child's strengths. Parents might also be asked whether their
child has had any serious physical injuries, medical problems, or recurring social or
behavioral problems.

As another assessment component, a psychologist, counselor, or special education teacher might observe the student in the classroom and other settings to learn
how he or she responds to teachers and peers in various school settings. For example, a special education teacher may have observed Chris, who usually plays with
younger students during recess and gets confused when playground games are too
complex. Chris also watches other students carefully and often seems to take cues
for how to act from how they are acting. These observations are all helpful for understanding Chris.

If a potential need exists for speech therapy or occupational or physical therapy,
another component is added to the assessment. The professionals in those areas complete assessments in their respective areas of expertise. A speech/language therapist
might use a screening instrument that includes having the student use certain words,
tell stories, and identify objects. The therapist also might check for atypical use of the
muscles of the mouth, tongue, and throat that permit speech and for unusual speech
habits such as breathiness in speaking or noticeable voice strain. Similarly, occupational or physical therapists might assess a student's gait, strength and agility, range
of motion, or ability to perform fine motor tasks such as buttoning and lacing.

Throughout the entire assessment process, IDEA-97 specifically gives parents
the right to provide information to be used as part of the evaluation. In addition, as
the general education teacher, you can provide details on the student's performance
in class, patterns of behavior, and discrepancies between expectations and achievement. Your informal or formal observations play an important role in assessment.

*What areas of individual as-
sessment are involved when
a team is deciding whether
a student is eligible for special education services? How
is the information from
these assessments used in
decision making?*

Assessment procedures.   The exact procedures for assessing a student's needs vary according to the areas of concern that initiated the assessment process. What is important is that the assessment be completed by individuals trained to administer the tests and other assessment tools used, that the instruments be free of cultural bias, that the student's performance be evaluated in a way that takes into account the potential disability, and that the assessment provide data that are useful for deciding an appropriate education for the student. School professionals are responsible for ensuring that these obligations are met.

Parent rights.   Throughout the assessment process, parents' rights to participate in their child's education must be respected as established in IDEA and reinforced in virtually all subsequent legislation and litigation (Rothstein, 1995). In addition to the rights already mentioned, parents have the right to be informed in a meaningful way about the procedures and processes of special education and the right to give permission before any individual assessment is completed (Salend & Taylor, 1993). Parents also have the right to request information from a school district representative about how to get an independent evaluation for their child and the right to bring information from an independent evaluation to a meeting to discuss the educational needs of the student. In some cases, parents are entitled to be reimbursed for their expense in obtaining an independent evaluation. These and other parent rights ensured through federal special education laws are outlined in Figure 2.4. If you teach older students, you also might be interested in knowing that, beginning at least one year before reaching the age of majority, students must also be informed directly of their rights (Johns, 1997).

Decision Making for Special Services

After a comprehensive assessment of the student has been completed, the multidisciplinary team, including the parent, meets to discuss its results and makes several decisions (Gritzmacher & Gritzmacher, 1995; Huefner, 2000; Rodger, 1995; Zetlin, Padron, & Wilson, 1996). The first decision they must make is whether the student is eligible under the law to be categorized as having a disability. If the team decides that a disability exists, they then determine whether the disability is affecting the student's education, and from that decide whether the student is eligible to receive services through special education. In most school districts, these decisions are made at a single meeting that includes the parents, other team members, and students as appropriate. As outlined in Figure 2.4, parents must agree with the decisions being made or the student cannot receive special education services. Most school districts have guidelines to direct team decision making, but the decisions ultimately belong to the team, and the team may decide that the formula or description does not exactly fit a particular case. For example, most states have guidelines specifying that students identified as having a mild cognitive disability have an IQ less than 70 as measured on an individual intelligence test, such as a WISC-III, and have serious limitations in adaptive behaviors. However, if a student's test scores are slightly above 70 and adaptive skills are particularly limited, a team can still decide that the student has a mild cognitive disability. Likewise, if this student has a measured IQ lower than 70 but seems to have many adaptive skills, the team might decide that the student does not have a disability.

If the multidisciplinary team determines that the student has a disability affecting his or her education and that the student is eligible for services according to

Cultural Awareness

Over the past 2 decades, efforts have been made to reduce the racial and cultural bias in assessment instruments and procedures, especially for African American and Hispanic students (Figueroa, 1989; Henry, 1992).

FYI

The Weschler Intelligence Scale for Children–Revised (WISC-III) is an individual intelligence test often used to assess the intellectual ability of students referred for possible education services.

WWW Resources

The Walter Reed Army Medical Center provides an overview of the entire process of obtaining, implementing, and monitoring special education services. The guide, available at http/www.wramc. amedd.army.mil/ departments/pediatrics/ efmp/handbook/CH4.htm, includes information on what parents should do when their child is moving to a new school.

Figure 2.4 Summary of Parent Rights in Special Education

IDEA-97 stipulates procedural safeguards to ensure that parents have the right to be active participants in their children's education. The following safeguards are some of the major ones provided to parents:

1. Parents are entitled to be members of any group that makes decisions about the educational placement of their child.

2. Parents are to be given written notice before the school initiates, changes, or refuses to initiate or change the identification or educational placement of a child.

3. Parents can participate directly in the determination of their child's eligibility for special education and in the development of the individualized educational program (IEP) and its periodic review, at least annually.

4. The school must obtain written, informed parental consent before conducting a formal evaluation and assessment and before initially placing a student in a program providing special education and related services. (*Note:* Written parental consent is required for initial evaluation and initial placement. Subsequent formal evaluation and placement actions require written notice, as described in item 1.)

5. Parents can inspect and review any educational records maintained by the school district or other agency providing service under IDEA. Access to educational records will be granted to parents without unnecessary delay and before any meeting regarding an IEP or before a hearing relating to identification, evaluation, or placement of the child, and in no case more than 45 days after the request has been made.

6. A parent may request, and the school district must provide, information on where independent educational evaluations may be obtained. A parent has the right to an independent educational evaluation at public expense if the parent disagrees with an evaluation obtained by the local school district or responsible public agency. However, the local school district or responsible public agency may initiate a due process

hearing to show that the original evaluation is appropriate. If the final decision is that the evaluation is appropriate, the parent still has the right to an independent educational evaluation, but not at public expense. The results of an independent evaluation obtained by the parents at private expense will be considered by the local school district in any decisions about the provisions of a free appropriate public education to the child. Such results may also be presented as evidence at a due process hearing.

7. Parents have the right to request mediation as a means to resolving conflicts with school districts concerning their children with disabilities. Mediation must be available to parents prior to a due process hearing, but it may not delay a hearing. Information shared during mediation is confidential and may not be used as evidence at any subsequent due process hearing. The state bears the cost of mediation, not the parents.

8. Parents have the right to request a hearing by an impartial hearing officer in cases in which they disagree with school district decisions regarding their children's education. Hearings may relate to any aspect of special education, including the fairness of the evaluation procedures used to determine the presence of a disability, the appropriateness of the disability label given the child, the adequacy of the services provided, and the suitability of proposed changes of placement. If parents fail to win a due process hearing at the local level, they may appeal the results of the hearing at the State Department of Education level. After this step, if parents are still dissatisfied with the outcome of the hearing, they may initiate court action.

9. Parents must be fully informed of their right and the procedural safeguards related to special education. They initially should receive this information in a readily understandable manner when their child is referred for evaluation. They should also receive it prior to each IEP meeting and reevaluation, and when a complaint is registered.

SOURCE: Adapted from "Questions and Answers about IDEA," *NICHCY NewsDigest 21* (2nd ed.), January 2000. Washington, DC: National Information Center for Handicapped Children and Youth, Retrieved June 9, 2000, from the World Wide Web: http://nichcy.org/pubs/newsdig/nd21txt.htm; and "Comparison of Key Issues: Current Law and 1997 IDEA Amendments," by the National Association of State Directors of Special Education, 1997, Alexandria, VA: Author.

federal, state, and local guidelines, the stage is set for detailed planning of the student's education and related services. This planning is recorded on the student's individualized education program (IEP). The IEP is the document that outlines all the special education services the student is to receive. Specific guidelines must be followed in developing an IEP. More details about IEPs and their preparation are provided later in this chapter.

The final decision made by the multidisciplinary team concerns the student's placement. **Placement** refers to the location of the student's education. For most students, the placement is the general education classroom, often with some type of supports offered. According to IDEA-97, when a placement does not have a significant general education component, justification must be provided for that decision. However, for a few students, the appropriate primary placement is a special education setting. Later in this chapter, special education services are discussed and placement options are outlined in more detail.

In your school district, the spirit of the procedures outlined above are followed, but the timelines used and the names for each part of the process will vary. However, all school district procedures are designed to ensure that students with disabilities are systematically assessed and that a deliberate and careful process is followed to provide for their education needs. Further, you are also a critical participant in the entire process. A description of your rights as they relate to the special education process is included in Figure 2.5.

Monitoring Special Education Services

In addition to specifying the procedures that must be followed to identify a student as needing special education services, federal and state laws also establish guidelines for monitoring student progress. The monitoring process is necessary to ensure that students' educational programs remain appropriate and that procedures exist for resolving disputes between school district personnel and parents.

Annual reviews. The first strategy for monitoring special services is the **annual review.** At least once each year, the student's progress toward his or her annual goals must be reviewed, and the IEP changed or updated as needed. The purpose of this annual review is to see that the student's best interests are being protected. Not all multidisciplinary team members who participated in the initial decisions about the student's disability and educational needs are required to participate in annual reviews. However, a teacher instructing the student and an administrator or other professional representing the school district must meet with the student's parents to discuss whether goals and objectives are met and, if not, what to do next. In practical terms, if your school district completes all annual reviews during a given month, you will find that the special education staff with whom you work are unavailable because of their other responsibilities, such as meeting with parents. Depending on local practices, you might be asked to attend annual reviews for some students. For many students, the general education teacher is the most knowledgeable about their day-to-day functioning. This concept was strengthened with the mandate in IDEA-97 that a general education teacher participate in the development of each student's IEP, not necessarily by writing it, but by contributing a classroom perspective.

Some advocates of students with significant disabilities, especially students nearly ready to leave the public school system for a job or postsecondary education, have expressed concern about the tendency for the annual review process to emphasize paperwork and rules more than the best interests of the student (Everson & Zhang, 2000). The Professional Edge on page 57 offers an alternative approach to conducting annual reviews. It meets the requirements of IDEA-97, but ensures even better than traditional approaches that the plan developed keeps the student as the clear focus.

Figure 2.5 General Education Teacher's Rights in Special Education

As a teacher, you play a crucial role in the design and delivery of special education services. The following is a set of rights that attorney and disability advocate Reed Martin has compiled to clarify what you can expect as you work with students with disabilities and other special needs:

- **Right of teachers to participate in self-evaluation of school district.** This self-evaluation would examine all the policies, practices, and procedures relating to students with disabilities and allow teachers to raise and answer their questions as interested parties. The self-evaluation was required to be completed under Section 504 (and renewed when needed) and completed under the Americans with Disabilities Act no later than January 26, 1993.

- **Right to seek assistance for a student in a classroom that is not receiving benefit.** It is illegal under federal special education law to leave a child to fend for himself in a classroom designed for others. The student has a right to be referred for necessary assistance and the teacher has a concomitant right to make the referral when assistance is needed. This is not a right to rid the classroom of that child but rather a right to bring additional information or assistance into the classroom.

- **Right to recognize the teacher as a child advocate.** The ADA recognizes teachers as advocates, and outlaws retaliation, intimidation, or reprisals for teachers who advocate for children.

- **The right to have the child fully evaluated.** The child has a right to be evaluated in every area that might adversely affect educational performance and the teacher has a right to know everything educationally relevant to that child.

- **The right to receive any training needed under the Comprehensive System for Personnel Development.** If the key to serving the student appropriately is teacher training, then the teacher has a right to receive that training.

- **The right to participate in the IEP that develops the plan for a student in their class.** The statute includes "the child's teacher" as a participant in the IEP meeting.

All questions a classroom teacher might have must be asked and answered before the child comes into the classroom. If the school's practice is simply to have "a representative of instruction" at the IEP, but they do not represent the interests of the classroom teacher, the classroom teacher should ask to have the IEP meeting reconvened to ask and answer the questions that have not been addressed. If the classroom teacher advocates in this way, they are protected from reprisal by school administrators.

- **The right to receive the related services that should honestly be on the IEP.** If needed supplemental aids and services are not discussed at the IEP, then it violates the teacher's, student's, and parents' rights. If services are decided on at the IEP, but they are not provided in the classroom, it violates the teacher's, student's, and parents' rights.

- **Right to be recognized as an advocate for all the children in the classroom.** A classroom teacher has a duty to all the children in the classroom. This duty is not antagonistic to a child with special needs. The cases on placing children in the least restrictive environment recognize that the interests of other children, and the ability of the teacher to teach the classroom, are balanced with the right of a child with special needs to be in that regular classroom.

- **The teacher has a right to participate in assessing the effectiveness of the program.** When the IEP committee leaves the IEP room, they must have an IEP that is reasonably calculated to confer benefit. Once the IEP is begun the teacher must have a role in assessing whether the IEP is working. During the year, and at the next IEP, the teacher's view is vitally important to determining whether that was an appropriate placement.

- **The teacher has the right to be treated as a professional.** Teachers are not just subordinate employees expected to carry out orders without questions. They are professionals with rights to ask for referral, for evaluation, for reevaluation, for an IEP meeting, and for further refinements of the IEP.

S O U R C E : From "Regular Teachers' Rights in Special Education," by R. Martin, (n.d.). Retrieved June 25, 2000, from the World Wide Web: http://www.reedmartin.com/teachers_rights.html. This information is educational and not intended to be legal advice. Reed Martin is an attorney with over 32 years of experience in special education law. He can be reached through e-mail at connie@westco.net or www.reedmartin.com.

Professional Edge

Person-Centered Planning

Although professionals intend the special education screening, referral, eligibility, program planning, placement, implementation, and monitoring process to be focused on the student, sometimes in the details of ensuring that all regulations are followed and all paperwork is completed, this focus is lost. A response to this problem, particularly for older students with significant disabilities, is person-centered planning, also called futures planning. Developed by professionals from both the United States and Canada, person-centered planning emphasizes the use of everyday events and activities in the student's life as the foundation for educational planning, the importance of family ties to the community, and the necessity of including individuals who know the student well as well as the student in setting goals.

Person-centered planning has these components:

- *Community presence.* The community setting the student uses and those that would benefit the student should be identified. The intent is to incorporate these settings into the educational planning process.
- *Choice.* Decisions made by the student and decisions made for the student should be identified. The goal of person-centered planning is to transfer as many choices to the student as possible.
- *Competence.* Skills that most assist the student to participate fully in the school and community and strategies that are most effective for teaching those skills should be identified.

- *Respect.* Roles the person has in the school and local community should be clarified. The goal is to strengthen and expand those roles and decrease or eliminate student characteristics that might cause the student to be perceived by others in a stereotypic way.
- *Community participation.* People with whom the student spends time at school and in other settings should be specified. The goal is to identify individuals who can advocate for the student and to foster friendships with age-appropriate peers.

A number of person-centered planning approaches have been developed, and you may find that one of these is used in your school district. These include Making Action Plans (MAPS), Planning Alternative Tomorrows with Hope (PATH), and Circle of Friends.

If you are interested in learning more about this approach to developing goals for individuals with disabilities, these websites include extensive information:

- Alaska Transition Initiative
  http://www.sesa.org/ati/pcpfaq.html
- REACH of Louisville
  http://www.reachoflouisville.com/person-centered/personplan.htm
- Training and Technical Assistance Center (T-TAC) at Old Dominion University
  http://www.ttac.odu.edu/Articles/PCentPl.html

S O U R C E : Adapted from information obtained from www.sesa.org, www.reachoflouisville.com, and www.ttac.odu.edu.

Three-year reevaluations. A second monitoring procedure required by law is the **three-year reevaluation.** At least every 3 years, and more often if deemed necessary by a multidisciplinary team, students receiving special education services must be reassessed to determine whether their needs have changed. This safeguard is designed to prevent students with disabilities from remaining in services or programs that may no longer be appropriate for them. In some cases, the reevaluation includes administering all the tests and other instruments that were used initially to identify the student as needing special education. However, IDEA-97 has streamlined the reevaluation process. It now permits existing information to be used for

Check Your Learning

How are annual reviews and three-year reevaluations similar and different?

reevaluation instead of requiring new assessments. In fact, with parent agreement and team agreement, reevaluations may not involve any new assessment at all (Huefner, 2000; Yell & Shriner, 1997). On the basis of the three-year reevaluation, the multidisciplinary team meets again to develop an appropriate IEP. According to current law, parents are informed that it is time for a three-year reevaluation, but school districts are not required to obtain written permission for this monitoring procedure. This practice enables school districts to continue providing high-quality services to students without interruptions that may be caused if new permission must be sought.

Additional reviews.   In addition to annual reviews and three-year reevaluations, IDEA-97 specifically stipulates that IEPs must be revised whenever there is a lack of expected progress toward achieving goals noted, reevaluation information is gathered, or parents bring to the attention of the MDT information that affects the IEP. This language, more specific than in prior laws, suggests that IEPs may need to be revised more frequently than before for some students.

Parents have one more formal mechanism for obtaining information about their child's learning. As established in IDEA-97, the parents of students with disabilities have the right to receive a progress report about their child as often as do parents of typical learners. In many school districts, this means that formal communication about student learning progress now occurs every six or nine weeks during the school year.

Due process.   Yet another strategy for monitoring students receiving special education services is **due process,** the set of procedures outlined in the law for resolving disagreements between school district personnel and parents regarding students with disabilities. Due process rights begin when a student is first brought to the attention of a team as potentially having a disability. Both school districts and parents are entitled to protection through due process, but parents typically exercise their due process rights when they fear that school districts may not be acting in the best interests of the child (Rothstein, 1995). For example, if parents have their child independently evaluated because they believe the assessment for special education did not accurately portray their child's needs, and if the school district does not agree with the findings of the independent evaluator, the parents may request a due process hearing. Or, parents could request a hearing if they disagree with the goals and objectives listed on the IEP and how services are provided to meet those goals and objectives. A hearing is conducted by an independent and objective third party selected from a list provided by the state, but the school district bears the expense. If either party disagrees with the outcome of a due process hearing, the decision can be appealed to a state-level review hearing officer. If disagreement still exists, either party can then take the matter to court. Due process hearings seldom address blatant errors on the part of schools or parents regarding special education; most often they reflect the fact that many decisions made about students with disabilities are judgment calls in which a best course of action is not always clear. For example, Mr. and Mrs. Schubat filed a due process complaint against their daughter's school district because they did not believe programs offered were addressing their daughter's needs. They wanted Judy to be more actively involved in general education activities despite her multiple disabilities. The school district personnel contended that the complexity of her needs prevented Judy from being reasonably accommodated in a classroom. They also indicated that she was part of a reverse tutoring program in which students without disabilities come to work in the special education setting. How do you think a hearing officer would decide this case?

In practice, most school districts and parents want to avoid due process hearings, which tend to be adversarial and can damage parent–school working relationships to the detriment of the student (Goldberg & Kuriloff, 1991). To foster a positive working relationship, IDEA-97 requires that all states have a system in place to offer **mediation** to parents at no cost as an initial means for resolving conflicts with schools (Yell & Shriner, 1997). In mediation, a neutral professional skilled in conflict resolution meets with both parties to help them resolve their differences informally. Mediation, however, cannot cause delay in parents' right to a due process hearing.

Although school districts work closely with parents to avoid due process hearings, if one occurs concerning a student you teach, you might be called to testify at the hearing. In such a case, you will be asked to describe the student's level of functioning in your classroom, the supports you provide, and your efforts with other special service providers to ensure the student is successful. An administrator and an attorney might help you prepare for the hearing, and they would answer any questions you might have about your role.

What Is an Individualized Education Program?

As mentioned earlier, the document that the multidisciplinary team uses to decide the best placement for a student with an identified disability and that serves as a blueprint for a student's education is called an individualized education program (IEP). The IEP addresses all areas of student need, including accommodations to be made in a general education class and the services and supports to be provided there; the IEP also documents that services are being provided (Rodger, 1995). Since the reauthorization of IDEA in 1997, classroom teachers must be involved as team participants in preparing IEPs if the student has any participation in the general education setting (Johns, 1997). Whether you are the teacher who serves in this role for particular students, if you have students with disabilities in your classroom, you will have opportunities to examine their IEPs or to meet with special educators to go over highlights of this important plan. If you are not provided with opportunities to review and discuss student IEPs, you should ask for the information you need. The Technology Notes explains how you can access this type of information as well as IEP forms and related materials from the Internet.

WWW Resources

Many statistics about students with disabilities and how they receive their education services come from the Twenty-First Annual Report to Congress on the Implementation of IDEA (U.S. Department of Education, 1999). If you would like to examine this voluminous report yourself, you can access the following site: http://www.ed.gov/offices/OSERS/OSEP/OSEP2000AnlRpt/.

Required Components of an IEP

The essential components of the IEP were established by P.L. 94-142, now IDEA. They were again modified in IDEA-97. Although specific state requirements for IEPs vary somewhat, the required elements of IEPs are described in the following sections.

Present level of functioning. Information about the student's current level of academic achievement, social skills, behavior, communication skills, and other areas of concern must be included on an IEP. Often, highlights of the information collected from the individual assessment of the student are recorded on the IEP to partially meet this requirement; that is, individual achievement test scores, teacher ratings, and summary assessments by specialists such as speech therapists or occupational

[Technology Notes]

Using Technology for IEPs

The preparation of IEPs has long been a time-consuming and labor-intensive activity, one that special education teachers were obligated to complete and general education teachers avoided. With the requirement in IDEA-97 that general education teachers be active team members in the IEP process, it is fortunate that a multitude of resources now exist on the Internet to facilitate their participation.

Computerized IEPs

A number of companies have produced IEP software that enables educators to write the IEP electronically, sometimes even incorporating information from a district database into the process so that basic demographic information already stored does not even have to be entered separately on the forms. One example of a computerized IEP program is Page 4 (http://www.page-4.com/pricing.htm), a program based on Florida's state-level special education policies and procedures. Additional IEP software packages are listed on the website of the Council for Exceptional Children at http://www.cec.sped.org/bk/catalog.htm.

State and Local IEP Policies and Forms

Many states and some large local school districts now make available online their policies and procedures related to special education as well as the forms that are

---

therapists can be used to report the present level of functioning. Another component of this assessment is information about how the students' disabilities affect their involvement in the general education curriculum. Including information on the **present level of functioning** serves as a baseline and makes it possible to judge student progress from year to year.

Annual goals and short-term objectives. The multidisciplinary team's estimate of what a student should be able to accomplish within a year, related to meeting the student's measured needs resulting from the disability, is referred to as **annual goals.** For some students, annual goals may refer primarily to academic areas and include growth in reading, math problem solving, and other curricular areas. A student with a learning disability might have an annual goal to read and comprehend books at a particular grade level or to demonstrate skills for finding and keeping a job. For other students, annual goals address desired changes in classroom behavior, social skills, or other adaptive skills. An annual goal for a student with a moderate intellectual disability, for example, may be to order a meal at a fast-food restaurant. A student with autism might have participation in a conversation as a goal. Annual goals may also encompass speech therapy, occupational and physical therapy, and other areas in which a student has specialized needs. There is no "right" number of annual goals. Some students have as few as 2 or 3, others as many as 8 or 10 (Epstein, Patton, Polloway, & Foley, 1992). However, IDEA-97 specifies that annual goals must be measurable, and increased emphasis is placed on annual goals that enable a student to progress in the general education curriculum.

Short-term objectives are descriptions of the steps to take to achieve an annual goal. For example, for a student to write a story that includes the elements of char-

needed for intervention assistance teams, special education referral, IEPs, and other special education activities. A website for the state of Nebraska is an example of how state information and forms are made available, at http://www.nde.state.ne.us/SPED/forms/iepnew.html. An example of how a local school district organizes information and forms is the San Diego City Schools website, at http://www.sdcs.k12.ca.us/specialed/Pages/IEP.html.

Information on Specific Issues Related to IEPs

When you are asked to attend an IEP meeting, you may have questions about particular aspects of a student's disability. Throughout this textbook many web sites are mentioned that fall into this category of specific information on special education issues, services, and disability types.

Questions

1. How might computerized IEPs affect your role as a general education teacher on a special education team?

2. Does your state or a local school district make information about special education and required forms available on the Internet? How could you find out? If so, what is available and how easily is it accessed?

3. What are aspects of special education that you are particularly curious about? What websites can you find that address these issues?

---

acter, plot, and setting, the student needs to understand each of those elements, recognize them in others' stories, and be able to complete the tasks that go along with writing a story. Each of these smaller steps that leads to accomplishing the annual goal would be a short-term objective. For a student with a severe physical disability whose annual goal is to feed herself, short-term objectives might include grasping a spoon, picking up food with the spoon, and using the spoon to transport food from plate to mouth. The number of short-term objectives for each annual goal relates to the type and severity of the disability, its impact on student learning, and the complexity of the goal. For some students, only a few short-term objectives may be needed; for others, each annual goal may be divided into several smaller steps. Examples of IEP goals and objectives are included in the Professional Edge on page 62.

Extent of participation in general education. In keeping with the trend toward inclusive practices, the IEP must include a clear statement of justification for placing a student anywhere but a general education classroom for all or part of the school day. Even for extracurricular and other nonacademic activities, an explanation of why such a placement is necessary must be part of the IEP.

Services and modifications needed. The IEP contains a complete outline of the specialized services the student needs; that is, the document includes all the special education instruction to be provided and any other related services needed to ensure instructional success. Thus, a student receiving adaptive physical education has an IEP indicating that such a service is needed. A student's need for special transportation is noted on the IEP, too. A student who is entitled to transition or vocational assistance has an IEP that clarifies these services. Perhaps most importantly, the

Professional Edge

Sample IEP Goals

IEPs have become complex documents with many required parts. However, the measurable annual goals related to assessed student needs that each IEP represents are the key to a student's education. They are supplemented by the short-term objectives that serve as benchmarks to measure progress toward achieving the annual goal. The following are sample IEP annual goals and objectives:

- Jerome will master math concepts and skills at the fourth-grade level as specified in the district math curriculum guide and assessed on the standardized end-of-grade assessment.

- Jerome will complete two-digit by two-digit multiplication problems with 80 percent accuracy.

- Jerome will complete word problems concerning multiple operations (for example, addition and multiplication) with 80 percent accuracy when they are presented orally to him.

- Susan will complete at least 80 percent of her homework assignments in English, algebra, and U.S. history.

- Susan will write down homework assignments 90 percent of the time with 90 percent accuracy.

- Susan will have in her backpack at the end of the day all needed materials to do assignments 90 percent of the time.

- Maria will make eye contact when communicating with adults in school at least 70 percent of the time.

- Maria will make eye contact with the speech/language therapist during individual sessions in 9 out of 10 interactions initiated by the therapist.

- Maria will make eye contact when the special education teacher calls Maria's name and looks at her in at least 9 out of 10 interactions.

- Maria will make eye contact when a classroom teacher calls Maria's name and looks at her in at least 4 out of 5 interactions.

statement of services must include information about the modifications and supports to be provided so that the student can progress in the general education curriculum.

One additional element of this IEP component concerns assessment. IDEA-97 stipulates that if students need modifications on district or state assessments (for example, extended time), these should be specified on the IEP. If a student is to be exempt from such assessments, the team must clarify why the assessment is not appropriate. Since the year 2000, students who are exempt from district or state assessments must have some type of alternative assessment that takes into account their functioning levels and needs (National Association of State Directors of Special Education, 1997).

Part of identifying services is indicating who is responsible for providing them. Any of the professionals introduced earlier in this chapter could be listed on the IEP to deliver special services. As a general education teacher, you will be included, too. For some students, you will be the teacher who completes most of the required instruction; for others, you will assist but will not be primarily responsible. For example, your student with a mild cognitive disability will probably be able to complete many class tasks with minor modifications that you can make. However, if your student has significant cognitive and physical disabilities requiring an alternative curriculum, other professionals will undoubtedly help develop the materials you will use when the student is in your classroom.

Behavior intervention plan. A critical aspect of the current regulations for educating students with disabilities concerns discipline and the need to respond to inappropriate behavior. All students with significant behavior problems, not just those labeled as having emotional disabilities, must have as part of their IEP an intervention plan based on a functional assessment of their behavior. This requirement, new in IDEA-97, reflects the increasing pressure for students to be supported in general education settings and the acknowledged difficulty of accomplishing that goal without appropriate student behavior.

Date of initiation and frequency and duration of service and anticipated modifications. Each IEP must include specific dates when specialized services and modifications begin, the frequency of the services and modifications, the types of modifications that are part of services, and the period of time during which services and modifications are offered. Because the law requires that student progress in special education be monitored at least once each year, the most typical duration for a service is a maximum of one year. If during the year a multidisciplinary team member sees a need to reconsider the student's educational plan, additional IEP meetings can be convened.

Strategies for evaluation. When a team develops an IEP, the members must clarify how to measure student progress toward achieving the annual goals and how to regularly inform parents about this progress. For each short-term objective, the team indicates the criteria to be used to judge whether the objective has been met and the procedures to be used to measure this. For the student learning to write a story, the criteria might include the actual production of a story, and a checklist might be used to judge whether the essential elements of plot, character, and setting are present. As with all aspects of special education, the evaluation criteria and procedures are individualized; they are as general or specific as needed to accomplish the student's educational goals.

Transition plan. For all students who are 14 years of age and older, part of the IEP is a description of strategies and services for ensuring that the student is prepared to leave school for adult life, called a **transition plan.** Students with disabilities who are college bound might have transition plans that include improvement of their study skills, exploration of different universities and their services for students with disabilities, completion of high school course requirements necessary to obtain admission to a university, and preparation in life skills such as responsibly using credit cards and checking accounts. For students who work after school, the transition plan might include skills such as reading employment ads, filling out job applications, and developing important job skills such as punctuality, pleasant manners, and respect toward people in authority and customers. As with IEPs, there is no single correct way to write a transition plan. It is tailored to meet the assessed strengths and needs of the particular student and it is updated annually, with participation by professionals from agencies outside the school typically increasing as the student nears graduation or school departure at age 21.

Check Your Learning

When did transition become part of special education law? Why is transition a major concern for students with disabilities?

In addition to their basic components, IEPs have several other requirements. For example, they are signed by the individuals who participate in their development, including the student's parent or guardian. They also list a justification for the placement recommended. For example, a decision that the student should receive some services in a pullout program might be justified on the basis of the student's need for one-to-one intensive instruction to succeed. In addition, if a student has specific types of needs, they must be addressed in the IEP. Examples of such needs include behavior, communication, braille (unless specifically excluded on the IEP), and assistive technology. In such cases, appropriate supports, services, and strategies must be specified (Johns, 1997).

To some educators, IEPs represent paperwork that mostly consumes time and energy (Smith, 1990). However, remember that IEPs guide the education of students with disabilities. The document helps you clarify your expectations for students and provides a means for you to understand the student's educational needs. An IEP also informs you about the types of services the student receives and when the student's educational plan will next be reviewed. Your job is to make a good-faith effort to accomplish the short-term objectives on the IEP. If you do that, you have carried out your responsibility; if you do not do that, you could be held accountable. For example, suppose an IEP indicates that a student should learn coins and make change for up to a dollar. If you can demonstrate that you are helping the student learn this by providing play money and opportunities to learn, you are carrying out your responsibility, even if the student does not master this skill. If you state that your students are no longer working on money skills and refuse to create opportunities for practice in this area, you are violating the IEP.

What Services Do Students with Disabilities Receive?

The services that students with disabilities can receive are comprehensive, limited only by the stipulation that they must be necessary as part of a student's education. These services are provided in a variety of placements. Both the services and placements are determined by the multidisciplinary team.

Special Education and Related Services

As noted in Chapter 1, the types of services students receive can be grouped into two categories: special education and related services. **Special education** refers to the specially designed instructional services students receive. These services may include adapted materials, alternative curriculum, access to a special education teacher qualified to teach students with a particular disability, and individualized instruction. When a student's special education teacher comes to the classroom and teaches with the general education teacher, that is special education. When a student leaves a classroom for 30 minutes three times each week for intensive tutoring, that is special education. When a middle school or high school offers a life skills class for students with disabilities, that is special education, too.

Related services refer to all the supports students may need to benefit from special education. Examples of related services are speech therapy, transportation, physical and occupational therapy, rehabilitation counseling, psychological services, and social work. A student's need to ride a special bus equipped with a wheelchair lift is a related service need. The student's need for assistance with personal care such as toileting is a related service need.

As you might guess, the range of possibilities for special education and related services is immense. Some students, particularly those with high-incidence disabilities, receive a limited number of special education services and perhaps no related services. For example, Lucas, a high school student with a learning disability in math, attends a geometry class in which a special education teacher teams with a math teacher. Lucas's assignments are sometimes shortened, and he is allowed extra time to complete tests. He is already looking into colleges that are known to be supportive of students with his special needs. Students with more complex or severe disabilities may have a more highly specialized special education as well as numerous related services. For example, Changyi, the student with physical disabilities and cognitive disabilities introduced at the beginning of the chapter, might have the services of a physical and occupational therapist, speech/language therapist, and inclusion specialist, as well as a special education teacher.

Student Placement

Until recently, any discussion of special education services typically began with a discussion of the least restrictive environment (LRE) and rapidly moved to a detailed discussion of the place in which the services would occur. This was because many students spent some, most, or all of the school day in a special education classroom where it was believed appropriate instruction could be delivered. Now, views about placements are changing rapidly (McLeskey, Henry, & Axelrod, 1999). It is true that many school districts still use special education classrooms, even for students with relatively mild disabilities, and that these are sometimes an appropriate LRE; however, the use of such classrooms is becoming more and more an exception as schools become more inclusive (U.S. Department of Education, 1999). In fact, with the passage of IDEA-97, students' placement in settings other than general education classes as the LRE must be specifically justified. As Figure 2.6 shows, the proportion of students with disabilities in various placements has changed over the past 5 years. The decision about placement is made by the multidisciplinary team and reviewed at least annually along with the IEP. Placements can be changed as often as appropriate, with parental permission. Generally, if parents and school district representatives disagree about placement, the student remains in the current placement until the disagreement is resolved. Exceptions to this occur when discipline issues arise. Administrators may unilaterally change a student's placement (e.g., suspension) for up to 10 days, provided such methods are used with other students, too. If students with disabilities bring a weapon or drugs to school, they can be placed in an alternative educational setting for up to 45 days while decisions are made concerning their long-term placement needs (Yell & Shriner, 1997).

> **Cultural Awareness**
>
> Concern has been expressed for many years about the disproportionate placement of minority students in special education programs. It appears that this practice is influenced by many variables in addition to ethnicity, including family size and structure and students' perceived social status (Artiles, Aguirre-Munoz, & Abedi, 1998).

Regular class. Nearly 46 percent of students with disabilities receive at least 79 percent of their education in a **regular class**—a general education classroom, with direct or indirect assistance provided (U.S. Department of Education, 1999). For example, a student in kindergarten with a communication disorder might be served by a speech/language therapist who comes to the classroom and teaches language lessons with the general education teacher. For a student with cognitive and physical disabilities in middle school, an inclusion specialist might adapt a lesson on fractions by helping the student learn how to cut simple shapes into halves. For a student with a learning disability in high school biology, a paraprofessional might assist the student in carrying out lab directions and recording and completing assignments. The student might have one class period of study skills and strategies assistance in a special education classroom.

Figure 2.6 **Percentage of Students Ages 6–21 Served in Various Special Education Settings, 1987–1988 and 1996–1997**

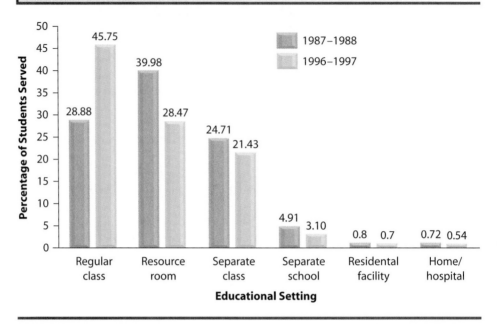

SOURCES: From *Twelfth Annual Report to Congress on the Implementation of the Education for the Handicapped Act,* 1990; and *Twenty-First Annual Report to Congress on the Implementation of the Individuals with Disabilities Education Act,* 1999, Washington, DC: U.S. Department of Education.

Resource room.   Approximately 29 percent of students with disabilities attend school mostly in general education settings but also receive assistance in a **resource room** between 21 and 60 percent of the day (U.S. Department of Education, 1999). In elementary schools, resource rooms are sometimes organized by the skills being taught; that is, from 10 A.M. until 10:45 A.M., basic math skills are taught, and all the second-, third-, and fourth-grade students needing math assistance come to the resource room at that time. Alternatively, some resource rooms are arranged as same-aged groups. In these programs, all fifth graders with disabilities in resource room programs go to the resource room together. In another approach, special education teachers negotiate with general education teachers about specific times students attend. In middle schools and high schools, students are scheduled to have resource periods in the same way that the rest of their classes are scheduled. That is, usually, students do not receive a grade for the instruction received there. How a resource room program is organized depends on many factors, including the number of students to be served, the nature and intensity of their needs, and local policies. One hallmark of resource room services is that they are supplemental to the instruction in the general education classroom.

Separate class.   Approximately 21 percent of students with disabilities attend **separate classes** for more than 60 percent of the school day (U.S. Department of Education, 1999). In this placement, a special education teacher has the primary instructional responsibility for the students, and the students probably spend a significant part of the day in that setting, receiving grades from the special educator for the subjects taught there. However, a separate class placement does not mean that students do not interact with nondisabled peers; they may have an assigned classroom for part of the day, and they may also participate in related arts and other school activities with peers. For example, although Kim is in a separate class most of the day at his high school, he takes a shop class with students without disabilities. A paraprofessional accompanies him because he has limited ability to understand directions and needs close guidance from an adult to operate equipment. At Kyle's elementary school, 45 minutes each day is called *community time*, during which students read and write together, share important events from their lives, and learn about their neighborhood and community. For community time, Kyle goes to Mr. Ballinger's fifth-grade class. The students are about Kyle's age and assist him with the community activities and learning. Kyle's special education teacher helps Mr. Ballinger plan appropriate activities for Kyle during that time.

Separate school. Approximately 3 percent of students with disabilities attend **separate schools** (U.S. Department of Education, 1999). Some separate schools exist for students with moderate and severe cognitive and physical disabilities, although such schools are rapidly becoming obsolete. Other separate schools serve students with multiple disabilities who need high levels of specialized services. For example, in a small community near Chicago, approximately 25 students are educated at a separate school. These students all need the services of a physical and occupational therapist; most have complex medical problems that must be closely monitored; and most cannot move unless someone assists them. These students have opportunities for contact with nondisabled peers who through a special program are brought to the separate school to function as "learning buddies."

Some students with serious emotional disabilities also attend separate schools. These students might harm themselves or others. They might not be able to cope with the complexity and social stress of a typical school, and so the least restrictive environment for them is a school where their highly specialized needs, including therapeutic supports, can be addressed.

Residential facility. A few students have needs that cannot be met at a school that is in session only during the day. If students in separate classes have even higher needs, they might attend school as well as live in a **residential facility.** Fewer than 1 percent of students with disabilities are educated in this manner (U.S. Department of Education, 1999). The students for whom this placement is the LRE are often those with severe emotional problems or severe and multiple cognitive, sensory, and physical disabilities. In some states, students who are blind or deaf might also receive their instruction in a residential facility, an approach that is supported by some and opposed by others.

A somewhat different group of students also can be considered under the residential placement option. For the first time in IDEA-97, children and young adults who are imprisoned are directly addressed. Generally, if a child is convicted of a crime and incarcerated as an adult, that child is still entitled to special education services unless the IEP team determines there is a compelling reason to discontinue services (National Information Center for Children and Youth with Disabilities, 1996). Other provisions in the law address the cessation of services for individuals aged 18 through 21 incarcerated as adults and the requirement for services for youth who had IEPs or who had been identified as disabled prior to dropping out of school who were then incarcerated as adults.

What special educational challenges arise when a student must be in a hospital for an extended period of time? How do these students receive their education?

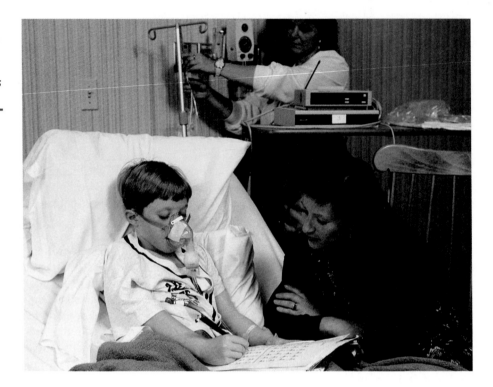

Home or hospital.   For half of 1 percent of students with disabilities, education occurs in a home or hospital setting (U.S. Department of Education, 1999). This placement is often used for students who are medically fragile or who are undergoing surgeries or other medical treatments, or for students who have experienced an emotional crisis. For a few students with limited stamina, school comes to the home because the student does not have the strength to come to school.

If parents and school representatives disagree about an appropriate educational placement, students are sometimes educated at home pending the outcome of a due process hearing. When students are educated at home or in a hospital, the amount of actual instruction is often limited. Home services might be as little as 4 or 5 hours per week, delivered by an itinerant teacher. Hospital services range from a few hours of itinerant teaching to a full school program delivered by teachers at the hospital.

If needed according to the team's judgment, any of the services in any of the placements just described can be extended into school breaks and summer vacations through *extended school year* programs.

As you can see, separate classes and schools for placement are rapidly becoming less important than supporting the education of students with disabilities in general education classrooms and schools. When placement includes a specialized setting, it often means that an alternative placement is appropriate for a specific skill or service, for a specific and limited period of time. However, "home" for most students with disabilities is the same classroom they would attend if they did not have a disability. As a general education teacher, you play a major role in the education of students with disabilities, so it is important for you to understand the kinds of special services your students receive.

Summary

Many individuals work to ensure that students with disabilities receive an appropriate education. These people include general education teachers; special education teachers; other specialists and related service providers such as school psychologists, counselors, speech/language therapists, social workers, physical and occupational therapists, adaptive physical educators, nurses, administrators, paraprofessionals, and other specialists; and parents, students, and advocates. Depending on need, a student with a disability may receive instruction from just one or two of these professionals, or from many of them.

To determine whether special services are needed, general education teachers begin a process of deciding whether to request that a student be assessed for the presence of a disability. They carry out this process by analyzing the nature and extent of a student's unmet needs, clarifying those needs by describing them through examples, determining that the need is chronic and possibly worsening over time, comparing the student's needs to those of others in the class, recognizing that no pattern seems to exist for the student's performance, and intervening to address the unmet needs and documenting those efforts. Based on these early strategies, the student's needs may be assessed by an intervention team or screening team, and, if warranted, special education referral and assessment steps are followed. This process includes completing an individualized assessment with parental permission, making decisions about the need for special education, developing an individualized education program (IEP), and monitoring the special education services.

When an IEP is developed, it includes the student's present level of functioning, goals and objectives, needed services, criteria for evaluation and the person(s) responsible for the services, and beginning and ending dates for service delivery. The IEP must be reviewed at least annually, and the student must be reevaluated at least every 3 years. The services students receive, as outlined by their IEPs, include special education and related services, and a designation of the placement for the student: a general education classroom, special education classroom, or separate special education setting. If parents and school personnel disagree on any aspect of a student's special education program or services and the disagreement cannot be resolved informally, due process procedures are used to ensure that the student receives the appropriate education.

General education teachers play an integral role in the education of students with disabilities. They are involved in the early identification of students who seem to have special needs, contribute during the assessment and identification process, and implement IEP goals and objectives as outlined by the multidisciplinary team.

Applications in Teaching Practice

A Visit to an MDT Meeting

Ms. Richards teaches science to sixth graders. Beginning in the fall, she and her team members will be working with Natasha, a student newly identified as having learning disabilities. Natasha enjoys many friends and extracurricular activities, but she has extraordinary difficulties with reading fluency, comprehension, and written expression. She also has significant problems organizing her work and remembering to complete and turn in assignments. To help set appropriate goals for the coming year, Ms. Richards is participating in a multidisciplinary team meeting to create an IEP for Natasha. Although it would be preferable for all the team members to attend the meeting, this is not feasible, and so Ms. Richards is there to represent her colleagues as well.

General education (sixth-grade) teacher: Ms. Richards
General education (fifth-grade) teacher: Mr. Tucker
Special education teacher: Ms. Hill
Principal: Ms. Hubbert
Psychologist: Ms. Freund
Speech/language therapist: Mr. Colt
Parent: Ms. Wright

Ms. Hubbert: Our next task is to develop goals and objectives for Natasha. I'd like to suggest that we discuss academics first, then social areas, and wrap up with related services needed. Let's look at Natasha's strengths first—in all those areas.

Mr. Colt: Natasha has a very strong speaking vocabulary. She is considerably above average in that realm.

Ms. Freund: Along with that, Natasha's general knowledge is very good. She also is near grade level in basic math skills.

Mr. Tucker: It's not really academics, but one strength Natasha has that I see is her willingness to help classmates. She really wants to help everyone in class learn. She was also very active in extracurricular activities this year—she participated in the service learning program, volunteered to read to the kindergarten class, and competed in the after-school sports program.

Ms. Hill: As we write academic goals and objectives, then, we need to remember that Natasha has high vocabulary and common knowledge and that she does not need help in math. Perhaps we can use her social skills and other interests to help in the academic arena. Ms. Wright, what strengths do you see in Natasha?

Ms. Wright: Hmmm. She minds me, that's for sure. And she helps out around the house with chores. She likes to help me watch her baby brother.

Ms. Hill: Helping really seems to be Natasha's thing—let's keep that in mind.

Ms. Hubbert: Let's focus for a minute on academic areas of need.

Ms. Freund: Reading comprehension and written expression are by far the areas that need the most work. Natasha's comprehension is just at a beginning third-grade level and her written expression is below that.

Ms. Wright: She says she doesn't like reading because the other kids make fun of her when she can't read the words and they tease her when Mr. Tucker gives her a baby book.

Ms. Richards: In middle school, that could be even more of a problem. We need to be sure that she uses the same textbooks as the other students next year. I'm sure we can also arrange to get some supplemental materials for her to use at home. Let's be sure that before we finish today we talk about that some more.

Ms. Freund: Ms. Richards and Ms. Hill, given what you know and have heard about Natasha, what might be the priorities for next year?

Ms. Hill: I agree that comprehension is the key. I think a goal should be for her to improve her comprehension to a fourth-grade level on reading tasks that include stories, textbooks, and other materials such as children's magazines.

Ms. Hubbert: Ms. Wright, how does that sound to you? [Ms. Wright nods.]

Before the meeting ends, the MDT has generated these additional goals in reading comprehension using materials at her instructional level: Natasha will identify the main characters and the problem and solution in literature that she reads at a third-grade level. She will comprehend 80 percent on both narrative and expository material she reads aloud; 80 percent on material she reads to herself.

Questions

1. What are the responsibilities of the professionals represented at the meeting? Which of the professionals are required to attend? How would your response be different if this were an annual review?
2. What role was Ms. Richards taking at the meeting? Why was her presence so helpful in creating an educational program for Natasha? How else might she contribute during this meeting?
3. What was the purpose in having both the fifth-grade teacher and a sixth-grade teacher attend the MDT meeting? How might this improve the quality of the IEP? What problems might it cause?
4. What steps do you think had occurred prior to the point at which this vignette began? What had the general education teacher done? What other team responsibilities had been met?
5. What part of the IEP was the team addressing? What other parts have to be completed before the meeting ends? What must occur for the IEP to be valid?
6. What would happen if Natasha's mother asked the school district for a separate class as Natasha's placement and the school district disagreed with this?

Professional Partnerships

After you read this chapter, you will be able to

1. Explain what the term *collaboration* means and describe how collaboration is part of providing services to students with disabilities.

2. Depict how an emphasis on collaboration in schools affects you as a general education teacher.

3. Describe inclusive programs and services in which collaboration is integral, including shared problem solving, co-teaching, teaming, and consulting.

4. Identify ways in which you can work effectively with parents to educate students with special needs successfully.

5. Outline your responsibilities in working with paraprofessionals and ways in which you can enhance collaboration with them.

Key Terms and Concepts

Collaboration (p. 75)

Consultation (p. 95)

Co-teaching (p. 87)

Paraprofessional (p. 103)

Shared problem solving (p. 82)

Teams (p. 92)

■ In Ms. Godina's biology class, 5 of her 42 students have IEPs. April, who has a mild learning disability, does not need assistance in the course. Enrico and Austen, both receiving services for emotional disabilities, are capable of completing the work but need a great deal of structure and support to do so. Carl, a student with a mild cognitive disability, does part of the course work, but he is not expected to master the extensive vocabulary nor to write lengthy lab reports. Janet, who has a physical disability that requires her to use a motorized wheelchair and who has limited stamina, often needs encouragement to keep up with the work. Twice each week during biology, Ms. Godina is joined by Mr. MacLean, a special education teacher. During these class periods, the two teachers share teaching responsibilities and group the students for instruction in a variety of ways—by skill needs, by interest, and by random assignment, among others. On two of the days that Mr. MacLean is not in class, Ms. Hugo, a teaching assistant, is available to help Ms. Godina and individual students. What happens when two teachers share instructional responsibilities in a classroom? What topics might Ms. Godina and Mr. MacLean need to discuss to ensure that their shared teaching is effective?

■ The three fourth-grade teachers are having a grade-level team meeting; Ms. Chiang, the special education teacher, is also present. They have discussed a curriculum issue related to social studies, and now the conversation has turned to a common problem. Mr. Balen states that the students with disabilities are taking a disproportionate amount of his time, especially in the morning. He explains that this group of students does not seem to be able to come into the classroom, put away their belongings, and settle into work without his close and constant supervision. Mrs. Dyer agrees but adds that many students without disabilities are having the same problem. After a few minutes of general conversation about this problem, the teachers begin generating ideas for dealing with it. Included in the list of ideas is letting students choose their own morning work, assigning all students a "morning study buddy," and reviewing expectations with all the classes. Even though Ms. Chiang does not teach fourth grade, she is in the classrooms to assist students, to observe, or to take part in lessons so often that she has several excellent ideas to contribute to the discussion. What is Ms. Chiang's role in the team? How can the team ensure that all the members feel committed to the team and valued as team members?

■ Chris's parents, Mr. and Mrs. Werner, arrived promptly for their after-school meeting with Ms. MacDougal, the middle school inclusion facilitator, and Mr. Saunders, the seventh-grade team leader. Mrs. Werner began by declaring that the school was discriminating against Chris because of her learning disability. Mr. Werner asserted that Chris was not to be singled out in any way because of her special needs and that he had learned that she was receiving tutoring during a lunch-period study hall. He strongly expressed that the family already provided tutoring for Chris so that this type of discrimination would not occur at school. Further, Mr. and Mrs. Werner showed the teachers modified assignment sheets, another example of discrimination. When Mr. Saunders started to explain that he was modifying Chris's work so she could learn more in his class, Mr. Werner cut him off, stating that a teacher's poor instructional practice was no excuse to destroy a child's self-concept through public humiliation. If you were Mr. Saunders, what type of assistance would you want from Ms. MacDougal during this difficult interaction? How can you prevent miscommunication in your work with parents of students with disabilities?

In the past, becoming a teacher—whether in general education or in special education—meant entering a profession frequently characterized by isolation and sometimes loneliness (Little, 1993; Lortie, 1975; Mitchell, 1997). Teachers typically spent most of the day alone in a classroom with students. They learned that they were expected to have all the skills to manage student learning and discipline issues, and they rarely had opportunities to discuss their questions, concerns, and misgivings with anyone, but especially not their colleagues at school.

That atmosphere of isolation is changing. Elementary school teachers are meeting on grade-level teams to share ideas and problem solve, and middle school and high school teachers are creating interdisciplinary teams to redesign curriculum and share instructional responsibility for smaller groups of students. School reform efforts are also characterized by partnerships. For example, professional development schools in which teacher trainees work with experienced educators and university instructors emphasize team approaches (Martin, Hutchinson, Whitehead, 1999). Likewise, entire schools are stressing the need to build a collaborative learning community (Million & Vare, 1997). As Barth (1990) comments, "The success of a school, I believe, depends above all on the quality of interactions between teacher and teacher, and teacher and administrator" (p. 15).

As the scenes that open this chapter illustrate, these emerging partnerships extend to special education and other support staff as well. Particularly as schools move toward increased inclusion, the working relationships among all the adults involved in the education of students with disabilities have become critical. For example, as a classroom teacher, you may find that you have questions about a student's behavior in class. A consultant might come to your class, observe the student and the overall classroom setting, and then meet with you to discuss how to address your concerns.

Similarly, you might find that some of your students cannot complete the grade-level work you are accustomed to assigning. To assist you, a special education teacher might meet with you to design the necessary modifications.

At first glance, these interactions seem like logical and straightforward approaches to optimizing education. However, because of the strong tradition in education of professionals working alone and the limited experience teachers have had in preparing to work effectively with other adults, problems sometimes occur (Friend & Cook, 2000). In some instances, support personnel are reluctant to make suggestions for fear that they may sound as if they are interfering with the classroom teacher's instruction. In other cases, the classroom teacher insists that no change in classroom activities is possible, even though a special education teacher is available for co-teaching. And often, when professionals in schools disagree, they are very uncomfortable discussing the issues.

Many personnel in inclusive schools assert that collaboration is the key to their success in meeting the needs of all students (Friend & Cook, 2000; Hudson & Glomb, 1997; Idol, 1997). The purpose of this chapter is to introduce you to the principles of collaboration and the school situations in which professionals are most likely to collaborate to meet the needs of students with disabilities. You also will learn how to develop strong working relationships with parents, an essential part of every teacher's responsibilities, and an especially important one when educating students with special needs. Finally, the special partnerships that are formed when teachers work with paraprofessionals also are considered.

What Are the Basics of Collaboration?

As a teacher, you will hear colleagues refer to many of their activities as *collaboration.* Sometimes they will be referring to a team meeting to propose ideas to help a student; sometimes they will mean sharing a classroom to teach a particular subject; and sometimes they will even use the term as a synonym for inclusion. How can all these things be collaboration? Actually, they are not. Collaboration is *how* people work together, not *what* they do. As Cook and Friend (1993) have clarified, **collaboration** is a style professionals choose to accomplish a goal they share. Professionals often use the term *collaboration* to describe any activity in which they work with someone else. But just the fact of working in the same room with another person does not ensure that collaboration occurs. For example, in some team meetings, one or two members tend to monopolize the conversation and insist that others agree with their points of view. Although the team is in proximity, it is not collaborative. Only on teams where all members feel their contributions are valued and the goal is clear, where they share decision making, and where they sense they are respected, does true collaboration exist.

Connections

Students experience many of the elements of adult collaboration through cooperative learning, a topic discussed in Chapter 13. This chapter's focus is adult interactions.

Characteristics of Collaboration

Collaboration in schools has a number of defining characteristics that clarify its requirements. Friend and Cook (2000) have outlined these key attributes.

Check Your Learning

If you are *required* to work with special education teachers and other colleagues, how can collaboration be voluntary?

Collaboration is voluntary.   Teachers may be assigned to work in close proximity, but they cannot be required to collaborate. They must make a personal choice to work collaboratively in such situations. You and another teacher could be told that you are expected to be part of an intervention assistance team. You could choose to keep your ideas to yourself instead of readily participating. On the other hand, you could conclude that even though you had not planned on volunteering for this activity, as long as you are a team member, you will contribute like a team player and collaborate. Your principal assigned the activity; you decided to collaborate. Because collaboration is voluntary, teachers often form close but informal collaborative partnerships with colleagues whether or not collaboration is a school-wide ethic.

Collaboration is based on parity.   Teachers who collaborate must believe that all individual contributions are valued equally. The amount and nature of particular teachers' contributions may vary greatly, but teachers need to recognize that what they offer is integral to the collaborative effort. If you are at a meeting concerning highly complex student needs, you might feel you have nothing to offer. However, you have important information about how the student responds in your class and the progress the student has made in developing peer relationships. The technical discussion of the student's disabilities are not your area of expertise, nor should it be; your ideas are valued because of your expertise in your classroom.

Collaboration requires a shared goal.   Teachers collaborate only when they share a goal. For example, if two third-grade teachers want to plan an integrated unit on the environment, their goal is clear. They can pool their knowledge and resources and jointly plan the instruction. However, if one wants to work on an environmental unit whereas the other prefers to stress weather, they cannot develop their units collaboratively. Teachers sometimes perceive that they share a goal when in fact their goals differ. For example, if the two third-grade teachers agree to work on an environmental unit, but one means global issues whereas the other means the pragmatics of recycling, either the content of the unit will have to be negotiated or the collaborative planning might not be possible.

Collaboration includes shared responsibility for key decisions.   Although teachers may divide the work necessary to complete a collaborative teaching or teaming project, they should share as equal partners the fundamental decision making about the activities they are undertaking. This shared responsibility reinforces the sense of parity that exists among the teachers. In the environmental unit example, the teachers share decisions about what topics to address within the unit, perhaps what order to cover them, learning objectives for students, and accommodations for students with special needs. However, they are likely to assign many tasks to just one person. One may contact the local zoo for information on tropical rain forests and arrange for a videotape on recycling. The other may duplicate the logs students use to record information they find in the newspaper about the environment and may contact the local nature preserve to arrange for a guest speaker.

Collaboration includes shared accountability for outcomes.   This characteristic follows directly from shared responsibility; that is, if teachers share key decisions, they must also share accountability for the results of the decisions, whether those results are positive or negative. If both the third-grade teachers carry out their assigned tasks, their unit will have a high probability of success. If one fails to contact a guest speaker, their shared unit is less effective. If something happens that is just wonderful (the classes begin a school recycling project that receives local and then national press attention), the teachers share the success. If something happens that is not so wonderful (the experiment to measure the impact of pollutants on climate fizzles and students become bored with it), they share the need to change their plans.

Collaboration is based on shared resources. Each teacher participating in a collaborative effort contributes some type of resource. This contribution increases commitment and reinforces each professional's sense of parity. Resources may include time, expertise, space, equipment, or other assets. The teachers working on the environmental unit contribute the time needed to make necessary plans, but they also pool their knowledge on teaching about the environment, share information on local resources to access for the unit, and share the equipment needed to show the recycling video.

Collaboration is emergent. Collaboration is based on belief in the value of shared decision making, trust, and respect among participants. However, although these qualities are needed to some degree at the outset of collaborative activities, they are not mature in a new collaborative relationship. As teachers become more experienced at collaboration, their interactions become characterized by the trust and respect that grow within successful collaborative relationships. If our third-grade teachers have worked together for several years, they may share freely, including offering constructive criticism to each other. If this is their first collaborative effort, they are much more likely to be a bit guarded and polite, or hesitant about sounding critical, because they are unsure how the other person will respond.

Check Your Learning

What is an example that illustrates each of the defining characteristics of collaboration?

Prerequisites for Collaboration

Creating collaborative relationships requires effort on everyone's part. Most professionals who have close collaborative working relationships note that it is hard work to collaborate—but worth every minute of the effort. They also emphasize that collaboration gets better with experience; when colleagues are novices at co-teaching or working on teams, their work seems to take longer and everyone has to be especially careful to respect others' points of view. However, with additional collaboration, everyone's comfort level increases, honesty and trust grow, and a sense of community develops. Here are some essential ingredients that foster the growth of collaboration.

Reflecting on your personal belief system. The first ingredient for collaboration is your personal beliefs. How much do you value sharing ideas with others? Would you prefer to work with someone to complete a project, even if it takes more time that way, or do you prefer to work alone? If your professor in this course offered the option of a small-group exam, would you be willing to receive a shared grade with your classmates? If your responses to these questions suggest that you prefer working with others, you will probably find professional collaboration exciting and rewarding. If your responses are just the opposite, you might find that you would rather do it yourself and experience collaboration as somewhat frustrating. For col-

Cultural Awareness

How might cultural differences affect collaboration? When people from very different cultures collaborate, what can you do to ensure that their collaboration is successful?

Special Emphasis On . . .

Collaboration for Secondary Teachers

Collaboration is important at every grade level and in every type of school, whether urban, suburban, or rural. One website dedicated to fostering effective educational practices, including collaboration, in secondary schools is the Secondary School Educators site on the About network, at http://7–12educators.tqn.com/education/ 7–12educators/library/weekly/aa120899.htm. This site includes an article about a secondary teacher's perspective on co-teaching, a discussion group in which you can pose questions on any pertinent topic, and links to many other websites that assist you in your work with students with special needs. For example, you can link to web-

laboration to occur, all those participating need to feel that their shared effort will result in an outcome that is better than could be accomplished by any one participant (DeBoer, 1995). They must also believe that a shared effort has value, even if the result is somewhat different from what each person envisioned at the outset (Friend, 2000; Phillips & McCullough, 1990).

Part of examining your belief system also concerns your understanding of and respect for others' belief systems. This tolerance is especially important for your collaborative efforts with special educators in inclusive programs. For example, what are your beliefs about changing the standards in your classroom for a single student to help that student succeed? You might at first say that changing your standards is no problem, but when you reflect on the consequence of that belief, you might have second thoughts. For example, it means that you must give alternative assignments to students needing them, that you must teach *students* not *subject matter*, and that you must grade on the basis of student effort and progress instead of according to a single standard. The special educators with whom you work are likely to believe strongly that alternative standards are not only helpful in inclusive settings, but that they are a requirement. How will you respond if you meet a colleague with this belief? Similarly, what if three teachers in your department are strongly opposed to alternative standards for students with disabilities? Will you debate the matter with them and hold your beliefs, or will you feel pressured to compromise? Teachers have faced these issues in the past. However, in schools in which collaboration is stressed, issues such as these tend to become more apparent and the need to resolve them more intense. Further, as collaboration becomes more integral to public schools, learning to value others' opinions and to disagree respectfully with them while maintaining a positive working relationship becomes more and more essential.

Refining your interaction skills.   The second ingredient you can contribute to school collaboration is effective skills for interacting. In many ways, interaction skills are the fundamental building blocks on which collaboration is based because it is through our interactions with others that collaboration occurs. There are two major types of interaction skills. The first are communication skills, some of which you may have already learned about in a speech or communication course. These skills include listening, attending to nonverbal signals, and asking questions and making statements in clear and nonthreatening ways. They also include paralanguage, for example, your

WWW Resources

The Center for Effective Collaboration and Practice (http://www.air.org/cecp/) is a federally funded organization designed to promote effective educational practices for students with emotional and behavior problems. It includes links for parents, teachers, and others on topics stressing working together on behalf of these students.

sites for working effectively with parents, for teaching students whose native language is not English, for effectively reaching teen parents, and for instructing in any subject area, including special education.

Another website just for secondary teachers and specifically aimed at creating successful heterogeneous classrooms is Help 4 Teachers, at http://www.help4teachers.com/articles.htm. This site provides a wide range of articles and tips for secondary teachers on working with students with learning and behavior problems and includes an invitation to receive an e-mail newsletter. The site also has a link to tips that secondary teachers offer for working effectively in classrooms with students with special needs. Examples for unit plan ideas by practicing teachers are also provided at this site.

tone of voice and your use of comments like "Uh-huh" and "okay." Additional information about communication skills is included in the Professional Edge on page 80.

The other type of interaction skill describes the steps that make interactions productive. Have you ever been in a meeting and thought that the same topic was being discussed repeatedly? Perhaps you wished someone would say, "I think we've covered this; let's move on." Or have you ever tried to problem solve with classmates or friends only to realize that every time someone generated an idea, someone else began explaining why the idea could not work? In both instances, the frustration occurred because of a problem in the interaction process, that is, the steps that characterize an interaction. The most needed interaction process for you as a teacher is shared problem solving. Other interaction–process skills include conducting effective meetings, responding to resistance, resolving conflict, and persuading others.

FYI

Communication skills are the words, paralanguage, and nonverbal signals you use to convey meaning to others. *Interaction processes* are the steps for using communication skills to accomplish a goal.

Collaboration often involves respectful differences of opinion. How do effective communication skills help you when disagreements arise?

Professional Edge

Barriers to Effective Communication

Mostert (1998), in his discussion of professional interactions, emphasizes that it is just as important to understand barriers to communication as to learn communication skills. He lists these barriers:

- **Advice.** When you offer unsolicited advice to a colleague or parent, that person may be confused by your intent, may reject the information and form an unfavorable opinion of you, or may feel obligated to follow it even if it seems inappropriate. In general, advice should be offered only when it is sought.

- **False reassurances.** If you offer parents or colleagues false reassurance about student achievement, behavior issues, or social skills, you are damaging your own credibility and setting the stage for additional future issues. Being truthful is the best strategy, even if you are concerned that a difficult situation may result.

- **Wandering interaction.** As another person communicates with you, it is sometimes easy to drift to peripheral topics that waste valuable time. For example, discussing a student's soccer team when the concern is academic performance is a distraction, which sometimes reflects avoidance of the key issues.

- **Interruptions.** When you interact with others, they are entitled to your full attention. When you are buzzed on the intercom or called to the door, you should politely decline until your interaction is concluded. During an interaction, it is important to avoid interrupting others. Especially when the person speaking has a language pattern that is slower than yours, you may have to make a concerted effect to wait until the person finishes speaking before adding your contribution.

- **Being judgmental.** If you tend to speak in absolutes (for example, "The only way to resolve this is to . . ." or "I don't see any way for him to complete the work . . ."), you may be perceived as a professional who only sees one right answer. One outcome may be that others minimize their meaningful conversation with you because they view it as futile.

- **One-way communication.** Communication is most effective when it involves all participants. If one person monopolizes the interaction, the others' points of view are not represented and any decisions made are likely to be questioned later.

- **Fatigue.** If you are so tired that you cannot accurately follow the thread of a conversation, your communication will be impaired. You may misspeak or misunderstand others' messages. In such cases, it may be best to request that the interaction be rescheduled.

- **Hot words or phrases.** In some communities and in some schools, certain words are "hot." For example, even the word *inclusion* is sometimes considered controversial. For productive interactions, such words (or even suspected words or phrases) are best avoided.

Do any of these barriers sound familiar? What examples of each can you and your classmates generate relating to your own communication experiences in an internship or field experience? What could you do to decrease the likelihood of these barriers occurring in your interactions with colleagues and parents?

SOURCE: Adapted from "Communication in Interprofessional Collaboration," by M. P. Mostert, 1998, Chapter 6, pp. 91–115, in *Interprofessional Collaboration in Schools*, Boston: Allyn & Bacon. Copyright © 1998 by Allyn & Bacon. Adapted by permission.

You need both types of interaction skills for collaboration to occur. If you are highly skilled in communicating effectively but cannot help to get an interaction from its beginning to its end, others will be frustrated. Likewise, even though you know the steps in shared problem solving, if you speak to others as though you know all the answers, they will withdraw from the interaction.

Contributing to a supportive environment.   The third ingredient for successful collaboration is a supportive environment (Pugach & Johnson, 1995). As a teacher, you will contribute to this atmosphere by your personal belief system and interaction skills, but this ingredient includes other items as well. For example, most professionals working in schools that value collaboration comment on the importance of administrative support. Principals play an important role in fostering collaboration (daCosta, Marshall, & Riordan, 1998; Johnson & Pajares, 1996). They can raise staff awareness of collaboration by making it a school goal and distributing information about it to staff. They can reward teachers for their collaborative efforts. They can urge teachers who are uncomfortable with collaboration to learn more about it and to experiment in small-scale collaborative projects, and they can include collaboration as part of staff evaluation procedures. When principals do not actively nurture collaboration among staff, collaborative activities are more limited, more informal, and less a part of the school culture. If you work in this type of school, you may find that you collaborate with specific teachers but that your efforts are considered a luxury or frill and are not rewarded or otherwise fostered.

Another component of a supportive environment is the availability of time for collaboration (Brownell, Yeager, Rennells, & Riley, 1997; Raywid, 1993). It is not enough that each teacher has a preparation period; shared planning time also needs to be arranged. In many middle schools, shared planning occurs as part of the middle school team planning period. In other schools, substitute teachers are employed periodically so that classroom teachers and special services staff can meet. In an increasing number of school districts, "early release" days are used. Once each week or month, students are dismissed in the early afternoon. Teachers use the time created to plan instructional units, confer about student problems, and attend professional development activities.

As a teacher, you will find that time is an important issue (Cole & McLeskey, 1997; Stump & Wilson, 1996). The number of tasks you need to complete during your preparation period will be greater than the number of minutes available. The time before and after school will be filled with faculty meetings, meetings with parents, preparation, and other assignments. You can help yourself maximize time for collaboration if you keep several things in mind. First, it may be tempting to spend the beginning of a shared planning time discussing the day's events or comparing notes on some school activity. But if you engage in lengthy social conversation you are taking away time from your planning. A trick discovered by teachers in collaborative schools is to finish the business at hand first and then to "chat" if time is left. Second, because you never truly have enough time to accomplish all that you would like to as a teacher, you must learn to prioritize. You have to choose whether collaborating about a certain student or teaching a certain lesson is justified based on the needs of students and the time available. Not everything can be collaborative, but when collaboration seems appropriate, time should be made available for it.

> **FYI**
>
> In our fieldwork with thousands of experienced teachers each year, lack of time is consistently noted as the most serious obstacle to collaboration.

What Are Effective Applications of Collaboration in Schools That Foster Inclusion?

The basic principles of collaboration are your guides to many types of partnerships in schools. These partnerships may involve other classroom teachers, special education teachers, support staff such as speech therapists or counselors, paraprofessionals, parents, and others. Four of the most common activities in which educators value and seek collaboration concerning students with disabilities are shared problem solving, co-teaching, teaming, and consultation.

Shared Problem Solving

Shared problem solving is the basis for many of the collaborative activities school professionals undertake on behalf of students with disabilities (Jayanthi & Friend, 1992; Johnson & Pugach, 1996). Although shared problem solving sometimes occurs when a classroom teacher and a special education teacher meet to decide on appropriate modifications or other interventions for a student, it occurs in many other contexts, too. For example, as you read the applications that follow this one, you find that some variation of shared problem solving exists in each. This happens because one way of thinking about co-teaching, teaming, and consultation is as specialized problem-solving approaches.

You might be wondering why problem solving is such a critical topic for professional partnerships. In fact, you may consider yourself adept at problem solving already because it is an ongoing responsibility of educators. However, as many authors have noted (for example, Friend & Cook, 2000; Pugach & Johnson, 1995), when professionals problem solve together the process is much more complex than when educators problem solve alone because the needs, expectations, and ideas of each participant must be blended into shared understandings and mutually agreed-on solutions. This is not a simple task!

Discover a shared need.   The starting point for problem solving is discovering a shared need, which demonstrates the point about the complexity of shared problem solving. If you face a problem that concerns only you, you try to resolve it by yourself. When you problem solve with colleagues and parents, all participants need to perceive that a problem exists. Further, it is important that all participants believe that they can have an impact on the problem, that they feel accountable for the results of problem solving, and that they can contribute constructively to resolving the problem. When these conditions exist, shared problem solving results in a high level of commitment. When these conditions do not exist, *shared* problem solving is not shared at all and may appear one-sided, with some participants trying to convince others to contribute. For example, many teachers report that they have been unable to enlist parents' help in resolving discipline problems. They then go on to describe meetings with parents in which school personnel describe the problem and the parents respond that they do not see such behavior occurring at home. Too often, instead of working to come to a shared understanding of the problem behavior, this type of meeting ends with the parents superficially agreeing to assist in a problem they do not believe exists and the school professionals perceiving the parents as only marginally supportive. The dilemma can be avoided if more effort is made to identify a shared need to problem solve.

Identify the problem.   Research on problem solving suggests that the most critical step in the process is problem identification (Rodgers-Rhyme & Volpiansky, 1991). However, when educators meet to share problem solving, they often feel pressured because of time constraints to resolve the problem; hence, they rush through this essential stage. Problem-solving experts suggest that up to half of the time available

WWW Resources

Sometimes your problem solving can be facilitated by obtaining more information. If you would like to explore resources available on the Internet that are related to disabilities, try the Comprehensive List of Disability-Related Web Sites at http://www.icdi.wvu.edu/Others.htm.

for problem solving should be devoted to this step (Bergan & Tombari, 1975). Problem identification includes gathering information, compiling it, analyzing it, and reaching consensus about the nature of a student's problem.

In a shared problem-solving situation, you can help emphasize the importance of problem identification by asking whether everyone has agreed on the problem, by asking someone else to restate the problem to check your understanding of it, and by encouraging participants who have not spoken to share their opinions. Consider the following situation, which shows what can happen when problem identification is not done correctly. A teacher in a shared problem-solving session says to the parent of a student whose attendance is irregular and who consistently comes to school without assignments or basic supplies, "We really need your help in making sure Rickie gets up when his alarm goes off so he can catch the bus. And we'd like to establish a system in which you sign off on his written assignments." The parent replies, "It's so hard. I work until midnight and I don't get up when it's time for the kids to go to school. I don't think he sees any point in the homework he's getting— that's why he doesn't bring it back." In this situation, the educator has identified the problem before the meeting has even started: Rickie needs to assume responsibility, and his parents need to provide more guidance for school activities. The teacher is further proposing a solution to the problem and not exploring the problem itself. The parent's response suggests that the parent does not see the same problem; in fact, the parent is implying that perhaps the problem does not belong to Rickie at all, but to the school staff.

As an alternative, consider how this interaction could have been handled: The teacher says to the parent, "Ms. Trenton, thanks so much for taking time off work to meet with us. We appreciate your concern for Rickie. Lately, we've seen a problem with Rickie's attendance. We asked you to come to school so we can learn about your perspective on this situation and to let Rickie know that we're working together to help him." When the parent replies with the comment about her working hours and Rickie's perception of the homework, the teacher replies, "That's important information for us. We're hoping we can find ways to motivate Rickie to come to school—and that includes assigning homework that he sees as valuable." In this situation, the school professionals are working *with* the parent to identify the problem, not against her.

Propose solutions. Once a problem has been clearly identified, the next step is to create a wide range of options that might be tried to solve the problem. One of the most common ways to come up with solutions is to **brainstorm.** VanGundy (1988) clarifies brainstorming as being based on two important principles. First, judgment is deferred; that is, to free the mind to be creative, we must suspend our predisposition to judge ideas. Second, quantity leads to quality; that is, the more ideas that are generated for solving a problem, the more likely it is that novel and effective solutions can be found. Brainstorming requires openness and creativity. The fourth-grade team you read about at the beginning of this chapter was engaged in proposing solutions. What other solutions might they have generated if they had stressed brainstorming principles?

Evaluate ideas. With a list of ideas, the next step in shared problem solving is to evaluate the ideas by considering whether they seem likely to resolve the problem and whether they are feasible. One way to evaluate ideas is to use a decision sheet as

Cultural Awareness

Nonverbal communication is partly influenced by culture. For example, some Navajos use peripheral vision when interacting because direct eye contact is considered confrontational. On the other hand, some African Americans use more eye contact when speaking and less when listening (Turnbull & Turnbull, 1997).

WWW Resources

The North Central Regional Educational Laboratory is dedicated to integrating services for students and their families. At their site, http://www.ncrel.org/sdrs/pbriefs/93/93-3guid.htm, you can learn about another dimension of collaboration, the complex issues that arise when school professionals work with individuals from social services, health services, and other community agencies.

[Technology Notes]

Electronic Collaboration

Collaboration traditionally has been thought of as the ways in which professionals interact when they are face to face or perhaps on the phone. However, more and more collaboration is occurring on the Internet, enabling professionals from all over the country and other countries as well to share ideas, ask questions, and provide support to others.

One of the most comprehensive web resources for learning to use electronic tools to interact with other professionals is Electronic Collaboration: A Practical Guide for Educators (http://www.lab.brown.edu/public/ocsc/collaboration.guide). Developed by the Northeast and Islands Regional Educational Laboratory (The Lab) at Brown University, the National School Network, and the Teacher Enhancement Electronic Community Hall through a project funded by the U.S. Department of Education, the site offers an online and downloadable guide that provides an explanation of what electronic collaboration is, a rationale for participating in electronic

Electronic Collaboration

A practical guide for educators

illustrated in Figure 3.1. On this decision sheet, the participants have listed the problem—helping Angela work independently on classroom tasks—and generated ideas for achieving this goal. They then selected criteria by which to judge the merits of each idea. They considered (1) how well the idea will work for increasing the amount of time Angela spends on her independent assignments; (2) the extent to which the idea has a low time cost; and (3) the extent to which the idea preserves classroom routines. Ideas not seriously considered were crossed out, and the criteria for decision making were applied to those remaining, with each idea being rated against each criterion. In Figure 3.1, the two ideas with the highest rating were assigning a study buddy and using picture directions.

Plan specifics.   Once one or two ideas are decided on using a process such as the one just described, more detailed planning needs to occur. For example, if you and others have decided that you would like to try having a high school service club provide volunteer tutoring in an after-school program, some of the tasks to assign include asking the club about their interests, arranging a place for the program, ensuring that needed supplies are available, obtaining permission to operate the program, establishing a schedule for students, determining who will provide adult supervision and scheduling it, advertising the program, and creating training sessions for the tutors and delivering them.

collaboration, sites with discussion groups, tools for electronic collaboration, and strategies for creating vehicles for electronic collaboration. For example, the guide discusses the use of videoconferencing as a means of collaborating, and it describes electronic "whiteboards" on which participants can sketch pictures or otherwise visually represent ideas to share with others.

Other sites also foster electronic collaboration. The Partnership for Family Involvement in Education, at http://pfie.ed.gov, is a federally funded website for parents and families designed to help them get more involved in their children's education. The site directs parents to links for building partnerships, for seeking information about what is new for education, and for publications and activities of the organization.

Parenting Special Needs, at http://specialchildren. about.com/parenting/specialchildren /msubeducation. htm?rnk=r6&terms=Special+Education, helps parents, educators, and others who work with children with disabilities to locate a vast array of resources on topics as diverse as attentional disorders, ear infections, law and legal procedures for special education, and juvenile delinquency. Although this site does not include an interactive format, it does include links to many sites that do, particularly sites related to specific disabilities.

Special Needs Opportunity Windows (SNOW), at http://snow.utoronto.ca/, is a Canadian initiative to support teachers and others working with students with special needs. The site includes not only curriculum materials and other resources, but also a discussion forum where educators can meet and share concerns and ideas.

The Integrated Network of Disability Information & Education, at http://indie.ca, features a discussion forum to learn about perspectives on specific disabilities and education related to students with disabilities from all over the world. The emphasis at this site is on the promotion of global understanding of individuals with disabilities.

If you explore the Internet, you will undoubtedly find other sites that focus on electronic collaboration. These sites can give you fresh ideas, basic knowledge, and a broader understanding of how you and others can make a profound difference in the lives of students with disabilities.

Typically, at this step of shared problem solving, participants not only list the major tasks that need to be completed to implement the solution, but they also decide who will take responsibility for each task. They also specify a timeline for completing all the tasks and usually decide how long to implement the solution before meeting to evaluate its effectiveness.

Implement the solution. If all the steps in the shared problem-solving process have been carefully followed, implementing the idea(s) decided on may be the most straightforward part of the process. When problem solving occurs concerning a student with a disability in an inclusive school, each team member may have some responsibility for implementing the solution. Occasionally, you will have much of the immediate responsibility. In other cases, parents will have a major role to play. What is critical is that each person involved does his or her part so that the solution has a high probability of success. During implementation, it is helpful to keep some type of record documenting your efforts and the impact of the intervention on the student.

Evaluate outcomes. After a period of time—anywhere from just a few days to two or more weeks—the professionals who are implementing the solution meet to evaluate its effectiveness. At this time, three possibilities exist. First, if the solution has been especially effective, it may be judged a success. It will then be either continued

Figure 3.1 A Sample Decision-Making Chart for Problem Solving

Problem Statement: How can we help Angela work independently on assigned classroom tasks?

Ideas:

Tape-record instructions	~~Don't give independent work~~
Have an assigned "study buddy"	Let her choose the assignment
Make the work easier	~~Make her stay in from recess to~~
Use pictures for directions	~~complete~~
Ask a parent volunteer to help	

Decision Making: (3 = high, 2 = medium, 1 = low)

Criteria

Idea	Angela will work for at least 5 minutes	Low time commitment for teacher	Doesn't disrupt class routine	Total	Rank
1. Taped instructions	3	1	2	6	
2. Study buddy	3	3	3	9	1
3. Easier work	2	2	2	6	
4. Picture directions	3	2	3	8	2
5. Parent volunteer	1	3	2	6	
6. Choose assignment	1	2	1	4	

to maintain the results, discontinued if no longer needed, or gradually phased out. Second, if the solution seems to be having a positive effect but is not ideal for some other reason, it may be modified. For example, a behavior management plan may be helping a student attend class rather than skip it, but the classroom teacher notes that the system is too time consuming. The problem-solving group may then try to streamline the plan to make it more feasible. Finally, even when the steps in problem solving are carefully completed, a solution is occasionally judged ineffective. The team then must decide what to do next: Should a different solution be selected from the list already generated? Should additional solutions be proposed? Is the problem accurately identified? The team needs to consider all these possibilities before additional problem solving occurs.

Professionals who regularly employ the strategies of shared problem solving are quick to acknowledge that the steps do not automatically lead to simple solutions that always work. What they report, however, is that when they problem solve in this fashion, they feel that their professional time is well spent and that the problem-solving process is truly a collaborative endeavor.

Check Your Learning

What are the steps in problem solving? As you observe others problem solve, can you recognize each step?

Co-Teaching

Co-teaching occurs when two or more educators, one a general education teacher and the other a special education teacher or other specialist, share the instruction for a single group of students, typically in a single classroom setting (Bauwens & Hourcade, 1995). Although any two teachers can teach together and this sometimes occurs at elementary, middle, and high school, we focus here on the unique arrangement of having two professionals with potentially very different points of view working together on behalf of all the students in a class.

Co-teaching is becoming a very popular strategy for achieving inclusion (Gerber & Popp, 1999; Walther-Thomas, Korinck, McLaughlin, & Williams, 1999). In a classroom with several students with disabilities, combining the strengths of the general education teacher and a special educator can create options for all students (Cook & Friend, 1995). Co-teaching typically occurs for a set period of time either every day (for example, every morning from 9:30 until 10:15) or on certain days of the week (for example, on Mondays and Wednesdays during third hour). Occasionally, especially in middle and high schools, a group of students with disabilities who used to attend a separate class for a specific subject join a general education class permanently. In such cases, the special education teacher may be available every day. For example, if a school used to have general science for students with disabilities, the group of eight students from that class and their teacher may become members

Co-teaching is an innovative and exciting way to provide special services to students with special needs. How can educators best use their collective expertise when they share instruction? What dilemmas might occur, and how can these be resolved?

Professional Edge

Tips for Successful Co-Teaching

Co-teaching is one approach that facilitates the inclusion of students who have disabilities in general education classrooms. The two teachers involved, often a general education teacher and a special educator, can together offer instructional options for all students. Keep in mind the following tips to make your co-teaching efforts successful.

1. **Planning is the key.** Make time to plan lessons and to discuss exactly how you will work together throughout your co-teaching experience.

2. **Discuss your views on teaching and learning with your co-teacher.** Experienced co-teachers agree that both teachers should share basic beliefs about instruction.

3. **Attend to details.** Clarify classroom rules and procedures, such as class routines for leaving the room, using free time, discipline, grading, and so on.

4. **Prepare parents.** If parents have questions, explain to them that having two teachers in the class gives every child the opportunity to receive more attention than before; it does not change the curriculum except to enrich it.

5. **Avoid the "paraprofessional trap."** The most common concern about co-teaching is that the special education teacher becomes a classroom helper, which quickly becomes boring for the special education teacher and awkward for the general education teacher. Using a variety of co-teaching approaches can help teachers avoid this predicament.

6. **When disagreements occur, talk them out.** To have some disagreements in co-teaching is normal. But be sure to raise your concerns while they are still minor and to recognize that both of you may have to compromise to resolve your differences.

7. **Go slowly.** If you begin with co-teaching approaches that require less reliance on one another, you have a chance to learn each other's styles. As your comfort level increases, you can try more complex co-teaching approaches.

S O U R C E : Adapted from "The New Mainstreaming," by M. Friend and L. Cook, 1992b, *Instructor, 101*(7), 30–32, 34, 36. Reprinted by permission of Scholastic, Inc.

Cultural Awareness

Kalyanpur and Harry (1999) postulate that the provisions of IDEA-97 represent the U.S. values of individualism, equity, and choice. How might families from other cultures differ from U.S. families in terms of the importance they place on these values and how these values shape the way they react to the special education procedures and services found in schools?

of a general education biology class of 25 students. The burden of extra students is more than offset by the advantage of two teachers being assigned to the class full-time. One other strategy for co-teaching is to have a special education teacher and a classroom teacher share instruction for a particular unit, often one that many students find difficult (for example, changing decimals to fractions). After the unit is completed, the co-teaching is stopped until another specific need arises. The Professional Edge offers suggestions for making co-teaching successful.

Effective as it is, co-teaching is not the answer for every student with a disability nor for every classroom in an inclusive school. Co-teaching is only one option for meeting the needs of students in inclusive schools (Reinhiller, 1996). Further, it is relatively expensive (that is, the cost of two teachers with one group of students) and should be reserved for situations in which the number of students with disabilities in a class justifies the presence of two teachers, or the class is one in which all students with disabilities enroll (for example, a high school U.S. history class).

Many approaches are available to teachers who decide to co-teach (Bauwens & Hourcade, 1995; Walther-Thomas et al., 1999). Cook and Friend (1995; 2000) have outlined some of the common ones, which are depicted in Figure 3.2.

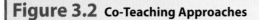

Figure 3.2 Co-Teaching Approaches

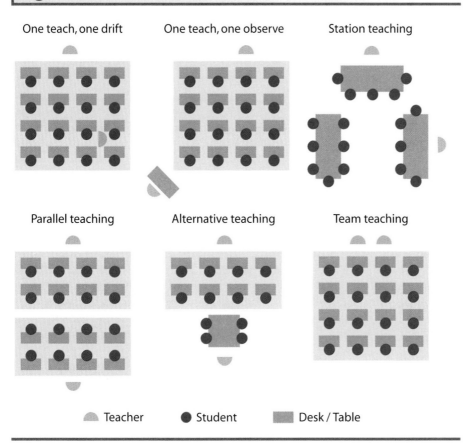

One teach, one drift One teach, one observe Station teaching

Parallel teaching Alternative teaching Team teaching

Teacher • Student ▬ Desk / Table

One teach, one observe. In this approach, one teacher leads the lesson and the other gathers data on students to understand them better and make instructional decisions. For example, while Ms. Tran, the general education teacher, leads a lesson in which students work in cooperative groups to answer questions about a map, Ms. Firestone, the special education teacher, might systematically observe three students who are known to struggle with social skills. Ms. Firestone might note on a chart the number of times each of those students initiates an interaction with a peer as well as how often other students direct comments or questions to them. How might this information be helpful to the teacher? Teachers can observe students' ability to pay attention, to work independently, to make productive use of spare time, and to seek assistance when they have questions. However this approach is used, it is essential that each educator sometimes leads the class while the other observes. In this way, both teachers have the opportunity to watch the class "in action," and both have credibility with students because of leading instruction.

One teach, one drift. Occasionally during instruction, it is appropriate for one teacher to be leading the lesson while the other quietly assists individual students. For example, while the special education teacher leads a lesson on a test review, the classroom teacher helps students individually as they have questions about the vocabulary.

FYI

Co-teaching is an instructional arrangement in which two or more teachers share responsibility for a group of students. In an inclusive setting, one of the co-teachers is a special education teacher or other special service provider.

Alternatively, while the classroom teacher leads a lesson on the causes of the Civil War, the special education teacher helps keep students on task, checks written work as it is being completed, and responds quietly to student questions. The key to using this approach successfully is to make it only one out of many approaches you use. With overuse, one of the teachers, often the special educator, may feel that he or she has no legitimate role in the class. In addition, if this approach to co-teaching is used too frequently, students may become overdependent on the extra help that always seems to be available.

Station teaching.   This approach is similar to the concept of stations found in many kindergarten classes. In **station teaching**, curricular content is divided into two parts. One teacher teaches half the content to half the students while the other teaches the other half to the rest. The groups then switch and each teacher repeats his or her part of the lesson. With classes of students able to work independently, a third group may be formed with "learning buddies" who tutor each other on a review assignment. Alternatively, a parent volunteer may provide instruction at a third station. In elementary schools, an entire lesson based on stations may be completed in a single day; in secondary schools, a station may take an entire class period or more. For example, in a ninth-grade math class, some of the students are working with the general education teacher on a new concept. A second group is meeting with the special education teacher to apply information taught last week to day-to-day situations. A third group of students is working in pairs on an assignment. Each station lasts the entire class period.

Connections

In Chapters 8, 9, 10, and 11, you are introduced to a wide variety of instructional strategies to use as you co-teach. Co-teaching requires two components: effective arrangement of teachers and students and effective instructional practices.

Parallel teaching.   Sometimes when two teachers are present, they find it advantageous simply to divide a heterogeneous class group in half and have each teacher instruct half the class separately. In this format, called **parallel teaching**, every student would have twice as many opportunities to participate in a discussion or respond to teacher questions. A teacher particularly skilled in presenting information through pictures could use this approach, while the other teacher could emphasize learning through listening. Students who prefer one method to the other could be placed with the appropriate teacher. In an elementary school classroom, this approach might be used to enable students to read different books based on their interests. In a secondary classroom, this approach could enable more students to have more opportunities to respond during a discussion of a current events topic.

Alternative teaching.   In most classrooms, dividing the class into one large and one small group is sometimes appropriate. This co-teaching option is referred to as **alternative teaching**. Traditionally, a small group has been used primarily for remediation, but many other options are possible and recommended. For example, some students may benefit from preteaching. In preteaching, one teacher works with a small group of students who may struggle to learn (whether or not they have IEPs), are shy, or need to feel a strong sense of success. Information to be presented the next day or later in the same day or class is taught to these students so that when questions are asked or vocabulary introduced, the students have a "jump start" on learning. Enrichment also works well in smaller groups. As a unit of instruction on space exploration is concluding, several students might have a strong interest in the topic. As the other students review and complete assigned tasks, this group might meet to discuss career opportunities related to the space industry, write letters to obtain more information on current U.S. space efforts, or explore websites on related topics. The members in this group could include high-achieving students, students who have average academic achievement but who have a strong interest in space topics, a student with a behavior disorder who would benefit more from this activity than from the assigned work, and a student with a moderate cognitive disability for whom the written work is not appropriate. Occasionally, grouping students for remediation is appropriate, but only when it is one among many grouping options. Otherwise, such an arrangement becomes the equivalent of running a special education program in the back of a general education classroom, an arrangement that completely belies the purpose and principles of inclusion.

Team teaching. In the co-teaching option of **team teaching,** the teachers share leadership in the classroom; both are equally engaged in the instructional activities. For example, one teacher may begin a lesson by introducing vocabulary while the other provides examples to place the words in context. Two teachers may role-play an important event from history or a science concept. Two teachers may model how to address conflict by staging a debate about a current event. One teacher may lecture while the other models note-taking strategies on the chalkboard. You reach the limits of team teaching only when you run out of exciting ideas for creating instruction with two teachers instead of one. Co-teachers who use this approach find it the most energizing, but you should also consider that you and a co-teacher might not be compatible enough in terms of teaching style to use this approach. If that is the case, using the other approaches might be more effective.

Co-teaching pragmatics. As you consider these co-teaching approaches, you might notice that many other factors need to be taken into account in addition to how the teachers arrange themselves and the students (Cook & Friend, 1995; Reinhiller, 1996; Walther-Thomas et al., 1999). First, in a co-taught class, students are heterogeneously grouped so students with disabilities are appropriately integrated with their peers without disabilities. Thus, in a station teaching arrangement, students with special needs are in each of the three station groups, and when alternative teaching occurs, the smaller group may or may not contain students with disabilities. Second, both teachers take on teaching and supportive roles. This principle is critical if students are to view both teachers as credible; without using it, the special education teacher may be seen as a helper who does not have teacher status. Third, the best approach to use depends on student needs, the subject being taught, the teachers' experience, and practical considerations such as space and time for planning. Novice co-teachers may prefer station teaching or parallel teaching over team teaching, especially in a class that includes several students with attention problems who would benefit from a smaller group structure. We make this recommendation because those approaches require less minute-to-minute coordination with another teacher. Sometimes, the type of curriculum dictates the approach. Curriculum that is hierarchical obviously cannot be taught in stations, especially in a cramped classroom; it might be best presented in a format of one teach, one support, followed by parallel-taught study groups. The Professional Edge on page 88 provides some additional guidelines for successful co-teaching.

Teaming

In Chapter 2, you learned that you have responsibility as a member of an intervention assistance team to problem solve about students before they are considered for

Research Note

Fisher, Pumpian, and Sax (1998) interviewed parents of students with significant disabilities about their high school experiences. Parents were generally supportive of inclusive practices even though they were concerned about teachers' preparation for this approach to services and the extent to which their children were receiving instruction to help them function in their communities.

special education. You also learned that you may be a member of the multidisciplinary team that determines whether a student is eligible to receive special education services and that writes the student's IEP. Now you need to understand the concepts and procedures that make those teams and other school teams effective.

When you think about highly successful teams, what comes to mind? Your favorite athletic team? A surgical team? An orchestra? What is it about these teams that makes them noteworthy? **Teams** are formal work groups that have certain characteristics. They have clear goals, active and committed members, and leaders; they practice to achieve their results; and they do not let personal issues interfere with the accomplishment of their goals. Can you think of other characteristics of effective teams?

The teams you will be part of at school have many of the same characteristics as other teams (Friend & Cook, 1997). Their success depends on the commitment of every member and the clarity of their goals (Welch, Brownell, & Sheridan, 1999). On effective school teams, members keep in mind why they are a team, setting aside personal differences to reach a goal, often designing the best educational strategies possible for students with disabilities or other special needs.

Team participant roles. Team members must assume multiple roles (Harris, 1995; Rankin & Aksamit, 1994). First, you have a **professional role.** In your role as a classroom teacher, you bring a particular perspective to a team interaction, as do the special education teacher, counselor, adaptive physical educator, principal, and other team members. You contribute an understanding of what students without disabilities are accomplishing in your grade or course, knowledge of curriculum and its pace, and a sense of the prerequisites of what you are teaching and the expectations likely to follow the next segment of instruction.

The second contribution you make is through your **personal role.** The characteristics that define you as a person shape this role. For example, are you an eternal optimist, a person who sees the positive aspects of almost any situation? You will probably be the person who keeps up the team's morale. Are you a detail-oriented person who is skilled at organizing? You will probably be the team member who ensures that all the tasks get completed and all the paperwork is filed.

Check Your Learning

What are the differences among professional, personal, and team roles? What team roles are you most likely to take?

Third, you have a **team role** to fulfill as well. You may be the individual who makes sure the agenda is being followed or who watches the time so that team meetings do not last too long. Or you may have the role of summarizing and clarifying others' comments or of suggesting ways to combine what seem to be contradictory points of view into integrated solutions to student problems. As an effective member, you will recognize your strengths and use them to enhance the team; you will also be vigilant so that your weaknesses do not interfere with the team accomplishing its tasks. Common formal team roles include team facilitator, recorder, and timekeeper. These roles might rotate so that every team member has the opportunity to experience each one. Informal team roles include being a compromiser, an information seeker, and a reality checker. These informal roles are not usually assigned, but team members ensure that they are being fulfilled as the need arises.

Team goals. One of the keys to effective teams is attention to goals (Friend & Cook, 1997). Being clear and explicit about goals is particularly important in educational settings because team goals are often assumed or too limited. For example, on some intervention assistance teams, teachers perceive the team goal to be to document interventions so that the special education assessment and identification procedures can begin. Others believe the team functions to help teachers problem solve so that the entire referral process can be avoided. Note how crucial this difference is! With the former, a team may function as a sort of "confirmation hearing" process for students with learning and behavior problems. In the latter, it may be a resource and idea support group. Without clear and specific goals, teams often flounder.

Another aspect of team goals is especially important. The goals just discussed are commonly referred to as **task goals;** that is, they are the business of the team. But teams have another set of goals as well, called maintenance goals. **Maintenance goals** refer to the team's status and functioning as a team. Maintenance goals may include beginning and ending meetings on time, finishing all agenda items during a single meeting, taking time to check on team members' perceptions of team effectiveness, improving team communication both during meetings and outside of them, and so on. These and other maintenance goals enable effective teams to accomplish the task goals they set.

One maintenance goal with which many teams struggle concerns how their meetings are scheduled, structured, and operated. Complaints frequently heard include some members' failure to arrive on time, the tendency of the group to wander off the topic, some members' habit of monopolizing the conversation while others seldom say anything, and the pattern of hurrying to finish meetings and in the process making hasty decisions. All these problems can be addressed and often alleviated through team attention to them.

The following example from an elementary school problem-solving meeting shows how each team member plays a vital role. The team included the principal, two general education teachers, a special education teacher, a speech/language therapist, a reading teacher, and a social worker. The reading teacher often spoke a great deal more than other team members, talking until others simply nodded their heads in agreement with whatever she wanted. At one team meeting, the reading teacher left early, just after the team had decided to assess a student for possible special education services. No sooner had the teacher left than the team members confronted the principal, explaining that they did not believe the referral for assessment was appropriate and asking the principal to make the reading teacher stop pushing through ideas other team members did not want. The principal made a wise reply. He said, "Wait a minute. If there's a problem, it's a team problem. If a poor decision was made, it was a team decision. It's not what am *I* going to do; it's what are *we* going to do."

In the conversation that followed, team members recognized that each of them had a responsibility to speak out when they disagreed with an idea that was presented. They also acknowledged that they were uncomfortable confronting the reading teacher about her interactions during team meetings. However, with the help of the principal, the team spent part of their next meeting talking about each team member's verbal contributions and establishing procedures for checking all team members' perceptions prior to making a decision. Although their actions did not completely change the reading teacher's style, they did bring the team closer together and dramatically increased the team's effectiveness.

The Case in Practice on page 94 lets you in on another team meeting, this time a problem-solving session that includes two teachers, a counselor, and a parent. Notice how each team member contributes to completing problem-solving steps using

C A S E   I N   P R A C T I C E

A Problem-Solving Meeting

Travis has been experiencing a variety of difficulties in his ninth grade English class. Although Travis states that he enjoys English, he has not been turning in his homework assignments, even though they are adapted for him. He also tends to be inattentive in class, watching other students and hallway traffic. Lately he has also begun talking out whenever he feels like it. Mr. Biernat, the English teacher, Ms. Antovich, the special educator, Mrs. Spence, Travis's mother, and Mr. Crain, Travis's counselor, are present at the meeting. They have completed introductions, they have sketched the overall situation, they have mentioned Travis's strengths, and they are now ready to directly address the problem.

Mr. Crain: Given what we've described, Mrs. Spence, I'm wondering what your reaction is.

Mrs. Spence: I don't know—I didn't realize there were all these problems.

Ms. Antovich: That's why we wanted to meet with you in person. This is just not like Travis. I'm sure there is a way to help Travis improve if we all put our heads together to come up with some ideas.

Ms. Biernat: It seems like we should start by looking at the most troublesome area. That's the homework not being turned in. This is affecting Travis's grades because of my grading system. I also know he can

do the work. He sometimes comments that it's easy.

Ms. Antovich: I think looking more closely at homework is a good idea. Mrs. Spence, what do you think?

Mrs. Spence: Yes, I'd like to discuss that some more. Travis tells me he has not had homework, and I checked his assignment notebook and none is written in it.

Mr. Crain: So we know that Travis is not writing down assignments in addition to not turning them in. I wonder whether it's the writing down that is the real problem. Because he has such difficulty remembering details, if the assignments aren't written down, he won't remember what he is to do.

Ms. Biernat: I noticed that Travis isn't writing down assignments, but he refuses to accept assistance with them.

Mr. Crain: I wonder whether we have something else going on here. Maybe this has become a matter of him being embarrassed with the classroom support he receives.

Ms. Antovich: Maybe we should check into a couple of things while we try to get to the bottom of this. I'll talk with Travis privately during his supervised study hall. He's usually pretty open with me. Then maybe we can develop an alternative way for him to get his assignments.

The meeting continues for a few more minutes. The group generates the idea of giving Travis an inexpensive voice recorder so that he can record his assignments orally instead of writing them. They also

consider the option of having another student write the assignments using carbon paper and giving one copy to Travis. Mrs. Spence is concerned that the issue is not the assignments at all, but that Travis's new friends, who are somewhat older than he is, are a negative influence on him. They agree to meet again in 2 weeks to continue their conversation.

1. What steps in a shared problem-solving process did this team complete? If you were asked to state succinctly the problem at hand, what would be your response? Is there more than one problem? If so, what are they?

2. Considering the topics that came up at the meeting, what additional information do you think the team needs to make decisions about Travis's work?

3. Travis was not present at this particular meeting. Why might that have occurred? How could Travis's input be included anyway? How might the meeting have been different with Travis present?

4. What are indicators that the individuals in this interaction used effective communication skills?

5. Consider another problem Travis is experiencing in English. Brainstorm ideas for addressing them. Create any additional details you need to complete this exercise (e.g., Travis's friends, the time of day he has English).

recommended communication skills. By doing so, the positive quality of their team effort comes through.

Consulting

In some cases, you may find that you do not have direct support for a student in your classroom. Perhaps the student does not have an identified disability, or perhaps the student's needs can be met with occasional supports. For example, you might have an outgoing student who suddenly begins acting very withdrawn. Or you may learn that for the next school year you will have a student who has a significant hearing impairment; you would like to know how to assist the student and whether you should enroll in a sign language class. If you have a student with autism in your class, you might find that both you and the special education teacher need assistance from someone else to help the student learn to transition from activity to activity. These are the types of situations in which you might seek support through consultation.

Consultation is a specialized problem-solving process in which one professional who has particular expertise assists another professional (or parent) who needs the benefit of that expertise (Erchul & Martens, 1997; Kampwirth, 1999). You may contact a behavior consultant for assistance when a student in your class is aggressive. You might meet with a vision or hearing consultant when students with those disabilities are included in your class. If you have a student who has received medical or other services outside of school, you may consult with someone from the agency that has been providing those services.

Although consultation is most effective when it is based on the principles of collaboration presented earlier in this chapter, it has a different purpose than collaboration. Even though the consultant working with you may learn from you and benefit from the interaction, the goal of the interaction is to help *you* resolve a problem or deal with a concern, not to foster shared problem solving, in which both or all participants share the problem. In consulting, the assumption is that you are experiencing a problem and that the consultant's expertise will enable you to solve the problem more effectively.

The process of consulting generally begins when you complete a request form or otherwise indicate that you have a concern about a student (Witt, Gresham, & Noell, 1996). The consultant then contacts you to arrange an initial meeting. At that meeting, the problem is further clarified, the teacher's expectations are discussed, and, often, arrangements are made for the consultant to observe in the teacher's room. Once the observation phase has been completed, the consultant and teacher meet again to finalize their understanding of the problem, generate and select options for addressing it, and plan how to implement whatever strategies seem needed. A timeline for putting the strategies into effect is also established. Typically, the teacher then carries out the strategies. Following this phase, the consultant and teacher meet once again to determine whether the problem has been resolved. If it has, the strategy either is continued to maintain the success or eliminated as no longer needed. If a problem continues to exist, the consultant and teacher may begin a new consulting process, or they may decide that some other action is needed. When appropriate, the consultant "closes" the case.

For consulting to be effective, both the consultant and the consultee (that is, you as teacher) need to participate responsibly. Your role includes preparing for meetings, being open to the consultant's suggestions, using the consultant's strategies systematically, and documenting the effectiveness of ideas you try.

How Can You Work Effectively with Parents?

The partnerships presented thus far in this chapter have focused primarily on your interactions with special education teachers and other professionals who will support you in meeting the needs of students with disabilities in your classroom. In this section, we emphasize your working relationship with parents.

The quality of your interactions with the parents of all your students is important, but it is vital for your students with disabilities (Sileo, Sileo, & Prater, 1996). Parents may be able to help you better understand the strengths and needs of their child in your classroom. They also act as advocates for their children, so they can help you ensure that adequate supports are provided for the child's needs. Parents often see their child's experiences in your classroom in a way that you cannot; when they share this information, it helps both you and the student achieve more success. Finally, parents are your allies in educating students; when you enlist their assistance to practice skills at home, to reward a student for accomplishments at school, to communicate to the child messages consistent with yours, you and the parents are multiplying the student's educational opportunities and providing a consistency that is essential to maximize student learning.

Understanding the Perspective of Family Members

You might be tempted to assume that because you work with a student with a disability in your classroom on a daily basis you understand what it would be like to be the student's parent. This assumption could not be further from the truth. For example, the parent of a high school student with a moderate cognitive disability as well as multiple physical disorders made this comment at a meeting of parents and teachers:

> You see my child in a wheelchair and worry about getting her around the building and keeping her changed. But remember, before you ever see her in the morning, I have gotten her out of bed, bathed her, cleaned her, washed her hair and fixed it, fed her, and dressed her. I have made sure that extra clothes are packed in case she has an accident, and I have written notes to teachers about her upcoming surgery. When she's at school I worry about whether she is safe, about whether kids fighting in the hall will care for her or injure her, and whether they are kind. And when she comes home, I clean up the soiled clothes, work with her on all the skills she is still learning, make sure that she has companionship and things to do, and then help her get ready for bed. And I wonder what will be the best option for her when she graduates in 3 years. You can't possibly know what it's like to be the parent of a child like my daughter.

As a teacher, you need to realize what this parent so eloquently demonstrated: that you do not understand what it is like to be the parent of a child with a disability unless you are the parent of one. That means that you should strive to recognize that the range of interactions you have with parents are influenced in part by the

W W W R e s o u r c e s

Many websites offer support to families of children with disabilities. For example, the National Institute on Life Planning for Persons with Disabilities, found at http://www.sonic.net/nilp, offers information to families on transition from school to work or other postschool activities, guardianship, advocacy, aging, housing, and other important topics.

How might the cultural heritage of a parent or family member of a child with a disability affect your interactions? How can you increase your sensitivity to parents' perceptions of their child?

stresses they are experiencing, their prior dealings with school personnel, and their own beliefs about their child's future. Apply this concept to Chris's parents, Mr. and Mrs. Werner, who were introduced at the beginning of the chapter. What might be influencing their interactions with the school professionals? How would knowing about their reluctance to have Chris identified as needing special education and their concerns about the stigma of the learning disability label help the teachers respond appropriately to them?

Parent Reactions to Their Child's Disability

Parents of children with disabilities have many reactions to their children's special needs, and these reactions may focus on positive or negative factors. Some parents go through several emotions roughly in a sequence, whereas others may experience only one or several discrete reactions. For some, the reactions may be minor and their approach pragmatic. For others, the child's disability might affect their entire family structure and life. Part of your work with parents includes recognizing that how parents respond to you may be influenced by these responses to their children's disabilities.

1. *Grief.* Some parents feel grief about their child's disability. Sometimes this is a sorrow for the pain or discomfort that their child may have to experience; sometimes it is sadness for themselves because of the added stress on the family when a child has a disability; and sometimes it is a sense of loss for what the child may not be able to become. Parents have a right to grieve about their child, a right educators should respect.

2. *Ambivalence.* Another reaction parents may have toward their child is ambivalence. This feeling may occur as parents attempt to confirm that the child's

> ### Cultural Awareness
>
> Many parents, but especially those from minority groups, can find school an intimidating place. You can promote participation by encouraging parents to come to school meetings with a friend or another family member and by asking them positive questions early during meetings (for example, "What does your child say about school at home?").

WWW Resources

The Center for Mental Health Services includes a link (http://www. mentalhealth.org/ publications/allpubs/ ca-0014/socare.htm) to information on the System of Care approach to working with students who have emotional disabilities. This highly collaborative model places the family at the center and assumes that effective services are based on the family's culture, community, and priorities.

disability is not temporary or "fixable," as they try to determine what the best educational options are for their child, and as they ponder how their child will live as an adult. The decisions that parents of children with disabilities have to make are often difficult, and these decisions continue throughout childhood and adolescence, and sometimes through adulthood. Parents often attend meetings at which tremendous amounts of information are shared with little time for explanations, and they often meet with representatives from many different disciplines. It is no wonder that they may feel ambivalent.

3. *Optimism.* One of our students was once interviewing the parent of a student with a mild cognitive disability. When asked what it was like having a child with a cognitive disability in the family, the parent replied, "Mary is my child. Just like any other child. I love her as my child. She is sometimes funny and sometimes clever and sometimes naughty. She can really get into trouble. She's just like my other children, except she's Mary." For this parent, her child's special needs are just part of the configuration of needs that the children in any family may have. In this family, the emphasis is on the person, not the disability. There are many families like this one. In these families, the special needs of the child are met without extraordinary reactions. Parents may work diligently to optimize their child's education, but they are hopeful about their child's future. They work closely with educators and others to ensure that the child's life, whatever it may be, is the best one possible.

How parents respond when they have a child with a disability depends on many factors. One is the intensity and complexity of the disability. The reaction of a parent whose child is diagnosed with a learning disability in third grade is likely to be somewhat different from that of parents who learned 2 months after their child was born that she could not see.

Another factor affecting how parents respond is how the information about the disability is shared with them. When such information is presented in a coldly clinical manner, without adequate sensitivity to the parents' emotions, their response can be quite negative. This is true even for mild disabilities. When a parent was told about her son's learning disability, the parent said, "Wait a minute. Stop and let me think. Do you realize what you've just said? You've just unraveled my whole way of thinking about my son. What do you mean a learning disability? What does that mean? Will it ever change? How can you sit there and keep talking as though it's no big thing?" A father related how he learned about his daughter's moderate cognitive disability: A physician simply said, "She's retarded. There's nothing we can do." The father left the office crying, partly because of the information and partly because of the insensitive way in which it had been communicated.

Yet another factor influencing a family's response to their child with a disability is culture (Kalyanpur & Harry, 1999). In some cultures, disability is a spiritual phenomenon that may reflect a loss of the soul or evidence of transgressions in a previous life. In other families, a child with a disability is considered a reflection on the entire family. In some families, a disability is accepted as just part of who the child is. In others, it is believed that a cure should be sought. It is important to listen to family members as they discuss their child to better understand their perspective on the child and perhaps their response to ideas and suggestions that you and the rest of the team make.

One other factor that affects parent response concerns resources, including financial support (Turnbull & Turnbull, 1997). If parents have the resources necessary to provide what they believe is the best set of support services for their child, they are less likely to experience negative emotions. However, when parents know that their child would benefit from some intervention, whether it is surgery, a piece of computer equipment, or tutoring, they are invariably frustrated when they cannot provide the needed support and have difficulty accessing it from school and community resources. The other type of resource is personal. In large families, families with many supportive relatives living in the same community, or families with a strong network of neighbors and friends, the stresses of having a child with a disability are greatly reduced. When parents are isolated or when friends and family are uncomfortable with the child, the parents will likely experience far more difficulties.

Collaborating with Parents

Your working relationship with parents will depend on the student's particular needs, the parents' desire to be actively involved in their child's education, and your efforts to make parents feel as though your partnership with them is important. In some cases, collaboration may be too ambitious a goal. For example, if you are going to interact with a parent only three or four times during the school year, you may simply not have adequate opportunity for collaboration to occur. Similarly, some parents may have so many other obligations and stressors that collaboration is not a realistic goal for them. Still, for others collaboration is not only appropriate, but recommended. Your first goal in working with parents, however, is to help them participate in meetings, conferences, and other interactions in a way that is meaningful and respectful (Friend & Cook, 2000). In this way, you create the opportunity to learn whether collaboration is an appropriate next step.

One of the most important factors that influence whether you can develop strong working relationships with parents and families is your sensitivity to the parents' point of view (Kalyanpur & Harry, 1999; Turnbull & Turnbull, 1997). For example, some parents find school an unpleasant or intimidating place. They may have had negative experiences when they were students, or, if they are from another country, they may be unfamiliar with expectations for involvement in U.S. public schools. If parents' primary language is not English, they may be uncomfortable because of the need for an interpreter, or they may misunderstand information communicated by school personnel, whether in face-to-face interactions or in writing. Some parents may consider the frequent written communication that comes from schools to be a nuisance (Harry, Torguson, Katkavich, & Guerrero, 1993).

Some parents may not be as involved as you would like because of pragmatic barriers. If a parent works at a job that is far from school, he or she may not be able to take time off to participate in activities at school and may not be able to afford the lost work time. For some parents, involvement is largely a matter of economics: The costs of child care and transportation may prevent them from being able to work with you.

In general, your attitude toward parents and their perceptions of their children greatly affect how you interact with them. If you telegraph through your choice of words, through your question-asking skills, and through your body posture that the parents are limited participants in their children's education, you will probably find that parents do not communicate with you and may, in fact, perceive you as an ineffective teacher. However, if you make parents feel welcome in your classroom, listen carefully to their perceptions and concerns, treat them as important, and work

Cultural Awareness

In schools with many bilingual students, parents are sometimes enlisted to work as paraprofessionals. In this way, students' language is present in the classroom. At the same time, parents gain a better understanding of the expectations for their children.

Connections

Information about working with parents is integrated in nearly every chapter of this textbook. For information on working with parents of students with specific disabilities, see Chapters 5 and 7.

with them to address student needs, many benefits will ensue for the student, for the family, and for you. With a positive approach, students learn more and your time is spent in creating options and opportunities, not in responding to parent complaints. The Professional Edge summarizes a range of barriers to collaboration with parents and offers ideas for overcoming them.

Parent Conferences

In addition to the informal, day-to-day communication in which you engage with parents, you also collaborate with them through conferences. Preparing effectively for parent conferences helps ensure successful conferences with the parents of all your students, including students with disabilities.

Prior to a conference. Before parent conferences, you should take several steps to prepare. First, you should clarify the purpose of the conference, both for yourself and for parents. If the purpose is to explain briefly a class or course and parents understand this, they are less likely to be disappointed when you do not share specific information about their child. If the purpose is to spend a specific amount of time discussing a child's progress and parents know this, they can come to school prepared for such a discussion. You can help parents prepare for a conference by sending home in advance a list of questions and suggestions. A sample of this type of conference–preparation flier is presented in Figure 3.3.

You should also prepare for conferences by organizing details to maximize the time available and create a comfortable atmosphere for both the parents and yourself. Specifically, you should plan to meet with parents at a conference table, not your desk, because your desk may be perceived as a symbol of power. If your class-

---

Figure 3.3 Sample Set of Questions to Help Parents Prepare for Conferences

1. What is your child's favorite class activity?
2. Does your child have worries about any class activities? If so, what are they?
3. What are your priorities for your child's education this year?
4. What questions do you have about your child's education in my class this year?
5. How could we at school help make this the most successful year ever for your child?
6. Are there any topics you want to discuss at the conference for which I might need to prepare? If so, please let me know.
7. Would you like other individuals to participate in the conference? If so, please give me a list of their names so that I can invite them.
8. Would you like me to have particular school information available? If so, please let me know.
9. Do you have other questions about our upcoming conference? If so, you can reach me by phone between 7:30 and 8:10 A.M. and between 3:00 and 3:45 P.M. at _____. If you prefer, you also can reach me by e-mail at _____.

room is equipped for young children, you should also arrange to have adult-sized furniture available for the meeting. A box of tissues should be within easy reach, and you should make sure that the conference is private, perhaps by posting a sign on your door that instructs parents to knock to indicate they have arrived and then to wait until you come to the door to greet them. Another part of planning a conference is preparing the questions and topics you want to discuss with parents. These might include specific questions regarding how a student behaves at home and how rewards are given, or they might be a list of academic strengths and concerns. Having samples of student work, your grade and plan books, and other pertinent student records easily available is also important.

During a conference. During the conference, your goal is to create a two-way exchange of information. To do this, greet parents positively, set a purpose for the conference, and actively involve parents in discussions. You should use all the collaboration skills you employ with colleagues in working with parents. In addition, you should use language respectful of the parents, their child, and their culture. Parents should be addressed as "Mr." or "Ms.," not as "Dad" or "Mom." Students should be referred to by name. Jargon should be avoided. In addition, teachers should work to understand that parents might interpret the meaning of *disability* and educators' response to it in ways that differ from the meanings given by educators. For example, low-income Puerto Rican parents have been found to think of disability in terms of family identity and the school's failure to provide for the student, not as an inherent student problem (Harry, 1992a). African American parents sometimes distrust school professionals and the decisions made about their children because of past segregation and discriminatory special education practices (Harry, 1992b). The Professional Edge on pages 102–103 suggests several strategies that a school or district could use to involve parents in conferences who are unfamiliar with or uncomfortable with public schools.

During a conference, you might meet both with parents and a special education teacher. As teachers, you share the responsibility for creating a collaborative environment as well as for ensuring that all critical information is presented to parents, that parents have ample opportunities to share information with you, and that any needed strategies are developed and follow-ups planned.

After a conference. After a parent conference, you should complete several additional responsibilities. First, you should write a few notes to remind yourself of the important points discussed. These notes help you improve the accuracy of your recollections. Second, if you made any major decisions regarding strategies that you and the parents will implement, you might want to write a brief note to the parents to confirm the decisions you made. Third, if you agreed to any action (for example, sending information to parents, asking a counselor to call parents), it is best to carry it out as soon as possible. Finally, if the special education teacher did not attend the conference, he or she may appreciate a brief note from you with an update on the conference outcomes.

Of course, you communicate with parents on many occasions, both formally and informally. If you keep in mind that your job is to work to understand parents' perspectives and to incorporate their priorities into your work with their child, your interactions with them will undoubtedly be successful. If you insist, either explicitly or implicitly, that you know best about the child, however, it is likely your interactions with parents will be either adversarial or minimal.

Professional Edge

Understanding Home–School Collaboration

Collaboration between parents or families and school professionals can be challenging. The following barriers may exist.

Barriers for Parents

- Some parents have feelings of inadequacy, failure, and poor self-worth. Many parents see themselves as not very smart and as school failures.
- Some parents have negative attitudes or bad experiences with schools.
- Parents may be suspicious or angry about schools not treating them fairly.
- Many low-income parents, as well as those from other cultures, see teachers as authority figures and leave it to the school to educate their children.
- Parents may experience cultural and language barriers.
- Parents may feel anxious about surrendering their children to strangers whose values differ from their own and who may inculcate those values in the children.
- Some parents experience economic hardship and unemployment. Financial pressure of making ends meet becomes primary to worrying about how children are doing in school.
- Many parents view schools as unsafe environments.
- Logistical problems may prevent parents from coming to the school because they lack access to or

are unable to afford transportation or child care for younger siblings.

- In many instances scheduling mismatches occur for parents and teachers.
- Many students who experience difficulties in school are from socially stressed homes. The stress may be such that it contributes to or exacerbates the difficulties students experience in school, or takes precedence over any difficulties students experience in school.

Barriers for Teachers and School

- School practices can discourage or completely block parent participation.
- School policies sometimes discourage home–school collaboration. For instance, in some schools union contracts specify that volunteers cannot be used for teaching functions.
- Schools may not make parents feel welcome.
- Schools may not be held accountable for implementing changes that produce high student achievement, and parents often are unaware of what should be happening for their children.
- Teachers may believe that certain parents do not care and will not keep commitments.
- Schools may focus on passive parent involvement, failing to recognize the multiple ways in which parents can participate effectively in school change.

How Can You Work Effectively with Paraprofessionals?

In our discussion throughout this chapter of forming partnerships with others in schools, an assumption has been made that everyone involved has equal status; that is, a general education teacher has approximately the same level of authority and equivalent responsibilities as a special education teacher, speech/language therapist, school psychologist, reading teacher, and so on. In many school districts, individuals in these types of positions are referred to as *certified staff*.

- Some teachers have low expectations for at-risk students.

- Some teachers worry that parent involvement in decision making decreases teacher independence and autonomy.

- Teachers may doubt their ability to work with some types of parents (e.g., parents who do not speak English, immigrant parents, single parents, parents from specific racial or ethnic groups, at-risk parents).

- Communication from schools may focus on the negative.

- Teachers may fail to reinforce the strengths that families have.

Mutual Barriers

- Teachers and parents may be confused about their roles in educating children. Teachers and parents may have stereotyped images of one another.

- Parents and teachers are busy. The pressure of having to get many things done in short periods of time interfers with collaboration.

- Teachers and parents may have concerns about turf and territory.

The following approaches may be useful in overcoming these barriers.

- A no-fault model in which parents and teachers do not blame each other for student difficulties.

- A nondeficit approach in which teachers respect families for who they are and look for assets and strengths rather than deficiencies and failures.

- Empowerment, or giving parents more control over their lives and their children's education. Parents thus are more able to influence those individuals who affect their lives and the lives of those they care about.

- An ecological approach in which schools and families together see all the connections in a child's world: family, neighborhood or community, church, school.

- Collaboration and partnership among school personnel and families to meet parenting, education, counseling, health care, housing, and other needs.

S O U R C E : From "Home–School–Agency Partnership," by J. E. Ysseldyke, B. Algozzine, and M. L. Thurlow, 1992, in *Critical Issues in Special Education* (2nd ed.), Boston: Houghton Mifflin. Copyright © 1992 by Houghton Mifflin Company. Adapted with permission. Adapted from *At-Risk Families and Schools: Becoming Partners*, by L. B. Liontos, 1992, Eugene, OR: ERIC Clearinghouse on Educational Management; *Beyond the Bake Sale: An Educator's Guide to Working with Parents*, by A. T. Henderson, C. L. Marburger, and T. Doms, 1986, Washington, DC: National Committee for Citizens in Education; *Urgent Message: Families Crucial to School Reform*, by A. C. Lewis and A. T. Henderson, 1997, Washington, DC: Center for Law and Education (ERIC Document Reproduction Service No. ED418480); and *Families and Larger Systems*, by E. Imber-Black, 1988, New York: Guilford.

One other partnership you may form involves another type of staff. As mentioned in Chapter 2, **paraprofessionals** are noncertified staff members who are employed to assist certified staff in carrying out the educational programs and otherwise helping in the instruction of students with disabilities. (Although some school districts also employ other types of paraprofessionals, for our discussion we refer only to paraprofessionals who are part of special education services.) When students with disabilities are members of your class, a special educator may not have adequate time or opportunity to assist them frequently, or the student might not need the direct services of that professional. Instead, a paraprofessional might be assigned to you for a class period or subject, or, depending on the intensity of student needs, for much of the school day (French, 1999a).

FYI

Some paraprofessionals are highly trained to work with students with specific disabilities. For example, a paraprofessional working with students who are deaf probably is expected to know sign language. A paraprofessional working with a student with autism probably has been prepared to respond to the student's behaviors using specific strategies known to be effective.

Understanding Your Working Relationship with Paraprofessionals

The partnerships you form with paraprofessionals are slightly different from those with certified staff because you have some supervisory responsibility for the paraprofessional's work, a situation that would not exist in your work with colleagues (Wadsworth & Knight, 1996). For example, you may be expected to prepare materials for the paraprofessional to use to work with a group of students; you may have the responsibility of assigning tasks to this person on a daily basis; and you may need to provide informal training to the paraprofessional regarding your classroom expectations.

Many classroom teachers have never been supervisors, and they worry about what types of tasks to assign to a paraprofessional and how to set expectations. Adding to the complexity is the fact that some paraprofessionals have extensive professional preparation, a teaching license, and years of classroom experience, which makes them want to do nearly everything you do, whereas others have a high school diploma and little training or experience in working with students (Marks, Schrader, & Levine, 1999). In Chapter 2 you learned about the types of responsibilities paraprofessionals may have in your classroom. If you will be working with a paraprofessional, you will probably receive a written description of that person's job responsibilities, which specifies the activities that individual is to complete. Also, you can arrange to meet with the special education teacher or other professional who has overall responsibility for the paraprofessional's job performance. Two general guidelines for working effectively with paraprofessionals are these: First, paraprofessionals generally enjoy working with students and want to participate actively in that process, and they should have the opportunity to do so. However, they also are appropriately expected to help teachers accomplish some of the "chores" of teaching, such as record keeping and instructional preparation tasks. Second, paraprofessionals always complete their assignments under the direction of a teacher who has either already taught the information or decided what basic work needs to be completed; that is, paraprofessionals should not engage in initial teaching, nor should they make instructional decisions without input from a certified staff member.

You have a key role in setting the expectations for paraprofessionals who work in your classroom, for ensuring that you and the paraprofessional are satisfied with your working relationship, and for resolving any problems that arise. At the beginning of the school year, you can orient the paraprofessional to your classroom by providing a place for the paraprofessional to keep personal belongings and instructional materials, explaining essential rules and policies for your classroom, clarifying where you want the paraprofessional to work, and asking the paraprofessional to voice questions and concerns. It is particularly important to touch base with the paraprofessional frequently early in the school year to be certain that expectations are clear. The paraprofessional may be working in several classrooms and trying to remember several sets of directions from different teachers, all with their own styles. You might even find that discussing these topics is best accomplished in a meeting that includes the special education teacher as well as you and the paraprofessional. Figure 3.4 outlines some guidelines for you to keep in mind throughout the school year as you work with paraprofessionals so that your experience is positive for you and your students as well as the paraprofessional.

Figure 3.4 Guidelines for Effective Teamwork with Paraprofessionals

1. Consider your paraprofessional an important member of the instructional team. Be sure to include him or her in team meetings whenever possible.

2. Treat your paraprofessional with dignity and respect. Provide support and backup.

3. Discuss goals, priorities, and plans with your paraprofessional on a daily basis.

4. Avoid interrupting the paraprofessional when he or she is engaged in an activity. Keep interruptions to a minimum.

5. Coordinate activities with the paraprofessional so you both accomplish as much as possible.

6. Provide as much lead time as you can. Avoid last-minute rush jobs for the paraprofessional.

7. Discuss problems and ideas with your paraprofessional. Ask for his or her ideas, suggestions, and opinions.

8. If you must leave the classroom temporarily, tell your paraprofessional where you are going, how you can be reached, and when you will return.

9. Keep the paraprofessional fully informed about what is happening in the school environment. Ask what he or she would like to know about your priorities.

10. Expect the best. Include the paraprofessional in staff development opportunities whenever possible.

11. If you are one of several teachers with whom a paraprofessional works, be alert for contradictory directions that may be given. Clarify expectations as needed.

12. Ask your paraprofessional whether you are wasting his or her time or hindering his or her performance. Make changes based on the feedback you receive.

S O U R C E : Adapted from *Strengthening the Partnership: Para-Educators and Teachers Working Together: Time Management for Teams,* by K. Gerlach, 1994, p. 18, Seattle: Pacific Training Associates.

To continue nurturing the working relationship you have with a paraprofessional, you should communicate clearly and directly all activities that you would like the paraprofessional to complete. Some paraprofessionals report that they enter teachers' classrooms only to find that the teacher is working with students and expects the paraprofessional to know what lesson to review with the students with special needs, assuming that the special education teacher has provided this direction. The special educator is assuming that the general education teacher is guiding the paraprofessional. Unfortunately, the paraprofessional may be left wondering how to proceed.

Although most paraprofessionals work diligently, have a tremendous commitment to working with students with disabilities, and manage their roles superbly, occasionally problems arise. If you teach older students, you might find that the paraprofessional does not have enough knowledge of the information being presented to reinforce student learning. A few paraprofessionals violate principles of confidentiality by discussing classroom or student matters away from school. Some paraprofessionals are disruptive in classrooms—their speech is too loud or their movements are too noticeable. If problems such as these occur and cannot be

How can you ensure that you establish and maintain a positive relationship with a paraprofessional? What topics might you decide to discuss with a paraprofessional to clarify your expectations and to make the paraprofessional comfortable working in your classroom?

Research Note

Whitworth (1999) used qualitative methods to examine factors that lead to the development of successful inclusive education in a school. The following are among the factors he identified: (1) principal leadership, (2) shared vision by all staff, (3) time for shared planning and other collaborative activities, and (4) commitment to collaboration by educators.

resolved directly between you and the paraprofessional, you should request that the special educator with whom you work meet with you and the paraprofessional to problem solve. If further action is needed, an administrator such as a principal or special education coordinator can assist.

Collaborating with Paraprofessionals

An often-asked teacher question regarding paraprofessionals is, Given the supervisory nature of teacher–paraprofessional work, is it possible to collaborate with this group of staff members? The answer is yes! Paraprofessionals can collaboratively participate in shared problem solving about student needs, in planning field trip details, and in making decisions regarding how best to adapt information for a specific student. Your responsibility as a teacher is to encourage this type of collaboration. At the same time, you should clearly inform the paraprofessional when a matter being discussed is *not* one in which the principles of collaboration are appropriate. It is also important that you tell paraprofessionals when they are meeting your expectations and that you promptly address any issues as soon as you become aware of them. For example, some paraprofessionals tend to hover over students with disabilities, preventing them from establishing social relationships with peers and fostering dependence instead of independence (Giangreco et al., 1999). You should discuss this well-intentioned but inappropriate activity with the paraprofessional and give clear, alternative directions for their interactions with students. By offering encouragement and addressing concerns, you can establish an environment that will make your collaboration with paraprofessionals invaluable. The suggestions presented in Figure 3.4 offer additional ideas for teaming with paraprofessionals.

Summary

Collaboration has become an important job responsibility for all educators and is especially important in educating students with special needs. Collaboration is the style professionals use in interacting with others, and it involves key characteristics such as voluntary participation, parity, shared goals, shared responsibility for key decisions, shared accountability for outcomes, shared resources, and the emergence of a collaborative belief system, trust, and respect. You help make your school's collaborative efforts more successful by identifying and clarifying your personal beliefs about collaboration, refining your interaction skills, and contributing to a supportive environment.

Collaboration can occur in many applications, but for students with special needs the most common ones are shared problem solving, co-teaching, teaming, and consulting. Each of these applications has its own set of guidelines and its own use in educating students.

Another collaborative responsibility teachers have relates to parents. You need to understand parents' perspectives on having a child with a disability, to work collaboratively with parents on the basis of your respect for their perspective, to communicate effectively with parents in conferences and in other ways, and to respond professionally to parents in team meetings, annual reviews, and other interactions at which you and they are present.

A final group with whom general education teachers collaborate is paraprofessionals. Understanding your roles and responsibilities and those of the paraprofessional, and basing your collaboration on these, leads to positive working relationships with paraprofessionals.

Applications in Teaching Practice

Collaboration at Lawrence Elementary School

Although the 23 teachers at Lawrence Elementary School have always worked together informally, when they began emphasizing inclusive programs for students with disabilities, they realized that they needed more than ever to work collaboratively. Dr. Tompkins, the principal, strongly agreed. Last spring, the teachers met on committees to decide what it would mean for them to be collaborative, what their collaborative priorities would be, and who would be involved in their efforts for the next school year.

First, the teachers reviewed their school mission statement as a starting point for discussions of their beliefs about how students learn, how teachers teach, and how schools can be learning communities. They quickly realized that their mission statement, although not bad, did not explicitly say that teachers in the school are expected to work together to meet the needs of all their students. During another after-school meeting, the mission statement was revised.

Next, the teachers began to discuss various forms their collaboration might take. Carole, a first-grade teacher anticipating a class group with many special needs, argued strongly for co-teaching. She stated that she needed someone to help her for at least a couple of hours each day. Peggy reminded her that with only two special education teachers and one paraprofessional for everyone, from kindergarten through fifth grade, she was asking for far too much, especially because these professionals also had other responsibilities. Jim, the special education teacher who works with students with moderate and severe disabilities, agreed. He noted that he had to reserve time to work individually with some of his students in a special education setting. Carole's reply to these comments was that she knew that when it really got down to it, there would not be enough resources to make their collaborative approach to meeting student needs work, and she referred to a situation that had happened 3 years earlier when one teacher inadvertently ended up with with several students with disabilities in her room and little support. She said little during the rest of the meeting.

For the next year, the teachers agreed that co-teaching should occur in four classrooms where student needs could best be met with that service delivery approach. Jim would co-teach with a fourth-grade teacher and a fifth-grade teacher because most of his assigned students were in those grade levels. Marta, the teacher for students with high-incidence disabilities, would co-teach in first grade and third grade because of the needs of her assigned students and other students in those grade levels. Kindergarten would not have co-teaching because parent volunteers seemed to provide positive assistance and no students with disabilities would be in the classes. Second grade would have the services of Stu, the paraprofessional, for an hour four times each week, and Marta would observe in the classes at least once every other week to ensure services were appropriate.

The teachers also decided to begin one more collaborative approach. They agreed to meet in grade-level teams at least once every other week. These separate teams would function as prereferral intervention teams for each grade level. They negotiated a schedule so that some grade levels met before school and others after school, and they staggered the meeting days so that either Jim or Marta could attend every team meeting. The teachers' goal for these teams was to renew their efforts to meet students' needs without relying on special education services, except when students clearly needed that extra assistance.

With much excitement and a little anxiety, the teachers finished their detailed planning. For example, they were a little concerned because fourth grade would have two new teachers who had not had the opportunity to participate in the planning. In the meantime, Dr. Tompkins lobbied for a few extra resources for the school's innovative plan so that the school could release the teachers for half a school day twice during the next year for evaluation of their efforts and problem solving.

Questions

1. Which characteristics of collaboration can you identify from the teachers' interactions and plans? Which are not evident?
2. How were the teachers working to ensure that their collaborative efforts would be successful? What was Dr. Tompkins's role?

3. How would you respond to Carole? What do you recommend that she do? What do you recommend that her colleagues do in their interactions with her?

4. What forms of collaboration did the teachers plan to try? What key concepts should the teachers keep in mind that relate to each form?

5. How could the teachers communicate with parents about their plans? What reactions might they expect from parents? Why? How could they involve parents in their programs?

6. How should the second-grade teachers and Stu plan for the year? What are some responsibilities Stu should have? What are some responsibilities that Stu should not assume?

7. How might decisions such as those made by these elementary teachers be made in a middle school? A high school? Considering how schools at those levels operate, how might collaborative services such as teaming, consulting, co-teaching, and problem solving be structured?

4

*Planning
Instruction
by Analyzing
Classroom and
Student Needs*

Learner Objectives

After you read this chapter, you will be able to

1. Explain what it means to make *reasonable* accommodations for students with special needs.

2. Describe the steps of a decision-making process for accommodating students with special needs in your classroom.

3. Identify and describe the key elements of an instructional environment.

4. Describe the major components of classroom organization and explain how they can be adapted for students with special needs.

5. Explain various ways that students can be grouped for instruction in an inclusive classroom.

6. Explain how the use of effective classroom materials and instructional methods can benefit students with special needs.

Key Terms and Concepts

Academic learning time (p. 125)

Assistive technology (AT) (p. 137)

Direct instruction (p. 139)

Discovery learning (p. 141)

Mixed-skill groupings (p. 130)

Same-skill groupings (p. 129)

Scaffolding (p. 144)

Transition time (p. 127)

■ Mr. Rodriguez teaches world history at a large urban high school. When he introduces new content to his students, he teaches to the whole class at once. First, he reviews material that has already been covered, pointing out how that material relates to the new content being presented. Next, he provides any additional background information that he thinks will help students understand the new material better. Before Mr. Rodriguez actually presents new material, he hands out a partially completed outline of the major points he will make. This outline helps students identify the most important information. Every 10 minutes or so, he stops his lecture and allows students to discuss and modify the outline and ask questions. When Mr. Rodriguez completes his lecture, he organizes students into cooperative learning groups of four to answer a series of questions on the lecture. Manuel is a student with a learning disability in Mr. Rodriguez's class. Manuel has a history of difficulty staying on task during lectures and figuring out what information to write down. He also has trouble remembering information from one day to the next. How well do you think Manuel will perform in Mr. Rodriguez's class? What changes in the classroom environment might help Manuel to succeed?

■ Josh has cerebral palsy. His scores on intelligence tests are in the normal range. However, he has lots of trouble with muscle movements, has little use of his lower body and legs, and also has problems with fine muscle coordination. As a result, Josh uses a wheelchair, has trouble with his speech (he speaks haltingly and is difficult to understand), and struggles to write letters and numbers correctly. Josh is included in Ms. Stewart's second-grade class. What aspects of the classroom environment do you think Ms. Stewart will need to adapt for Josh? How do you think she could use technology to facilitate Josh's inclusion?

Disabilities and other special needs arise when characteristics of individual students and various features of students' home and school environments interact. Effective teachers analyze their classroom environment in relation to students' academic and social needs and make accommodations to ensure student success in the classroom. For example, Manuel has difficulty staying on task and retaining new information. However, features of Mr. Rodriguez's class make it easier for Manuel to function. The partially completed lecture outlines help Manuel focus his attention on specific information as he tries to listen and stay on task; the pauses help him catch any lecture information he might have missed. The review sessions are intended to help Manuel retain information by giving him a mechanism for rehearsing newly learned material. Josh has some serious motor problems, but he may be able to function quite independently if Ms. Stewart makes her classroom accessible to a wheelchair and works with special educators to use assistive technology to meet Josh's needs in handwriting and oral communication.

This chapter introduces you to a systematic approach to adapting instruction for students with special needs, called INCLUDE. Although there are other ways to adapt instruction for students with special needs, this strategy gives teachers a systematic way of matching the needs of students, classroom demands or expectations of the teacher, and accommodations that can help when gaps exist. The rest of the text—especially Chapters 8 through 13, in which specific strategies are presented—expands and elaborates on this approach. Later chapters also present a more in-depth look at the relationship between your classroom environment and the diverse needs of learners. An important assumption throughout the text is that the more effective your classroom structure is, the greater the diversity you are able to accommodate and the fewer individualized adaptations you need to make.

How Can the INCLUDE Strategy Help You Make Reasonable Accommodations for Students with Special Needs?

At a recent conference presentation that included both classroom teachers and special education teachers, one of the authors of this text asked the audience how many of those present worked with students with disabilities. A music teacher at the back of the room called out, "Everyone in schools works with students with disabilities!" He is right. Although the professionals who have specialized in meeting the needs of students with disabilities are valuable and provide critical instructional and support systems for students, you and your peers will be the primary teachers for many students with disabilities and other special needs, and you will form partnerships with special educators to meet the needs of others. That makes it critical for you to feel comfortable making accommodations for students.

The **INCLUDE** strategy is based on two key assumptions. First, student performance in school is the result of an interaction between the student and the instructional environment (Lilly, 1979; Smith, 1997; Ysseldyke & Christensen, 1987). In other words, students do have problems, but sometimes the task or the setting causes or magnifies the problems. Second, by carefully analyzing students' learning needs and the specific demands of the classroom environment, teachers can *reasonably* accommodate most students with special needs in their classrooms. You can maximize student success without taking a disproportionate amount of teacher time or diminishing the education of the other students in the class. For example, Mr. Chavez provided Royce, a student with a mild hearing impairment, an outline of lecture notes to help him keep up with the lesson. Soon, other students who had been struggling to recognize the important lecture points requested and also benefited from the outlines. Such a reasonable accommodation assists many students in the class.

The INCLUDE strategy for accommodating students with special needs in the general education classroom follows seven steps:

Step 1. **I**dentify environmental, curricular, and instructional classroom demands.

Step 2. **N**ote student learning strengths and needs.

Step 3. **C**heck for potential areas of student success.

Step 4. **L**ook for potential problem areas.

Step 5. **U**se information gathered to brainstorm instructional adaptations.

Step 6. **D**ecide which adaptations to implement.

Step 7. **E**valuate student progress.

These steps are designed to apply to a broad range of special needs and classroom environments.

Step 1: Identify Classroom Demands

Because the classroom environment significantly influences what students learn, analyzing classroom requirements allows teachers to anticipate or explain problems a student might experience. Then, by modifying the environment, teachers can solve or lessen the impact of these learning problems. Common classroom demands may relate to classroom organization, classroom grouping, instructional materials, and instructional methods.

Classroom organization. The ways in which a teacher establishes and maintains order in a classroom are referred to as **classroom organization** (Doyle, 1986). Classroom organization includes a number of factors: physical organization, such as the use of wall and floor space and lighting; classroom routines for academic and nonacademic activities; classroom climate, or attitudes toward individual differences; behavior management, such as classroom rules and reward systems; and the use of time for instructional and noninstructional activities. LaVerna is a student who needs adaptations in physical organization; she uses a wheelchair and requires wide aisles in the classroom and a ramp for the step leading to her classroom. DeShawn would benefit from a behavior management system; he might move from class to class prior to the end of each period to eliminate many potential opportunities to fight with classmates. He would also benefit from an efficient use of time; minimizing transition times or the amount of time between activities would eliminate further opportunities to engage in inappropriate interactions with his classmates.

Classroom grouping. Teachers use a variety of **classroom grouping** arrangements. Sometimes they teach the whole class at once, as when they lecture in a content area such as social studies. Other times teachers may employ small-group instruction. For example, they may teach a small group of students who have similar instructional needs, such as a group of students who all require extra help on multiplication facts. They may also group students of differing interests and abilities in an effort to foster cooperative problem solving and/or peer tutoring. Finally, classroom groups may be either teacher centered, in which the teacher is primarily responsible for instruction, or peer mediated, in which much of the instruction is carried out by students. Mike needs adaptations in classroom grouping to succeed; for example, he might do better in a small group in which other students read assignments aloud so that he can participate in responding to them.

Instructional materials.   The types of **instructional materials** teachers use can have a major impact on the academic success of students with special needs. Although many teachers are choosing to develop or collect their own materials, published textbooks are most commonly used. Published textbooks include basic-skills texts called *basals* and texts that stress academic content in areas such as history and science. Other materials commonly used by teachers include concrete representational items, such as manipulatives and technological devices, including audiovisual aids, telecommunications systems, and computers. Roberta's use of large-print materials to assist her in seeing her work and Carmen's use of a study guide to help her identify important information in her history text are both examples of adaptations in instructional materials.

Instructional methods.   The ways in which teachers teach content or skills to students and evaluate whether learning has occurred are the essence of teaching and are crucial for accommodating students with special needs. Teachers use a number of different approaches to teach content and skills. Sometimes they teach skills directly, whereas other times they assume the role of a facilitator and encourage students to learn on their own. Instructional methods also involve student practice that occurs in class, through independent seatwork activities, or out of class, through homework. Ms. Correli's decision to use the overhead projector and then give Lon a copy of the transparency to help his learning is an example of adapting the presentation of subject matter. Using a paraprofessional to write a student's words is an example of adapting student practice.

Finally, **student evaluation,** or determining the extent to which students have mastered academic skills or instructional content, is an important aspect of instructional methods. Grades are frequently used to communicate student evaluation. When evaluating students with disabilities, teachers must focus on measuring what a student knows rather than the extent of his or her disability. For example, Alex, who has a severe learning disability in writing, may need to answer test questions orally to convey all he knows; if he gives written answers, you may only be measuring his writing disability. For some students, grading is an appropriate evaluation strategy. But for others, such as Anita, a fifth-grade student who has a moderate cognitive disability and is learning to recognize her name, a narrative report might be a better evaluation tool.

Step 2: Note Student Learning Strengths and Needs

Once instructional demands are specified, the *N* step of INCLUDE calls for identifying student strengths and needs. Remember that students with disabilities are a very heterogeneous group; a label cannot communicate a student's learning profile.

For example, some students with cognitive disabilities can learn many life skills and live independently, whereas others continually need daily assistance. Also keep in mind that students with disabilities are more like their peers without disabilities than they are different. Like their nondisabled peers, they have patterns of learning strengths and weaknesses. Focusing on strengths is essential (Aune, 1991; Epstein, Rudolph, & Epstein, 2000; Epstein & Sharma, 1997). Three areas describe student learning strengths and needs: academics, social-emotional development, and physical development. Problems in any one of these areas may prevent students from meeting classroom requirements.

Academics. The first part of academics is basic skills, including reading, math, and oral and written language. Although these skills might sometimes be bypassed (for example, through the use of a calculator in math), their importance in both elementary and secondary education suggests you should consider them carefully. For example, a student with a severe reading problem is likely to have trouble in any subject area that requires reading, including math, social studies, and science, and on any assignment with written directions.

Cognitive and learning strategies make up the second part of academics. These strategies involve "learning how to learn" skills such as memorization, textbook reading, note taking, test taking, and general problem solving. Such skills give students independence that help them in adult life. Students with problems in these areas experience increasing difficulty as they proceed through the grades. For example, students who have difficulty memorizing basic facts have trouble learning to multiply fractions, and students who cannot take notes could fall behind in a history course based on a lecture format.

Survival skills, the third area of academics, are skills practiced by successful students, such as attending school regularly, being organized, completing tasks in and out of school, being independent, taking an interest in school, and displaying positive interpersonal skills (Brown, Kerr, Zigmond, & Harris, 1984). Students lacking in these areas usually have difficulty at school. For example, disorganized students are not likely to have work done on time, nor are they likely to deliver parent permission forms for field trips to their parents or return them to school. Survival skills also help some students compensate for their other problems. For example, given two students with identical reading problems, teachers sometimes offer more help to the student who has good attendance and tries hard.

Social-emotional development. Students' social-emotional development involves classroom conduct, interpersonal skills, and personal/psychological adjustment. Classroom conduct problems include a number of aggressive or disruptive behaviors, such as hitting, fighting, teasing, hyperactivity, yelling, refusing to comply with requests, crying, and destructiveness. Although most of these behaviors may be exhibited by all children at one time or another, students with special needs may engage in them more frequently and with greater intensity. Conduct problems seriously interfere with student learning and can lead to problems in interpersonal relations and personal psychological adjustment. For example, students who are disruptive in class are less likely to learn academic skills and content; their outbursts also may be resented by their peers and lead to peer rejection, social isolation, and a poor self-image.

Interpersonal skills include but are not limited to initiating and carrying on conversations, coping with conflict, and establishing and maintaining friendships. Although these skills are not ordinarily part of the explicit school curriculum, their overall impact on school adjustment makes them important. For example, students lacking in peer support may have difficulty completing group projects (an example of student practice) or finding someone to help with a difficult assignment (an example of homework).

Personal/psychological adjustment involves the key motivational areas of self-image, frustration tolerance, and proactive learning. For example, students with a poor self-image and low tolerance for frustration may do poorly on tests (an example of student evaluation); students who are inactive learners may have difficulty pursuing an independent science project (an example of student practice).

Physical development.   Physical development includes vision and hearing levels, motor skills, and neurological functioning. Students with vision problems need adapted educational materials. Students with poor fine motor skills may need a computer to do their homework, an adaptation for student practice. Finally, students with attention deficits may need a wider range of approaches for presenting instruction, including lecture, discussion, small-group work, and independent work.

Step 3: Check Potential Areas of Student Success

The next INCLUDE step is *C*, analyzing student strengths in view of the instructional demands identified in Step 1 and checking for activities or tasks students can do successfully. Success enhances student self-image and motivation. Look for strengths in both academic and social-emotional areas. Reading the Current Levels of Performance section of the IEP is a good way to begin identifying student strengths. For example, Jerry doesn't read but can draw skillfully. In social studies, his teacher asks him to be the class cartographer, drawing maps for each region of the world as it is studied. Kurt has a moderate cognitive disability and learns very slowly, but he always comes to school on time. His second-grade teacher appoints him attendance monitor. Dwayne has attention deficit–hyperactivity disorder, is failing all his classes in school, and is beginning to become difficult to handle at home. His parents and teachers have noticed, however, that he is able to identify personal strengths, has a good sense of humor, and can enjoy a hobby. They support Dwayne's positive interests by enrolling him in the school band.

Step 4: Look for Potential Problem Areas

In the *L* step of the INCLUDE strategy, student learning needs are reviewed within a particular instructional context, and potential mismatches are identified. For example, Susan has a learning need in the area of expressive writing; she is unable to identify spelling errors in her work. This is an academic learning need. When evaluating students' work, her history teacher deducts one letter grade from papers that contain one or more spelling errors. For Susan to succeed in writing, this mismatch needs to be addressed. Similarly, Sam has a severe problem that prevents him from speaking fluently. This physical problem creates a learning need. His fourth-grade teacher requires that students present book reports to the class, a demand for student practice. Again, a potential mismatch exists that could prevent Sam from succeeding.

Step 5: Use Information to Brainstorm Adaptations

Once potential mismatches have been identified, the *U* step of INCLUDE is to use this information to identify possible ways to eliminate or minimize the effects of them. Adaptations could include bypassing the student's learning need by allowing the student to employ compensatory learning strategies, making a modification in classroom teaching or organization, and teaching the student basic or independent learning skills. The Professional Edge box on page 118 summarizes points to keep in mind when making instructional adaptations for students.

Bypass strategies. Bypass strategies allow students to gain access to or demonstrate mastery of the school curriculum in alternative ways. For example, a bypass strategy for Claire, who has a serious problem with spelling, would be a computerized spell checker. Alternatively, a peer could help her proofread her work. However, bypassing cannot be used in a primary area of instruction: Susan cannot spell check her spelling test. Also, bypassing a skill does not necessarily mean that the skill should not be re-mediated. Susan may need spelling instruction as part of her English class. Finally, bypass strategies should encourage student independence. For example, Susan might be better off learning to use a spell checker rather than relying on a peer proofreader.

Classroom teaching and organization. Teachers can make adaptations in their classroom organization, grouping, materials, and instruction to help students succeed. For example, if Ramos has attention problems, he might be seated near the front of the room, and he might benefit from a special system of rewards and consequences and a classroom in which "busy" bulletin board displays are removed. All these are classroom organization adaptations. A change in classroom instruction would be to call on Ramos frequently during class discussions and to allow him to earn points toward his grade for appropriate participation.

Intensive instruction on basic skills and learning strategies. A third option for including students with special needs is to provide intensive instruction designed to address basic skills or learning strategies in which the student is deficient. Often a special education teacher carries out this instruction in a resource room. This approach assumes that basic skills and learning strategies are prerequisites for successful general education experiences. Unfortunately, the results of research on whether skills taught in pullout programs transfer to the general education class are mixed; some studies show positive results (Marston, 1996; Snider, 1997), whereas others show minimal effects (Wang, Reynolds, & Walberg, 1988). Studies do suggest that teachers play an important role in determining whether skills taught in a separate setting transfer to their classrooms (Ellis, Lenz, & Sabornie 1987a; 1987b). For example, Ms. Henry had a student in her English literature class who was receiving pullout services on taking effective lecture notes. First, Ms. Henry found out from the special education teacher what strategy for note taking the student was learning. Then she reminded the student to perform the strategy before she delivered a lecture, and sometimes even during a lecture. Finally, Ms. Henry collected

What classroom demands might this student have difficulty meeting? What bypass strategies or adaptations might help him demonstrate that he has learned his assignment as well as his classmates have?

FYI

Bypass strategies are techniques students with special needs use to learn or demonstrate mastery of curriculum in a way that minimizes the impact of their disability.

Professional Edge

Selecting Appropriate Instructional Adaptations

The following list of general guidelines can help you make reasonable accommodations in instruction.

- Employ an adaptation only when a mismatch occurs. Your time and energy as a teacher are limited; make changes only when necessary.

- Be certain that the student's problems are not physical in origin before you make any adaptations. This concern relates particularly to students with no obvious physical or sensory needs. Prior to adapting your class for a student with an attentional problem, be sure that the problem is not the result of a hearing loss, seizure disorder, or other physical problem.

- Determine whether you are dealing with a "can't" or a "won't" problem. Blankenship and Lilly (1981) describe a "can't" problem as one in which the student, no matter how highly motivated, is unable to do what is expected. A "won't" problem implies that the student could do what is expected but is not motivated to do so. Each type of problem may require a different adaptation.

    A student unable to do what is expected might need a bypass strategy; a student unwilling to do the work might need a behavior management strategy. This distinction can also save you time. For example, if a student fails a test because she doesn't feel like working on the day of the test, a teacher's attempt to provide extra tutorial assistance is likely to be wasted effort. The "can't" and "won't" problems are particularly relevant for adolescents, who are often less likely than younger students to work to please their teachers.

- Keep adaptations as simple as possible. A good rule of thumb is to try the intervention that requires the least time and effort on your part and is likely to affect the student positively. Try a more involved adaptation only when needed.

FROM THE RESEARCH

A number of recent studies show that students with disabilities have definite preferences for certain adaptations in the areas of homework (Nelson, Epstein, Bursuck, Jayanthi, & Sawyer, 1998), testing (Nelson, Jayanthi, Epstein, & Bursuck, 2000), and grading (Bursuck, Munk, & Olson, 1999) and that student acceptance of an adaptation can affect its implementation and effectiveness (Reimers, Wacker, & Koeppl, 1987). Further, students believe that particular adaptations can affect their emotional well-being, their interactions with teachers and peers, their success in school, and their desire to learn in ways suitable to them (Nelson et al., 1998). Therefore, we suggest that you actively seek student input when choosing adaptations for your students.

the student's notes on a weekly basis to see whether she was performing the strategy correctly, giving specific feedback to the student as needed and reporting her progress to the special education teacher.

An alternative is to provide this type of instruction yourself. This option is feasible when many students have similar instructional needs and when you can easily monitor skill development. For example, Mr. Higgins, a seventh-grade science teacher, lectures frequently. As a result, students need to be proficient note takers. At the beginning of the school year, Mr. Higgins noticed during a routine check of student notebooks that many students were not taking adequate notes. With assistance from the special education teacher, he taught note taking as part of science. Three students for whom note taking was especially difficult handed in their notes each day so Mr. Higgins could monitor their progress.

Step 6: Decide Which Accommodations to Implement

After you have brainstormed possible bypass strategies or instructional adaptations, you can implement the *D* step in INCLUDE, which involves selecting strategies to try. A number of guidelines are suggested here to help you decide which accommodations best suit your students' needs.

Select age-appropriate adaptations.   Students' adaptations should match their age. For example, using a third-grade book as a supplement for an eighth-grade science student reading at the third-grade level would embarrass the student. In such a situation, a bypass strategy such as a taped textbook would be preferable if the student has the necessary background and cognitive skills to listen to the book with understanding. A good rule of thumb is to remember that no students, whether in first grade or twelfth and regardless of their special needs, want to use what they perceive as "baby" books or materials.

Select the easiest accommodations first.   Accommodations need to be feasible. Although making adaptations often means some additional work for you, it should not require so much time and effort that it interferes with teaching the entire class. It is easier to circle the 6 out of 12 math problems you want Maria to complete than to create a separate worksheet just for her.

Select adaptations you agree with.   You are more likely to implement an approach successfully if you believe in it (Polloway, Bursuck, Jayanthi, Epstein, & Nelson, 1996), especially in the area of behavior management. For example, in selecting rewards for students, if you are uncomfortable with candy, try activities such as time on the computer. However, adaptations should not be considered only in light of teacher beliefs. IDEA-97 is clear that the unique needs of students take precedence over the convenience of schools. With imagination and some input from special educators, you will undoubtedly find strategies that match your teaching approach while maximizing your students' learning.

Select adaptations with demonstrated effectiveness.   Over the past 25 years, a massive body of professional literature on effective teaching practices has accumulated. This research can help you avoid fads and other unvalidated practices. The strategies suggested throughout this text are based on research and form a starting point for your understanding of validated practices. Another means of staying professionally current is to read relevant professional journals.

Step 7: Evaluate Student Progress

Although many effective teaching practices exist, it is impossible to predict which will be effective for a given student. As a result, once an adaptation is implemented, the *E* step of INCLUDE is essential: evaluate strategy effectiveness. You can track effectiveness through grades; observations; analysis of student work; portfolios; performance assessments; and teacher, parent, and student ratings. Evaluating this information helps you decide whether to continue, to change, or to discontinue an intervention.

> **Check Your Learning**
>
> What are three examples of age appropriate interventions? Why is age appropriateness a key concept for thinking about students with special needs in general education classes?

> **Connections**
>
> A list of general education and special education publications appeared in Chapter 1.

> **Check Your Learning**
>
> What are all the steps in INCLUDE? What is an example of each?

In the next section, the relationship between your classroom and the diverse needs of learners is examined. As we have said, the use of effective practices allows teachers to accommodate more diversity in their classrooms while at the same time lessening the need for making more individualized adaptations. The key aspects of classroom environments are shown in Figure 4.1. These features include classroom organization, classroom grouping, instructional materials, and instructional methods.

FYI

The rest of this chapter aims to help you answer two questions: (1) How can I teach my whole class so that students' individual difficulties are minimized? (2) What adaptations of the instructional environment might I still need to make to meet individual students' special needs?

How Is an Inclusive Classroom Organized?

Your classroom organization involves physical organization, routines for classroom business, classroom climate, behavior management systems, and the use of time. You may need to use the INCLUDE strategy to make reasonable accommodations for students with special needs in all these areas.

Physical Organization

Although the direct effects of physical organization on student academic performance are open to interpretation (Doyle, 1986), how a classroom is physically organized can affect student learning and behavior in a number of areas. For example, carefully arranged classrooms can decrease noise and disruption, improve the level and quality of student interactions, and increase the percentage of time that students spend on academic tasks (Paine, Radicchi, Rosellini, Deutchman, & Darch, 1983). Classroom organization influences learning conditions for all students and the accessibility of instructional presentations and materials for students with sensory and physical disabilities. Physical organization includes the appearance of the classroom and the use of space, including wall areas, lighting, floor space, and storage.

Wall areas can be used for decorating, posting rules, displaying student work, and reinforcing class content, sometimes through the use of bulletin boards. For example, one teacher taught a note-taking strategy and posted the steps on a bulletin board to help her students remember them. In using wall space, keep in mind two possible problems. First, wall displays may divert students with attention problems from concentrating on your instruction. Place these students where they are least likely to be distracted by displays. Second, students may not notice that important information appears on a display, and you may need to direct their attention to it. For example, Ms. Huerta posted a display showing graphic representations of the basic fractions. She reminded her students to look at these fractions while they were doing their independent math work.

Lighting, either from windows or ceiling lights, also can be problematic for students with special needs. Students with hearing impairments might need adequate light to speech read; they also are likely to have problems with glare in areas where the light source comes from behind the speaker. Students with visual impairments also have difficulty working in areas that are not glare-free and well lighted. Occasionally, students with learning disabilities or emotional disturbances may be sensitive to and respond negatively to certain types of light. In most cases, problems with lighting can be remedied easily by seating students away from glare caused by sunshine coming through the classroom windows.

Figure 4.1 Overview of Classroom Environments

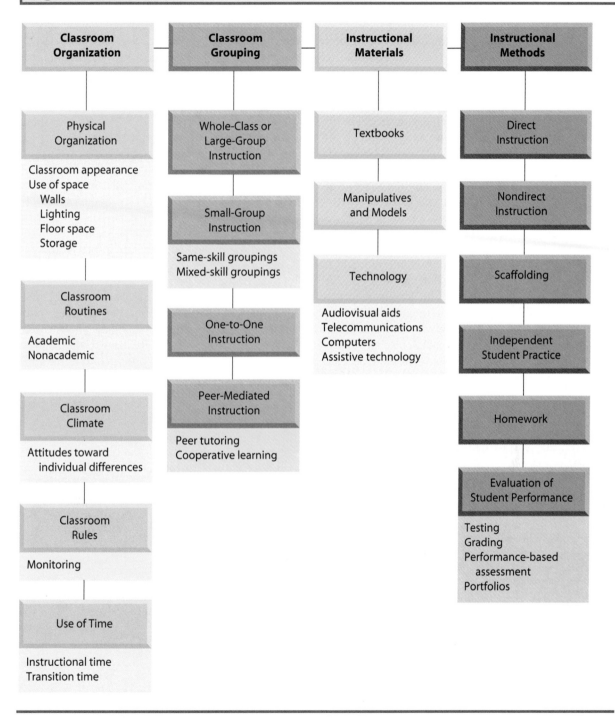

The way in which floor space is organized and the kinds and placement of furniture used also need to be considered. For example, floors that do not have a nonslip surface can make wheelchair travel difficult. Furniture that is placed in lanes can block access to the chalkboard or materials such as computers and make mobility difficult for students in wheelchairs or students with visual impairments. Tables, pencil sharpeners, and chalkboards that are too high may prove inaccessible to students who use wheelchairs. Desks that are too low can interfere with students who have prostheses (artificial limbs). Placement and configuration of special equipment in science labs, computer centers, and vocational areas also can present difficulties in accessibility for students with special needs. For example, the lathe in the woodworking room might be positioned too high for a person in a wheelchair to operate; the space between work areas in the science lab might not be wide enough for a wheelchair to pass.

Finally, the arrangement of your class should be predictable. This means that you should not make major changes without first considering their impact on students with special needs and then informing these students so they have time to adapt. For example, Mr. Tate decided to move one of the bookshelves in his classroom. He noticed, however, that the new location blocked the passageway from the door to the desk of a student in his class who was blind. Mr. Tate informed the student of the move in advance, and together they worked out an alternative route to the student's desk.

The arrangement of student desks, whether in rows, circles, or small groups, can have considerable impact on students with special needs. For example, traditional row configurations, which provide students with an immediate, unobstructed view of the teacher, have been shown to help students with attention disorders focus better when the teacher is instructing the whole group at one time. On the other hand, the placement of desks into clusters of four works better when you are using mixed-ability, cooperative learning groups to help integrate a student who is so-

This is a teacher-centered grouping arrangement for large-group instruction. What are some advantages and disadvantages of this strategy for students with special needs? What other ways of grouping students should be part of a teacher's instructional repertoire?

cially withdrawn. Another important consideration about floor space concerns student monitoring: Teachers should be able to see all parts of the classroom at all times, whether they are teaching large or small groups, or are working at their desks. Designing such visual access means that all specially designated areas in the classroom, such as learning/interest centers, computer stations, small-group instructional areas, or study carrels, need to be positioned so they can be monitored.

An additional area of physical organization is storage. For example, students with visual disabilities may need to store equipment such as tape recorders, large-print books, braille books, and magnifying devices. For students with severe disabilities, space might be needed to store book holders, paper holders, page turners, braces, crutches, and communication boards.

Routines for Classroom Business

Establishing clear routines in both academic and nonacademic areas is important for two reasons. First, routines that are carefully structured (that is, clear to students and used consistently) reduce nonacademic time and increase learning time. Second, you can prevent many discipline problems by having predictable classroom routines.

Most students, especially those with special needs, find stability in knowing that classroom activities will be similar each day. In the absence of this stability, misbehavior often follows. You can find many examples of breaks in school routines. On the day of a field trip, elementary school students are more likely to hit or push, to delay beginning assignments, and to do poor work. In middle schools and high schools, teachers often dread shortened schedules for assemblies and other school programs because of increased student behavior problems.

You can create daily classroom routines that help students learn. For example, you might expect fourth graders to enter your classroom each morning, begin their morning work, and read quietly if they finish before instruction begins. Having routines for sharing time, for setting up science experiments, for preparing to go to physical education, for moving to the computer lab, and so on helps students meet your expectations. Routines are especially helpful to students who need a strong sense of structure in classroom life. In secondary schools, routines might include having specific lab procedures, starting each class with a 5-minute review, or scheduling a particular activity on the same day every week. For example, in a geometry class, students who complete their assignments might choose to begin the day's homework, complete a Math Challenger worksheet from the activity file, or work on research papers or other long-term projects.

Classroom Climate

A number of authors have noted that classroom climate contributes significantly to the number and seriousness of classroom behavior problems (Jones & Jones, 1990; Morse, 1987). The classroom climate concerns the overall atmosphere in the classroom—whether it is friendly or unfriendly, pleasant or unpleasant, and so on. Climate is influenced by the attitudes of the teacher and students toward individual differences: Is the classroom characterized by a cooperative or a competitive atmosphere? Is the classroom a safe place for all students to take risks? Are skills for interacting positively with children and adults actively supported in the classroom?

Teachers who communicate respect and trust to their students are more successful in creating positive classroom environments in which fewer behavior problems occur (Deluke & Knoblock, 1987). For example, Mr. Elliott reprimanded a student who talked out of turn by saying, "I know you have a question about your work, and I'm glad you care enough to ask for help; but I need to have you raise your hand because I can only help people one at a time." Mr. Elliott showed respect for the student and built the student's trust by not putting her down. Yet, Mr. Elliott stuck to his rule about not speaking before being called on and explained why it was important. Similarly, Harriet's teacher, Ms. Belson, asked Harriet to define the word *diffident*. Harriet gave an incorrect definition, saying it meant "being bored." Ms. Belson said, "Harriet, I can see how you might think the meaning is 'bored' because *diffident* looks a lot like *indifferent*. The word actually means 'lacking in confidence.' "

F Y I

Classrooms in which instruction is relevant, interesting, and active are classrooms with fewer behavior problems. Strategies to design instruction effectively to maximize student learning are covered in Chapters 9 and 10.

You build the overall quality of your communication with your students in many small ways. For example, finding the time each week to speak privately with students lets them know that you care about them as individuals. Asking older students sincere questions about their friends, out-of-school activities, or part-time jobs also conveys your interest in them. Taking the time to write positive comments on papers lets students know that you appreciate their strengths and do not focus only on their needs. When you encourage each student to achieve his or her own potential, without continually comparing students to one another, you are communicating the idea that each class member has a valuable contribution to make. Teachers who fail to take these small steps toward positive communication with students, or who publicly embarrass a student or punish a group for the behavior of a few, soon may create a negative classroom climate that thwarts appropriate and effective learning.

Classroom Rules

What rules do you intend to establish in your classroom? Rules help create a sense of order and expectations for a classroom, and they form a significant first step in setting up a learning environment based on preventive classroom management. Teachers who are effective classroom managers have well-defined rules for their classrooms (e.g., Bullara, 1993; Smith & Mirsa, 1992).

R e s e a r c h N o t e

Research suggests that the most effective classroom rules are ones that students develop themselves and express with teacher guidance (Bullara, 1993).

Effective classroom rules share three key characteristics: they are brief and specific, positively worded, and clearly understood by students (Doyle, 1990). First, rules should be few in number but as specific as possible. For example, a list of 10 or 12 general rules that urge students to be fair, kind, and respectful are not as useful as 3 or 5 specific rules such as "Speak one at a time," "Keep your hands to yourself," and "Be prepared to start class when the bell rings by having all your learning materials ready."

Second, rules should be worded in a positive way (Bullara, 1993). In some classrooms, rules sound punitive because they are so negative. Consider the difference between a rule that states, "Don't call out answers" and one that says, "Raise your hand to speak." If students assist in making classroom rules, you can encourage positive wording by rephrasing any rules that students have inappropriately worded. Keep in mind that students who participate in rule making might be more motivated to obey rules.

Third, rules should be explained carefully to your students. Post rules during the first weeks of school, explain and discuss them, and model them for students. Violations of the rules should be pointed out and corrected immediately. For example, after you and your students have established and reviewed classroom rules, explain their use, congratulate students for following them, and ask students whom you reprimand to explain why their behavior violated the rules. Younger students could draw pictures about their classroom rules and procedures. Older students could write about the necessity for rules. This early attention to setting your classroom expectations has a year-long payoff. By rehearsing and focusing student attention on them, you make the rules part of students' understanding of their classroom interactions. If you do not take this time to teach the rules, too often they become merely a bulletin board display, ignored by teachers and students alike.

Finally, you need to be sure that your rules accommodate students from different cultures. For example, rules about respecting other students' property may be puzzling for Hispanic students, for whom sharing one's belongings is a highly valued activity. Similarly, rules related to aggressive behavior may need to be enforced with care for students whose parents expect them to stand up for themselves, especially when someone says something derogatory about their family (Grossman, 1995). It is important to note that taking cultural differences into account does not necessarily mean that the rules need to be changed, only that the rules may need to be more carefully explained and enforced.

Cultural Awareness

If your classroom includes students who are not native English speakers, you need to make sure that these students understand classroom expectations.

Monitoring

In addition to having clear expectations, you also need to monitor student classroom behaviors frequently. For example, scan the room to check that students are following the rules. To do this, you always need to have a clear view of the entire class, regardless of the activity in which you or the class are engaged. When student behavior is not carefully monitored, students choose not to follow the rules consistently. For example, Charmaine is a student in Ms. Patrick's fifth-grade class who has behavior problems. Ms. Patrick has a rule that students need to complete all their independent work before they can go to the computer station to play a problem-solving game. Ms. Patrick did not have time to monitor Charmaine's behavior. One day, she saw Charmaine at the computer station and asked her whether she had completed her assignments. Not only had Charmaine not completed her assignments on that day, but she hadn't done any work for the past 3 days. Thereafter, Ms. Patrick was careful to monitor the work progress of all her students.

Connections

Strategies for effective classroom management programs are presented in more detail in Chapter 12.

Use of Time

How teachers use time in the classroom is one of the most important aspects of classroom organization. Effectively using instructional time and managing transition time constitute two particularly important tasks.

Use of instructional time. The amount of time that students are meaningfully and successfully engaged in academic activities in school is referred to as **academic learning time** (Arends, 1991). Research has shown that the greater the academic learning time in a classroom is, the more students learn (Fisher et al., 1980). Time usage is particularly important for students with special needs, who may need more time to learn than their peers.

Paine and colleagues (1983) suggest several ways in which teachers can maximize instructional time. One way is to minimize the time spent on organizational activities such as lunch counts, opening activities, getting drinks, sharpening pencils,

WWW Resources

Ideas to simplify your job, including a variety of classroom management and other teaching tips can be found at http://www.classroom.net.

cleaning out desks, and going to the bathroom. Another way is to select activities with the greatest teaching potential and that contribute most to students achieving the core school curriculum. Although learning activities can be fun, they should ultimately be selected for the purpose of teaching students something important. Finally, the strategies described in this chapter and throughout this book for organizing your classroom, grouping your students, and adapting your methods and materials also help ensure the productive use of your students' time. Another way to increase the academic learning time of your students is described in the Professional Edge.

Professional Edge

Using "Sponges" to Increase Academic Learning Time

You almost always have times during the day when you have a minute or two before a scheduled academic activity or before the class goes to lunch, an assembly, or recess. You can fill that extra time with productive activities by using "sponges." Sponges are activities that fit into brief periods of time and that give students practice or review on skills and content you have already covered in class. The following lists of sponges can help you "soak up" that extra classroom time.

Lower-Grade Sponges

1. Tell children to be ready to state one playground rule.
2. Tell children to be ready to list the names of children in the class that begin with *J* or *M*, and so on.
3. Tell children to be ready to draw something that is drawn only with circles.
4. Tell children to be ready to think of a good health habit.
5. Flash fingers—have children tell how many fingers you hold up.
6. Say numbers, days of the week, months—and have children tell what comes next.
7. Ask what number comes between two numbers: for example, 31–33, 45–47, and so forth.
8. Ask children what number comes before or after 46, 52, 13, and so on.
9. Write a word on the board. Have children make a list of words that rhyme with it.

10. Count to 100 by 2s, 5s, 10s, and so on, either orally or in writing.
11. Think of animals that live on a farm, in the jungle, in water, and so forth.
12. Name fruits, vegetables, meats, and the like.
13. List things you can touch, things you can smell, and so on.

Dismissal Sponges

1. "I Spy"—Ask children to find something in the room that starts with *M*, *P*, and so on.
2. Ask children to find something in the room that has the sound of short *a*, long *a*, and so forth.
3. Number rows or tables. Signal the number of the table with fingers, and allow children to leave accordingly.
4. Count in order or by 2s, 5s, and so on.
5. Say the days of the week, the months of the year.
6. Ask what day it is. What month it is. What the date is. What the year is. Ask how many months are in a year, how many days are in a week, and so on.
7. Use reward activities:

"We have had a good day! Who helped it to be a good day for all of us? Betty, you brought flowers to brighten our room. You may leave. John, you remembered to rinse your hands, good for you. You may leave. Ellen showed us that she could be quiet coming into the room today. You may leave, Ellen. Bob remembered his library book all by

Managing transition time. Just as important as the amount of time spent in academic activities is the management of transition time. **Transition time** is the time it takes to change from one activity to another. Transition time can occur when students remain at their seats and change from one subject to another, move from their seats to an activity in another part of the classroom, move from somewhere else in the classroom back to their seats, leave the classroom to go outside or to another part of the school building, or come back into the classroom from outside or another part of the building (Paine et al., 1983).

himself. Dawn walked all the way to the playground—she remembered our safety rules. Lori brought things to share with us. Tom surprised us with a perfect paper—he must have practiced. . . ."

Students' good deeds can be grouped together to speed up dismissed. The teacher can finish with, "You're all learning to be very thoughtful. I'm very proud of all of you and you should be very proud of yourselves."

8. Use flashcards. A first correct answer earns dismissal.

9. Review the four basic shapes. Each child names an object in the room in the shape of either a triangle, circle, square, or rectangle.

Upper-Grade Sponges

1. List the continents.

2. Name as many gems or precious stones as you can.

3. List as many states as you can.

4. Write an abbreviation, a Roman numeral, a trademark, a proper name (biological), or a proper name (geographical).

5. Name as many countries and their capitals as you can.

6. List the names of five parts of the body above the neck that are spelled with three letters.

7. List one manufactured item for each letter of the alphabet.

8. List as many nouns in the room as you can.

9. List one proper noun for each letter of the alphabet.

10. Name as many parts of a car as you can.

11. List as many kinds of trees as you can.

12. List as many personal pronouns as you can.

13. Name as many politicians as you can.

How many sponges can you think of for your grade or subject area? Additional ideas for sponges can be found at the Busy Teacher website: www.ceisnc.gatech.edu/busyt/k12wel.html

FROM THE RESEARCH

The effectiveness of sponges shows how important it is to use school time wisely. A recent study by Muyskens and Ysseldyke (1998) shows that how teachers structure school time is even more important for student learning than time of day. For example, children are often thought to be more receptive to learning in the morning when they are fresh. Because of this belief, many teachers schedule more important subjects such as reading in the morning. Muyskens and Ysseldyke observed 122 students with and without disabilities in 10 urban and suburban school districts. They found that when classrooms were appropriately structured, learning occurred, regardless of the time of day in which the instruction was delivered.

SOURCE: From "Effective Teaching for Higher Achievement," by D. Sparks and G. M. Sparks, 1984, *Educational Leadership*, *49*(7). Copyright 1984 by Association for Supervision and Curriculum Development ASCD. All rights reserved.

Research studies show that teachers sometimes waste instructional time by not managing transitions carefully (Ornstein, 1990). Paine and colleagues (1983) suggest that you have rules devoted specifically to transitions and that you teach these rules directly to students. The following are among the rules they suggest:

1. Move quietly.
2. Put your books away and get what you need for the next activity. (You may need to state what that activity is and what materials students need for it.)
3. Move your chairs quietly. (In some classes with small-group instruction, students carry their desk chairs to the group for seating there.)
4. Keep your hands and feet to yourself. (p. 85)

As with all rules, those for transitions need to be consistently monitored and reinforced.

How you organize classroom materials also can affect the management of transitions. For example, you need to have all materials ready for each subject and activity. In addition, materials should be organized so that they are easily accessible. No matter how well organized your transitions are, you still may need to adapt them for some students with special needs. Students with physical disabilities may need more time to take out or put away their books. Students with physical and visual disabilities may have mobility problems that cause them to take more time with such transitional activities as getting into instructional groups or moving from room to room. You may need an individualized system of rewards or other consequences to guide students with attention deficit–hyperactivity disorder or behavior disorders through transition times.

How Can You Group All Your Students for Instruction in Inclusive Classrooms?

Students with special needs benefit from a variety of classroom grouping arrangements, including large- and small-group instruction, mixed- and same-skill groupings, and teacher-centered or peer-mediated group instruction. It is important to remember that the particular arrangement you choose depends on your instructional objectives as well as your students' particular needs.

Whole-Class or Large-Group Instruction

Students with special needs benefit from both whole-class and small-group instruction. One advantage of whole-class instruction is that students spend the entire time with the teacher. In small-group instruction, on the other hand, students spend part of the time with the teacher and also spend time working independently while the teacher works with other small groups. Research shows that the more time students spend with the teacher, the more they learn (Rosenshine & Stevens, 1986). This increase in learning may be because students are more likely to go off task when they are working on their own, particularly when they have learning or behavior problems. Whatever grouping arrangements you use, try to make sure that students spend as much time as possible working with you.

Another advantage of whole-group instruction is that it does not single out students with special needs as being different from their peers. However, you may need to adapt whole-group instruction for students with special needs. For example, students in a fourth-grade class were reading *Charlotte's Web* as a large-group instructional activity. One student in the class read more slowly than the rest of the class. To help her keep up, the teacher provided a book on tape. The teacher also gave the student more time to answer comprehension questions about the story in class because it took her longer to look up some of the answers. In another example, a high school science teacher identified before his lecture technical words he was going to use and worked before school with a small group of students with vocabulary problems to help them learn the words.

Small-Group Instruction

You may encounter situations in which small-group instruction is more appropriate for students with special needs. You can use either same-skill groupings or mixed-skill groupings in setting up your small groups.

Same-skill groupings are helpful when some but not all students are having trouble mastering a particular skill and need more instruction and practice. For example, a teacher was showing her students how to divide fractions that have a common denominator. She gave her class a miniquiz to see who had learned how to do the problems. She found that all but five students had mastered the skill. The next day, the teacher worked with these five students while the rest of the class did an application activity. It is important to recognize that small-group instruction is not only for special education or remedial students; most students benefit from extra help in a small group at one time or another. In fact, many times students with special needs do not need extra instruction.

Small same-skill groups have also been proven effective in basic skill areas when students are performing well below most of the class (Mosteller, Light, & Sachs, 1996). For example, Lori is in Ms. Hubbard's fourth-grade class and is reading at the second-grade level. Lori is learning decoding and vocabulary skills in a small group with other students who are at her level. Because the group is small and homogeneous, Ms. Hubbard is able to proceed in small steps, present many examples, and allow students to master skills before they move on. Lori is making progress and feels good about herself because she is becoming a better reader. However, keep in mind that small, same-skill groups should be used only when attempts to adapt instruction in the large group have been unsuccessful.

Same-skill groups tend to become permanent and take on a life of their own, and students are more likely to become stigmatized when they are entrenched in low groups. Although some students do require instruction that is more individualized and intensive than can be provided in the large group, the ultimate goal of any small group should be its eventual dissolution. Also, on many days, students can benefit from instruction with the rest of the class. For example, Lori's group participates in large-group reading when the teacher is reading a story and working on listening comprehension. Another potential problem in using same-skill groupings is the danger that students who are in a low-achieving group in one area will be placed in low-achieving groups in other areas even though their skill levels do not justify it. For example, just because Lori is in the lowest reading group does not automatically mean she needs to be in low-achieving groups in other areas such as math.

The major advantage of **mixed-skill groupings** is that they provide students with special needs a range of positive models for both academic and social behavior. In mixed-skill groupings, students often help each other, so such groups can also be a vehicle for providing direct instruction to individual students, something for which classroom teachers often do not have the time. In addition, mixed-skill groups, like large groups, tend not to single out students with special needs.

One-to-One Instruction

Providing **one-to-one instruction** for students with special needs can be very effective under some circumstances. In this grouping arrangement, students work with either a teacher, a paraprofessional, or a computer in well-sequenced, self-paced materials that are geared to their specific level. For example, Waldo is having trouble with addition and subtraction facts. For 15 minutes each day, he works at the classroom computer station on an individualized drill-and-practice program. Right now he is working on addition facts through 10. When he masters these, the machine automatically places him into more difficult problems. Shamika, a student with a moderate to severe cognitive disability, works with a paraprofessional on selecting food items for a balanced lunch while the rest of the class listens to a presentation on the process of performing a nutritional analysis.

Although one-to-one instruction may be appropriate in some circumstances, it is not necessarily the grouping arrangement of choice. First, it is inefficient; when it is carried out by the classroom teacher, the extensive use of one-to-one instruction will result in less instructional time for everyone. Second, the logistics of one-to-one instruction sometimes require that students complete much independent work while the teacher moves from student to student. This can lead to high levels of off-task behavior, a problem many students with special needs experience (Hardman, Drew, Egan, & Winston, 1999; Mercer, 1997). Third, the lack of peer models in one-to-one instruction makes it more difficult to motivate students, a problem particularly relevant at the high school level (Ellis & Sabornie, 1990). Sometimes, its exclusive use can exclude students from critical social interactions. Finally, when a student requires one-to-one instruction for extended periods of time, further analysis of his or her needs and instructional setting is needed.

Connections

The grouping strategies in this chapter are all teacher centered. Strategies for using groupings that are peer mediated, such as peer tutoring and cooperative grouping, are covered in Chapter 13.

How Can You Evaluate Instructional Materials for Inclusive Classrooms?

The nature of the instructional materials you use is another very important consideration in accommodating students with special needs in your classroom. Classroom instructional materials include textbooks, manipulatives and models, and technology.

Textbooks

Basal textbooks (often called **basals**) are books used for instruction in any subject area that contain all the key components of the curriculum being taught for that subject. The careful evaluation of basals is vital because the selection of well-designed textbooks that require fewer adaptations for students with special needs can save you much time and energy. For example, a math basal that contains plenty of practice activities does not need to be adapted for students who require lots of practice to master a skill. Similarly, a history textbook that highlights critical vocabulary and includes clear context cues to help students figure out the words on their own may make it unnecessary for teachers to prepare extensive vocabulary study guides.

Fortunately, over the past 20 years, guidelines for distinguishing well-designed texts have been developed (Armbruster & Anderson, 1988; Kameenui & Simmons, 1991). A set of questions to help you evaluate basals and other basic-skills materials is included in the Professional Edge on pages 132–133. Carefully evaluating basals helps alert you to any adaptations you may need to make. For example, a spelling basal with little provision for review can be troublesome for students who have problems retaining information. You may want to develop review activities for every three lessons rather than every five as is done in the book.

Many teachers are choosing to develop or collect their own materials rather than depending on published basal series. For example, some teachers have their students read trade books instead of traditional reading books; others have their students engage in the actual writing process rather than or in addition to answering questions in a book. Still others involve their students in real-life math problem solving rather than use basal math books. Even if you choose not to use basals, however, the guidelines for teaching basic skills discussed here apply.

Content-area textbooks, which are books used for instruction in subject matter areas such as science or social studies, also need to be evaluated. In secondary schools, students are often expected to read their textbooks to access curriculum content (Armbruster & Anderson, 1988; Deshler, Putnam, & Bulgren, 1985). Because students are required to read and understand their texts, often without previous instruction, the texts should be written at a level at which students can easily understand them. Armbruster and Anderson (1988) refer to readable textbooks as "considerate." Considerate textbooks are easier for students to use independently and require fewer teacher adaptations. The following guidelines refer to features involving content, organization, and quality of writing.

Check the content covered in the text to see whether it stresses "big ideas" rather than facts in isolation.   Big ideas are important principles that enable learners to understand the connections among facts and concepts they learn (Carnine, Crawford, Harniss, Hollenbeck, & Miller, 1998). For example, in a text that stressed facts in isolation, students learned that Rosa Parks was an important figure because she led the Montgomery bus boycott in 1955. In a text that stressed big ideas, students learned that the bus boycott, led by Rosa Parks in 1955, was carried out in response to a problem of segregation in the South in the early 1950s and that the boycott was the first in a series of civil rights protests eventually leading to the Civil Rights Act of 1965.

Check to see whether support is provided for student comprehension.   Support for student comprehension can be detected in the following ways:

1. **Check the organization of the headings and subheadings.** Make an outline of the headings and subheadings in a few chapters. How reasonable is the structure revealed? Is it consistent with your knowledge of the subject matter?

2. **Check the consistency of organization in discussions of similar topics.** For example, in a science chapter on vertebrates, information about the different groups of vertebrates should be similarly organized; that is, if the

---

Research Note

Elbaum, Moody, and Schumm (1999) asked 53 third-grade students, 27 of whom had learning disabilities, what they thought of mixed-skill grouping in reading. Students were concerned that small group work was often noisy, encouraged disruptive students, and made it harder to get individual help from the teacher. Children who had lower reading skills, including some children with learning disabilities, were often anxious when working in small mixed skill groups because it made their problems more obvious. Some higher-achieving children felt that working with lower readers hindered the progress of faster students.

FYI

Workbooks are commonly used to practice skills taught in basal materials. The material on practice activities in this chapter and in Chapter 9 applies to workbooks as well.

Connections

Ways to adapt content-area texts are described in Chapter 9. Student strategies for reading texts are covered in Chapter 10.

WWW Resources

The Internet School Library Media Center provides a massive index to Internet lesson plan sites for K–12 educators at http://falcon.jnu.edu/ ~ramseyil/index.html.

Professional Edge

Guidelines for Evaluating Basals or Other Basic-Skills Curricula

Before evaluating any material, read the evaluative questions following and place an asterisk next to those that are critical for the type of material you are examining. Answer each question with yes or no. Examine all your responses in a single area, paying special attention to the questions you designated as critical. Rate each area inadequate (1), adequate (2), or excellent (3). If the area is inadequate, designate whether the features can be easily modified (M).

Rating Scale:	Inadequate	Adequate	Excellent	Easily modified
	1	2	3	M

1 2 3 M   Effectiveness of Material

Yes No   Is information provided that indicates successful field testing or class testing of the material?
Yes No   Has the material been successfully field tested with students similar to the target population?
Yes No   Are testimonials and publisher claims clearly differentiated from research findings?

1 2 3 M   Prerequisite Skills

Yes No   Are the prerequisite student skills and abilities needed to work with ease in the material specified?
Yes No   Are the prerequisite student skills and abilities compatible with the objectives of the material?
Yes No   Are the prerequisite student skills and abilities compatible with the target population?

1 2 3 M   Content

Yes No   Are students provided with specific strategies rather than a series of skills in isolation?
Yes No   Does the selection of subject matter, facts, and skills adequately represent the content area?
Yes No   Is the content consistent with the stated objectives?
Yes No   Is the information presented in the material accurate?
Yes No   Is the information presented in the material current?
Yes No   Are various points of view, including treatment of cultural diversity, individuals with disabilities, ideologies, social values, gender roles, and socioeconomic status, represented objectively?
Yes No   Are the content and the topic of the material relevant to the needs of students with disabilities?

1 2 3 M   Sequence of Instruction

Yes No   Are the scope and sequence of the material clearly specified?
Yes No   Are facts, concepts, and skills ordered logically?
Yes No   Does the sequence of instruction proceed from simple to complex?
Yes No   Does the sequence proceed in small, easily attainable steps?

1 2 3 M   Behavioral Objectives

Yes No   Are objectives or outcomes for the material clearly stated?
Yes No   Are the objectives or outcomes consistent with the goals for the target population?
Yes No   Are the objectives or outcomes stated in behavioral terms, including the desired behavior, the conditions for measurement of the behavior, and the desired standard of performance?

Rating Scale:	Inadequate	Adequate	Excellent	Easily modified
	1	2	3	M

1 2 3 M   Initial Assessment and Placement

Yes No   Does the material provide a method to determine initial student placement in the curriculum?

Yes No   Does the initial assessment for placement contain enough items to place the learner accurately?

1 2 3 M   Ongoing Assessment and Evaluation

Yes No   Does the material provide evaluation procedures for measuring progress and mastery of objectives?

Yes No   Are there enough evaluative items to measure learner progress accurately?

Yes No   Are procedures and/or materials for ongoing record keeping provided?

1 2 3 M   Instructional Input (teaching procedures)

Yes No   Are instructional procedures for each lesson either clearly specified or self-evident?

Yes No   Does the instruction provide for active student involvement and responses?

Yes No   Are the lessons adaptable to small-group and individualized instruction?

Yes No   Are a variety of cueing and prompting techniques used to gain correct student responses?

Yes No   When using verbal instruction, does the instruction proceed clearly and logically?

Yes No   Does the material use teacher modeling and demonstration when appropriate to the skills being taught?

Yes No   Does the material specify correction and feedback procedures for use during instruction?

1 2 3 M   Practice and Review

Yes No   Does the material contain appropriate practice activities that contribute to mastery of the skills and concepts?

Yes No   Do practice activities relate directly to the desired outcome behaviors?

Yes No   Does the material provide enough practice for students with learning problems?

Yes No   Are skills systematically and cumulatively reviewed throughout the curriculum?

FROM THE RESEARCH

Guidelines such as those shown here have been recently confirmed in a review of 34 research studies (Adams & Engelmann, 1996; Forness, Kavale, Blum, & Loyd, 1997; Fischer & Tarver, 1997). Overall, programs that employed many of these features showed large gains for both general and special education students, in both elementary and secondary classes.

These gains were in a variety of subject matter areas, were measured using norm-referenced or criterion-referenced measures, and lasted up to 1 year or more.

SOURCE: From *Instructional Materials for the Mildly Handicapped: Selection, Utilization, and Modification*, by A. Archer, 1977, Eugene, OR: University of Oregon. Northwest Learning Resources System. Used by permission of the author.

section on amphibians discusses structure, body covering, subgroups, and re-production, the section on reptiles should discuss the same topics, in the same order.

3. **Look for clear signaling of the structure.** A well-designed text includes in-formation headings and subheadings. The most helpful headings are those that are the most specific about the content in the upcoming section. For ex-ample, the heading Chemical Weathering is a more helpful content clue than Another Kind of Weathering. A well-signaled text also includes format clues to organization. Page layouts, paragraphing, marginal notations, graphic aids, and the use of boldface, italics, or underlining can all serve to highlight or re-inforce the structure. For example, a discussion of the four stages in the life cycle of butterflies could be signaled by using a separate, numbered paragraph for each state (that is, 1. Egg; 2. Larva; 3. Pupa; 4. Adult) and by including a picture for each stage. Finally, look for signal words and phrases that desig-nate particular patterns of organization. For example, the phrases *in contrast* and *on the other hand* signal a compare-and-contrast organization whereas the words *first*, *second*, and *third* indicate an enumeration or list pattern.

Check to see that important background knowledge is activated.   Despite the im-portance of background knowledge for comprehension (McKeown, Beck, Sinatra, & Loxterman, 1992), many textbooks assume unrealistic levels of students' back-ground knowledge (McKeown & Beck, 1990). A failure to activate important back-ground knowledge may be especially problematic for students with special needs, who are more likely to be lacking this information (Lenz & Alley, 1983). A number of textbook features indicate adequate attention to background knowledge. For ex-ample, social studies texts often activate background knowledge by providing de-finitions for important vocabulary content, displaying geographical information on maps, and featuring time lines delineating when key events took place (Har-niss, 1996).

Check for quality of writing.   The quality and clarity of writing can also affect stu-dent comprehension. Quality of writing can be evaluated in a number of ways.

1. **Look for explicit or obvious connectives, or conjunctions.** The absence of connectives can be particularly troublesome when the connective is a causal one (for example, *because*, *since*, *therefore*), which is frequently the case in con-tent-area textbooks. Therefore, look especially for causal connectives. For ex-ample, the sentence *Because the guard cells relax, the openings close* is a better explanation than the sentences *The guard cells relax. The openings close.*

2. **Check for clear references.** One problem to watch for is confusing pro-noun references when more than one noun is used. For example, consider the following: *Both the stem of the plant and the leaf produce chloroform, but in differ-ent ways. For one, the sun hits it, and then. . . .* Here, the pronouns *one* and *it* could be referring either to *the stem* or *the leaf.* Also, look out for vague quan-tifiers, those that do not indicate the noun being quantified (for example, *some*, *many*, *few*). For example, the clause *Some whales have become extinct* is clearer than *Some have become extinct.* In addition, check for definite pronouns without a clear referent (for example, *She saw the man*, in which the identity of *him* is not specified).

3. **Look for transition statements.** Transitions help the reader move easily from idea to idea. Given that a text covers many topics, make sure that the topic shifts are smooth.

4. **Make sure the chronological sequences are easy to follow.** In a discussion of a sequence of events, the order of presentation in the text should generally proceed from first to last; any alteration of the order could cause confusion if not clearly signaled.

5. **Make sure graphic aids are clearly related to the text.** Graphic aids should contribute to understanding the material rather than simply providing decoration or filling space, should be easy to read and interpret, and should be clearly titled and labeled and referenced in the text so the reader knows when to look at them.

Manipulatives and Models

Manipulatives and models can help students make connections between the abstractions often presented in school and the real-life products and situations these abstractions represent. **Manipulatives** are concrete objects or representational items, such as blocks and counters (for example, base-10 blocks for math), used as part of instruction. **Models** are also tangible objects; they provide a physical representation of an abstraction (for example, a scale model of the solar system). Strategies to help students make these connections have great potential benefit for students with special needs, who may lack the background knowledge and reasoning skills to understand abstractions (Hutchinson, 1993). Still, manipulatives and models should be used carefully (Clements & McMillen, 1996). When using these valuable tools, consider the following guidelines (Marzola, 1987; Ross & Kurtz, 1993).

> **Research Note**
>
> Research shows that manipulatives do not guarantee student success in math (Baroody, 1989). More important is whether skills are explicitly taught in a meaningful way (Evans & Carnine, 1990).

1. **Select materials that suit the concept and the developmental stage of the student.** When you are first introducing a concept, materials should be easy to comprehend. Generally, the order in which you introduce materials should follow the same order as students' understanding: from the concrete to the pictorial to the abstract. However, not all students need to start at the same level. For example, in a biology lesson on the heart, many students benefit from viewing a three-dimensional model of a human heart, whereas other students are able to understand how a heart works just by seeing a picture of one.

2. **Use a variety of materials.** Students with special needs may have trouble transferring their understanding of a concept from one form to another. For example, Wally's teacher always demonstrated place value using base-10 blocks. When Wally was given a place-value problem using coffee stirrers, he was unable to do it. Wally's teacher could have prevented this problem in the first place by demonstrating place value using a range of manipulative materials such as coffee stirrers, paper clips, and so on.

3. **Use verbal explanations whenever possible to accompany object manipulation.** Models and manipulative demonstrations should be preceded and accompanied by verbal explanations of the concept or skill being demonstrated. Verbal explanations are valuable because students may not be able to identify the important features of the model on their own. For example, Ms. Balou put a model of a

two-digit by two-digit multiplication problem on the board. She verbally explained to her students all the steps in computing the problem and wrote each step on the chalkboard as it was completed.

4. Encourage active interaction. It is not enough just to have the teacher demonstrate with manipulatives or models and students observe. Allow your students to interact actively with models and manipulatives. Hands-on experience helps them construct their own meaning from the materials.

5. Elicit student explanations of their manipulations or use of models. Encourage your students to verbalize what they are doing as they work with models and manipulatives. This is a good way for you to assess whether they really understand the concept or skill. For example, Ms. Conway had her students name the main parts of the human heart using a model. Mr. Abeles had his students explain out loud how they would subtract 43 from 52 using base-10 blocks. Although explanations can help you evaluate how your students process information, students with special needs may not be able to articulate concepts right away because of language problems or a lack of reasoning skills. These students may require frequent demonstrations of how to articulate what they are doing.

6. Present clear guidelines for handling manipulatives to prevent management problems. Although manipulatives can be helpful instructional tools, they also can create management problems, particularly in larger groups when your physical access to students is limited. For example, Ms. Leifheit wanted her students to manipulate blocks to show the sounds in words. Each child received three blocks. When the children heard a word such as man, they were to move a block as they said each sound: *m–a–n*. Ms. Leifheit had trouble getting students' attention at the beginning of the lesson because they were busy handling the blocks. She also found that students were not listening to her say the words, again because they were playing with the blocks. Ms. Leifheit decided to break the class into smaller groups so she could more carefully monitor student use of the blocks. She also established a simple rule: When the teacher is talking, students are not to touch their blocks.

7. Move your students beyond the concrete level when they are ready. Some students with special needs may have trouble moving from one learning stage to another. One effective way to help students make the transition from the concrete to the abstract is to pair concrete tasks with paper-and-pencil tasks. For example, Ms. Washington had her students label a picture of a human heart after they had observed and discussed a physical model. Mr. Parks had his second graders solve subtraction problems using manipulatives and then record their answers on a traditional worksheet. However, Marsh and Cooke (1996) found that students with learning disabilities who were taught to solve story problems using manipulatives were able to solve similar problems at an abstract level without having to go through the representational stage.

Technology

Teachers today have available to them a broad array of technology to enhance the presentation of material to their students. These technologies range from more traditional audiovisual aids, such as audiotape, videotape, and overhead projectors, to the more advanced technologies of computers, videodiscs, and telecommunications and electronic networks.

A number of guidelines for using all types of technology in your classroom have been suggested (Schuller, 1982). First, you should have clearly defined objectives for why you are using the technology. You should also know the content of the film, software, or other materials you are using. Being familiar with the content makes it easier to decide which technologies work for you and how you can best use them. You should also guide learners on what to look for. This guidance is especially relevant for students with disabilities, who often have trouble focusing on the essential information. Finally, evaluate the results to see whether the technology has helped students meet your instructional objectives.

One common use of computers in inclusive classrooms is to provide instruction to students through drill-and-practice programs, tutorials, and simulations. In general, drill-and-practice programs are used most often with students with special needs. Drill-and-practice programs have been shown to be effective for students with special needs largely because they allow students to learn in small steps, provide systematic feedback, and allow for lots of practice to mastery. Still, not all drill-and-practice programs are created equal (Okolo, 1993). Some guidelines for what to look for and what to avoid in these programs are given in the Professional Edge on page 138.

Computers can also provide initial, sequenced instruction for students, using **tutorials,** as well as instruction in problem solving, decision making, and risk taking, using **simulations.** Each of these forms of computer-assisted instruction has potential advantages and disadvantages (Roblyer, Edwards, & Havriluk, 1997). For example, tutorials can present instruction to mastery in small, sequential steps, an instructional approach shown to be effective with students with special needs. Tutorials can also provide one-to-one instruction at varying levels of difficulty, something teachers usually do not have time to do. On the other hand, you need to check to be sure that students have the necessary prerequisite skills to benefit from the tutorials. In addition, tutorials may not provide sufficient review for students, and students may not be motivated enough to work through them independently (Roblyer et al., 1997). Simulations are of great potential benefit in teaching students to be active learners by confronting real-life situations. However, simulations may be difficult to integrate with academic curriculum, may require much teacher assistance, and can be time consuming (Roblyer et al., 1997).

Computer technology is an important part of an inclusive classroom. A great variety of **assistive technology** (AT) is available to enable students with both low- and high-incidence disabilities to communicate or to access information by allowing them to bypass their disability. Students with physical disabilities such as Josh, whom you read about at the beginning of the chapter, can operate computers with a single key or switch rather than through a regular keyboard. Students with physical disabilities can use voice command systems to enter information into a computer verbally. Students who are deaf can communicate with hearing students or other deaf students using computer-assisted telecommunication devices such as those described in Chapter 5. Computer-generated large print, braille translations, and synthesized speech can assist students with visual disabilities in communicating. Students with communication problems can benefit from augmentative communication devices, which are computers equipped with speech synthesizers that can type text and produce speech heard by everyone. These devices can also be programmed with words and phrases for particular situations. Students with learning disabilities can compensate for poor

Professional Edge

Features of Effective Drill-and-Practice Software

The introduction of technology in the classroom has given teachers a new array of tools to use in presenting material to students. Students with special needs can especially benefit from using drill-and-practice software, which allows them to learn at their own pace. Keep in mind the following guidelines when choosing an effective drill-and-practice program for your students who have special needs.

What to Look for	What to Avoid	Rationale
Programs that provide high rates of responding relevant to the skill being learned	Programs that take too much time to load and run or that contain too many activities unrelated to the skill being learned	The more time students spend on task, the more they learn.
Programs in which animation and graphics support the skill or concept being practiced	Programs with animation or graphics that are unrelated to the program's instructional objective	Although animation and graphics may facilitate student interest in an activity, they may also distract students, interfere with skill mastery, and reduce practice time.
Programs in which reinforcement is clearly related to task completion or mastery	Programs in which the events that occur when students are incorrect (for example, an explosion) are more reinforcing than the events that occur when the student is correct (for example, a smiling face)	Some programs may inadvertently encourage students to practice the incorrect response to view an event they find more interesting.
Programs in which feedback helps students locate and correct their mistakes	Programs in which students are told merely whether they are right or wrong or instructed to try again	Without feedback that informs them of the correct answer after a reasonable number of attempts, students may become frustrated and make random guesses.
Programs that store information about student performance or progress that can be accessed later by the teacher	Programs without record-keeping features	Students may encounter difficulties with the skills covered by a program that requires teacher intervention. However, teachers often find it difficult to monitor students as they work at the computer. Access to records of student performance enables the teacher to determine whether a program is benefiting a student and whether the student needs additional assistance.
Programs with options for controlling features such as speed of problem presentation, type of feedback, problem difficulty, and number of practice trials	Programs that must be used in the same way with every student	Options are cost effective; they enable the same program to be used with a broad range of students. Furthermore, they permit a teacher to provide more appropriate individualized instruction.

FROM THE RESEARCH

Sands and Bucholz (1997) report numerous studies showing the effective use of well-designed drill-and-practice software to teach reading to persons with severe reading disabilities such as dyslexia. These students benefit from the repeated activities that are multisensory (visual, auditory, motoric) in nature.

SOURCE: From "Features of Effective Instructional Software," by C. M. Okolo, 2000, in *Technology and Exceptional Individuals*, 3rd ed., edited by J. Lindsey. Austin, TX: PRO-ED.

Assistive technology promises to revolutionize education in U.S. schools. In what ways might technology serve as a "great equalizer" in inclusive classrooms?

handwriting, spelling, and grammatical skills using word-processing equipment. Guidelines for using the INCLUDE strategy to match students with disabilities to appropriate assistive technology are in the Technology Notes feature on pages 142–144. More examples of assistive technology are shown in the Chapter 5 Technology Notes feature on page 166.

How Can You Analyze Instructional Methods in Relation to Student Needs?

Teachers use a number of instructional methods in class, including direct instruction, nondirect methods of instruction, scaffolding, independent student practice, and evaluation of student performance. Each of these methods should be analyzed in relation to student needs and then used and/or adapted as needed.

Elements of Direct Instruction

Several decades of research in teaching effectiveness have shown that many students learn skills and subject matter more readily when it is presented explicitly, often referred to as **direct instruction** (Christenson, Ysseldyke, & Thurlow, 1989; Rosenshine & Stevens, 1986; Stein, Carnine, & Dixon, 1998). Direct instruction consists of six key elements.

1. Review and check the previous day's work (and reteach if necessary). This aspect of direct instruction may include establishing routines for checking

WWW Resources

The National Center to Improve Practice has gathered and synthesized information about technology, disabilities, and instructional practices through a broad range of resources. This site also provides opportunities for teachers to exchange information, build knowledge, and practice through collaborative dialogue: http://www2.edc.org/ncip.

WWW Resources

Interested in learning more about direct instruction? Consult Association for Direct Instruction at http://darkwing.uoregon.edu/~adiep/.

homework and reviewing relevant past learning and prerequisite skills. These procedures are important because students with special needs might not retain past learning and/or know how to apply it to new material. For example, on Thursday Ms. Guzik taught her students how to round to the nearest whole number. On Friday she gave her class a story problem to solve that required rounding. Before the students solved the problem, she pointed to a chart in the front of the room that displayed a model of how to round numbers and suggested that they refer to this chart when they finished solving the problem.

2. Present new content or skills. When content or skills are presented, teachers begin the lesson with a short statement of the objectives and a brief overview of what they are going to present and why. Material is presented in small steps, using careful demonstrations that incorporate illustrations and concrete examples to highlight key points. Included within the demonstrations are periodic questions to check for understanding.

3. Provide guided student practice (and check for understanding). At first, student practice takes place under the direct guidance of the teacher, who frequently questions *all* students on material directly related to the new content or skill. You can involve all students in questioning by using unison oral responses or by having students answer questions by holding up answer cards, raising their hands when they think an answer is correct, or holding up a number to show which answer they think is right. For example, when asking a yes-or-no question, tell your students to hold up a 1 when they think the answer is yes and a 2 when they think the answer is no. This approach can be used with spelling, too. Have your students spell words on an index card and then hold up their answers. Unison responses not only give students more practice, but they also allow you to monitor student learning more readily. Prompts and additional explanations or demonstrations are provided during guided practice when appropriate. Effective guided practice continues until students meet the lesson objective. For example, Mr. Hayes was teaching his students how to add *es* to words that end in *y*. After modeling two examples at the board, he did several more examples *with* the students, guiding them as they applied the rule to change the *y* to *i* before they added *es*. Next, Mr. Hayes had them do a word on their own. Students wrote their answers on an index card and held up the card when directed by the teacher. Mr. Hayes noticed that five students did not apply the rule correctly. He called these students up to his desk for additional instruction and had the rest of the students work independently, adding *es* to a list of words on a worksheet.

4. Provide feedback and correction (and reteach when necessary). When students answer quickly and confidently, the teacher asks another question or provides a short acknowledgment of correctness (for example, "That's right"). Hesitant but correct responses might be followed by process feedback (for example, "Yes, Yolanda, that's right because . . . "). When students respond incorrectly, the teacher uses corrections to draw out an improved student response. Corrections can include sustaining feedback (that is, simplifying the question, giving clues), explaining or reviewing steps, giving process feedback ("The reason we need to regroup in this subtraction problem is because the top number is smaller than the bottom number"), or reteaching last steps ("Remember, at the end of this experiment you need to tell whether the hypothesis was accepted or rejected. Let me show you what I mean"). Corrections continue until students have met the lesson

Connections

Presenting new content also involves using strategies for activating students' prior knowledge. These strategies are explored further in Chapter 9.

Research Note

Research shows that students are usually more attentive to varied, fast-paced presentations (Darch & Gersten, 1985). The key to providing a fast-paced presentation is to begin the directions for the next question (or for correction of the current task) immediately after the students make a response. It also helps to limit your own talk to give your students as many opportunities to respond as possible.

objective, with praise used in moderation. Specific praise ("I'm impressed by how you drew a picture of that story problem!") is more effective than general praise ("Good boy, Leon").

5. Provide independent student practice. Students practice independently on tasks directly related to the skills taught until they achieve a high correct rate. Practice activities are actively supervised and students are held accountable for their work.

6. Review frequently. Systematic review of previously learned material is provided, including the incorporation of review into homework and tests. Material missed in homework or tests is retaught (Rosenshine & Stevens, 1986).

Rosenshine and Stevens (1986) are careful to note that for older students or for those who have more subject-matter knowledge or skills, these six steps can be modified, such as by presenting more material at one time or spending less time on guided practice. For example, when a second-grade teacher presented a unit on nutrition, she spent a whole week defining and showing examples of complex carbohydrates, fats, sugar, and protein. In an eighth-grade health class, this material was covered in one day, largely because students already had much background information on this topic. Although each of the direct instruction steps is not required for every lesson you teach, they are particularly helpful to students with learning and behavior problems, who have been shown to benefit greatly from a high level of classroom structure (Algozzine, Ysseldyke, & Campbell, 1994; Christenson et al., 1989; Kameenui, Carnine, & Dixon, 1998).

The Case in Practice on page 145 presents an example of a direct instruction lesson.

Nondirect Methods of Instruction

Nondirect instruction is based on the belief that children are naturally active learners and that given the appropriate instructional environment, they actively construct knowledge and solve problems in developmentally appropriate ways (Harris & Graham, 1996). This type of teaching is often referred to as being *constructivistic* because of the belief that students are capable of constructing meaning on their own, in most cases without explicit instruction from the teacher (Hallahan, Kauffman, & Lloyd, 1999; Poplin, 1988). Nondirect instruction is used by classroom teachers for both basic skills and content areas.

A common nondirect method is called **inquiry,** or **discovery learning** (Hoover & Hollingsworth, 1982; Jarolimek & Foster, 1993; Putnam & Wesson, 1990). Unlike direct instruction, which is very teacher centered, in the inquiry approach, the teacher's role is "that of a guide-stimulator, a facilitator who challenges learners by helping them identify questions and problems and who guides their inquiry" (Jarolimek & Foster, 1993, pp. 142–143). The learners, therefore, are placed "in a role that requires considerable initiative in finding things out for themselves. They must be actively engaged in their own learning" (Jarolimek & Foster, 1993, p. 143).

You can see these elements of inquiry learning in a social studies lesson on Inuit people developed by Lindquist (1995). The goal of the lesson was for students to "realize that there are many different groups of Inuit people, each having unique customs and traditions, but whose culture has been shaped by the Far North" (Lindquist, 1995, p. 54). First, the teacher gave the students 5 minutes to list everything they

FYI

Whole language represents a nondirect, constructivistic approach.

[Technology Notes]

Using INCLUDE to Determine Assistive Technology Needs

According to IDEA, the IEP team must consider whether a child needs assistive technology devices and services as part of his or her plan for an appropriate education. We believe that the steps in the INCLUDE strategy can assist greatly in helping the team make this decision. What follows is a series of questions related to assistive technology (AT) that teams may want to incorporate into the INCLUDE process. These questions were adapted from ones originally suggested by Beigel (2000) and Pedrotty-Bryant, Bryant, and Raskind (1998).

Identify Classroom Demands

1. How do you present information? For example, teachers who use a lot of classroom discussions place a particular demand on children's speaking abilities; teachers who lecture frequently place a strain on students' writing and organizational skills.

2. What types of grouping arrangements do you use? For example, an emphasis on cooperative learning places a burden on student communication skills.

3. What types of assignments do you make? For example, a project-driven class requires students to find and organize resource materials and then present them to the class in a clear, orderly way.

4. What are the primary ways you assess and evaluate your students? For example, oral assessments can place a strain on student verbal communication skills; written assessments place demands on written language skills such as handwriting, spelling, and sentence and paragraph construction.

5. How comfortable are you with having a learner who uses AT in the classroom? Your role in this process is very important. Without your support for learning to use AT and then continuing its use, a student may abandon his/her device.

6. What is the physical structure of your classroom and school? Issues such as whether there are ade-

How is technology enhancing the instruction and learning in this classroom?

quate electrical outlets or tables large enough to accommodate a computer and various peripherals need to be considered.

Note Learner Strengths and Needs and Check for Potential Success and Problem Areas

1. What purposeful motoric movement does the student have? A purposeful movement is one that the learner controls in a conscious, consistent manner (Beigel, 2000, p. 240). Examples of purposeful motoric movement include raising an eyebrow, moving the fingers of one hand in a motion similar to that of typing, and using a pen or pencil to write or draw.

2. How willing is the student to try new activities or tasks? Using the AT requires a willingness to change on the part of the student. Your knowledge of the student in this area can help determine the nature of the equipment selected (e.g., easy to use or hard to use) as well as the amount of time needed to achieve independent usage.

3. What does the student desire from the use of AT? The personal goals of the learner can greatly influence AT usage. Relevance of the material is an important factor in learning to perform any skill. For example, Tamra had an expressed desire to

write poetry and was quite receptive to learning to use a laptop with a large keyboard especially designed for her.

4. What emotional and psychological supports does the student need when learning to use the device? Some students may require considerable emotional and psychological support as they learn and use an AT device. You or other staff working with the student should provide such support when it is needed or students are not likely to use the device. It is important to remember that students cannot be forced to use AT; they can only be encouraged and supported whenever using the device.

5. What level of training does the student and others who interact with the student need? You, the student, and other staff working with the student need to be given the opportunity to see how the various devices work and to see who needs training and in what areas.

6. What impact, if any, does the student's socioeconomic status and cultural background have on the use of AT? Students who live in poverty and their parents are less likely to have previous experience with technology and may need more extensive training. There is also the question of the impact of culture on the acceptance of AT by students and their families.

Brainstorm and Then Decide on Adaptations

You need to consider the features of the technical devices as well as the extent to which they help students meet identified IEP goals.

1. How durable is the device? All devices that are used in schools should be able to withstand minimal bumps and jars common in schools.

2. What set-up and maintenance issues must be addressed? How easy is the device to update or repair? Do compatibility issues with other technology already in the classroom exist that must be addressed? Devices that are difficult to maintain, take a long time to repair, are not easily upgraded, or are incompatible with other technology should be avoided because eventually they are abandoned.

3. How willing is the vendor of the device to provide a trial or loaner period of use for the student? You

often need to try several devices in the school environment before a final AT decision can be made.

4. What is the reputation of the company in terms of construction, service, training, and reliability? These questions can be answered by consulting publications that deal with AT (*Team Rehab, TAM Connector*), contacting organizations (Council for Exceptional Children, Center for Applied Special Technology), and asking others who use AT. A number of websites that also may be helpful are listed at the end of this feature.

5. Does the student have the psychomotor skills needed to use the device in a functional manner? This question should be answered during student assessment. Many devices can be adapted for students with limited motoric control; if not, then it is unrealistic to expect that the device will be used.

6. Is the device aesthetically acceptable to the student? Some students may prefer a certain color or type of mouse; others may prefer a brightly colored exterior as opposed to the typical colors of blue, black, and beige; still others may want to decorate their equipment (as long as it doesn't interfere with its function). If students' aesthetic needs are not addressed, they may feel the device doesn't fit into their social milieu and are not likely to use it.

7. Does the device meet the student's needs in a way that is easily understood by others? Students should be able to use their devices without causing a distraction. In addition, the device should not be so complex that only the vendor is able to program the device or explain how it can be used.

8. How portable is the device? For AT to be useful, the student or support person must be able to move the device from one class to another—from an elementary classroom to a special class such as art or physical education or between various academic classes in a middle or high school environment.

Evaluate Student Progress

The ultimate goal of AT is to enable students to more readily meet their IEP goals. Pedrotty-Bryant, Bryant, and Raskind (1998) suggest that teachers ask

continued

the following questions when determining whether the assistive technology selected is an appropriate match for the student.

To what extent does the AT assist the student in compensating for the disability?

To what degree does the technology promote student independence?

What is the student's opinion of the technology adaptation?

What is the family's opinion of the AT?

Is the AT efficient and easy for the student to use?

Does the device promote meeting IEP goals and objectives in the least restrictive environment? (p. 55).

For additional information on assistive technology, consult the following websites.

ABLEDATA
http://www.abledata.com

Alliance for Technology Access
http://www.ataccess.org

Apple Disability Resources
http://www.apple.com/education/k12/disability/

Closing the Gap
http://www.closingthegap.com/

Dreamms for Kids
http://www.dreamms.org

Microsoft's Accessibility Web Site
http://www.microsoft.com/emble/default.htm

---

knew about the Inuit people. The teacher then had some students share their lists with the class. Student sharing of their background knowledge was followed by a short film on the Inuit people. After the film, the students were asked to cross out anything on their lists that the film caused them to change their minds about. When the children had revised their lists, the teacher divided the class into pairs; each pair was asked to research a different Inuit tribe. They were to gather information about food, shelter, clothing, and language. Each pair of students recorded information about their particular tribe on a data sheet and reported their information to the class. As each group reported, the teacher synthesized the information on an overhead chart, creating a graphic display for comparing similarities and differences among the various tribes.

Scaffolding

Nondirect methods of instruction have great potential for use with students with disabilities, many of whom are characterized as being passive learners who lack skills in these areas. Still, to succeed in a discovery format, students with special needs require support from the teacher. An approach that has been used successfully to support students as they develop problem-solving skills is called **scaffolding** (Pearson, 1996). Scaffolds are "forms of support provided by the teacher (or another student) to help students bridge the gap between their current abilities and the intended goal" (Rosenshine & Meister, 1992, p. 26).

Before using scaffolding, you need to find out whether students have the necessary background ability to learn a cognitive strategy (Rosenshine & Meister, 1992). For example, a strategy for helping a student read a physics textbook is not useful if the student lacks basic knowledge of mathematics and physical properties. Similarly, teaching a strategy for solving math word problems cannot succeed if the student does not have basic math computation skills. Using scaffolding to teach higher-order cognitive strategies consists of six stages:

Connections

Ways to use scaffolding to teach students study skills are described in the discussion of learning strategies in Chapter 10.

C A S E   I N   P R A C T I C E

A Direct-Instruction Lesson

This direct-instruction lesson is designed to teach two-digit subtraction problems that involve renaming. Notice that the teacher first reviews the preskills of knowing when to rename. Then she guides students through several problems.

Teacher: Yesterday we learned a rule about renaming with subtraction problems. What is that rule?

Students: When we take away more than we start with, we must rename.

Teacher: Great! Now tell me whether we need to rename in doing this problem. [Teacher writes on the board.]

$$\begin{array}{r} 42 \\ -37 \\ \hline \end{array}$$

Students: Yes, we need to rename.

Teacher: Why is that?

Students: Because we're taking away more than we start with. We start with 2 and take away 7. Seven is more, so we have to rename.

Teacher: Okay. Today we're going to learn how to rename in subtraction.

[Teacher writes on the board.] Read this problem.

$$\begin{array}{r} 53 \\ -26 \\ \hline \end{array}$$

Students: 53 take away 26.

Teacher: The 1s column tells us to start with 3 and take away 6. What does the 1s column tell us to do?

Students: Start with 3 and take away 6.

Teacher: Do we have to rename?

Students: Yes.

Teacher: Right! We start with 3 and have to take away more than 3. Here's how we rename: First we borrow a 10 from the five 10s. What do we do first?

Students: Borrow a 10 from the five 10s.

Teacher: How many 10s will be left?

Students: Four 10s.

Teacher: So I cross out the 5 and write 4 to show that the four 10s are left. [Teacher crosses out 5 and writes 4.]

Teacher: We borrowed a 10. What do we do next?

Students: Put the 10 with the three 1s.

Teacher: Right. Put 10 with the three 1s. [Teacher writes 1 in front of 3.] Now we have 13 in the 1s column. Figure out what 13 minus 6 is. [Pause] What's 13 minus 6?

Students: Seven.

Teacher: We write 7 in the 1s column. [Teacher writes 7 under the 1s column.]

Teacher: The 10s column says four 10s minus two 10s. How many is four 10s minus two 10s?

Students: Two 10s.

Teacher: What is 53 minus 26?

Students: 27.

[Teacher repeats with two more problems.]

R E F L E C T I O N S

What direct-instruction steps did the teacher use here? Why do you think direct instruction is particularly effective for students with learning and behavior needs? Can you think of some situations in which you would not want to use direct instruction?

---

1. Present the new cognitive strategy. In this stage, the teacher introduces the strategy concretely, using a list of strategy steps. The teacher then models the strategy, including all *thinking* and *doing* steps. For example, Mr. Bridges is teaching his history class how geographic features and natural resources affect the growth and location of cities. First, he introduces the problem-solving strategy to his students: (1) define the problem, (2) propose hypotheses to explain the problem, (3) collect data to evaluate your hypotheses, (4) evaluate the evidence, and (5) make a conclusion. These steps are posted on the chalkboard for easy reference. Mr.

With the appropriate support, nondirect instruction can be effective for students with special needs. What steps should this teacher take to ensure effective instruction using scaffolding?

Bridges then models the strategy steps by showing students a map of the state of Illinois and saying the following:

> The problem here is finding out why Chicago came to be located where it is and not anywhere else in Illinois. Some possible factors that might affect where big cities are located are the presence of water (rivers and lakes); mountains, valleys, or other land forms; climate; access to other cities; and whether mineral or oil deposits are nearby. Next, I'm going to collect some data or information to determine which factors had an influence on the development of Chicago. Chicago is on a large lake, Lake Michigan. This makes it easier for people and goods to travel in and out. It is also centrally located in the middle of the country; people from other cities can get to it easily. It is also easy to get to because no mountains are around it. No major mineral deposits are nearby, so that is not a factor. The climate is cold, so I don't think people came to Chicago for the weather. All this evidence leads me to conclude that Chicago is where it is because of Lake Michigan and because it is easy to get to from a lot of places.

FYI

Scaffolding is a helpful strategy for teaching basic skills too.

2. Regulate difficulty during guided practice. At this stage, students begin practicing the new strategy using simplified materials so they can concentrate on learning the strategy. First, the strategy is introduced one step at a time. Students are guided carefully through the steps, with the teacher anticipating particularly difficult steps and completing these difficult parts of the task as necessary. Before tackling difficult problems, such as the geography of Chicago, Mr. Bridges has his students use the problem-solving steps to solve simpler problems on topics familiar to them. For example, he had them solve problems such as why the cookies someone made were dry, why a hypothetical student was late for school every day, or why the school lunches tasted awful. He also helped students brainstorm ideas for how to collect data, a step that can be difficult. Mr. Bridges did this by compiling an initial list of data collection procedures for each problem. For the problem of why the cookies were dry, Mr. Bridges gave his students a list of possible data collection procedures, such as identifying the ingredients, finding out how long the cookies were baked, and figuring out how old the cookies were.

3. Provide varying contexts for student practice. Students practice the strategy on actual classroom tasks under the teacher's direction. The teacher starts out leading the practice, but the students eventually carry out the practice sessions in small cooperative groups. In Mr. Bridges's class, students practiced the problem-solving strategy using examples from their history textbooks.

4. Provide feedback. The teacher provides corrective feedback to students using evaluative checklists based on models of expert problem solving carefully explained to the students. Students are encouraged to evaluate their performance using these checklists. For example, each time Mr. Bridges's students used the problem-solving strategy, they evaluated their performance by asking themselves questions such as, Did we clearly state the problem? Did we state a complete list of hypotheses? How thorough were our data collection procedures? Were we able to evaluate all the hyptheses using the information collected? Did we interpret the results accurately? Were our conclusions consistent with our results?

5. Increase student responsibility. Next, the teacher begins to require students to practice putting all the steps together on their own. Student independence is encouraged by removing elements of the scaffold. For example, prompts and models are diminished, the complexity and difficulty of the materials are increased, and peer support is decreased. The teacher checks for student mastery before going to the last step, independent practice.

6. Provide independent practice. Finally, the teacher provides the students with extensive practice and helps them apply what they have learned to new situations. For example, Mr. Bridges showed his students how problem solving could be used in other subjects, such as science (Rosenshine & Meister, 1992).

Check Your Learning

How can scaffolding be used to make nondirect instruction more effective for students with special needs?

Independent Student Practice

The major purpose of practice is to help students refine or strengthen their skills in various areas. Consider the following guidelines for using practice activities effectively in your classroom:

1. **Students should practice only skills or content they have already learned.** This guideline is particularly important for students to be able to perform practice activities independently. Tasks that are too difficult can lead to high levels of off-task behavior.

2. **Practice is more effective when students have a desire to learn what they are practicing.** Whenever possible, point out to students situations in which they can use the skill in other phases of learning. For example, you may explain to your students that if they learn to read more quickly, they will be able to finish their homework in less time.

3. **Practice should be individualized.** Exercises should be organized so that each student can work independently.

4. **Practice should be specific and systematic.** Practice should be directly related to skills and objectives you are working on in class. This guideline is

Special Emphasis On . . .

Teaching Vocabulary to English Language Learners with Learning Disabilities

Content-area instruction requires teaching new vocabulary words, many of which can be technical. Gersten, Baker, and Marks (1998) suggest the following research-based strategies when teaching vocabulary to your English language learners who have learning difficulties.

Focus Vocabulary Instruction on a Small Number of Critical Words.

Providing extensive drill on lengthy word lists is ineffective for students with learning difficulties. Instead, focus on several critical words at a time and emphasize these for several days. Enhance understanding of vocabulary by showing how the words are used in a variety of contexts, including below-grade-level books in the same subject area, texts in different content areas, and personal writing projects.

Provide Multiple Exposures.

You need to expose students to the word in a variety of contexts before they begin to develop a deeper understanding of the meaning of the word and use the word as part of their expressive vocabulary. Multiple exposures can include how the words are used in below-grade-level books in the same subject area, texts in different content areas, and in personal writing projects.

Introduce New Words before They Are Encountered in Reading.

The introduction of vocabulary should be done explicitly during a short segment of class time, usually around 5 minutes (Echevarria, 1998). During these 5 minutes you would say the vocabulary word, write it on the board, ask students to say and write it, and then define the word using pictures, demonstrations, and examples familiar to students. (See "Teaching Vocabulary through Modeling Examples, Synonyms, and Definitions" in Chapter 9.)

Practice with New Words.

Give your students many opportunities to practice the new words they are learning. Gersten et al. (1998) report an example of teaching the word *audience* in *Mr. Popper's Penguins*. After teaching the definition of *audience,* the teacher discussed other kinds of audiences with the

particularly important for students with special needs, who require more practice to master academic skills.

5. **Students should have much practice on a few skills rather than little practice on many skills.** Focusing on one or two skills at a time is less confusing and gives students more practice on each skill.

6. **Practice should be organized so that students achieve high levels of success.** Correct answers reinforce students and encourage them to do more. Most students need at least 90 percent accuracy when doing practice activities, though higher-achieving students can tolerate a 70 percent rate as long as the teacher is present to assist them (Good & Brophy, 1986).

7. **Practice should be organized so that students and teacher have immediate feedback.** You need to know how students are progressing so you can decide whether to move to the next skill. Students need to know how they are doing so they can make meaningful corrections of their work (Ornstein, 1990).

class, such as an audience at a Madonna concert, an audience at a *Star Wars* movie, an audience at a wrestling match, and an audience with the Pope. It is critical that English language learners have lots of practice so they can go from a basic understanding of a word to actually being able to use the word in classroom conversation.

Focus on Idioms.

Idioms may be hard for English language learners to understand because their overall meaning can be quite different from their individual parts. Still, idioms can be used effectively to focus students' attention on important differences between standard and contextual definitions of words, as well as to increase student comprehension. For example, in a history class devoted to the rise of labor unions, a union leader was quoted as using the idiom "hit them in the pocketbook where it hurts." The teacher explained carefully that this expression was not to be taken literally and that it simply meant the unions wanted to hurt management by causing them to lose money.

Develop Word Banks.

A word bank is a place where key vocabulary is stored and posted for students' reference throughout a teaching unit or beyond. Selection of words for word banks should be based on their relevance for understanding key concepts, high frequency of use, and relevance for students' lives. For example, in a unit on the topic of the green house effect, explaining what the ozone layer is would be more important than presenting the definition of fluorocarbons. Word banks can be created by groups of students or by students individually. They can also be visually displayed. For example, as a word is introduced, its meaning and key attributes can be written on chart paper and posted in the room. The displays can then become reference points for students, can help students remember definitions and relationships among words, and can provide guides for correct spelling. Word banks can also be dynamic; as students learn more about words, this new information can be added to existing definitions. For example, the class that was learning the word *audience* came across the term *audience share* in an article they read about a current television show. The class added this use of *audience* to their visual display.

Use Visual Organizers.

Visual organizers can help students access and understand vocabulary that they could not otherwise understand if presented only verbally. Examples of using visual organizers to teach vocabulary are described in Chapter 9.

For students with special needs, consider these additional questions. First, what are the response demands of the activity? Do students have to answer orally or in writing? How extensive a response is required? Do the students have enough time to finish the activity? Response demands are important because students who are unable to meet them will not be able to do the practice activity independently. For example, Mr. Edwards is having his class practice weekly vocabulary words by orally stating their definitions. Ross stutters and is unable to answer out loud. Mr. Edwards allows him to submit a written list of definitions. Ms. Osborne is having her students complete short-answer questions in their history books. Clarice has a physical disability and is unable to write her answers independently. She uses an adapted classroom computer to prepare her answers. Mr. Nusbaum asked his students to write a paragraph summarizing the reasons for the stock market crash of 1929. Maurice cannot write a coherent paragraph but can answer orally into a tape recorder. Amanda writes very slowly, so Mr. Nusbaum gave her more time to complete the activity. Ways in which direct instruction and scaffolding can be used to teach vocabulary to English language learners are in the Special Emphasis On . . . feature.

Connections

Strategies for adapting
seatwork, independent
practice activities, and
homework for students
with special needs are presented in Chapter 9.

Homework. Perhaps the most common form of practice used by teachers is
homework. Research shows that homework can have a positive effect on student
achievement when it is properly assigned (Cooper, 1989; Cooper & Nye, 1994).

Homework is often a challenge for students with special needs. For example, most
teachers expect homework to be completed independently, and students must have the
sensory, academic, and organizational skills to do so. A student with a severe reading
disability might be unable to read a chapter in a history book and answer the questions
without some form of adaptation such as a peer reader or taped text. Similarly, a student with fine-motor difficulties might be unable to answer the written questions unless allowed to do so orally or with an adapted word processor. In addition, you may
need to provide this same student more time or to assign fewer problems. Therefore,
it is important that you carefully examine your own particular homework requirements and adapt them to ensure full participation by all your students.

Evaluation of Student Performance

Connections

Chapter 11 explores strategies for adapting classroom
tests and report card grades
for students with special
needs. It also covers potentially valuable additions to
testing and grading, such as
performance-based assess-
ments and portfolios.

The major purpose of student evaluation is to determine the extent to which students have mastered academic skills or instructional content. The results of student
evaluations often are communicated through grades, which are determined in a
number of ways, including tests and assignments. Because student evaluation is so
important, you need to consider how classroom tests and assignments may interact
with student learning needs. Most critical is that the method of evaluation measures
skill or content mastery, not the student's disability. For example, Carson, a student
who has an attention deficit, should be given tests in small segments to ensure that
the test measures his knowledge, not his attention span. Similarly, Riesa, a student
with a severe learning disability in writing, needs to take an oral essay test in history
if the test is to be a valid measure of her history knowledge, not of her writing disability. The type of report card grade used as well as the system used to arrive at that
grade might also need to be adapted for some students. For example, Hal was dis-
couraged about always getting a C in English no matter how hard he tried. His
teacher decided to supplement his grade with an A for effort to encourage Hal to
keep trying. Mr. Henning encouraged his students to come to class on time by giving them credit for punctuality.

Summary

Various aspects of classroom environments can affect the learning of all students, including those with special needs. Fewer individualized accommodations for students
with special needs are required in classrooms that are well structured and organized.
However, even in the best situations, some adaptations are needed.

The INCLUDE strategy is a decision-making process to help teachers make
reasonable accommodations for students with special needs. Reasonable accommodations are those that maximize student success without taking a disproportionate
amount of time or diminishing the education of the other students in the class. The
steps in INCLUDE are *i*dentify environmental, curricular, and instructional classroom demands; *n*ote student learning strengths and needs; *c*heck for potential areas
of student success; *l*ook for potential problem areas; *u*se information gathered to

brainstorm instructional adaptations; *d*ecide which adaptations to implement; and *e*valuate student progress.

An important part of the INCLUDE strategy is analyzing classroom demands. Demands covering four major areas should be analyzed: classroom organization, classroom grouping, instructional materials, and instructional methods. Classroom organization includes physical organization, classroom routines, classroom climate, classroom rules, monitoring, and the use of time. Key aspects of classroom grouping involve the use of whole-class and small instructional groups, same-skill and mixed-skill groups, and one-to-one instruction. Instructional materials that need to be considered are basic skills materials, content-area textbooks, manipulatives and models, and instructional and assistive technology. With regard to teaching demands, two common instructional models used in schools are direct and nondirect instruction. Sometimes students with special needs may require support or scaffolds when participating in nondirect teaching. Finally, consider the demands of your practice activities and follow guidelines for using practice effectively.

Applications in Teaching Practice

Planning Adaptations in the Instructional Environment

Consider two scenarios.

- Verna is a student with a learning disability in Ms. Chang's fourth-grade class. Ms. Chang uses whole-group instruction in math. This method is sometimes hard for Verna, who is behind her peers in math; Verna is slow to answer math facts, has trouble keeping numbers straight in columns, and sometimes forgets a step or two when she is computing a problem that requires several steps.

- Mr. Howard wanted to teach the following textbook reading strategy to his freshman history students:

    R *Review* headings and subheadings.

    E *Examine* boldface words.

    A *Ask* "What do I expect to learn?"

    D *Do* it: Read!

    S *Summarize* in your own words (Bartelt, Marchio, & Reynolds, 1994).

Questions

1. What can Ms. Chang do to help Verna succeed in the large group?
2. How can Ms. Chang use direct instruction to teach students to round numbers to the nearest 10? Design such a lesson.
3. How can Mr. Howard use scaffolding to teach his history students the READS strategy?
4. Find a drill-and-practice computer program for elementary or high school students and evaluate it. Does it meet the criteria discussed in this chapter?

5

Students with Low-Incidence Disabilities

After you read this chapter, you will be able to

1. Describe what it means to say that a student has a low-incidence disability.

2. Depict the characteristics of students with moderate, severe, or multiple disabilities, including mental retardation, and the accommodations general education teachers can make for them.

3. Explain the characteristics of students with sensory impairments and the accommodations general education teachers can make for them.

4. Describe the characteristics of students with physical or health impairments and the accommodations general education teachers can make for them.

5. Outline the characteristics of students with autism and the accommodations general education teachers can make for them.

Key Terms and Concepts

Asperger's syndrome (p. 189)

Assistive technology (p. 166)

Augmentative communication (p. 164)

Autism (p. 187)

Down syndrome (p. 159)

Functional curriculum (p. 159)

Hearing impairments (p. 168)

Low-incidence disabilities (p. 154)

Orthopedic impairments (p. 177)

Other health impairments (p. 177)

Traumatic brain injury (p. 177)

Visual impairments (p. 168)

■ Kamil is a first-grade student with a moderate cognitive disability. She is described by her teachers and her mother as a "bundle of energy," and she is enthusiastic about school and all the activities that occur in her classroom. Although Kamil is just learning to recognize colors and to identify shapes and is a prereader, she receives nearly all her instruction in the first-grade classroom. Because Ms. Atkins often uses cutouts, puppets, or other concrete strategies to illustrate the literature being read, Kamil follows along without much difficulty. When other students work on writing or editing, Kamil works with a computer program, either practicing shapes and colors, or learning to recognize her name. What are the learning characteristics and needs of students like Kamil? What are appropriate expectations for Kamil's teacher to have for her this year? What accommodations does Kamil need to succeed in first grade? If Ms. Atkins has a question about Kamil, how can she find an answer?

■ Jesús is a fifth-grade student. According to federal guidelines, he is eligible to receive special education because he has multiple disabilities. Jesús uses a motorized wheelchair, and he has limited use of his arms. His wheelchair is specially equipped to provide support for his head because his neck muscles are weak. Because writing is not possible for Jesús, he does assignments by dictating his answers to a peer scribe or his assistant, a paraprofessional employed to ensure that Jesús' personal and mobility needs are met. Sometimes Jesús composes stories with a computer program that translates his spoken words into print. He is becoming quite proficient in using this technology. Although Jesús also has a mild cognitive disability, he is learning, with accommodations, most of the same curriculum as his classmates. His general education teacher and special education teacher meet regularly to discuss upcoming units of instruction and the types of adapted materials and alternative assignments most beneficial for Jesús. How are decisions made about what Jesús should be learning in fifth grade? What can Jesús' teacher do from both an instructional and social perspective to include Jesús in classroom activities?

■ Carter is a seventh-grade student diagnosed with autism who has some remarkable skills. His math achievement is far above grade level, and he has a prodigious ability to remember facts and figures, particularly about his favorite subjects—currently presidents of the United States and

South American countries. Carter has many personally determined routines that he follows in school. For example, before he leaves the classroom, he counts the books in his backpack, reties his shoes, and says as he leaves the room, "That's my final answer." Any change in the schedule of the day or interference with his personal routines can lead to disruptive behavior. What is autism? What should Carter's teacher do to help him learn? What accommodations might Carter need now, in middle school, and later, in high school?

■ Martina is a senior this year. She plans to become a special education teacher someday, and she is studying hard to improve her chances of succeeding in college. Martina has had a profound hearing loss since she was 3 months old. Martina did not learn sign language until she began high school. She now prefers signing as a communication approach, and she has an interpreter who accompanies her to core academic classes. Martina's most difficult subject is English. She has problems writing down her ideas logically and elaborating on them. How do hearing impairments affect learning for students like Martina? What are Martina's responsibilities for self-advocacy? What can her teachers do to help her prepare for college?

Students like Kamil, Jesús, Carter, and Martina have the same rights as other students to be part of a classroom community with nondisabled peers. For Kamil and other young children with significant disabilities, attending first grade with peers prepares them for the demands of school and also creates the expectation that they can fully participate in typical educational environments and live as valued and contributing members of communities after their school years. For Martina, success in college depends on her receiving the strong academic background available in general education classes. Because of their disabilities, however, these and other students in inclusive schools might need specialized equipment or assistance.

Connections

In Chapter 1, all the categories of disabilities are listed and the concept of high- and low-incidence disabilities is explained.

In this chapter, you learn about the characteristics and needs of students with **low-incidence disabilities,** that is, moderate, severe, or multiple disabilities; sensory impairments; physical or health disabilities; and autism. The federal terms for these disabilities and the proportion of students with low incidence served through IDEA are summarized in Table 5.1. You also learn about accommodations specific to the unique needs of these students that general education teachers can make to enable them to learn.

What Are Low-Incidence Disabilities?

When you work with students with low-incidence disabilities, you are struck by the diversity of their needs, the range of educational services they access, and the variety of specialists who ensure they receive an appropriate education. Typically, individuals within any categories of disability do not exhibit all the characteristics of that

Table 5.1 School-Age Students with Low-Incidence Disabilities Receiving Special Education Services in 1997–1998[a]

Federal Disability Category	Defining Characteristics	Total Number of Students	Percentage of All Students Receiving IDEA Services
Mental retardation	Significant below-average general intellectual functioning with deficits in adaptive behavior	602,111	11.6[b]
	Identified between birth and 18 years of age		
	Adversely affects educational performance		
Multiple disabilities	Two or more disabilities so interwoven that none can be identified as the primary disability	106,758	1.8
	Adversely affects educational performance		
Hearing impairments	Hearing loss is permanent or fluctuating, mild to profound in nature, in one or both ears	69,537	1.3
	Loss may be referred to as *hard of hearing* or *deaf*		
	Adversely affects educational performance		
Orthopedic impairments	Physically disabling conditions that affect locomotion or motor functions	67,422	1.2
	May be the result of a congenital anomaly, a disease, an accident, or other causes		
	Adversely affects educational performance		
Other health impairments	Condition resulting in limited strength, vitality, or alertness and caused by chronic or acute health problems	190,935	2.2
	Adversely affects educational performance		
Visual impairments	Vision loss in which student cannot successfully use vision as a primary channel for learning or has such reduced acuity or visual field that processing information visually is significantly inhibited and specialized materials or modifications are needed	26,015	0.5
	Adversely affects educational performance		
Deaf–blindness	Presence of both a vision and a hearing disability that causes severe communication and related problems	1,454	0.0
	Adversely affects educational performance		
Autism	Developmental disability characterized by impairments in communication, learning, and reciprocal social interactions	42,487	0.5
	Usually identified in infancy or early childhood		
	Adversely affects educational performance		
Traumatic brain injury	Impairments manifested by limited strength, vitality, alertness, or other impaired development resulting from a traumatic brain injury	11,895	0.1
	Adversely affects educational performance		

[a]Students age 6–21 receiving services through IDEA, Part B (U.S. Department of Education, 1999). Additional students receive services under Part H of the same law, under Chapter I. Approximately 1,935 students who received services through this law were categorized as having developmental delays.

[b]Because federal categories of disability do not distinguish among students with various degrees of mental retardation, it is difficult to provide a precise estimate of the number of students with moderate or severe cognitive disabilities. However, approximately one-third of the students in this category have moderate or severe cognitive disabilities.

SOURCE: From *Twenty-First Annual Report to Congress on the Implementation of the Individuals with Disabilities Education Act,* 1999, Washington, DC: U.S. Department of Education.

WWW Resources

One valuable source of information about students with Down syndrome is the website of the organization called Downs City, at http://www.nads.org. This site includes resources, news, and information about this syndrome.

disability, but they display them much more than other students do. The following points can help you keep in perspective students' needs and your role in their education.

First, students with low-incidence disabilities together make up only about 10 percent of all the students with disabilities in schools. That means that you may teach students with these needs some years, but not others, and make accommodations described in this chapter for a small number of students. An exception to this situation could occur if your school district operates **cluster programs,** in which students with low-incidence disabilities from throughout the district are bussed to a single school. In such cases, you might find that your school has a "class" of students with low-incidence disabilities, making it likely that you will teach more students with such needs.

Second, students with low-incidence disabilities often have received some type of special education services from birth or shortly thereafter. They might come to kindergarten already having attended an infant stimulation program or a preschool program in which their special needs were addressed in a day care, inclusive preschool, or special education setting. You may find that many supports and extensive technical assistance are available for students with low-incidence disabilities.

Third, students with low-incidence disabilities need the same basic attention from you that other students do. If you are unsure about a student need, it is nearly always best to rely on the same professional judgment you would use in working with other students. If you encounter difficulty, you can access the technical support that special education professionals offer. Students with certain disabilities, especially severe or complex ones, are often accompanied by a paraprofessional or personal assistant who might work with them for several years. Such an individual may be able to offer insight about responding to the student.

You may have many concerns about meeting the needs of a student with a low-incidence disability in your classroom. The Professional Edge features questions you can ask to prepare yourself for a student with a low-incidence disability to join your class. The questions address the student's strengths and potential, learning and social needs, and physical or health needs. They also cover domains in which accommodations might be needed, including the physical arrangement of the classroom. What other questions would you add to these lists?

Connections

The INCLUDE strategy (see Chapter 4) can also guide you through the process of providing appropriate instruction for students with moderate or severe disabilities.

If you look ahead in this textbook, you find that this chapter as well as Chapter 6, on high-incidence disabilities, address students with cognitive disabilities. This dual consideration occurs because the federal category of mental retardation is used for all students with this disability, whether the disability is mild, moderate, or severe. This chapter addresses only students with moderate or severe cognitive disabilities. Students with mild cognitive disabilities have characteristics and needs more similar to those of students with learning and behavior disabilities, and they are discussed with those groups.

What Accommodations Can You Make for Students with Moderate, Severe, or Multiple Disabilities?

Students with moderate, severe, or multiple disabilities include those whose cognitive impairments and adaptive behavior deficits are so significant and pervasive that considerable support is needed for them to learn. This group also includes students

Professional Edge

Questions to Ask When Working with Students with Low-Incidence Disabilities

If you will be teaching a student with a low-incidence disability, you will probably have questions about the student's needs and your responsibilities for helping the student succeed. You might ask in your conversation with a special education teacher or administrator the following key questions to help both you and the student feel more comfortable.

Student Needs

1. What is the student's greatest strength?
2. What activities or rewards does the student most enjoy?
3. What is the student's level of functioning academically, socially, emotionally, behaviorally, and in other domains?
4. Does the student have physical or health needs that require my attention? For example, does the student need to take medication? Is the student likely to have a reaction to medication? Does the student tire easily? Does the student need assistance in moving from place to place?

Student Goals

1. What are the three or four most important instructional goals for this student in my class? What are the academic, social, emotional, or other goals?
2. What are the goals for this student in each subject (for elementary teachers)? How do the goals for this student interface with the instructional goals of this course (for secondary teachers)?
3. What are the goals that this student is working on throughout the day? Which of those are emphasized during different periods of the day?

Student Supports and Accommodations

1. If I have a question about the student, who is my primary contact person? How do I reach that person?
2. Does the student have an assistant or interpreter? If there is an assistant, what are his or her major responsibilities? Can that person help other students in the class as well?
3. What other services (for example, speech/language services) will the student access? How often? Who will be in touch to help arrange these services? Will they be delivered in the classroom or in another location?
4. Do I need to adapt the physical environment for this student? How?
5. Do I need to adapt my expectations for this student because of physical or health needs? How? Are there restrictions on this student's participation in any class activities?
6. How can I adapt my teaching approach to accommodate the student's needs?

with multiple disabilities, that is, students who have more than one disabling condition. Both groups of students typically have a curriculum that differs significantly from that of other students in your class, but many students with such significant disabilities can still learn in a general education setting and can benefit from social interactions with classmates that occur there.

Students with Moderate to Severe Cognitive Disabilities

Students with moderate to severe cognitive disabilities have ongoing needs for supports during their school years and into adult life. Some students are able to learn the academic, social, and vocational skills that enable them to live independently or semi-independently as productive adult citizens. Others' learning will be more limited, and they may need intensive services throughout their lives. In most school districts, some students with moderate or severe disabilities are being integrated into general education classrooms, particularly at the elementary school level.

Most states use scores on intelligence tests and adaptive behavior scales to determine the presence of a cognitive disability. Although intelligence tests must be interpreted carefully and are not helpful in designing instruction for students, an overall IQ score of less than 70 with significant difficulty in the area of adaptive behaviors (for example, ordering a meal in a restaurant) leads to eligibility for special education in the category of mental retardation. Students with moderate or severe cognitive disabilities generally have IQ scores of approximately 55 or below. It is important to realize that leaders in the field argue that a more appropriate strategy for identifying individuals with cognitive disabilities is to define the disability on the basis of its impact on daily life activities and student needs for services (Beirne-Smith, Patton, & Ittenbach, 1994).

Generally, students with moderate or severe cognitive disabilities have several noticeable characteristics. First, the amount of information they can learn may be quite limited and the rate at which they learn it may be quite slow. These two factors suggest that considerable repetition of skills particularly essential for adult functioning are needed. For example, Noemi, a middle school student with a severe cognitive disability, is working to learn to communicate her needs to others. She has a communication device that enables her to indicate that she needs a drink of water, that she needs to use the bathroom, and that she is hungry. The paraprofessional sometimes works with her on this skill, but her classmates also ask her questions related to these needs. Martin, an elementary student with a moderate cognitive disability, is learning a variety of preacademic skills within his general education classroom, including telling a story from a picture book, recognizing his name and address, and understanding directional prepositions such as *up*, *down*, *inside*, and *outside*. He rehearses these as opportunities arise during general instruction, and when other students are completing individual assignments that are beyond his capability, he works on his skills on the computer, sometimes with a peer assistant.

Students with moderate or severe cognitive disabilities need to learn many other essential skills. One example is social skills. Several IEP goals and objectives may relate to participating in one-to-one or small-group interactions with peers, responding to questions asked by others, and sharing toys, games, or materials. Another example is recreational skills. In one recent study, high school juniors who were typical learners worked with their English teacher and a special education teacher to teach students with moderate cognitive disabilities how to play cards, select a television program, play a sports videotape, and play a computer game (Collins, Hall, & Branson, 1997). The English students used the project as the basis for a series of writing assignments. Results indicated that not only was the project successful in teaching these useful leisure activities to students with cognitive disabilities, but the typical students became more understanding of and positive toward individuals with disabilities.

A second characteristic of individuals with moderate or severe cognitive disabilities is that they may have difficulty maintaining their skills; without ongoing practice, they are likely to forget what they once learned. To ensure that these students continue to practice necessary skills, teachers should stress skills they need both in and outside school. This learning characteristic commonly worries general education teachers having students with these disabilities in their classrooms: What is the student going to do while in the classroom? Students with such significant

---

FYI

Another term you may hear in conversations about students with moderate or severe disabilities is *developmentally delayed.* This term is broad, including students with cognitive disabilities, multiple disabilities, and autism.

needs practice repeatedly a small number of skills. Teachers will not find it necessary to provide new alternatives for each day. For example, the student mentioned previously who is learning to recognize his name and address will need computer practice on that skill for many days. In addition, once the student has identified the information, the student should practice printing it on cards, writing it on the chalkboard, and saying it aloud. Extensive practice on a single skill using many approaches is commonly appropriate.

A third characteristic of students in this group is that they may have difficulty generalizing skills learned in one setting or situation to another setting or situation. It is thus critical that they learn as many skills as possible in context. For example, rather than have these students practice buttoning and unbuttoning out of context, as part of a segregated classroom exercise, have them apply this skill in the morning and afternoon as they enter and leave school wearing coats or sweaters. Older students need to learn how to greet classmates and teachers appropriately, for example, with a handshake or by just saying hello instead of shouting or tightly hugging them. Obviously such a skill is most easily taught as students meet and greet people throughout the school, not in a special education classroom.

One additional characteristic of students with moderate to severe cognitive disabilities is difficulty combining small skills into a larger one. For example, a student may be taught each step involved in making a sandwich, but unless the steps are taught in an integrated way, the student is probably going to have difficulty carrying them out in a logical sequence. In the study of teaching leisure skills just summarized, the English students outlined clear steps for each activity (i.e., turn on the TV set, turn on the videocassette recorder, select channel 4 on the television, and so on), and taught them so that each one built on the one before.

Helen is a young woman with **Down syndrome,** a condition that often includes a moderate cognitive disability. She illustrates a typical experience for such a student in a school district committed to inclusive education. She attended elementary school with her peers even though she did not always learn the same things they were learning. Her teachers expected her to behave appropriately, and her peers helped her when she got confused by classroom directions or otherwise needed support in the classroom. As she moved to middle school, she participated with peers in co-taught science and social studies and in elective classes such as foods and computers, and she received some of her reading and math instruction in a special education classroom. In high school, she took several classes, including choir, U.S. history, home economics, career exploration, and family living. She also entered a vocational preparation program so she would be ready to get a job after high school. At 21, Helen graduated from high school. She now works in a local medical office. Her job includes duplicating medical records, doing simple filing tasks, running errands, and helping get mail ready to send. Helen's success as an adult is in large part a result of learning many skills fostered in inclusive schools.

Three principles usually guide instruction for students with moderate or severe cognitive disabilities (Hickson, Blackman, & Reis, 1995). The first is the principle of a **functional curriculum.** In a functional curriculum, the goals for students, whether they attend a general education classroom or receive supports elsewhere, are based on real-life skills they need to succeed. For example, such a student might benefit more from learning to make purchases than learning to write a story because most adults make purchases regularly but not all have to have writing skills. The most important job skills Helen learned during her school career were punctuality, following multiple-step directions, and keeping her voice appropriately low. Jesús,

Cultural Awareness

In rural areas, parents of children with severe or multiple disabilities face the problem of isolation. They are likely to be the only parents in the area with a child with complex needs, and they may not have a network to provide support and information. Advances in telecommunications can help alleviate this dilemma.

Research Note

Many factors affect families of children with disabilities. Hughes (1999), in her ethnographic study of 34 families, found that those who participated in church activities were less stressed and better able to cope with their children with developmental disabilities.

Special Emphasis On . . .

Physical Education

Across grade levels, physical education is often the first area considered for the inclusion of students with low-incidence disabilities. In many schools, physical education teachers work with every student attending the school, both those with disabilities and those without.

From the Research

No one would disagree with the fact that students with low-incidence disabilities need as much as any student to participate in physical activities. Evidence supports inclusive approaches. Lorenzi, Horvat, and Pellegrini (2000) studied typical elementary students and those with mental retardation as they shared unsupervised recess time. They found that for both groups, boys tended to have a higher level of activity and to raise their heart rates more than girls, but they also found that both boys and girls with cognitive disabilities raised their heart rates more than their classmates. The authors concluded that inclusive recess settings fostered healthy physical activity for students with cognitive disabilities. Similar results are found when students with disabilities participate in integrated physical education programs (Downing & Rebollo, 1999). However, in a study of parent perspectives of inclusive physical education for students with physical disabilities, it was found that smaller class sizes, support for teachers, and teacher interest were critical factors for predicting success (Downing & Rebollo, 1999).

Strategies and Approaches

The key to including successfully students with low-incidence disabilities into physical education classes is careful planning with the students' IEP teams using the INCLUDE strategy. By determining student goals related to physical education, student stamina and other health variables, and the extent of appropriate participation, accommodations can be developed to match student characteristics and needs (Block, 1994; Block & Burke, 1999). The following is a sample of accommodations that can be made for students participating in a dance activity.

whom you read about at the beginning of the chapter, was taught fire safety as a functional skill within the context of a much broader science curriculum.

The second principle is **community-based education;** that is, what is learned in school should be related to what occurs in the community and other settings in which the student may function. Many students, both those with and those without disabilities, benefit from applying skills learned in school to real-life settings and activities. For some, systematic instruction in the community is necessary to teach skills needed to live, work, recreate, and continue to learn there. Lessons about the local community might include going to the bank, visiting people who live in a retirement center, and exploring job possibilities in local restaurants, hotels, and other businesses. Part of Helen's community-based instruction was learning how to ride the bus from her home to her job.

The third principle is that education should be **chronologically age appropriate.** This concept conveys the idea that individuals with disabilities, even very significant disabilities, should use materials that look appropriate for their age and should learn skills or variations of skills that typical learners their age are acquiring. This idea can be explored in more than one way. First, it implies that students with significant cognitive disabilities in high schools should not be using materials designed for young children. Second, it highlights the idea that the life skills appro-

General

- Use colored markers or cones on the floor for direction.
- Use colored markers on hands and feet for left and right.
- Practice small portions of dance and gradually add more steps.
- Slow down music

Students who use wheelchairs (normal upper body strength)

- Substitute arm movements for leg movements.
- Allow partner to push person's wheelchair as needed.

Students who use wheelchairs (limited upper body strength and control)

- Substitute any controllable movements the student has for more traditional movements.
- Allow peers to assist student in movements.
- Allow students to push wheelchair.
- Encourage student to maintain proper posture and to focus eyes on partner.

Students with visual impairments

- Use brightly colored markers on the floor.
- Have partner wear brightly colored pinny or shirt.
- Have partner wear bells on wrist.
- Have partner tell student in which direction to stand and where to move.
- Have partner provide physical assistance as needed.

Students with mental retardation

- Have peers assist student (extra verbal and physical cues).
- Encourage proper technique.

If you are interested in learning more about physical education for students with disabilities, two resources are useful:

- American Alliance of Health, Physical Education, Recreation, and Dance (AAHPERD) at http://www.aahperd.org
- National Consortium on Physical Education and Recreation for Individuals with Disabilities (NCPERID) at http://ncperid.usf.edu

priate for young children, including taking turns, sharing, following directions, and others, occur most appropriately in the school setting with other children. Specific vocational skills such as operating a cash register or stocking shelves should be reserved for older students who are chronologically much closer to using such skills.

Instructional Accommodations for Students with Moderate to Severe Cognitive Disabilities

Experience shows that teachers in many school districts are looking for a single strategy to make including students with moderate and severe disabilities in their classrooms clear and simple. Unfortunately, such a strategy does not exist. Most successful inclusive programs use many strategies and many variations of them (Janney, Snell, Beers, & Raynes, 1995). What is emerging more and more clearly, however, is the fact that attending school as members of general education classrooms is beneficial for many students with these needs. In one review of 36 studies on including students with cognitive disabilities in general education settings, the authors found that students did better there both academically and socially than comparable students did in self-contained special education classrooms (Freeman & Alkin, 2000). In fact, many

WWW Resources

The ARC, an organization on mental retardation, has a website filled with information for understanding students with cognitive disabilities. You can find the site at: http://thearc. org/welcome.html.

of the adaptations and general school conditions needed by students with moderate and severe disabilities are the same ones that make learning more successful for all students (McDonnell, 1998). A few of them are unique and designed for the abilities and special needs of the individual student.

Clarify expectations and use instructional approaches that match those expectations.   As a teacher, you should know what a student is expected to learn, whether or not that student has a disability. For example, in a social studies class, the goal for a student with a moderate cognitive disability might be to locate on a map states where relatives live, whereas the goal for other students might be to understand detailed topographical maps. For a student with a severe disability, a pertinent activity might be to identify photos of local community businesses. A fundamental ingredient for adaptation is to make learning standards appropriate for the student as well as a natural part of the instructional environment. You should work with a special educator to arrange learning activities suitable for reaching those standards using age-appropriate materials (Giangreco, Dennis, Cloninger, Edelman, & Schattman, 1993; Williams & Fox, 1996). One detailed system designed to accomplish this plan examines overall goals for the student and clarifies expectations that should exist all day (for example, approaching adults and peers in an age-appropriate fashion) as well as those for specific subject areas (for example, making choices between two items during math) (Forest & Lusthaus, 1990). Table 5.2 illustrates this blending of the IEP goals and the typical curriculum for one student.

Check Your Learning

How does meeting the needs of students with moderate or severe disabilities in your class help you meet the needs of your other students?

Use heterogeneous classroom groups.   Most professionals who write about adapting general education classrooms to include students with moderate and severe disabilities stress the importance of strategies such as peer tutoring, cooperative learning, and friend support systems in classrooms with a heterogeneous group of learners, including a few students with disabilities (Wisniewski & Alper, 1994). By structuring your teaching so that students work with each other, you foster a sense of classroom community and help students learn to value and respect classmates with disabilities as individuals (York, Vandercook, MacDonald, Heise-Neff, & Caughey, 1992).

Identify optimal times for specialized instruction.   Students with moderate or severe disabilities sometimes need to learn skills that are unlikely to arise as part of the traditional school curriculum. For example, a fifth grader who needs to learn how to tell time on a digital clock may not have enough opportunities to practice in class. However, if a peer, special educator, or related services provider works with her as classmates are entering the room during the morning or for a few minutes between lunch and the beginning of afternoon activities, critical instruction in telling time can occur in context instead of out of context in an isolated setting. Jesús, introduced at the beginning of this chapter, has some specialized needs that are met in this way. Research suggests that this practice of arranging for brief periods of one-to-one or small-group instruction is necessary for student success (Logan & Malone, 1998b). It also indicates that if special educators are providing specialized support, they should ensure that they also co-teach, work with more diverse groups, and assume other roles in the classroom so that they do not inadvertently provide too much assistance to the students (Logan & Malone, 1998a).

Enlist natural support systems.   Peers, older students, parent volunteers, student teachers, interns, and other individuals at school can all assist a student with a mod-

Table 5.2 Sample Communication Skills Mapped onto Elementary School Subjects

Communicative Skills	Subjects			
	Daily Oral Language (DOL)	**Social Studies**	**Math**	**Spelling**
Rejecting	Says no to the activity	Rejects one topic for another	Rejects certain manipulatives for others	Rejects one picture for another
	Rejects certain pictures to illustrate sentence	Rejects the offer of help from a peer	Rejects the offer of help from a peer	Rejects the offer of help from a peer
Social interaction skills	Exchanges visual glances	Exchanges visual glances	Exchanges visual glances	Exchanges visual glances
	Smiles in response to a comment	Smiles in response to a comment	Smiles in response to a comment	Smiles in response to a comment
	Teases others between activities	Teases others between activities	Teases others between activities	Teases others between activities
	Asks others to come talk	Asks others to come talk	Asks others to come talk	Asks others to come talk
Making comments	Decides on what picture goes best with the DOL sentence	Makes comments about topic of study	States whether it is fun to do math	Decides which picture/item goes with each spelling word
	States whether the sentence is funny	Responds to direct questions from teachers/peers	Beginning and end of school	States whether sentence using word and written by peer is okay or not
Greetings/ departures	Beginning and end of school	Beginning and end of school	Beginning and end of each class (secondary)	Beginning and end of school
	Beginning and end of each class (secondary)	Beginning and end of each class (secondary)	As new people enter a room	Beginning and end of each class (secondary)
	As new people enter a room	As new people enter a room	Errands to the office	As new people enter a room
	Errands to the office	Errands to the office		Errands to the office
Requesting activity/items/ information	Asks for help during activity	Chooses to do one activity over another	Asks for help to solve problems	Requests that spelling end or continue
	Asks for certain paper, pen, or pictures to do assignment	Requests different writing materials	Asks for manipulatives to do math	Asks for another spelling word
		Asks for help or more information	Asks whether problems are correct	Asks for specific partner to work with
			Asks for calculator	

S O U R C E : Adapted from "Analyzing the Communication Environment," by J. E. Downing, 1999, p. 59, in *Teaching Communication Skills to Students with Severe Disabilities*. Baltimore: Paul H. Brookes Publishing Co. Reprinted with permission.

erate or severe disability (Fulton, LeRoy, Pinckney, & Weekley, 1994). Peers can often answer simple questions or respond to basic requests without adult intervention. In some cases, they understand their classmate with a disability better than adults do (Hendrickson, Shokoohi-Yekta, Hamre-Nietupski, & Gable, 1996). They sometimes also can make needed adjustments in equipment, retrieve dropped articles, and get needed instructional materials for the student. Older students can serve as peer tutors or special buddies, both for instruction and for the development of appropriate social skills. Parents, student teachers, interns, and others can all assume part of the responsibility for supporting students. For example, an administrative intern who reads a story to the class releases the classroom teacher to observe the student with a moderate or severe cognitive disability or to work briefly with that student. A student teacher can work with a small instructional group that includes both typical learners and the student with a moderate or severe cognitive disability.

Create a collaborative effort with families.   When you teach a student with a moderate or severe disability, you should communicate regularly with the student's parents. Families know their children better than school professionals, and parents can provide valuable information about teaching them. They might also have questions about how to reinforce at home skills learned at school. Occasionally, you may encounter a family that does not want to be actively involved in the education of their child. In these cases, it is your responsibility to accept their decision without judging it.

As with all parents, it is also essential to remember that their responses to their children are based on many factors, including their culture. Alvarez (1998) clarifies this point in her discussion of children with disabilities in Hispanic families. Although acknowledging that many variations in families exist, she noted that Hispanic families' responses to their children with disabilities are likely to be influenced by their generally strong religious beliefs. If they believe their child's disability is a punishment from God or fate, and unchangeable, they may not assertively seek services for him. Hispanic mothers may assume nearly all responsibility for caring for a child with a moderate or severe cognitive disability whereas fathers may be seen as family decision makers. This means that mothers, who often come alone to school meetings concerning their child, may feel pressured if not given the opportunity to discuss the matter with their husbands before agreeing to any action.

Take advantage of assistive technology.   Consider, for example, the many low-tech and high-tech means for enhancing learning. Some students experience success when you provide them with pictures that remind them of key concepts, and with the widespread availability of digital cameras, infinite opportunities are created to take photos of signs, locations, people, and other items that can be used as tools for contextual learning. In another example, many students who cannot use language to communicate use various forms of **augmentative communication,** that is, alternative communication forms that enable students to convey their messages. Other students use technology to aid movement. Assistive technology can be either simple or complex, as shown in the Technology Notes feature on pages 166–167.

Multiple Disabilities

Because students with multiple disabilities often have extraordinary needs, they are considered a distinct group in IDEA-97. Most students with multiple disabilities have a cognitive disability and a physical or sensory impairment. Jesús, the kindergartner you met at the beginning of this chapter, has a cognitive disability and a physical disability. The needs of these students and the accommodations that help them succeed can be similar to those for students with moderate and severe cognitive disabilities, differences being a matter of degree and complexity. For example,

Connections

In Chapter 2, you learned about strategies for communicating with parents of students with disabilities. Such strategies can foster a positive educational experience for students with moderate or severe disabilities.

Cultural Awareness

Sensitivity to cultural values must be a constant consideration for special education services, even in the selection of assistive technology. If a family values "blending in," members may not wish their child to use devices or equipment that draws attention to the child.

in one school integrating students with multiple disabilities into general education classes, teachers faced the following primary challenges:

- Providing a functional curriculum within the context of the general education class
- Providing community-based instruction for all students
- Scheduling staff coverage
- Promoting social integration between students with multiple disabilities and other students (Hamre-Nietupski, McDonald, & Nietupski, 1992)

Other teachers have added concern about the number of special service providers who come to the classroom to work with students with multiple special needs and the potential disruption this causes for other students. Yet others have discovered that in a crowded setting the wheelchair, computer equipment, other therapeutic equipment, and specialized materials (for example, large books in three-ring binders made with many pictures) of a student with multiple disabilities can pose obstacles to classroom traffic patterns, safety, and storage capacity.

Because many students with multiple disabilities have limited speech and do not easily convey their preferences and needs, communicating with them can be a challenge. One strategy for communication is using augmentative communication systems, the same systems that are sometimes used by students with moderate or severe cognitive disabilities.

As a teacher, you can expect some but probably not all students with multiple disabilities to participate in general education activities in your school. They are likely to receive considerable support from a special education teacher or a paraprofessional who thus becomes available for co-teaching and other classwide integration activities (McDonnell, 1998). These professionals and other members of the multidisciplinary team can assist you in setting expectations for students, planning appropriate educational experiences, monitoring their performance, and problem solving when concerns arise (Williams & Fox, 1996). In an elementary school, a student with multiple disabilities might attend your class for morning activities, remain in the room for language arts, and participate in art and music with other students. That student might also receive some services in other building locations (for example, the library, gym, learning center, or special education classroom). In a secondary school, a student with multiple disabilities might attend some core classes with peers, some classes with a vocational emphasis (for example, consumer and food sciences), and might spend part of the school day learning to function in the broader community and to perform job-specific skills.

Deaf-Blindness

Although students with dual sensory impairments typically are not totally blind or deaf, they do have extraordinary needs related to staying in touch with the environment, making sense of events that most teachers and students take for granted, and learning with limited access to vision and hearing (Engleman, Griffin, Griffin, & Maddox, 1999). These students sometimes have average or above-average intelligence (as did Helen Keller), but they often have cognitive or other disabilities. How a student with **deaf-blindness** is educated in any particular school varies considerably. Some professionals, paraprofessionals, and parents judge that these students

[Technology Notes]

Assistive Technology

Many students with disabilities use **assistive technology** to help them learn. Assistive technology devices can include adaptive clothing and toys, seating systems, communication devices, and many other items. In your classroom, students might use a wide variety of computer devices and systems, special tables or chairs, and alternative communication systems such as communication boards. A student's needs for assistive technology support are written into the IEP. School districts are responsible for providing such equipment or devices if a student needs them, unless insurance or some other funding source is available.

To give you a sense of how many technology options exist, the following are some items available for computers. All of these, along with many others, are described in more detail at the website of Don Johnston, Incorporated, an organization based in Volo, IL, which is committed to making available computer access products that let students with disabilities use the computer to learn to read and write. They also provide critical intervention products for literacy instruction. The website address is http://www.donjohnston.com.

Discover:Board

This all-in-one keyboard and mouse combination allows students with disabilities to use the reading and

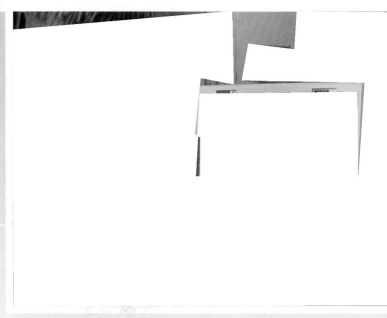

This student uses a communication board to interact with his peers.

writing software you may already have in your classroom. It is designed for students who cannot use a

can be successful in inclusive environments with extensive supports (Giangreco, Edelman, MacFarland, & Luiselli, 1997), but they disagree somewhat on the types and approaches to service delivery. In addition to instructional support in general education settings, these students often need extensive training to learn to communicate, through sign language, signals and gestures, touch cues, or other means (Engleman et al., 1999; Engleman, Griffin, & Wheeler, 1998). In addition, students who are deaf-blind need assistance in social interactions with their peers. Teachers can facilitate interactions by doing the following (Goetz & O'Farrell, 1999):

- Arranging the classroom to promote active participation by students who are deaf-blind

standard keyboard, and the keys can be adjusted to change size, color, and "touch."

Big Area Switches (BASS)

Some students operate their toys and even their computers with simple switches. This example of a switch has a large surface so that students with limited motor control can still press it. This type of switch is intended to be used on the floor or on a table.

Discover Switch

This second example of a switch is designed especially for students who use their computers to write, but who operate them with a switch. All the keyboard and mouse functions are in the switch. These functions are displayed on the screen with keys that scan; the student presses the desired key. This device includes a picture bank for non–readers/writers, a wordbank for those needing assistance. It also can display a full keyboard on the screen so that students can independently write their ideas.

Write:OutLoud

This software is a talking word processor that speaks while students write, highlighting the word being spoken. For students with physical disabilities as well as other special needs, it provides a means for increasing writing confidence, a means for checking written work, and a strategy for spell checking. There are even different voice options (male, female, child).

- Prompting both the students with special needs and the typical learners to interact with each other
- Interpreting for typical students the behaviors of the student with deaf-blindness (for example, the pushing and shoving may be an indication that the student is excited about playing with the other students)

In other schools, a student who is deaf-blind may be a member of your class, accompanied by a special education teacher or personal assistant, only on some field trips, at assemblies, in selected class activities, or for particular school programs. The specialists working with the student can prepare both you and your students, letting you know how to approach and greet the student, telling you what to expect in terms of behavior, and explaining why inclusive activities are important for the student and what learning or social objectives are being addressed.

What Accommodations Can You Make for Students with Sensory Impairments?

Students with **sensory impairments** have vision or hearing disabilities so significant that their education is affected. Their specialized needs can range from slight to complex. Because school learning relies so heavily on seeing and hearing, students with these disabilities often experience academic problems and need both teacher accommodations and adaptive equipment. Some of the vocabulary used to describe sensory disabilities is included in the Professional Edge.

Students with **visual impairments** cannot see well enough to use vision as a primary channel for learning without significant assistance. Some students are considered **legally blind,** which means that the vision in their best eye, with correction, is 20/200 or less, or their visual field is 20 degrees or less. What a person with normal vision could see at 200 feet, these students can see only at 20 feet. Students legally blind because of a limited visual field can see just a 20 percent or less "slice" of what a person with normal vision would see within his or her range of vision.

Although the concept of legal blindness is an important one that helps students access special services throughout their lives, a different set of terms is used in schools. For educators, the term **blind** is generally reserved to describe the few students who have little useful vision. They use touch and hearing for most learning. Most students with visual impairments are **partially sighted,** meaning that they have some useful vision; their vision is between 20/70 and 20/200, or they have another vision problem that has a serious negative effect on their learning.

Students with **hearing impairments** cannot hear well enough without significant assistance to use hearing as a primary channel for learning. Because a huge proportion of formal and incidental learning occurs through informal conversations, formal presentations, and overheard information, and relies on understanding language, many consider hearing impairments primarily language or communication impairments. A small number of students with hearing impairments are **deaf.** They cannot process linguistic information through hearing, with or without hearing aids. Most students, however, are **hard of hearing,** meaning that they have some residual hearing that lets them process linguistic information through hearing, usually by using hearing aids or other assistive devices.

To determine the severity of a hearing loss, professionals check the loudness of sounds as measured in **decibels** (dB) and the pitch or tone of the sound as measured in **hertz** (Hz). Normal speech is usually in the 55–60 dB range at 500–2000 Hz. In contrast, a whisper is about 15–25 dB, and a rock band plays at about 110 dB. Students with a hearing loss of 25–40 dB are considered to have a mild loss; they might not hear every word in a conversation or might not distinguish between words with similar sounds (*breathing, breeding*). Those with a loss of 40–60 dB have a moderate loss; they typically cannot hear enough of a conversation to follow it auditorily. Those with 60–80 dB have a severe loss, and those with more than 80 dB have a profound loss. Students with severe and profound hearing losses typically cannot pro-

FYI

Although a few students have guide dogs, more adults use them because of the training and expense involved.

Professional Edge

The Vocabulary of Sensory Impairments

To be effective in making adaptations for your students with sensory impairments, you should understand the terminology used to describe these disabilities. The following terms are some you may encounter in your dealings with students who have sensory impairments and the special educators who work with them.

Visual Impairment

- *Refractive disorders.* The way the eye focuses light is impaired, as in myopia (near-sightedness), hyperopia (far-sightedness), and astigmatism (blurred vision).

- *Muscle disorders.* The ability to control eye movements is impaired, as in strabismus (crossed eyes).

- *Receptive disorders.* The ability to receive and process signals from light is impaired, as in retinal detachment caused by glaucoma or a blow to the eye.

Hearing Impairment

- *Conductive disorders.* The way the ear transmits sound is impaired; these disorders are generally correctable through surgery or medication.

- *Sensorineural disorders.* The auditory nerve, by which we receive and process signals from sound, is impaired; these disorders are generally not correctable through amplification or hearing aids.

- *Mixed losses.* A combination of conductive and sensorineural impairments.

cess speech, even when amplification is used. They rely on sight as an alternative means of learning.

Another factor professionals consider in judging the seriousness of a student's hearing loss is when the loss occurred. Students who have been hearing impaired since birth are often at a disadvantage for language learning because they did not go through the natural process of acquiring language. These students can speak, but because they learned to talk without hearing how they sounded, their speech may be difficult to understand. They might prefer sign language and an interpreter for communicating with you and others. Students who lose their hearing after they learn language, after about age 5, sometimes experience fewer language and speech difficulties.

Accommodations for Students with Visual Impairments

Although students with visual impairments have the same range of cognitive ability as other students, they typically have had fewer opportunities to acquire information usually learned visually. For example, students generally learn about maps by looking at them. Although students who are blind can learn by feeling a raised map, this method is not as efficient as seeing it. The same problem can occur with academics. Students with visual impairments often experience learning difficulties simply because they cannot easily use vision to process information. Think about how you read this text: You probably scan the pages, focus on words and phrases in boldface print, and visually jump between reading the type and looking at a figure or photo. If you could read this book only by magnifying it 15 times, or by listening to it on

Check Your Learning

What common classroom arrangements and items might prove hazardous for a student with a visual impairment?

audiotape, or by reading it in braille, you would find it much more tedious to scan, to select important words and phrases, and to go back and forth between components. If you multiply this dilemma across all the visual learning tasks students face, you can begin to understand the challenges of learning with a visual impairment.

As is true for all individuals, students with visual impairments vary in their social and emotional development. Some students encounter little difficulty making friends, interacting appropriately with peers and adults, and developing a positive self-concept. Other students need support in these areas (Barclay, 1999; Sacks, Wolffe, & Tierney, 1998). For example, it is important to teach some students who cannot see to adhere to social norms such as facing a person when talking, taking turns, and keeping an appropriate social distance. Conversely, teachers should keep in mind that some students might miss another student's or a teacher's puzzled expression about something they had said and continue to interact as if they understood. They should also help other students to understand that a student with a visual impairment cannot help a wiggling eye, or that they stand a little too close during interactions because they have difficulty judging distance.

Accommodations needed by students with visual impairments depend on many factors. First, take into account students' overall ability level, use of learning strategies and other learning skills, and attentional and motivational levels, just as you would for any other student. Then make accommodations depending on the amount of students' residual vision and the nature of their vision problems, keeping in mind that these students have many essential life skills to master that other students take for granted and that time must be made in their school careers for these skills (for example, proper eating manners, appropriate social distance during interactions, keyboarding, signature writing, and proficiency in using adaptive technology) (Lueck, 1999). Some specific adaptations you can make and unique needs you must consider for students with visual impairments are covered in the following paragraphs.

W W W R e s o u r c e s

You can learn more about sensory impairments by accessing the American Foundation for the Blind at http://afb.org.

One important area of need for students with visual impairments is **orientation and mobility,** that is, the sense of where they are in relation to other objects and people in the environment and the ability to move about within a space. For example, students with visual impairments need to understand where furniture, doorways, bookshelves, and the teacher's desk are in the classroom, in relation to their location. In addition, they need to be able to move from the classroom to the auditorium to the cafeteria and out to the bus in a timely manner. Your first task in preparing for a student with a visual impairment might be to arrange your classroom carefully, leaving adequate space for all students to move about. Depending on the amount of sight the student has, you might need to keep furniture and supplies in the same places, and make sure the student has an opportunity to learn where everything is. If you decide to rearrange the room or move your supplies, alert your student with a visual impairment to the changes and allow opportunities to adapt to them. Another orientation and mobility issue is safety. Half-open doors or trash cans inadvertently left in aisles can be serious hazards for students with visual impairments. For fire drills or emergencies, pair all students with buddies to assist each other so as to avoid singling out any individual student.

You might also be asked to modify your teaching slightly to accommodate a student with a visual impairment. For example, you might need to identify the novels you plan to use in class prior to the start of the school year so they can be ordered in **braille,** large-print, or audiotape format. For visual clarity, you might need to use a whiteboard with a black felt-tipped marker instead of a traditional chalkboard, or to provide the student with paper that has heavy black lines instead of the traditional light blue ones. In addition, you should be sure to recite what is written on the chalkboard; call students by name so the student with a visual impairment can learn the sounds of everyone's voices and where they are seated; allow the student to move close to demonstrations and displays; give specific directions instead of using general words such as *here* or *there*; and seat the student so as to optimize visual learning (for example, away from bright light or near the front of the room). Usually, an itinerant vision specialist or other special educator will alert you to these types of accommodations and arrange for any classroom modification.

Some general modifications in your classroom can also help a student with a visual impairment. Meet with the itinerant vision specialist or other resource persons to discuss the student's needs and the extent of assistance required, including the important matter of problems related to storing students' specialized equipment. Based on that information, some or many accommodations might be appropriate. Assign a buddy to assist a new student at the beginning of the school year, especially in dealing with the cafeteria, moving from room to room, and locating supplies. This assistance might be discontinued later in the school year to avoid creating unneeded dependence.

Some students with visual impairments need additional time to complete assignments, either during class or as homework. Monitor closely to ensure that the student is not spending too much time on a single task; this might be a signal that the task needs to be shortened or otherwise modified. Be alert for a student's need for a change-of-pace activity. A student who is fidgeting or refusing to work might be fatigued, a common problem for students who have to make extraordinary efforts to learn using vision. Letting the student take a break or substitute an alternative activity both helps the student and prevents discipline problems. Also keep in mind how to plan alternative learning opportunities for students. If you are talking about history and using a timeline, if you use white glue or some other means of marking points on the timeline, a student with a visual impairment can participate meaningfully in the discussion by touching the points in time and feeling the distance between them. A vision specialist can help you develop such alternative learning opportunities. Finally, teachers sometimes worry about the impact on a student with a visual impairment of words and phrases such as *Do you see my point?* or *That's quite a sight*. Generally, you should just use the vocabulary you normally would; avoiding words related to seeing is not necessary.

Learning Tools for Students with Visual Impairments

Students with visual impairments use a wide variety of equipment or devices to facilitate their learning. If they have some residual vision, they can use devices to help them acquire information visually. Some use simple devices such as magnifying lenses or bright light to read or do other school work. Others might hold their books close to their eyes or at an unusual angle to see the print. Many students with visual impairments use computers. For example, if students use a speech synthesizer or text enlarger with a standard word processing program, they may be able to type their assignments exactly like their peers. For students who read braille, assignments can be printed on a braille printer as well as a standard printer so that both the teacher and student can read them. A further sample of the learning tools available for students with visual impairments is included in the Professional Edge on page 172.

Professional Edge

Learning Tools and Technology for Students with Visual Impairments

Students with visual impairments can benefit from a variety of learning tools and technology. The following list describes some of these items:

- **Large print materials.** Books or other materials are printed somewhat larger than typical print, which is 14- to 18-point for children's books.
- **Low vision devices.** Specially designed optical devices enable students to read print and to see distant objects such as writing on the chalkboard. One example of this learning tool is a specially designed magnifying glass that students slide across their work. Another is a monocular that magnifies like binoculars but is for just one eye.

A student with a visual impairment uses specialized books and equipment.

- **Braillewriter.** A mechanical device developed in the 1950s facilitates efficient writing of braille. It has six keys, a spacebar, a carriage return, and a paper advance. To produce braille, the student simultaneously presses down various key combinations.
- **Slate and stylus.** This method for producing braille is the oldest. The slate is a frame of two metal strips containing braille cells composed of a rectangle with six notches in the four corners and two sides. The stylus is positioned to press raised dots in the braille paper, which is held in place by the slate.
- **Closed circuit television.** This system used by students enlarges print information. A television camera is mounted on a stand to input the print, and the student reads the enlarged print from a monitor. Letters can be displayed as white on a black background or as black on a white background, depending on student need. A single letter can fill the entire screen if necessary.
- **Portable notetaker.** This small device is equipped with six keys and a spacebar, but also a speech synthesizer. It is used to take notes or to compose written information and to print it in braille or print.
- **Specialized computers.** Computers are equipped with special software and devices: (1) screenreading software and a speech synthesizer enable the student to listen to information presented on the screen; (2) braille translation software and a braille printer enable the teacher or student to convert information on the screen to braille and to print it; (3) screen enlargement software enables a student with significant sight to read information directly from the computer screen.

Accommodations for Students with Hearing Impairments

Students with hearing losses have the same range of cognitive ability as other students. However, if intelligence is assessed using a test based on language, they might have depressed scores. Academically, many students struggle because their hearing loss affects their ability to understand language and this affects their learning. Martina, the student with a hearing impairment introduced at the beginning of the chapter, finds this problem especially frustrating. Students might have difficulty learning vocabulary and as a result understanding the materials they read and the lessons you present, although evidence suggests that students with hearing impairments educated in general education settings usually read better than their peers educated in special education classrooms (Easterbrooks, 1999). For example, students with hearing impairments often miss subtle meanings of words, which can affect both their learning and their social interactions. One simple example can illustrate the complexity of learning language. Think of all the meanings you know for the word *can*. As a noun, it refers to a container made of metal for storing food, for example, a can of peas. But it also means a container with a lid—as in the type of can that tennis balls are packaged in. *Can* also has slang meanings, as a synonym for *bathroom* and *prison*. As a verb, it means "to be physically able," as in "I can do that by Tuesday." It also refers to preserving produce from the garden, as in "I plan to can green beans this year"; to losing a job, as in "I just got canned"; and to the state of being likely, as in "Can that be true?" If you think about all the words in the English language that have multiple and sometimes contradictory meanings, it becomes easier to understand the difficulties faced by students who are deaf or hard-of-hearing.

Socially and emotionally, students who are deaf or hard-of-hearing are sometimes immature. This lack of maturity occurs for two reasons. First, much of the etiquette children acquire comes from listening to others and modeling what they say and do. This learning is not available to many students with hearing impairments. Second, these students can become confused in interactions that involve many people and multiple conversations. Because these types of situations are often uncomfortable for them, they sometimes avoid them and fail to develop social skills needed in group interactions. For example, Jim is a seventh-grade student with a moderate hearing loss. When students work in lab groups in Mr. George's science class, Jim tends to tune out because he cannot follow what everyone is saying. Sometimes he tries to participate in the activity, but he often does so by making an exaggerated face or drawing a cartoon to show others. He does this even when the other students are working intently, and they become annoyed with his antics. When Jim realizes his attempts to participate are not being successful, he withdraws from the group and becomes passive. Mr. George and the hearing specialist are working to address this problem. Mr. George makes sure that he monitors the group's work, and he sometimes intervenes by asking Jim a question that helps him participate. Mr. George reminds his students that unless every group member understands a science experiment, the group is not finished. Jim also receives help on his social interactions in a support group that he attends with several other students led by a social worker twice each week.

Accommodations for students with hearing impairments emphasize helping them use whatever residual hearing they may have and accessing language to promote formal and informal learning. Although the specific types of accommodations needed by a student you teach are determined by the multidisciplinary team that writes the student's IEP, following are some common ones.

Because many students with hearing impairments get some information through **speech reading**, or watching others' lips, mouth, and expressions, teachers should always face the class when presenting information and stand where no glare or shadow makes it difficult for a student to see. They should also stand in one location instead of moving around the room. The student should sit near them. These adjustments facilitate speech reading but are also necessary if an interpreter is present. Teachers should avoid exaggerating sounds or words; doing this makes it more difficult for the student, not easier. Because some students with hearing impairments do not use speech reading, and because even those who do get only part of the message that way, teachers should use as many visual aids as possible. Important directions can be written on the chalkboard, either with words or, for younger students, pictures. Major points in a lecture for older students can be written on an overhead projector or on the chalkboard. With an overhead projector, the teacher can face students while writing, thus enabling students with hearing impairments to speech read. If teachers talk and write on a chalkboard at the same time, students with hearing impairments can become confused because they cannot see the teacher's lips or facial expression when the teacher is facing the board to write.

If a student with a hearing impairment speaks to you and you do not understand what has been said, ask the student to repeat the information. If you still do not understand or the student becomes frustrated, switching to paper and pencil is sometimes appropriate. When a student appears confused following directions or answering a question you ask, the difficulty might be vocabulary. Try substituting a simpler word or offering a word you think the student might be trying to convey. Above all else, be patient when communicating with students who are deaf or hard-of-hearing.

As with students with visual impairments, safety also needs to be kept in mind. Assigning a buddy to assist the student during a fire, tornado, or earthquake drill is a simple strategy for addressing this issue. For other specific adaptations regarding safety, a hearing specialist can assist you.

If a student with a hearing impairment uses sign language, you might consider enrolling in a sign class yourself and inviting a deaf education teacher to your class to teach some signs to the entire group. Students generally enjoy this experience, and both you and they will be better able to communicate with the student who cannot hear. The Case in Practice highlights a little more about what it is like to teach a student who is deaf or hard-of-hearing.

Finally, you should be aware that the field of deaf education is one facing complex issues about whether oral language, sign language, or a combination of approaches is most appropriate for educating students who are deaf or hard-of-hearing (Easterbrooks, 1999). Controversy exists, too, about Deaf Culture, that is, individuals who view deafness as a cultural phenomenon rather than a disability (Baker & Baker, 1997). Some individuals believe students who are deaf should be educated in separate schools with specially designed curricula and experiences. Others believe that all opportunities for using oral language should be explored. It is unlikely that you will be pulled into heated discussions concerning these topics, but knowing about them may help you better understand the range of perspectives among professionals, parents, and students.

Adaptive Devices for Students with Hearing Impairments

Students with some residual hearing are likely to use amplification devices such as hearing aids. If you have a student who wears hearing aids, you should be alert for signs of inattention that signal the hearing aid is not turned on or the battery needs to be replaced. Other students might use an FM system consisting of a microphone worn by the teacher and a receiver worn by the student. When the teacher talks, the sound is converted into electrical energy carried on a specific radio frequency

C A S E   I N   P R A C T I C E

Including Students Who Are Deaf or Hard-of-Hearing

Ms. Skinner is a fifth-grade teacher at Lunar Elementary School. This year in her class of 31 she has 2 students with hearing impairments. The girls, who are twins, have profound hearing losses present since birth. Because they use sign language as their primary means of communication, they are accompanied by Ms. Mohammed, their interpreter.

Ms. Skinner discussed what it is like to teach in this class:

> When I first heard I was going to get Jenna and Janice this year, I was worried. I knew they'd been in fourth grade and done well, but there's so much more cur-riculum at this level. I didn't know how I was going to teach everything and also do all the work necessary for Jenna and Janice and at the same time deal with end-of-grade testing and all that pressure.
>
> As it turns out, it hasn't been much of an adjustment at all. Ms. Mohammed interprets for the girls, and she adds explanations if they need it. The hardest part for me was learning to stay in one place when I talk—for a teacher like me, who is constantly moving around the room, that has been very difficult. Ms. Mohammed has taught all of us some basic signs—that puts us all in touch.
>
> Jenna and Janice have some serious academic problems mostly related to vocabulary, but the other kids just think of them as classmates. I've learned a lot this year. I'm a lot more confi-dent that I really can teach any student who comes through my door!

R E F L E C T I O N S

Why might teachers be worried about having students like Jenna and Janice in their classrooms? What is the best way to get over this worry? What might be particu-larly challenging for you if you had students like Jenna and Janice in your classroom? How would you help them compensate for their dif-ficulty in vocabulary? What do you imagine is the impact of having an interpreter in a classroom most of the time? What might the inter-preter need from you to feel com-fortable? What type of assistance might you ask from the twins' par-ents to help them master the sub-jects you will be teaching?

---

through the air. The receiver converts the electrical energy back to sound, amplifies it, and sends it to the student's ear. A third type of device is also becoming more common. Cochlear implants and related technology are creating options for some students to "hear" electronically.

Keep in mind that hearing aids and FM systems both amplify sounds, but they do not discriminate from other sounds important sounds like the teacher's voice. Thus, a student wearing hearing aids can be distracted by the amplified noise of someone typing on the computer keyboard, a door slamming, or chairs scraping on the floor. A student using an FM device also hears amplified sounds of a teacher's jewelry hitting the microphone or the static from a teacher fingering the micro-phone. Any of these extraneous noises can interfere with the student's understand-ing of spoken information and can distract from learning. Amplification clearly assists some students with hearing impairments, but it also has limits.

Students who have a severe or profound hearing impairment often use sign lan-guage. Sometimes they use **American Sign Language (ASL),** a separate language not based on standard English grammar and structures. Learning ASL is like learn-ing Spanish, French, or another language. Other students use **signed exact English (SEE),** that is, spoken English converted to a set of signs. Students sometimes use

Professional Edge

Families and Assistive Technology

The wide and rapidly expanding range of assistive technology devices available to students with disabilities is creating opportunities never before possible. However, both general education teachers and special educators should keep in mind that assistive technology solutions to the challenges students face can only be effective if they are consistent with the family's knowledge base, value system, and acceptance of the device or equipment. The following checklist can help you remain aware of the fundamental issues that should be addressed when discussing assistive technology for one of your students.

Family and Cultural Issues Questionnaire

Question	Yes	No	Notes
1. Has the family clearly communicated concerns, needs, and goals about the child?			
2. Are the family's and child's daily routines identified?			
3. Would the family like a support group to convey information or training regarding assistive technology devices?			
4. Would the family prefer a community leader or liaison to convey information regarding assistive technology devices?			
5. Has a range of possible technology solutions for the child and family been explored?			
6. Do family members and the child want an assistive technology device?			
7. Are family expectations of the assistive technology assessment process clearly understood?			
8. Does the family understand issues related to funding and ownership of the assistive technology device?			
9. Do all family members understand how assistive technology devices may affect family routines?			
10. Have the various settings where the child might use assistive technology devices, and resulting demands/consequences of device usage there, been identified?			
11. Do families want to use device in community settings?			
12. Are the family expectations of the assistive technology device clearly understood prior to purchase?			

S O U R C E : From "Family and Cultural Alert: Considerations in Assistive Technology Assessment," by J. J. Hourcade, H. P. Parette, and M. B. Huer, 1997. *Teaching Exceptional Children,* 30(1), pp. 40–44. Questionnaire from H. P. Parette, 1997. Copyright 1997 by Howard P. Parette. Used with permission.

finger spelling, in which every letter of a word is spelled out. For example, finger spelling is needed for names or technical terms for which no signs exist.

Students who use sign language are often accompanied by an interpreter who translates your words and those of classmates into sign language (Jones, Clark, & Soltz, 1997). The interpreter needs to sit facing the student and near you so that the student can both watch you and follow the interpreter. Some older students also use a note taker (who could be a classmate) because they cannot both watch an interpreter and a teacher and take notes. Even if a student uses an interpreter, however, you should speak directly to the student when asking questions, giving directions, or otherwise conversing. Do not speak to the interpreter instead of the student. The interpreter will make sure the student understands what you say. For example, you should say to Paige, a student with a profound hearing loss, "Do the first five examples on the page." You should not direct your remarks to the interpreter by saying, "Tell Paige to do the first five examples on the page." Also keep in mind that interpreters need breaks; you might be asked to make small changes in your instructional pattern to ensure that the interpreter can take a break without negatively affecting student learning.

What Accommodations Can You Make for Students with Physical or Health Disabilities?

Some students receive special education and related services because they have physical disorders, chronic or acute medical problems, or health impairments that interfere with their learning. In IDEA, three categories of disabilities can be loosely grouped in this area: orthopedic impairments, other health impairments, and traumatic brain injury. **Orthopedic impairments** are diseases or disorders related to the bones, joints, or muscles. **Other health impairments** include medical or health conditions such as AIDS, seizure disorders, and asthma. **Traumatic brain injury** is any insult to the brain caused by an external force and includes injuries sustained in auto accidents and during play. Students with these kinds of disabilities, caused by a wide variety of physical or health problems, differ greatly in their level of innate ability and academic achievement and in their needs, which can range from mild to severe.

Orthopedic Impairments

The largest group of students with orthopedic impairments in public schools are those who have **cerebral palsy** (CP) (Sirvis, 1988). Some 5000 infants and babies and 500–1500 preschoolers are diagnosed each year as having this condition (United Cerebral Palsy Associations, n.d.; WebDoctor, 2000). Cerebral palsy occurs because of injury to the brain before, during, or after birth and results in poor motor coordination and abnormal motor patterns. These problems can occur in just the arms or legs, in both the arms and legs, or in a combination of limbs, and with varying degrees of severity. For some students, CP also affects other muscle groups, such as those controlling the head and neck. Thus, some students with cerebral palsy walk on their toes with their knees close together. Their arms may be positioned with their elbows bent and their hands near shoulder height. Other

Cultural Awareness

Parents of students in your class might have disabilities, including orthopedic impairments, vision or hearing impairments, or cognitive disabilities. What special considerations do you need to take into account to interact effectively with parents with disabilities?

FYI

Cerebral palsy is the most frequently occurring orthopedic disability among children and youth. Students with cerebral palsy often have cognitive disabilities as well.

WWW Resources

Information about the causes, classification, prognosis, treatment, and psychological aspects of cerebral palsy can be found at the website for the United Cerebral Palsy Association at http://www.ucpa.org.

students with CP need braces or a walker to move about. Yet others use wheelchairs. For some students, head supports prevent their heads from lolling side to side. Cognitively and academically, students with CP can be gifted, average, or below average, or they might have a cognitive disability.

Don is a student with CP. His arms and hands are drawn up close to his body and he does not control their movement. He moves around school in a motorized wheelchair and Mike, his personal assistant, helps with personal care (going to the bathroom, eating) and tasks such as writing. Don has low-average ability, but his physical disabilities sometimes cause others to think he has a cognitive disability as well, especially because his speech is difficult to understand. Don's teacher has learned to engage him in class activities by asking yes or no questions to which he can respond fairly easily. If she asks a question requiring a longer answer, she gives Don time to form the words needed and does not let other students speak for him.

Another orthopedic impairment is **muscular dystrophy,** a disease that weakens muscles. Students have increasing difficulty walking and otherwise actively moving about. Gradually, they lose their ability to stand and they require a wheelchair. They also tire more and more easily. Students with muscular dystrophy usually die during their late teens (Sirvis, 1988). Frank was a student with muscular dystrophy. When he began elementary school, he seemed no different from any other student. However, he began middle school using a wheelchair when he became tired. By the end of that year, he was using the wheelchair all the time. By late in his sophomore year, Frank was too weak to attend school and received instruction from an itinerant teacher at his home. He died in late September of his junior year of high school.

A third orthopedic impairment is **spinal cord injury.** As the term implies, these injuries exist when the spinal cord is severely damaged or severed, usually resulting in partial or extensive paralysis (Kirk, Gallagher, & Anastasiow, 1997). Spinal cord injuries are most often the result of automobile or other vehicle accidents. The characteristics and needs of students with this type of injury are often similar to those of students with cerebral palsy. Judy suffered a spinal cord injury in a car accident. She was hospitalized for nearly half the school year, and at the time she returned to school she could not walk and had the use of only one arm. She is as bright and articulate as ever and still gets in trouble when she challenges teachers' authority. What has changed is how she moves from place to place.

Cerebral palsy, muscular dystrophy, and spinal cord injuries are just a sample of the range of orthopedic impairments students can have. You are likely to teach students who have physical disabilities caused by amputations or birth defects that result in the absence of all or part of a limb. Likewise, you might have a student with **spina bifida,** a birth defect in which an abnormal opening in the spinal column results in some degree of paralysis. Whatever the orthopedic impairment a student has, your responsibility is to learn about the student's needs and work with special education professionals to ensure those needs are met through various adaptations.

The adaptations you make for students with orthopedic impairments will depend on the nature and severity of the disability and on the students' physical status. For example, you need to be alert to changes you might need to make in the physical environment so that students can comfortably move into, out of, and around the classroom. Such changes include rearranging classroom furniture and adding supports such as handrails to walls. Other physical adaptations, such as creating adapted work spaces with large tables and lowering chalkboards, can facilitate student learning.

Cultural Awareness

The value placed on independence and self-sufficiency in the United States is not universal. In some cultures, families may not put as high a priority on fostering independence in their children as special education staff typically do. Concerns about care may predominate.

A second area of adaptation to consider for students with orthopedic impairments involves their personal needs (Kirk et al., 1997). Many students become fatigued and might have difficulty attending to learning activities late in the school day. A few take naps or otherwise rest. Other students need to stop during the school day to take medication. Some students need assistance with personal care, such as using the bathroom and eating. Students who use wheelchairs might need to reposition themselves because of circulation problems. This repositioning can be done readily for young children, who can be moved to sit or lie on the classroom floor during stories or other activities. Paraprofessionals typically assume personal-care responsibilities and those related to moving students. If you have questions about these areas, a special educator can assist, or the student's parent can explain what is needed.

Academically and socially, it is not possible to generalize about student needs. Some students with orthopedic impairments enjoy school and excel in traditional academic areas. Some students with cerebral palsy are gifted. Others experience problems in learning. Some are charming and gregarious students who are class leaders; others have a low self-concept and are likely to have problems interacting with peers. If you think about a student like Judy, the student introduced previously who has a spinal cord injury, you can imagine that her reaction to her accident and her need to use a wheelchair is influenced by many factors, including her family support system, her self-concept, and her peers' reactions. The suggestions throughout this text for working with students to help them learn and succeed socially are as applicable to this group of students as to any other.

Check Your Learning

What accommodations is a student with orthopedic impairments likely to need? Who is responsible for ensuring that the accommodatins are made?

Other Health Impairments

Students with health impairments often are not immediately apparent to a casual observer. For example, one common group of health impairments is seizure disorders, or **epilepsy,** a physical condition in which the brain experiences sudden but brief changes in functioning. The result is often a lapse of attention or consciousness and uncontrolled motor movements. A single seizure is not considered a symptom of epilepsy, but if several seizures occur, the disorder is diagnosed. About 75,000 new cases of epilepsy in children occur each year, and for most cases no specific cause is ever determined (Epilepsy Foundation of America, 1986). Overall, between 1 and 2 percent of the entire population is affected by epilepsy (Speigel, Cutler, & Yetter, 1996).

Epilepsy can produce different types of seizures. **Generalized tonic-clonic seizures** involve the entire body. A student experiencing a generalized tonic-clonic seizure falls to the ground unconscious; the body stiffens and then begins jerking. Breathing may become shallow, and the student might lose bladder or bowel control. After a minute or two, the movements stop and the student regains consciousness. Steps you should take when a student has a generalized tonic-clonic seizure are summarized in the Professional Edge.

Other seizures do not involve the entire body. **Absence seizures,** sometimes called petit mal seizures, occur when students appear to temporarily blank out for just a few seconds. If they are walking or running, they might stumble because of their momentary lapse of awareness. When you observe a student with these symptoms, alert the school nurse or another professional who can further assess the student. It is not unheard of for students to attend school for several years before someone realizes that their inability to pay attention is actually the result of a seizure disorder.

FYI

Nationwide, some 500,000 individuals have epilepsy. It can occur in anyone of any age, sometimes for no apparent reason, but also as a result of illness or injury.

WWW Resources

If you are looking for more detailed information about epilepsy, you might find what you need at the site of the University of Washington's Regional Epilepsy Center at http://elliott.hmc.washington.edu.

Professional Edge

What to Do When a Student Has a Seizure

As a teacher in an inclusive school and as a responsible citizen, you should know how to respond when someone has a seizure. The American Epilepsy Foundation recommends these steps:

1. Keep calm and reassure other people who may be nearby.

2. Clear the area around the person of anything hard or sharp.

3. Loosen ties, scarves, or anything around the neck that may make breathing difficult.

4. Put something flat and soft, like a folded jacket, under the head.

5. Turn the individual gently onto his or her side. This will help keep the airway clear. Do *not* try to force his or her mouth open with any hard implement or with your fingers. It is not true that a person having a seizure can swallow his or her tongue, and efforts to hold the tongue down can injure the teeth or jaw.

6. Do not hold the person down or try to stop his or her movements.

7. Do not attempt artificial respiration except in the unlikely event that an individual does not start breathing again after the seizure has stopped.

8. Stay with the person until the seizure ends naturally.

9. Be friendly and reassuring as consciousness returns.

10. Follow whatever procedures have been established for notifying parents that a seizure has occurred.

11. Call for medical assistance if
    - The seizure lasts more than 5 minutes
    - The person is not wearing an "epilepsy/seizure disorder" I.D.
    - There is a slow recovery, a second seizure, or difficult breathing afterwards
    - The person is pregnant or is carrying other medical I.D.
    - Any signs of injury are apparent

Further information about what to do in the case of seizures and more information about this disorder are available from the Epilepsy Foundation of America at http://www.efa.org/answerplace.

S O U R C E : From *Epilepsy: First Aid for Seizures.* Landover, MD: Epilepsy Foundation of America. Retrieved September 5, 2000, from http://www.efa.org/answerplace/recognition/poster.html.

Check Your Learning

Review the steps for treating a person having a seizure. Can you name each one? In what circumstances should you seek medical help?

Most students who have seizures take medication to control their disorder, and if necessary you should monitor the consistency with which the medication is taken because that greatly affects its effectiveness. If the medication is carefully monitored and student size and status is not changing, you might not even be aware of the student's disability. However, when children are growing rapidly and gaining weight, and when they approach puberty and undergo many physical and hormonal changes, seizures may occur as the student's body changes.

Although no relationship exists between having a seizure disorder and academic performance (Huberty, Austin, Risinger, & McNellis, 1992), you may find that a student with this disability is reluctant to engage in interactions with peers out of fear of peers' reactions to seizures (Speigel et al., 1996). Students may also experience low self-esteem. If a student is likely to have recurring seizures, you may want (with student and parent support) to explain epilepsy to your class, or ask a specialist to do that. What is important is that typical learners understand that, although somewhat frightening, epilepsy is not dangerous, not controlled by the student with the disorder, and not contagious.

Another health impairment is **sickle-cell anemia.** This disorder is inherited and occurs most often in African American individuals, with an incidence of 1 in 500. One out of every 12 African Americans carries the gene for the disorder. The disease is occasionally found in other groups, including Greeks and Italians (Operation Sickle Cell, 2001). Sickle-cell anemia occurs when normally round blood cells are abnormally shaped liked sickles. This makes the blood thicker and prevents it from efficiently carrying oxygen to tissues. The result for individuals who have this disorder is fatigue and reduced stamina along with mild to severe chronic pain in the chest, joints, back, or abdomen; swollen hands and feet; jaundice; repeated infections, particularly pneumonia; and sometimes kidney failure (Operation Sickle Cell, 2001). No reliable treatments are currently available for individuals who have this disease. In children, sickle-cell anemia can affect growth. Students with sickle-cell anemia experience crises in which their symptoms are acute and include high fevers, joint swelling, and extreme fatigue; they are likely to miss school during these times. A student with this health impairment, then, often needs assistance in making up for missed instruction and encouragement for dealing with the pain and discomfort.

A third health impairment is **acquired immune deficiency syndrome (AIDS).** AIDS results when students are infected with the **human immuno deficiency virus (HIV)** and their bodies lose the ability to fight off infection (Shea & Bauer, 1994). At the end of 1999, some 3,622 children under the age of 13 were reported as having AIDS, and, in addition, 1,876 children were reported to have HIV (Centers for Disease Control and Prevention, 2000). The latter is considered a significant underestimate of the incidence of this disease because several states, including some with a high incidence of reported AIDS infections, do not release HIV statistics to the Centers for Disease Control. Students with AIDS can often attend school with little assistance until their illness progresses to the point that they lack the stamina to complete school work or that the risk of catching an infection or illness from a classmate becomes too great. As you probably know, no medical cure currently exists for AIDS. Studies of the impact of AIDS on children are just beginning.

A fourth example of a health impairment is **asthma.** Children with asthma comprise the largest group of chronically ill children in the United States: Approximately 5 million youngsters have this illness, and at any single time, most educators have two students in their classrooms who have asthma (Getch & Neuharth-Pritchett, 1999). Asthma is the leading cause of absenteeism among schoolchildren. When asthma occurs, airways become inflamed because of sensitivity to certain substances called *allergens,* and the airflow is reduced, leading to breathing difficulty (Bender, 1999). Although only students with moderate or severe asthma are likely to be receiving special education services, any student with asthma may need special consideration in your classroom. For example, these students probably miss more school than other students and need assistance in mastering missed concepts. When in school, they sometimes feel tired or generally unwell, and they may need to be excused from some activities (Madden, 2000). For students who use inhalers to treat their condition, you should monitor that the student carries this medication as needed.

Students may have many other health impairments. For example, you may have a student who has been badly burned and is undergoing medical treatment and physical or occupational therapy to restore range of movement in affected limbs. Other

WWW Resources

At the Sickle Cell Information Center at Emory University (http://www.cc.emory.edu/PEDS/SICKLE/index.htm), you can find news, research updates, and worldwide resources related to this genetic disorder.

Research Note

Some students with low-incidence disabilities require specialized health care at school; this care is often provided by the paraprofessional or special education teacher. In a survey of more than 500 individuals who provide health care assistance to students with physical or medical disabilities in public schools, Heller, Fredrick, Best, Dykes, and Cohen (2000) reported that only about half the respondents were knowledgeable about the procedures they perform.

Orthopedic disabilities and other health impairments can include a great variety of conditions, illnesses, and injuries, including cerebral palsy, seizure disorders, asthma, and AIDS. What special considerations may general education teachers need to make when working with these students?

health impairments your students might have include **hemophilia,** a genetically transmitted disease in which blood does not coagulate properly; **diabetes,** a condition in which the body does not produce enough insulin to process the carbohydrates eaten; and **cystic fibrosis,** a genetically transmitted disease in which the body produces excessive mucus that eventually damages the lungs and causes heart failure.

As noted throughout this discussion, the adaptations you make for students with health impairments often relate to helping them make up for work missed because of an absence or hospitalization and to recognizing their social and emotional needs and responding to them (Lynch, Lewis, & Murphy, 1993b). In one study of parents' and educators' perceptions of problems faced by children with chronic illness, parents reported that their children's most frequent problems were "feeling different," undergoing constant medical procedures, experiencing pain, and facing death. Educators listed absences, falling behind in school, lack of interaction with peers, school's inability to meet the student's needs, and social adjustment as the most serious problems (Lynch, Lewis, & Murphy 1993a).

General strategies for working with students with health impairments include these:

1. Find out students' most difficult problems and help students work through them. Strategies include having students write or draw about their concerns or referring students to the school counselor or social worker as you see a need.

2. Provide materials for the students about others who have a similar disease or disorder. Books, videotapes, movies, and informational materials can help students with health impairments understand how others have successfully coped with their illnesses, and they can be useful for explaining the needs of these students to peers without disabilities.

3. Consider including death education in your curriculum if you have a student with a life-threatening condition such as cancer (Peckham, 1993). A special educator, counselor, or social worker can probably prepare a unit and help you present it.

4. Work closely with families. Parents can often be the most valuable source of information concerning their child's status and needs. They can also alert you to upcoming changes in medications and emotional problems occurring at home, and they can help their children work on missed school assignments (Lynch et al., 1993b).

In terms of academic and curricular adaptations, you should respond to students with health impairments as you would to other students with disabilities. Using the INCLUDE strategy, you can identify their needs. If modifications in the environment, curriculum, or instruction are needed, you can carry them out using the suggestions made throughout the remainder of this text.

Traumatic Brain Injury

Traumatic brain injury (TBI) occurs when a student experiences a trauma to the head from an external physical force that results in an injury to the brain, often including a temporary loss of consciousness. TBI has many causes, including child abuse and gunshot wounds (Savage & Wolcott, 1994). The most common causes of TBI, however, are falls; bicycle and motor vehicle accidents; sporting accidents; and, increasingly, accidents on playground equipment. Approximately 1 million children and adolescents sustain a TBI each year. Whereas most of these injuries are mild, some 200,000 of these youngsters require hospitalization (Clark, Russman, & Orme, 1999). Whether TBI is the result of a severe injury or a mild one, it can have a pervasive and significant impact on the student's educational performance (Hux & Hacksley, 1996).

Recovery from a TBI can take months or even years, and some students with severe TBI spend time in rehabilitation after their hospitalization and before returning to school. Other students with mild or moderate injuries are likely to go directly from the hospital back to their homes and schools (Clark et al., 1999). Students with TBI often return to school at some point during the recovery process, but predicting their abilities and the point at which they will reach their best outcome is impossible given the length of recovery time and the varioius patterns for treatment.

One of the most perplexing aspects of teaching students with TBI is that they can appear just as they did prior to their injuries and yet have significant learning and social problems. They can also seem to be "back to normal" one day only to seem lethargic and incapable of learning the next day. Because of the extreme variability in needs of students with TBI, the information presented in this section should be considered illustrative; if you teach a student with TBI, seeking input from a specialist is essential.

Cognitively, students with TBI might have the same abilities they had before, or they might experience a loss of capacity. For example, after an automobile accident Michael, a high school honor student who used to be a class leader, was left struggling to remaster basic math facts. His injury affected his school learning. Students might experience difficulty initiating and organizing their learning tasks, remembering what they have learned, and reasoning or problem solving. They might also have difficulty processing verbal information and producing spoken and written language.

Connections

Students with mild forms of health impairments in which there is no ongoing adverse effect on education might receive services through Section 504. Such cases are explained further in Chapter 7.

Check Your Learning

What accommodations are students with health impairments likely to need? How do these students' needs vary based on the nature and severity of their disorders?

FYI

Working with students with TBI has become an important topic because of many recent advances in medical technology. Many students who used to die from their injuries now survive and return to school.

[Technology Notes]

Working with Technology

Teachers in inclusive classrooms can be overwhelmed by the number and variety of options their students may have. As you consider the use of technology for your students with disabilities, as well as other students, these are points to keep in mind:

- Opt for open-ended devices whenever possible, ones that permit customizing for the student and tasks.

- Try the lowest technology solution before assuming that high technology is needed. A larger mouse may accommodate a student; an entirely different keyboard or computer may not be needed.

- Collaborate with other teachers. Keeping abreast of all new developments is an impossible task for one person to accomplish. If you learn how to use a program or device, share your knowledge with others, and they can do the same for you.

- Collaborate with parents to be sure that technology devices that go home are used for the purpose intended.

- Ensure that devices used by students are age and gender appropriate. For example, a high school student using a talking word processor should use the adult voice option, not the child voice.

- Avoid the belief that you have to understand completely a piece of assistive technology before you can use it and help your students use it. In many cases, "jumping in," even when you are uncertain, is the strategy of choice.

- Check on your school district policy concerning equipment use (home versus school), maintenance, and repairs. Although you are not responsible for these areas, being knowledgeable can help you and parents avoid problems.

- Ask for training on equipment or devices that your students will use. You are the primary teacher for the student, and you should not rely on the special educator to provide all expertise.

- Experiment with assistive technology. It is a very young field, and everybody is learning.

SOURCE: Adapted from "Using Assistive Technology in the Inclusive Classroom," by J. B. Merbler, A. Hadadian, & J. Ulman, 1999, *Preventing School Failure, 43*, pp. 113–117. Reprinted with permission of the Helen Dwight Reid Educational Foundation. Published by Heldref Publications, 1319 Eighteenth St., N.W., Washington, DC 20036-1802. Copyright © 1999.

Students with TBI also have physical needs. Depending on the severity of the injury and the extent of recovery, some students have limited use of their arms and legs. Others have problems in fine motor movements such as those needed to grasp a pencil or turn the pages of a book. Yet others have limited strength and stamina. Students with these needs sometimes attend school only part of the day.

Socially and emotionally, students with TBI experience many difficulties. One comment made about students with TBI is that they sometimes have changes in their personalities, that they are not who they used to be (Kehle, Clark, & Jenson, 1996). For example, they often remember what they were able to do prior to their injuries and sometimes become depressed as they recognize their current limitations (D'Amato & Rothlisberg, 1996). Because they often need a high degree of structure and do not respond well to change, they can display behavior problems when a sudden change in schedule occurs, as when an assembly interrupts an accustomed routine. Some students lose their ability to interpret and to respond appropriately to social cues. As a result, they might laugh at inappropriate times, speak loudly when everyone else has realized a whisper is needed, or wander off when distracted by something. Their behaviors can be puzzling or frustrating unless you understand how to respond to them. Some of the most common characteristics and related behaviors of students with TBI, along with potential responses teachers can make, are included in Table 5.3.

It is especially important to mention families as part of considerations about TBI. Often, parents or siblings have witnessed the student in a totally unresponsive state, and they have psychologically prepared for the possibility of death. They might be tremendously relieved that the student survived, but at the same time traumatized by the amount of physical care the student needs and by the drain on financial and psychological family resources. Depending on the amount of uncertainty about the extent to which the student can eventually recover, the impact of the TBI on the student's intellect and personality, and the family's ability to provide for the student's needs, families can experience a range of emotions, including shock, denial, sorrow, and anger (Wade, Taylor, Drotar, Stancin, & Yeates, 1996). Eventually, many adapt. You need to be sensitive to the family's stress and their changing capacity to follow up on homework as well as schoolwork to support your efforts.

If you teach a student with TBI, you might attend at least one planning meeting to discuss the details of the student's abilities and needs and to prepare you for helping the student in the classroom. This transition planning, which typically occurs when a student is moving from the hospital or rehabilitation center back to school, is essential to ensure that appropriate expectations are set for the student, procedures are established for responding to changes in the student's condition, and all services are coordinated (Clark, 1996).

In your classroom, adaptations relate to physical needs, instructional and organizational routines, academic content, and the social environment. Because students with TBI need structure and routine, you should follow the same pattern in classroom activities, expect the same types of student responses, and keep supplies and materials in the same place in the classroom. If a break in routine is necessary, you can prepare the student by alerting him or her, assigning a buddy, and staying in close proximity.

You may need to make changes in the academic expectations for a student with TBI. Because students might know information one day but forget it the next, or learn with ease sometimes but struggle to learn at other times, the need for flexibility is ongoing. Students are also likely to become frustrated with their inability to learn the way they did in the past, so your patience in reteaching information, providing additional examples and exercises, and using strategies to help them focus attention can be essential.

Socially, emotionally, and behaviorally, students with TBI rely on you to set clear expectations but to be supportive and responsive to their changing needs. One student, Gary, had been in a coma but gradually regained enough ability to function to return to his middle school, at first for only an hour or two each day and eventually for the entire day. However, he continued to forget common words and grew increasingly frustrated when he could not convey his message. His teachers began providing the words he needed. Because many students with TBI seem unable to form a realistic picture of how they are functioning, you might need to confront them gently about socially inappropriate behavior. Frustrated with his language skills, Gary yelled at friends, yet his sentences remained unclear. Teachers intervened to help him

Check Your Learning

What characteristics of students with TBI create challenges for teachers working with them?

Connections

Information on communicating with families was emphasized in Chapter 3. Review the strategies that promote positive interactions with families.

WWW Resources

The Brain Injury Association, Inc. website, at http://www.biausa.org, includes information about causes, cost, prevention, and treatment of TBI. It even has a kid's corner.

Table 5.3 Classroom Behaviors of Students with Traumatic Brain Injury

Characteristics	Behavior	Solutions
Overestimates abilities	Student brags to friends that he or she is still the fastest runner or will win the spelling bee.	Do not challenge the student. Reassure him or her that individuals change after a head injury.
Lowered social inhibition and judgment	Student tries to touch and hug everyone.	Redirect student's attention to an appropriate behavior. Model correct or alternative behavior for student.
Lowered impulse control	Student interrupts teachers and peers at inappropriate times.	Verbally remind student of rules. Provide alternative ways to have his or her needs met (raises hand or other private signal).
Faulty reasoning	Student confronts peers and teachers with unfair accusations.	Do not feel obligated to respond immediately. Reassure student and move on. Return later to resolve the problem.
Lowered initiative	Student will not begin a task without a reminder or assistance.	Be proactive and impose organization before assigning tasks. Cognitive behavior modification techniques may be beneficial.
Depression	Student appears uninterested and passive, even in activities once considered highly enjoyable. The emotional stress of the injury may be prolonged and can be overwhelming.	Involve the student directly in the activity. Assign a specific role to hook the student's interest. Individual counseling or support group participation can be beneficial.
Fatigue	Student may be fatigued as a result of both the injury and the medication. Sleep disorders are common.	Review medical information regarding physical limitations. Provide variety by changing tasks often and giving frequent breaks. Consider a shortened school day.
Acting-out behavior	Student may yell or curse about being asked to do a task he or she does not want to do. He or she may walk out of class or knock over a desk.	First protect other students and yourself from physical injury. The student may need to be removed to another location (with adult supervision) in the school.
Impulsivity	Student may be unable to wait his or her turn at a drinking fountain or in the cafeteria. He or she may talk out during a test or speak before being called on.	Restate the classroom rules or limits. Reassure the student that there is plenty of time for the activity.
Rigidity	Student may be unable to adapt to changes in schedule or routine. Student may be unwilling to go to an assembly if it is scheduled during regular academic subjects.	Alert the student in advance to anticipated changes in each day's accustomed routine.
Flat affect	Student seems to have no voice inflections. Face seems expressionless; eyes seem vacant; he or she does not laugh or smile appropriately.	Try to remember that this behavior is characteristic of a person with a head injury and not necessarily a demonstration of low motivation or apathy. Use novel or stimulating learning activities that are relevant to the student's interests and goals.
Low motivation	What appears as low motivation may actually be confusion and inability to conceptualize and plan how to do the task.	Ask the student to verbalize the first step toward completing the task. Ask for succeeding steps if necessary.
Agitation and irritability	Varying degrees of agitation and irritability may manifest. Student may become annoyed over picky things or become aggressive toward self or teachers.	Try to redirect the student's attention away from the source of agitation, offer an alternative activity, or move him or her to another area or room where it is quiet and he or she can regain control.

S O U R C E : From "Traumatic Brain Injury: An Overview of School Re-Entry," by B. F. Tucker and S. E. Colson, 1992, *Intervention in School and Clinic,* 27(4), pp. 198–206. Copyright © 1992 by PRO-ED, Inc. Reprinted by permission.

learn to control his anger and to assist friends to understand him. Students with TBI might also overestimate their abilities. Informally, you can assist in this area by discussing realistic options for the near future and, with older students, for career choices.

In general, the adaptations needed by students with TBI are much the same as those needed by students with physical or health disabilities, learning disabilities, and emotional disabilities (Adams et al., 1991). The uniqueness of students with TBI and the reason they are grouped as a separate category in IDEA is that their needs are difficult to predict, change either slowly or rapidly, and vary in intensity. With patience and a willingness by teachers to meet the student wherever he or she is and work forward from there, students with TBI can achieve school success.

What Accommodations Can You Make for Students with Autism?

Autism was first identified as a disorder in 1943 by Dr. Leo Kanner. Since then, it has been the source of much research and ongoing professional debate. Autism has been considered part of various emotional disabilities, including schizophrenia, and has been addressed as a form of mental retardation. Currently, however, autism is considered a unique disorder that affects boys more than girls in a ratio of approximately 4:1. Between 1995 and 1999, the number of children identified with autism has climbed 120 percent (Sack, 1999). Autism frequently occurs with other disorders. In particular, it is estimated that 70 percent of individuals with autism also have mental retardation; but that number could be an overestimate because of the communication difficulties that accompany the disability and the resulting problems in obtaining accurate estimates of ability (Freeman, 1994). At least some of the 30 percent of individuals with autism who do not have cognitive disabilities are gifted or talented (Cash, 1999). If you teach a student with autism, you will find that it is both rewarding and challenging, that sometimes the student is a frustrating enigma and others times the student's progress in learning and contributions to the school community are exciting.

Although autism is like most of the other low-incidence disabilities in that it can exist in many forms, from mild to severe, and cannot be treated as a single disorder with a single set of adaptations, it does have specific characteristics. First, students with autism have seriously impaired social relationships. Many students with autism resist human contact and social interactions from a very early age, and they have difficulty learning the subtleties of social interactions (Donellan, 1999). They often do not make eye contact with others, and they can seem uninterested in developing social relationships. For example, young children often ask teachers to watch them do something ("Look at me!"), and they bring interesting items to share with the teacher and their classmates. A young child with autism would not seek out such opportunities for social interactions. Albert, a 13-year-old with autism, discussed his problems in the social domain. He maintained that others viewed him as extremely ugly, but he did not understand why he did not have friends. When an interviewer asked him what he talked about with others, the two topics he mentioned were wind and smells in the environment (Cesaroni & Garber, 1991). He did not take on the perspective of others, and he did not understand that others' interests, so different

Cultural Awareness

Children with low incidence disabilities, including TBI, who live in rural areas have advantages and disadvantages. Because of a strong sense of community, they are likely to be welcomed in classrooms and strongly supported in their communities. However, specialized services such as special transportation and advanced technology options may be difficult to arrange, and the turnover rate among special educators and other support staff tends to be quite high.

from his own, are also part of social interaction. Ideas for teaching social skills to students with autism are included in the Professional Edge on pages 190–191.

Students with autism also experience problems in both verbal and nonverbal communication (Paneri, Ferrante, Caputo, & Impellizzeri, 1998). They often have significantly delayed language development, and, if they have language skills, they struggle to maintain a conversation with another person. In writing about her experiences of being autistic, Temple Grandin provides a clear example of her communication problems (Grandin, 1984). She explains that once when her mother wanted her to wear a hat while riding in the car, she didn't have the words to refuse. Instead, she screamed and threw the hat out the window, causing her mother to hit another car. Unlike Temple Grandin, many students with autism cannot write or otherwise clearly communicate about their experiences, although some can communicate by typing their thoughts. Often, however, students with autism use inappropriate behaviors instead of words to convey many needs. Unless taught alternative behaviors, they might hit a peer as a way of saying hello, or run from a classroom instead of saying they do not like the assignment just given. Some students with autism have **echolalic speech.** They repeat what others have said instead of producing original communication.

Another characteristic of students with autism is a very limited range of interest, such as a student who is fascinated with radios to the exclusion of nearly everything else. When students with autism have such an interest, they can spend literally hours and hours absorbed in a private world of exploration. They might act bored with every topic and every activity unless it relates to their special interest. Such a narrow range of interest often has a negative impact on social relationships with peers and adults because the student does not discern that others are not as interested in the preferred topic.

Students with autism have a low threshold for and difficulty in dealing with stress (Grandin, 1984). A change in a class schedule could be difficult for a student with autism, as could be the introduction of a new route from the classroom to a bus or an alternative order for the day's activities. Particular noises or odors or a noisy environment also can be stressful. Many students with autism respond to stress with **stereotypic behaviors.** They complete the same action or motion again and again. For example, they may rock rapidly in their chairs, spin an object repeatedly, or twirl themselves or their arms. In other situations, students might develop a ritual to complete a task. For example, they might need 10 minutes to prepare to complete an assignment because they need to arrange paper and pencil on the desk in a precise pattern, check that all books in the desk are also stored in a specific order, and make sure their desk is aligned precisely at the intersection of tiles on the classroom floor. In your classroom, you should be aware of potentially stressful situations for a student with autism. You can either allow time for the student to prepare for the situation, talk about the situation well in advance, assign a peer partner to assist the student, or enlist the assistance of a special educator or paraprofessional. If a student's response to stress is demonstrated with aggressive or extremely disruptive behavior, you should work closely with a special educator, behavior consultant, or other specialist to address the problem. In some instances, the student might need to spend part of the school day in a more structured, less stressful environment, such as the school library or learning center.

In the past, nearly all students identified as autistic had noticeable behaviors and serious problems in social relationships and communication. Recently, however, professional attention has turned to students with milder forms of autism, including **Asperger's syndrome.** These students sometimes seem like "perfect students" (Coppola, 1987), somewhat like Carter, the middle school student described at the beginning of the chapter. These students usually develop speech at a normal age, but they sometimes have problems knowing whether to use a first-person, second-person, or third-person pronoun. They have limited facial expression, seem inept at interpreting others' nonverbal communication, and are awkward in social situations, as though they do not quite understand the unspoken rules for social interactions. They sometimes have problems in gross motor coordination but are highly intelligent, with intense interest in one or two topics (Atwood, 1993). Because these students may be quiet and do not seek out interactions with others, they often have trouble forming friendships.

Supporting Appropriate Behavior

Students with autism often have behaviors that are unusual and can be disturbing to teachers and students who do not understand this disorder. However, many of the behaviors can be corrected with highly structured behavior support programs, and some can be ignored. Many students with autism can receive some or all of their education in a general education classroom, provided that needed supports are in place for them (Pratt & Moreno, 1994; Simpson, 1995).

Generally, the adaptations you make for students with autism involve creating a structured and predictable environment and encouraging appropriate social interactions (Clark & Smith, 1999). To create a positive learning environment, establish clear procedures and routines for classroom tasks and follow them consistently. For example, in an elementary classroom, you can create procedures for students to retrieve their coats at lunchtime, or begin each day with the same activities in the same order. For secondary students, you can set a clear pattern in your instruction by beginning each class with a 3-minute review followed by a 20-minute lecture followed by a 15-minute individual or small-group work session.

In addition to providing structure, students with autism may need opportunities during the day to work alone and be alone (Christof & Kane, 1991). This time serves as a break from the stresses of the classroom and the social and communication demands of that setting. A special education teacher can probably advise you about whether this is necessary for a particular student and assist in making arrangements for a quiet place for the student to work.

To help students with social interactions and communication, you can observe student behavior to understand its purpose from the student's perspective (Christof & Kane, 1991). For example, if a student with autism withdraws from classroom activities and begins rocking every day at about 11:00 A.M., it could be a signal that the student is too hungry to work until a 12:15 P.M. lunchtime. Providing a snack in a quiet corner of the classroom could reduce the problem. If a student has been working in a small group but suddenly leaves the group and runs to the room next door, it could be a signal that the student has reached the limits of his or her tolerance for social interactions. It might be appropriate to work with another teacher to provide a safe and isolated location where the student can take a break from classroom social demands. With these understandings, you can communicate to a special educator or paraprofessional the behaviors of concern and possible explanations for them, thus setting up a positive approach for problem solving. Other social areas in which general education

Check Your Learning

What alternative communication approaches have you learned about in this chapter that students with autism might use? What augmentative communication devices might they use?

Professional Edge

Teaching Social Skills to Students with Autism

Students with autism have a great need to develop appropriate social skills that will serve them well in school and throughout their lives. These are some useful skills and ideas for addressing them.

Behavior	Examples	Strategies for Teaching
Waiting	Waiting in line	Establish clear rules, such as "Stand up when the teacher calls your name."
	Waiting for someone else to answer	Teach the student to occupy wait time doing a favorite activity of choice.
	Waiting for a program to start	Try to keep wait time as short as possible at first; reward the student for successfully waiting.
Taking turns being first	Being first in line	Create a chart to show who is to be first in line each day and put marks on the floor as a guide if needed.
	Being first to answer	Set rules about answering questions; for example, the student can be the first to answer every sixth time only.
Transitioning before completing something	Stopping before a workbook page is completed	Try to avoid this problem by allowing enough time for the student to finish a game or activity.
	Leaving the computer in the middle of a game	Give the student warnings when time is about to run out. For example, alert the student 5 minutes before the end of the time period, and again at 2 minutes and 1 minute before the end using visual cues.
Changing topics	Asking endless questions about what is going to happen	Set a time limit on the amount of time a student can talk about a topic. Use a visual timer.
	Talking endlessly about favorite topics	Give the student three or four picture cards of alternative topics.
	Repeating that others do not like him or her	Create a rule about the number of times you will respond to the same questions. For example, after two times, say, "You know the answer to that." Write the answer for the student.
		Write a story or script to give specific information.

teachers can accommodate students with autism include teaching them to wait, to take turns, to stop an activity before it is complete, to negotiate, to change topics, to finish an activity, to be more flexible, to be quiet, and to monitor their own behavior.

Communicating with Students with Autism

Communication with students with autism is accomplished through a wide variety of strategies (Brown, 1994). Some students with autism can communicate adequately with speech, especially when they do not feel pressured. With young chil-

Behavior	Examples	Strategies for Teaching
Finishing	Finishing lunch Finishing an assignment	Define "finished" in concrete terms. For example, finishing a paper might be defined as putting an answer in every space or filling a specific amount of the page with writing.
	Finishing a game or activity	Finishing games or activities might be cued by all the cards being drawn, everyone having had a turn, or a bell or buzzer.
Being flexible	Teacher absence Art class canceled because of an assembly Field trip delayed because of rain	Use pictures to show the expected routine, and cross out the part of the routine that is changing. If possible, prepare the student for the change by describing it verbally and visually and asking the student to explain it to you.
Being quiet	Being quiet while working Being quiet when others are being quiet Being quiet while others are talking	Teach a specific and concrete strategy for being quiet, either by setting a time limit or setting rules such as, "When someone else speaks, keep completely quiet."
Monitoring behavior when excited	Learning to stop clapping or laughing when others have done so Learning when it is okay to run and talk loudly and when it is not okay	Teach a student to watch others and stop clapping or laughing as soon as they do. Set rules for when and where loud talking and running are okay. Use visual cues to remind the student.

S O U R C E : From *Some Social Behaviors That Students with Autism Need Help to Learn and Apply in Everyday Situations*, by N. Dalrymple, 1990, Bloomington, IN: Indiana Resource Center for Autism, Institute for the Study of Developmental Disabilities. Used by permission of the author.

dren, this sort of communication can sometimes be prompted by interrupting the child during a favorite activity (for example, playing with a toy), then permitting the child to resume the activity after communicating with you (Sigafoos & Littlewood, 1999). Other students learn to communicate through sign language, just as many students who are deaf or hard-of-hearing do. For some students, the motor activity of signing seems to help them successfully convey their needs and preferences. For yet other students, communication boards are useful tools: By simply touching pictures, students can communicate with others even when they cannot speak the appropriate words. Other communication devices that help students with limited speech, including those with autism, were described previously in this chapter.

Students with autism have a range of cognitive abilities, and some are gifted. What strategies help students with autism succeed in general education classrooms?

Some students now use a widely publicized and controversial technique called **facilitated communication** (Biklen, 1993; Graley, 1994). A person trained in this technique sits next to the student with autism and provides touch support to the wrist, elbow, or shoulder as the student types responses or other information on a typewriter, computer, adapted keyboard, or communication board. The purpose of the touching is not to guide the student's hand, but instead to provide steadiness and support for it. Some professionals and parents have found this technique helpful in enabling students with autism to communicate, often for the first time in their lives. They report many examples of students who previously had been thought to have significant cognitive disabilities who through facilitated communication now can type (sometimes independently) and share their thoughts, feelings, and needs (Beirne-Smith, Patton, & Ittenbach, 1994). Others question whether the written work produced represents the student's thinking or that of the facilitator. The best communication strategies for a student with autism are generally determined by the multidisciplinary team. A special educator or paraprofessional informs you about a student's communication needs and strategies and helps you develop an effective communication system.

Summary

Students with low-incidence disabilities comprise only about 10 percent of all students with disabilities, but they account for eight of the federal categories of disabilities and part of the mental retardation category. Together, these students have tremendously diverse abilities, challenges, and needs. Many of them can succeed in your classroom if you take into account that you will teach only one or two students with these disabilities at any single time and that they are students first and have disabilities second. Many teaching strategies you have already learned are effective in teaching these students, and other professionals and parents are available to assist you in creating successful learning experiences for them.

One group of students with low-incidence disabilities is composed of those with moderate or severe cognitive disabilities, multiple disabilities, and deaf-blindness. These students learn slowly, and they usually need assistance to maintain and generalize their skills, and to combine skills to complete complex activities. They need a functional and community-based education that can be accomplished in general education settings with appropriate supports and a commitment to effective teaching and learning practices such as multiple levels of instruction occurring in one classroom, heterogeneous student groupings, natural support systems, and development of partnerships with families.

Students with sensory impairments are those with significant limitations for processing information using visual or auditory channels. The impact of these students' disabilities on their education can be slight or significant. They often have needs related to academic learning, social and emotional skills, and skills for living in their environments. They also use adaptive equipment or materials to help them learn.

Some students have orthopedic impairments or other health impairments, including traumatic brain injury. Their special supports and services are determined by their needs. Students in these groups often have medical needs that directly or indirectly affect their learning. Their cognitive levels can include an entire range. Most students in this group have social and emotional needs because of their illnesses, and accommodations in these areas are likely to be necessary.

Autism is another low-incidence disability. Students with autism have a wide range of cognitive and other abilities, and they have impairments in their social relationships, communication, range of interests, and capacity to respond to stressful events. They need highly structured learning environments with clear procedures and routines. Recently, more attention is being paid to students with mild forms of autism, including Asperger's syndrome.

Applications in Teaching Practice

Planning Adaptations for Students with Low-Incidence Disabilities

Mr. Guidroz teaches English to ninth graders. This year he has several students with learning disabilities and emotional disabilities in his class, but his primary concern is Viral, a young man who has cerebral palsy and limited vision. Mr. Guidroz has been told that Viral has average intelligence and is quite capable of following the standard course of study for English, but with accommodations. Mr. Guidroz is meeting with Ms. Bickel from the special education department to ask questions about Viral.

Mr. Guidroz: I need more information about Viral. Can he really do the work? How much can he see? How is he going to take tests? What is his assistant supposed to be doing? Am I accountable if Viral has a medical problem during class? Is it likely that will happen? I hear that Viral has all sorts of computer equipment and a motorized wheelchair—I have 32 other students in that class period and I'm concerned about just fitting everyone in the door!

Ms. Bickel: It sounds like you haven't gotten the information I thought you had. Let me try to clarify. Viral is quite a good student. He usually gets A's and B's in his core academic classes, and he is highly motivated to learn. He has every intention of going to college, and right now he hopes to be an editor. Because he can't use his voice, he "talks" using his communication board. I'll be working with you to be sure the board includes all the key words you want it to contain. All Viral has to do is point his head toward the answer he wants and the laser pointer activates the board, which "says" the answer out loud. Probably one adaptation Viral will need is extra time to answer; he really wants to participate but might need a moment to get the laser beam focused on the answer he wants to give. His equipment is all adapted to take into account his limited vision.

Mr. Guidroz: I'll have to see how that works. What does his assistant do?

Ms. Bickel: Mr. Owen is responsible for Viral's personal care and for making sure he gets from class to class. He also takes notes for Viral and records answers Viral gives on his communication board. He can help you out in class if there's a chance, but Viral needs his attention much of the time.

Mr. Guidroz: Oh, I wasn't trying to get more help. I just need a picture of what this will be like. I need an extra place for Mr. Owen in class, don't I?

Ms. Bickel: Yes, he'll need to sit right next to Viral.

The teachers continued talking for another 45 minutes, problem solving about the space issue and trying to ensure that Viral would experience success and that Mr. Guidroz understood Viral's needs. The next week, Ms. Bickel asked Mr. Guidroz how it was going with Viral. Mr. Guidroz commented that he was surprised how smoothly and easily things were going. Viral "spoke" in class on the first day, and the other students asked a few questions about the equipment, but that was all. He asked if Ms. Bickel could help him deal with two other students who already seemed to have behavior problems.

Questions

1. What type of disability does Viral have? Why is he included in Mr. Guidroz's English class?
2. What accommodations should Mr. Guidroz make in his classroom and his instruction to address Viral's special needs?
3. If you were meeting with Ms. Bickel, what additional questions would you ask? About Viral? About needed accommodations?
4. What assistance would you need from Ms. Bickel to feel comfortable teaching Viral?

5. What would your expectation be for working with Viral's parents? What might you learn from them that would help you be more effective in teaching Viral? What expectations might you have for them for working with you?

6. Review the entire chapter and all the information about students with low-incidence disabilities presented in it. What are the benefits of inclusive practices related to students in this group? What are the concerns and questions you still have for working with students with low-incidence disabilities?

Students with High-Incidence Disabilities

Learner Objectives

After you read this chapter, you will be able to

1. Explain what is meant by *high-incidence disabilities*, including their prevalence and the key elements of the federal definitions for each of the high-incidence categories.

2. Describe the characteristics and needs of students with communication disorders and explain how you can make classroom adaptations for them using the INCLUDE strategy.

3. Describe the characteristics and needs of students with cognitive, learning, and emotional disabilities and the adaptations you can make for them using the INCLUDE strategy.

Key Terms and Concepts

Academic survival skills (p. 215)

Attribution retraining (p. 227)

Emotional disturbance (p. 205)

Expressive language (p. 200)

High-incidence disabilities (p. 198)

Learned helplessness (p. 222)

Learning disabilities (p. 205)

Mild cognitive disabilities (p. 205)

Receptive language (p. 200)

Self-control training (p. 226)

Social skills training (p. 224)

Speech articulation (p. 198)

Stuttering (p. 200)

■ Seth is an eighth-grade student at King Middle School. Most people who know Seth outside of school would never guess that he has a learning disability. He converses easily with children and adults, has a great sense of humor, and is renowned among his peers for his "street smarts." Things don't go as well for Seth in school; basic academic skills are particularly problematic. He reads slowly, struggling with each word, and as a result he often cannot tell you what he has read. Seth's written language is also a problem. His handwriting is illegible, his spelling is inconsistent, and his written essays lack organization. In math, Seth still doesn't know basic math facts, and when faced with answering word problems, he simply gives up. What disability does Seth have? What factors do you think may have contributed to Seth's academic problems? What kinds of adaptations should Seth's teacher make for him? What other kinds of support do Seth and his teacher need?

■ Rick is heading toward his 15th birthday and major trouble in and out of school. Rick's behavior in school has never been easy to manage. In the primary grades, he was disruptive in class but responded well when his parents gave him rewards at home for good behavior in school. When Rick was in fifth grade, his parents divorced and behavior problems in school began to worsen. Rick began to talk abusively to peers in class and to refuse loudly to do any work. He began to bully other students, particularly those least likely to be able to defend themselves. In seventh and eighth grades, Rick attended an alternative school. Although his school behavior improved somewhat, he became involved in gang activities in eighth grade. This year, Rick is a freshman in high school and is attending all general education classes in addition to seeing a special education teacher once a day in the resource room. His school and class attendance has been spotty, and he occasionally engages in disruptive behavior in his classes. What is Rick's disability? How do you think his general education teacher can accommodate his behavior? What kinds of support do Rick and his teacher need?

Students like Seth and Rick have high-incidence disabilities. These students' disabilities affect their language, learning, and behavior. You probably will teach students with high-incidence disabilities in your classroom. These students can benefit from being in a general education setting, but they require support from general and special education professionals. Seth is learning word-processing skills to help him overcome his problems with spelling and handwriting. He is also using texts on tape in his science and social studies classes, which are sometimes co-taught. Rick and his teachers have developed an individualized behavior contract in which Rick is allowed extra access to the auto mechanics shop for attending class and complying with teachers' requests. This chapter covers characteristics and needs of students with high-incidence disabilities and classroom accommodations that enable these students to learn.

What Are High-Incidence Disabilities?

Connections

Compare Table 6.1 with Table 5.1 on page 155. How do these tables support the concept of high-incidence and low-incidence disabilities? How do the concepts of mild, moderate, and severe disabilities also contribute to a cross-categorical view of students with special needs?

Students with **high-incidence disabilities** have speech or language disabilities, learning disabilities, emotional disturbance, or mild cognitive disabilities. The federal terms for high-incidence disabilities and the proportion of students with these disabilities served through IDEA are summarized in Table 6.1. Students with high-incidence disabilities share a number of important characteristics. These students are often hard to distinguish from peers without disabilities, particularly in nonschool settings. In addition, students with high-incidence disabilities often exhibit a combination of behavioral, social, and academic problems. Finally, students with high-incidence disabilities benefit from systematic, highly structured instructional interventions such as those discussed in this chapter and throughout the remainder of this book.

FYI

Students with mild cognitive disabilities comprise two-thirds of the federal category of mental retardation. The federal definition of mental retardation is in Table 5.1 on page 155.

What Accommodations Can You Make for Students with Communication Disorders?

Malcolm and Clarissa are part of a large group of students who have communication disorders. Communication is the exchange of ideas, opinions, or facts between people. Effective communication requires a sender to send a message that a receiver can decipher and understand. Students with communication disorders have problems with speech and/or language that interfere with communication. They need accommodations that help them better understand and express oral language.

FYI

Stuttering is the most common kind of speech problem involving fluency. *Stuttering* is a speech impairment in which an individual involuntarily repeats a sound or word, resulting in a loss of speech fluency.

Understanding Speech Problems

Speech is the behavior of forming and sequencing the sounds of oral language (Hallahan & Kauffman, 2000). One common speech problem is **speech articulation,** or the inability to pronounce sounds correctly at and after the developmentally appropriate age. For example, Stacey is in second grade but cannot pronounce the *s* sound, a sound most students master by age 5. Other speech difficulties involve **voice** and **fluency.** Examples of these speech problems are shown in Figure 6.1.

Table 6.1 **Proportion of Students with High-Incidence Disabilities Receiving Special Education Services in 1997–1998**[a]

Federal Disability Category	Defining Characteristics	Total Number of Students	Percentage of All Students Receiving IDEA Services
Learning disabilities	General intellectual functioning within the normal range	2,748,497	51.0
	Significant difference between ability and school achievement		
	Difference in ability/achievement *not* due to (a) a visual, hearing, or motor handicap; (b) mental retardation; (c) emotional disturbance; and (d) environmental, cultural, or economic disadvantage		
Emotional disturbance	Inability to learn that cannot be explained by intellectual, sensory, or health factors	454,363	8.4
	Inability to build or maintain satisfactory interpersonal relationships with peers and teachers		
	Inappropriate types of behavior or feelings under normal circumstances		
	General pervasive mood of unhappiness or depression; or tendency to develop physical symptoms or fears associated with personal or school problems		
Speech[b] or language[c] impairments	Speech is disordered when it deviates so far from the speech of other people that it calls attention to itself, interferes with communication, or causes the speaker or listeners distress.	1,065,074	19.8
	Three kinds of speech disorders are articulation (abnormal production of speech sounds), voice (absence of or abnormal production of voice quality, pitch, loudness, resonance and/or duration), and fluency (impaired rate and rhythm of speech, for example, stuttering).		
	Language is disordered when comprehension and/or use of a spoken, written, and/or other symbol system is impaired or does not develop normally.		
	Language disorders may involve form (word order, word parts, word usage), content (word meaning), and function (words that communicate meaningfully).		

[a]Students age 6–21 receiving services through IDEA, Part B (U.S. Department of Education, 1996). Additional students receive services under Part H of the same law, and under Chapter I.

[b]From definitions developed by Van Riper and Emerick (1984).

[c]From definitions developed by the American Speech-Language-Hearing Association (1982).

S o u r c e : From *Twent-First Annual Report to Congress on the Implementation of the Education of the Handicapped Act,* 1999, Washington, DC: U.S. Department of Education.

Figure 6.1 Speech Problems

Articulation

1. Difficulty pronouncing sounds correctly (at and after the developmentally appropriate age). Frequent articulation errors include *f, v, k, g, r, l, s, z, sh, ch,* and *j.* Sounds may be distorted or omitted, or one sound may be inappropriately substituted for another.

2. Speech may be slurred.

Voice

1. Speech is excessively hoarse.

2. May use excessive volume or too little volume.

3. Speech has too much nasality.

4. Speech lacks inflection.

Fluency

1. Stutters when speaking.

2. May have excessively slow rate of speech.

3. May exhibit uneven, jerky rate of speech.

S o u r c e : *Adapting Instruction in General Education for Students with Communication Disorders,* by D. Barad, 1985, unpublished manuscript, DeKalb, IL: Northern Illinois University.

WWW Resources

For more information about stuttering, visit the National Center for Stuttering, at www.stuttering.com.

Because communication is social, students with speech disorders, such as **stuttering,** often experience social problems. Students who can clearly communicate draw positive attention from peer relationships, but students who cannot are often avoided by their peers and sometimes ridiculed. The experience of peer rejection can be devastating, leading to a lack of confidence, a poor self-image, social withdrawal, and emotional problems later in life (Cowen, Pederson, Babijian, Izzo, & Trost, 1973). For example, after years of being ridiculed by peers, a high school freshman, who stutters, speaks infrequently and has no friends. He would like to ask a girl in his math class to a dance but is petrified that he will not be able to do so without stuttering.

Understanding Language Problems

Cultural Awareness

Learning English is particularly challenging for students with learning disabilities whose native language is not English (Lerner, 2000). For these students, teachers need to draw on instructional methods from both bilingual education and special education.

Language is a system of symbols that we use to communicate feelings, thoughts, desires, and actions. Language is the message contained in speech. Language can exist without speech, such as sign language for people who are deaf, and speech without language, such as birds that are trained to talk (Hardman, Drew, Egan, & Winston, 1999). Students who have language problems have trouble with either or both of two key parts of language: receptive language and expressive language. **Receptive language** involves understanding what people mean when they speak to you. **Expressive language** concerns speaking in such a way that others understand you. Receptive language problems occur when students are unable to understand what their teachers and peers are saying. For example, students with receptive language difficulties may not understand questions, may have trouble following directions, and may not be able to retain information presented verbally. Students with expressive language problems are unable to communicate clearly; their spoken language may include incorrect grammar, a limited use of vocabulary, and frequent hesitations. Some common receptive and expressive language problems are listed in Figure 6.2.

Students with language problems may also have difficulty using language in social situations. For example, they may be unable to vary their conversation to match the person with whom they are talking or the context in which it is occurring, to maintain a topic during conversation, to take turns during a conversation, to recognize when a listener is not understanding and take action to clarify, and to be a considerate speaker and listener (Bos & Vaughn, 1998). As with problems in communicating clearly, problems in using language appropriately can seriously impede students' social development and peer relationships. General education teachers can intervene in the classroom to help such students socially.

Early language development forms the underpinning for much of the academic learning that comes when students go to school. It is not surprising, then, that students with speech and language disorders are likely to have trouble with academics as well. Problems with sounds can result in students having difficulties acquiring word analysis and spelling skills. Receptive language problems can make comprehension very difficult and can result in trouble understanding mathematical terms such as *minus*, *regroup*, and *addend* and confusion sorting out words with multiple meanings, such as *carry* and *times* (Mercer, 1997). Language disabilities can seriously impede the content-area learning stressed in middle, junior high, and high school. In these settings, much information is provided orally using lecture formats, the vocabulary and concepts covered are much more abstract, and students are expected to learn with less support from the teacher. These task demands are difficult for students with language disorders.

Another part of learning independently is solving problems. Students with language disorders may have difficulty verbalizing the steps to solve a problem. For example, when a language-proficient student solves story problems, she talks to herself as follows: "First I need to find the key words. Okay, here they are. Now, do these key words tell me to add or subtract? I think they tell me to subtract because the problem asks me how many are left." A student with language problems cannot talk herself through problems.

Accommodations for Students with Communication Disorders

As discussed in Chapter 4, the INCLUDE strategy suggests that before you make adaptations, you carefully consider potential student problems in view of your instructional demands. For students with speech and language problems, note especially any areas in which students are required to understand oral language (for example, listening to a lecture or a set of verbal directions) or to communicate orally (for example, responding to teacher questions or interacting with classmates when working in cooperative groups). The following discussion highlights specific suggestions for working with students with speech and language disorders.

Create an atmosphere of acceptance. You need to help students who have difficulty expressing themselves believe they can communicate without worrying about

FYI

In remembering the distinction between receptive and expressive communication disorders, think of the root words *receive* and *express*.

Cultural Awareness

It is incorrect to view students as having communication disorders when they use ethnic or regional dialects, speak a form of nonstandard English learned at home, or are native speakers of languages other than English and have limited English proficiency.

Figure 6.2 Language Problems

Expressive Language Problems

1. Uses incorrect grammar or syntax ("They walk down together the hill"; "I go not to school").

2. Lacks specificity ("It's over there by the place over there").

3. Frequently hesitates ("You know, uhm, I would, uhm, well, er, like a, er, Coke").

4. Jumps from topic to topic ("What are feathers? Well, I like to go hunting with my uncle.").

5. Has limited use of vocabulary.

6. Has trouble finding the right word to communicate meaning (word finding).

7. Uses social language poorly (inability to change communication style to fit specific situations, to repair communication breakdowns, and to maintain the topic during a conversation).

8. Is afraid to ask questions, does not know what questions to ask, or does not know how to ask a question.

9. Repeats same information again and again in a conversation.

10. Has difficulty discussing abstract, temporal, or spatial concepts.

11. Often does not provide enough information to the listener (saying, "*We* had a big fight with *them*," when *we* and *them* were not explained).

Receptive Language Problems

1. Does not respond to questions appropriately.

2. Cannot think abstractly or comprehend abstractions as idioms ("mind sharp as a tack"; "eyes dancing in the dark").

3. Cannot retain information presented verbally.

4. Has difficulty following oral directions.

5. Cannot detect breakdowns in communication.

6. Misses parts of material presented verbally, particularly less concrete words such as articles (*the* book; *a* book) and auxiliary verbs and tense markers (He *was* going; She *is* going).

7. Cannot recall sequences of ideas presented orally.

8. May confuse the sounds of letters that are similar (*b, d; m, n*) or reverse the order of sounds and syllables in words (*was, saw*).

9. Has difficulty understanding humor or figurative language.

10. Has difficulty comprehending concepts showing quantity, function, comparative size, and temporal and spatial relationships.

11. Has difficulty comprehending compound and complex sentences.

S O U R C E S : *Adapting Instruction in General Education for Students with Communication Disorders,* by D. Barad, 1985, unpublished manuscript, DeKalb, IL: Northern Illinois University; and *Strategies for Teaching Students with Learning and Behavior Problems* (3rd ed.), by C. S. Bos and S. Vaughn, 1994. Copyright © 1994 by Allyn and Bacon. Reprinted by permission.

making mistakes. You can foster this nonjudgmental atmosphere in several ways. First, when students make an error, model the correct form instead of correcting their mistakes directly:

> *Teacher:* Kareem, what did Jules do with the frog?
>
> *Kareem:* Put pocket.
>
> *Teacher:* Oh. He put it in his pocket?
>
> *Kareem:* Yes.

Second, try to allow students who stutter or have other fluency problems more time to speak, and do not interrupt them or supply words that are difficult for them to pronounce. Offering praise or other reinforcement for successful efforts to communicate, as you would for your other students, is also helpful. Sometimes, you should praise even an attempt.

> *Teacher:* Anthony, what did you do when you went home yesterday?
>
> *Anthony:* Television.
>
> *Teacher:* Great, you told me one thing you did. You watched television.

Finally, try to minimize peer pressure. One effective way to do this is to model and reinforce tolerance of individual differences in your classroom.

Encourage listening and teach listening skills. Even though students spend more time listening than doing any other school activity, very little time is devoted to teaching listening skills (Mandlebaum & Wilson, 1989). Stressing listening is particularly important for students with receptive language disorders. First, listen carefully yourself and praise listening among your students. For example, when Ms. Hernandez listens to a student speak, she leans forward and nods. Many of her students copy these listening actions. Second, be sure to engage your students' attention before you begin speaking by increasing your proximity to the listeners, by giving direct instruction (such as, "Listen to what I'm going to say"), and by reducing competing stimuli (have only one activity going on at one time, or have only one person speak at a time). You can also use verbal, pictorial, or written advance organizers to cue students when to listen (for example, "When we get to number 3 on this list, I want you to listen extra carefully for an error I am going to make") (Lenz, Alley, & Schumaker, 1987; Robinson & Smith, 1981). Third, make oral material easier to understand and to remember by simplifying vocabulary, simplifying syntax, using high-frequency words, repeating important information, giving information in short segments using visual aids for emphasis, having students rehearse and summarize information, and using cues that signal when you are going to say something important (Mandlebaum & Wilson, 1989). Finally, teach listening skills directly. Provide practice on skills such as predicting what might be heard, following directions, appreciating language, identifying main ideas and supporting details, drawing inferences, differentiating fact from fiction, and analyzing information critically (Brent & Anderson, 1993).

When you speak, you can also enhance your students' listening skills by stressing words that are important to meaning. For example, say "He *hit* the *ball*" or "*He* hit the ball," depending on what you want to emphasize. Stressing inflectional patterns, such as using an upward inflection when asking a question, also helps students better understand what you are saying.

Connections

Using modeling, providing meaningful learning contexts, and developing other instructional methods are discussed in greater detail in Chapters 9–11.

Use modeling to expand students' language. You can expand the language of students with expressive language problems by adding relevant information to student statements:

> *Student:* John is nice.
>
> *Teacher:* Yes, he is very nice, and polite, too.

You can also expand language by broadening a minimal statement:

> *Student:* My shoe.
>
> *Teacher:* Your shoe is pretty.

Modeling to expand students' language is most effective when it is done as an ongoing part of your everyday communications with students.

Cultural Awareness

Teaching language in meaningful contexts is also an effective strategy for students with limited English proficiency. Strategies for building background information help all students comprehend what they read.

Provide many meaningful contexts for practicing speech and language skills.
The goal of successful language programs is to teach students to use appropriate language in a variety of social and academic situations both in and out of school. You can help students with all types of speech and language problems meet that goal by providing as many opportunities as possible to practice language skills within meaningful contexts (Hardman, Drew, Egan, & Winson, 1999). Practice helps students refine language skills and make them more natural and automatic. When students practice in many different contexts, they can apply what they learn more readily. For example, Ms. Crum just taught her class the meaning of the word *ironic*. During health class, the students discussed the irony of the government warning people against fat consumption and then funding school lunches that are high in fat. During a trip to the museum, Ms. Crum pointed out the irony of the guard telling them to be quiet when he was wearing shoes that squeaked loudly when he walked.

To help students develop communication skills, provide many "safe" and meaningful contexts for students to learn and practice listening skills, speaking skills, interaction skills, and self-expression skills. What are some specific strategies for teaching students with communication disorders?

It is also helpful to encourage students with communication disorders to talk about events and experiences in their environment, describing them in as much detail as possible (Hardman et al., 1999). For example, Ms. Cusak, a first-grade teacher, starts every Monday by having two students tell about something they did over the weekend. Mr. Drake, a sixth-grade teacher, uses a "Saturday Night Live" format whereby students in his class act out something funny that happened to them over the weekend.

Finally, whenever possible, instruction should be embedded in the context of functional areas. For example, in Ms. Taylor's consumer math class, she has students go out to appliance stores, talk to salespeople about service contracts, and then describe and compare the various service contracts that are available. In Ms. Ellen's second-grade class, students invite and converse with classroom visitors.

Check Your Learning

What are the differences between language disorders and speech disorders? How can you modify instruction to promote success among students with communication disorders?

What Are the Learning Needs of Students with Learning and Behavior Disabilities?

Students with learning and behavior disabilities have learning disabilities, emotional disturbance, and mild cognitive disabilities. These are the students who are most likely to be included in your classroom, because they comprise more than 80 percent of all students with disabilities in the United States (U.S. Department of Education, 1999). Students with **learning disabilities** are students who achieve less academically because they have trouble with processing, organizing, and applying academic information. Students with learning disabilities are of normal intelligence, have presumably received adequate instruction, and have not been shown to be sensory impaired, emotionally disturbed, or environmentally disadvantaged. Students with **mild cognitive disabilities** are students who have some difficulty meeting the academic and social demands of general education classrooms, due in large part to below-average intellectual functioning (i.e., 55–70 on an IQ test). Students with mild cognitive disabilities can meet at least some of the academic and social demands of general education classrooms. Students with **emotional disturbance** are of average intelligence but have problems learning primarily because of external (acting out; poor interpersonal skills) and/or internal (anxiety; depression) behavioral adjustment problems.

Students with learning disabilities, mild cognitive disabilities, and emotional disturbances differ in a number of ways (Hallahan & Kauffman, 2000). The behavior problems of students with emotional disturbance are more severe, and students with mild cognitive disabilities have lower levels of measured intelligence. Students with learning disabilities may have more pronounced learning strengths and weaknesses than students with mild cognitive disabilities, who are likely to show lower performance in all areas. Still, the academic and social characteristics of students with these disabilities overlap considerably. All three groups may experience significant problems in academic achievement, classroom behavior, and peer relations.

The causes of these disabilities are largely unknown because learning and behavior result from a complex interaction between students' individual characteristics, the various settings in which they learn, and the tasks or other demands they face in those settings (Ysseldyke, Algozzine, & Thurlow, 2000). It is often difficult to identify the primary cause of a learning or behavior problem. For example,

FYI

Students with emotional disturbance often are referred to as **behavior disordered (BD)**. Another term for students with mild cognitive disabilities is **educable mentally handicapped (EMH)**.

Research Note

Glassberg, Hooper, and Mattison (1999) studied a sample of 233 students aged 6–16 years who were newly identified with behavior disorders to see how many of them also had learning disabilities. Overall, they found that 53 percent of the students had a learning disability based on criteria for at least one of four accepted definitions for learning disabilities.

FYI

Some advocacy groups prefer the term *specific learning disability* because it emphasizes that only certain learning processes are affected.

Cultural Awareness

African American students, especially those in urban middle schools, are at risk of being overidentified for behavior disorders; children from Hispanic or Asian American families are at risk of underidentification (Peterson & Ishi-Jordan, 1994). Why do you think this is so?

WWW Resources

The Learning Disabilities Association (LDA) is a helpful support group for parents of students with learning disabilities. Valuable information on parental rights and tips for parenting are available on their website at http://www.ldanatl.org.

Cultural Awareness

Research from the National Institute of Child Health and Human Development has shown that reading disabilities affect boys and girls at roughly the same rate. Boys, however, are more likely to be referred for treatment, as they are more likely to get teacher's attention by misbehaving. Girls may escape the teacher's attention, as they may withdraw into quiet daydreaming (Bock, 1999).

Thomas is lagging behind his classmates in acquiring a sight-word vocabulary in reading. Learning disabilities tend to run in his family, but Thomas's school district also changed from a basal to a literature-based reading program last year. In addition, Thomas's parents separated in the middle of the school year and divorced several months later. Why was Thomas behind in reading? Was it heredity? Was it the new reading program? Was it his parents' marital problems? All these factors may have contributed to Thomas's problem.

The most important reason students with high-incidence disabilities are grouped together for discussion is that whatever behaviors they exhibit and whatever the possible causes of these behaviors, students benefit from the same instructional practices (Algozzine, Ysseldyke, & Campbell, 1994; Christenson, Ysseldyke, & Thurlow, 1989). These practices are introduced in this chapter and covered in considerable depth throughout the rest of this book. For example, Raeanna has a mild cognitive disability. She has difficulty reading her classmates' social cues. As a result, she does not recognize when she is acting too aggressively with her classmates and often is rejected by many of them. Del is a student with learning disabilities. He also has trouble reading the social cues of his peers. Although Raeanna and Del may learn new social skills at different rates, both can benefit from social skills training that provides considerable guided practice and feedback on how to read social cues.

The point to remember is that categorical labels are not particularly useful in describing specific students or developing instructional programs for them (Hardman et al., 1999). For example, both Damon and Aretha have learning disabilities, yet their areas of difficulty differ. Damon has a severe reading problem but excels in mathematics and various computer applications. Aretha, on the other hand, is reading at grade level but has significant problems with math. Though both students are categorized as having learning disabilities, they have very different needs. You must analyze each individual student's needs and then make adaptations as necessary. This individualization is at the heart of the INCLUDE strategy introduced in Chapter 4.

Students with learning and behavior disabilities have many learning needs. They have difficulty acquiring basic skills in the areas of reading, math, and written language. They also may lack skills necessary for efficient learning, such as attending to task, memory, independent learning skills, language skills, reasoning, conceptualization and generalization, motor, and school survival skills.

Reading Skills

Students with learning and behavior disabilities have two major types of reading problems: **decoding** and **comprehension.** Decoding problems involve the skills of identifying words accurately and fluently. They are most readily observed when students read orally, mispronouncing words, substituting one word for another, or omitting words (Lerner, 2000). Students with reading fluency problems can read words accurately but do not recognize them quickly enough. They read slowly, in a word-by-word fashion, without grouping words together meaningfully (Lerner, 2000). Many of these reading decoding problems are exemplified in the following oral reading sample by a student with a learning disability.

> Then Ford had uh other i . . . a better idea. Take the worrrk to the men. He deee. . . . A long rope was hooked onto the car . . . wheels. . . . There's no rope on there. The rope pulled the car . . . auto . . . the white wheels

along . . . pulled the car all along the way. Men stood still. Putting on car parts. Everybody man . . . put on, on, a few parts. Down the assembly line went the car. The assembly line saved . . . time. Cars costed still less to buh . . . bull . . . d . . . build. Ford cuts their prices on the Model T again. (Hallahan, Kauffman, & Lloyd, 1985, p. 203)

Here is the actual passage the student was to read:

Then Ford had another idea. Take the work to the men, he decided. A long rope was hooked onto a car axle and wheels. The rope pulled the axle and wheels along. All along the way, men stood still putting on car parts. Down the assembly line went the car. The assembly line saved more time. Cars cost still less to build. Ford cut the price on the Model T again. (Hallahan et al., 1985, p. 203)

Students who have serious difficulties decoding written words are sometimes referred to as having *dyslexia*. The Professional Edge on page 208 discusses the meaning of this term and suggests instructional approaches.

Students with learning and behavior disabilities often have problems comprehending stories in the elementary grades and content-area textbooks and advanced literature in the upper grades. Although these difficulties result in part from poor decoding skills, they may also occur because these students lack strategies for identifying the key elements of stories and content-area texts. For example, Todd's teacher asked him questions about a book he had just read as part of his classroom literature program. Todd was unable to tell her where the story took place (setting) or the lesson of the story (moral) because the answers to these questions were not directly stated in the story and Todd lacked the necessary inference strategies to figure them out. Patsy was unable to answer a study question comparing the causes of World Wars I and II because she could not locate key words, such as *differences* and *similarities*. In addition, students may not be able to adjust their reading rate to allow for skimming a section of text for key information or for reading more slowly and intensively to answer specific questions. For example, Dennis takes a lot of time to locate key dates in his history book because he thinks he needs to read every word in the chapter while he is looking for the dates.

Written Language Skills

The **written language difficulties** of students with learning and behavior disabilities include handwriting, spelling, and written expression. Handwriting problems can be caused by a lack of fine motor coordination, failure to attend to task, inability to perceive and/or remember visual images accurately (Smith, 1997), and inadequate handwriting instruction in the classroom (Graham, 1999). Students may have problems in the areas of letter formation (is the letter recognizable?), size, alignment, slant, line quality (heaviness or lightness of lines), straightness, and spacing (too little or too much between letters, words, and lines).

Students with learning and behavior disabilities also have trouble with spelling. The English language consists largely of three types of words: those that can be spelled phonetically, those that can be spelled by following certain linguistic rules, and those that are irregular. For example, the words *cats*, *construction*, and *retell* can be spelled correctly by applying phonics generalizations related to consonants, consonant

Research Note

Research shows that fewer than one child in eight who is failing to read by the end of first grade ever catches up to grade level (Juel, 1988). Many at-risk readers benefit from early intervention that includes the explicit teaching of our letter–sound system, often referred to as *phonics* (Lyon, 1998).

Connections

Assessment strategies to identify at-risk readers in kindergarten and first grade are described in the Professional Edge in Chapter 8 on page 292.

FYI

Graham (1999) suggests that you can make spelling engaging by including student choice as part of the selection and study of words, allowing peers to study and work together, helping students discover patterns in the spelling of words, and using games to learn and practice spelling skill approaches.

WWW Resources

The website for LD in Depth: Individualized Education Program, www. ldonline.org/ld_indepth/ iep/iep.html, provides many links to help parents and teachers develop IEPs.

Understanding Dyslexia

The term *dyslexia* is used a lot these days. You hear that a friend's child has dyslexia, or you see a person who is dyslexic on television, or you read that Albert Einstein and Thomas Edison had dyslexia. The word *dyslexia*, which means developmental word blindness, has a medical sound to it, so you may automatically assume that it is medically based. Yet we really do not know what dyslexia is. Some people believe dyslexia is a brain disorder, that people with dyslexia have a different brain structure that leads to difficulties in processing oral and visual linguistic information, and that this faulty brain structure is genetically based (Flowers, 1993). Although research using more sophisticated technology provides some support for a genetic, neurological basis for reading problems (Filipek, 1995; Pennington, 1995; Shaywitz, Pugh, Jenner, Fulbright, Fletcher, Gore, & Shaywitz, 2000), the evidence is still largely circumstantial (Kender & Kender, 1998). In any case, knowing the cause of severe reading problems is one thing; knowing what to do to help students who have these problems is another altogether. Perhaps the best way to describe dyslexia at this point is to say that it is a term used to describe any serious reading difficulty.

Put very simply, students with dyslexia have serious problems learning to read despite normal intelligence, normal opportunities to learn to read, and an adequate home environment. Although the precise organic cause of dyslexia is unknown, considerable evidence suggests that reading problems associated with dyslexia are phonologically based (Lyon, 1998; Stanovich & Siegel, 1994). Students with dyslexia have difficulty developing phonemic awareness, the understanding that spoken words are comprised of sounds. Phonemic awareness problems make it hard for them to link speech sounds to letters, ultimately leading to slow, labored reading characterized by frequent starts and stops and multiple mispronunciations. Students with dyslexia also have comprehension problems largely because the struggle for them to identify words leaves little energy for understanding what they read.

Students with dyslexia also have trouble with the basic elements of written language, such as spelling and sentence and paragraph construction. Finally, students with dyslexia may have difficulty under-standing representational systems, such as telling time, directions, and seasons (Bryan & Bryan, 1986). Dyslexia commonly is considered a type of learning disability, and students with dyslexia are served under the learning disability classification of IDEA.

It is important to identify students with dyslexia or other severe reading disabilities early, before they fall far behind their peers in word-recognition reading skills. Students who appear to be learning letter names, sounds, and sight words at a significantly slower rate than their classmates are at risk for developing later reading problems.

FROM THE RESEARCH

A large body of research (Blackman, 2000; Oakland, Black, Stanford, Nussbaum, & Balise, 1998; Snow, Burns, & Griffin, 1998; Swanson, 2000) shows that many students with severe reading disabilities benefit from a beginning reading program that includes the following elements:

1. **Direct instruction in language analysis.** For example, students need to be taught skills in sound segmentation or in orally breaking down words into their component sounds.

2. **A highly structured phonics program.** This program should teach the alphabetic code directly and systematically using a simple-to-complex sequence of skills, teaching regularity before irregularity, and discouraging guessing.

3. **Writing and reading instruction in combination.** Students need to be writing the words they are reading.

4. **Intensive instruction.** Reading instruction for at-risk students should include large amounts of practice in materials that contain words they are able to decode.

5. **Teaching for automaticity.** Students must be given enough practice so that they are able to read both accurately and fluently.

For students who are dyslexic, visit Dylsexia: The Gift, at www.dyslexia.com, for curriculum aids, a bookstore, discussion board, and links to further information.

blends (*str*), vowels, root words (*tell*), prefixes (*re*), and suffixes (*ion, s*). The word *babies* can be spelled by applying the linguistic rule of changing *y* to *i* and adding *es*. Words such as *said, where*, and *through* are irregular and can be spelled only by remembering what they look like. Students with learning and behavior disabilities may have trouble with all three types of words.

Students with learning and behavior disabilities have two major types of written expression problems: product problems and process problems (Isaacson, 1987; Ellis & Colvert, 1996). Their written products are often verb–object sentences, characterized by few words, incomplete sentences, overuse of simple subject–verb constructions, repetitious use of high-frequency words, a disregard for audience, poor organization and structure, and many mechanical errors, such as misspellings, incorrect use of punctuation and capital letters, and faulty subject–verb agreements and choice of pronouns (Isaacson, 1987).

These students also have trouble with the overall process of written communication. Their approach to writing shows little systematic planning, great difficulty putting ideas on paper because of a preoccupation with mechanics, failure to monitor writing, and little useful revision (Ellis & Colvert, 1996; Isaacson, 1987). A writing sample from a student who has a disability is shown in Figure 6.3. What types of product problems do you see in this sample? What process problems do you think might have led to these problems?

Math Skills

Math also can be problematic for students with learning and behavior disabilities. Their problems tend to occur in eight key areas (Cawley, Parmar, Yan, & Miller, 1998; Smith, 1997; Strang & Rourke, 1985).

1. **Spatial organization.** Students may be unable to align numbers in columns, may reverse numbers (write a 9 backwards; read 52 as 25), or may subtract the top number from the bottom number in a subtraction problem such as

$$\begin{array}{r} 75 \\ -39 \\ \hline 44 \end{array}$$

2. **Alertness to visual detail.** Students misread mathematical signs or forget to use dollar signs and decimals when necessary.

3. **Procedural errors.** Students miss a step in solving a problem. For example, they may forget to add the carried number in an addition problem or subtract from the regrouped number in a subtraction problem:

$$\begin{array}{r} 29 \\ +53 \\ \hline 72 \end{array} \qquad \begin{array}{r} 41 \\ -28 \\ \hline 23 \end{array}$$

4. **Failure to shift mind set from one problem type to another.** Students solve problems of one type but, when required to solve another type of problem, inappropriately solve them in the way they did the first type. For example, Kristy just completed several word problems that required addition. The next problem required subtraction, but she continued to use addition.

FYI

Teachers often mistake natural stages of child and adolescent development for signs of the presence of learning disabilities or emotional problems. Reversing letters or confusing *b* and *d*, for example, is common among children first learning to write.

Connections

Specific strategies for teaching written language skills are given in Chapter 10.

FYI

Adaptations of materials and formats for math instruction include keeping models on the board, providing graph paper to align problems, and using visual cues, such as color-coded or boldfaced signs and arrows, as reminders of direction, and frames, to set off problems and answers.

Figure 6.3 **Written Expression Sample of a 14-Year-Old Student with a Learning Disability**

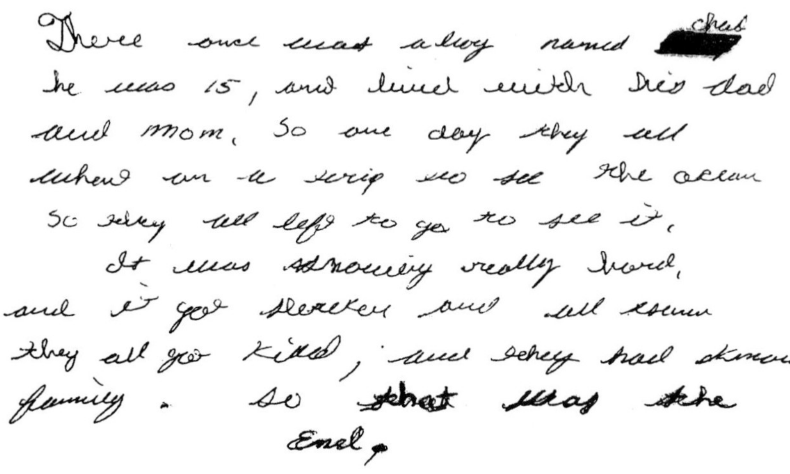

5. **Difficulty forming numbers correctly.** Students' numbers are too large or poorly formed, which makes solving computational problems awkward, particularly when the students are unable to read their own numbers.

6. **Difficulty with memory.** Students are frequently unable to recall basic math facts.

7. **Problems with mathematical judgment and reasoning.** Students are unaware when their responses are unreasonable. For example, they do not see the obvious errors in 9 − 6 = 15 or 4 + 3 = 43. They may also have trouble solving word problems. For example, they may be unable to decide whether to add or subtract in a word problem.

8. **Problems with mathematical language.** Students may have difficulty with the meanings of key mathematical terms such as *regroup*, *place value*, or *minus* (Cawley, Fitzmaurice, Shaw, Kahn, & Bates, 1979). They may also have trouble participating in oral drills or verbalizing the steps in solving word or computational problems (Cawley, Miller, & School, 1987).

Students from culturally and linguistically diverse backgrounds may have additional problems learning math skills. Some potential trouble spots and strategies for dealing with these trouble spots are shown in the Professional Edge. In addition, the Technology Notes feature on pages 212–213 presents a multimedia program that fosters student skills in technology, communication, and problem solving within the area of mathematics.

Connections

Approaches to adapting instruction for students with ADHD, which are covered in Chapter 7, are also applicable here.

Learning Skills

Students with learning and behavior disabilities have difficulty performing skills that could help them learn more readily. One such skill is attention. Students may have difficulty coming to attention or understanding task requirements (Hallahan et al.,

Professional Edge

Adapting Math Instruction for Students Who Are Linguistically and Culturally Different

Math can be a challenging subject for all students, including students with learning and behavioral difficulties. Students from linguistically and culturally diverse backgrounds may face additional challenges when learning math. In the following table, Scott and Raborn (1996) present some potential trouble spots and suggested strategies for teaching math to students from linguistically and culturally diverse backgrounds.

Trouble Spot	Recommendation
Learning a new language	• Determine the student's level of proficiency in both English and the native language.
	• Assess math abilities in both languages.
	• If a student is stronger in math than in English, provide math instruction in the primary language.
	• Listen to the words you most frequently use in teaching math. Work together with the ESL teacher to help the student learn these words or to help you learn them in the student's language.
	• Use a variety of ways to communicate such as gesturing, drawing sketches, writing basic vocabulary and procedures, rewording, and providing more details.
	• Provide time and activities that will allow students to practice the English language and the language of math.
Cultural differences	• Use story problem situations that are relevant to students' personal cultural indentity (e.g., ethnicity, gender, geographical region, age).
	• Share examples of the mathematical heritage of students' cultures (e.g., folk art, African and Native American probability games, measurement systems).
	• Involve family and community members in multicultural math.
Tricky vocabulary	• Use concrete activities to teach new vocabulary and the language of math.
	• Use only as many technical words as are necessary to ensure understanding.
	• Give more information in a variety of ways to help students understand new vocabulary.
	• Develop a picture file; purchase or have students make a picture dictionary of math terms and frequently used vocabulary.
Symbolic language	• Allow students to draw pictures, diagrams, or graphic organizers to represent story problems.
	• Make clear the meanings and function of symbols.
	• Point out the interchangeable nature of operations.
	• In algebra, teach students to translate phrases to mathematical expressions.
Level of abstraction and memory	• Allow students to develop mathematical relationships using concrete representations accompanied by verbal descriptions.
	• Develop mathematical understanding from concrete to abstract form.
	• Use visual and kinesthetic cues to strengthen memory.
	• Keep distractions to a minimum.

S O U R C E : From "Realizing the Gifts of Diversity Among Students with Learning Disabilities," by P. Scott and D. Raborn, 1996, *LD Forum, 21*(2), pp. 10–18. Reprinted by permission of the Council of Learning Disabilities.

[Technology Notes]

Teaching Mathematics in a Multimedia Environment

Bottge and Hasselbring (1999) have developed a mutimedia program that fosters student skills in technology, communication, and problem solving within the subject of mathematics. The program uses video-based mathematical "anchors" to improve students' problem-solving ability. Anchors are real-world problems depicted in short dramatic videos within authentic contexts. The anchors focus student attention on problems confronting the main character of the story. Students must clearly describe the problem situation and then search for possible solutions, just as ordinary persons solve problems in their lives. The theory behind the anchors is that real-life situations motivate students to apply mathematics in meaningful contexts. In addition, working on real-life problems is more understandable than working with traditional story problems, particularly for students with reading problems. Students may spend up to five class periods trying to solve the overall problem. Typically, the 7–20-minute anchors are presented using videodisc technology that allows students to search and retrieve information almost immediately. The most popular setup for classroom use is a large-screen monitor and a videodisc player operated with a handheld controller (Bottge & Hasselbring, 1999, p. 113).

One example of such anchor software is entitled Bart's Pet Project, which involves two boys who want to buy a pet and keep it in a cage. The problem is that they have only enough money to buy one pet and have none left over to buy a ready-made cage. When teaching using this anchor, the students are first shown how to operate the videodisc equipment. This is done by showing them the scenario and then questioning them to be sure they understand the challenge. Students are then directed to solve two problems. First they must decide which pet they can afford. Then they must figure out how to make a cage with the money they have left. The solution requires several skills, including computing whole numbers, adding fractions, counting money, reading a tape measure, and interpreting a schematic drawing.

An important aspect of problem solving is that students show how they arrive at a solution. To help them do this, they are given "proof sheets" that help them organize their thoughts and allow the teacher to see how they are progressing. The teacher makes sure that students are able to complete these sheets prior to solving the problem on their own. (See the sample proof sheet in Figure 6.4.)

Students are told that they are free to use whatever resources they can find when solving the anchor problems, just as they would in solving any important problem. An important role of the teacher at this time is to closely monitor student discussions to ensure that they stay on task and do not wander too far from the central question. If this happens, the teacher needs to steer them back on track by redirecting student questions to justify their hypotheses. The effectiveness of the anchors depends largely on the ability of the teacher to provide such redirection. When students have solved the entire problem, they record all their problem-solving steps on the procedural checklist in Figure 6.5. Bottge and Hasselbring (1999) suggest that students can also report their findings in technology-based formats such as Hyperstudio (1996), a simple yet powerful tool that integrates sound, graphics, and text into a sophisticated presentation.

Bottge and Hasselbring (1999) reported positive findings for the middle school students with disabilities who participated in Bart's Pet Project. The students improved their computation skills, such as adding whole numbers and fractions; demonstrated their ability to work together in groups, drew on each other's suggestions and reasoning skills to solve a complex problem, and showed persistence in sticking to a task. Video anchors more sophisticated than Bart's Pet Project have been shown to be effective with high school students with disabilities and general education elementary students (Learning and Technology Center, Vanderbilt University, 1996).

Figure 6.4 Video Anchor Problem-Solving Proof Sheet

| Name: _____ Page _____ |
| Videodisc: _____ |

Important Information (in words)	Frame Number	Calculations

SOURCE: From "Teaching Mathematics to Adolescents with Disabilities in a Multimedia Environment," by B. A. Bottge and T. S. Hasselbring, 1999, *Intervention in School and Clinic, 35,* pp. 113–116. Copyright © 1999 by PRO-ED, Inc. Reprinted with permission.

Figure 6.5 Procedural Checklist

Procedural Checklist for "Bart's Pet Project"				
Money	Money Available $5.00 bill 1.00 bill 1.00 bill .50 quarters .10 dime .05 nickel + .03 pennies $7.68	$ 7.68 −5.99 $ 1.69	Store-bought cage/tank Not feasible	
Pet prices	Parakeet $9.95 Not feasible	Snake $99.95 Not feasible	Iguana $69.95 Not feasible	Rat $5.99
Cage option #1	Has 55¼" 20¾ 20¾ +13 54½"	Has 47" 15½ 15½ +15½ 46½"	Needs 20¾ 20¾ 15½ 13 13 +13 96"	
Cage option #2	Has 55¼" 13 13 13 +15½ 54½"	Has 47" 15½ 15½ +15½ 46½"	Needs 20¾ 20¾ 20¾ 20¾ +13 96"	
Cage option #3	Has 55¼" 20¾ 20¾ +13 54½"	Has 47¼" 20¾ 13 +13 46¾"	Needs 20¾ 15½ 15½ 15½ 15½ +13 95¾"	
Wood	Needs 96" 96" = 8'	8' × 2 × 2 = $1.20	$1.69 −1.20 $ .49 change	

SOURCE: From "Teaching Mathematics to Adolescents with Disabilities in a Multimedia Environment," by B. A. Bottge and T. S. Hasselbring, 1999, *Intervention in School and Clinic, 35,* pp. 113–116. Copyright © 1999 by PRO-ED, Inc. Reprinted with permission.

1999). For example, Janice frequently fails essay tests; she is unable to focus on key words in the questions to help her organize a response. As a result, she loses valuable writing time just staring at the question and not knowing how to begin. Benito misses important information at the beginning of science lectures because he takes 5 minutes to attend to the teacher's presentation. Students may also have trouble focusing on the important aspects of tasks. For example, Anita can tell you the color of her teacher's tie or the kind of belt he is wearing, but nothing about the information he is presenting. When Arman tries to solve word problems in math, he is unable to tell the difference between information that is needed and not needed to solve the problem. Finally, students with learning and behavior disabilities may have trouble sticking to a task once they have started it.

Memory problems may also make learning difficult for students (Wong, 1996). Some problems occur when information is first learned. For example, Carla cannot remember information when it is presented just once. Sal has practiced math facts many times but still cannot remember some of them. Students may also fail to retain what they learn. For example, Abby had learned addition facts in the fall but remembered only about 50 percent of them when tested in the spring. Finally, students sometimes learn something but do not remember to use the information to solve problems or to learn other information. For example, a student who learned a note-taking strategy in a resource room failed to use the strategy in her content-area classes.

Students with learning and behavior disabilities may have trouble organizing and interpreting oral and visual information despite adequate hearing and visual skills (Lerner, 2000). For example, Rodney is a student with a learning disability who has trouble with visual tasks. He frequently loses his place while reading and copying; has trouble reading and copying from the chalkboard; does not notice details on pictures, maps, and photographs; is confused by worksheets containing a great deal of visual information; and often cannot remember what he has seen. LaTonya, on the other hand, has trouble with auditory tasks. She has difficulty following oral directions, differentiating between fine differences in sounds (*e/i; bean/been*), taking notes during lectures, and remembering what she has heard.

Students also may lack **reasoning** skills necessary for success in school. Important reasoning skills include reading comprehension, generalization (the ability to recognize similarities across objects, events, or vocabulary), adequate background and vocabulary knowledge, induction (figuring out a rule or principle based on a series of situations), and sequencing (detecting relationships among stimuli) (Salvia & Ysseldyke, 1998). For example, Stu has difficulty understanding a lecture on the civil rights movement because he lacks necessary background information; he is unsure what a civil right is. Tamara has trouble recognizing a relationship on her own, even after repeated examples; her teacher presented five examples of how to add *s* to words that end in *y*, but Tamara still could not figure out the rule.

Some students with learning and behavior disabilities may have motor coordination and fine motor impairments (Lerner, 2000). For example, Denise is a first-grade student who has some fine motor and coordination problems. She has trouble using scissors, coloring within the lines, tying her shoes, and printing letters and numbers. Cal is in third grade. His handwriting is often illegible and messy. He is also uncoordinated at sports, which has limited his opportunities for social interaction on the playground because he is never selected to play on a team.

Independent learning also can be a challenge for students with learning and behavior disabilities. They have been referred to as **passive learners,** meaning that

---

Connections

Specific strategies for helping students remember information are described in Chapter 11.

Research Note

Many educators claim that students have certain learning preferences or styles and that teaching to accommodate these styles enhances instruction, particularly in reading. In a review of more than 40 research studies on learning styles, Kavale and Forness (1987) found no evidence for teaching based on learning styles. Yates (1999), in a more recent review of the literature, concluded that learning style questionnaires cannot reliably differentiate instructional groups, have not generated a consistent body of research verifying their effectiveness, and may distract teachers from approaches that do have a sound research base. Our advice is to meet individual needs by always teaching to as many senses as possible.

they do not believe in their own abilities; have limited knowledge of problem-solving strategies; and even when they know a strategy, cannot tell when it is supposed to be used (Hallahan et al., 1999; Lerner, 2000). Being a passive learner is particularly problematic in the upper grades, where more student independence is expected. For example, when LaVerne reads her science textbook, she does not realize when she comes across information that she does not understand. So instead of employing a strategy to solve this problem, such as rereading, checking the chapter summary, or asking for help, she never learns the information. As a result she is doing poorly in the class. When Darrell studies for tests, he reads quickly through his text and notes, but does not use, strategies for remembering information, such as asking himself questions, saying the information to himself, or grouping into meaningful pieces the information he needs to learn.

Students with learning and behavior disabilities may also have problems in the area of **academic survival skills** such as attending school regularly, being organized, completing tasks in and out of school, being independent, taking an interest in school, and displaying positive interpersonal skills with peers and adults (Brown, Kerr, Zigmond, & Harris, 1984). For example, Duane is failing in school because he rarely shows up for class; when he does attend class, he sits in the back of the room and displays an obvious lack of interest. Nicole is always late for class and never completes her homework. Her teachers think she does not care about school at all.

As you can see, students with learning and behavior disabilities have problems in a number of academic and learning areas. In the Special Emphasis On . . . feature on pages 216–217, strategies for working with these students in the area of art are described. Some parents and teachers have tried unproven interventions in search of quick fixes for students with learning and behavior disabilities. The issue of using unproven, controversial therapies is discussed in the Professional Edge on pages 218–219.

Check Your Learning

What learning needs might students with learning and behavior disabilities share? How might you modify instruction for basic academic skills for these students?

What Are the Social and Emotional Needs of Students with Learning and Behavior Disabilities?

Considering students' social needs is crucial because students who have social adjustment problems in school are at risk for academic problems (Epstein, Kinder, & Bursuck, 1989; Lane, 1999) as well as serious adjustment problems when they leave school (Cowen et al., 1973). Students with learning and behavior disabilities may have needs in several social areas, including classroom conduct, interpersonal skills, and personal and psychological adjustment.

Students with learning and behavior disabilities may engage in a number of aggressive or disruptive behaviors in class, including hitting, fighting, teasing, hyperactivity, yelling, refusing to comply with requests, crying, destructiveness, vandalism, and extortion (Deitz & Ormsby, 1992; Hallahan & Kauffman, 2000). Although many of these behaviors may be exhibited by all children at one time or another, the classroom conduct of students with behavior disorders is viewed by teachers as abnormal, and their behavior has a negative impact on the other students in class (Cullinan, Epstein, & Lloyd, 1983). For example, Kenneth is an adolescent with learning and behavior problems. His father died last year, and his mother has been working two jobs just to make ends meet. Kenneth has begun to hang out with a rougher crowd

FYI

Estimates of the number of students with learning disabilities who are at risk for social problems range from 34 to 59 percent (Bryan, 1997).

Connections

The use of strategies for responding to student behavior, including punishment, is the topic of Chapter 12.

Special Emphasis On . . .

Inclusive Practices in Art, Music, and Physical Education

The visual arts, music, and physical education have always been considered disciplines that reach out to all students, including those who have disabilities. Visual arts, physical education, and music teachers can use the INCLUDE strategy to make commonsense adaptations for students with special needs without having to water down the standard curriculum. Specific adaptations suggested by Pappalardo (1999) for students with learning, behavior, emotional, mild cognitive, and communication problems are described in the following lists. These adaptations can also be helpful for students in vocational classes.

Learning Problems

- Establish and maintain consistent routines (time patterns).
- Give directions in single units. For instance, consider a teacher saying: "Take out your journal, and using pencil and white paper, copy the vocabulary words in column 1." Instead, use a short sentence for each unit of the directions: "Take out your journal. Now open to a clean page and find vocabulary column 1" (demonstrate). "Now take your pencil and copy the words into your journal." This rule applies to older students as well as to younger ones.
- Provide secluded and/or quiet areas for students with distractibility problems.

- Offer a choice of media for exploring techniques and skills. Allow for individual needs.
- Be aware of low frustration levels. Help the student address the problem and deal with it.
- Be positive and praise when necessary, always considering a student's self-esteem.
- Use a buddy or an aide to help keep the student on task. Be sure the person helps the student with a disability understand the problem but does not do the task for him or her.

Behavior Problems

- Be as positive as possible.
- Give the student activities that are within his or her capabilities. Provide positive reinforcement when appropriate and possible.
- Follow exactly the disciplinary plan specified by support personnel and administration.
- Establish procedures, rules, and expectations.

Emotional Problems

- Have lessons as structured as possible but flexible, allowing for individual expression.
- Give the student small amounts of work at a time, with praise at each step to encourage completion.

and has been getting into fights in school. He has also been talking back to his teachers frequently and refusing to comply with their demands. Kenneth's behavior has gotten so bad that other students and their parents are complaining about it to the teacher. Some cautions involved in disciplining students like Kenneth are presented in the Professional Edge on pages 220–221.

Interpersonal Skills

Students with learning and behavior disabilities are likely to have difficulty in social relations with their peers. Evidence for these problems comes from more than 20 years of research showing that these students have fewer friends, are more likely to

- Provide the student with activities for which he or she is able to expend energy positively in order to achieve success quickly, foster confidence, and build on that confidence.
- Have a minimum of supplies within reach, particularly if they can be spilled or broken.
- Give verbal and nonverbal recognition for efforts. Give the student extra attention when he or she responds, but do not force attention on the student when he or she withdraws. Reward positive behavior with concrete or nonverbal (i.e., wink, smile) expression.
- Encourage group discussions on personal expression through art to help the student learn to express his or her emotions (anger, joy, sadness) in appropriate ways.
- Identify each person's individual space where the student feels safe and cared about.
- Establish procedures, rules, and expectations, and follow them consistently. Be prepared by planning alternatives and appropriate steps for discipline. If a student's behavior becomes too disruptive, send for help. Do not leave the group.
- Look at the student when you ask short questions. Listen attentively.

Mild Cognitive Problems

- Keep directions simple; break the task into progressive steps; demonstrate each task.

- Be patient and allow extra time to observe and think.
- Use repetition in directions and actions. Identify all materials verbally.
- Use concrete ideas and terms that are familiar to students; don't assume ability to generalize or associate from past experience.
- Allow and encourage students to do their own work; step-by-step procedures ensure this.
- Take a student's hands and guide him or her through the motions if the process is too difficult.
- Avoid paying attention to distractions.
- Encourage discussing music or art forms, how they were created, how they make you feel.
- Remember, students with mild cognitive problems will give honest, simple answers. Accept them with praise.

Communication Problems

- Be sure that he or she understands what is to be done.
- Use short, simple verbal directions and provide written ones as well.
- Clarify understandings, especially word meanings.
- Keep auditory and visual distractions to a minimum.
- Try to establish eye contact when conversing with him or her.
- Use visual images to explain a procedure.
- Use visual images created by the student to express his or her feelings or ideas.

be rejected or neglected by their peers (Bryan, 1997), and are frequently rated as socially troubled by their teachers and parents (Smith, 1997). Many of these problems can be traced to the failure of students to engage in socially appropriate behaviors or social skills in areas such as making friends, carrying on conversations, and dealing with conflict.

There are a number of explanations for why students have social skills problems. Some students may simply not know what to do in social situations. They may lack knowledge because they do not learn from naturally occurring models of social behavior at home or in school. Students also may have trouble reading **social cues** and may misinterpret the feelings of others (Bryan & Bryan, 1986). For example, a story was told recently about five boys sitting on the floor of the principal's office, waiting to be disciplined. Four of the boys were discussing failing or near-failing grades and

Cultural Awareness

Social skills are learned in cultural contexts. Teach your students about the variance in social behavior within all cultures and emphasize the notion that families and individuals experience their cultures in personal ways.

Professional Edge

Controversial Therapies in Learning and Behavior Disabilities: What Does the Research Say?

Being the parent or teacher of a student with learning disabilities is not easy. Students with learning disabilities often do not respond favorably to the first approach tried—or, for that matter, to the first several. Failure and frustration can lead to the search for miracle cures. This problem is compounded by the fact that journals that publish research about the effectiveness of various treatments are not normally read by parents and teachers. Unfortunately, this void is readily filled by a steady stream of information, much of it not substantiated by research, from popular books, lay magazines, television talk shows (Silver, 1998), and now the Internet.

As a teacher, you need to be well informed about these therapies so you can give parents reliable, up-to-date information when they come to you for advice. The best way to get this information is to read professional journals. Any treatment may work for a few students, but this is not the same as demonstrating effectiveness in a controlled research study. If you or a student's parents decide to use a controversial therapy, you must monitor its effectiveness carefully and discontinue it if necessary. Several controversial therapies are summarized here, including the latest research findings for their effectiveness.

Neurophysiological Retraining

In this group of approaches, learning difficulties are seen as the result of dysfunctions in the central nervous system that can be remediated by having students engage in specific sensory or motor activities. One common example of this approach is patterning (Doman & Delacato, 1968), in which students are taken back through earlier stages of development (creeping and crawling). Another approach is optometric visual training, in which students do eye exercises designed to improve their visual perception and hence their reading skills. A third approach, vestibular training, takes children through tasks involving spatial orientation, eye movements, and balance with the goal of improving their academic performance,

especially in reading. No research evidence suggests that patterning, optometric visual training, or vestibular training improve students' cognitive functioning or reading ability (Silver, 1998).

Diet Control Therapies

A number of therapies involve using diet to control hyperactivity and other learning disorders. One of these (Feingold, 1975) claimed to decrease student hyperactivity by eliminating various artificial flavors, colors, and preservatives from the student's diet. Most research studies have shown that the Feingold Diet is not effective in controlling hyperactivity (Smith, 1997). Others have suggested that refined sugars in the diet lead to hyperactivity. Again, these claims have not been proven by research (Barkley, 1995; Connors & Blouin, 1982/1983). Another diet therapy for learning disorders involves using megavitamins to treat emotional or cognitive disorders (Cott, 1977; 1985). This therapy has not been verified by research (American Academy of Pediatrics, 1976). Another theory purports that deficiencies in trace elements such as copper, zinc, magnesium, manganese, and chromium along with the more common elements of calcium, sodium, and iron cause learning disorders; but these claims remain unsubstantiated (Silver, 1998). Finally, one theory claims hypoglycemia (low blood sugar levels) causes learning disabilities. Clinical studies on this theory have been inconclusive (Rappaport, 1982/1983).

Scotopic Sensitivity Syndrome

This syndrome has been defined as a difficulty in efficiently processing light, which causes a reading disorder (Irlen, 1991; Lerner, 2000). Symptoms include abnormal sensitivity to light, blinking and squinting, red and watery eyes, frequent headaches, word blurriness, print instability, slow reading, skipping and rereading lines, and difficulty reading at length because of general eye strain and fatigue (Irlen, 1991). Following a screening test, students identified as having scotopic sensitivity are treated with plastic overlays or colored lenses, which can be expensive. Although many people treated with tinted lenses claim that the lenses eliminate their symptoms and help them read better, research shows that tests for scotopic sensitivity are flawed (Silver, 1998; Woerz & Maples, 1997), and the effects of the lenses have not been verified (Fletcher & Martinez, 1994). Caution is advised.

Allergies

Although there seems to be a relationship between allergies and brain functioning, no clear cause-and-effect relationship has yet to be established (Silver, 1998). Two persons who have written a lot about the relationship between allergies and learning disabilities and ADHD are Dr. Doris Rapp and Dr. William Crook. Dr. Rapp suggests the elimination of certain foods from the diet, such as milk, chocolate, eggs, wheat, corn, peanuts, pork, and sugar. She performs an "under-the-tongue" test (not validated) that she claims determines whether a child is allergic to any or all of these foods. Dr. Crook's recent work has focused on child reactions to a specific yeast and the development of specific behaviors following a yeast infection. According to Silver (1998), neither Crook nor Rapp support their findings with research. In addition, the established profession of pediatric allergies does not accept either of these treatments (Silver, 1998).

Controversial Therapies and the Internet

As the number of Internet sites created for specific disabilities or related health issues increases, so too does information about controversial therapies. Because information on the Internet is not reviewed for quality, Ira (2000) suggests that you do the following to determine the credibility of the various websites you visit.

1. Click on the About Us or Contact Us links or buttons at a website. These links may inform you of who is on the team of people running a particular website. Many sites, particularly those that want to prove their credibility, feature a page describing their background, history, and affiliations (the About Us section) and an address, e-mail, and phone number (the Contact Us section).

2. Try to establish links with other sites. Sites with reliably usable information may have endorsements from prominent special needs organizations or may have links to other websites with more information on the subject. Look for links to other associations or educational or even government-supported institutions related to the subject. The more independent sites that validate a recommendation, the more credible it is. The following are specific sites that may address doubts about the credibility of a particular controversial therapy.

   www.intedys.org   International Dyslexia Society

   www.ldanatl.org   The Learning Disabilities Association of America

   www.ncld.org   National Center for Learning Disabilities, Inc.

   www.cldinternational.org   The Council for Learning Disabilities

3. Ask friends and special needs associations to recommend websites that are informative. You can also e-mail people you think can clue you in on the credibility of a particular site.

4. Examine the content of the site for typographical or grammatical errors. As with books, magazines, and journals, credibility is often reflected in editorial excellence.

5. Check to see how often the site is updated. A site that is updated regularly with new research findings is most likely to be run by people interested in learning the truth rather than perpetuating their own point of view.

6. Check to be sure that a given finding has been validated by a credible, refereed research publication. Many of these publications are available on the web.

Professional Edge

Disciplining Students with Emotional Disturbance

Students with emotional disturbance sometimes behave in ways that disrupt the education of other students in the class or threaten their safety. When this happens, you may need to punish the student both to defuse the situation and to deter the student from acting out again. Punishment involves decreasing inappropriate behavior by either presenting something negative or taking away something positive. Although the courts have held that it is permissible to punish students with emotional disturbance, they have also held that the punishment must be delivered according to the following principles (Hartwig & Ruesch, 2000; Yell, 1990; Yell, Clyde, & Puyallup, 1995):

1. Teachers must be careful not to violate the due process rights of their students. This means that you need to communicate clearly to parents and students the behaviors you expect and the specific consequences for inappropriate behaviors. As needed, these items should be written in the student's IEP as part of the behavioral intervention plan.

2. When using punishment, do not violate the educational rights of students with emotional disturbance. Punishments such as expulsion, serial suspensions (successive, consecutive suspensions), prolonged in-school suspensions, and prolonged periods of time-out (removing students from classroom activities; see Chapter 12) constitute a change of placement and therefore cannot be done without due process. Temporary suspensions of 10 days or fewer are permissible; possession of a weapon or illegal drug, or

other extraordinary situations, can result in a suspension of up to 45 days. To expel a student for more than 10 days, a committee, including the student's parents, must determine that the misconduct had nothing to do with the disability. Finally, in the case of any suspension, students must be presented with the evidence against them and given the opportunity to present their side of the story.

3. The punishment of students with emotional disturbance must serve a legitimate purpose. Its use must serve an educational purpose, and clearly written guidelines for its use must exist. For example, Calvin is told that his verbal outbursts in class are preventing him and his classmates from learning. He is handed a written contract indicating that if he engages in more than one verbal outburst in class he will be required to sit in the back of the room and not participate in any classroom activities for 3 minutes.

4. The punishment procedure used must be reasonable according to these guidelines:

   a. Was the rule being enforced reasonable?

   b. Did the punishment match the offense?

   c. Was the punishment reasonable in light of the student's age and physical condition?

   d. Did the teacher deal out the punishment without malice or personal ill-will toward the student?

5. More intrusive punishments should be used only after more positive procedures have been tried. For

the trouble they were going to be in when the fifth boy, a student with a learning disability, chimed in to say that his grandparents were coming to visit the next week.

Other students may know what to do—but not do it. For example, some students with learning and behavior disabilities are **impulsive**; they act before they think. In Del's sessions with the school social worker, he is able to explain how he would act in various social situations, but in an actual social setting he gets nervous and acts without thinking. Other students may choose not to act on their knowledge because their attempts at socially appropriate behavior may have gone unrecognized and they would rather have negative recognition than no recognition at all. For ex-

example, Calvin's teacher had first tried giving Calvin 5 minutes of free time for *not* having a verbal outburst. When this approach did not work, he tried a different reward. When this positive procedure failed Calvin's teacher resorted to sitting him by himself for a period of time.

6. When you use punishment, keep records of all the procedures you try. Write down the behavior that precipitates the punishment, the procedures used, the length of time they were used, and the results. This information can help you make informed decisions about a student's behavior management program. It can also help clarify for parents why you used a particular procedure.

7. Punishment procedures for students with emotional disturbance should be carried out in conjunction with the special education teacher as agreed on in the student's IEP. Any major changes in punishment should be decided on only in collaboration with these same people. For example, Calvin's teacher consulted with Calvin's special ed-

Students who are experiencing emotional problems might be withdrawn, anxious, or depressed. What can you do to help these students in your classroom?

ucation teacher and parents each time he tried a different punishment procedure.

8. Remember that punishment should always be used in conjunction with positive consequences for appropriate behavior. The use of positive consequences can greatly reduce the need for using punishment in the future and can help build positive behaviors that benefit students throughout their lives.

ample, James was rebuffed by one group of students so often that he began to say nasty things to them just to provoke them. He also began to hang out with other students who chronically misbehaved because, according to James, "at least they appreciate me!" Finally, still other students may know what to do socially but lack the confidence to act on their knowledge in social situations, particularly if they have a history of social rejection or lack opportunities for social interactions. Consider Holly, a student who is socially withdrawn. Holly worked for a year with her school counselor to learn how to initiate a social activity with a friend but is afraid to try it out for fear of being rejected.

W W W R e s o u r c e s

The website for Internet Mental Health, www. mentalhealth.com, is a virtual encyclopedia of mental health information.

R e s e a r c h N o t e

Maag and Reid (1994) found the incidence of depression in a sample of 95 adolescents with learning disabilities to be about 10 percent. Carmanico et al. (2000) found that 59 percent of a sample of 185 adolescents with emotional disturbance were depressed.

Personal and Psychological Adjustment

Students with little success at academics and/or social relationships may have personal and psychological problems as well (Kerschner, 1990; Torgesen, 1991). One common personal problem is **self-image.** Students with learning and behavior disabilities often have a poor self-concept; they have little confidence in their own abilities (Licht, Kistner, Ozkaragoz, Shapiro, & Clausen, 1985). Poor self-image, in turn, can lead to **learned helplessness.** Students with learned helplessness see little relationship between their efforts and school or social success. When these students succeed, they attribute their success to luck; when they fail, they blame their failure on a lack of ability. When confronted with difficult situations, students who have learned helplessness are likely to say or think, "What's the use? I never do anything right anyway." For example, Denny is a 15-year-old sophomore in high school. He has been in special education since the second grade. He has never received a grade better than a C, and has received quite a few D's and F's. Last quarter, Denny started to skip classes because he felt that even when he went to class he did not do well. Denny is looking forward to dropping out of school on his 16th birthday and going to work for a fast-food chain, where at least he is able to do the work.

Students with learning and behavior problems may also have severe **anxiety** or **depression** (Cullinan & Epstein, 1994; Wright-Strawderman, Lindsey, Navarette, & Flippo, 1996). Depressed or anxious students may refuse to speak up when in class, may be pessimistic or uninterested in key aspects of their lives, may be visibly nervous when given an assignment, may become ill when it is time to go to school, or may show a lack of self-confidence when performing common school and social tasks. For example, Barrett is a 9-year-old boy with a consistent history of school failure. Barrett is sick just about every morning before he goes to school. At first his mother let him stay home, but now she makes him go anyway. When at school, Barrett is very withdrawn. He has few friends and rarely speaks in class. Barrett's teachers tend not to notice him because he is quiet and does not cause problems. If you have a student in your class who exhibits the signs of depression shown in Figure 6.6, get help for him or her by contacting your school counselor, psychologist, or social worker.

Figure 6.6   **Diagnostic Criteria for Major Depression**

Depression is a dysphoric mood (unhappy; depressed affect), a loss of interest or pleasure in all or almost all usual activities. At least four of the following symptoms also must have been present consistently *for at least 2 weeks.*

a. change in appetite or weight
b. sleep disturbance
c. psychomotor agitation or retardation
d. loss of energy
e. feelings of worthlessness
f. complaints of difficulty to concentrate
g. thoughts of death or suicide

S o u r c e : *Diagnostic and Statistical Manual of Mental Disorders* (4th ed., Text Revision), 2000, Washington, DC: American Psychiatric Association. Reprinted by permission.

What Accommodations Can You Make for Students with Learning and Behavior Disabilities?

As you have just read, students with learning and behavior disabilities have a range of learning and social-emotional needs. Although these needs may make learning and socializing difficult for them, students with learning and behavior disabilities can succeed in your classroom if given support. Some initial ideas about how you can accommodate students with learning and behavior disabilities in your classroom are discussed next. A more in-depth treatment of such accommodations can be found in Chapters 8–13.

Addressing Academic Needs

As we have already discussed, you can discern whether students with learning and behavior disabilities need adaptations by using the INCLUDE strategy to analyze their learning needs and the particular demands of your classroom. You can try three different types of adaptations: bypassing the student's need by allowing the student to employ compensatory learning strategies; making an adaptation in classroom organization, grouping, materials, and methods; and providing the student with direct instruction on basic or independent learning skills. For example, Jessica, who has learning disabilities, is enrolled in Mr. Gresh's high school general science class. Mr. Gresh uses a teaching format in which the students first read the text, then hear a lecture, and finally conduct and write up a lab activity (demands). Jessica has severe reading and writing problems. She is reading at about a sixth-grade level and has difficulty writing a legible, coherent paragraph (student learning needs). However, she does have good listening skills and is an adequate note taker (student strength). In

WWW Resources

LD Online is an interactive guide to learning disabilities for parents, students, and teachers. This site offers newsletters, teaching tips, and more at www.ldonline.org.

Connections

Review all the steps of the INCLUDE strategy (see Chapter 4). What are they? How can you use them for students with high-incidence disabilities?

In what ways might students with cognitive, emotional, and behavioral disorders have difficulty learning? How can teachers address each of these areas of difficulty?

Research Note

Sutherland, Wehby, and Copeland (2000) found that the rate of on-task behavior of nine fifth-grade students with emotional and behavior disorders was significantly increased by simply increasing the number of times their teacher praised them for appropriate behavior.

Check Your Learning

What social-emotional needs might students with learning and behavior disabilities share? Why is it important to address students' social and emotional needs?

WWW Resources

The Center for Effective Collaboration and Practice promotes collaboration among federal agencies serving children with emotional disabilities or at risk of developing emotional disabilities. This site provides many links to resources on issues of emotional and behavioral problems in children and youth. Visit http://cecp.air.org/index.htm.

Mr. Gresh's class, Jessica will have difficulty reading the textbook and meeting the lab writing requirements independently (problem). She will be able to get the lecture information she needs because of her good listening skills (success). Mr. Gresh, with help from Jessica's special education teacher, brainstormed a number of possible adaptations for Jessica and then agreed to implement three of them. He developed a study guide to help Jessica identify key points in the text (adaptation). He also set up small groups in class to review the study guides (adaptation) and assigned Jessica a buddy to help her with the writing demands of the lab activity (bypass). Finally, Mr. Gresh and the special education teacher set up a schedule to monitor Jessica's progress in writing lab reports and reading the textbook. Several more examples of how the INCLUDE strategy can be applied are provided in Table 6.2.

Addressing Social and Emotional Needs

One of the most important reasons given to explain the trend toward inclusive education is the social benefits for students with and without disabilities (Schaps & Solomon, 1990; Stainback & Stainback, 1988). Unfortunately, experience shows that many students with learning and behavior problems do not acquire important social skills just from their physical presence in general education classes (Sale & Carey, 1995). Although much of the emphasis in your training as a teacher concerns academics, your responsibilities as a teacher also include helping all students develop socially, whether or not they have special needs. As with academics, the support students need depends largely on the specific social problem each student has.

Students who have significant conduct problems benefit from a classroom with a clear, consistent behavior management system. In classrooms that are effectively managed, the rules are communicated clearly and the consequences for following or not following those rules are clearly stated and consistently applied. Conduct problems can also be minimized if students are engaged in meaningful academic tasks that can be completed successfully. Still, conduct problems may be so significant that they require a more intensive, individualized approach. For example, Rick, whom you read about at the beginning of this chapter, repeatedly talked out and loudly refused to carry out any requests his teachers made of him. His school attendance was also spotty. Rick's general education teachers got together with Rick's special education teacher to develop a **behavior contract.** According to the contract, each teacher was to keep track of Rick's attendance, talk-outs, and refusals to comply in class. The contract specified that when Rick talked out or refused to comply once, he would be given a warning. If he engaged in these behaviors again, he would be required to serve 5 minutes of detention for each violation. The contract also specified that for each class Rick attended without incident, he would receive points that his parents would allow him to trade for coupons to buy gasoline for his car.

Adaptations depend on the types of interpersonal problems your students have. You can use **social skills training** for students who do not know how to interact with peers and adults (Goldstein, Sprafkin, Gershaw, & Klein, 1980). For example, Tammy is very withdrawn and has few friends. One day her teacher took her aside and suggested that she ask one of the other girls in class home some day after school. Tammy told her that she would never do that because she just would not know what to say. Tammy's teacher decided to spend several social studies classes working with the class on that skill and other skills such as carrying on a conversation and using the correct words and demeanor when asking another student whether he or she

Table 6.2 **Making Adaptations for Students with Learning and Behavior Disabilities Using Steps in the INCLUDE Strategy**

Identify Classroom Demands	Note Student Strengths and Needs	Check for Potential Successes Look for Potential Problems	Decide on Adaptations
Student desks in clusters of four	*Strengths* Good vocabulary skills *Needs* Difficulty attending to task	*Success* Student understands instruction if on task *Problem* Student off task—does not face instructor as she teaches	Change seating so student faces instructor
Small-group work with peers	*Strengths* Good handwriting *Needs* Oral expressive language—problem with word finding	*Success* Student acts as secretary for cooperative group *Problem* Student has difficulty expressing self in peer learning groups	Assign as secretary of group Place into compatible small group Develop social skills instruction for all students
Expect students to attend class and be on time	*Strengths* Good drawing skills *Needs* Poor time management	*Success* Student uses artistic talent in class *Problem* Student is late for class and frequently does not attend at all	Use individualized student contract for attendance and punctuality—if goals met, give student artistic responsibility in class
Textbook difficult to read	*Strengths* Good oral communication skills *Needs* Poor reading accuracy Lacks systematic strategy for reading text	*Success* Student participates well in class Good candidate for class dramatizations *Problem* Student is unable to read text for information	Provide taped textbooks Highlight student text
Lecture on women's suffrage movement to whole class	*Strengths* Very motivated and interested in class *Needs* Lack of background knowledge	*Success* Student earns points for class attendance and effort *Problem* Student lacks background knowledge to understand important information in lecture	Give student video to view before lecture Build points for attendance and working hard into grading system
Whole class instruction on telling time to the quarter hour	*Strengths* Good coloring skills *Needs* Cannot identify numbers 7–12 Cannot count by fives	*Success* Student is able to color clock faces used in instruction *Problem* Student is unable to acquire telling time skills	Provide extra instruction on number identification and counting by fives

continued

Table 6.2 Continued

Identify Classroom Demands	Note Student Strengths and Needs	Check for Potential Successes Look for Potential Problems	Decide on Adaptations
Math test involving solving word problems using addition	*Strengths* Good reasoning skills *Needs* Problems mastering math facts, sums of 10–18	*Success* Student is good at solving problems *Problem* Student misses problems due to math fact errors	Allow use of calculator
Multiple choice and fill-in-the-blanks test	*Strengths* Memory—good memory for details *Needs* Attention—cannot identify key words in test questions Weak comprehension skills	*Success* Student does well on fill-in-the-blank questions that require memorization *Problem* Student is doing poorly on multiple choice parts of history tests	Use bold type for key words in multiple choice questions Teach strategy for taking multiple choice tests

Connections

Ways of teaching students self-control are covered in Chapters 10 and 12.

Cultural Awareness

Altwerger and Ivener (1996) suggest that teachers can build up the self-esteem of English language learners by embracing the common and diverse strengths brought from their home culture, by considering all learners capable of constructing and reconstructing meaning over time, and by providing opportunities for students to share their knowledge and questions and to view themselves as important contributors to their own language.

would like to play a game. She felt that many of the students in class besides Tammy would benefit from these lessons. First, Tammy's teacher posted the steps involved in performing these skills on a chart in front of the classroom. Then, she and several students in the class demonstrated the social skills for the class. She then divided the class into small groups, and each group role-played the various skills and were given feedback by their classmates and peers. To make sure that Tammy felt comfortable, the teacher put her in a group of students who had a positive attitude and liked Tammy. An example of how to carry out social skills training is presented in the Case in Practice.

For students who know what to do in social situations but lack the self-control to behave appropriately, **self-control training** can be used (Kauffman, 1997). Self-control training teaches students to redirect their actions by talking to themselves. For example, Dominic does not handle conflict very well. When his friends tease him, he is quick to lose his temper and verbally lash out at them. His outbursts only encourage the students, and they continue teasing and taunting him any chance they get. Dominic's teacher taught him a self-control strategy to help him ignore his friends' teasing. Whenever he was teased, Dominic first counted to 5 to himself to get beyond his initial anger. He then told himself that what they were saying wasn't true and that the best way to get them to stop was to ignore them and walk away. When he walked away, Dominic told himself he did a good job and later reported his efforts to his teacher.

Some students may know what to do socially but lack opportunities for using their social skills. For example, students who are newly included in your classroom and/or new to the school need opportunities to interact with classmates to get to know them better. One way to create opportunities for social interaction is to allow students to work in small groups with a shared learning goal. For example, Thomas is a student with a mild cognitive disability who is included in Mr. Jeffreys's sixth-grade class. This is Thomas's first year in general education; until this year, he had

C A S E   I N   P R A C T I C E

A Social Skills Training Session

Ms. Perez and her fourth-grade class are working on a unit on social skills in social studies. They are learning the skill of listening to someone who is talking by doing the following:

1. Look at the person who is talking.
2. Remember to sit quietly.
3. Think about what is being said.
4. Say yes or nod your head.
5. Ask a question about the topic to find out more.

Jeanine, a student in the class, has just practiced these listening skills in front of the class by role-playing the part of a student who is talking to her teacher about an assignment. In the role-play, Ms. Perez played herself. The class is now giving Jeanine feedback on her performance.

Ms. Perez: First, did Jeanine look at me when I was talking? Before you answer, can someone tell me why it's important to look at the person who is talking?

Lorna: You don't want the other person to think you're not listening even though you are. So you really have to *show* them you are listening.

Ms. Perez: That's right, Lorna. Well, how did Jeanine do on this one?

Charles: Well, she looked at you at first but while you were explaining the assignment she looked down at her feet. It kind of looked like she wasn't listening.

Jeanine: I was listening, but I guess I should have kept good eye contact all the way through.

Ms. Perez: Yes, Jeanine. To be honest, if I didn't know you better, I would have thought that you didn't care about what I was saying. You need to work harder on that step. The next step is to remember to sit quietly. How did Jeanine do with this one?

Milton: I think she did well. She remembered not to laugh, fidget, or play with anything while you were talking.

Ms. Perez: I agree, Milton. Nice work, Jeanine. Now, can someone tell me what the next listening step is?

Kyrie: It's to think about what the person is saying.

Ms. Perez: Right, Kyrie. Let's let Jeanine evaluate herself on this one.

Jeanine: Well, I tried to think about what you were saying. Once I felt my mind start to wander, but I followed your suggestion and started thinking about a question that I could ask you.

Ms. Perez: Good, Jeanine. Trying to think of a question to ask can be very helpful. How did you think you did on the next step? Did you nod your head or say yes to show you were following me?

Jeanine: I think I did.

Ms. Perez: What do the rest of you think? Did Jeanine nod her head or say yes?

Tara: Well, I saw her nod a little, but it was hard to tell. Maybe she needs to nod more clearly.

Ms. Perez: Jeanine, you need to nod more strongly or the teacher won't realize you are doing it.

R E F L E C T I O N S

What teaching procedures is Ms. Perez using to teach her students listening skills? Do you think they are effective? What could she do to make sure that her students use this skill in their classes? For what settings outside of school would these and other social skills be important?

been in a self-contained special education classroom. Mr. Jeffreys decided to use peer learning groups in science because he thought it would be a good way for Thomas to get to know his classmates and make some friends. Every 2 weeks, Thomas has the opportunity to complete various lab activities with a different group.

Students who exhibit learned helplessness can benefit from **attribution retraining** (Ellis, Lenz, & Sabornie, 1987). The idea behind attribution retraining is that if you can convince students that their failures are due to lack of effort rather than ability, they will be more persistent and improve their performance in the face of difficulty (Schunk, 1989).

You can enhance student self-image by using the following strategies suggested by Mercer (1997):

1. **Set reasonable goals.** When setting goals for students, make sure that they are not too easy or too hard. Self-worth is improved when students reach their goals through considerable effort. Goals that are too ambitious perpetuate failure. Goals that are too easy can give students the idea that you think they are not capable of doing anything difficult.

2. **Provide specific feedback contingent on student behavior.** Feedback should be largely positive, but it should also be contingent on completion of tasks. Otherwise, students are likely to perceive your feedback as patronizing and just another indication that you think they are unable to do real academic work. Do not be afraid to correct students when they are wrong. Providing corrective feedback communicates to students that you think they can succeed if they keep trying and that you care about them.

3. **Give the student responsibility.** Assigning a responsibility demonstrates to students that you trust them and believe they can act maturely. Some examples include taking the class pet home on weekends, taking the lunch count, being a line leader, taking messages to the office, and taking attendance.

4. **Teach students to reinforce themselves.** Students with poor self-images say negative things about themselves. You can help students by reminding them of their strengths, encouraging them to make more positive statements about themselves, and then reinforcing them for making these statements.

5. **Give students a chance to show their strengths.** Part of the INCLUDE strategy is to identify student strengths and then help students achieve success by finding or creating classroom situations in which they can employ their strengths. For example, Cara cannot read very well but has an excellent speaking voice. After her group wrote a report on the 1960 presidential election, Cara was given the task of presenting the report to the whole class.

Summary

Students with high-incidence disabilities are students who have speech and language disabilities, learning disabilities, emotional disturbance, or mild cognitive disabilities. Students with high-incidence disabilities make up about 90 percent of all students who have disabilities. They are often hard to distinguish from their peers; exhibit a combination of behavioral, social, and academic problems; and are likely to benefit from systematic, highly structured interventions.

Students with communications disorders have a number of learning, social, and emotional needs. Their language problems can affect their performance in all academic areas, including reading, math, written expression, and content-area instruction. Socially, they may be withdrawn, rejected by their peers, and have considerable difficulty using language in social situations. The academic and social performance of students with speech and language problems can be enhanced through a number of adaptations, including creating an atmosphere of acceptance, actively encouraging listening skills, stressing words that are important to meaning, presenting many examples of vocabulary and concepts being taught and presenting them several times, using modeling to teach students to expand their language, and teaching within a context that is meaningful for students.

Students with learning and behavior disabilities receive special education services within the categories of learning disabilities, emotional disturbance, and mental retardation (mild). Students with learning and behavior disabilities have many learning needs. They have difficulty acquiring basic skills in the areas of reading, math, and written language. They may also lack skills necessary for efficient learning, such as attending to task, memory, independent learning skills, language skills, reasoning, conceptualization and generalization, motor, and school survival skills. You can make adaptations for these students in academic areas using the INCLUDE strategy.

Students with learning and behavior disabilities have social and emotional difficulties in classroom conduct, interpersonal skills, and personal and psychological adjustment. Their classroom conduct may be characterized by disruptive behaviors in class, including hitting, fighting, teasing, refusing to comply with requests, crying, destructiveness, and vandalism. Students with learning and behavior disabilities are also likely to have interpersonal problems. They are at risk for being rejected or neglected by classmates, and they may have a number of social skills deficits. The personal/psychological adjustment of students with learning and behavior disabilities may also be problematic. They sometimes have a poor self-image, are not proactive in academic and social situations, and may experience bouts of depression or anxiety. Adaptations for students with learning and behavior disabilities in social areas include individualized behavior management, social skills training, self-control training, and attribution retraining.

Applications in Teaching Practice

Using the INCLUDE Strategy with Students with High-Incidence Disabilities

Answer the following questions to show how you would apply the INCLUDE strategy to accommodate the students described in the vignettes at the beginning of this chapter. To help you with this application, refer to Table 6.2 on pages 225–226 and to the section on the INCLUDE strategy in Chapter 4.

Questions

1. What communication, academic, behavior, and social and emotional needs does each student have?
2. Keeping in mind the major aspects of the classroom environment, including classroom organization, classroom grouping, instructional materials, and instructional methods, what kinds of problems are these students likely to have?
3. What types of adaptations would you make for each of these problems?
4. Are these adaptations reasonable in terms of teacher time and ease of implementation? What support (if any) would you need to carry them out?
5. How can you monitor the effectiveness of your adaptations? What can you do next if your first adaptation is ineffective?

Other Students with Special Needs

After you read this chapter, you will be able to

1. Describe students protected through Section 504 and the accommodations general education teachers can make for them.

2. Explain accommodations general education teachers can make for students with attention deficit–hyperactivity disorder.

3. Outline the adaptations that students who are gifted and talented may need in general education classrooms.

4. Explain how general education teachers can address the needs of students from diverse cultural backgrounds.

5. Describe how general education teachers can make adaptations for students at risk for school failure, including students who live in poverty, those who are abused or neglected, and those who live in homes in which drugs, including alcohol, are abused.

Key Terms and Concepts

Section 504 (p. 233)

Attention deficit–hyperactivity disorder (ADHD) (p. 236)

Bilingual education programs (p. 258)

Child abuse (p. 261)

Fetal alcohol effects (p. 261)

Fetal alcohol syndrome (p. 261)

Gifted and talented (p. 245)

Multicultural education (p. 258)

■ Victor is a student in Mr. Steinberg's seventh-grade computer class. Mr. Steinberg says Victor just cannot attend to the work at hand, even though students usually enjoy the computer class and all the specialized technology they can access there. Victor is constantly looking around, distracted by almost anything, including computers operating, students conversing, changes in the light when a cloud momentarily blocks the sun, or a passerby outside the classroom door. Instead of raising his hand during class discussions, Victor just blurts out what is on his mind, and he is as likely to make a comment about his visit with his aunt last weekend as he is to contribute a comment relevant to the topic being presented.

■ Victor also has a habit of acting first and thinking later. It almost seems that he is incapable of reversing this process. For example, in class the other day, as Mr. Steinberg cautioned students not to remove a disk from the floppy drive while the drive light was on, Victor was already in action. He ruined the disk he was using and didn't seem to understand how he had caused this to happen. Mr. Steinberg is convinced that Victor is likely to do this again because he doesn't seem to learn from experience. Victor's parents report that he is "all boy," much like his father. They readily admit, however, that keeping up with him can be an exhausting task. Does Victor have a disability? What are Victor's special needs? What is the responsibility of school personnel for meeting those needs?

■ Lydia is a fourth-grade student who is gifted and talented. She has been reading since age 3, and she frequently borrows her sister's high school literature anthology as a source of reading material. She knew most of the math concepts introduced in fourth grade before the school year began. She has a strong interest in learning Spanish and playing flute and piano, and she would like to volunteer to read to residents of a local nursing home. Lydia's idea of a perfect afternoon is to have a quiet place to hide, a couple of wonderful books, and no one to bother her. Lydia's teacher, Mr. Judd, enjoys having her in class because she is so enthusiastic about learning, but he admits that Lydia's abilities are a little intimidating. He has also noticed that Lydia doesn't seem to have much in common with other students in class. She is a class leader but does not appear to have any close friends as other students do. Is Lydia entitled to receive special services because of her giftedness? Is Lydia typical of students who are gifted or talented? What can Mr. Judd do to help Lydia reach her full potential? What social problems do students like Lydia encounter?

■ Tejal is a sophomore in high school, but he doubts that he'll finish the school year. He describes school as pointless, and he sees that he has more important things to do than sit in classrooms learning about topics he believes have no relevance in his life. Although he still attends school, he is absent more and more often and usually does not bother to do homework or read assignments. He does not have a history of behavior problems in school, but during the past month he has received in-school suspension for a fight just outside school during lunch and for profane comments he made to a teacher who confronted him about being out of class without a pass. His teachers describe him as unmotivated, a student who has vastly more potential than they see him using. He excels as a basketball player, but he is academically ineligible to participate. He is currently working at a local car wash at minimum wage, but makes extra money in tips. After hours he likes to visit with his friends in the parking lot behind a local convenience store, so he often stays out until after midnight. Those friends influence Tejal tremendously. One of them has offered to get Tejal a gun so that he can defend himself in his neighborhood, and several friends use drugs. One friend is hoping Tejal will agree to work as a distributor. Tejal has a juvenile record; he is on probation for stealing a car with yet another of his friends. How common are students like Tejal? What other characteristics and behaviors might Tejal display in school? What should his teachers do to help Tejal stay interested in school?

Although special education services are available to students who have documented disabilities, most educators agree that many more students than those served through IDEA-97 have special needs. In fact, some teachers comment that they have students in their classes not eligible for special education services whose needs are greater than those of students protected by the federal law. For example, even though Victor has a significant attention problem, he does not qualify for special education. Lydia's teacher is concerned that he cannot possibly make time to provide the advanced instruction that would benefit her. Tejal's teachers worry about his future and are frustrated that they cannot make his life better and help him reach his potential. They sometimes feel powerless to influence students like Tejal who have so many difficulties in their young lives, and they question how traditional academic standards and activities can be made relevant for them.

This chapter is about students who are not necessarily eligible for special education but who have special needs and often require special attention from general education teachers. In fact, you may find that you have characteristics similar to those of students described in this chapter or that you have had similar experiences. If that is the case, you bring to your teacher preparation program knowledge other teachers may not have, and you may have a perspective on student diversity that you can draw on in understanding student needs. The students examined in this chapter include those who have functional disabilities addressed by Section 504 but not IDEA, including those with attention deficit–hyperactivity disorder; those who are gifted and talented; those whose native language is not English and whose cultures differ significantly from that of most of their classmates; and those who are at risk because of special situations, including poverty, child abuse, and drug abuse.

The rationale for discussing Victor, Lydia, Tejal, and other students like them in this text has four parts. First, students with these types of special needs often benefit greatly from the same strategies that are successful for students with disabilities. Thus, one purpose is to remind you that the techniques explained throughout this text are applicable to many of your students, not just those who have IEPs. Second, it is important for you to understand that you will teach many students with a tremendous diversity of needs resulting from many different factors, disability being just one potential factor. Creating appropriate educational opportunities for all your students is your responsibility. Third, students with special needs often are referred for special education services because caring teachers recognize that they need help. It is important to realize that special education is much more than help and is reserved for just the specific group of students already described in Chapters 5 and 6. Finally, although many special educators are committed to helping you meet the needs of all your students, including those at risk, they cannot take primary responsibility for teaching students like Victor, Lydia, and Tejal. These are not students who "should be" in special education. They represent instead the increasingly diverse range of students that all teachers now instruct, and they highlight the importance of creating classrooms that respect this diversity and foster student learning, regardless of students' special needs.

This chapter also highlights how complex student needs have become (Reynolds & Heistad, 1997). For example, you probably realize that students with disabilities can also have the special needs described here. A student with a physical disability might also be academically gifted. A student with a cognitive disability might also live in poverty. A student with a learning disability might speak a language other than English at home. You probably also recognize that the student groups emphasized in this chapter are not necessarily distinct, even though it is convenient to discuss them as if they are. Students who live in poverty can also be gifted and from a cultural minority. An abused student can be at risk from drug abuse. Keep in mind as you read this chapter that your responsibility as a teacher for all students, regardless of their disabilities or other special needs, is to identify strengths and needs, arrange a supportive instructional environment, provide high-quality instruction, and foster student independence. When students have multiple special needs, these tasks can be especially challenging, and you should seek assistance from professional colleagues, parents, and other resources.

> **Connections**
>
> Review the information about IDEA and the procedures for serving students through special education in Chapters 1 and 2.

Which Students Are Protected by Section 504?

> **Connections**
>
> Section 504 was defined in Chapter 1. It is civil rights legislation protecting students with functional disabilities.

In Chapter 1, you learned that some students with special needs do not meet the eligibility criteria for receiving services through IDEA, but they are considered functionally disabled as defined by **Section 504** of the Vocational Rehabilitation Act of

1973. Students in this group are entitled to receive reasonable accommodations that help them benefit from school. These accommodations can include many of the same types of services and supports that students eligible through IDEA receive, but there are crucial differences between the two statutes as well (Rosenfeld, 2000). First, the definition of a disability in Section 504 is considerably broader than it is in IDEA. Any condition that substantially limits a major life activity, such as the ability to learn in school, is defined as a disability (Katsiyannis & Conderman, 1994). This definition means that students with a wide range of needs who cannot receive IDEA special education services are eligible for assistance through Section 504. For example, a student who is photophobic (that is, highly sensitive to bright light) might receive services through Section 504, and so also might students with significant attention problems, drug addiction, chronic health problems, communicable diseases, temporary disabilities resulting from accidents or injury, environmental illnesses, and alcoholism (Rosenfeld, 2000). Second, unlike IDEA, no funds are provided to school districts to carry out the requirements of Section 504 (Henderson, 2000). The expectation is that schools should take whatever steps are necessary, even if additional funds are required, to eliminate discrimination as defined through this statute. Third, the responsibility for making accommodations for students who qualify as disabled through Section 504 belongs to general education personnel, not special education personnel. Special educators might provide some informal assistance, but their aid is not mandated as it is in IDEA, nor can IDEA funds, including those for teachers, be used to provide assistance to students who only receive Section 504 plans. The types of accommodations required vary based on student needs, but could include alterations in the physical environment, such as providing a quiet workspace or a room with specialized lighting; modifications in instruction, such as decreasing an assignment or allotting additional time to complete it; organizational assistance, such as checking a student's backpack to ensure all materials for homework are there; and changes in the student's schedule, such as allowing a rest period. Individual school districts establish policies for meeting the requirements of Section 504.

WWW Resources

If you are interested in reading more about Section 504, you can find the text of this statute at the following website: http://www.specialedlaw.net/PDF/specialedlaw.net.504.statute.pdf.

For students to receive assistance through Section 504, their needs must be assessed and a decision made concerning their eligibility. The regulations for Section 504 advise that a team be convened to manage this process, but this is not required. The assessment procedures can be similar to those used for IDEA, but school districts probably should assess some students for Section 504 assistance who would not be assessed at all for special education services. Students determined eligible have a Section 504 plan that covers their instructional program as well as after-school programs, field trips, summer programs, and other extracurricular activities (Advocacy Incorporated, 2000). The plan outlines the accommodations needed, who is to implement them, and how they will be monitored. A sample of the types of accommodations that may be incorporated into a Section 504 plan is presented in the Professional Edge.

Although many students can qualify for assistance through Section 504, two common groups are addressed in this chapter: students with medical or health needs and students with attention deficit–hyperactivity disorder (ADHD). (The first group is discussed here; students with ADHD are covered in the following major section of this chapter.)

Students with chronic health or medical problems, for example, those with communicable diseases, who are not eligible for IDEA services according to established

Professional Edge

Section 504 Plan Accommodations

The types of accommodations that can be written into a Section 504 plan are almost without limit. Some accommodation may relate to physical changes in the learning environment (for example, ensuring that the doorway in the media center is wide enough for the student's wheelchair, or that air filters are installed to remove allergens). However, many students who have Section 504 plans have functional impairments related to their learning or behavior, and their needs are somewhat similar to those of students with disabilities. The following is a sample of instructional accommodations that could be incorporated into a Section 504 plan:

- Seat the student nearest to where the teacher does most of his/her instruction.

- Have the student sit next to a peer who can help as needed.

- Seat the student away from the distractions of doorways or windows.

- Fold assignments in half so that the student is less overwhelmed by the quantity of work.

- Make directions telegraphic, that is, concise and clear.

- Allow use of a calculator or tape recorder.

- Use voice recognition software on the computer for written assignments.

- Mark right answers instead of wrong answers.

- Send a set of textbooks to be left at home so that the student does not have to remember to bring books from school.

- Provide books on tape so that the student can listen to assignments instead of reading them.

If you review these items, you can see that many of them just make good instructional sense. They are effective instructional practices that help learners with special needs succeed in your classroom.

SOURCE: Adapted from "Ideas for an IEP or Section 504 plan," by D. Simms, 2000. Retrieved on September 13, 2000, from the World Wide Web: http://www.angelfire.com/ny/Debsimms/education.html.

criteria and as determined by a multidisciplinary team, comprise one of the major groups that can qualify for assistance through Section 504. For example, a student who has asthma might have a Section 504 plan. The plan could address accommodations related to the student's need for occasional rest periods, opportunities to take medication, exemption from certain physical activities, and provisions to make up assignments and tests after absences. A student with severe allergies might have a plan that addresses materials in school that cannot be used (for example, paints, chalk, peanut products), guidelines for participation in physical education, and requirements for providing assignments that can be completed at home if necessary. A student who is photophobic might have a Section 504 plan that calls for darkening shades on classroom windows and for providing a shaded area in which the student can work. A student with diabetes might need a Section 504 plan that spells out procedures to be followed in case of an insulin reaction or other health problems.

As you can tell, some of the responsibility for implementing Section 504 plans belongs to administrators, who authorize physical modifications to classrooms and make arrangements for students to have rest periods or take medications. Your responsibility is to implement instructional adaptations outlined in the plan, such as providing assignments in advance and allowing extra time for work completion. Your

WWW Resources

At the website for LD Online (http://www.ldonline.org), you can find an in-depth discussion of similarities and differences between Section 504 and IDEA-97.

interactions with students protected by Section 504 differ from your interactions with other students only in your responsibility to make the accommodations required. However, you may find that some students with Section 504 plans have learning and behavior problems that at times seem very similar to those of students with disabilities. These students benefit from the many strategies presented in this text.

How Can You Accommodate Students with Attention Deficit–Hyperactivity Disorder (ADHD)?

Students with attention problems have long been a concern of teachers, especially at the elementary school level. In fact, labels such as *hyperkinesis* and *minimal brain dysfunction* have been applied to these students since the 1940s (Barkley, 1998). In recent years, concern about student attention seems to have escalated. One special education clearinghouse reported that it is receiving thousands of requests each year for information about attention problems (Fowler, 1994). Even popular magazines are tackling the topic of children who cannot pay attention (for example, Wallis, 1994). A few students with significant attentional problems, as described in this section, are eligible for services through IDEA, but others receive assistance through Section 504 (Weaver & Landers, 1998).

The term for significant attention problems is **attention deficit–hyperactivity disorder (ADHD),** a condition defined in the *Diagnostic and Statistical Manual of Mental Disorders (DSM-IV)* (American Psychiatric Association, 1994). ADHD is characterized by chronic and serious inattentiveness, hyperactivity, and/or impulsivity. You might also hear the term **attention deficit disorder (ADD)** being used to label the condition. *ADD* is an earlier term for describing attention problems, and some professionals use the terms *ADHD* and *ADD* interchangeably. Some authors use *ADD* as a general term to describe all serious attention problems and *ADHD* only for students who display symptoms of hyperactivity.

Estimates of the prevalence of ADHD range from less than 1 percent to more than 20 percent of school-age children (Centers for Disease Control and Prevention, 2000), but experts seem to agree that it affects no more than 3 to 5 percent of students (Loechler, 1999). Because most of the studies of ADHD have been clinical, assessing relatively small numbers of students, and because there is no systematic national monitoring of this disorder nor clear standards for research about it, any figures about it are at best rough estimates. Adding to the controversy is the fact that in many other countries, especially in Europe where the study of ADHD has been ongoing, the disorder generally is not identified at all or is relatively rare (Reid & Maag, 1997).

The causes of ADHD are not clear, and opinions have been changing over the past several years. Currently, many professionals believe that ADHD is not a matter of attention per se, but that it occurs when the brain fails to develop properly, leading to deficits in inhibition and self-control (Barkley, 1998). These deficits result in the behavioral symptoms of inattention and impulsivity. In addition to researchers investigating a neurological basis for ADHD, a few authors have suggested that ADHD is the result of food additives or food allergies, inner ear problems, vitamin deficiencies, or bacterial infections, but none of these causes has been demonstrated to be valid (Lerner, Lowenthal, & Lerner, 1995). Usually, a diagnosis of ADHD is the result of individualized testing for cognitive ability and achievement, a medical screening, and behavior ratings completed by family members and school professionals (Maag & Reid, 1994).

ADHD is one of the most commonly diagnosed disorders of childhood (Frazier & Merrell, 1997), and some evidence indicates a genetic link (*ADHD Owner's Manual*, 2000). It appears to be three to five times more common in boys than in girls (Barkley, 1998), and some evidence suggests that the disorder is more common in some racial or ethnic groups than in others (Livingston, 1999; Reid et al., 1998). However, as is true with the assessment of many types of special needs, the latter bit of information may be inaccurate because instruments designed to detect ADHD may have culture bias that leads to overidentification (Reid et al., 1998).

Characteristics and Needs of Students with Attention Deficit–Hyperactivity Disorder

The characteristics and needs of students with attention deficit–hyperactivity disorder can vary considerably. For example, some students with ADHD have primarily an **attention disorder.** They have difficulty sustaining attention to schoolwork or play activities, they often lose things, and they appear forgetful. Other students with ADHD have a **hyperactive-impulsive disorder.** They tend to fidget constantly, need to move around a room even when other students can stay seated, and frequently interrupt others. A third group of students with ADHD have a **combination disorder,** with both the inattentive and hyperactive-impulsive characteristics. Figure 7.1 provides additional examples of behavioral characteristics of students who are inattentive, hyperactive, or impulsive.

FYI

Parents and teachers often misuse the term *hyperactive* to refer to any students whose high activity levels and easy distractibility make them challenging to teach.

Figure 7.1 **Behavior Characteristics of Students with Attention Deficit–Hyperactivity Disorder**

Inattention
- Making careless mistakes
- Having difficulty sustaining attention
- Seeming not to listen
- Failing to finish tasks
- Having difficulty organizing
- Avoiding tasks requiring sustained attention
- Losing things
- Becoming easily distracted
- Being forgetful

Hyperactivity
- Fidgeting
- Being unable to stay seated
- Moving excessively (restless)
- Having difficulty engaging quietly in leisure activities
- Being "on the go"
- Talking excessively

Impulsivity
- Blurting answers before questions are completed
- Having difficulty awaiting turn
- Interrupting/intruding upon others

S O U R C E : Adapted from "The Practical Aspects of Diagnosing and Managing Children with Attention Deficit Hyperactivity Disorder," by M. L. Wolraich and A. Baumgaertel, 1997, *Clinical Pediatrics, 36,* pp. 497–504.

Although all students might occasionally demonstrate some symptoms of ADHD, students diagnosed with this disorder display many of them prior to 7 years of age. Further, their symptoms are chronic and extraordinary. For example, Joyce, the mother of 8-year-old Matt, who has been diagnosed with ADHD, described one memorable morning like this:

> Matt was 4 years old. He had spilled an entire box of breakfast cereal on the kitchen floor and then had a screaming tantrum when Joyce instructed him to help her pick it up. He then knocked over a vase of flowers and announced sincerely that he didn't do it. Joyce believed he meant what he said even though she saw him do it. Part of the reason Matt was home that day was because his preschool had asked Joyce not to bring him back. He was too disruptive in class and the parents of other students were complaining that he often hit, kicked, or bit their children. The final straw that morning came when Matt ran upstairs after being asked to sit down. He slammed the bathroom door, locking himself in; in his haste to shut the door, he broke the lock mechanism. After an hour of trying to dismantle the lock to open the door, while Matt opened drawers and cabinets, taking apart the bathroom, Joyce declared defeat and called the fire department. The firefighters extricated Matt by entering the bathroom through a window and bringing him down the ladder.

Check Your Learning

What characteristics of ADHD does Matt display? What strategies might help him in a school setting?

Joyce called this just one more day that made her question her own parenting skills and even her sanity. She said that there were far too many days like that. Matt's home behavior is somewhat like the behavior of Victor, whom you read about at the beginning of this chapter. Both Matt and Victor seem incapable of controlling their actions and of learning from past experiences.

Cognitively, students with ADHD can function at any level, although the disorder is usually diagnosed for students who do not have cognitive disabilities. Students who are below average in ability and achievement, students who are average learners, and students who are gifted and talented can all have ADHD. Some students with the disorder experience very serious learning problems. They sometimes receive special services under the learning disabled category, or they might be classified as having other health impairments. Other students experience low achievement apparently because of extremely low self-esteem or other emotional or behavior problems. In some cases, students with ADHD receive the same services as for students who are emotionally disturbed. Some authors assert that more than half of all students with attention deficit–hyperactivity disorder already receive services through special education (Centers for Disease Control and Prevention, 2000). The remaining students may or may not have serious learning problems. Problems can occur in reading, especially with long passages in which comprehension demands are high; in spelling, which requires careful attention to detail; in listening, especially when the information presented is highly detailed; and in math, which often requires faster computational skills than students with ADHD can handle (Zentall, 1993). All these learning problems can be related to students' inability to focus on schoolwork for extended periods of time and their difficulty in attending selectively only to important aspects of information.

Socially and emotionally, students with ADHD are at risk for a variety of problems (Frazier & Merrell, 1997). For example, they are more likely to be depressed or to have extremely low confidence or self-esteem. Likewise, they are likely to have conflicts with parents, teachers, or other authority figures. They are often unpopular with peers, frequently rejected by them, and have difficulty making friends. Students with ADHD may feel demoralized, but they may also be bossy and obstinate.

The frequency of behavior problems of students with ADHD varies. Students whose disorder is inattention might not act out in class, but they can be disruptive when they try to find lost items or constantly ask classmates for assistance in finding their place in a book or carrying out directions. Students with hyperactive-impulsive disorder often come to teachers' attention immediately because they have so many behavior problems. Their constant motion, refusal to work, and other behaviors can be problematic even in the most tolerant environments.

ADHD also has a physical component. As noted previously, recent research suggests that brain dysfunction might contribute to the disorder (Riccio, Hynd, Cohen, & Gonzalez, 1993). First, a neuroanatomical perspective proposes that ADHD is caused by a dysfunction in part of the brain, especially the frontal lobe, possibly because this area is developing more slowly or abnormally. Second, a neurochemical perspective suggests that a chemical imbalance exists that affects neurotransmitters, the chemicals that regulate how the brain controls behavior. Because of the imbalance, students with attention deficit–hyperactivity disorder are not capable of rapidly monitoring and controlling their behavior; hence they are impulsive and inattentive.

FYI

Behavior rating scales are frequently used to determine whether a student has ADHD. Commonly used rating scales include the Achenbach Behavior Checklist for Parents, the Connors Rating Scale, and the Behavior Problems Checklist.

Interventions for Students with Attention Deficit–Hyperactivity Disorder

Academic interventions.   Students with ADHD typically struggle with academic achievement, although the extent of their learning problems varies considerably (Marshall, Hynd, Handwerk, & Hall, 1997). To assist students with ADHD academically, you can emphasize key features of their learning and eliminate unnecessary information (Zentall, 1993). For example, keep oral instructions as brief as possible. Rather than giving directions, providing multiple examples, and then recapping what you have said, instead list directions by number using very clear language (for example, "First, put your name on the paper; second, write one sentence for each spelling word; third, put your paper in your spelling folder"). When reading for comprehension, students with ADHD tend to perform better on short passages than on long ones. Thus, it would be better to ask a student with ADHD to read just a small part of a long story and check comprehension at that point, then have him or her read another part and so on, rather than read an entire story or chapter. In spelling, using color cues to highlight words to be learned can be helpful, but only after students have practiced the words without the color cues. In math, students should be given extended periods of time to complete computational work because their attentional problems interfere with their efficiency in this type of task.

In addition to the types of interventions just outlined, most recommendations for helping students with ADHD academically are similar to those used for students with learning and emotional disabilities, and for other students who need highly structured and especially clear instruction. The following chapters feature many instructional approaches that meet the needs of students with ADHD. For example, DuPaul, Ervin, Hook, and McGoey (1998) found that using Classwide Peer Tutoring (CWPT), a highly structured peer-tutoring program found to be extraordinarily effective with students with emotional disabilities, was also successful in improving

FYI

Because interest in ADHD is so high, parents may ask if you think their child has this disorder. It is essential for you to remember *not* to offer a diagnostic opinion. Refer parents to their family doctor or pediatrician for this information.

Special Emphasis On . . .

Adolescents with Attention Deficit–Hyperactivity Disorder (ADHD)

Because the definition of ADHD includes onset at an early age and many students with ADHD are identified early in elementary school, most information about ADHD has focused on children. In addition, questions have been raised about whether ADHD disappears as children reach puberty and whether medication or other treatments are even necessary as students enter middle school or high school. Recently, though, more professionals have become interested in ADHD in adolescents, and they are finding out that adolescents with attention deficit–hyperactivity disorder should continue to receive the special attention of parents and teachers. Did you know these facts about ADHD and older students and young adults?

- Of all students diagnosed with ADHD by the end of elementary school, approximately 20 percent seem to outgrow the disorder. However, that means that 80 percent of students with ADHD continue to have the disorder as they go through secondary school (Klorman, 1991).

- The effects of medication are virtually the same for children, adolescents, and young adults with ADHD. A number of studies have demonstrated that medication should be continued, possibly for a lifetime, with many individuals with ADHD (Klorman, 1993; Robin, 1998).

- During adolescence, the symptoms of ADHD may be more subtle than they were during earlier years (National Health and Medical Research Council, 2000).

- After leaving high school, individuals with ADHD tend to overcome many of their social problems. Although they report more encounters with law enforcement than individuals without attention deficit–hyperactivity disorder, they do not seem to have more legal problems than others (Hansen, Weiss, & Last, 1999).

- During high school, individuals with ADHD continue to have significantly more problems in reading, spelling, and mathematics than other students (Claude & Firestone, 1995).

- Several studies have found that individuals with attention deficit–hyperactivity disorder are at greater risk than other students for having problems with social interactions. This problem is particularly significant for individuals who as children were considered to be quite aggressive (Dumas, 1998).

the academic and behavior outcomes for students with attention deficit–hyperactivity disorder. This strategy is discussed more fully in Chapter 12. Additional simple strategies for assisting students with ADHD are included in Figure 7.2.

Behavior interventions. For responding to behavior, professionals generally recommend interventions that emphasize structure and rewards, such as specific verbal praise ("Martin, you began your work as soon as I gave the assignment"), stickers or other symbols of appropriate behavior ("Tamatha, you will earn a sticker for each five math problems you complete"), and games that emphasize rewards for positive classroom behaviors (Anholt, McNeil, & Bahl, 1998). Reprimands or consequences may be needed at times, but these should be mild and used less often than rewards. As the INCLUDE strategy outlines, you should first consider environmental demands and address these as a means of preventing behavior problems (Yehle & Wambold, 1998). For example, students with ADHD exhibit less acting-out behav-

- Drug use among individuals with ADHD is higher than for other individuals, but this fact seems accounted for by a subgroup of individuals who were aggressive as children (Claude & Firestone, 1995).

Taken together, this information suggests that teachers in middle and high school can still play a crucial role in helping students with ADHD succeed. Recommended interventions include behavioral programs in which students are rewarded for appropriate behavior and academic effort; continued, consistent use of medication (which may require monitoring by teachers); and careful transition planning so that students with ADHD consider attending college or prepare to enter the workforce (Abramowitz & O'Leary, 1991; Shapiro, DuPaul, & Bradley-Klug, 1998).

Resources on Adolescents with Attention Deficit–Hyperactivity Disorder

If you are interested in this topic, the following materials can help you learn more.

Flick, G. L. (2000). *Managing teens with ADHD.* **New York: Prentice-Hall**

This book includes detailed information on many topics of interest to those who work with adolescents with at-

tention deficit–hyperactivity disorder. It addresses the diagnosis of ADHD, family issues, preparation of teens with attention deficit–hyperactivity disorder for adulthood, and networks and resources for teens with this disorder.

Robin, A. L. (1998). *ADHD in adolescents: Diagnosis and treatment.* **New York: Guilford Press**

This book is divided into three main sections. The first addresses the definition of ADHD and theories regarding it; the second considers diagnosis; and the third includes educational, medical, and family interventions for ADHD.

Adolescents' Questions about ADHD

(http://users.aol.com:80/jimams/answers2.html)

This website includes questions and answers for teens on topics such as taking medication, the impact of medication, the decision to tell friends about having ADHD, and other topics of interest to students in middle school and high school.

About.com

(http://www.add.about.com/health/add/library/weekly/aa022600a.htm)

This website includes information for graduating high school seniors written by a young adult with attention deficit–hyperactivity disorder.

---

ior when they sit near the front of the room, and they often benefit from working in an area with few visual or auditory distractions (for example, away from bulletin board displays and computers signaling with tones and music). Likewise, using study carrels, allowing a student to move from one desk to another in the classroom, and permitting the student to stand while working are examples of simple strategies that may help prevent serious behavior problems.

If a student needs to be corrected, provide a clear and direct but calm reprimand. If you say, "Tamatha, I know you are trying hard, but you have to try harder to raise your hand before speaking," Tamatha might not even realize that you are correcting her. A preferred response would be to say quietly to her, "Tamatha, do not call out answers. Raise your hand." This message is much clearer.

Both to address behavior issues and to teach social skills, some professionals recommend that students with ADHD learn strategies for monitoring their own behavior through self-talk. Whether these types of strategies are actually effective,

Check Your Learning

What cognitive, academic, social and emotional, and behavior characteristics of students with ADHD does Victor, the student you met at the beginning of the chapter, display? What types of interventions might help Victor learn?

Figure 7.2 **Strategies to Help Students with Attention Deficit–Hyperactivity Disorder Stay Attentive during Instruction**

- Begin your lesson with an attention grabber (e.g., joke, experiment, question).
- Prepare and distribute an outline of your lesson, including objectives.
- Pace the lesson to maintain student attention.
- Use visual images as much as possible.
- Draw students' attention to important concepts (e.g., vary your voice tone).
- Establish a signal to silence students and gain their attention.
- Repeat and highlight key concepts many times during presentation (e.g., have students repeat ideas by chorally responding).
- Allow students to respond frequently, and direct questions to students when they seem to be getting off task.
- Allow students a few seconds of think time before prompting them for an answer.
- Provide students with short breaks between long lessons.
- Alternate between high- and low-interest activities.
- Try to include activities that require movement, and be as interactive as possible.
- Frequently use students' names and interests in examples.
- Use lots of eye contact and proximity control.
- End each class or lesson with a clear closure, by highlighting important concepts, giving reminders about homework, exams, or other class business

S O U R C E : Adapted from "An ADHD Success Story: Strategies for Teachers and Students," by A. K. Yehle, and C. Wambold, 1998, *Teaching Exceptional Children, 30*(6), pp. 8–13.

however, has been questioned, especially for younger students (Abikoff, 1991). One area in which self-talk strategies are generally recommended is anger control. Students with ADHD often need to learn to control their anger because they experience much frustration that can lead to angry outbursts. If you teach a student who needs to learn anger management, a special education teacher, counselor, or social worker would probably design a program to meet this need; your responsibility would be to provide follow-through in your classroom.

Use of medication.   The most common intervention for students with ADHD is the prescription of psychostimulant medications. Approximately 750,000 students, 2 percent of the school-age population, take such medication each year (DuPaul, Barkley, & McMurray, 1991). Stimulant medications, the most common being the drug **Ritalin,** have been demonstrated to be effective in approximately 80 percent of cases in decreasing students' activity level and increasing their compliance (Swanson et al., 1992). How knowledgeable are you? Other common medications prescribed for ADHD are described in Table 7.1.

Despite the apparent effectiveness of stimulant medications in treating ADHD, their use remains somewhat controversial. For example, teachers often encounter the problem of students not consistently taking their medication, or sharing their medication. This situation can endanger other students, or at least result in a loss of learning (Howell, Evans, & Gardner, 1997). Another issue concerns the proper dosage. Some researchers contend that dosages high enough to cause an improvement in behavior can negatively affect students' academic learning and performance (Swanson et al., 1992). A third area of concern pertains to side effects. For example, approximately 30 percent of students have a **rebound effect** from their medication

FYI

The three medications most frequently administered to students with ADHD are Ritalin (methylphenidate), Dexedrine (dextroamphetamine), and Cylert (pemoline).

Table 7.1 Overview of Medications Commonly Used for ADHD

Brand Name [generic name]	Type of Medication	Positives	Negatives	Comments
Ritalin (tablets) [Methylphenidate]	Psychostimulant	Excellent safety record. Easy to use and evaluate. Works in 15–20 minutes.	Lasts only 4 hours. Must be administered frequently.	The most frequently prescribed medication. Watch for tics or Tourette's syndrome.
Ritalin SR20 (sustained release) [Methylphenidate]	Psychostimulant	Excellent safety record. Easy to use and evaluate. Longer lasting (6–8 hours).	Does not work as well as Ritalin tablets.	Can be used along with regular Ritalin.
Dexedrine (tablets) [Dextroamphetamine]	Psychostimulant	Excellent safety record. Rapid onset (20–30 minutes).	Lasts only 4 hours. Must be administered frequently.	Some patients do well on Dexedrine tablets.
Dexedrine (spansules) [Dextroamphetamine]	Psychostimulant	Excellent safety record. Longer lasting (6–8 hours).	Slower onset (takes 1–2 hours).	Can be used along with Dexedrine tablets. Some patients do well.
Cylert (tablets) [Pemoline]	Psychostimulant	Long lasting (6–8 hours).	Slower onset (several hours).	Not as safe as the other stimulants. Requires liver function blood test every 6 months.
Tofranil and Norpramin (tablets) [Imipramine and desipramine]	Antidepressant	Long lasting (12–24 hours). Can be administered at night. Often works when stimulants do not.	Has possible side effects. May take 1–3 weeks for full effects. Should not be started and stopped abruptly.	High doses may improve depression symptoms and mood swings.
Catapress (patches or tablets) [Clonidine]	Antihypertensive medication	Patches long lasting (5–6 days). Can be used with Tourette's syndrome.	Tablets are shorter lasting (4 hours). Patches are expensive.	Tablets cost less. Often has positive effect on defiant behavior.

S O U R C E : From *Attention Deficit Disorders: Assessment and Teaching,* by J. W. Lerner, B. Lowenthal, and S. R. Lerner. © 1995. Reprinted with permission of Wadsworth, an imprint of the Wadsworth Group, a division of Thomson Learning. Fax 800-730-2215.

(DuPaul et al., 1991). As the medication wears off, the student displays behaviors that may be worse than those that existed before the medication was administered. Some students can also experience a loss of appetite accompanied by suppressed weight and height gain (Reeve, 1990). However, once the medication is discontinued, students catch up in height and weight. Ultimately, a student's physician decides whether to prescribe medication. However, you are likely to be asked to provide educational input into this decision. These are some guidelines to consider when you are thinking about whether medication is likely to have a positive effect:

1. The student's attention is extremely limited, and his or her behavior is extremely disruptive.
2. Other interventions, in both academic and behavior domains, have been systematically attempted and have failed.

W W W   R e s o u r c e s

You can access the website for Children and Adults with Attention Deficit Disorder (CHADD) at http://www.chadd.org. CHADD is a nonprofit organization dedicated to bettering the lives of those with ADD and their families.

3. The student does not display symptoms of emotional problems such as anxiety.

4. The parents are supportive of trying medication.

5. The student can be adequately supervised so that medication is taken consistently.

6. The student understands the purpose of the medication and does not have a strong negative opinion about taking it (DuPaul et al., 1991).

Families of Children with Attention Deficit–Hyperactivity Disorder

WWW Resources

The website of the Developmental Disabilities Branch of the Centers for Disease Control and Prevention, at http://www.cdc.gov/ncbddd/adhd/, contains detailed information about the characteristics of ADHD and the effect it may have on families and communities.

Just like families of other students with disabilities or special needs, families of students with ADHD cannot be described using a single set of characteristics. However, it is fair to say that for many families, having a child with ADHD affects virtually every area of family functioning and adds significant stress for parents and siblings both at home and in interactions with school personnel (Erk, 1997). For example, Tate is a student with ADHD. Nearly everyday at school, he has some sort of negative experience, either because of inattention during instruction or a behavior disruption during lunch or passing periods. Because of this, Tate's parents receive quite a few late-afternoon phone calls from school personnel, and they, trying to respond to the teachers and keep clear their expectations for his school performance, often punish him by taking away computer time or some other privilege. Tate dislikes school, dreads the phone ringing when he gets home, and feels like all his parents ever do is criticize him. His parents are very concerned that they are having a more and more difficult time "getting through" to Tate about his behavior. What seems to be developing is a negative cycle of teacher–parent–child interactions that is likely to lead to frustration and ineffective intervention. When working with families like Tate's, your job as a teacher is to try to build positive relationships by encouraging parents to reward their children for their successes and by helping parents see their children's strengths.

Some parents of children with attention deficit–hyperactivity disorder struggle with their own role in their children's disorder, particularly when they believe that the child is "just like his father." Teachers have to be careful not to blame parents for their children's attention deficit–hyperactivity disorder, but, at the same time, not to condone inappropriate student behavior that a parent might excuse by saying that the child can't help it. Kilcarr and Quinn (1997) specifically addressed the difficulty that fathers sometimes have in their responses to their children with attention deficit–hyperactivity disorder. They note that fathers sometimes get very frustrated because they can't make the child behave the way they believe they are supposed to, and their attempts to impose harsher and harsher discipline just leads to more and more misbehavior. They encourage fathers to work diligently at understanding the disorder and their own role in dealing with it.

Before we close this discussion of ADHD, it is important to mention that this disorder still spurs heated discussions. Although most educators and physicians acknowledge the existence of ADHD (for example, Adams, 1994), others question whether ADHD is a distinct condition (for example, Reid, Maag, & Vasa, 1994) and whether it exists with distinctly different subtypes (e.g., Hall, Halperin, Schwartz, & Newcorn, 1997; Purvis & Tannock, 2000). Questions about the existence of ADHD usually center on the widely different prevalence rates reported, the difficulty in distinguishing ADHD from disabilities such as learning and emotional disabilities, and the absence of a consistent or unique approach for intervening for students with ADHD. Further, some professionals fear that medication has become too easy an intervention for students with attention problems. They comment that giving a pill can be perceived as more efficient than teaching students behavioral or cognitive strategies to monitor their own actions (Swanson et al., 1992) and that even though best practice demands that medication be accompanied by other interventions, too often this does not occur.

How Can You Accommodate Students Who Are Gifted and Talented?

In addition to students who are not able to meet typical curricular expectations, you also will have in your classroom students who have extraordinary abilities and skills. The term used to describe these students is **gifted and talented.** The federal definition for this group of students is stated in the 1988 Gifted and Talented Students Education Act (P.L. 100-297), which pertains to students who possess demonstrated or potential high-performance capability in intellectual, creative, specific academic and leadership areas, or the performing and visual arts. The federal definition further clarifies that these students need services in school that other students do not. However, unlike services offered through IDEA, federal legislation does not require specific services for gifted and talented students, and so the extent to which programs exist is largely determined by state and local policies.

An ongoing discussion in defining giftedness and serving these students concerns prevalence. As you have learned about several other groups of students with special needs, the reported prevalence of giftedness varies considerably from location to location. For example, the state of Wisconsin identifies 15 percent of its students as gifted, whereas North Dakota identifies only 1 percent (Council of State Directors of Programs for the Gifted, 1996). This variability is probably due to many factors, including funding, variations in state definitions of giftedness, and the procedures used to identify students for gifted services.

Prevalence of giftedness is also greatly affected by two other factors. First, researchers and writers now question traditional concepts of intelligence (Armstrong, 1994; Gardner, 1993). They argue that measured IQ is far too narrow a concept of intelligence and that a person's ability to problem solve, especially when in a new situation, is a more useful way of thinking about intelligence. Gardner (1993) has proposed that there are **multiple intelligences** that describe the broad array of talents that students possess. These intelligences are discussed in the Professional Edge. Because they range from the ability to use words and language effectively through the ability to produce and appreciate music, this concept of intelligence suggests that many individuals can be gifted and that their talents need to be developed in schools.

The second factor that affects the number of students identified as gifted is the notion of potential. Although some students who are gifted can be easily identified because they use their special abilities and are willing to be recognized for them, it is widely acknowledged that some gifted students go unnoticed. These students mask their skills from peers and teachers because low expectations are set for them

Connections

The use of performance-based assessments, often helpful in identifying students who are gifted and talented, is discussed in more depth in Chapter 11.

Professional Edge

Teaching to Diverse Student Needs through Multiple Intelligences (MI)

Over the past 2 decades, some professionals have reconceptualized intelligence from the traditional notion to one that emphasizes its multidimensional nature (Gardner, 1993). One strategy for reaching the range of diverse needs in many of today's classrooms is to arrange instruction to take into account eight intelligences.

1. *Verbal-linguistic.* This is the ability to use words effectively in prose, poetry, formal speech, informal conversation, and other forms, as well as the ability to understand others' words.

2. *Visual/spatial.* This is the ability to visualize forms, shapes, patterns, and designs, whether or not they exist in concrete form, as well as the ability to discern position in space and directionality.

3. *Logical/mathematical.* This is the ability to understand through the use of patterns as well as symbolic representations, and the ability to apply reasoning.

4. *Bodily/kinesthetic.* This is the ability to use the body effectively through athletics, dance, movement, and other activities, as well as the ability to use the body skillfully (for example, for delicate or intricate tasks, as must a surgeon or sculptor use his or her hands).

5. *Musical.* This is the ability to perceive, analyze, create, and perform through music, including culminating in practicing professions such as composer, critic, and musician.

6. *Intrapersonal.* This is the ability to analyze and understand oneself and to be able to take actions based on that understanding.

7. *Interpersonal.* This is the ability to observe, grasp, and act on the moods, emotions, perceptions, and other aspects of relationships with people.

8. *Naturalist.* This is the ability to understand, respond to, and explain phenomena encountered in nature as illustrated by the work performed in professions such as farmer, hunter, and veterinarian.

If you are interested in learning more about multiple intelligences, the following websites, as well as many others, can help you explore this fascinating and useful way of thinking about teaching and learning.

http://www.ThomasArmstrong.com
Dr. Thomas Armstrong has written extensively about multiple intelligences. At his website, you can learn about the development of the theory of multiple intelligences, find more detailed explanations of the eight intelligences, and locate resources to help you learn more.

http://www.multi-intell.com
At the New Dimensions of Learning website, you can find detailed information about the eight intelligences as well as ways of exploring each of them yourself and with students.

http://edweb.gsn.org/edref.mi.intro.html
The EdWeb website is dedicated to educational technology and school reform. The site includes discussions of traditional versus contemporary thinking about intelligence; additional information about Howard Gardner, developer of MI theory; and Project Zero, a Harvard University project designed to enhance creativity and complex thinking among students, particularly those living in urban, low-income areas.

http://www.harding.edu/~cbr/midemo/mifirst.html
The Resources in Teaching Multiple Intelligences website includes information similar to that of other sites, but it also has a newsletter and links to related sites.

or their unique needs are not nurtured. Groups at risk for being underidentified include young boys, adolescent girls, students who are highly gifted or talented who might be considered geniuses, students from minority groups, and students with disabilities (e.g., Kloosterman, 1998; Reis, Gentry, & Park, 1996).

Characteristics and Needs of Students Who Are Gifted and Talented

Students who are gifted and talented have a wide range of characteristics, and any one student considered gifted and talented can have just a few or many of these characteristics. Although early studies presented a limited number of descriptors, the studies were frequently completed with high achievers from privileged backgrounds and did not take into account the diverse nature of today's society (Terman, 1925). More recently, especially with the increasingly recognized need to address giftedness among the entire population, including students from diverse cultural groups, deciding whom to identify as gifted or talented and how to describe them has become complex. For example, as noted in the preceding section, some students with gifts or talents have gone unrecognized (Cline & Schwartz, 1999). Some of these students have avoided identification because of low self-esteem leading to avoidance of academic tasks (Davis & Rimm, 1994). These students sometimes have very poor academic test scores and may have poor relationships with peers. Other students have not been identified because of cultural bias in assessment and other identification procedures (Cline & Schwartz, 1999). The following information about student characteristics is intended to provide an overview of students who are gifted and talented and should be viewed as a sample of what is known, not as a comprehensive summary.

Cultural Awareness

Research has repeatedly demonstrated that African American students, particularly males, are overrepresented in special education classes and underrepresented in gifted programs (Graybill, 1997).

Cognitive abilities and academic skills. The area of cognitive functioning and academic skills is the most delineated aspect of gifted education. Students who are gifted and talented in the area of cognitive functioning generally have an extraordinary amount of information, which they retain easily; a wide variety of interests; and high levels of language development and verbal ability. They also have advanced ability to comprehend information using accelerated and flexible thought processes, a heightened ability to recognize relationships between diverse ideas, a strong capacity to form and use conceptual frameworks, and an exceptional degree of persistent, goal-directed behavior (National Foundation for Gifted and Creative Children, 1996). These students tend to be skilled problem solvers because they are better able than other students to pick out important information that helps them solve the problem and are more likely to monitor their problem-solving efforts (Westberg & Archambault, 1997).

The cognitive abilities of students who are gifted and talented sometimes lead them to high academic achievement, but not always. Consider these two students who are gifted and talented: Belinda was identified as gifted and talented in second grade. She has been reading since the age of 3, seems as comfortable interacting with adults as with her peers, and invariably becomes the leader of the groups of children with whom she plays, even if they are older. She enjoys school immensely and wants to be a university professor when she grows up. Omar is also identified as gifted and talented. He has been taking violin and piano lessons since the age of 5, and his first music teacher recommended him to a local university program. In the sixth grade, Tomas is a veteran pianist, and he already plans to major in music theory when he goes to college. He has an unusual grasp of the subtleties of music, and he already offers his own interpretations of both classical and contemporary music. In his academic studies, however, Tomas is just slightly below average in achievement. He is also somewhat shy; he appears more comfortable with his musical instruments than with his peers.

Students who are gifted and talented are often difficult to identify and challenging to teach. What kinds of intelligence might you recognize in your students? Within your inclusive classroom, how might you address the academic and social-emotional needs of students who are gifted and talented?

Social and emotional needs.

Socially and emotionally, gifted and talented students can be well liked and emotionally healthy, or they can be unpopular and at risk for serious emotional problems. Affectively, they tend to have unusual sensitivity to others' feelings as well as highly developed emotional depth and intensity, a keen sense of humor that can be either supportive or hostile, and a sense of justice (Clark, 1992). They often set high expectations for themselves and others, which can lead to frustration when those expectations are not met (Mendaglio & Pyryt, 1995).

WWW Resources

You can learn about resources for students who are gifted or talented at The World Council for Gifted and Talented Children website at http://www.WorldGifted.org/.

Because some gifted students have a superior ability to recognize and respond to others' feelings, they can be extremely popular with classmates and often sought after as helpmates. However, if they tend to "show off" their talents or repeatedly challenge adult authority, they may be perceived negatively by peers and teachers and have problems developing appropriate social relationships (Clark, 1992). For example, Ms. Ogden is concerned about eighth grader Esteban. On some days, Esteban seems to have just a four-word vocabulary: "I already know that." He says this to teachers, to peers, and to his parents about nearly any topic under discussion. Although it is often true that Esteban does know about the subjects that are being discussed, Ms. Ogden finds herself becoming annoyed at Esteban's style of interacting, and she knows the other students don't want to be grouped with Esteban because of it.

Students' emotional status is one factor that contributes to their social skills. Some gifted and talented students are self-confident, have a strong positive self-concept, and are generally happy (Hoge & Renzulli, 1993). Others, however, feel isolated or alienated and can experience depression, low self-concept, and other emotional problems. If they find school boring and have difficulty forming friendships, students who are gifted and talented can also have poor attitudes toward learning and school activities in general. These students are at risk for dropping out of school (Davis & Rimm, 1994).

Behavior patterns.

Students who are gifted and talented display the entire range of behaviors that other students do. They can be model students who participate and seldom cause problems, often serving as class leaders. In this capacity, students are sensitive to others' feelings and moderate their behavior based on others' needs (Winebrenner, 1992). However, because students who are gifted and talented often have an above-average capacity to understand people and situations, their negative behavior can sometimes be magnified compared with that of other students. This behavior can be displayed through an intense interest in a topic and refusal to change when requested by a teacher (Smith & Luckasson, 1995). Other behavior problems some students who are gifted and talented display include being bossy in group situations, purposely failing, and valuing and participating in counterculture activities (Van Tassel-Baska, Patton, & Prillaman, 1991; Winebrenner, 1992).

Interventions for Students Who Are Gifted and Talented

Although some school districts operate separate classes and programs for students who are gifted and talented, you will likely be responsible for meeting some or all of the needs of these students in your classroom (Torrance & Sisk, 1998). The concept used to think about meeting the needs of students who are gifted or talented is *differentiation* (Dinnocenti, 1998), the same concept that is suggested for thinking about the instruction of students with academic and behavior problems. Four differentiation strategies often used to challenge gifted and talented students are *enrichment, acceleration, sophistication,* and *novelty* (Gallagher & Gallagher, 1994).

Enrichment is an instructional approach that provides students with information, materials, and assignments that enable them to elaborate on concepts being presented as part of the regular curriculum and usually require high levels of thinking (Dinnocenti, 1999). This option requires you to find related information, prepare it for the students who need it, and create relevant activities for them. One teacher provided enrichment to her students in math (Winebrenner, 1992). She gave a pretest for each unit to the students who were gifted and talented, and if they had already mastered all the concepts, they were given a choice of alternative activities and assignments. If any concepts had not yet been mastered, the students were required to participate in the lesson on the days those concepts were taught. Students excused from lessons were expected to take a unit test with the rest of the class. The expectations for student work, options for enrichment, lessons to attend, and testing requirements were all summarized on a student learning contract. For enrichment to be effective, you need to ensure that students have opportunities to complete alternative assignments designed to encourage advanced thinking and product development, that they do such assignments in lieu of other work instead of as additional work, and that many learning resources are available to them both in and out of the classroom (Maker, 1993).

Acceleration is providing students with curriculum that takes them from their current level of learning and moves them forward (Feldhusen, Van Winkle, & Ehle, 1996). For example, Stephen is a student who is gifted in math. In middle school, he worked in an individualized and independent program to advance his skills. In high school, he completed the available curriculum during his freshman year and then began taking math courses at a local university. Stephen's program is based on acceleration. Acceleration can occur in one area, as is the case with Stephen, or can be total. For a few students, acceleration includes entering kindergarten early, skipping grades, taking correspondence courses, and attending residential high schools designed to enable students to work at their own rate through an advanced curriculum (Davis & Rimm, 1994).

FYI

Students with disabilities have been underrepresented in gifted and talented programs. It is essential that students with learning disabilities, emotional disabilities, communication disorders, orthopedic impairments, sensory impairments, and other disabilities not be overlooked in nurturing giftedness.

Research Note

A 1993 U.S. Department of Education study found that gifted and talented elementary schoolchildren master 35 to 50 percent of the grade curriculum in five basic subject areas before starting the school year.

Sophistication is a strategy in which teachers help students to see the principles or systems that underlie the content being learned by the rest of the class (Dinnocenti, 1999). For example, in an elementary school classroom, as students are reading stories and answering questions about vocabulary or the main idea, a student who is gifted might analyze how character, plot, and setting are intertwined in the story. In a music class, a student who is talented might be assigned to add harmony to a basic melody other students are learning.

Novelty is an approach in which teachers give students opportunities to explore traditional curricular content in alternative and unusual ways (Gallagher & Gallagher, 1994). For example, students might develop interviews with historical figures to gain their perspectives on world events of the past instead of simply reading about them. They might likewise be asked to create multimedia presentations that capture concepts being taught in a science class. Working with a mentor, using problem-based learning, and creating learning materials that other students can use are examples of novelty approaches for teaching students who are gifted and talented (Savoie & Hughes, 1994; Winebrenner, 1992).

Further examples of these four approaches to intervening with students who are gifted and talented are summarized in Table 7.2. The Case in Practice illustrates a teacher using some of these strategies.

Some professionals contend that strategies for instructing students who are gifted or talented are appropriate for most students (Culross, 1997; Reis, Gentry, & Park, 1996). They suggest that your job as a general education teacher is to design effective instruction for all students, and that this instruction also meets the needs of students who are gifted and talented. To reach all your students, you need to offer activities that address several ability levels at one time, that accommodate a variety of interest areas, and that enable students to integrate their learning. You must also have an overall plan for your instruction (Cline & Schwartz, 1999; Torrance & Sisk, 1998).

Check Your Learning

What strengths might students who are gifted and talented have in the social-emotional area? What problems might they face?

FYI

Two variations on the instructional approaches presented here are *accelerated integrated learning* and *curriculum compacting*, in which students study the same themes and topics as the rest of the class but in greater detail or depth and with enhanced opportunities for application.

Table 7.2 Sample Content Modification for Gifted Students

| Modification | SUBJECT | | | |
	Math	Science	Language Arts	Social Studies
Acceleration	Algebra in fifth grade	Early chemistry and physics	Learning grammatical structure early	Early introduction to world history
Enrichment	Changing bases in number systems	Experimentation and data collecting	Short story and poetry writing	Reading biographies for historical insight
Sophistication	Mastering the laws of arithmetic	Learning the laws of physics	Mastering the structural properties of plays, sonnets, and so on	Learning and applying the principles of economics
Novelty	Probability and statistics	Science and its impact on society	Rewriting Shakespeare's tragedies with happy endings	Creating future societies and telling how they are governed

S O U R C E : From *Teaching the Gifted Child* (4th ed., p. 100), by James J. Gallagher and Shelagh A. Gallagher, 1994, Boston: Allyn and Bacon. Copyright © 1994 by Allyn and Bacon. Reprinted by permission.

C A S E   I N   P R A C T I C E

Meeting the Needs of a Gifted Student

It is Wednesday morning and Ms. Ollendorf is preparing for the school day. She is thinking about what to do with Mary Jo, a student in her class who is clearly gifted in a number of areas. Mary Jo writes with surprisingly sophisticated vocabulary, and she seldom makes any type of error. Her true talents, however, lie in math, science, and music. She either knows or masters within minutes any math concept introduced, and she has a grasp of science that is just a little intimidating to Ms. Ollendorf. Mary Jo most likes searching for information on the Internet related to topics addressed in school.

Yesterday Mary Jo's mother came in for a conference. She said that Mary Jo's love of science was waning and was concerned. Mary Jo's mother offered this explanation:

> Mary Jo has said probably 20 times during the past month that science is boring. She thinks the book is too simple and doesn't explain "interesting" things. She says she could finish her reports on the experiments before doing

them because they are not complex enough to challenge her. She also said that she doesn't do the extra-credit work that you give students as an option because she can get perfect scores on everything anyway. Why would she want to do extra work?

In thinking about Mary Jo, Ms. Ollendorf has to admit that the child has made a few good points. What concerns Ms. Ollendorf most, though, is the possibility of Mary Jo becoming uninterested in science when she so clearly has the potential to pursue a science-related career if she so chooses.

A week later, Ms. Ollendorf introduces a different sort of science to Mary Jo. She has gathered advanced supplemental science textbooks and has contacted several friends who work in local businesses to be mentors for Mary Jo. She has also spoken with a friend who is a science education professor about how to challenge Mary Jo. She offers Mary Jo these options:

1. She will take unit tests prior to instruction.
2. If she scores at least 80 percent on a unit test, she can work 4 days per week in the alternative

science materials. If she does not achieve 80 percent, she will participate in the lessons on the parts of the unit she has not mastered.
3. For each unit of instruction completed in this manner, Mary Jo is to select and create a product that demonstrates the science concepts she has explored.
4. Mary Jo will have a once-per-month visit with a mentor. Mentors might include a high school student, one of the local businesspeople, or another teacher.

R E F L E C T I O N S

What type of gifted student is Mary Jo? If you had to make a prediction, how do you think she behaves in other subject areas? What did Ms. Ollendorf do to make science a more challenging subject for Mary Jo? Which of the four approaches to providing appropriate instruction to gifted and talented students did Ms. Ollendorf use? What other strategies could Ms. Ollendorf implement to expand Mary Jo's science instruction further?

What Are the Needs of Students from Culturally Diverse Backgrounds?

The racial, cultural, and linguistic diversity of U.S. classrooms has been increasing steadily, and all indications are that it will continue to do so. For example, in 1972 just 15 percent of students enrolled in grades 1 through 12 were members of minority groups. In 1998, that number had risen to 37 percent. Hispanic students account for the greatest part of the change: In 1972 they accounted for 6 percent of school enrollments, but in 1998 they accounted for 15 percent of enrollment. The percent of African American students enrolled in schools changed during that same time period from 15 percent to 17 percent. Other minority student enrollments increased 4 percent (National Center for Education Statistics, 2000).

Evidence suggests that students from cultures other than Anglo European sometimes experience an extraordinarily high failure rate in school. For example, in 1996 only 11.1 percent of all young adults in the United States ages 15 through 24 did not have a high school diploma and were not enrolled in school; however, this number included 29.4 percent of Hispanic young adults and 13 percent of African American young adults (National Center for Education Statistics, 1998). The dropout rate has been decreasing slightly, but only for white students. The reasons for these students' failure to complete school are complex and interrelated, but involve several identifiable factors (Stephen, Varble, & Taitt, 1993). First, students from racial and ethnic minority groups often lack role models because most teachers are from the majority Anglo European culture. Second, when students are not born in this country, they are far more likely to drop out of school. For example, 44.1 percent of Hispanic students who are born outside the United States drop out of school—double the rate of 16.7 percent for students with at least one parent born in this country (National Center for Education Statistics, 1998). Third, societal expectations and realities for these students are often contradictory. Although they are told that they can meet high educational standards, they may be discriminated against in assessment for and access to advanced programs. Fourth, instructional practices can negatively affect students. In particular, textbooks with cultural biases can promote stereotypes and omit culturally important information. Teaching practices that do not allow opportunities for student-centered learning also can put students from different cultures at a disadvantage, because students' background and experiences may lead them to learn more effectively from small-group peer interactions. A mix of teaching approaches is needed. Finally, school policies and organization can penalize students. For example, few schools operate mentor programs specifically designed to connect students from diverse cultures with leaders in business, industry, and education. These contacts can be essential for helping students succeed.

The relationship among school failure, special education, and diverse student needs is not a comfortable one (Grossman, 1995). Historically, students from racial or cultural minorities were sometimes inappropriately placed in special education programs based on discriminatory assessment practices (Drew, Logan, & Hardman, 1992). Evidence suggests that this unfortunate bias may still be in play today (Benner, 1998; Obiakor, 1999). This practice can be attributed at least partly to an inappropriate school perspective that students with non-Anglo European values or those who speak languages other than English need to be remediated in some way (Benner, 1998). Current programs that emphasize multicultural education for both teachers and students are designed to increase sensitivity to cultural and linguistic diversity, which should counteract this bias (Pohan & Mathison, 1999).

Cultural Awareness

Understanding the characteristics of students who are members of racially and culturally diverse groups involves recognizing that the contradictions between some of these students' home and community experiences and the expectations placed on

---

Check Your Learning

Why are students with culturally and linguistically diverse backgrounds given special attention in a textbook about students with special needs?

Cultural Awareness

By the year 2020, it is estimated that 28 percent of the population under the age of 18 will be Hispanic, up from the current 11 percent. Some 40 percent of Hispanic children live in poverty, and, at least in some cases, the children and mothers may be homesick for their family, language, and customs (Holman, 1997).

Cultural diversity offers rich opportunities for learning but it is also a source of misunderstandings that can lead to school failure. What steps can you take to ensure that you are responding appropriately to all your students as individual members of diverse cultural groups? How can you promote student acceptance of cultural differences in your classroom?

them at school can lead to learning and behavior problems. It also includes acknowledging that teachers sometimes misunderstand students and their parents, which can lead to miscommunication, distrust, and negative school experiences.

The makeup of today's general education classrooms reflects the racial, linguistic, and cultural diversity of the communities they serve. The Technology Notes feature on page 256 describes how computers can be used to foster students' cultural awareness. However, as the preceding discussion of cultural bias suggests, such awareness and sensitivity also must be cultivated among general and special education teachers.

If you live in an area in which many different cultures are represented in a single classroom, the thought of learning about all of them can be intimidating. It is probably not possible, nor necessary, to learn many details about all the cultures of your students (Benner, 1998). However, it is your responsibility to learn fundamental characteristics students might have because of their backgrounds. For example, some students might keep their questions to themselves instead of asking you because of concern about interacting with the teacher, who is perceived as an authority figure. If you understand this reticence, you can make a special effort to initiate interactions with those students. Further, when a student displays behavior that you find troublesome, you should determine whether a cultural reason prompted the behavior before responding to it or before assuming it represents misbehavior. This information can be learned by talking with students, with their families, or with teachers experienced in working with students from that culture, or by consulting your district's print or video resources on cultural diversity. Of course, you should also keep in mind that not all students from diverse backgrounds encounter these problems, nor do all families from racial or ethnic minority groups use discipline practices different from those schools use.

The INCLUDE strategy can be a valuable tool for making decisions about instruction for students from culturally and linguistically diverse groups. First, you

Cultural Awareness

Cultural awareness includes understanding that individuals and families experience various degrees of assimilation and that the United States has been a culturally diverse society for hundreds of years. Teachers should not assume cultural traits on the basis of ethnic identity alone.

should consider the demands of the classroom setting, and then identify strengths and interests that students bring to the learning environment. Next, you should look for potential problem areas throughout your entire instructional program and use that information to brainstorm ideas for ameliorating the problems and select those with the most potential for success. As you go through this process, it is essential to monitor student progress and make adjustments as needed.

The impact of cultural and linguistic diversity in educational settings can be examined from three perspectives: how cultural factors affect student behavior, how teaching approaches can be tailored to culturally diverse groups, and how communication with non-native English speakers can be enhanced. We examine each perspective briefly.

Cultural values and student behavior.   Various cultural values have an impact on students' behaviors and the way educators interpret these behaviors. For example, for some Native American students, time is a fluid concept not necessarily bound by clocks. A student might come to school "late" by Anglo European culture standards that measure time precisely, but "on time" according to events happening at the student's home. Another example of the differences between Anglo European standards and some students' cultures concerns school participation. Hispanic American students sometimes are more likely to participate when they have established a close relationship with their teachers and peers (Wallis, 1993). Contrast this fact with the common high school structure in which one teacher sees as many as 180 students each day and often uses an instructional format that minimizes interactions. In such settings, Hispanic American students can be at a great disadvantage. Similarly, recent research suggests that some African American students learn better in cooperative situations (Wallis, 1993). If these small-group learning experiences are not offered in the classroom, some students are being denied access to a potentially powerful learning opportunity.

Informed instructional decision making.   Decisions about teaching approaches occur by matching the needs of students from culturally diverse backgrounds to instructional approaches (Banks, 1993). For example, not only do many African American students respond well to cooperative rather than competitive learning environments, but also many Hispanic American and Asian American students (Guild, 1994). Such approaches should become integral to your teaching. Likewise, because traditional Native American students dislike responding individually and out loud in a large-group situation, you may need to create opportunities for individual contacts and quiet participation.

Cross-cultural communication.   For students who do not speak English as their native language, school can be a frustrating experience, resulting in some common problems. First, students who do not use English proficiently can easily be discriminated against when they are assessed. As noted earlier, students may be identified as needing special education just because their English skills are limited; particular care must be taken to ensure that non-native speakers are not mistakenly labeled. Second, students with limited English skills are sometimes perceived by teachers and classmates as deficient; teachers might have difficulty understanding students and might assume they have limited ability, and peers may exclude students from social activi-

Connections

The role of cultural awareness in teacher–parent communication and in professional collaboration is introduced in Chapters 2 and 3.

ties because of language differences. Third, language-related issues sometimes lead to a belief that students must be segregated from other students to learn when English is not their primary language.

For students from culturally and linguistically diverse backgrounds, home–school communication is critical. You might have difficulty even in basic communication, though, because of language differences and the lack of availability of an interpreter. A second problem you may face concerns cultural values and parent responses to school personnel (Dennis & Giangreco, 1996). For example, in traditional Asian American families, pride and shame are often emphasized, and indirectness is valued. Imagine a parent conference in which an insensitive teacher describes in detail the academic and learning problems an Asian American child is having and directly asks the parents whether they can assist in carrying out a home–school behavior change program. If they follow traditional Asian values, the parents might be humiliated by the public accounting of their child's failures and embarrassed at the teacher's direct and unnecessary request for their assistance.

A third example of the importance of communication relates to the parents' perceptions of school and how they should interact with school personnel contrasted to school staff expectations for parent involvement. For example, the parents of some students may find school foreign and intimidating, and they may believe that their role is to listen passively to what school personnel say. For students from diverse cultural backgrounds who have disabilities, it is particularly important to be sure that adequate information is communicated to parents about the student's instructional program and the procedures used in special education (Sontag & Schacht, 1994). You share this responsibility with special education professionals.

Another example of potential home–school misunderstanding related to cultural diversity concerns discipline. Some discipline practices Anglo European educators might consider abusive are widely accepted in some cultures (McIntyre & Silva, 1992). In some low-income Hispanic American families from the Caribbean Islands, children kneel on uncooked rice as a punishment for misbehavior. In some unassimilated Asian American families, children are locked out of the house as punishment when they are perceived as forgetting their own cultural values. In some Vietnamese American families, children with pierced ears are tied by their ear to a doorknob when they misbehave (McIntyre & Silva, 1992). Practices such as these are not typical in Anglo European American culture, and teachers might consider them a reason to report the family for abuse or neglect. Further, teachers' perceptions can easily be telegraphed to parents, leading to less than ideal home–school interactions. Of course, discipline practices such as these are not common in all families from cultural and ethnic minority groups. Through clear communication and a willingness to understand your students' backgrounds, you can avoid stereotyping.

Families and Diversity

Not only may you find that it takes a great effort to understand students and family members because of language barriers and global cultural difference, but also you may learn that you simply do not grasp the day-to-day realities of your students' and their families' lives. Probably the single most recommended strategy for gaining a better understanding is to set aside books and lesson plans, to release your conceptual ideas about diversity and multiculturalism, and simply to listen to families

Check Your Learning

What types of communication problems can occur between school professionals and parents of students from racially and ethnically diverse groups?

[Technology Notes]

Using Computer Technology to Foster Cultural Awareness

Technology can be used effectively to build a greater understanding of world politics and cultural differences. In the following lesson plan, developed by Roblyer, Edwards, and Havriluk (1997), the teacher assists students in using a variety of technologies as they develop a multicultural resource center for the employees of an international business.

Computers with access to the World Wide Web offer a wealth of multicultural learning opportunities.

Activity: Training for Cultural Awareness

Level: Grades 9–12

Purpose of Activity: To familiarize students with the intricacies of other cultures through the development of a project

Instructional Activity: **Setting the Stage: The Training Department Dilemma.** Over the past 2 years your company, NUTECH, has experienced a surge in overseas business. This has resulted in a tremendous increase in the amount of foreign travel for NUTECH employees, who have conducted business in locales where they knew very little about the local cultures. The employees report that they believe that this has put them at a distinct disadvantage, and they would like to get training on how to relate more effectively to indigenous populations when traveling abroad.

Your training team has been assigned the task of putting together a multicultural center to provide employees with an easy-to-access compilation of resources. At a team meeting, a brainstorming session identified several ideas for potentially valuable resources.

(Ladson-Billings, 1999). In addition to being willing to make the time to learn about families, Sánchez (1999, pp. 354–357) recommends the following:

1. Be willing to step outside your comfort zone, going into the community to learn about families.
2. Adopt the unequivocal view that all families are involved in and significant to their children's education, and that schooling is only one source of education.
3. Be willing to examine your own story more deeply.

<table>
<tr><td>Ideas for Multicultural
Resource Center:</td><td>Brochure. The brochure should include a brief description of the history of the country along with relevant geographic and cultural data. It would be helpful to stress any cultural difference that visitors should recognize; for example, in Thailand it is considered very rude to sit with one leg crossed over the other with a foot pointing at another person. Students should use a desktop-publishing or word-processing program to develop the brochure. Graphics should enhance the layout.</td></tr>
</table>

Videotape. Create a videotape that provides useful information to a traveler in a specific country. The information should enable that person to function more effectively in the local culture by stressing customs, values, and historical perspectives.

Bar-coded videodisc presentation. Develop a bar-code–driven program that accesses relevant segments of a videodisc that pertain to a specific culture. Students should use a bar-code generator and a word processor for the project materials, which they should mount on tagboard and laminate.

Multimedia display. Create a multimedia display that provides suggestions for travelers in a particular country. Video segments would enhance the program, either imported into the program or through interaction with a videodisc player.

Database. Develop a database of resources for each country to which employees might travel. This should include magazine and newspaper articles, videos, books, and so forth. Students can access much of this information via the Internet.

Suggestions for Teacher: For this activity, students choose a country on which to focus. They must understand the purpose of the product—to provide a resource for someone who needs help functioning in another country's culture. To develop a quality product, students will need to strive to truly understand the culture of the chosen country. Encourage students to use telecommunications resources to locate information. The Internet may offer them an opportunity to actually converse with citizens of the chosen country. They may also have access to foreign nationals living nearby.

S O U R C E : *Integrating Educational Technology into Teaching*, by M. D. Roblyer, J. Edwards, and M. A. Havriluk, 1997, Columbus, OH: Merrill.

---

4. Be willing to challenge stereotypes and reduce prejudice.
5. Be willing to explore the sociocultural context in the lives of families and teachers.
6. Be willing to examine your own teaching practices from a family perspective.
7. Be willing to distribute power.

By carefully listening to families and by recognizing that the most important factor about working with others is that, unless you have been in the same situation, you *cannot* completely understand, you can respond with respect and sensitivity to your students as well as their families.

Multicultural and Bilingual Education

WWW Resources

You may wish to locate more resources related to multicultural education. One good site that has many listed resources, including information about African American and Native American children, is http://curry.edschool.virginia.edu/go/multicultural/teachers.html.

Creating a classroom in which students' cultures are acknowledged and valued is a fundamental characteristic of **multicultural education,** that is, curriculum and instruction that reflects the diversity of our society. Multicultural education begins with examining how you decorate your classroom and how you select learning materials (Banks, 1993). Do your bulletin boards display the work of students from ethnic and cultural minority groups? When you portray historical events, do you include information about members of several cultural groups? Does your classroom contain stories or literature about successful individuals from a variety of cultures? Is respect for diversity infused throughout your curriculum? Two points are especially noteworthy regarding multicultural education. First, professionals agree that multicultural education should not be an event that occurs for 1 week out of each school year. It is better addressed through ongoing inclusion of multicultural information in students' education activities. Second, multicultural education is not a topic that is confined to social studies, as some educators believe. It should pervade all subject areas, being reflected in the stories or literature addressed in language arts or English, in assignments given in science and math classes, and in the community contacts students make in vocational classes.

WWW Resources

The National Association of Bilingual Education is an organization concerned with the quality of education received by students whose native language is not English. You can learn more about this organization by visiting their website at http://www.nabe.org/.

The school in which you teach might also offer **bilingual education programs.** Bilingual education programs are based on the assumption that students need to learn English by being immersed in the language environment, but that until a level of proficiency in English is achieved, many students do not learn concepts and skills from English language instruction (Bennett, 1995). In bilingual programs, students spend part of the school day receiving instruction in core academic areas in their native language and the remainder of the day with English-speaking students. For students receiving special education services, a **bilingual special education program** staffed by a bilingual special education teacher may be provided in which students receive individualized services designed to strengthen their learning and demonstrate respect for their language and culture (Díaz-Rico & Weed, 1995). Yet other students, especially in elementary schools, who are English language learners (ELLs) participate fulltime in the typical classroom, with a bilingual teacher joining the class for all or part of the day (Bahamonde & Friend, 1999).

If you develop curiosity about your students' cultures and languages, you can be sensitive to their learning needs and responsive to them. To guide you in looking at the curriculum and instruction you will use, the Professional Edge provides a list of questions for successful teaching in a diverse classroom.

Ｈow Can You Meet the Needs of Students Who Are at Risk?

In addition to all the other special needs you find among students, you are likely to encounter one that is found in virtually every public school classroom in the country. That special need is being at risk for school failure. Students who are at risk are

Professional Edge

Assessing Your Effectiveness as a Teacher in a Culturally Diverse Classroom

As a teacher, it is your responsibility to respond positively to the cultural and linguistic diversity in your classroom. The following questions can help you focus on making your teaching culturally sensitive:

- Do I have an understanding of the cultures that are represented in my classroom?
- Am I aware of culture-based learning styles?
- Are my expectations as high for students of color as for Anglo students?
- Do I make conscious efforts to engage all students in learning activities?
- Do I make conscious efforts to give equivalent attention and encouragement to all students?
- Do I participate in staff development programs that help teachers better understand student diversity?
- Do the staff development programs for my school and district address multicultural and bilingual education issues?

- Am I open to identifying racial and cultural biases in myself, my students, and my curriculum materials?
- Do I use methodology that fosters integration (for example, cooperative learning)?
- Do my instruction and methodology conflict with the cultural beliefs of any students in my classroom?
- Do I use a variety of tasks, measures, and materials in assessing student competencies to avoid inadvertent bias in assessment?

S O U R C E : Adapted from *How to Respond to Your Culturally Diverse Student Population*, by Sarah LaBrec Wyman, 1993, Alexandria, VA: Association for Supervision and Curriculum Development.

those who have been exposed to some condition that negatively affects their learning. Most teachers include in this list students who have been prenatally exposed to drugs, including alcohol; students who are homeless; and students who have been neglected. Others include students who are bullies and those who are victims, as well as those who have recently experienced the death of someone close to them. Students who are school phobic are at risk, as are those considering suicide, those who are considered physically unattractive, and those who are socially underdeveloped. Slow learners are a group of particular concern for professionals (MacMillan, Gresham, Bocian, & Lambros, 1998). It is difficult to understand the range of problems students face and the tremendous impact these problems have on their lives. One school district committee, formed to identify the district's at-risk learners and to create options for helping them succeed, became overwhelmed at the enormity of their task. One teacher finally suggested that all at-risk students were students who were not achieving in the way teachers thought they could.

You might be wondering why students who are at risk are discussed in a text about students with disabilities. Three reasons are these: First, with a well-designed education, many students who are at risk for school failure succeed in school. The strategies for accommodating the needs of students with disabilities are usually effective for students at risk; these strategies are discussed in the remaining chapters of this text. Second, it is well known that effective early-school experiences for students who are at risk can establish a pattern of success in school learning (Bowman, 1994).

Without such experiences, students at risk are more likely to be identified as having learning or emotional disabilities. Third, many students with disabilities also are students at risk. Many students with disabilities have been abused, some live in poverty, others use illegal drugs. Increasing your understanding of risk factors and approaches for working with students at risk benefits all students at risk for school failure.

Characteristics and Needs of Students at Risk

Cognitively, socially and emotionally, behaviorally, and physically, students considered at risk are as diverse as students in the general school population. What distinguishes them from other students is the high likelihood that they will drop out of school prior to earning a high school diploma and that they will experience difficulty throughout their lives. Some also share other characteristics and needs, including a tendency to be noncompliant, problems in monitoring their learning and behavior, language delays, difficulties with social relationships, and problems understanding the consequences of their behaviors (Wenz-Gross & Siperstein, 1998). To illustrate further the needs these students have, three representative groups of at-risk students are briefly discussed: children living in poverty, including those who are homeless; children who have been abused or neglected; and children who live in homes in which substance abuse occurs. Keep in mind that even though this discussion treats each group as distinct for the sake of clarity, any single student could be in all three groups.

Students who live in poverty. The United Nations Children's Fund defines poverty as living in a household with an income less than half a country's median income. By this definition, approximately 22 percent of U.S. children live in poverty (Canadian Scholars' Press, 2000). Students who live in poverty often come to school tired and preoccupied from the stresses they experience in their lives away from school (Kirst, 1991). They might not have nutritious meals, a safe and warm place to play and sleep, or needed supplies to complete homework. They are sometimes worried about their family's circumstances, and older students might be expected to work evenings and weekends to help support the family or to miss school to babysit for younger siblings. Students living in poverty also are more likely than advantaged students to experience parental neglect, to witness violence, and to change schools and residences frequently.

Some poor families are homeless; it is now estimated that more than 700,000 people are homeless each night (National Law Center on Homelessness and Poverty, 1999), and that this number is rising dramatically. Approximately 25 percent of homeless individuals in urban areas are children under the age of 18 (National Coalition for the Homeless, 1999). In addition to homelessness, many families are in temporary living arrangements with relatives or friends. Homelessness results in many educational problems. Students sometimes leave their neighborhood school or transfer from school to school when they move to a shelter or stay with family or friends. This can leave gaps in their learning. Other students are placed in foster care when the family is homeless, and this arrangement affects their social and emotional adjustment. In addition to learning problems, students who live in poverty or who are homeless sometimes (although not always) display acting-out, restless, or aggressive behavior; depression; regressive behaviors; and anxiety (Linehan, 1992).

Students who are abused or neglected. A second group of students at risk are the approximately 4 million who are physically abused, sexually abused, psychologically

Research Note

Fujiura and Yamaki (2000) used large data sets to analyze the relationship between poverty and disability. They found that the two are clearly linked, and that when poverty is controlled as a factor, links between ethnicity or culture and disability do not exist.

FYI

Homeless children have to make many educational and personal adjustments as a result of four conditions in their lives: constant moving, frequent change of schools, overcrowded living quarters, and lack of basic resources such as clothing and transportation.

abused, and neglected each year (Lonergran, 2000). Some 2000 children die each year as a result of abuse. Although the precise meaning of the term **child abuse** varies from state to state, it generally refers to situations in which a parent or other caregiver inflicts or allows others to inflict injury on a child, or permits a substantial risk of injury to exist (Bear, Schenk, & Buckner, 1992/1993). **Child neglect** is used to describe situations in which a parent or other caregiver fails to provide the necessary supports for a child's well-being, whether these are basic food and shelter, education, medical care, or other items. Figure 7.3 summarizes demographic characteristics of students who are abused and of the individuals who abuse them.

Some students who have been abused or neglected have visible signs such as bruises, burns, or other untreated physical problems. They might also complain of hunger. The following student characteristics might signal to school professionals the presence of abuse or neglect ("Child Abuse Characteristics," 2000):

- Wears clothes inappropriate for weather
- Cries excessively or shows little or no response to pain
- Seems wary of physical contact
- Appears apprehensive when approached by other students
- Engages in vandalism
- Arrives early to or departs late from school, or is frequently absent
- Attempts to explain away unusual injuries
- Is fatigued, falls asleep
- Shows precocious or bizarre sexual behavior

You should be aware that you have a legal and ethical obligation to report any suspected child abuse among your students (Pearson, 1996). Although the specific reporting requirements for teachers vary from state to state, federal law requires that every state maintain a hotline and other systems for reporting abuse, and every state has statutes that define abuse and neglect and establish reporting procedures. If you suspect that one of your students is being abused, you should follow your school district's procedures for reporting it. If you are unsure about those procedures, you should notify your principal, school social worker, or school nurse.

Students who live with substance abuse. A third group of students at risk for school failure are those involved in substance abuse. Some students' parents have abused drugs and alcohol. The impact on students begins before they are born and often affects them throughout their lives. Babies born to mothers who drink heavily during pregnancy may have a medical condition called **fetal alcohol syndrome (FAS)**, or a milder form known as **fetal alcohol effects (FAE)**. Babies with FAS or FAE are smaller than expected, may have facial and other slight physical abnormalities, and often experience learning and behavior problems when they go to school. The prevalence estimate for these disorders is 1 in 500 to 600 children born for FAS and 1 in 300 to 350 children born for FAE. Some researchers estimate that as many as 1 in 8 children in the United States has some type of permanent brain damage related to the mother's alcohol use during pregnancy (Fasworld, 2000). Students with FAS or FAE tend to use poor judgment, leaving a situation when things do not go as planned or failing to predict the consequences of their behavior (Burgess & Streissguth, 1992). Babies born to mothers who have been abusing cocaine or other

FYI

Because poverty affects life chances in so many ways, students often face multiple risk factors simultaneously. Some children experience both poverty and abuse, for example. Family dysfunction, crime, youth violence, teen pregnancy, and sexually transmitted diseases also place students at risk.

WWW Resources

The National Clearinghouse on Child Abuse and Neglect Information website, at http://www.calib.com/nccanch/index.html, provides updated information on prevention, identification, and treatment of child abuse and neglect.

Figure 7.3 Child Abuse: A National Profile

In 1998, more than 2.8 million children were reported to child protective services because of abuse or neglect. Some 903,000 of these cases were substantiated. This was a slight decrease (12.9 cases per 1000 children versus 13.9 cases per 1000 children) from 1997.

Racial and Ethnic Backgrounds of Abused and Neglected Children
Cases per 1000 children

Breakdown by Type of Abuse
Substantiated cases: 1995

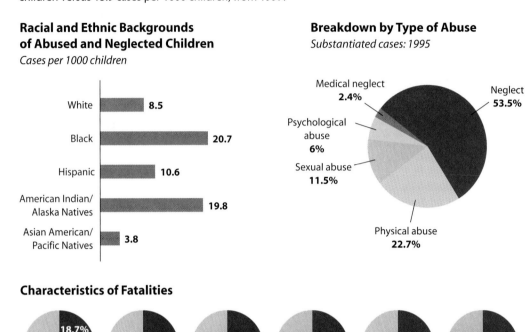

Characteristics of Fatalities

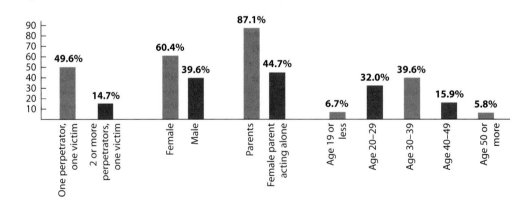

Perpetrator Profile

S o u r c e : *Reports from the States to the National Children Abuse and Neglect Data System,* by the National Child Abuse and Neglect Reporting System, 1998, Washington, DC: U.S. Department of Health and Human Services, Administration of Children, Youth, and Families, National Clearinghouse on Child Abuse and Neglect Information. Retrieved September 13, 2000, from the World Wide Web: http://www.acf.dhhs.gov/programs/cb/stats/ncands98/98ndsrpt/index.htm

drugs are often low in weight. They also are likely to become overstimulated, which leads to an array of irritable behaviors. When these children reach school age, they are likely to experience a wide variety of learning and behavior problems. Some are low achievers, and others may become eligible for special education services. They may be inattentive, hyperactive, and impulsive.

Researchers estimate that some 12 million children grow up in homes where alcohol or drugs are abused (Germinario, Cervalli, & Ogden, 1992). They are at risk because of a number of factors. For example, they are at risk for being neglected or abused. In homes in which drugs are abused, these students may be passive recipients of drugs that can be inhaled or may accidentally ingest other drugs. Students who live in homes in which alcohol or drugs are abused often display at least several of the following characteristics at school:

- Poor or erratic attendance
- Frequent physical complaints and visits to the nurse
- Morning tardiness, especially on Mondays
- Inappropriate fear about the possibility of parents being contacted
- Equating any drinking with being drunk or being alcoholic
- Perfectionistic and/or compulsive behavior
- Difficulty concentrating, hyperactivity
- Sudden emotional outbursts, crying, temper tantrums
- Regression (for example, thumb sucking)
- Friendlessness, isolation, withdrawn behavior
- Passivity but becoming active or focused during drug/alcohol awareness lesson
- Lingering after drug/alcohol awareness lessons to ask unrelated questions
- Signs of abuse or neglect (Germinario et al., 1992, p. 106)

A third group of students affected by substance abuse includes students who themselves abuse drugs or alcohol. It is estimated that 9.9 percent of youth ages 12 through 17 reported currently using illicit drugs in 1998, a decrease from the 1997 figure of 11.4 percent (Substance Abuse and Mental Health Services Administration, 1999). During the same year, 10.5 million youth ages 12 through 20 indicated they were current drinkers, with 20 percent of those classified as heavy drinkers. Among youth ages 12 through 17, 18.2 percent were current cigarette smokers. The individuals in this group are 11.4 times more likely to use illicit drugs and 16 times more likely to drink heavily than nonsmokers (Substance Abuse and Mental Health Services Administration, 1999). It should be noted that students with emotional disabilities are at particularly high risk for alcohol and drug abuse. Students who are substance abusers often have poor diets, sleep disturbances, feel a great deal of stress, and are at risk for depression and suicide. In school, they typically recall only information taught while they are sober, interact poorly with peers and teachers, and display excessive risk-taking behavior.

As you can see, students who live in poverty, who are abused or neglected, or who live with substance abuse, as well as other at-risk students, collectively have many characteristics and needs that affect their learning. Although some of them are resilient and do not suffer long-term consequences because of their stressful lives (Henderson & Milstein, 1996), the majority do not thrive without the support of an understanding school system and knowledgeable and committed teachers.

Interventions for Students at Risk

As a classroom teacher, you will be faced with the sometimes frustrating situation of not being able to take away from your students the stresses that often prevent them from learning to their potential. However, you can offer them a safe environment, with clear expectations and instructional support, that might become an important place in their lives.

Generally, recommendations for intervening to teach students at risk include four goals, none of which is completely unique to these students: set high but realistic expectations, establish peers as teaching partners, seek assistance from other professionals, and work closely with parents or other caregivers. Each recommendation is discussed briefly here.

Set high but realistic expectations. When you are teaching students who are at risk, it is tempting to make assumptions about how much they are capable of learning. For example, you might think that because the student does not have books at home and the parent is either unable or unwilling to read with the student, the student cannot be a successful learner. The result of such thinking is often inappropriately low expectations—which students might "live down" to (Ramirez-Smith, 1995). Low expectations can also lead to overusing teaching strategies that emphasize drilling students on lower-level academic skills. Although drill activities have a place in educating at-risk students, they must be balanced with other approaches as well. For example, students need to learn thinking processes along with basic skills, and they need to learn to construct their own knowledge along with receiving it from you. This more balanced approach is illustrated in Project Achievement (Mercure, 1993), an after-school program designed to provide students with an enriching and challenging learning environment. Activities included in the project occur mainly in heterogeneous groups and involve photography, television production, and even the creation of a pond ecosystem. This project demonstrates that when students have challenging tasks that are interesting and provide them with opportunities to make decisions, they can be successful and motivated learners.

One other strategy for setting high expectations should be mentioned. Many professionals now believe that the still-common practice of **tracking,** that is, grouping students for instruction by perceived ability, can discriminate against students at risk. Tracking leads to a sense of failure among some students, and it tends to lead to lowered expectations for at-risk students. Grouping students heterogeneously generally does not place high-achieving students at a disadvantage, but it may help raise the achievement of at-risk learners (Wheelock, 1992). Although teachers appropriately group students by their need for instruction in specific skills as part of their overall instructional plan, and some secondary schools offer advanced classes that lead to a limited amount of tracking, you should be aware of the potential negative effects of tracking. As a teacher, you can ensure that you do not overuse this type of grouping in your classroom, and you can work with your colleagues to create a school in which students of many different abilities learn together.

One word of caution about setting standards is necessary. Some students who are at risk have such high stresses outside school that they might not have much support from their parents and other family members for school assignments and work. Two examples from teachers help to illustrate this point. One talked about a student who was not returning homework. The teacher was penalizing the student by giv-

Research Note

According to data gathered in 1998 by the National Child Abuse and Neglect Reporting System (NCANDS), two-thirds of the 2.8 million referrals to child protective services were determined to be valid enough to merit investigation. One-third of those investigations resulted in evidence of abuse or neglect.

ing her lower grades and making her complete the work during recess. She later found out that the family was penniless and had a single light bulb in their tiny apartment. When the bulb burned out, there was no light after sunset, and homework was not the priority. Another teacher described a high school student who always slept in class. Detention did not help, nor did attempts to contact parents. The teacher later learned that this student left school each day, cooked dinner for her younger siblings, and then worked at a fast food restaurant until midnight. Thus, high expectations are important, but they need to be tempered with understanding of the circumstances in the student's life outside school.

Effective instruction for students at risk includes the same strategies you would use for other students, with particular attention to the physical and social-emotional challenges these students often face. Students at risk need a structured learning environment, systematic instruction in basic skill areas, and strategies for learning independence. The Technology Notes feature on page 266 provides specific strategies on how to use computers to maximize at-risk students' learning.

Establish peers as teaching partners. Peers learning from one another is a strategy recommended earlier for students from diverse cultural and linguistic backgrounds; it is also useful for at-risk students. For example, in the Success for All Program (Slavin et al., 1994), an intensive early reading program designed to help at-risk learners acquire foundational learning that helps them throughout their school careers, a key ingredient is a cooperative learning approach. Students work with each other in structured groups to learn vocabulary, writing, comprehension, and other reading skills. This program appears to have great potential for helping students achieve school success.

Collaborate with other professionals. A third strategy for teaching at-risk students involves increasing your problem-solving capability by adding the skills and resources of your colleagues. In a survey of teachers' and principals' preferences for providing support to students at risk, these individuals were mentioned as potential resources: special education teachers, other special education professionals, psychologists, social workers, reading teachers, and paraprofessionals. Other programs for at-risk students enlist the assistance of volunteers, counselors, and administrators.

The purpose of problem solving with your colleagues about at-risk students is that you can check your own perspectives against theirs, gain access to their expertise, and coordinate your efforts. For example, if you are teaching Shaneal, a student whom you suspect has been abused, you can first ask the counselor or social worker whether there is any past documentation of abuse, and you can request that one of these professionals speak with the student. If you are teaching Jack, a student who is missing quite a few school days and increasingly refuses to complete assignments, you might want to consult with colleagues about the causes of Jack's behavior and how to address them.

Support family and community involvement. As with all students, it is essential that you maintain positive contact with parents or other caregivers of your at-risk students. However, the level of participation you can expect will vary considerably. Some parents are anxious to ensure that their children have all the advantages a positive education can give them, and they will do all they can to assist you in teaching.

Connections

Peer teaching and other forms of peer-mediated instruction are discussed in Chapter 13.

High expectations and family involvement contribute to the greater academic success of some students at risk. In your classroom, how can you identify students who are at risk? What other interventions and instructional strategies can you use to help them succeed in school?

[Technology Notes]

Technology and Students at Risk

Have you ever considered how access to technology could make a positive difference to at-risk students and how those students may have less access to technology than other students? Brown (2000) included students of color, those who live in poverty, and those with limited English proficiency in her review of scholarly literature on access and barriers to technology. She found that whereas nearly 33 percent of white students used computers at home, only 11 percent of black students and 10 percent of Hispanic students used home computers. She also found that computers in schools typically are placed in locations more readily used by high achievers than struggling learners (e.g., in library and media centers instead of in classrooms). She provided evidence that the instructional uses of computers for students at risk tended to be for remedial and routine tasks instead of complex and challenging ones. She also raised issues related to the role models for technology use available to students of color and females.

The following table lists suggestions for fostering equitable access to technology for all students.

Problem	Suggestions
Location of labs	• Create mini-labs throughout the building (McKenzie, 1998). • Have roving computer stations that stay in classrooms for extended periods (McKenzie, 1998). • Create computer labs for each department (e.g., math, science, English).
Promote technology use by different groups	• Offer and allow the typically underserved students opportunities to take technology courses and earn credits toward graduation. • Invite guest speakers who will serve as role models for students of color and female students. • Encourage all students to join technology clubs (e.g., meet during lunch). • Encourage students to use technology during their own time and for their own purposes. Technology does not always have to be used for academics. • Actively encourage students of color and female students to use technology to help overcome some of the negativisms they may hold about technology (e.g., have a female students' technology day, use female students and students of color as technology monitors, and have more technology sign-up slots for female students during free time). • Seek software that meets the needs and special interests of all students (e.g., instructionally sound simulations). • Encourage students of color and female students to attend summer technology camps (Wolfe, 1986).
Quality access for the entire student body	• Assure equal technology use regardless of gender, ethnicity, or achievement level by removing some of the biases and stereotypes associated with technology use (Martin, 1990; Wolfe, 1986). • Target all students for higher-level cognitive skills by having them use more problem-solving tools and learn programming (Emihovich, 1992). • Consider summer school courses that meet at atypical times to accommodate students who work after school.
Computer scheduling	• Blend technologies into the daily routines to promote learner-centered environments. • Schedule individual and group time for students. • Offer evening classes to involve parents and other community members. • Provide appropriate activities for each special population in the school and classroom.

SOURCE: From "Access Instruction and Barriers: Technology Issues Facing Students at Risk" by M. Brown, 2000, *Remedial and Special Education, 21*, p. 188. Copyright © 2000 by PRO-ED, Inc. Reprinted with permission.

Other parents are themselves not functioning well, and they probably cannot be expected to participate actively in their children's education. To involve families and communities in their children's education, you might try these ideas. Sometimes it might be more appropriate for a student to bring to school something important from home and to base an assignment on that, rather than being assigned more traditional homework. It can also be helpful to assist parents in connecting with community resources such as health clinics and social service agencies. One school district, struggling because of the rapidly increasing number of at-risk students, worked with local church leaders to connect families with resources and improve the communication between school personnel and families.

When you think about the diversity of students you may teach, it is easy to become overwhelmed by the challenge of meeting all students' instructional needs. Keep in mind that classrooms structured to celebrate diversity rather than treat it as a deficiency or an exception are classrooms with many options for learning and a blend of structure and flexibility.

FYI

Effective prevention and intervention programs exist for all grade levels. Programs for students at risk are most effective when family and community support are present.

Summary

In addition to students with disabilities, you will teach many other students who have extraordinary learning needs. Some students receive specialized services through Section 504, federal legislation requiring that accommodations be provided by general educators to students who have functional disabilities that might limit their access to an education.

One major group of students who receive Section 504 assistance is students with attention deficit–hyperactivity disorder (ADHD), a medically diagnosed problem characterized by chronic and severe inattention and/or hyperactivity-impulsivity. Students with attention deficit–hyperactivity disorder are served through a variety of academic and behavior interventions, and they often are helped by medication. Most other students protected through Section 504 have physical conditions or medical problems, and their plans outline needed academic, behavioral, and physical or medical accommodations.

Students who are gifted and talented comprise a second group with special needs. Students who are gifted and talented include those with generally high intellectual ability as well as those with specific talents in areas such as music. The interventions most often used to help them achieve school success are enrichment, acceleration, sophistication, and novelty.

A third group with special needs includes students from culturally and linguistically diverse backgrounds. These students and their families sometimes have values that differ from those of schools. Teachers need to learn about students' cultures, teach in a manner that is responsive to the cultures, and acknowledge and value diverse cultures in the classroom to teach students from diverse cultural backgrounds effectively.

Finally, students at risk for school failure because of environmental influences such as poverty, child abuse, and drug addiction also have special needs. Because students at risk often live in unpredictable and stressful environments, strategies for teaching them include setting appropriate expectations, understanding the often-fluctuating range of their needs, and stressing structure and accomplishment in their classroom instruction.

Applications in Teaching Practice

Diversity in a High School Class

Ivan Robinson is a high school teacher in a suburban school district. Although it is only the fourth week of school, he is concerned. He is confident of his knowledge of history and civics as well as his teaching skills, and he has a strong commitment to teaching all the students assigned to him, but he is worried that he won't be able to meet the vast array of needs represented in his second-block class this year.

He is well aware that student needs in school are becoming increasingly diverse, and this current class group clearly demonstrates that fact. For example, Thuan, who just emigrated to the United States from Vietnam, speaks very little English and seems overwhelmed by nearly everything at school. Mr. Robinson can't recall ever seeing Thuan smile. As he discusses U.S. history, he knows that much of the information is beyond Thuan's understanding, and he knows that Thuan does not have the context for grasping the themes in history.

Then there is Sonny. Sonny is supposed to be taking medication for ADHD, but it doesn't seem to be having the right effect on him. At an after-school meeting, Mr. Robinson, the school psychologist, the counselor, and the assistant principal discussed the matter with Sonny, and it was noted that Sonny recently had decided he had outgrown the need for medication and was sometimes not taking it. He did say, though, that a few times he decided to "catch up" by taking a double dose. The counselor is supposed to follow up on this unhealthy and potentially dangerous thinking about medication and keep Mr. Robinson informed. In the meantime, Sonny is in his class and, as Mr. Robinson puts it, "bouncing off the walls or drugged out of his mind."

Jenny is a concern as well. She and her twin sister, Jenna, are struggling academically despite lots of individual attention and supportive parents. Neither girl is reading well enough to complete the chapters in the history text. Both girls have been referred in the past for special education services, but neither is eligible to receive them. Mr. Robinson knows that the twins' father has been out of work for nearly a year, that the girls both work after school and have little time for homework or any type of tutoring assistance, and that the family is barely getting by on donations from friends and their church. He wonders how much of the twins' learning problems are related to their home situation.

He also teaches Kimberly, who just moved into the district, and who is so far ahead of other students that Mr. Robinson wishes she was taking his course through the local community college. Two other students—Lisa and Paul—are from families that have very little; they come to school without supplies and seem reluctant to interact with the other children.

In thinking about his class, Mr. Robinson realizes that at least half the students have special needs of one sort or another. He wants to reach them all to share his love of history, but he is not sure he can accomplish his goal.

Questions

1. How typical is the type of class group Mr. Robinson has? What other types of diverse needs might you expect to have represented in a class you are responsible for teaching?
2. What general strategies might Mr. Robinson use in his class that would benefit many students with special needs and harm none?
3. For each student with special needs Mr. Robinson has identified, consider what strategies he might use by making a chart specifying at least one strategy in each pertinent domain. The chart should include these parts:

Intervention Area	Thuan	Sonny	Jenny	Kimberly	Lisa and Paul
Academic					
Social/emotional					
Behavioral					
Medical/physical					

4. There are four special education teachers in Mr. Robinson's school, and he works extensively with Mr. Settle. What is Mr. Settle's role in assisting Mr. Robinson and other teachers in the school to meet the diverse needs of students, including those who do not have IEPs?
5. How might Mr. Robinson work with the parents of his students to help ensure their needs are addressed? How likely is it that some of the students about whom Mr. Robinson is concerned are living without parental supervision?
6. What realistic expectations can Mr. Robinson set for himself as a teacher for this school year? How can he reach his goal of meeting the needs of all his students?

Assessing Student Needs

After you read this chapter, you will be able to

1. Explain how general education teachers can contribute significantly to the assessment process.

2. Describe the uses of standardized achievement and psychological tests in making educational decisions for students with special needs.

3. Define curriculum-based assessment and explain how it can help general education teachers.

4. Describe how alternative assessments for students with significant cognitive disabilities can be developed and scored.

5. Construct and use probes of basic academic skills, content-area prerequisite skills, and independent learning skills.

6. Use curriculum-based assessments to make special education decisions.

Key Terms and Concepts

■ Ms. Lyons is concerned that Rob, a student in her second-grade class, is not keeping up with the rest of the class in math. Mr. Blair, the special education teacher, suggests that Ms. Lyons do some informal assessment herself before going through the special education referral process. What kind of assessments can Ms. Lyons use to clarify Rob's problems in math? How might these assessments help Ms. Lyons make adaptations for Rob in math? Under what circumstances should she refer Rob for special education?

■ Mr. Blount teaches a high school U.S. history class. He has learned that three special education students will be in his class next fall. Mr. Blount was told that these students have some reading problems and may have trouble reading the textbook. Mr. Blount decided to make up a test to give at the beginning of the year to see how well the students were able to use the textbook. Using a section of a chapter from the text, Mr. Blount wrote questions to test how well students could figure out the meaning of key vocabulary words, use parts of the book (for example, the table of contents, glossary, or index), read maps, and read for information (for example, note main ideas, draw conclusions). When Mr. Blount gave the test in the fall, he found that the three identified students had trouble reading the text, but that many other students also had difficulty. What decision might Mr. Blount make on the basis of the assessment?

■ Roberto is a student with moderate to severe disabilities who is in Ms. Benis's sixth-grade social studies class. As a result of Roberto's cerebral palsy, he has significant cognitive, language, and motor deficits. Roberto can read his name, as well as some high-frequency sight words. He uses a wheelchair, and he has trouble with fine motor movements such as cutting and handwriting. Roberto speaks with the aid of a communication board. Ms. Benis is doing a unit on recycling with her class. The students are working in small, mixed-skill groups, with each group constructing a graphic of the recycling process for either paper products, plastic, or metal. What assessment process can Ms. Benis carry out to help her develop a plan for including Roberto in this unit?

As more and more students with disabilities are being served in general education classes, teachers need to make many important decisions that can greatly affect these students' success. For example, in the preceding vignettes, Ms. Lyons was trying to find out whether Rob needed intensive math instruction from a special education teacher or whether his needs could be met through adaptations in her regular math program. Mr. Blount wanted to find out whether his students with disabilities could read the textbook for his history class to help him decide whether he would need to adapt the book. Ms. Benis wants to include Roberto, who has moderate to severe disabilities, in her social studies class. To answer questions such as these, teachers need accurate, relevant information. Thus, they need to develop informal measures to help them make a number of instructional decisions as well as participate in special education decision making. This chapter explores assessment strategies that help general education teachers contribute to the process of decision making for students with special needs. This decision making involves, for example, determining whether a student needs special education services, when a student is ready to learn in inclusive settings, and what classroom accommodations to try, continue, or change.

How Do Your Student Assessments Contribute to Special Education Decisions?

Connections

The assessment types and procedures described in this chapter are an integral part of the INCLUDE model presented in Chapter 4.

As a classroom teacher, you make an important contribution to the process of identifying and meeting the needs of students with special needs. A major part of that contribution involves assessing student needs. **Assessment** has been defined as the process of gathering information to monitor progress and to make educational decisions when necessary (Overton, 1999). The two most common ways of collecting information are through standardized, commercially produced tests and informal tests devised by the teacher. Much of the information in this chapter is about ways in which these measures can be used to make decisions about students with special needs.

General education teachers contribute assessment information for six important decisions about students with special needs: screening, diagnosis, program placement, curriculum placement, instructional evaluation, and program evaluation.

Screening

Check Your Learning

What questions are involved in making a screening decision?

The major **screening** decision is whether a student's performance differs enough from that of his or her peers to merit further, more in-depth assessments to determine the presence of a disability. For example, to clarify Rob's problems in math, Ms. Lyons, whom you read about at the beginning of this chapter, examined the most recent group achievement test scores for her class in math and found that Rob's total math score was 1 to 2 years below grade level. Ms. Lyons then gave Rob and his classmates some minitests on various math computation skills she had taught to see whether Rob was behind his peers in these skills. Using this information, Ms. Lyons found that a number of students were performing similarly to Rob. She therefore decided not to refer Rob for a more comprehensive evaluation until she tried some adaptations in the classroom first, with Rob and several other students.

Connections

Legal requirements for assessing students with disabilities are covered in Chapters 1 and 2.

Diagnosis

The major decision related to **diagnosis** concerns eligibility for special education services. Does the student meet established federal guidelines for being classified as

272

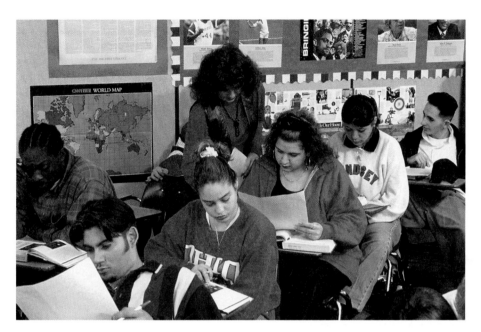

having a disability? If so, what is the nature and extent of the student's disability? For example, Ms. Clark referred Paula for a case-study evaluation because she suspected that Paula had a learning disability. The school psychologist administered an individual intelligence test and found that Paula's performance was in the above-normal range. The school psychologist also gave Paula a test on cognitive functioning, including a test of memory, attention, and organization, and an individual achievement test. She found that Paula was slow in processing visual information (letters, numbers, shapes) and that her achievement in reading was significantly lower than that of other students her age. Her achievement in math was at grade level. Ms. Clark evaluated Paula's classroom reading performance by having her and five "average" students read orally and answer questions from a grade-level trade book that was part of the classroom literature program. Paula read slower and with less accuracy than her peers, and she was able to answer only 40 percent of the comprehension questions. Because Paula showed problems processing visual information quickly enough, and because her potential as measured by the intelligence test and her achievement as measured by both a standardized achievement test and informal classroom reading tests differed significantly, Paula was declared eligible to receive services for learning disabilities.

Check Your Learning

What questions are involved in diagnosing a student?

Program Placement

The major **program placement** decision involves the setting in which a student's special education services take place (for example, in a general education classroom, resource room, or full-time special education classroom). The IEP team must make this decision with great care. In the past, the tendency was to pull students out of general education classrooms without carefully considering whether they could be supported within the general education program instead. In this book, the emphasis is on doing all that you can within the general education class first. Still, students

Check Your Learning

What questions are involved in making a program placement?

FYI

Program placement
decisions for students
with moderate to severe
cognitive disabilities
should be based on the
supports needed to meet
the curricular goals
outlined in their IEPs.

have different needs, and some may require instruction in an area at a level of intensity that cannot be delivered in the general education classroom. That is why it is important to make placement decisions based on measures that accurately reflect student performance in class. For example, Carlos has been shown to be eligible for receiving services for learning disabilities in math. His IEP team is trying to decide whether his learning needs can be met by adapting the math methods and materials in the general education classroom or whether he should be provided more intensive instruction in a resource room setting. Carlos's classroom teacher gave Carlos and his classmates a series of informal math tests. She found that Carlos was significantly behind his peers on some but not all of the tests; his math problem solving was very deficient compared to that of his classmates, but his math computational skills were fine. The IEP team decided to keep Carlos in his general education class and support his instruction in problem solving by providing him extra teacher-guided practice whenever a new problem-solving skill was introduced. The team also decided that they would carefully monitor Carlos's problem-solving skills; if those skills showed little improvement, they would consider other options.

Curriculum Placement

**Check Your
Learning**

What questions are
involved in placing
students into the class-
room curriculum?

Curriculum placement involves deciding at what level to begin instruction for students. For an elementary school teacher, such a decision may mean choosing a reading or math book. For example, Ms. Tolhurst has her students read orally and answer questions to find the appropriate trade books in which to place them (that is, the level of difficulty at which the books are neither too easy nor too hard in her literature-based reading program). At the secondary level, curriculum placement decisions are likely to involve which class in a sequence of classes a student should take. For example, Mr. Nowicki, Scott's math teacher, is trying to decide whether to place Scott in his Algebra 1 class. Mr. Nowicki identifies basic math skills that he feels all students entering algebra should have. He constructs a test based on those skills and gives it to Scott as well as other incoming freshmen.

Instructional Evaluation

Decisions in **instructional evaluation** involve whether to continue or change instructional procedures that have been initiated with students. For example, Ms. Bridgewater is starting a peer tutoring program to help Cecily, a student with severe cognitive disabilities, read her name and the names of her family members. Each week, Ms. Bridgewater tests Cecily to see how many of the names she has learned. Mr. Jackson decides to accompany each of his history lectures with a graphic organizer of the material. He gives weekly quizzes to find out whether his students' performance is improving.

**Check Your
Learning**

What questions are
involved in evaluating
the program of a student
with special needs?

Program Evaluation

Program evaluation decisions involve whether the special education program should be terminated, continued as is, or modified. A key consideration is whether students are meeting their IEP goals. For example, Amanda is receiving social work services twice per week. Her IEP goal is to decrease the number of times she has a verbal confrontation with Mr. Alvarez, her teacher. Mr. Alvarez is keeping track of the number of times daily that Amanda refuses to comply with his requests to see whether sessions with the social worker are improving Amanda's behavior.

What Information Sources Are Used in Programming for Students with Special Needs?

A number of information sources are used in programming for students with special needs. The use of multiple assessment sources is consistent with the principle of nondiscriminatory testing, discussed in Chapter 2, which says that no single measure should be used to establish eligibility for special education services. The measures described in this section include standardized achievement tests, reports of psychological tests, the environmental inventory process, and curriculum-based assessments.

Standardized Achievement Tests

A common source of information for making educational decisions is the **standardized achievement test.** These tests are designed to measure academic progress, or what students have retained in the curriculum. Standardized achievement tests are norm referenced. In a norm-referenced test, the performance of one student is compared to the average performance of other students in the country who are the same age or grade level. Student performance is often summarized using grade equivalents and/or percentile ranks. Grade equivalents simply indicate the grade level, in years and months, for which a given score was the average, or middle, score in the norm group. For example, a score of 25 with the grade equivalent of 4.6 means that, in the norm group, 25 was the average score of pupils in the sixth month of fourth grade. Percentile ranks represent the percentage of students who scored at or below a given student's score. A percentile score of 75 percent, then, means that the student scored higher than 75 percent of all students in his or her age group that took the test. Keep in mind that grade-level equivalencies and percentiles look at student performance only from the standpoint of how different they are from average, *not* according to how well they performed a skill from the standpoint of mastery. For example, a grade equivalent score of 3.2 in reading comprehension means that the student achieved the same score as the average of all students in the third grade, second month, who were in the normative sample; it does not say anything about how well the student is able to answer the various kinds of comprehension questions that may be in the third-grade reading curriculum.

Group-administered tests. Two major types of standardized achievement tests are group-administered and individually administered diagnostic tests. As the name implies, group-administered standardized achievement tests are completed by large groups of students at one time; this usually means that the general education teacher gives the test to the entire class. These tests assess skills across many areas of the curriculum, none in much depth. For this reason, they are intended to be used solely as

WWW Resources

In the Pathways to School Improvement website, at http://www.ncrel.org/sdrs/pathwayg.htm, click on the assessment topic button to find information about critical issues in assessment and links to other assessment pages. Also, click on the search button to do a keyword search for articles about critical issues in assessment.

FYI

Criterion-referenced tests compare student performance to a standard rather than a norm. They are used when we want to know how well students meet the requirements of a task and are particularly helpful when making day-to-day instructional decisions.

screening measures. Nonetheless, information obtained from group-administered achievement tests may be inappropriate for making some decisions, even in screening, for the following list of reasons:

1. Administration in a group environment does not allow students to ask the teacher questions about directions or to clarify test questions (Overton, 1999). For example, Alicia has a learning disability in reading and has problems comprehending written directions. When Alicia obtained a low score on a social studies subtest, it was hard to determine whether her low score was due to a lack of knowledge or her inability to follow the directions.

2. Many group tests are timed, which may limit the responses of students with disabilities. For example, Carmen has a problem with eye–hand coordination and makes errors in transferring her answers to a computer-scored answer sheet. Corrine has an attention deficit and is unable to complete a reading subtest in one 45-minute sitting.

3. National or even local norms might not match actual distribution of classroom achievement (Deno, 1985; Marston, 1989; Salvia & Ysseldyke, 1998). For example, Darryl is in fourth grade and scored at the second-grade level on a standardized achievement test in reading, a score that was at least 6 months below the rest of his classmates. However, the results of an informal reading probe of his classroom literature-based program revealed that four other students in class were reading at a level roughly equivalent to Darryl's. The teacher decided to form an instructional group made up of these students to help them with their literature books and did not refer Darryl for special services.

4. The results of standardized tests provide little useful data to guide instruction (Bursuck & Lessen, 1987; Deno, 1985; Marston, 1989; Salvia & Ysseldyke, 1998; Shinn, Collins, & Gallagher, 1998). For example, Ellen's math achievement scores showed that she was 1 year below grade level in math computation. However, the test contained too few items to ascertain the particular kind of errors she was making.

Check Your Learning

What are the drawbacks in using group-administered standardized achievement tests to make educational decisions for students?

5. Standardized achievement tests might be culturally biased, and they can lead to the overrepresentation of minorities in special education classes (Garcia & Pearson, 1994; Oakland, 1981). For example, Bill comes from a single-parent home in a high-rise apartment building in the city. When he read a story on a standardized achievement test about an affluent two-parent family in the suburbs, he had difficulty predicting the outcome.

6. The content of a standardized achievement test might not match what is taught in a particular classroom (Deno, 1985; Deno & Fuchs, 1987; Marston, 1989; Jitendra & Kameenui, 1993). For example, one teacher stressed problem solving in his science class, whereas the standardized achievement test given in his district stressed the memorization of facts. Therefore, he had to give his own tests to determine whether students were learning the material. The reading achievement test used at another teacher's school had the students identify words in lists. The teacher found that the words tested were quite different from the words in her literature-based program, which stressed reading in context using syntactically predictable books. She decided to develop her own test to place students with appropriate books as well as to monitor progress in her program.

7. Because it is not possible to administer standardized tests frequently, their utility as a tool for evaluating day-to-day instruction is limited (Bursuck & Lessen, 1987; Deno, 1985). For example, James was mainstreamed into a second-grade class for math. After 1 month, the teachers wanted to check his progress. Because the standardized tests were not to be given for another 3 months, James's teacher gave him her own informal test based on what she taught in class. In another instance, Clark was not allowed into Algebra 1 because of his poor performance on a standardized achievement test in math. After 1 month, Clark's teacher felt he was ready for Algebra 1. Because the achievement test could not be given again until May, the algebra and basic math teachers developed their own test of skills prerequisite for Algebra 1 and gave it to Clark.

Group-administered standardized achievement tests can be useful in some circumstances. One such situation involves making administrative and policy decisions on a school-district or even national level. For example, a district found that their students were below the national average on the problem-solving portion of a math achievement test and decided to spend more time on math problem solving at all levels in the district. However, the validity of group-administered achievement tests for making decisions about individual students at the classroom level is limited. These tests should be used with great caution and only in conjunction with informal, classroom-based measures.

In the past, school districts have not always included students with disabilities in their testing programs. Goals 2000 and IDEA-97 require that all students be included in school district assessments of progress toward goals and that appropriate accommodations for students with disabilities be used during these assessments. Common accommodations include changing the setting of the test (for example, allowing students to take tests in special education classrooms), changing the timing of the test (for example, providing extended time or more frequent breaks), changing the response format (for example, allowing students to mark responses in test books rather than on scantron sheets), and changing the presentation format (for example, using a braille edition of a test or giving directions in sign language) (Thurlow, Elliott, & Ysseldyke, 1998; Thurlow, Ysseldyke, & Silverstein, 1995).

Individually administered tests. A special education teacher or the school psychologist usually gives **individually administered diagnostic tests** as part of a student's case-study evaluation. Although these tests may screen student performance in several curricular areas, they tend to be more diagnostic in nature. For example, an individually administered diagnostic reading test may include subtests in the areas of letter identification, word recognition, oral reading, comprehension, and phonetic skills; a diagnostic test in math might include math computation, fractions, geometry, word problems, measurement, and time. Because individually administered diagnostic tests provide information on a range of specific skills, they can be useful as an information source in making educational decisions. For example, Tamara scored 2 years below grade level on the comprehension subtest of an individually administered diagnostic test in reading. Yet in an oral reading sample taken from her fourth-grade reader, she read both fluently and accurately. On the basis of these two findings, her teacher placed her into a literature-based reading program that stressed skills in reading comprehension.

Connections

More ideas for adapting tests for students with disabilities are described in Chapter 11.

WWW Resources

For more information on the topic of state and national testing policies, access the web page for the National Center on Educational Outcomes (NCEO) at http://www.coled.umn.edu/nceo.

What are some advantages of individually administered diagnostic tests? What are other sources of assessment information used in educational decision making for students with special needs?

Although individually administered diagnostic tests may be more helpful than group-administered achievement tests, they are still subject to many of the same problems. Again, you should always verify findings from these tests using more informal measures based on what you teach.

Psychological Tests

Psychological tests are used as part of the process of evaluating students with special needs, particularly to determine whether a student has cognitive or learning disabilities. Reports of the results of these tests are often written by school psychologists and consist of a summary of the findings and the implications for instruction. **Psychological tests** can include intelligence tests and tests related to learning disabilities (Overton, 1999; Salvia & Ysseldyke, 1998).

The overall purpose of psychological tests is to measure abilities that affect how efficiently students learn in an instructional situation. These abilities are inferred based on student responses to items that the test author believes represent that particular ability. For example, comprehension, an important learning ability, is often assessed on psychological tests (Salvia & Ysseldyke, 1998). To test their comprehension, students may be asked to read and answer questions about a series of directions or other printed material. Student scores are then compared to a norm group of other same-aged students, with an average score being equal to 100. Other abilities commonly assessed by psychological tests include generalization (the ability to recognize similarities across objects, events, or vocabulary), general or background information, vocabulary, induction (the ability to figure out a rule or principle based on a series of situations), abstract reasoning, and memory (Salvia & Ysseldyke, 1998).

Psychological tests can be helpful if they clarify why students may not be learning in class and lead to effective changes in instruction. For example, the results of Amanda's test showed that she had difficulty with visual memory. Her teacher, Ms. Fasbacher, felt that this was related to her poor performance in spelling. As a result, Ms. Fasbacher provided Amanda with extra practice on her weekly spelling lists. Interpreting the results of psychological reports seems less daunting if you follow the general guidelines suggested here. First, do not be intimidated by the sometimes generous quantity of technical terms and jargon. You have the right to expect that reports be translated into instructionally relevant language. Second, the results of psychological tests are most valid when corroborated by classroom experience. Further, in the event of discrepancies between psychological reports and your experience, do not automatically discount your experience. Keep in mind that your impressions are the result of many more hours of classroom observation than are psychological evaluations, which are based on fewer samples of student behavior and on samples that represent behavior that takes place outside the classroom. Third, be sure to check the technical adequacy of the psychological tests included in your report. You may be surprised to find that many of these tests are not acceptable. Fourth, psychological tests may discriminate against students from culturally different or disadvantaged backgrounds. The various ways in which psychological and other tests can be biased, along with suggestions for making them more fair, are presented in the Professional Edge on page 280. Finally, the primary purpose of psychological tests is to establish possible explanations for particular learning, behavioral, or social and emotional problems. Keep in mind that such explanations should be springboards for helping students overcome these problems, not excuses for a student's lack of achievement.

The Professional Edge on page 281 contains lists of standardized tests commonly used in special education decision making. These include standardized group and individual achievement tests and psychological tests used to assess intelligence or cognitive functioning.

Alternative Assessments

The 1997 Amendments to the Individuals with Disabilities Education Act (IDEA, 1997) require states to include students with disabilities in statewide and districtwide educational assessments. Most students with disabilities are able to participate in the assessments when they are given appropriate accommodations. These accommodations have made possible the creation of **alternative assessments.** For example, Clara, a student who is blind, takes her state tests using a version written in Braille. Kareem, a student with a reading disability, takes the social studies section of the state exam with extended time. However, a small percentage of students are typically working on a more functional curriculum and do not have to meet the same requirements as those students graduating with a standard diploma. They are required to meet the same broad standards as your other students, but they meet them in different, more basic ways. For example, one of the standards in Ms. Barber's state is that students develop an appreciation for literature. One of the ways that Darrell, a student with a significant cognitive disability, meets that standard is by watching a video of *Oliver Twist* and answering a few basic questions using his communication board.

Cultural Awareness

Psychological tests can be biased against students from diverse backgrounds. Use them only in conjunction with other formal and informal measures.

WWW Resources

The home page for the National Council on Measurement in Education (NCME), at http://www.ncme.org, provides information on the organization and links to other relevant measurement-related websites.

FYI

The National Center on Educational Outcomes offers these recommendations for developing alternative assessment systems: (1) define the purpose of the alternative assessment system and identify who is qualified to participate in it; (2) identify the common core of learning, for example, what students need to know and be able to do; (3) develop participation guidelines; (4) determine how results will be organized and summarized; and (5) integrate these results with those from the general assessment.

Professional Edge

Strategies for Fair Assessment of Diverse Students

Grossman (1995) reports that although today's teachers are much more knowledgeable about the presence of bias in assessing poor students and students from culturally diverse backgrounds, bias and discrimination continue to exist. The following two lists present areas that can be problematic when assessing diverse students and strategies for assessing and interpreting their performance more accurately, respectively.

Problem

1. Students may exhibit test anxiety due to lack of familiarity with the assessment process.
2. Students may lack motivation to perform well on tests because of differing cultural expectations.
3. Students may not respond to traditional motivators.
4. Students' test scores may be depressed because assessor is unfamiliar or speaks a different language.
5. Students may have different communication styles; for example, they may not feel comfortable asking for help with directions or may respond using fewer words.
6. Students may be unwilling to take risks; for example, they may be reluctant to guess on a test even though it is to their benefit.
7. Students may be accustomed to working at a slower pace.

8. Students may lack exposure to test content.
9. Students may not be proficient in the language used for a test.
10. Students may speak with a dialect that differs from the assessor's.

Recommendation

1. Give students practice tests. Teach test-taking skills.
2. Qualify test performance with class performance.
3. Individualize reinforcers; use individualistic, competitive, and cooperative goal structures.
4. Allow more time to establish rapport and gain trust.
5. Check for understanding of directions; avoid automatically penalizing students for not saying enough or not giving details.
6. Teach students strategies for when and how to make a best guess on a test.
7. Extend test-taking time to accommodate students' pace.
8. Eliminate unfamiliar content or don't give the test.
9. Assess students using both English and students' native language.
10. Do not count dialectical differences as errors; examine your attitudes about nonstandard dialects for potential bias.

Teachers of students with moderate, severe, and profound disabilities from five states recently identified the following five important considerations when using alternative assessments (Ysseldyke & Olsen, 1999).

1. The focus should be on authentic skills and on assessing experiences in community/real-life environments. For a younger child the community might mean the school, playground, or home; for a high school senior the community might mean the store, bank, or other commercial sites.
2. School personnel should measure skills that are integrated across many areas; personal and social skills, for example, should be assessed right along with academic and functional literacy skills, rather than separately. For example, Ms. Halpern assesses Thomas's literacy and social skills when he is ordering fast food from a clerk at a fast-food restaurant.

Professional Edge

Standardized Tests Commonly Used in Special Education Decision Making

You can choose from many standardized tests to help you make decisions for special education assessment. When selecting an instrument, make sure it is appropriate for the student being tested. If you have questions about the suitability of a particular test, consult your school psychologist or special education teacher. The following lists provide the names and sources of commonly used standardized tests for special education decision making.

Standardized Achievement and Diagnostic Tests

Woodcock-Johnson Revised Tests of Achievement (Chicago: Riverside)

Peabody Individual Achievement Test–Revised/ Normative Update (Circle Pines, MN: American Guidance Service)

Kaufman Test of Educational Achievement/ Normative Update: (Circle Pines, MN: American Guidance Service)

KeyMath Diagnostic Arithmetic Test–Revised/ Normative Update (Circle Pines, MN: American Guidance Service)

Woodcock Reading Mastery Tests–Revised/ Normative Update (Circle Pines, MN: American Guidance Service)

Wechsler Individual Achievement Test II (San Antonio, TX: Psychological Corporation)

Test of Written Language—3 (Austin, TX: PRO-ED)

Test of Written Spelling—4 (Austin, TX: PRO-ED)

Test of Reading Comprehension—3 (Austin, TX: PRO-ED)

Gray Oral Reading Test—3 (Austin, TX: PRO-ED)

Intelligence Tests and Tests of Cognitive Functioning

Wechsler Intelligence Scale for Children–III (San Antonio, TX: Psychological Corporation)

Woodcock-Johnson Revised Tests of Cognitive Abilities (Chicago: Riverside)

Stanford-Binet IV (Chicago: Riverside)

Kaufman Assessment Battery for Children (Los Angeles: Western Psychological Services)

3. Assessments should involve multiple measures over time rather than one-shot measures given at the beginning and/or end of the school year because students with severe disabilities can change so much from day to day that a skill that is not observed one day might be fully in place the next. For example, one of Eduardo's IEP objectives is being able to signal when he has had enough food by shaking his head rather than his previous behavior of spitting out his food. The paraprofessional who feeds Eduardo daily marks a yes–no checklist to assess whether Eduardo has acquired the new skill, and regularly thereafter to be sure that Eduardo has maintained this important communication skill.

4. Alternative assessments should measure district accountability by including as one of the criteria for success the extent to which the school system provides supports that allow the student maximum independence. For example, one of Ms. Engram's objectives for Darlene is to have her participate in small-group activities in science class. For Darlene to meet this objective, she needs the assistance of a paraprofessional as well as an augmentive communication device. The provision of the aid and augmentive communication device is an important part of evaluating Darlene's success and is thus included as part of the criteria for Darlene's alternative assessment measure.

Students with more severe disabilities participate in alternate assessments that stress authentic skills and experiences in real life environments. What skills do you think are being assessed here?

Connections

More information on how to develop, score, and use portfolios for students with special needs is covered in Chapter 11.

Research Note

Kleinart, Kennedy, and Kearns (1999) surveyed 331 teachers in Kentucky who were involved in carrying out the Kentucky Alternative Assessment portfolios to determine whether the system was benefitting students. Teachers felt a number of outcomes were positive; students learned how to follow their own individualized schedules, assess their own performance, and use augmentative communication devices. Some teachers expressed concern about the amount of time the assessments required and felt that more training on how to score the portfolios was needed.

5. Teachers should continually monitor the extent to which alternative assessments lead to better outcomes for students. Alternative assessments should inform the need for services which in turn should lead to more productive, independent lives for students with severe disabilities in the community. For example, Eduardo's teacher checks Eduardo's communication skills in other settings to see whether what he has learned in his feeding program is leading to important outcomes in other settings.

The state of Kentucky has developed an alternative assessment system that meets many of these guidelines using portfolio assessments (Kleinart, Kearns, & Kennedy, 1997). All students, regardless of disability, are required to meet standards in a range of areas including using patterns to understand past and present events and predict future events, using technology effectively, demonstrating knowledge and skills and values that have lifetime implications for involvement in physical activity, and completing a postsecondary opportunities search (Kearns, Kleinert, Clayton, Burdger, & Williams, 1998). Although the portfolios reflect the same set of outcomes for all students, students with significant cognitive disabilities meet them in different ways. For example, Damon met the standard of completing a postsecondary opportunities search by compiling a list of his work preferences and specific jobs aligned with his preferences. Sibilie demonstrated her effective use of technology by using an augmentative communication device across a range of school and community settings. Carolyn, a student with multiple disabilities, demonstrated achievement in skills and values related to physical activity by participating in a volleyball game in physical education class. Linus demonstrated his ability to use patterns to understand events by recognizing that on days his paraprofessional wasn't in school he had less time to get ready for recess.

Each student's portfolio has six essential components: evidence of how the student communicates, the student's daily or weekly schedule, a student letter to the reviewer indicating why the student has chosen the portfolio entries and naming the student's best or favorite entry, a resume of work experiences for twelfth graders, a letter from the student's parents indicating the parents' level of satisfaction with the student's portfolio, and five academic entries that serve as evidence of meeting academic expectations. Academic entries for all levels need to include language arts; only twelfth graders need a vocational entry (Kearns et al., 1998).

Student performance is evaluated according to a rubric based on five dimensions. These include performance of targeted skills within the context of academic expectations, appropriate supports that lead to independence, performance in multiple settings to ensure the transfer of skills, social relationships that support the development of appropriate social interaction skills and the development of social networks, and age-appropriate social interaction with opportunities for making choices and decisions (Kearns, Kleinert, & Kennedy, 1999, p. 36).

Curriculum-Based Assessments

Because of the limited utility of standard achievement tests and psychological reports for day-to-day instructional decisions, you need other tools to be a partner in the evaluation process. **Curriculum-based assessment (CBA)** is an effective option, and in many instances can be an alternative to standardized tests. CBA has been defined as a method of measuring the level of achievement of students in terms of what they are taught in the classroom (for example, Bursuck & Lessen, 1987; Choate, Enright, Miller, Poteet, & Rakes, 1995; Tucker, 1985). CBA has a number of attractive features. When using CBA, you select the skills that are assessed based on what you teach in class, thus ensuring a match between what is taught and what is tested. CBA compares students within a class, school, or district to show learning differences, not national norms (Marston, Tindal, & Deno, 1984), thus ensuring that a student referred for special education services is significantly different from his or her peers (Bursuck & Lessen, 1987). For example, in the vignettes at the beginning of this chapter, Ms. Lyons, before referring Rob to special education, gave him some curriculum-based assessments in math to determine the specific kinds of problems he was having. She then implemented a peer tutoring program and used these same tests to measure its effectiveness. Mr. Blount used an informal reading assessment based on his U.S. history textbook to see how well his students were able to read this text. Finally, research shows that when teachers use CBA to evaluate student progress, and adjust their instruction accordingly, student achievement increases significantly (Fuchs, Fuchs, Hamlett, & Stecker, 1991; Shinnet, Colins, & Gallagher, 1998). The Case in Practice on page 284 illustrates a scenario in which both standardized and curriculum-based assessments are used to help make a special education decision.

What Kinds of Curriculum-Based Assessments Can You Create for Your Students?

Two major kinds of curriculum-based assessments are commonly used: probes of basic academic skills (for example, reading, math, and writing) and probes of content-area strategy assessments (for example, prerequisite skills, textbook reading, and note taking). Although probes of basic academic skills relate more directly to elementary school teachers and probes of content-area strategy assessments to middle and high

Assessments in Special Education Decision Making

Darnell is 9 years old. He was referred for testing for a learning disability by his fourth-grade teacher, Ms. Davis. Ms. Davis was particularly concerned about Darnell's lack of progress in written language (for example, paragraph writing and spelling). Following an evaluation, a meeting was held to discuss Darnell's eligibility for special education. Present at the meeting were the school psychologist, Mr. Earl; the learning disabilities teacher, Mr. Bryant; Darnell's fourth-grade teacher, Ms. Davis; and Darnell's mother, Mrs. Lewis. The following information was presented after introductions were made.

Mr. Earl: We're all here today to take a careful look at some of the problems Darnell has been having with his writing to see whether he may have a learning disability and be eligible for some extra help. I'll start by sharing the results of Darnell's intelligence test. Then, Mr. Bryant will discuss the results of a standardized achievement test in writing that he gave Darnell. Ms. Davis will share the results of some informal testing she has been doing in her class. Finally, Mrs. Lewis will tell us about Darnell's language use at home.

I gave Darnell the commonly used Wechsler Intelligence Scale for Children—III. His overall score was 105, well within the average range. I think it's also important to point out that Darnell's verbal IQ of 103 was also in the normal range; he may be having trouble

with his written language, but his oral language seems okay. Darnell seems to have the ability to be successful in writing.

Mr. Bryant: I gave Darnell the Woodcock-Johnson–Revised Tests of Achievement. His scores in all areas of written expression were well below what we might predict based on the IQ scores presented by Mr. Earl. His overall grade equivalence score in written expression is grade 2, month 3. Darnell scored particularly low in writing mechanics such as spelling, proofing, capitalization, punctuation, and fluency. His score in this area was grade 1, month 8.

Ms. Davis: At the end of last month, I was teaching my class to write "how to" papers, such as how to make a peanut butter and jelly sandwich. After about a week, I no-

school teachers, each of these measures is relevant for both groups. For example, high school students need to perform basic skills fluently if they are to have ready access to curriculum content; elementary school students need early training in learning strategies to make the difficult transition to high school instruction easier.

Probes of Basic Academic Skills

Probes are quick and easy measures of student performance in the basic skill areas of reading, math, and written expression. They consist of timed samples of academic behaviors and are designed to assess skill accuracy and fluency.

Probes can sample a range of skills in a particular area, such as a mixed probe of fifth-grade math computation problems in addition, subtraction, multiplication, and division; or they can sample one skill area, such as letter identification or writing lowercase manuscript letters.

Check Your Learning

What are the four major types of probes? Give an example of each.

Typically, students work on probe sheets for 1 minute. The teacher then records the rate of correct and incorrect responses as well as any error patterns. Student performance rates have been shown to be useful for making many of the important eval-

gave the students five minutes to write their paragraphs. This is what Darnell wrote:

waat you haist and not sopo in haid

First, I wanted to see whether Darnell wrote as much as the rest of the class. As you can see, Darnell wrote 8 words, which is less than 2 words per minute. The average for the rest of the class was 30 words, or about 6 words per minute. I also judged Darnell's paragraph for quality; his paragraph lacked features such as title, topic sentence, closing sentence, and the use of signal words; "*First* you do this, and *next* you do that." The papers of all the other students in class except one had these features.

Mrs. Lewis: This sounds a lot like how Darnell is at home. He has never had trouble following oral directions, but his handwriting and spelling have always been a problem. Getting him to write a letter to his grandmother is like pulling teeth.

REFLECTIONS

What different kinds of assessment were used here? What other measures might have been used? What instructional changes did Ms. Davis try before referring Darnell? Can you think of some other interventions that she could have tried? Do you think Darnell should be declared eligible for receiving special education services for learning disabilities on the basis of this information? Why or why not?

uation decisions described earlier in the chapter, such as screening, diagnosis, program placement, curriculum placement, instructional evaluation, and program evaluation (Bursuck & Lessen, 1987; Deno & Fuchs, 1987; Shinn et al., 1998; Tindal & Marston, 1990). The Professional Edge on page 286 describes the importance of considering both student accuracy and student fluency when assessing basic academic skills.

Probes are classified according to how students take in task information (seeing, hearing) and how they respond (writing, speaking). They include four major types: see–say, see–write, hear–write, and think–write (Bursuck & Lessen, 1987). For example, when reading orally from a textbook, students *see* the text and *say* the words. Hence, oral reading is referred to as a see–say probe. Similarly, in a spelling probe, students *hear* the teacher dictate words and *write* the words as they are dictated. This is a hear–write probe.

As you develop curriculum-based assessments, keep in mind the following suggestions:

1. Identify academic skills that are essential in your particular room or grade. In the elementary grades, include skills in handwriting, spelling, written expression, reading (for example, letter identification, letter sounds, oral reading accuracy,

Connections

Probes of academic skills help you evaluate the instructional progress of students with special needs, an application of the *E* step of the INCLUDE strategy, as discussed in Chapter 4.

Professional Edge

Assessing Student Rates on Basic Academic Skills

When basic skills or other academic content are assessed informally in the classroom, **student accuracy** is usually stressed. For example, we say that Jill formed 85 percent of her cursive letters correctly, John was 90 percent accurate on his addition facts, or Al identified key pieces of lab equipment with 100 percent accuracy. Although accuracy is important because it tells us whether a student has acquired a skill or section of content, accuracy is not the only useful index of pupil performance. **Student fluency,** or how quickly a student is able to perform a skill or recall academic material, is also relevant. Before you consider the reasons for assessing student fluency provided here, consider this: If your car needed service and you had your choice between two mechanics, both of whom did accurate work and charged $35 an hour, but one of whom worked twice as fast as the other, which mechanic would you choose?

The Rate Rationale

1. Students who are proficient in a skill are more likely to remember the skill, even if they do not need to use it very often. If they forget the skill, they need less time to relearn it.

2. Students who are proficient in a basic skill are better able to master more advanced skills. For example, students who can perform addition problems fluently often acquire advanced multiplication skills more easily.

3. Performance of basic skills at an "automatic" level frees students to perform higher-level skills more readily. For example, students who can read fluently with understanding are more likely to be successful in high school classes that require reading lengthy textbook assignments in little time. Students who know their math facts without counting on their fingers can solve word problems more efficiently.

4. Students with special needs are often so labeled because they work more slowly than their peers. Fluency scores allow teachers to compare these students directly with their classmates on this important dimension of speed; they also provide a useful index of student progress, including, for

some students, readiness for inclusion in general education classes.

USING THE RESEARCH

If you are interested in learning how your students' oral reading rates compare to national norms, Hasbrouck and Tindal (1992) have compiled national norms based on student oral reading fluency scores from multiple school districts across the country. These norms are shown in Table 8.1. Notice that separate norms are presented for fall, winter, and spring to account for student growth during the year. So, if Simone is reading 80 words correct per minute in February of second grade, she is reading at just above the 50th percentile for winter of grade 2.

Table 8.1 National Norms for Student Oral Reading Fluency

Grade	Percentile	Fall (August–December) WCPM*	Winter (January–March) WCPM	Spring (April–June) WCPM
	75	82	106	124
2	50	53	78	94
	25	23	46	65
	75	107	123	142
3	50	79	93	114
	25	65	70	87
	75	125	133	143
4	50	99	112	118
	25	72	89	9
	75	126	143	151
5	50	105	118	128
	25	77	93	100

*WCPM = words correct per minute

SOURCE: From "Curriculum-Based Oral Reading Fluency Norms for Students in Grades 2–5," by J. E. Hasbrouck and G. Tindal, 1992, *Teaching Exceptional Children, 24* (3), pp. 41–44.

comprehension), and math (for example, number identification, computation, problem solving, time, and money).

2. Select skills representing a *sample* of skills that are taught, not necessarily every skill. Performance on these skills then acts as a checkpoint for identifying students in trouble or measuring student progress. For example, in assessing reading performance, having students read a passage aloud from their reading or literature books and answer comprehension questions may not represent all reading skills you have taught (for example, words in isolation), but it does include a representative sample of many of these skills.

Probes of reading skills. The critical reading skills in the elementary years include letter identification, letter sounds, word recognition, and comprehension. Student ability to identify letter names and sounds can be assessed using a see–say probe. Word recognition and comprehension can be assessed using a see–say oral passage reading probe such as the one in Figure 8.1.

Although the easiest method for assessing comprehension is to use the questions that accompany most classroom reading series, if you are using a literature-based reading program, you may need to design your own questions, which can be a difficult task. Carnine, Silbert, and Kameenui (1997) have suggested one practical model for designing comprehension questions based on story grammar. A **story grammar** is simply the description of the typical elements found frequently in stories. These include theme, setting, character, initiating events, attempts at resolution, resolution, and reactions. These elements of story grammar can be used to create comprehension questions that may be more appropriate than traditional main idea and detail questions, because story grammar describes the organization of most stories that elementary school students are likely to read. The Case in Practice on pages 290–291 shows how a teacher uses a story grammar with one of her second-grade students.

At times, you might not wish to ask questions about a story. Specific questions can give students clues to the answers, and they especially help students identify the kind of information you think is important to remember or the way you organize this information. One way to solve this problem is to have students retell stories after they read them. Students then must organize the information they think is important. You can then evaluate the completeness of their recall. Such a situation has two requirements for effective evaluation to occur: a standard set of criteria to evaluate the completeness of the retelling, and the opportunity to evaluate each student's retelling individually. The Professional Edge on page 292 offers additional means of assessing students' reading skills.

Probes of written expression. Written expression can be assessed using a think–write probe. In this probe, the teacher reads the students a story starter. The students then have 1 minute to plan a story and 3 minutes to write it. This probe is scored according to the number of intelligible words the student is able to write per minute. Intelligible words are those that make sense in the story. This way of scoring is useful for screening students for serious writing difficulty (Shinn & Hubbard, 1992). If you are interested in more diagnostic information, such as grammar usage, spelling, handwriting, punctuation, vocabulary, or ideas, you can score this probe differently or give another probe designed to measure these areas specifically (see Choate et al., 1995; Ellis & Colvert, 1996; Evans, Evans, & Mercer, 1986; and Howell & Morehead, 1993, for sample informal assessments in these areas).

Research Note

Fuchs, Hamlett, and Fuchs (1990) have developed a computer program to monitor reading fluency and comprehension. Students are presented with a passage in which words are omitted and replaced with blanks. Students answer by filling in each blank from a choice of three words. Jenkins and Jewel (1993) found that this measure was closely related to student performance on standardized measures of reading achievement.

Research Note

Allinder, Bolling, Oats, & Gagnon (2000) found that students of teachers who regularly asked themselves the following questions when giving curriculum-based measures made more academic progress in math computation: On what skills has the student done well during the last 2 weeks? What skills should be targeted for the next 2 weeks? How will I attempt to improve student performance on the targeted skills?

Figure 8.1 See–Say: Oral Passage Reading

Time	1 minute
Materials	*Student*—Stimulus passage
	Examiner—Duplicate copy of stimulus passage, pencil, timer
Directions to Student	"When I say 'Please begin,' read this story out loud to me. Start here [examiner points] and read as quickly and carefully as you can. Try to say each word. Ready? Please begin."

Scoring   Place a slash (/) on your copy of the materials where the student started reading. As the student reads, place a mark (X) on your copy over any errors (mispronunciations, words skipped, and words given). (If student hesitates for 2–3 seconds, give him or her the word and mark it as an error.) If student inserts words, self-corrects, sounds out, or repeats, do not count as errors. When the student has read for 1 minute, place a slash (/) on your copy to indicate how far the student read in 1 minute. (It is usually good practice to let students finish the paragraph or page they are reading rather than stopping them immediately when 1 minute is over.) Count the total number of words read during the 1 minute (the total number of words between the two slashes). Tally the total number of errors (words mispronounced, words skipped, and words given) made during the 1-minute sample. Subtract the total number of errors from the total words covered to get number correct (total words – errors = correct words).

If students complete the passage before the minute is up, compute student rate using this formula:

$$\frac{\text{\# Correct words}}{\text{Seconds}} \times \frac{60}{1} = \text{Correct words per minute}$$

Note   Probe administered individually.

Billy decided to go down by the river and	(9)
demonstrate his fishing ability. He always could deceive	(17)
the fish with his special secret lure. He had his best	(28)
luck in his own place, a wooded shady spot downstream	(38)
that no one knew about. Today he was going to try	(49)
to catch a catfish all the boys called Old Gray. Old Gray	(61)
was a legend in this town, because even though many boys	(72)
had hooked him, he always managed to get away.	(81)
This time Billy knew that if he sat long enough, he could	(93)
catch his dream fish!	(97)

1. Who is the main character in this story?
2. Where does the story take place?
3. What problem is Billy trying to solve?
4. How is Billy going to try to solve the problem?
5. What do you think is going to happen?

SOURCE: From *Curriculum-Based Assessment and Instructional Design,* by E. Lessen, M. Sommers, and W. D. Bursuck, 1987, DeKalb, IL: DeKalb County Special Education Association. Used with permission.

Probes of math skills. Teachers in the primary grades need to measure student identification of numbers, coins, and geometric figures. This assessment can be done as a see–say probe using numbers and symbols.

Content-Area Assessments

While content-area teachers can use curriculum-based assessment probes to test student knowledge of subject matter (see Figure 8.2), they may need to take a somewhat different approach to student assessment. Content-area classrooms are characterized by increased curricular demands with fewer opportunities for individualization; students are expected to learn more material and to take responsibility for learning much of it on their own. Students who enter a class significantly behind their classmates either in background knowledge or independent learning skills are likely to struggle. Thus, it is important to identify these students early so that they can be better prepared when they enter a content class. For example, at the beginning of this chapter, Mr. Blount assessed his history students' ability to read the class textbook independently because students in his class were expected to read much of the material on their own.

Probes of prerequisite skills. The decision to place a particular student in a given middle school or high school class depends on identifying which skills or content are prerequisite. For example, the English department at a high school developed a test of prerequisite skills for freshman English. Clarise, a student with a learning disability, was given this test at the end of eighth grade to find out whether this class was appropriate for her to take. For skill-oriented classes such as math and English, prerequisite skills would be those covered in elementary school or previously taught courses, such as computation skills for algebra and sentence writing for English. For classes that stress content rather than basic skills (for example, science), having the necessary background information to understand the material currently being presented is also vital.

Unfortunately, the process of determining whether students have necessary prerequisite skills can be problematic. A key problem involves identifying these

FYI

King-Sears, Burgess, & Lawson (1999) suggest using the following steps for the mnemonic APPLY when using CBAs in your classroom: **A**nalyze the curriculum, **P**repare items to meet curriculum objectives, **P**robe frequently, **L**oad data using a graph format, and **Y**ield to results for making revisions and decisions.

Connections

Using probes of prerequisite skills is a good way to identify classroom demands as part of the INCLUDE strategy.

Figure 8.2	**Using Curriculum-Based Assessment (CBA) Probes in Content Areas**

Content Area	CBA Probe Examples
Geography	Identify each state's location on a map by writing the correct state abbreviation. Match the terrain of an area to corresponding industry and products. Compare and contrast regions so that two similarities and two differences are provided.
Science	Given science terms to define, write the correct definitions. Identify steps in the scientific process, and describe how to apply each step to a given hypothesis. Describe the human body systems so that each system's function and relationship to other systems is stated.

SOURCE: From "Applying Curriculum-Based Assessment in Inclusive Settings," by M. King-Sears, M. Burgess, and T. Lawson, 1999, *Teaching Exceptional Children, 32* (1), pp. 30–38.

CASE IN PRACTICE

Using Story Grammars

Ms. Padilla's second-grade students have just read the story *The Funny Farola* by Ann Miranda and Maria Guerrero. The story is about a girl and her family participating in an ethnic festival in their city. The girl, Dora, makes a farola, which is a type of lantern people carry while marching in a parade. Dora's family laughed at her farola because it was in the shape of a frog. However, her unusual farola saves the day when it helps Dora and her parents find Dora's lost brother and sister.

Ms. Padilla is assessing Chantille's comprehension of the story using the story grammar retelling format.

Ms. Padilla: Chantille, you have just read *The Funny Farola*. Would you tell me in your own words what the story is about?

Chantille: The story is about a girl named Dora who made this funny frog that she carried in a parade. You see, her brother and sister got lost at the parade 'cause they were having such a good time, but they got found again 'cause they could see Dora's frog.

Ms. Padilla: Chantille, where does this story take place?

Chantille: It took place in a city and the people were having a big festival. That's why they were having the parade.

Ms. Padilla: Chantille, what was the problem with Dora's frog?

Chantille: Well, it was called a farola, which is a kind of lantern. Everyone was making them for the parade. Dora's family laughed at her farola 'cause they had never seen a frog farola before.

Ms. Padilla: You said that Dora's sister and brother got lost. What did they do to solve that problem?

Chantille: Well, they saw Dora's frog so they knew where to find them.

Ms. Padilla: How did you feel at the end of the story?

Chantille: I felt happy.

Ms. Padilla: Why did you feel happy?

Chantille: Well, 'cause Dora's brother and sister found their mom and dad.

Ms. Padilla: Chantille, what lesson do you think this story teaches us?

Chantille: Not to get lost from your mom and dad.

A score sheet that Ms. Padilla completed for Chantille is shown in Figure 8.3. A plus (+) means that Chantille responded accurately to that element without any prompting or questioning; a checkmark (✓) means that Chantille mentioned the element after she was questioned or prompted; a minus (–) means that she failed to refer to the element even after questioning or prompts.

Look at Chantille's scores. As you can see, she had a good idea of who the main characters were and received a plus for this component (Characters). Chantille named two problems in the story: Dora making a farola that her family laughed at and Dora's brother and sister getting lost. Chantille identified the problem of the lost kids without being prompted, and the problem of the funny farola with prompts; thus, a + and a ✓ were scored for Goal/Problem. It was unclear from Chantille's response exactly how the characters tried to solve their problem, so she received a – for Attempts. Chantille did say the problem was solved when Dora's brother and sister saw the frog; she received a + for this element of Resolution. However, she did not say how this resolved the problem of

skills. Teachers' choices of prerequisite skills often include skills that a student can bypass yet still have access to course content, such as reading in a history class (which can be bypassed by using an oral text) or written expression in a science class (which can be bypassed by using oral tests and reports). When testing for prerequisite skills, you must be careful that you do not inadvertently exclude students with special needs, many of whom are capable of passing content classes despite their problems in certain basic skills areas.

This and other problems suggest the need for a fair way of making placement decisions for students with special needs at the high school level. A potentially useful

her family laughing at the farola so she received a –. Chantille's reaction to the story was appropriate, so a + was scored. For Setting, Chantille received a ✓; she identified the setting after Ms. Padilla prompted her. Finally, Chantille received a – for Theme. This response was lacking, even after prompting.

Notice that Ms. Padilla's prompts included explicit refer-ences to the various story grammar components. For example, she asked, "You said that Dora's sister and brother got lost. What did they do to solve that problem?" as op-posed to asking a more general question, such as, "What happened to Dora's sister and brother?" This use of specific language makes the story grammar components more clear, a necessary structure for younger, more naïve learners.

Figure 8.3 Story Retelling Checklist

Student Name	Story Grammars Evaluated													
	Theme		Setting		Characters		Goal/Problem		Attempts		Resolution		Reactions	
Chantille	–		✓		+		+	✓	–		+	–	+	

+ Responded correctly without prompting
✓ Responded correctly after prompting
– Did not identify relevant story grammar component

method is for teachers to develop probes to evaluate student performance on critical prerequisite skills. The probe-development process, which is similar to the process of developing curriculum-based assessments described previously in this chapter, consists of the following steps:

1. Identify critical content learning or skills for your class.
2. Identify entry-level content or skills needed. Be certain these are not skills for which a bypass strategy would be possible.
3. Develop a probe to measure the identified skills.

Professional Edge

Using Probes to Identify Children at Risk for Reading Problems

More than 20 years of research show that two early language skills are highly predictive of reading success in school: letter-naming fluency and phonemic segmentation (Kaminski & Good, 1996). Assessing both these skills from the middle of kindergarten to the end of first grade can help you identify children who are at risk for having reading problems later on.

Letter-naming fluency can be measured by giving a 1-minute see–say letter-naming probe using guidelines discussed in this chapter. Although clear-cut national norms are not available, students who perform in the bottom 25 percent of their kindergarten class are more likely to be at risk for reading problems later (Chard & Dickson, 1999).

Phonemic segmentation involves the understanding that speech is composed of individual sounds (Snider, 1995). Phonemic segmentation involves the ability to say the individual sounds in words that are presented orally. For example, the teacher says *sad,* and the student says *ssss . . . aaaa . . . dd.* To get a rough estimate of student skill in phonemic segmentation, dictate 10 one-syllable words and have students say the individual sounds in each word. Note that this task is completely oral; no written words are presented to students. If students are not able to say *all* of the individual sounds in *most* words, they may be at risk for

reading problems and in need of segmentation instruction. Students who do poorly on both letter-naming fluency and phonemic segmentation are even more likely to have trouble learning to read.

Research shows that teaching your students to identify letters more quickly does not necessarily improve their chances of being better readers, but teaching them phonological awareness skills does (Blachman, 2000; Nation & Hulme, 1997; Smith, Simmons, & Kameenui, 1995). Snider (1995) suggests teaching sound segmentation and blending as follows:

> Use a Say It and Move It activity to model how to say the sounds in a word. For example, "Watch me. Every time I say a sound, I'm going to move one of these chips down. Fffffaaaaatt."
>
> Model how to blend sounds into words. For example, "I'm going to say a word the slow way and then I'll say it fast. Mmmmmaaaaannnnn. Man. Now you try. If you can say the word fast, I'll show you a picture." (p. 448)

For more information on how to assess and teach phonemic segmentation, see Carnine, Silbert, and Kameenui (1997), Chard and Dickson (1999), and Snider (1995).

4. Administer the probe to current classes to make sure that students passing the class are able to pass the probe test.

5. Set a minimum score necessary for student course entry based on the results of the preceding step. You may want to use an acceptable range rather than a single score, particularly during the initial stages of this process.

6. As with all educational decisions, no one score should be the sole basis for a decision. Other factors, such as student motivation and level of supportive assistance, need to be considered.

Measures of independent learning skills.   When students enter high school, they find an environment often not as supportive as the smaller elementary and junior high or middle school environments they left. The student body is often larger and more diverse. Daily routines change and curriculum is more difficult (Schumaker & Deshler, 1988). High schools also demand a much higher level of student indepen-

What curriculum goals might a physical education teacher observing this class be assessing?

dence through the application of a range of **independent learning skills.** These skills, often referred to as *learning strategies* or *study skills*, include note taking, textbook reading, test taking, written expression, and time management. Student ability to perform these various skills independently can make the difference between passing or failing a class. For example, at the beginning of the chapter, Mr. Blount decided to assess textbook reading skills because these were important for success in his class. A sample instrument to measure textbook reading skills, which was originally developed by Voix (1968) and later adapted by Lessen, Sommers, and Bursuck (1987), is shown in Figure 8.4. Notice that the reading tasks for this measure are taken directly from the students' history and science textbooks. Doing so ensures that the results are relevant for the particular classroom situation. Note also that this textbook reading assessment can be given to the entire classroom at once, enabling the assessment of many students who have trouble reading their textbooks, not just students with special needs. A strategy for assessing higher-level thinking skills, an important part of independent learning skills, is described in the Special Emphasis On . . . feature on page 296.

As with the basic and prerequisite skills mentioned previously, probes can be developed to assess independent learning. A key consideration is that the tasks used for assessment should parallel the tasks students are faced with in your classroom: If you are evaluating textbook reading, the reading task should come from the textbook you are using in class; if you are measuring a student's ability to take lecture notes, the task should involve elements similar to a typical lecture delivered in your class.

Once the task has been selected, decide what kind of measure to use. Three possible choices are direct observation checklists, analysis of student products, and student self-evaluation. With direct observation checklists, a list of observable steps necessary to perform a given strategy is developed. Next, the teacher has a student perform a classroom task that requires him or her to use the strategy and records on the checklist which behaviors the student did or did not perform.

FYI

A less informative but easier way to measure student textbook comprehension is to use the cloze procedure (Jongsma, 1980). Simply select a 250-word passage from your text and delete every fifth word. Have your students read the passage and fill in the blanks. To score, count the number of blanks in the passage and then the number of blanks completed with the exact word that was omitted. If a student has correctly completed about 45 to 50 percent of the blanks, the material is probably at his/her instructional level. If the student has correctly completed 60 percent or more of the blanks, the material is likely to be at his/her independent reading level.

Figure 8.4 Evaluating Content-Area Textbook Reading Skills

Suggestions for specific types of questions are included here. The information in parentheses explains or offers additional information about a particular item.

Using Parts of the Book

1. On what page would you find the chapter called _____? (Tests ability to use table of contents.)
2. Of what value to you are the questions listed at the end of each chapter? (Tests understanding of a specific study aid.)
3. How are the chapters arranged or grouped? (Tests knowledge of text organization.)
4. What part of the book would you use to find the page reference for the topic _____? (Tests knowledge of index.)
5. On what page would you find the answer to each of the following questions? (Tests ability to use index.)

Using Source Materials (examples)

1. What library aid tells you the library number of a book so that you are able to find the book on the shelves? (Tests knowledge of functions of card catalog and computerized cataloging systems.)
2. What is a biography? (Tests knowledge of a type of reference book.)
3. Explain the difference between science fiction and factual science materials. (Tests knowledge of important types of science materials.)

Comprehension

The following questions would be based on a three- or four-page selection from the textbook.

Vocabulary

1. Turn to page _____. How does the author define the word _____? (Tests ability to use context clues and the aids the author uses to convey the meaning of the word.)
2. Define _____.
3. What is a _____?
4. *Vocabulary in context:* From the paragraph on page 584 beginning "In Poland, the Soviet Union . . . ," write an appropriate and brief definition of each of the following words: _____ , _____ , and _____ .

Noting Main Ideas

These questions would ask for main points of information, such as main ideas of longer, important paragraphs of the chapter or summary of an experiment. (*Examples:* What are atoms composed of? What reason was given for the conservation of human resources? What is the result of the photosynthetic process?)

Noting Details

These questions would ask for specific bits of information, such as an aspect of a process, the application of a law, the principal steps in an experiment, a life cycle, or incidents in the life of a scientist. (*Examples:* Describe the photosynthetic process. What are the different stages in the cycle of precipitation and evaporation? List the major incidents in the life of Mme. Marie Curie.)

Drawing Conclusions

Ask questions about the significance or value of a finding, the implication of a description of some species or natural phenomenon, causes and effect, or a comparison of two or more types of organisms. The questions should call for answers that are not stated in the text. (*Examples:* Illustrate the term *balance of life.* What conclusion can you draw from the importance of the photosynthetic process? What is the principal difference between mitosis and meiosis?)

Applying Theoretical Information

These questions would ask for examples of practical uses of scientific law and principles. (*Examples:* Explain the relationship of photosynthesis to the conservation of plant life. Explain the idea that air confined in a small area exerts pressure in all directions, in relation to the action of air in a football.)

Following Directions

These questions would ask learners to show the sequence of steps or ideas for solving a problem or performing an experiment or the sequence of a chain of events. (*Examples:* What is the second step of the experiment? What should you do after you have placed the flask over the burner?)

Understanding Formulas and Symbols

These questions test student understanding of how symbols and formulas are used with scientific data. (*Examples:* What does the H refer to in the symbol H_2O? What does 40# mean?)

Maps and Graphs

Use questions that require knowledge of map and graph symbols and how to use them. (*Examples:* Use the graph on page 602 to answer these questions: By 1925, how many millions of people inhabited Earth? How many times will the world population have increased from 1900 to 2000? Use the map on page 174 to answer these questions: Who ruled Gascony in the 12th century? Who governed the major portion of Flanders after 1550?)

Study Reading

Directions: Read pages 584–586. Take notes. Then, close your book and keep it closed. However, you may use the notes you made to help you answer the following questions. (Have questions on a separate sheet for distribution after notes have been made.) *Note:* Ask detail, main idea, and inference questions.

Although direct observation of student behavior can provide much useful information, it is time consuming, particularly when you are a high school teacher who teaches many students each day. For most students, you can use analysis of student products or student self-evaluations. Nonetheless, if you have the luxury of a free moment with an individual student, such as before or after school or during a study hall, the time spent directly observing a student perform a task is very worthwhile.

Analysis of student products involves looking at student notebooks, tests, papers, and other assignments or written activities to find evidence of effective or ineffective strategy performance. In most cases, you can evaluate your whole classroom at once, and you do not have to score the products while you are teaching.

In **student self-evaluations,** students perform a task such as taking a test, are given a checklist of strategy steps, and are then asked to tell which of these steps they

Connections

Sample direct observation checklists can be found in Chapter 11.

Cultural Awareness

Student-centered assessment strategies such as self-evaluation are an important part of empowering students through multicultural education.

Special Emphasis On . . .

The Assessment of Higher-Level Thinking Skills

With the exception of English and math teachers, middle and high school teachers are concerned primarily with teaching subject matter rather than basic academic skills. However, learning subject matter knowledge involves more than just the ability to recall specific information; students also need to be able to access information, plan responses, organize information, and monitor their performance. These skills are commonly referred to as *higher-level thinking skills,* and they can be assessed using the content that you are covering in your particular curriculum.

What to Measure

Tindal and Nolet (1995) suggest that you measure thinking skills by assessing your students in five areas: reiteration-summarization, illustration, prediction, explanation, and evaluation. In reiteration-summarization, students are asked to recite facts, recall definitions, restate relationships, or follow procedures. Reiteration involves having students reproduce material exactly as it was originally presented ("Recite the preamble to the Bill of Rights"). When summarizing, students paraphrase, reword, or condense content already presented ("Describe the main problem engineers encountered when they first tried to extract oil from shale"). With illustration, students are expected to recognize or produce previously unused examples of concepts and principles already presented ("From your own experience, provide an example of the consequences of procrastinating"). Prediction involves describing or selecting a likely outcome given a set of conditions that have not been presented previously ("If all the plankton in a lake die, describe what happens to the other

organisms living in the lake"). Explanation is the reverse of prediction; students are given an outcome (effects) and some beginning state, and then figure out the causes that brought about the outcome ("Use what you have learned about plate tectonics to explain the existence of the Cascade mountain range"). Evaluation focuses on decision making; students first identify possible courses of action and then use a set of guidelines or criteria for choosing among them ("Of the alternatives to using fossil fuels listed above, select the one you think would work the best, and justify your answer"). Some additional sample questions from Tindal and Nolet (1995) follow.

Prediction

Question

1. The air contains a certain amount of water vapor. What do you think happens to the water vapor as the air cools?

2. An air mass that forms over northern Canada is cold and dry. What would be the characteristics of an air mass that forms over tropical Hawaii? Tell why you think so.

3. What would the earth's climate zones (tropical, temperate, polar) be like if the earth was not tilted on its axis? Tell why you think so.

Explanation

1. Suppose a planet in another solar system has a higher gravity than on earth and is colder than earth. Do you think it would have an atmosphere? Why or why not?

2. One morning the ground in your neighborhood is wet and saturated with water. The night before it

did or did not use (Bursuck & Jayanthi, 1993). Student self-reports are useful for several reasons. They can provide information about strategy behaviors that cannot be directly observed. Student evaluations also stimulate student self-monitoring, a behavior critical for independent learning. Self-report measures can also include interview questions that further clarify strategy usage. For example, one teacher asked,

rained heavily. That same rain used to be in the form of groundwater at an earlier time. What do you think happened to change this water from groundwater to rain and back to groundwater again? Explain why you think so.

3. Pretend that when you leave for school one morning, you notice a small puddle in your driveway. The entire day is steamy and hot. When you get home that afternoon, the mud puddle is gone. Explain what you think happened to the puddle of water while you were at school. (No, the dog didn't drink it.) Use what you know about how water changes form.

Evaluation

1. Does the atmosphere on earth differ from the moon's? Why do you think so or why not? What affects the atmosphere of a planet?

2. Many different types of research are carried out today. Equipment has been developed to study many aspects of the ocean, from the surface to the ocean floor. If money for research became limited, which one of the following would you choose as the most important to continue studying: ___ minerals ___ plants and animals ___ ocean floor?

3. Which do you think might cause more destruction on earth: ___ a volcano with silica magma ___ a volcano with basaltic magma? Choose one and tell why you think so.

Ways to Get Accurate Assessment Results

Tindal and Nolet (1995) suggest that you use these strategies when assessing thinking skills to ensure obtaining accurate results.

- For more complicated questions, try to include enough background information so that students have an equal chance of answering questions correctly.
- End each question with directions for how the answer should look and include some qualifying guidelines. For example, tell students that although they should write legibly, their answers will not be scored for penmanship and spelling, and that if they don't know how to spell the word, they should do their best. It is important that the score obtained reflects their ability on the thinking skills you have targeted, not their ability to write or spell.
- Encourage students to take a few minutes before they begin writing to review questions and plan answers. Have students use a graphic organizer to help them plan their answers.
- Tell students to work for the entire time allowed and to review their answers if they finish early.
- Give a running time notice to help students pace themselves so that they don't spend too much time on any one part of the test.
- Provide a motivating statement that encourages everyone to perform with equal effort and care.

Ways to Measure Thinking Skills Using Computers

Guptill (2000) has listed numerous ways technology can be used to measure and reinforce higher-level thinking skills. A list of these suggestions is shown in Figure 8.5.

continued

"What was the first thing you did when you received your test?" As with all measures, student self-evaluations need to be corroborated by information from other sources (for example, direct observation checklists and student products). Such corroboration may be particularly important for students with special needs, many of whom have difficulty evaluating their own behavior.

Connections

Examples of student self-evaluation are shown in Chapter 10.

Special Emphasis On . . . Continued

Figure 8.5 Measuring Student Thinking Skills through Computer Applications

Thinking Skills	Computer Application
Knowledge	Search and reinforce Knowledge of major ideas Knowledge of dates, events, places Technological and academic concepts
Comprehension	Surf (and sift) through information on the Web, and read for understanding Identify valuable websites, record sites Group websites into categories Interpret, compare, and contrast facts Predict consequences—use interactive websites to develop understanding of concepts Contact experts to clarify understanding Interpret information, provide perspectives
Application	Draw together associations between prior knowledge and a search of the Web Collect information as individual or team Classify information Predict outcomes based on website search Refine outline search, as needed Select photographs, quotations, sound clips, virtual reality tours for use in presentation Select format of presentation: newspaper, collage, web page
Analysis	Organize information (text, graphics, sound clips) Sort and discern quality information from outdated or biased information Find solutions to questions using collaboration and investigations with peers and experts
Synthesis	Combine information from different websites Modify information to meet assignment guidelines Create and design websites, interactive projects, visual displays, and written text Prepare essays, projects, visual displays, interactive presentations Compare meaningful text from information gathered Explain findings/synthesize findings
Evaluation	Assess value and quality of presentation Compare and discriminate between information from different sites Verify value of information from various sources Recognize the difference between subjective versus objective information Support information with prior knowledge Summarize findings

S O U R C E : From "Using the Internet to Improve Student Performance," by A. M. Guptil, 2000, *Teaching Exceptional Children, 32* (4), pp. 16–20.

How Are Learning Probes Used to Make Special Education Decisions?

Academic probes can help teachers make many of the assessment decisions discussed previously in this chapter. Several examples are discussed in the following sections.

Peer Comparison in Screening

The key question involved in screening is whether the student is different enough from his or her peers on important skills in a given academic area (or areas) to indicate that some form of classroom accommodation is necessary. If the difference between a student and his or her peers continues or worsens despite repeated attempts in the classroom to remediate, a referral to special education and a more comprehensive assessment *may* be called for.

The **peer comparison method** suggested here was originally developed by Deno and his colleagues at the University of Minnesota (Deno, 1985, 1989; Deno & Fuchs, 1987; Marston, Tindal, & Deno, 1984). First, probes are selected in the area(s) of suspected difficulty. Next, the probes are given to the entire class or a representative subsample of the class (for example, five "average" performers).

Figure 8.6 shows probe results for oral reading in context. The scores are ranked from high to low, and then the class median is determined. The median, or middlemost score, is used to summarize the scores because it is affected less by extreme scores than the mean, or average, which could over- or underestimate the performance of the group as a whole.

> **Connections**
>
> The national norms for oral reading in Table 8.1 on page 286 can also be used to screen students with reading problems.

> **FYI**
>
> Peer comparison and other classroom assessment procedures developed by Deno and colleagues are referred to as *curriculum-based measurement*.

Figure 8.6 Classroom Performance on Academic Skill Probe in Reading

Reading Orally in Context

Number of correct words per minute read orally

190	136	103
189	128	99
172	125	97
160	123	96
159	120	94
151	119	90
139	119	50*
136	117	

Median	123
Median/2	61.5

*Denotes score of Median/2 or lower

Figure 8.6 also gives a score equal to one-half of the median (Median/2). This score can be used as a cutoff for identifying students having trouble with that particular skill (Shinn & Hubbard, 1992). Such a cutoff point typically identifies 6 to 12 percent of a class or grade level who may be experiencing difficulty with a particular skill (Bursuck & Lessen, 1987; Marston et al., 1984). Some probes may identify more students in trouble. For example, we would expect a higher percentage of third graders to be discrepant on basic multiplication facts in the fall than in the spring because these facts have not yet been covered in class. Similarly, many first graders score low on probes given during the first half of the year because many of the skills being assessed are being presented for the first time.

To see how these scores are used to make decisions about screening, look again at Figure 8.6. Oral reading in context represents the number of correct words read orally from a grade-level passage in a basal reader or in books used in a classroom literature-based reading program. As shown, the class scores range from a high of 190 words read correctly per minute to a low of 50 words read correctly per minute. The median, or middlemost, score for the class is 123 words read correctly per minute. A score of 61.5 words read correctly per minute is half of the median. One student is below this point. Although this student may be in need of a classroom accommodation or a referral to special education, other factors should also be considered, including the student's performance across other academic skills assessed and whether other students in the class are having similar problems. The Technology Notes feature illustrates a way you can use software to help you assess your students.

Fluency and Accuracy in Diagnosis

Check Your Learning

What kinds of diagnostic information can you learn by checking student rates of performing academic skills?

Curriculum-based assessment probes also can help teachers diagnose specific skills deficits. For example, a student who performs poorly on a math facts probe may not know the math facts or may simply be unable to write numbers fast enough. You can figure out which situation exists by examining the student's rates, or **fluency,** on think–write number writing. Likewise, keeping track of the number of errors per minute, or **accuracy,** in oral reading can help you detect a particular student's reading problem. Figure 8.7 shows the results of an oral reading probe for two third-grade students. The correct reading rate for both students was 53. However, Student 1 was more accurate in her reading than Student 2. Student 1 seems to have a problem with reading rate. What she reads, she reads accurately; the problem is that 53 words correct per minute is slow for a third-grade student. Student 2, on the other hand, is

Figure 8.7 Reading Rate Information for Two Students

Student 1		Student 2	
Number of words correct per minute	Number of words incorrect per minute	Number of words correct per minute	Number of words incorrect per minute
53	2	53	16

making many word identification errors as well and needs to be further assessed to ascertain whether these errors are part of a pattern or are due to carelessness.

The fact that curriculum-based assessment probes measure rate as well as accuracy adds an important diagnostic dimension. For example, if the reading performance of the two students just discussed had been reported solely as a percentage, the results would have looked like those shown in Figure 8.8. Using percentages alone, Student 1 does not appear to have a problem at all. However, as previously shown, she is reading much more slowly than Student 2.

Skill Mastery and Curriculum Placement

As we have already discussed, inclusive education involves the use of a variety of instructional grouping arrangements: same-skill groups, mixed-skill groups, and individualized instruction. Students with special needs benefit from all three of these arrangements. You can use curriculum-based assessment probes to form all of these grouping types by rank ordering and then visually inspecting your students' probe scores. For example, Mr. Glass wanted to form mixed-skill cooperative groups in math. He used probe scores on a problem-solving task form by picking one lower performer, two middle performers, and one higher performer for each group. Ms. Robins, on the other hand, found that three of her students were having difficulty with capitalization but the rest of the class was not. She formed a small group to review capitalization rules.

Monitoring Student Progress and Instructional Evaluation

Although education has come a long way in terms of researching what constitutes effective teaching, predicting whether a given technique will work for a given student in a particular situation is still difficult. It is thus important that we carefully monitor the results of our teaching. This monitoring is particularly relevant for students with special needs who, by definition, are less likely to respond favorably to commonly used instructional methods.

Curriculum-based assessment probes, because they are time-efficient, easy to give, and match what is taught in the classroom, are ideal for monitoring student progress in class. For example, Mr. Harris was interested in whether Maria, a student

Check Your Learning

How can probes be used to monitor student progress?

Figure 8.8 **Percentage of Accuracy in Passage Reading for Two Students**

Student 1	Student 2
Percentage of Accuracy	Percentage of Accuracy
96	70

[Technology Notes]

Computerized Curriculum-Based Measurement

You may be wondering how you are going to assess your students systematically and still have time to prepare and teach your lessons. Researchers have developed a product that may help you (Fuchs, Fuchs, Hamlett, Philips, & Bentz, 1994). They have developed software that makes scoring and interpreting curriculum-based measures in math much easier. In the Fuchs et al. system, students take a weekly probe test that measures required math operations for a given grade level. Students then are taught to enter their own data into a computer program that scores their test and summarizes the results.

The software program summarizes student performance using a display like the one shown in Figure 8.9. The graph shows the student's rate and accuracy on weekly math tests over time. This student (Sheila Hemmer) went from a score of 10 digits correct per minute at the beginning of October to a score of more than 30 digits correct per minute in March. The skills profile chart shows which skills (A1 = first skill in addition; S2 = second skill in subtraction) have been mastered and which may require more instruction.

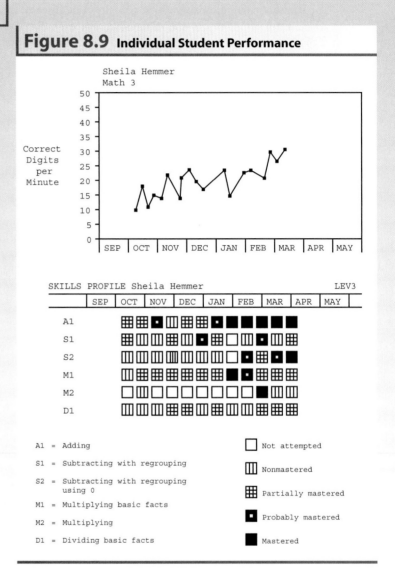

Figure 8.9 Individual Student Performance

with learning disabilities, was retaining any of the words featured on weekly spelling lists. She had scored 90 and above on her weekly tests, but Mr. Harris was still unsure whether she was remembering the words from week to week. He developed a spelling probe using words from previous spelling lists. He gave the probe to his entire class and found that Maria and 10 other students were retaining only 20 percent of the words. As a result, he started a peer tutoring program to help students review

Teachers also receive a display like the one in Figure 8.10. The graph shows the teacher, Mr. Martin, how his students progressed from October through March. The top line indicates scores at the 75th percentile; the middle line, scores at the 50th percentile; and the bottom line, scores at the 25th percentile. The lists below the graph provide information about which students should be watched, or monitored; areas in which the class has improved or not changed; and recommendations for skills that could be covered in whole-group instruction (most of the class needed instruction) or small-group instruction (only one or two students).

Figure 8.10 **Summary of Class Performance**

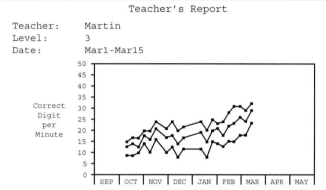

Teacher's Report

```
Teacher:    Martin
Level:      3
Date:       Mar1-Mar15
```

STUDENTS TO WATCH (LOWEST 25%):

Raymond Goldsmith   Leigh Cawthorne   Betsy Dalton
Michael Larson   Aline Jackson   Amanda French

AREAS OF IMPROVEMENT: Subtracting with
                               regrouping (S1)
                               Multiplying (M2)

AREAS OF LITTLE CHANGE: Adding (A1)
                               Subtracting with
                               regrouping using 0 (S2)

WHOLE GROUP INSTRUCTION: Subtracting with
                               regrouping using 0 (S2)

Because over half your class has difficulty with this skill, we recommend you teach it to your entire class.

SMALL GROUP INSTRUCTION: Adding (A1)
Two of your students show continued difficulty on this skill:

Leigh Cawthorne   Amanda French

We recommend that you work with these students to determine the source of their difficulty and try to remediate the problem.

their words. Mr. Harris also set up group competitions and awards for groups scoring the highest on the review probes. Implementing these two activities improved Maria's and the other students' retention significantly.

A final example is worthy of mention. Mr. Rock recently switched his reading program from a basal series to a literature-based program. He wanted to make sure that several of the lower-performing students in his class were adding new words to

WWW Resources

For the latest research on student testing, curriculum, and achievement, go to National Institute on Student Achievement, Curriculum and Assessment at http://www.ed.gov/offices/OERI/SAI/index.html.

their sight vocabularies. He randomly selected three 300-word passages from a literature book that all these students had recently completed. He found that two of the students read the passages at mastery levels, but one student was reading at the frustration level. Mr. Rock decided to drop the student to an easier level of book and to use a peer tutor to provide some high-frequency word drills for the student. Again, teaching approaches, no matter how promising, may not work for all students. By monitoring his students' progress using CBA probes, Mr. Rock was able to make a helpful adaptation in a student's instructional program.

Summary

General education teachers can make assessments that contribute to six special education decisions: screening, diagnosis, program placement, curriculum placement, instructional evaluation, and program evaluation. Screening involves determining whether a student's performance differs enough from that of his or her peers to merit further, more in-depth assessments to ascertain whether the student has a disability. Diagnosis relates to eligibility for special education services; namely, does the student meet federal guidelines for being classified as having a disability? If so, what is the nature and extent of the student's disability? The major program placement decision involves determining the instructional setting where a student's special learning needs can be met. Curriculum placement decisions concern the level at which to begin instruction for students. Decisions in instructional evaluation involve whether to continue or change instructional procedures that have been initiated with students. The purpose of program evaluation decisions is to determine whether a student's special education program should be terminated, continued as is, or modified.

General education teachers can go to a number of information sources to help them program for students with special needs. Group-administered standardized achievement tests can be used to screen students in difficulty, but they have serious drawbacks for making other types of decisions. Individually administered diagnostic tests provide more specific information but are susceptible to many of the same problems as group-administered tests. Psychological tests, such as tests of intelligence and tests related to learning disabilities, measure abilities that affect how efficiently students learn in an instructional situation. These tests can clarify why students may not be learning in class, but they are most helpful when corroborated by classroom experience. Be aware that psychological tests may discriminate against students from culturally diverse or disadvantaged environments. A small percentage of students who are typically working on a more functional curriculum do not have to meet the same requirements as those students graduating with a standard diploma. These students are eligible for alternative assessments based on their more functional curriculum. Curriculum-based assessments measure student achievement in terms of what they are taught in the classroom. As such, they are helpful in making a range of special education decisions, particularly those involving day-to-day instruction.

There are two major kinds of curriculum-based assessments: probes of basic academic skills and probes of content-area strategy assessments. Probes of basic academic skills consist of timed samples of academic behaviors and are designed to assess skill accuracy and fluency. Probes can be developed for all basic skills areas, including reading, written expression, and math. Content-area assessments include probes of prerequisite skills and measures of independent learning skills. Probes of prerequisite skills help teachers make decisions about whether to place students in particular high school classes. Measures of independent learning skills, often referred to as learning strategies or study skills, include note taking, textbook reading, test taking, written expression, and time management. Three ways to measure skills in these areas include direct observation checklists, analysis of student products, and student self-evaluations.

Curriculum-based assessment probes can be used to help make special education decisions. A peer comparison method can help screen students who are in academic difficulty. Probes can also be used to help teachers diagnose specific skill deficits by determining whether academic problems involve accuracy, fluency, or both. In addition, academic assessment probes can be used to help form instructional groups. Finally, curriculum-based probes can help teachers monitor the progress of students in class by measuring student performance over time.

Applications in Teaching Practice

Collecting and Using Assessment Information

It is November 1, and you are concerned about two students in your literature-based reading program. The students' parents have commented that they have not seen improvement in their children's reading at home. You have also noticed that both of these students seem to pick trade books that are too hard for them. In addition, you have concerns about what progress they have made in their word identification and comprehension skills. You wonder whether you should make some changes in their reading program.

Questions

1. What areas of reading would you want to assess here? Why?
2. How would you assess each area using the curriculum-based assessment procedures described in this chapter? What probes would you give? What would your probes look like? How would you score them?
3. What additional assessment information (for example, standardized tests, psychological tests) would you collect?
4. How would you use the information you obtained in questions 2 and 3? Under what circumstances would you decide to adapt the current program? Use an alternative program? Advocate for intensive instruction from a special education teacher?
5. What would you do to evaluate the changes suggested in question 4? What measures would you give? How often? What kinds of decisions would you be making?

Yolanda is a student with a learning disability in your class who has been receiving indirect support in the area of (pick one: reading, math, written expression). You are interested in knowing how she is doing in relation to the rest of the class.

Select a subject area in which Yolanda has been receiving indirect support. Then, select a particular skill in that subject matter that you have been working on in your class (for example, in reading—sight-word reading, passage reading, comprehension, letter or letter–sound identification; in math—any math computation skill, word problems, money, geometry; in written expression—writing mechanics, writing productivity, quality of ideas). Next, describe a curriculum-based assessment strategy you would use to judge how well Yolanda is doing on that skill as compared with her classmates. Respond to the following questions in your description.

Questions

1. How would you use peer comparisons to measure the extent of Yolanda's problem?
2. What additional information would you collect to clarify Yolanda's problem?
3. How would you use probe information to measure the effectiveness of classroom supports for Yolanda?
4. How would you use probe information to help you instruct the rest of the class?

The high school resource room teacher has suggested that Antoine, who has a learning disability, be included in your second semester class. He has asked you to help collect some information to assist him in deciding what support service (if any) Antoine should receive. Assuming you are a math teacher, describe a strategy for determining whether Antoine has the prerequisite skills for your class. Your strategy should respond to the following questions.

Questions

1. What skills would you include on your probe and why?
2. Are all these skills essential, or could some of them be bypassed?
3. How will you design, administer, and score your probe?
4. How will you determine whether Antoine is experiencing academic difficulty?
5. How would you use the information collected to determine needed support services for Antoine?
6. How might the information collected help you in teaching the rest of the class?

If you are teaching a class for which the ability to read the textbook is an important skill, select a sample textbook from your content area. Then, develop a probe of content-area reading skills using the model shown in Figure 8.2 on page 289.

Questions

1. How did you select the skills to be included on your measures?
2. How would you use the information collected to determine the nature and extent of classroom support needed for students with disabilities? For the rest of the class?

Design a 1- or 2-day lesson in the area of your choice describing briefly all the instructional activities involved. Be sure to specify objectives for as many of the following student outcome areas as possible: using patterns to understand past and present events and predict future events, using technology effectively, demonstrating skills and values for physical activity, and completing a postsecondary education search. Tell how you would use an alternative assessment to measure the progress of Darrell, a student with a severe cognitive disability who is in your class.

Questions

1. What outcomes would you expect for your students without disabilities?
2. What outcomes would you expect for Darrell?
3. Describe how you would assess the outcomes for Darrell using alternative assessment devices. Include evaluation criteria for each of the assessments described.

 **chapter**

Instructional Adaptations

After you read this chapter, you will be able to

1. Adapt lessons when students do not have the preskills necessary to learn new skills.

2. Select and sequence instructional examples to help students acquire basic skills.

3. Adapt instruction by providing the direct instruction, practice, and review needed to help students acquire basic skills.

4. Describe adaptations you can make in providing background knowledge, organizing content, and teaching terms and concepts to help students acquire academic content.

5. Implement strategies for improving the clarity of your written and verbal communication with students.

6. Adapt independent practice activities for students.

7. Describe how you can make adaptations in your classroom materials and activities for students with moderate to severe disabilities.

Key Terms and Concepts

■ Ms. Diaz was teaching her fourth-grade class how to write percentages for fractions using this example from her math book:

Write a percent for $\frac{7}{8}$.

$\frac{7}{8}$ means $7 \div 8$.

$$0.87\frac{4}{8} = 0.87\frac{1}{2} = 87\frac{1}{2}\%$$

$$8\overline{)7.00}$$

$\underline{64}$	Divide until the answer is
$\overline{60}$	in hundredths. Give the
$\underline{56}$	remainder as a fraction.
4	

$\frac{7}{8} = 87\frac{1}{2}\%$, or 87.5%

To show her students how to do this problem, Ms. Diaz wrote the example on the board, pointing out that the fraction $\frac{7}{8}$ means 7 divided by 8. She then explained that they would have to divide until the answer was in hundredths and would have to give the remainder as a fraction. Following this instruction, Ms. Diaz assigned the students 15 similar problems to do independently. Abdul, who is a student in this class, has a learning disability. He has difficulty learning new skills unless he is given many opportunities for instruction and practice. Abdul answered none of the 15 problems correctly. He missed converting the fractions to percentages because he forgot that $\frac{7}{8}$ means 7 divided by 8; Abdul divided 8 by 7 instead. How could this lesson have been taught to Abdul to prevent this misunderstanding?

■ Cecily is a student with a hearing impairment who is in Ms. Boyd's U.S. history class. Cecily is failing history because the tests are based mainly on the textbook and she has trouble picking out main ideas in the text and understanding important vocabulary words. Cecily can read most of the words in the text but she reads very slowly, word by word. Last week, she was assigned a chapter to read for homework; she spent almost 2 hours reading 15 pages, and when she was done, she couldn't remember what she had read. The key words are highlighted, but Cecily can't figure them out from the context and doesn't know how to use the glossary. What can Ms. Boyd do to help Cecily read and remember key ideas in her textbook? What can she do to help Cecily understand new vocabulary words?

■ Albert has ADHD and is included in Ms. Olivieri's second-grade class. Albert has trouble following written directions and doing independent practice assignments that have more than one part. He also complains that his seatwork assignments are too hard for him. During seatwork, Albert is frequently out of his chair, either getting help from or bothering other students in the class. Ms. Olivieri feels that she is already spending too much time helping Albert. What should she do to make seatwork a more successful experience for Albert and give herself more time to work with other students?

FYI

This chapter presents guidelines for steps 5 and 6 of the INCLUDE strategy presented in Chapter 4:

Step 5. Use information from steps 1–4 to brain-storm instructional adaptations.

Step 6. Decide which adaptations to use.

As you have already learned, the curriculum methods and materials teachers use have a strong influence on how readily students learn in the classroom. In fact, the better the materials and teaching, the fewer the adaptations required for students with special needs. However, for a variety of reasons, you may not have control over the materials used in your school. Furthermore, despite your best teaching efforts, some students still need **instructional adaptations** to master important skills and content. For example, in the vignettes just described, merely showing Abdul how to do one problem is not enough. He needs guidance through a number of examples before he is ready to do problems independently. You can help Cecily focus on important information in her textbook by giving her a study guide that has questions pertaining to the most important content in each chapter. You can also have Cecily identify words she does not know and ask a classmate to help her with the meanings before she reads. For Albert, you can make sure all directions are clearly written using words he can decode; you can also give the directions orally and guide students through several practice examples before they are required to work independently. Of course, you also want to be sure that Albert has the necessary academic skills to complete assignments independently.

The purpose of this chapter is to provide you with strategies for adapting curriculum materials, teacher instruction, and student practice activities that are reasonable to carry out and that increase the likelihood of success for students with special needs. Remember, reasonable accommodations are those adaptations that can help a student without taking so much time and effort that they interfere with the teacher's responsibilities to other students. Furthermore, these accommodations may be helpful for other students in class who don't have formally identified special needs.

How Can You Adapt Basic-Skills Instruction for Students with Special Needs?

Basic-skills instruction primarily means instruction in the academic skills of reading, writing, and math. However, you may also apply effective principles for adapting basic-skills instruction to content areas such as science. Four aspects of basic-skills instruction that may need to be adapted for students with special needs are preskills, selection and sequencing of examples, rate of introduction of new skills, and direct instruction, practice, and review.

Teaching Preskills

Darrell is in Ms. Rayburn's second-grade class. In language arts, he is experiencing a problem common to many students with special needs. On Tuesday, Darrell was at his desk reading a book on his favorite topic: magic. However, when Ms. Rayburn asked Darrell specific questions about the book, he was unable to answer them. It turned out that Darrell was unable to decode most of the words in the book and was just pretending to read.

 Preskills are basic skills necessary for performing more complex skills. Prior to teaching a skill, you should assess students on the relevant preskills and, if necessary, teach these skills. Darrell was unable to comprehend the magic book because he lacked the word-identification skills needed to read the words. He may need instruction in word-attack skills; he may also need to be encouraged to read trade books at his reading level. Because commercially produced materials do not generally list preskills, you need to ask yourself continually what preskills are required, and you need to be on the lookout for students who lack them. This may mean informally assessing such skills. For example, before Mrs. Tompkins taught her kindergartners to tell time, she checked to see whether they could identify the numbers 1–12 and count by fives to 60. Before teaching students to look up words in a dictionary, Mr. Thurman checked to see whether his students could say the letter in the alphabet, could alphabetize words to the third letter, and knew whether to turn to the front, middle, or end of the dictionary when looking up a certain word.

 If you are teaching a skill and find that most of your students lack the necessary preskills, teach these preskills directly before teaching the actual skill. If only one or two students lack preskills, you can provide these students with extra practice and instruction through a peer or parent volunteer, or with the help of a special service provider. For example, Ms. Cooper is preparing a lesson on how to find the area of a rectangle. Before beginning the lesson, she gave her students a multiplication probe and found that almost half the class was still having problems with their multiplication facts. Ms. Cooper set up a peer tutoring program in which students who knew their facts were paired with students who did not; they practiced facts for 10 minutes each day for a week. Ms. Cooper still introduced finding areas as scheduled, but she allowed students to use calculators until they had mastered their facts in the peer tutoring sessions.

Selecting and Sequencing Examples

The way you select and sequence instructional examples can affect how easily your students learn. For example, Alex's practice activities for a week in Mr. Huang's third-grade math class are shown in Figure 9.1. Mr. Huang has been covering two-digit subtraction with regrouping. On Monday through Thursday, Alex was given five of these problems and got them all right. On Friday, he was asked to do a mixture of problems, some requiring regrouping and some not. Alex got only three of

Figure 9.1 Alex's Math Work

Monday's Seatwork

$^2\!\!\!/\!\!5^1$	$^3\!\!\!/\!\!2^1$	$^2\!\!\!/\!\!8^1$	$^3\!\!\!/\!\!1^1$	$^6\!\!\!/\!\!4^1$
-17	-15	-19	-22	-49
18	27	19	19	25

Tuesday's Seatwork

$^5\!\!\!/\!\!4^1$	$^6\!\!\!/\!\!0^1$	$^8\!\!\!/\!\!1^1$	$^5\!\!\!/\!\!8^1$	$^7\!\!\!/\!\!2^1$
-38	-32	-58	-39	-28
26	38	33	29	54

Wednesday's Seatwork

$^8\!\!\!/\!\!4^1$	$^5\!\!\!/\!\!1^1$	$^2\!\!\!/\!\!3^1$	$^6\!\!\!/\!\!6^1$	$^7\!\!\!/\!\!1^1$
-57	-45	-19	-38	-47
37	16	14	38	34

Thursday's Seatwork

$^4\!\!\!/\!\!5^1$	$^2\!\!\!/\!\!0^1$	$^6\!\!\!/\!\!2^1$	$^8\!\!\!/\!\!6^1$	$^7\!\!\!/\!\!3^1$
-29	-18	-28	-59	-38
26	12	44	37	45

Friday's Seatwork

$^8\!\!\!/\!\!6^1$	$^3\!\!\!/\!\!3^1$	$^7\!\!\!/\!\!9^1$	$^5\!\!\!/\!\!7^1$	$^6\!\!\!/\!\!5^1$
-53	-18	-33	-28	-57
313	25	416	39	18

the problems correct because he was unable to discriminate between subtraction problems that required regrouping and those that did not. He was unable to differentiate these two types of problems in part because his daily practice pages had included only one problem type. Carefully preparing the **example selection** you use when you teach can help students learn to differentiate among problem types.

Help students make key discriminations between current and previous problem types by using examples that at first require only the application of that particular skill (Carnine, Silbert, & Kameenui, 1997). When students can perform these problems without error, add examples of skills previously taught to help students discriminate between the different problem types. Doing this also provides students with needed review. An easy adaptation for Alex would have been to add several problems that did not require regrouping to each daily practice session once he had shown that he could accurately compute the regrouping problems accurately when presented alone.

Ms. Owens ran into another example-related problem when teaching her students word problems in math. In her examples, when a word problem included the word *more*, getting the correct answer always involved subtracting, such as in the following problem:

Alicia had 22 pennies. Juanita had 13. How many more pennies does Alicia have than Juanita?

However, on her test, Ms. Owens included the following problem:

Mark read 3 books in March. He read 4 more books in April. How many books did Mark read?

Several students with special needs in Ms. Owens's class subtracted 3 from 4 because they thought the presence of the word *more* signaled to subtract. Ms. Owens needed to include problems of this latter type in her teaching to prevent such misconceptions. Consider this example: When Mr. Yoshida taught his students how to add *ed* to a word ending in *y*, he demonstrated on the board as follows:

carry + ed = carried   hurry + ed = hurried

Next, Mr. Yoshida had his students add *ed* to five words ending in *y*. Finally, he assigned students 10 practice problems in their English books that looked like this:

Write the past tense of *marry*.

A number of students were unable to answer the questions in the book, even though they knew how to add *ed* to words ending in *y*, because the practice examples in the book required students to know the meaning of *past tense* and how to form the past tense by adding *ed*. The book's practice activity was very different from the instructional examples Mr. Yoshida used, which only required students to add *ed* to words ending in *y*. Both these examples demonstrate an important part of selecting instructional examples: The range of your instructional examples should match the range of the problem types used when you assess student learning. Ms. Owens could have prevented problems in her class by expanding her range of examples to include word problems that contained the word *more* but that were not solved by subtracting. Mr. Yoshida could have better prepared his students for the practice activities in the English book by using examples that referred directly to forming the past tense by adding *ed*.

The following example shows a different example selection problem. Tawana's class was covering several high-frequency sight words that appeared in trade books they used in their literature-based reading program. On Wednesday Tawana learned the word *man*, but on Tuesday, after the word *men* was presented, she was unable to read *man* correctly. Tawana's word-identification problem illustrates another example selection problem, namely, **example sequencing.** The visual and auditory similarities of *man* and *men* make learning these words difficult for many at-risk students and students with learning disabilities, who may have trouble differentiating words that look and/or sound the same. One way to prevent this problem is to

FYI

Student errors and misconceptions also stem from the over- or undergeneralization of concepts. Careful selection and sequencing of a range of examples can help prevent these kinds of errors.

separate the introduction of *man* and *men* with other, dissimilar high-frequency words, such as *dog*, *house*, and *cat*.

This same sequencing idea can be applied to teaching letter sounds. For example, when deciding on the order in which to teach the sounds, consider separating letters that look and sound the same, such as *b* and *d*, *m* and *n*, and *p* and *b*. The careful sequencing of instruction can also be applied to teaching higher-level content. For example, when Mr. Roosevelt, a high school chemistry teacher, taught the chemical elements, he separated those symbols that looked and/or sounded similar, such as bromine (Br) and rubidium (Rb), and silicon (Si) and strontium (Sr).

Deciding the Rate of Introduction of New Skills

Students sometimes have difficulty learning skills when they are introduced at too fast a rate. For example, Mr. Henry is teaching his sixth-grade students how to proofread rough drafts of their writing for errors in using capital letters and punctuation marks. He reviews the rules for using capital letters, periods, commas, question marks, and exclamation points. Next, he has students take out their most recent writing sample from their portfolios to look for capitalization and punctuation errors. Carmen found that he had left out capital letters at the beginning of two sentences, but he did not find any of the punctuation errors he had made. He missed them because Mr. Henry taught his students to proofread their papers for capital letters and punctuation marks simultaneously. A better pace would have been first to work on proofreading for capitalization errors and then to add one punctuation mark at a time (first periods, then commas, followed by question marks, and then exclamation points).

WWW Resources

The Homework Central website, at http://www.homeworkcentral.com, provides lesson plans that include modifications for students with special needs.

In another example of the **rate of introduction** of new skills, Ms. Stevens is working on reading comprehension with her students. She introduces three new comprehension strategies at once: detecting the sequence, determining cause and effect, and making predictions. Carlos is a student who has a mild cognitive disability; he learns best when he is taught one strategy at a time. Ms. Stevens adapted Carlos's instruction by forming a group with three other students who, like Carlos, will benefit from learning these comprehension strategies one by one. She also deleted cause-and-effect and prediction questions from these students' written comprehension exercises until they had been taught these strategies directly in their small group. When Mr. Wallace, the special education teacher, came to co-teach, he worked with these students on detecting the story sequence.

These examples demonstrate an important principle about introducing new skills to students with special needs: New skills should be introduced in small steps and at a rate slow enough to ensure mastery prior to the introduction of more new skills. Furthermore, you may want to prioritize skills and even delete some, as Ms. Stevens did. Many commercially produced materials introduce skills at a rate that is too fast for students with special needs. As just illustrated, a common adaptation is to slow down the rate of skill introduction and provide more practice. Other students in the class, including those with no formally identified special needs, often benefit from such adaptations as well. If a student happens to be the only one having a problem, you can seek additional support from special needs staff, paraprofessionals, peers, and/or parent volunteers. Slowing down the rate of skills introduced is an adaptation in the way curriculum is presented, but it is not the same as reducing the amount of curriculum to be learned. For some students, though, you may need to decrease the amount of curriculum. For example, Ms. Evers reduced Robin's curriculum by shortening her spelling lists from 15 to 5 words and selecting only words that Robin used frequently in her writing.

Providing Direct Instruction and Opportunities for Practice and Review

Students with special needs may require more direct instruction and review if they are to acquire basic academic skills. Consider the following example. Lashonda is in Ms. Howard's spelling class. On Monday, Ms. Howard gave students a pretest on the 15 new words for the week. On Tuesday, the students were required to use each word in a sentence. On Wednesday, the teacher scrambled up the letters in all the words and had the students put them in the correct order. On Thursday, students answered 15 fill-in-the-blank questions, each of which required one of the new spelling words. On Friday, Lashonda failed her spelling test even though she had successfully completed all the spelling activities for that week. She did poorly on her spelling test because the daily spelling activities did not provide her with enough direct instruction and practice on the spelling words. Although activities such as using spelling words in sentences are valuable in the right context, they do not provide practice on the more primary objective of this particular lesson, which is spelling all 15 words correctly from dictation. One way to help Lashonda would be to have a peer tutor give her a daily dictation test on all 15 words, have Lashonda write each missed word three times, and then retest her on all 15 words again.

These examples demonstrate another problem that students with special needs have when learning basic skills: **retention.** Melissa had mastered addition facts to 10

Connections

Direct instruction may help Abdul, whom you read about at the beginning of the chapter. His teacher could teach the skill directly by listing the steps in solving these problems on the board; having students say all the steps; solving several sample problems for students by following the listed steps; leading students through solving similar problems using the steps until they are able to do them independently; and assigning problems for students to do independently, reminding them to follow the steps listed on the board.

Some students need additional instruction and practice when they are learning new skills. What prerequisite concepts and skills might you teach for this assignment on addition and subtraction facts. What kinds of additional practice might you provide?

as measured by a probe test in October, but when she was given the same test in January, she got only half of the facts correct. Thomas could state the major causes of the Civil War in November, but he could not remember them when asked to compare them to the causes of World War I in February. A common adaptation you can use for these students is to schedule more skill review for them. This review should be more frequent following your initial presentation of the skill, and then can become less frequent as the skill is established. For example, instead of waiting until January to review addition facts, Melissa's teacher could first provide review weekly, then every other week, and then every month. Thomas's teacher could periodically review key concepts and information that he may need to apply later, either through homework, an instructional game or contest, or an activity in a co-taught class.

A related concern is that nondirect instructional approaches may be appropriate for some students but may need to be supplemented for others. For example, Felix and Bill are learning to read in Ms. Farrell's class. Neither boy has mastered the *ch* sound (as in *chin*). On Monday, Felix came across the word *chair* in his trade book. His teacher pronounced the word and stated, "When *c* and *h* are together in a word, they usually say *ch*." The next day, Felix came to the word *chip* in his book, and he figured it out, remembering what Ms. Farrell had told him the day before. For Felix, one example in his book and a brief teacher explanation was enough for learning to occur. On Monday, Bill also came across a *ch* word, and he, too, was told what the word was and what sound *c* and *h* make when they come together in a word. Unlike Felix, however, when Bill came across another *ch* word the next day, he could not remember the sound of these letters. Having the teacher tell him once the sound *ch* made was not enough. Bill requires more direct instruction and practice than Felix, such as that provided in the activity shown in Table 9.1.

This discussion of Felix and Bill raises an important issue: General education teachers need to know more than one approach to meet the needs of individual students. Felix can learn sounds with minimal instruction, while reading books; Bill cannot. Bill's teacher may need to supplement the literature-based program with some direct instruction on letter–sound correspondences.

Another example reinforces the idea that some of your students with special needs may need more direct instruction and practice. Mr. Thomas is teaching his sixth-grade students the format for writing a letter to a friend, including where to put the date and inside address and how to write a salutation and closing using correct punctuation. First, he reviewed the various circumstances in which people write letters to friends. Next, he showed a sample letter using the overhead projector and wrote a letter with the class. Finally, he asked the students to write a letter for homework. Brenda handed in her letter the next day; although her ideas were good, she had the inside address in the wrong place, left out commas in the salutation, and forgot to include a closing. Brenda needed more instruction and guided practice on how to format a letter than Mr. Thomas had provided. He had shown the students one letter and had written one letter with them before assigning them to write a letter on their own for homework. Mr. Thomas could have continued to write letters with the class until even the lower performers seemed comfortable performing the task. He could also have had the students write a letter independently in class so that he could monitor their performance and provide corrective feedback if necessary.

Finally, it is important to remember that practice is most effective when it follows direct instruction; practice is never an adequate substitute for direct instruc-

Research Note

Research shows that many students with learning disabilities need direct instruction in letter sounds to learn to identify words systematically (Snow, Burns, & Griffin, 1998).

Cultural Awareness

In Native American cultures, children learn new skills by first observing them and then doing them. Native American students can benefit from direct teaching approaches that stress first modeling or demonstrating skills. You can make demonstrations particularly effective for your Native American students by showing them what the final product looks like before the demonstration (Sparks, 2000).

Table 9.1 Direct Instruction of *ch* Sound

Teacher	Students
1. Teach directly the *ch* sound in isolation.	
Teacher writes on the board: *ch, or, ee, ch, th, sh, ch,* and *ing.*	
1. Teacher models by saying the sound of the new letter combination and tests by having the students pronounce it. Teacher points to *ch.* "These letters usually say *ch.* What sound?"	"ch"
2. Teacher alternates between the new combination and other combinations. Teacher points to a letter combination, pauses 2 seconds, and asks, "What sound?"	Say the most common sound.
3. Teacher calls on several individual students to identify one or more letter combinations.	
2. Teach directly *ch* sound in words.	
Teacher writes on the board: *chin, chair, chip, boot, beam, chomp, stain, chum, moon, chat.*	
1. a. Students identify the sound of the letter combination, then read the word. Teacher points under the underlined letters and asks, "What sound?"	"ch"
b. Teacher points to left of word. "What word?"	"chin"
c. Teacher repeats step 1(a–b) with remaining words.	
2. a. Students reread the list without first identifying the sound of the letter combination. Teacher points to *chin,* pauses 2 seconds, and asks, "What word?"	"chin"
b. Teacher repeats step 2(a) with remaining words.	
3. Teacher calls on individual students to read one or more words.	

S o u r c e : From *Direct Instruction Reading* (3rd ed.), by Douglas Carnine, Jerry Silbert, and Edward J. Kameenui. Copyright © 1997. Reprinted with the permission of Prentice-Hall, Inc.

tion. For example, Mr. Hanesworth designs a board game in which students get to move ahead if they can answer a division fact problem. The problem is that five students in his class still do not understand the concept of division. For them, this practice activity is likely to result in failure. Mr. Hanesworth can solve this problem by providing additional instruction on division for those students who need it while allowing the rest of the class to play the board game independently. Of course later on Mr. Hanesworth can reward the hard work of the small group by allowing them to practice a skill they know using a gamelike format.

Clearly, you may need to adapt instruction to enable students with special needs to acquire basic skills. These adaptations include teaching preskills, selecting and sequencing examples, adjusting the rate of introduction of new skills, and providing additional direct instruction, practice, and review. Students may also need adaptations in the presentation of subject-matter content, the primary teaching focus as students move into the upper grades.

Check Your Learning

How can basic-skills instruction be adapted for students with special needs through attention to preskills, example selection and sequencing, rate of introduction of new skills, and direct instruction with opportunities for practice and review?

Professional Edge

Providing Differentiated Instruction in Reading

The idea behind differentiated instruction is that a variety of teaching and learning strategies are necessary to meet the range of needs evident in any given classroom. According to Tomlinson (2000), students' diverse needs can be met by "providing materials and tasks at varied levels of difficulty, with varying degrees of scaffolding, through multiple instructional groups, and with time variations" (p. 9). Nowhere is the need for differentiated instruction more evident than in the area of beginning reading. Research tells us that many students acquire reading skills readily without the need for extensive support. However, the literature also tells us that many students need more intensive support if they are to learn to read (National Reading Panel, 2000; Snow, Burns, & Griffin, 1998). Dickson and Bursuck (1999) developed and implemented a four-tier model of differentiated beginning reading instruction in grades K–3 in two rural schools. The literature-based reading program at these schools was meeting the needs of about 75 percent of the students very well, but staff felt that more explicit instruction needed to be added for the remaining 25 percent. The purpose of the four-tier model was to provide more intensive reading supports for students who needed them while maintaining the more naturalistic, less intensive programs for those who did not. The model is shown in Figure 9.2.

Tier 1 is the standard general education reading program. As just mentioned, this was a literature-based reading program in Dickson and Bursuck's schools. The performance of students in tier 1 is continually monitored using curriculum-based measures of key literacy skills such as phonemic awareness, letter sounds, listening comprehension, and word identification. Students who are not acquiring key literacy skills according to the assessments remain in tier 1 but are provided with 10 minutes of extra practice daily on these skills. These booster sessions are represented in tier 2 of the model and are delivered by the classroom teacher or a trained paraprofessional using either one-to-one or small-group instruction. The progress of tier-2 students continues to be regularly monitored. If these students continue to show problems acquiring beginning reading skills, they move to more intensive instruction in tier 3.

Tier 3 is an alternative reading program designed for at-risk readers (Wilson, 1996). The program stresses carefully designed, highly structured phonics instruction. Tier-3 instruction is carried out in small groups by the Title 1 teacher. Students in tier 3 still participate in many of the general education reading activities, but care is taken to coordinate those activities with the students' tier-3 reading program. Dickson and Bursuck (1999), similar to other researchers (O'Connor, 2000; Torgesen, 2000), found that approximately 5 percent of the students continued to struggle to acquire beginning reading skills, even with

How Can You Adapt the Instruction of Subject-Area Content for Students with Special Needs?

The instruction of academic content includes areas such as history and science. This instruction mainly involves the use of textbooks and lecture–discussion formats, but

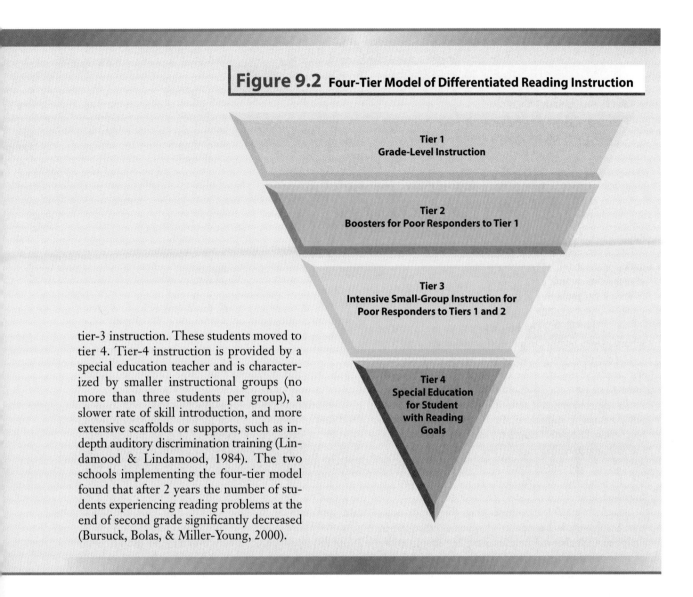

Figure 9.2 **Four-Tier Model of Differentiated Reading Instruction**

Tier 1
Grade-Level Instruction

Tier 2
Boosters for Poor Responders to Tier 1

Tier 3
Intensive Small-Group Instruction for
Poor Responders to Tiers 1 and 2

Tier 4
Special Education
for Student
with Reading
Goals

tier-3 instruction. These students moved to tier 4. Tier-4 instruction is provided by a special education teacher and is characterized by smaller instructional groups (no more than three students per group), a slower rate of skill introduction, and more extensive scaffolds or supports, such as in-depth auditory discrimination training (Lindamood & Lindamood, 1984). The two schools implementing the four-tier model found that after 2 years the number of students experiencing reading problems at the end of second grade significantly decreased (Bursuck, Bolas, & Miller-Young, 2000).

also can include other activities, such as videos, films, and cooperative learning. Although content-area instruction generally is associated with instruction in secondary schools, the information presented here is relevant for elementary teachers as well. In this section, you learn how you can adapt your teaching and materials to help students with special needs learn subject-area content. Strategies for making adaptations are stressed for the areas of activating background knowledge, organizing information, and teaching terms and concepts.

[Technology Notes]

Supporting Student Journal Writing Using Word Recognition and Speech Synthesis Software

Dialogue journals are written conversations between the teacher and each individual student (Staton, Shuy, Kreeft-Peyton, & Reed, 1988). Dialogue journals can benefit students with special needs in a number of ways. Journals can provide students with an opportunity to practice writing without the fear of being continuously corrected. Teacher responses to students' journal entries can also model good writing for students. Dialogue journals also motivate student writing by giving them a specific reason to write.

Although journals can benefit students with special needs, problems with basic skills can disrupt the journaling process. Illegible handwriting and severe spelling problems can render student work unreadable, making it impossible for the teacher to respond to entries. Dictation can help, but that takes a lot of individual attention, more than you may be able to provide. A word processor with a spell checker can also be used, but the spelling errors of some students may be too severe for a spell checker to help.

MacArthur (1998) has researched the use of assistive technology as a support for students engaging in dialogue journals with their teachers. He equipped the computers of third-grade students with special needs with speech synthesis and word prediction capabili-

How might speech synthesis and word prediction programs help this student with her journal entries? What other types of assistive technology might help her with her writing?

ties. **Speech synthesis** translates words typed by students into speech. Speech synthesis helps students read their teachers' messages without having to ask for help. It also helps students read their own writing, allowing them to detect more spelling and grammatical errors than by reading alone. **Word prediction programs** help students "predict" words they intend to write based on the first letters typed. Students type the first letter, or first few letters, and then choose from a list of predictions instead of having to type the whole word. Word prediction can help students with severe spelling problems. MacArthur (1998) used a word prediction program called My Words (1993) in his research. My Words makes its predictions from an al-

Activating Background Knowledge

The amount of background knowledge students have can greatly influence whether they can read subject matter with understanding. To illustrate, read this list of words:

are	making	between
only	consists	often
continuously	vary	corresponding
one	curve	points
draws	relation	variation

phabetical word list that is visible on the screen. A sample screen display is shown in Figure 9.3. As students type the first letter(s) of a word, the word list automatically scrolls to the first word beginning with that letter(s). Students can then click on the word in the list to insert it in their story. They can also hear the word pronounced by the speech synthesizer before selecting it.

MacArthur (1997) found that the speech synthesizer and word prediction program greatly improved the spelling accuracy and legibility of the journal entries of four of the five students with severe writing problems who participated in the study. However, student spelling performance reverted to previous problematic levels when the synthesizer and word prediction programs were taken away. This shows that programs such as the speech synthesis and word prediction ones described here are useful as bypass or compensatory strategies but do not by themselves result in improved independent spelling skills. Such skills need to be directly and systematically taught.

Figure 9.3 My Words Software

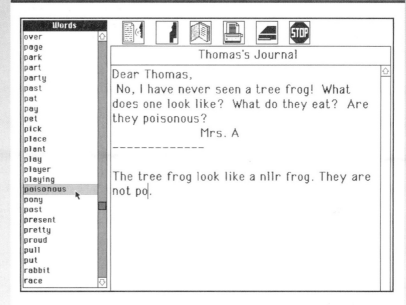

Thomas has typed the first two letters of *poisonous;* the word list has scrolled to the first word beginning with those letters; and Thomas is about to double-click on the word to insert it in his text.

S O U R C E : "From Illegible to Understandable: How Word Recognition and Speech Synthesis Can Help," by C. A. MacArthur, 1998, *Teaching Exceptional Children, 30*(6), p. 67. From *My Words* software published by Hartley. Copyright © CompassLearning, Inc. Used by permission.

set	graph	table
if	values	isolated
variables	known	

Were you able to read all of them? Do you know the meanings of all these words? Now read the following passage:

> If the known relation between the variables consists of a table of corresponding values, the graph consists only of the corresponding set of isolated points. If the variables are known to vary continuously, one often draws a curve to show the variation. (From Michaelson, 1945, cited in Lavoie, 1991)

Cultural Awareness

Relating subject-area content to students' background knowledge makes material more relevant for students. Relevance is particularly important for students who do not come from families with high educational attainment (Cortes, 1978).

Chances are, if you were asked to summarize what you just read, you would be unable to do so despite the fact that you probably answered yes when asked whether you could read and understand all the words individually. You may lack the background knowledge necessary to understand this very technical paragraph. The knowledge students bring to a content-area lesson is often as important for understanding as the quality of the textbook or instructional presentation (Langer, 1984). For students to understand content material, they need to relate it to information they already know. Unfortunately, teachers often fail to consider background information. Students with disabilities and students who are at risk may have two problems with background knowledge: They may simply lack the necessary knowledge, or they may know the information but be unable to recall it or relate it to the new information being presented.

Using the PReP strategy.   A teaching strategy for determining how much knowledge students already have about a topic so that you can decide how much background information to present in class prior to a reading assignment is called the **PReP** (*Pre-Reading Plan*) **strategy** (Langer, 1984). The PReP strategy has three major steps:

Research Note

Several studies of second-language speakers' reading comprehension show that prior cultural experiences are extremely important in comprehending text (Johnson, 1982; Steffensen, Joag-Dev, & Anderson, 1979). In some cases, cultural origin plays a greater role in comprehension than does language complexity (Johnson, 1981).

1. **Preview the text or lesson and choose two to three important concepts.** For example, for a science lesson, Mr. Amin chose the concept of photosynthesis and the key words *cycle* and *oxygen.*

2. **Conduct a brainstorming session with students.** This process involves three phases. In Phase 1, students tell you what comes to mind when they hear the concept. This gives you a first glance at how much they already know about the topic. In Phase 2, students tell you what made them think of their responses in Phase 1. This information can help you judge the depth and/or basis for their responses, and it also provides a springboard for students to refine their responses in Phase 3. In Mr. Amin's class, two of the students mistakenly thought that photosynthesis had to do with photography because of the presence of *photo* in the word. This error provided an opportunity to build on students' knowledge—Mr. Amin explained that *photo* means light and that in photography, a camera takes in light and combines it with certain chemicals on film to make pictures. He then said that plants take in light, too, and when the light combines with chemicals in the plant, carbohydrates and oxygen are made. This process is called photosynthesis. In this way, Mr. Amin used what the students already knew to teach them a concept they did not know. In Phase 3, students can add to their responses based on the discussion in Phase 2.

3. **Evaluate student responses to determine the depth of their prior knowledge of the topic.** During this step, you can decide whether students are ready to read the text and/or listen to a lecture on photosynthesis or whether they first need more information. In Mr. Amin's class two students continued to have trouble understanding that photosynthesis was something plants did with light to make carbohydrates and oxygen. They needed more information before they were ready to read the chapter. Mr. Amin showed them a video illustration of photosynthesis including concrete examples.

WWW Resources

Education World, at http://www.education-world.com, provides a searchable database of more than 50,000 sites related to curriculum ideas. Many of the resources are geared especially to students with exceptionalities.

Preparing anticipation guides.   Anticipation guides can help you activate student knowledge about a particular topic and construct bridges to new information by encouraging students to make predictions (Moore, Readance, & Rickleman, 1989; Vacca

& Vacca, 1986). **Anticipation guides** consist of a series of statements, some of which may *not* be true, related to the material that the student is about to read (Burns, Roe, & Ross, 1992). Before teaching, students read these statements that either challenge or support ideas they may already have about the subject. This process catches their interest and gives them a reason for listening and reading. Providing questions or statements prior to reading also aids comprehension for all students, including those with special needs.

For example, Ms. Henry constructed an anticipation guide prior to teaching a unit on the nervous system. Her anticipation guide included the following statements:

> A person cannot function without the nervous system.
> Our nervous system helps us study and learn about new things.
> There are gaps between the nerve cells in our body.
> Nerve cells do different jobs in the body.
> The central nervous system is only one part of our nervous system.
> Our brain does not control our reflexes.
> A person cannot hold his breath until he dies.
> Some people can swim without thinking about it.

Providing planning think sheets. Activating background information and building bridges to current knowledge is also of concern to teachers when asking students to write. Some researchers recommend a **planning think sheet** to help writers focus on background information as well as on the audience and purpose of a paper (Englert et al., 1988). For audience, students are asked to consider who will read the paper. For purpose, students clarify why they are writing the paper (for example, to tell a story, to convey information, or to persuade someone). Finally, students activate background knowledge and organize that knowledge by asking themselves questions such as, What do I know about the topic? How can I group/label my facts? (Englert et al., 1988). A planning think sheet for a paper assignment might contain write-on lines for students to answer the following questions:

- What is my topic?
- Why do I want to write on this topic?
- What are two things I already know that will make it easy to write this paper?
- Who will read my paper?
- Why will the reader be interested in this topic? (Raphael, Kirschner, & Englert, 1986)

Organizing Content

Research shows that many students, including students with special needs, have difficulty understanding important ideas and their interrelationships in content areas such as social studies (Lawton, 1995) and science (Scruggs & Mastropieri, 1994). These students can benefit from the use of supports or scaffolds that help them identify and understand important information (Carnine et al., 1997). As we discussed in Chapter 4, one form of support is to organize the curriculum according to big ideas rather than facts in isolation. Another form of support is to make these big ideas more evident to students through the use of advance organizers, cue words for organizational patterns, study guides, and graphic organizers.

FYI

Advance organizers help
activate prior learning,
keep students on task, and
provide reference points
for remembering tasks that
need to be completed.

Cultural
Awareness

Direct teaching of organizational patterns can greatly
assist second-language
learners in comprehending
content-area textbooks
(Schifini, 1994).

Using advance organizers.   **Advance organizers** include information that makes content more understandable by putting it within a more general framework. They are particularly effective for students with special needs who may have limited background knowledge and reading and listening comprehension skills. Examples of advance organizers include the following:

- Identifying major topics and activities
- Presenting an outline of content
- Providing background information
- Stating concepts and ideas to be learned in the lesson
- Motivating students to learn by showing the relevance of the activity
- Stating the objectives or outcomes of the lesson (Lenz, 1983)

Employing cue words for organizational patterns.   Big ideas are often the central focus of an **organizational pattern** of information. The most common patterns of information include the descriptive list and the sequence of events in time, comparison/contrast, cause/effect, and problem/solution (Ellis, 1996). Each of these patterns of information can be made more conspicuous for students through the use of cue words. For example, cue words for a list, description, or sequence might include *first, second,* or *third;* cue words for comparison/contrast would be *similar, different, on the other hand;* cue words for cause/effect might be signaled by *causes, effects, because, so that;* and cue words for problem/solution would be *problem, solution,* and *resolve.* Cue words are important for students with special needs, many of whom have difficulty telling the difference between important and unimportant information (Kinder & Bursuck, 1991).

Consider the following two passages, about the formation of the two-party system, which are taken from two different social studies textbooks.

Text 1

Ordinary People Formed a Political Party

The problem.   You have learned how the policies of the Federalist party of the wealthy business people did not directly help the ordinary people. Small farmers had to pay the Whiskey Tax, but wealthy farmers who grew other crops did not. Ordinary people had lost a great deal of money when they sold their bonds to speculators. Government money was being paid primarily to wealthy people. The Alien and Sedition Acts were passed to keep ordinary people from gaining political power. A serious problem for the first few years in our country's history was that the party of the wealthy business people ignored the **viewpoint** of ordinary people.

What was a serious problem during the first few years of our country's history?

The solution.   Although Thomas Jefferson didn't like the idea of political parties, Jefferson felt that ordinary people needed to be brought together and organized to get the political power that would result in the government doing things to help the ordinary person. Thomas Jefferson was a popular leader who gathered up the support of a great number of skilled workers, such as carpenters, blacksmiths, and other craftsmen, as well as shopkeepers and small farmers.

Jefferson began to organize a political party before the Presidential election of 1800. He felt confident that a political party of ordinary people could win elections because there were many more common people than wealthy business people. The political party of the ordinary people wanted to elect enough representatives to control Congress and to elect Thomas Jefferson to be President in the next Presidential election in 1800. That new political party was called by several names: the Democratic-Republicans, the Republicans, and also the Jeffersonian party. During the election campaign, the political party of the ordinary people made an issue of the unpopular Whiskey Tax and also the unpopular Alien and Sedition Acts. In the election of 1800, the party of the ordinary people won, and **Thomas Jefferson,** who also wrote the Declaration of Independence, became the third President of the United States. Also, enough legislators from the party of the ordinary people were elected to make those legislators the new majority in charge of Congress.

Why was Thomas Jefferson important to the development of political parties in the United States? (Carnine, Crawford, Harniss, & Hollenbeck, 1995, p. 207)

Text 2

The Constitution said nothing about the political parties that Washington had warned against. As early as the presidential election of 1792, however, something resembling two major parties appeared in American politics. These parties centered around Alexander Hamilton and Thomas Jefferson.

Rise of the two-party system.   In the election of 1792, Washington was re-elected by unanimous vote. Vice-President John Adams was also re-elected but against strong opposition. He was opposed by George Clinton of New York, a candidate backed by Thomas Jefferson and his followers.

Hamilton's followers came to be called Federalists. The Federalist Party was strongest in New England and along the Atlantic seaboard. It included many wealthy merchants, manufacturers, lawyers, and church leaders. John Adams, himself a Federalist, said that Federalists represented "the rich, the well-born, and the able."

The opposition party was led by Thomas Jefferson. Its members called themselves Republicans. Although some wealthy people were Republicans, most of Jefferson's supporters were the owners of small farms or wage earners in the growing towns. (Todd & Curti, 1982, p. 212)

Which passage is easier to understand? Most teachers would say the first one. The major heading is specific. The relationship between Federalist legislation and the formation of the Republican party is clear. This relationship is cast in the form of a problem/solution framework; the formation of the Republican party was the solution to a problem involving the Federalists trying to grab power from the ordinary people. This problem/solution structure is clearly signaled by boldface headings. Notice, too, that each section in the first passage is followed by a question that helps students sort out the main idea.

The second passage contains no explicit signals of the relationship between Federalist policies and the formation of the Republican party. It is also unclear why ordinary people so hated these policies. Students reading this passage are required to make a number of inferences, inferences that may be difficult for students with special needs to make. Although rewriting the book is obviously not a reasonable adaptation here, you can help make the key concepts more explicit. Two additional options for assisting students in organizing content material are study guides and graphic organizers.

Constructing study guides.   The general term **study guide** refers to outlines, abstracts, or questions that emphasize important information in texts (Lovitt & Horton, 1987). Study guides are helpful in improving comprehension for students with special needs in content-area classrooms (Lovitt, Rudsit, Jenkins, Pious, & Benedetti, 1985). For example, at the beginning of this chapter, Cecily was having trouble picking out key ideas in her American history text, a common problem for students at all educational levels. She might benefit from study guides that cue students to important information by asking them questions about it. Procedures for constructing study guides are shown in the Professional Edge. A sample study guide for a section of a social studies text on Truman's Fair Deal is shown in Figure 9.4.

Horton (1987) has suggested the following additional modifications you might want to try:

1. Allow 2 or 3 inches of margin space in which students can take notes. Draw a vertical line to indicate the margin clearly. For example, in the study guide in Figure 9.4, the answer to the first vocabulary question is, *Consumables are products that cannot be used over again.* You may want to have students write the word along with its complete definition in the margin. Some students with special needs find new words easier to understand if you first use the overhead to discuss the definition along with a series of positive and negative examples. Specific strategies for presenting new vocabulary are presented later in the chapter.

2. Print page numbers next to the sentences in the study guide to show where to find the missing word in the textbook.

3. Print the missing words at the bottom of the page to serve as cues.

4. Leave out several words for more advanced students and fewer for students with special needs. For example, the **effect** part of the big idea could be simplified as, The **effect** of strikes such as the railroad strike was that the stability of the American economy was threatened, and _____.

5. Arrange for peer teaching situations; pair students and have them take turns being the teacher and the student.

6. Use the study guide for homework assignments. Assign students a passage in the text and give them accompanying study guides (either with or without the pages marked for easy reference). Have them complete the guides and study the material for homework.

7. Ask students to keep and organize their study guides from a number of passages and to study them as they review for unit or end-of-semester tests.

8. Place reading passages, study guides, and tests on a computer.

9. Whenever possible, write the study guide at a reading level that fits most of your students. Students with reading and writing problems may need to have the study guide read to them or may need to respond to the questions orally.

10. Include only key information on the guide. When necessary, reduce the content load by having students complete fewer items. For example, Ms. Hall required that Al, a student with a mild cognitive disability in her fourth-grade class, answer only 4 out of 10 questions on a study guide. When the students were tested on the content covered in the guide, Al was held responsible for answering questions related only to the four items he had studied.

WWW Resources

The web page for The National Center for Improving Practice, at http://www2.edc.org/ncip, provides many ideas on how to implement research-based teaching practices with students with special needs.

Professional Edge

How to Develop Study Guides

Study guides help improve the comprehension of all students, especially those with special needs who are included in content-area classrooms. The following steps show you how to develop a study guide from a content-area textbook.

1. Go through the entire book and mark the chapters you want to cover for the term and those you do not.

2. Indicate the sequence in which you will assign the chapters; that is, note the one that comes first, second, and so forth.

3. Read the material in the first chapter carefully. Mark the important vocabulary, facts, and concepts that you expect students to learn. Cross out any material you do not intend to cover.

4. Divide the chapter into logical sections of 1,000- to 1,500-word passages. (The length will depend, of course, on how detailed the material is and how much of it you deem important.)

5. Write brief sentences that explain the main ideas or emphasize the vocabulary, facts, or concepts from the passage. Write 15 sentences per passage.

6. Place those sentences in order so that the material in one leads to the next, and so forth.

7. To create questions, either leave out a few words in each sentence or change each sentence into a

question. For example, the following statement was identified as important in a chapter on natural disasters:

> A 2 percent sales tax was passed to pay for relief efforts after the massive floods of 1993.

This statement could be turned into a question by leaving out several words:

> _____ was passed to pay for relief efforts after the massive floods of 1993.

You could also change the statement into a question:

> How did the people pay for the relief efforts after the massive floods of 1993?

8. Make a transparency of sentences and/or questions using large type.

9. Prepare sheets for the students, using regular type.

10. Prepare an answer sheet for the teacher.

11. Develop a multiple-choice test to cover the material in the study guide. The test should have 10–15 items, with four possible choices for each question.

SOURCE: From *Study Guides: A Paper on Curriculum Modification*, by S. V. Horton, 1987, Seattle: University of Washington.

Of course, study guides are not a substitute for direct instruction. The amount of direct instruction necessary varies with the difficulty of the material. In general, students need more help completing study guides for texts that assume high levels of student background knowledge and in which key information needs to be inferred as opposed to being explicitly presented.

Creating graphic organizers. Another way teachers can help students organize content is to use **graphic organizers.** This strategy gives students a visual format to organize their thoughts while looking for main ideas. Archer and Gleason (1997) suggest the following guidelines for constructing graphic organizers:

1. Determine the critical content (for example, vocabulary, concepts, ideas, generalizations, events, details, facts) that you wish to teach your students. Help-

FYI

Teachers successfully use graphic organizers at all phases of instruction, from advance organizers to review. Graphic organizers, sometimes called concept maps or semantic webs, can make your lessons multisensory and are helpful for students with special needs.

Figure 9.4 Sample Study Guide for Truman's Fair Deal

VOCABULARY

Consumables are products that _____ .

Some examples of consumables are _____ , _____ ,

and _____ . A nonexample of a consumable is _____ .

BIG IDEAS

The **problem** was that after World War II, price controls were lifted and the cost of

_____ , _____ , and other consumer goods

went _____ .

The **solution** was for workers to _____ .

The **effect** was that _____ and _____ .

---

ing students focus on the most critical information is important for several reasons. First, students with special needs may have trouble identifying the most important information in an oral lesson or textbook chapter. Second, it is easier for students to remember several main ideas than many isolated details. Third, putting too much information on a graphic organizer can make it so visually complex that students may have trouble interpreting it.

2. Organize the concepts in a visual representation to reflect the structure of the content, such as stories, hierarchies (top-down and bottom-up), feature analysis, diagrams, comparison–contrast, timelines. Because the purpose of a graphic organizer is to clarify interrelationships among ideas and information, you should keep the visual display as simple as possible. Figure 9.5 shows a completed comparison–contrast graphic organizer.

3. Design a completed **concept map.** Completing the map before you teach with it ensures that the information is clear and accurate and can be presented to your students in a timely manner.

4. Create a partially completed concept map (to be completed by students during instruction). Having students fill out the map as you present your lesson is an excellent way to keep them on task. Also, many students with special needs benefit from a multisensory approach; seeing the information on the graphic, hearing it from the teacher, and writing it on the map helps them better retain the information presented.

5. Create a blank concept map for students to use as a postreading or review exercise. This structure for review is easy for students to use.

Figure 9.5 Comparison–Contrast Graphic Organizer

Attribute	Native Americans	Colonists
Land	Shared	Owned
	Lived close to it without changing it	Cleared it
	Respected it	Used it

Summarize

Native Americans and colonists had different ideas about land. Native Americans shared the land while the colonists owned individual pieces of it. Native Americans lived close to the land; they respected it and did not change it. Colonists used the land for their own gain.

Once you have constructed graphic organizers, you can use them as follows:

1. Distribute partially completed concept maps to your students.

2. Place a transparency of the completed map on an overhead projector. Place a piece of paper under the transparency so that you expose only those portions you wish students to attend to. Limiting the amount of information you present at one time helps students with attention problems who have trouble focusing on more than one piece of information at a time.

3. Introduce the information on the concept map, proceeding in a logical order; stress the relationships between the vocabulary, concepts, events, details, facts, and so on.

4. At natural junctures, review concepts you have introduced. You can do this by placing the blank map on the overhead and asking students questions about the content. This review is essential for students who have difficulty learning large amounts of information at one time.

5. At the end of the lesson, review the critical content again using the blank concept map. You can also have students complete the blank maps for homework. These maps help students organize their studying and also help you find out what they have learned. (Carnine et al., 1997)

The Case in Practice on pages 332–333 illustrates how one teacher uses a graphic organizer called a *story map* to help her students better comprehend a particular story.

Teaching Terms and Concepts

Content-area instruction is often characterized by a large number of new and/or technical vocabulary words and concepts. Students who have special needs or who are at risk are likely to have difficulty with the vocabulary and concept demands of many content-area texts and presentations. For example, consider the following passage from a general science text:

> Thousands of years ago, Scandinavia was covered by a thick ice sheet. The mass of the ice forced the crust deeper into the denser mantle. Then the ice

Special Emphasis On . . .

Using the Lesson Organizer Routine in Math

Many students with special needs have difficulty recognizing important features of the content or skills to be taught. The Lesson Organizer Routine developed by Lenz, Marrs, Schumaker, & Deshler (1993) can help you convert the content you teach into understandable formats and present the content in ways that help all children learn. The routine has three major components: the Lesson Organizer device, the Linking Steps, and the Cue-Do-Review sequence.

The **Lesson Organizer** is a graphic organizer that teachers and students develop and use together. The device helps focus their attention "on the important outcomes of a lesson, the relationships between abstract ideas and concrete objects and situations, and the relationship of the content to students' background knowledge and experience" (Mittag & Van Reusen, 1999, p. 70). A sample Lesson Organizer for a math lesson on estimating populations is shown in Figure 9.6. Notice how the students and the teacher used words and graphics that students could easily understand by applying keywords, webs, ovals, lists, and arrows showing relationships. A section called Task-Related Strategies shows strategies the

students can also use to meet the goals of the lesson. The lesson also allowed the class to develop self-assessments (Self-Test Questions) and required assignments and tasks (see section called Tasks, p. 70).

The **Linking Steps** involve the class in creating the Lesson Organizer. A series of questions is presented using the mnemonic, CRADLE. The questions help provide students with the big picture of the lesson. The CRADLE steps are as follows:

C Consolidate goals.
R Review knowledge.
A Assemble a visual anchor.
D Describe and map the content.
L Link to students' lives.
E Explore questions and tasks.

Cue-Do-Review represents the most important part of the lesson. In the **Cue** phase, you tell the class about the lesson organizer. The **Do** phase involves using the CRADLE steps to design the lesson. During the **Review** phase, the students check their understanding of the lesson.

---

melted. The mantle has been slowly pushing the land upward since then. This motion will continue until a state of balance between the crust and mantle is reached again. This state of balance is called *isostasy* (ie-soss-tuh-see). (Ramsey, Gabriel, McGuirk, Phillips, & Watenpaugh, 1983)

Although the term *isostasy* is italicized for emphasis, other technical terms and concepts, such as *crust* and *mass*, also may pose a problem for students and require special attention. These words may be particularly difficult because students are likely to be familiar with their nonscientific meanings, which are quite different from their technical meanings (for example, *mass* as in church; *crust* as in bread). You need to check student understanding and teach vocabulary directly, if necessary, using one of the strategies covered in the next section.

Modeling examples, synonyms, and definitions. An approach to teaching terms and concepts has been proposed by Carnine and colleagues (1997). They suggest three related ways of teaching new vocabulary to students: modeling examples,

Figure 9.6 Lesson Organizer

Lesson Organizer   Date: _____ Name: _____

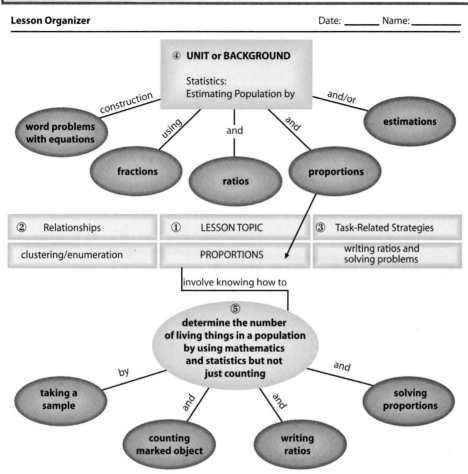

Challenge Question: What other real-life situations require the use of the estimation procedure?

⑥ **Self-Test Questions:**
1. How do you write a ratio?
2. How do you solve a proportion?
3. How is an estimate different from an actual answer?
4. What is the class average estimate for the population of goldfish?

⑦ **Tasks:**
1. Complete the worksheet after taking a sample and counting living things in the object.
2. Compare your estimate to others in your group.
3. Compare your estimate to the real answer.

S O U R C E : From "Learning Estimation and Other Advanced Mathematics Concepts in an Inclusive Class," by K. C. Mittag and A. K. Van Reusen, 1999, *Teaching Exceptional Children, 31*(6), p. 70.

Teaching with Story Maps

Story maps are graphic organizers that provide students with a visual guide to understanding and retelling stories. They have been shown to help students with special needs read with better comprehension (Bos & Vaughn, 1998). In the account that follows, Ms. Barrows, a second-grade teacher, is using the story map in Figure 9.7 to teach her students the story "The Funny Farola" (Miranda & Guerrero, 1986). She has demonstrated using the maps for a week now, so her students are familiar with the format. Today, she is providing guided practice for her students on how to use the maps.

Ms. Barrows: Boys and girls, today we're going to read a story entitled "The Funny Farola." A farola is a lantern used to give light. What do you think the story is going to be about?

Juliane: Maybe it's going to be about a lantern that looks funny.

Lee: Maybe it's about something funny happening to someone who has a farola.

Figure 9.7 Story Map

Characters	**Setting**
Dora	A city on the day of a parade
Dora's mom and dad	
Dora's brother Ramon and her sister Rosa	

Problems
Dora's brother and sister got lost at the parade.
Dora's family laughed at her farola.

Attempts
Dora got on her father's shoulders to see whether she could find her brother and sister.

Resolution
Dora found her brother and sister because they were holding her funny farola and she was able to see it.

Theme
Just because other people think something is not any good doesn't mean that they're right.

Ms. Barrows: Well, before we read and find out, who can tell me what a story map is?

Darwain: Well, it's a map that guides us through a story kind of like a regular map tells us where we're going when we're driving a car.

Ms. Barrows: That's right, Darwain. Now let's read the first page and find out who the main characters in this story are and where the story takes place. When you find out, we'll fill them in on our story maps. [She distributes a blank story map to each student.]

Harley: I know, the story is about Dora Rivers, her sister Rosa, her brother Ramon, and her mom and dad. I think Dora is the main character.

Ms. Barrows: That's right, Harley. Let's all fill in the main characters on our maps.

Ms. Barrows: Where do you think the story takes place? It's hard to tell because they don't come right out and say it.

Lovell: I think it takes place in a city.

Ms. Barrows: Why do you think so, Lovell?

Lovell: Because it sounds like it's a big parade, and cities have big parades.

Ms. Barrows: Good thinking, Lovell. When stories don't come out and say things, we have to figure it out by thinking hard, and that's what you did. Let's all fill in the setting on our maps. [They do.] Remember, we said last week that all stories have a problem that needs to be solved. Read the next four pages and find out what the

problem is here. [The students read the passage.] What's the problem?

Harley: Well, Dora's little brother and sister got lost at the parade.

Ms. Barrows: Right. That's one problem. Write it on your maps. Now, does anyone see another problem?

Eliseo: I know. Dora made a farola that looked like a frog and everybody laughed at her.

Ms. Barrows: Eliseo, what's wrong with a farola that looks like a frog? I thought it looked cute.

Eliseo: Well, I think it was because Dora's was different from everyone else's. In the pictures in the story, there were no farolas that looked like animals.

Ms. Barrows: That's right, Eliseo. Let's all put this problem on our maps. [They do.] Let's read the next page and find out what Dora and her mom and dad attempted to do to try to find her brother and sister.

Lovell: Dora got up on her father's shoulders to see whether she could see her brother and sister.

Ms. Barrows: Do you think this will help Dora find her brother and sister?

Lesa: I don't think so. There are so many people there.

Ms. Barrows: Well, let's all finish the story and find out. [They finish reading the story.] So, did Dora find her brother and sister?

Juliane: Yes. She found them because they were carrying her funny farola and it really made them stand out in the crowd.

Ms. Barrows: That's right. Let's fill in how Dora solved the problem on

our story maps. [They do.] What about Dora's other problem? Was it solved, too?

Juliane: Yes. They didn't think Dora's farola was so funny anymore because it helped them find Dora's brother and sister.

Ms. Barrows: That's right. How do you think Dora felt at the end?

Lovell: I think she felt happy.

Ms. Barrows: Why do you think that, Lovell?

Lovell: Well, because she found her brother and sister and no one thought her farola was stupid anymore.

Ms. Barrows: Good thinking, Lovell. I'd like the rest of you to put how *you* think Dora felt, and why, on your maps. Remember, we said a part of stories is a lesson that they teach us. What lesson do you think this story teaches?

Harley: Well, just because something is different doesn't mean it's no good.

Ms. Barrows: Good thinking, Harley. Let's all put down the lesson of this story on our maps.

R E F L E C T I O N S

How did Ms. Barrows use the story map to help her students comprehend the story? Which students do you think would benefit most from this approach? What should Ms. Barrows do to get her students ready for completing story maps on their own? How could you incorporate the use of story maps into a literature-based classroom reading program?

synonyms, and definitions. Although there is some variation from method to method, all three use the following five steps:

1. Pick a range of both positive and negative examples to teach your new word. Example selection is most important. A range of positive examples is used to make sure students can apply the word to a variety of contexts or forms. For example, if you are teaching your students to identify a *rectangle*, you want them to identify a rectangle whether it is big, small, empty, or shaded. Therefore, when showing students examples of rectangles, show them big rectangles, small rectangles, empty rectangles, and shaded rectangles. If you are teaching your students what a *vehicle* is, you want them to recognize a vehicle whether it is a car, boat, or bicycle. Whereas positive examples help students learn the range of a word, nonexamples help them discriminate the new word from other words that may be similar. For example, for teaching *rectangle*, use figures such as triangles, circles, and trapezoids as nonexamples. For teaching *vehicle*, use chair, house, or even an exercise bike as nonexamples. Generally, you should use at least six examples to teach a new word and include at least two nonexamples.

2. If you are teaching a word using a synonym, students must already know the synonym. For example, when teaching the word *gigantic* using the synonym *huge*, first make sure students know what *huge* means. If you are teaching a word using a definition, the definition should be stated simply and clearly and should contain only words for which students know the meaning. Consider the following definition of *vehicle* for third grade:

> *Vehicle:* A method of transportation that takes a person from one location to another.

This definition uses a number of words that third graders might not know. Instead, consider a simpler definition that younger students can understand:

> *Vehicle:* An object that takes you from place to place.

3. Tell students the meaning of the words either through modeling positive and negative examples or by presenting positive and negative examples using a synonym or a definition. For example, if you are teaching *rectangle* by modeling positive and negative examples, you might say the following as you pointed to your examples:

> This is a rectangle. . . . This is a rectangle. . . . This is *not* a rectangle. . . . This is a rectangle.

If you were teaching *vehicle* using a definition, you might say:

> A vehicle is an object that takes you from place to place. What is a vehicle? [Point to a picture of a car.] This is a car. It is an object that takes you from place to place. It is a vehicle. . . . This is a boat. It is an object that takes you from place to place. A boat is a vehicle. . . . This is a chair. A chair is an object but it doesn't take you from place to place. It is *not* a vehicle.

Finally, if you were teaching the word *gigantic* using the synonym *huge*, you might say:

> Today we're going to learn the meaning of the word *gigantic*. What's the word? *Gigantic* means huge. [Point to picture of an elephant.] An elephant is a gigantic

This teacher is modeling positive and negative examples to clarify the meaning of a new concept. How can using both examples and nonexamples help make the meaning of new terms and concepts clear?

animal. It is huge. [Point to a picture of a redwood tree.] This is a redwood tree. It is gigantic. It is huge. [Point to a smallish dog.] This is a dog. The dog is not gigantic. The dog is not huge.

4. Ask students a series of yes or no questions to ascertain whether they can discriminate examples from nonexamples. For example, Is this a rectangle? If students have been taught a word using a definition or synonym, follow your question with, How do you know? Their reasons for answering yes or no will reveal whether the students are correctly using the definition or just guessing. For example, to test whether students know what a vehicle is, you might say:

> What is this? (A car.) Is a car a vehicle? (Yes.) Why do you say that? (Because it is an object that takes you from place to place.) What is this? (A chair.) Is a chair a vehicle? (No.) Why do you say that? (Because it doesn't take you from place to place.)

5. The purpose of this step is to discover whether students can discriminate the new word from words they have learned previously. This step is carried out through a series of open-ended questions. For example, in teaching *rectangle*, the teacher points to a rectangle along with other figures already taught and asks, What is this?

Teaching vocabulary by modeling examples or by using synonyms and definitions can benefit all your students. Use modeling examples when students may not understand words that explain the meaning of the new word (for example, teaching students what a herringbone design is). Use synonyms when students already know another word with a meaning similar to the new word; for example, you could teach the word *bow* using the synonym *front*. Use definitions when a longer explanation is needed to define a word and students already understand the words that make up the explanation.

Figure 9.8 Concept Diagram

Concept Name: Nonviolent resistance
Definition: Protesting in a peaceful way

Always	Sometimes	Never
Peaceful	Done in a group	Violent
	Done individually	

Examples	Nonexamples
Picketing	Shouting match
Boycott	Physical attack
Sit-in	Revolutionary war
Hunger strike	Riot

Making concept diagrams. Constructing **concept diagrams** is a method that combines graphic organizers with the methods just described using definitions, synonyms, and examples and nonexamples (Bulgren, Schumaker, & Deshler, 1988). A sample concept diagram for the concept of nonviolent resistance is shown in Figure 9.8. First, the teacher selects key words from a story or lecture. Next, he or she constructs a diagram that features the definition of the word; the characteristics that are always present, sometimes present, or never present; and examples and nonexamples that can be used to model the word. Finally, the concept diagram is presented to students as follows:

1. Present the word and its definition.
2. Discuss which characteristics are always, sometimes, or never present.
3. Discuss one of the examples and one of the nonexamples in relation to the characteristics.
4. Check other examples and nonexamples to discover whether they match the characteristics. (Carnine et al., 1997)

How Can You Improve Clarity in Written and Oral Communication?

Check Your Learning

What are the major areas for making adaptations in subject-area instruction?

In effective instruction, ideas are clearly tied together, which enables students to understand them more easily. The need for instructional clarity applies to both written communication and oral communication. Written communication, in many school situations, involves the use of textbooks. Oral communication can include instructional behaviors such as giving directions, asking questions, and delivering lectures. When a textbook is not written clearly or a lecture is not presented clearly, students have to make critical connections between ideas on their own, a skill that many at-risk students may not have. Students with special needs may not be able to recognize that they do not understand the material, or they may not be aware of strategies to try when instruction is difficult to understand. For example, when reading a text, they may not know how to use key words and headings or to look at the end-of-chapter questions to get main ideas. During oral presentations, students may not feel comfortable asking questions to clarify the information presented because often they are not sure what to ask and are afraid of looking stupid. Finally, students with special needs may lack the background knowledge necessary to construct meaning on their own. If you communicate clearly and use materials that do so as well, students with special needs can be more successful.

Clarity in Written Communication

The importance of clearly written communication is illustrated by these two textbook passages about western migration in the United States:

> Many of the farmers who moved in from New England were independent farmers. Land cost about a dollar an acre. Most men could afford to set up their own farms. Livestock farming was quite common on the frontier. Hogs could be fed in the forests. The cost of raising hogs was low. (Senesh, 1973, cited in Armbruster, 1984)

> Most of the farmers who moved in from New England were independent farmers. Being an independent farmer means that the farmer can afford to own his own farm. Around 1815, most men could afford their own farms because lands were cheap—it cost only about a dollar an acre. Many of these independent farms were livestock farms. For example, many frontier farmers raised hogs. Hog farming was common because hogs were inexpensive to keep. The cost of raising hogs was low because the farmer did not have to buy special feed for the hogs. The hogs did not need special feed because they could eat plants that grew in the surrounding forests. (Armbruster, 1984)

The second paragraph is much easier to understand; it requires fewer inferences by the reader and requires less adaptation by the teacher. The second passage defines *independent farmer* for the reader. If students were reading the first passage, you might have to provide this definition—which you could do orally or in a study guide. The reason farmers turned to raising livestock can be inferred from the first paragraph, but it is stated directly in the second. For students reading the first paragraph, teachers may need to pose questions prior to reading to establish an understanding of this relationship: for example, Why did the farmers turn to raising livestock? Obviously, adapting every paragraph like this is not feasible. But this example underscores the need for adopting structurally and organizationally coherent textbooks. However, adaptations may still be needed, but should be made only for sections containing the most important information.

Problems with textbook organization and clarity can also occur in explanations, especially when a sequence of events is being described. The ease with which students can understand the sequence depends on a number of factors, including the number of steps, the format used (list or paragraph), and the presence of distracting information or of material not related to the sequence. For example, students with special needs may struggle to understand the following passage about how baby alligators are hatched.

> Adult female alligators make large cone-shaped nests from mud and compost. The female lays from 15 to 100 eggs with leathery shells in the nest and then covers it. The heat from both the sun and the decaying compost keeps the eggs warm. The eggs hatch in about 9 weeks. Unlike other reptiles that hatch from eggs, baby alligators make sounds while they are still in the shell. The mother then bites off the nest so the baby alligators can get out. When first hatched, baby alligators are about 15 to 25 cm long. (Berger, Berkheimer, Lewis, & Neuberger, 1979, p. 55, cited in Armbruster, 1984)

WWW Resources

Get practical ideas about specific teaching problems from actual teachers in the field from Teachers Helping Teachers at http://www.pacificnet.net/~mandel/.

As you can see, the passage states a sequence of events leading up to the hatching of a baby alligator. It is written in paragraph format, which is harder to decipher than a list. Although the events are described in chronological order, the presence of a distractor, the sentence "Unlike other reptiles that hatch from eggs, baby alligators make sounds while they are still in the shell," breaks up the sequence and makes it harder for students to comprehend. A relatively easy adaptation would be to highlight the sentences in the sequence, or have students put numbers next to each key sentence in the sequence. Of course, if a number of students in your class are having trouble with distracting information, you can provide direct instruction on how to identify and/or ignore distracting or irrelevant information.

Another aspect of written language that can make comprehension more difficult is the use of pronoun referents. A general rule of thumb is the closer the pronoun is to its referent, the easier it is to translate. Consider the following section of text:

> Now life began to change. The Eskimo hunters could see that these tools were useful. So they became traders, too. They trapped more furs than their families needed.
>   Then they brought the furs to the trading posts. There they could trade the furs for supplies they had never had before. Because the new tools helped Eskimo hunters get along better, they became part of the Eskimo environment. (Brandwein & Bauer, 1980)

Many readers may have trouble figuring out who *they* refers to in this passage. Although the placement of most pronouns is not this problematic, understanding pronouns can be difficult for students with special needs. However, students can be taught to make sense of pronouns (Carnine et al., 1997). Before students read, identify unclear pronouns. Have students underline the pronouns in a passage. Then show them how to find the pronouns referents by asking questions. Study the following example:

Passage

Curtis and Dorva skipped school. They were grounded for a week. He was sorry. She got mad.

Student Questioning

Teacher: "Curtis and Dorva skipped school." Who skipped school?
Students: Curtis and Dorva.
Teacher: "They were grounded for a week." Was Curtis grounded?

Students: Yes.

Teacher: Was Dorva grounded?

Students: Yes.

Teacher: "He was sorry." Was Curtis sorry?

Students: Yes.

Teacher: Was Dorva sorry?

Students: No.

Teacher: "She got mad." Did Dorva get mad?

Students: Yes.

Clarity in Oral Communication

Just as the quality of textbook writing affects student learning, so, too, does the quality of teachers' oral language. Three particularly important areas of oral language are giving directions, asking questions, and presenting subject matter (such as in a lecture).

Giving oral directions. Giving oral directions is the most common way that teachers tell their students what they want them to do. When directions are not clear, valuable instructional time is wasted having to clarify them repeatedly. Consider this set of directions given by a middle school teacher at the beginning of a social studies lesson:

Unclear Instruction

> All right, everyone, let's settle down and get quiet. I want you all to get ready for social studies. Shh. . . . Let's get ready. Alice and Tim, I want you to put those worksheets away. We need our books and notebooks. (Evertson et al., 1983, p. 143)

How clear is the teacher about what she wants her students to do? Now read this alternative set of directions:

Clearer Instruction

> All right, everyone, I want all of you in your seats facing me for social studies. Now, I want you to get out three things: your social studies book, your spiral notebook, and a pencil. Put everything else away so that you just have those three things—the social studies book, the spiral notebook, and the pencil—out on your desk. [As students get out their materials, the teacher writes "Social Studies, page 55, Chapter 7 on Italy" on the chalkboard. She waits until students have their supplies ready and are listening before she begins talking.] (Evertson et al., 1983, p. 143)

In the first example, the teacher does not get the students' attention before giving them directions. She is also unclear about what she wants her students to do. For example, the words *settle down* and *get ready* are not defined for the students. In the second example, the teacher first gets her students' attention, and then very specifically states all the things they need to do. Lavoie (1989) has suggested a number of guidelines for giving directions that are helpful for students with special needs:

1. State commands specifically, using concrete terms. In the Clearer Instruction example, the teacher was very specific about what the students needed to do

to get ready for social studies. They had to get out three things: their book, notebook, and pencil. The first teacher told them only to "get ready."

2. Give "bite-size" directions; avoid a long series of directions. The second teacher first had her students sit down and face her; then she had them take out their materials; finally, she had them turn to the chapter they were going to read that day.

3. Whenever possible, accompany explanations with a demonstration. For example, Mr. Gaswami asked his students to take out their science books, turn to the beginning of the chapter, identify five key words, and define them using the glossary. Mr. Gaswami showed his students what he wanted them to do by opening his book to the chapter, pointing out that the key words are italicized, and then defining several key words to demonstrate how to find and paraphrase the meanings using the glossary in the back of the book. He also wrote these directions on the board to help students remember all the steps.

4. Use cueing words such as *Look up here* and *Listen, please* before giving directions. Gestures such as a raised hand are also effective in getting students' attention.

Asking questions. Asking students questions is a vital part of instructional clarity. The way you question your students is important for several reasons. Questioning is a quick way of assessing what your students have learned. In addition, questioning through the use of follow-up probes can help you analyze your students' errors. For example, Ms. Dilworth's third-grade class was given the following math problem:

> Three-fourths of the crayons in Bob's box of a dozen crayons are broken. How many unbroken crayons are there?

Ms. Dilworth asked Kareem what the answer was, and Kareem answered that there are four unbroken crayons left. Ms. Dilworth asked Kareem to explain how he got that answer. Kareem said, "Because three-fourths means three groups of four and because there is only one group left, that group has four in it." By asking a question, Ms. Dilworth found out that Kareem did not know the concept of three-fourths. Questions can also be used to redirect students to the correct answer when they make mistakes. For example, Ms. Dilworth might have asked Kareem a number of follow-up questions:

> How many crayons did you start with? How many is a dozen? What fraction of the crayons were broken? What does three-fourths mean? What would one-fourth of twelve be?

Last, and perhaps most important, it is through effective questioning that your students can learn thinking skills. Well-constructed questions provide students with a model for effective thinking; in time, students learn to ask themselves these same questions as they solve problems. For example, Ms. Collins wanted her students to ask themselves key questions while they read stories to help improve their comprehension. At first she asked them questions while they read, such as, What is the story about? What is the problem? What is the solution? What's going to happen next? Is your prediction still good? Do you need to change your prediction? What makes you think so? In time, she taught the students to ask themselves these questions as they read independently.

FYI
Another use of cueing is to let a student know that he or she can expect to be called on to respond orally when you present a particular cue that only the student knows. This way the student can attend to a lesson with less anxiety about speaking in class.

Cultural Awareness
Strategies for questioning students with limited English proficiency are covered in Chapter 7.

Connections
Students with special needs benefit from being taught to think because efficient thinking may not come naturally to them or they may not have been exposed to good models of thinking. Strategies for teaching students thinking skills are described further in Chapter 10.

Although asking questions can be a very potent teaching strategy, to achieve maximum benefit, questioning needs to be carried out correctly. Kindsvatter, Wilen, and Ishler (1988) have suggested the following guidelines for using questions in your classroom:

1. Phrase questions clearly to ensure that students know how to respond. For example, a vague question, such as, What about the Great Depression? forces students to guess rather than to consider carefully a direct response to the question. Better wording would be, What were the two primary causes of the Great Depression?

2. Provide a balance between higher- and lower-level questions. The important point to keep in mind is that both kinds of questions are important. Lower-level, or convergent, questions help you find out whether students have the basic understanding necessary for higher-level thought. Further, critical and creative thinking can be developed by using convergent and evaluative questions. Although the current emphasis on incorporating more higher-level skills into the curriculum is positive, it is important to realize that lower-level knowledge is still important, particularly for students with special needs. Students with special needs may not readily acquire lower-level knowledge. Failing to help them acquire these understandings can prevent them from ever developing higher-level understandings. Also, lower-level questions can give students an opportunity to succeed in class. Finally, research suggests that lower-level questions may be most appropriate in teaching basic skills to students who are at risk (Emmer, Evertson, Sanford, Clements, & Worsham, 1983; Berliner, 1984).

3. Adapt questions to the language and skill level of the class, including individual students in the class. Your questions should accommodate a range of needs, from lower-performing students to gifted students. For example, a question for a lower-performing student might be, From what you have just read, how does the demand for a product affect its supply? For students with more skills, the question might become, Going beyond the article a little, how does price affect supply and demand and at what point is market equilibrium reached?

4. Vary the "wait time" you give students to answer questions. Wait time is the amount of time you give students to respond to questions in class.

5. Involve all students in classroom questioning by calling on nonvolunteers as well as volunteers. Calling on all students also allows you to monitor student learning efficiently. In addition, calling on nonvolunteers (who frequently are students with special needs) demonstrates that you hold them accountable for listening and leads to higher levels of on-task behavior. However, as mentioned before, you should match questions with student ability to maximize the likelihood of student success. Finally, for lower-level questions, consider using **unison responding,** or having all students respond at once, together. Unison responding allows more student opportunities for practice and recitation and can lead to higher levels of correct responses and on-task behavior (Carnine, 1981).

Presenting content orally. Communicating clearly to your students when you are presenting subject-matter content orally, such as in a lecture, also is important. The following section of a lecture was delivered during a geography lesson on Italy:

Teacher 1

Italy is in southern Europe, down by France and the Mediterranean Sea. It's a peninsula in the Mediterranean. There are a lot of beautiful islands in the Mediterranean off of Italy and Greece as well. Sardinia and Sicily are islands that are part of Italy. Corsica, Capri, and some other islands like Crete and Cyprus are in the same part of the world, but they don't belong to, although they may be close to, Italy. You could turn to the map of Europe that's in your text to see where Italy is. (Evertson et al., 1983, pp. 143–144)

Check Your Learning

List general and specific strategies for improving the clarity of your written and oral communication.

The language used by this teacher lacks clarity. For example, he presents information about a number of islands but is unclear how these islands relate to the main topic, which seems to be the location of Italy. The teacher is also vague when he says, "[the islands] don't belong to, although they may be close to, Italy." In addition, the teacher uses the word *peninsula* but does not define it. Finally, this explanation needs the visual display of a map to bring clarity to it, but the teacher refers to a map only at the end of the explanation, almost as an afterthought, and rather than requiring students to refer to it, leaves students with the impression that its use is voluntary. The only students who will know where Italy is after this lecture is over are those who already knew in the first place. Many students with special needs may be left behind. An example of another lecture on the same topic is much clearer:

Teacher 2

Now, I want all eyes on me. [The teacher then gestures to the world map next to her.] Raise your hand if you can show the class where Italy is. [Several students raise their hands. The teacher then has Maria read the names and show the class where France, Switzerland, Austria, Slovenia, and the Mediterranean Sea border on Italy.] Italy is in Europe. It is a large peninsula shaped like a boot that extends into the Mediterranean Sea. [She writes *peninsula* on the board, sounding the syllables as she writes. Because students have studied the word once before, she calls on a student to define it.] Agnes, what is a *peninsula*?

How Can You Involve Parents in Teaching Their Children?

Teachers are always looking for ways to find extra help for students who take more time to learn new content or skills. That is why we often hear teachers say, "If only his parents would work with him more at home." Although we know parents can promote learning by showing affection for their child, displaying interest in their child's schoolwork, and expecting academic success, the effectiveness of parents tutoring their children at home is less clear. The results of research on the effectiveness of parent teaching is mixed; some experts say it is effective whereas others question it (Mercer, 1997). When determining whether to involve parents in tutoring their children, Mercer (1997) suggests that the following factors be taken into account.

1. Are there reasons for deciding against tutoring (for example, mother–father disagreement over the necessity of tutoring, health problems, financial problems, marital problems, or a large family with extensive demands on parental authority)?

2. Do parents have the resources of a professional (for example, a teacher) to assist them? The success of home tutoring may depend on cooperative efforts.

3. Can the sessions be arranged at a time when there is no interruption from siblings, callers, or other demands? These children need sustained attention in order to learn.

4. Will the child become overwhelmed with academic instruction and resent the home sessions or feel overly pressured?

5. Do the parents become frustrated, tense, disappointed, or impatient during the tutorial sessions? These parents may spend their time better with the child in activities that are mutually enjoyable.

6. Do the tutorial sessions create tensions among family members? For instance, do the siblings view the sessions as preferential treatment?

7. Does the parent resent tutoring the child or feel guilty every time a session is shortened or missed? Are the sessions usually enjoyable or rewarding? (p. 125)

Of course, if you decide to have parents tutor their child, the same strategies for teaching skills and content to students with special needs covered earlier in this chapter still apply. For example, only skills or content at the student's level should be presented, and the progression of skills or content should be gradual and based on student mastery. In addition, parents should be carefully trained to present new information or skills clearly and enthusiastically, and to provide appropriate corrections and encouragement as needed. Parents should also limit the length of the tutoring sessions to 15 minutes for children up to grade 6, and 30 minutes for older students (Cummings & Maddux, 1985), and should periodically alternate the tutoring with everyday chores and games that incorporate skills and content being taught (Kronick, 1977). Too, care must be taken to select the most appropriate time to tutor and to select a place that does not restrict the activities of other family members and is not too distracting. Finally, tutoring should be held at the same time and place to establish a clear routine (Mercer, 1997).

What Adaptations Can You Make to Help Students Succeed in Independent Practice?

As discussed in Chapter 4, the main purpose of practice activities is to provide students with opportunities to refine skills or solidify content that they have already learned and to allow you to monitor their performance. To achieve these purposes, students should be able to complete practice activities such as seatwork and homework independently.

Even under ideal circumstances and with the best intentions, it is difficult to design practice activities that meet the needs of all students in your class. Problems arise because of individual characteristics, and adaptations need to be made. For example, students with severe reading problems may have difficulty reading directions that are quite clear to everyone else. Students with attention problems may have trouble answering questions that have multiple steps. Students with physical disabilities may be unable to perform the writing requirements of their assignments. In the case of students with severe cognitive disabilities, practice activities may need to be revamped totally so that they are consistent with the students' skill levels and the goals and objectives on their IEPs.

Adapting Seatwork Assignments

One problem with seatwork is that the practice activities may not contain enough items. This limitation is important because students with disabilities often require more practice to master skills or content. For example, Ms. Jennings has just taught her students to solve two-step story problems in math that first require adding and then subtracting. She demonstrated three problems in front of the class and then guided her students through three more. Ms. Jennings then had students independently complete five problems in the math book. She found that only half the students answered all the problems correctly and that the rest of the class needed more practice. Many math books have extra problems for students who need more practice, but some do not. You may need either to make up your own items or to find similar items from other books.

Another common problem with seatwork is that the directions are too difficult. Complicated or confusing directions can prevent students from completing their seatwork successfully. For example, some directions are excessively wordy: "Use the words letters stand for and the sense of the other words to find out what the new word in heavy black print is" (Center for the Study of Reading, 1988, p. 14). This is just a convoluted way of saying *read*. Other directions have too many steps: "Read the first sentence, and fill in the missing word. Read the second sentence. Find the word from the first sentence that makes sense in the second sentence and print it where it belongs. Then, do what the last sentence says. Repeat for all the other sentences" (Center for the Study of Reading, 1988, p. 14).

Affleck, Lowenbraun, and Archer (1980) have suggested a number of adaptations you can make to directions to ensure that students with special needs know what to do prior to working independently.

1. Verbally present the tasks. This adaptation can be applied to the whole class, particularly when many students are having problems with the directions. You can accommodate the needs of individual students by pairing a worksheet with an auditory tape that explains the directions.

2. Add practice examples that you can do with the whole class or a small group of students who are having particular difficulty.

3. Write alternative sets of directions. You can project these onto a screen using an overhead projector or distribute individual copies to students.

4. Highlight the important words in the directions.

5. Have students help each other when the directions are difficult.

Students may also have trouble when single pages of seatwork contain a number of different tasks. This combination of tasks can cause problems for students with special needs, who often have difficulty making the transition from one task to another. Consider the example shown in Figure 9.9. This worksheet has three different tasks. Students need to make a number of transitions within one worksheet to complete the activity successfully. Also, students are required to use words circled in part A as answers to part C. Using answers from one part of a worksheet as answers to questions on another part is confusing and assumes that students answered the first part correctly. You could adapt this worksheet by visually cueing the change

Figure 9.9 Seatwork Activity

Name _____

The Sound of Short *i*

A. Say each word. Circle the words that have the vowel sound you hear in *hit.*

lick	milk	cane	time
might	away	drink	gone
rabbit	house	sing	girl
this	come	five	fish

B. Make new words by changing the first letter or letters.

pick   _____   _____   _____

wing   _____   _____   _____

slip   _____   _____   _____

C. Fill in each blank with one of the words that you circled above to complete the sentences.

1. The boys and girls will _____ a song in school.

2. My father and I went to the river and caught a big _____ .

3. _____ is not the book I want to read.

4. The fluffy little _____ ran across the road.

5. My mother gave me a glass of _____ .

---

of task on the page (for example, draw a line between tasks), and by correcting part A before the students do part C.

Finally, seatwork should provide opportunities for students to practice functional skills. When seatwork tasks are nonfunctional, much valuable practice time is wasted. For example, in part A of the seatwork activity shown in Figure 9.9, students are required to circle the words that contain the same vowel sound as in the word *hit*. This task is nonfunctional because students must already be able to read the words to tell whether they have the short *i* sound. The exercise does not teach students to read the words; students can be successful only if they already can perform the skill. A more direct way to have students practice reading words that have the short *i* sound would be to have them orally read to you words in passages and lists and to provide them with corrective feedback on missed words. Before you give a seatwork assignment to your students, ask yourself what is the objective and whether this task meets the objective. If you have a hard time answering either question, consider using a different worksheet.

Providing Feedback on Independent Practice Activities

You can also adapt student practice by providing feedback on students' performance. It makes good sense to correct and return students' work as soon as possible. Timely feedback allows you to find out right away where students are making mistakes so

F Y I

Before starting independent practice, complete sample items for the students. Talk through each step, modeling your thought process and decision making. Use questioning to check that students understand directions. What other strategies can you use for adapting seatwork and homework?

you can reteach material if necessary. Providing feedback as quickly as possible is particularly important for students with special needs, who are less likely to learn material the first time it is presented. Returning papers soon after they are handed in also helps students know what they are doing correctly or incorrectly, and gives them the opportunity to make corrections while the material is still fresh in their minds and before they have forgotten why they responded as they did. In addition, regular feedback makes students feel more accountable for their work.

Although providing timely feedback to students is a good practice, as a professional teacher and as an individual with a personal life as well, you may have limited time during and after school. Therefore, in grading your students' papers, efficiency is imperative. The following list of suggestions are designed to help you save time.

1. Correct papers as you circulate. You can correct some papers as you circulate throughout the room during the seatwork period. First, carry a pen with different color ink than those used by students when they correct their own papers. Begin correcting the papers of students with special needs first. This ensures that those who are most likely to need your help receive it. Each time you stop at a student's desk, correct at least two items. Correct answers can be marked with a *C*, star, happy face, or whatever you prefer. Mark errors with a dot. When you find an error, try to determine whether the student simply made a careless mistake or did not know how to do the item correctly. If the student does not know how to do the item, show him or her how to do it, assign several similar problems, and say that you will be back to check the work in several minutes (Paine, Radicchi, Rosellini, Deutchman, and Darch, 1983).

2. Use spot checking. Reading 3 of the 10 comprehension answers assigned should give you a fairly good idea of whether students understand the material (Lavoie, 1989).

3. Use shared checking. Allow the first two students finished with an assignment to go to a corner and compare their answers. When they reach agreement on the answers, they can design a "key." They can then check the other students' answers. If you have students exchange papers, have the corrector sign the paper at the bottom. This strategy helps ensure that students correct fairly and accurately (Lavoie, 1989).

4. Use easy checking. Design assignments in a way that makes them easy to correct. For example, put problems or questions in neat, orderly rows. When checking assignments from consumable workbooks, cut off the corners of the pages you have checked or corrected. This helps you (and the student) find the next page quickly (Lavoie, 1989).

5. Use self-checking. Dictate or display answers using an overhead projector while students correct their own papers. Require that pencil assignments be corrected in pen and vice versa. Making corrections in a different shade or color enables you to monitor the number of mistakes students make before completion of their final corrected copy. Having students color over each answer with a yellow crayon before the correction activity serves the same purpose because their original answers are impossible to erase. After collecting papers, spot check them for accuracy and provide corrective feedback for errors and positive feedback for correct answers (Lavoie, 1989).

Adapting Homework Assignments

As with in-class practice activities, students with special needs may have difficulty completing traditional homework assignments. A major reason for student failure to complete homework assignments independently, successfully, and without undue stress is that the assignments are too difficult to begin with. Before you give your students an assignment, ask yourself the following questions:

1. What skill (for example, reading, written expression, math) demands does the assignment make on the students? Are the students capable of meeting these skill demands?

2. What background knowledge (for example, knowledge of vocabulary, concepts) demands does the assignment make on the students? Are the students capable of meeting these demands for background knowledge?

3. Is the purpose of the assignment made clear to the students?

4. If the assignment involves skill practice, does it include much practice on a few skills rather than little practice on many skills?

5. Are clear, written directions provided for how to complete the assignment?

6. Is enough time allotted for completion of the assignment?

Homework problems may also be related to how the homework process is managed and how independently students are capable of working. A list of effective homework practices for each of these areas is shown in Figure 9.10.

Even if you answered yes to all these questions, students with special needs may still require adaptations. For example, students with reading problems may need extra assistance with homework directions. Students with physical disabilities may need assignments shortened, or they may need to respond orally rather than in writing.

WWW Resources

For homework help, students simply click on one of the links on this site's home page, at http://www.startribune.com/homework.shtml, and are instantly linked to a general discussion on the academic subject of their choice, including math, English, literature, social studies, and science. Students are free to browse the questions and responses and also to ask questions of their own. Actual teachers monitor the discussions and post answers to the questions within 24 hours. Students are directed to related websites and provided guidance to answer many of their questions on their own. This site contains enormous collections of weblinks listed by subject.

All students can benefit from homework and other independent practice activities. What are some strategies you can use to adapt homework and other assignments for students with special needs?

CHAPTER 9

Figure 9.10 Recommended School-Based Homework Practices

Management Considerations
- Communicate clear expectations for homework from the beginning of the year.
- Establish a routine for assigning, collecting, and evaluating homework.
- Write assignments on the board so students can easily record them.
- Remind students of assignment due dates.
- Communicate consequences for completing/not completing homework.
- Present homework instructions clearly and verify student understanding.
- Allow students to start homework in class.
- Use assignment organizers or homework planners.
- Implement classroom-based incentive programs.
- Coordinate homework assignments with other teachers.

Student Competencies
- Teach interdependent learning skills (how to do homework with others).
- Teach independent learning or study skills.
- Teach time management skills.
- Teach self-advocacy skills, including the ability to ask for help if needed.

SOURCE: Adapted from "Practical Recommendations for Using Homework with Students with Disabilities," by J. R. Patton, 1994, *Journal of Learning Disabilities, 27*(9), pp. 570–578; "Home School Communication about Homework: What Do We Know and What Should We Do?" by J. R. Patton, M. Jayanthi, and E. Polloway, in press, *Reading and Writing Quarterly;* and "Homework Practices of General Education Teachers," by E. A. Polloway, M. H. Epstein, W. D. Bursuck, M. Jayanthi, and C. Cumblad, 1994, *Journal of Learning Disabilities, 27*(8), pp. 100–109.

Connections

Select a commercially prepared student workbook page in the subject area and grade level you plan to teach. Critique a worksheet in light of the guidelines for adapting seatwork. How might you adapt this worksheet for a student with special needs?

Remember to use the INCLUDE strategy introduced in Chapter 4 to make adaptations that fit your assignments and the individual characteristics of your students with special needs. A survey of general education teachers (Polloway, Epstein, Bursuck, Jayanthi, & Cumblad, 1994) showed that teachers favored the following homework adaptations: adjusting the length of assignments; providing extra teacher help; providing a peer tutor for assistance; setting up student study groups; providing auxiliary learning aids (for example, computers and calculators); checking more frequently with students about assignments (for example, when they are due and what is required); and allowing alternative response formats (for example, oral or written).

Of course, successful homework also depends on individual student skills. Not only do students need to be proficient in basic academic skills, but also they need to be able to learn independently. For example, they need to recognize their homework problems and seek help when necessary. They also need to manage their time effectively. Strategies for teaching these and other independent learning skills are covered in more depth in Chapter 10.

FYI

Sometimes, homework is not a viable option, as in the case of students who work so hard during the day that they need a break, or students whose life circumstances make homework irrelevant.

Involving Parents in the Homework Process

The success of homework depends in large part on the successful involvement of parents. Parents play two key roles: overseeing the homework process while their child is at home and communicating with the school regularly and clearly regarding homework exceptions.

Oversight of homework completion.   One way parents oversee the homework process is by having daily discussions about homework with their child (Bursuck et al., 1999). For example, every night after dinner, Mr. Rojas asks his son Juan what assignments he has for that day, when they are due, and whether he thinks he is going to need some help with any of them. Mr. Rojas also asks his son whether he has any tests coming up or long-term assignments due and asks Juan what his plan is for getting things done. Parents can also create an environment at home that is conducive to getting homework done. For example, at the beginning of the school year Ms. Lange and her son Damon determined how much time Damon needed to set aside each night for homework, identified a set time each night, and materials needed, and then selected a setting in which Damon could complete his homework relatively free of distractions. Parents also need to supervise homework activities periodically during the time scheduled for homework and provide support and encouragement for their child's homework completion. For example, Mr. and Mrs. Brown frequently praise their child's efforts to complete his homework, and take him out from time to time for ice cream when he completes a particularly difficult assignment.

Home–school communication.   The quality of home–school communication about homework is very important to a successful homework process (Polloway, Bursuck, & Epstein, in press). Yet, despite its importance, home–school communication about homework is likely to be a problem (Buck, Bursuck, Polloway, Nelson, & Whitehouse, 1996; Epstein et al., 1997; Harniss, Epstein, Bursuck, Nelson & Jayanthi, in press; Munk et al., in press). Parents feel the need for much more communication with teachers about homework and feel that teachers need to make more of an effort to initiate such communication (Munk et al., in press.). Likewise, teachers feel that parents do not (a) initiate communication about homework often enough, (b) take homework seriously enough, and (c) follow through with commitments they make about helping their children with homework. Teachers also feel they lack the time to communicate often enough with parents due to large class sizes and increased paperwork demands. In addition, teachers feel they lack knowledge and training about adapting homework for students with special needs (Epstein et al., 1997).

Contacts with parents about homework can be increased by conducting parent–teacher meetings in the evening for working parents, and taking advantage of the ever-increasing use of e-mail, a great potential time-saver (Harniss et al., in press). Another strategy for increasing communication is to establish homework hotlines that can be accessed by phone, or websites that provide certain types of homework assistance. You can also involve parents in the homework process from the beginning of the school year and on an ongoing basis thereafter. For example, at the open house at the beginning of the school year, Ms. Ordonez gives parents information about course assignments for the semester, homework adaptations available in the classroom, and policies on missed homework and extra-credit assignments. She then sends home school progress updates every 4 weeks; the progress reports include a section on homework completion. It is also important to understand that homework may be a lower priority for families when compared to other home issues. For example, Mr. Gentry knew that Dominique's family had recently been evicted from their apartment and were living in their car. Until Dominique's family was able to find another place, Mr. Gentry arranged for him to complete his homework before or after school.

R e s e a r c h   N o t e

Nelson et al. (1998) surveyed middle school students of varying achievement levels about their preferences for homework adaptations. The most preferred adaptations were completing assignments entirely at school, working on assignments in small groups, beginning homework in class with the teacher checking understanding, and allowing extra-credit assignments. The least preferred adaptations were making changes to assignments for individual students and using assignment notebooks.

Adapting Materials for Students with Moderate to Severe Disabilities

Students with moderate to severe disabilities often cannot perform some or all of the steps in tasks performed every day by students without disabilities. In the past, this inability to perform tasks in the same way as other students was interpreted to mean that students with moderate to severe disabilities could not benefit from these activities. Today, the emphasis is on making adaptations and providing support for these students so that they can increase their participation level or level of independence in performing classroom activities (Lowell-York, Doyle, & Kronberg, 1995).

One way to adapt materials and activities for students with moderate to severe disabilities is to conduct an **environmental inventory.** The purpose of an environmental inventory is to find out what adaptations or supports are needed to increase the participation of these students in the classroom as well as in community environments (Vandercook, York, & Forest, 1989). The environmental inventory process involves asking yourself three questions:

1. What does a person who does not have a disability do in this environment?
2. What does a person who has a disability do in this environment? What is the discrepancy?
3. What types of supports and/or adaptations can be put in place to increase the participation level or independence of the person who has a disability label?

An example of how this process is used in a classroom environment is shown in Figure 9.11. This example involves Roberto, the student with moderate to severe disabilities whom you read about at the beginning of the chapter. Roberto is in Ms. Benis's sixth-grade social studies class. The class is working in small groups on depicting the steps in the recycling process for paper, metal, and plastic. Each group is studying a different recycled material. Roberto lacks the motor and cognitive skills necessary to participate like everyone else. Ms. Benis has decided to assign Roberto to the group that his friend Seth is in. She also decides to use different materials for Roberto. Ms. Benis will have a paraprofessional help Roberto find pictures of recycled products; Seth will help Roberto paste these pictures onto the group's diagram. Mr. Howard, Roberto's special education teacher, will help Roberto identify recycled products in grocery stores and restaurants. Roberto's parents will help him sort the recycling at home.

Summary

Teachers who communicate clearly through the curriculum materials they use or the information they present orally in class can meet the needs of a broad range of students without having to make adaptations. Nonetheless, despite your best efforts, you still need to make some adaptations for students who are at risk or have other special needs.

In teaching basic skills, you may need to make adaptations in the areas of preskills, selecting and sequencing examples, rate of introduction of new skills, and the amount of direct instruction, practice, and review. Preskills are basic skills necessary for performing more complex skills. Before teaching a skill, you should assess the relevant preskills, and, if necessary, teach them. The range of examples you present

Figure 9.11 Environmental Inventory Process

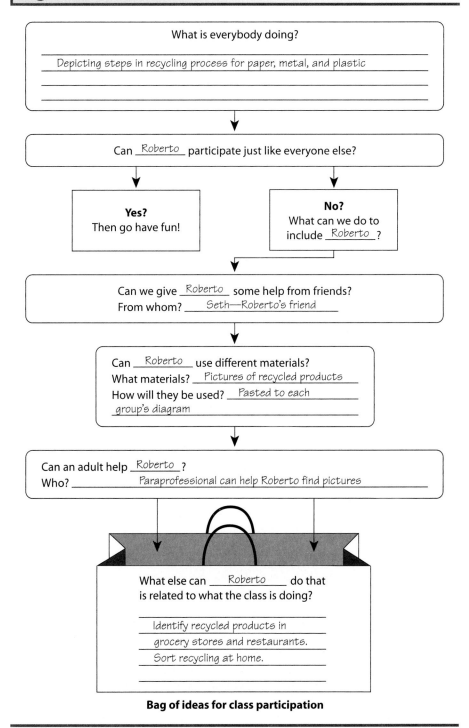

What is everybody doing?

Depicting steps in recycling process for paper, metal, and plastic

Can Roberto participate just like everyone else?

Yes?
Then go have fun!

No?
What can we do to
include Roberto ?

Can we give Roberto some help from friends?
From whom? Seth—Roberto's friend

Can Roberto use different materials?
What materials? Pictures of recycled products
How will they be used? Pasted to each
 group's diagram

Can an adult help Roberto ?
Who? Paraprofessional can help Roberto find pictures

What else can Roberto do that
is related to what the class is doing?

Identify recycled products in
grocery stores and restaurants.
Sort recycling at home.

Bag of ideas for class participation

S O U R C E : From "The McGill Action Planning System (MAPS): A Strategy for Building the Vision," by
T. Vandercook, J. York, & M. Forest, 1989, *Journal of the Association for Persons with Severe Handicaps,*
14(3), pp. 205–218.

should correspond directly with the types of problems you want students to solve, in and out of class. Examples can also be sequenced to make learning easier for students. Students sometimes have difficulty learning skills when they are introduced at too fast a rate. Introduce skills in small steps and at a slow enough rate to ensure mastery before you present more new skills. Finally, in learning basic skills, students at risk or with special needs may need more direct instruction, practice, and review.

In teaching subject-matter content to students with special needs, adaptations may need to be made in the areas of activating background knowledge, organizing content, and teaching terms and concepts. Students who have disabilities may lack background knowledge necessary for learning a content area, or they may know the information but be unable to recall it and relate it to the new information being presented. The PReP strategy, anticipation guides, and planning think sheets can help activate students' background knowledge. When content is well organized, students' understanding of important ideas and their interrelationships is enhanced. Student understanding also increases when study guides and graphic organizers are used. Students may also need help comprehending the large number of new and/or technical vocabulary words and concepts in content-area instruction. Strategies for teaching vocabulary that are effective for students with special needs include modeling examples, using synonyms and definitions, and creating concept diagrams.

Your oral and written communication with students must be clear. Clear written communication requires fewer inferences by the reader, a help for students with special needs, who may lack the background knowledge and reasoning skills to make such inferences. Effective written communication also explains sequences of events logically and uses obvious pronoun referents. Clear oral communication involves the effective use of directions, questions, and lectures.

You may also need to make adaptations for students in independent practice activities. Seatwork can be adapted by increasing the number of practice items, by clarifying the directions, and by reducing the number of different activities on a page. Providing feedback on independent practice activities can be facilitated by correcting papers as you circulate and by using spot checking, shared checking, easy checking, and self-checking. You can use homework more effectively by carefully managing the homework process, building student independence, giving assignments of appropriate difficulty, and communicating clearly and often with parents. Effective homework adaptations for students with special needs include adjusting assignment length; providing extra teacher help; providing a peer tutor; setting up student study groups; providing auxiliary learning aids, such as calculators and computers; and allowing alternative response formats, such as oral or written responses.

Students with moderate to severe disabilities often cannot perform some or all of the steps in tasks. You can use the environmental inventory process to adapt your classroom activities for these students.

Applications in Teaching Practice

Developing a Repertoire of Instructional Adaptations

You want to teach a group of at-risk students to spell the following contractions: *can't, aren't, couldn't, shouldn't, wouldn't, don't, won't,* and *isn't.*

Questions

1. How can you evaluate whether your students have learned the contractions?
2. What preskills should you be concerned with, how can you assess them, and what can you do with students who do not know them?
3. How can you sequence your instruction? Why did you choose this particular sequence?
4. How can you provide direct instruction, practice, and review for your students?
5. At what rate should you introduce the contractions?

Design a study guide for a section of Chapter 2 of this text.

Questions

1. What steps did you go through in constructing your study guide?
2. How did you select the vocabulary and concepts that you included?
3. How would you use the study guide to teach at-risk students or other students with special needs?

Develop a graphic organizer for a major concept in Chapter 1 of this text.

Questions

1. How did you select the concept? Is it a big idea?
2. How would you use the graphic organizer to teach at-risk students or other students with special needs?

Design a lesson to teach the concept of reasonable accommodations using a definition.

Questions

1. Is your definition stated clearly, simply, and concisely?
2. What examples and nonexamples did you use?
3. How can you find out whether your students know the meaning of the concept?
4. How can you find out whether your students can differentiate this concept from other concepts presented in the text?
5. How would you teach the concept using a concept diagram format?

You are teaching a lesson on the respiratory system. First you describe the respiratory process (for example, diaphragm contracts; air rushes into nose/mouth; air travels down windpipe/trachea; air enters lungs through bronchial tubes, and so forth) using a chart showing the key parts of the respiratory system (for example, nose, throat/esophagus, bronchial tubes, lungs). Next you plan to have students work in small heterogeneous groups on labeling a model of the respiratory system and describing all the key steps in the respiratory process.

Questions

1. Based on this lesson, complete an environmental inventory for Timothy, a student with a moderate cognitive disability described at the beginning of Chapter 5 in your text.
2. What other adaptations might you make for Timothy?

10

Strategies for Independent Learning

After you read this chapter, you will be able to

1. State ways that teachers can encourage student self-awareness and self-advocacy.

2. Describe ways that learning strategies can be developed and taught.

3. List and describe successful learning strategies in the areas of reading comprehension, note taking, written expression, math problem solving, and time management.

4. Describe ways that students can learn to use learning strategies independently.

■ Gerald is a student with learning disabilities in Mr. McCrae's ninth-grade English class. Gerald has had problems in the area of written expression throughout his school years. It is not that he does not have good ideas. When Gerald talks about what he is going to write, it sounds great. However, when he tries to get his ideas on paper, writing becomes a very frustrating experience for him. First of all, Gerald's papers lack organization. They rarely have a good introduction and conclusion, and the body is usually out of sequence. Gerald also makes a lot of mechanical errors; his papers are full of misspellings, and he frequently leaves out punctuation marks and capital letters. When asked by Mr. McCrae why he does not proofread his papers, Gerald responded that he does. What can Mr. McCrae do to help Gerald learn to organize his papers better? What can be done to help Gerald proofread his papers better for mechanical errors?

■ Traci is a student in Ms. McCord's third-grade class. Although Traci was referred for special education services last year, she was not eligible for them. Traci has trouble solving story problems in math because she does not have a systematic way of working on them. When Traci starts a problem, she looks for the numbers right away rather than first reading the problem carefully. For example, one day she saw the numbers 23 and 46 in a problem and automatically added them to get a sum of 69. The problem called for subtraction, but Traci did not know that because she had not read the problem. What can Ms. McCord do to help Traci solve math word problems more successfully? How can Ms. McCord help Traci become a more independent problem solver?

■ Ronald is a student with a moderate cognitive disability who has problems with organization. He is often late for school because, according to his parents, he rarely plans ahead and is always getting his materials ready for school at the last minute. Ronald is usually late for class as well. He says that he cannot keep track of what he needs to bring to each class, so he is constantly going back to his locker, which makes him late. His locker is a complete mess. Afternoons, Ronald has a part-time job bagging groceries as part of a work–study program. His supervisor has expressed concern that Ronald has been late for work several times, has frequently forgotten his uniform, and several times has missed his bus and had to be driven home by one of the clerks. What can Ronald's teachers do to help him become better organized?

Connections

How does this chapter relate to the INCLUDE model presented in Chapter 4?

Cultural Awareness

The value placed on student independence may differ depending on a student's culture. For example, compared to European American students, many Hispanic, Native American, Filipino, and Southeast Asian students are more interested in obtaining teacher direction and feedback than in working on their own (Grossman, 1995). Because being independent and taking direction are both important behaviors, you should teach your students to function in both manners.

Connections

Strategies for achieving independence that are relevant for students with moderate to severe cognitive disabilities are discussed in Chapters 5 and 9.

All these students share a common problem: They are unable to meet the academic and organizational demands of school independently. Being able to work independently is a skill that becomes increasingly important as students move through the grades. Gerald needs to be able to organize his papers better, not just in English but in all areas, because teachers often judge quality on the basis of organization, neatness, or the number of spelling or punctuation errors. Traci needs to solve problems more systematically, not just in math but in other classes and out of school as well. Ronald needs a strategy for managing his time: Being punctual and having the necessary supplies or materials are essential in school as well as in the world of work. The fact is, as students move through the grades and on to careers or postsecondary education, more and more independence is expected by teachers and is necessary for student success.

Students need to perform independently in five key areas: gaining information, storing and retrieving information, expressing information, self-advocating, and managing time (Ellis & Lenz, 1996). Gaining information involves skills in listening to directions during lessons and on the job, or in reading and interpreting textbooks, source books, or other media. Storing information consists of strategies for taking notes and preparing for tests or other evaluations. Students also need to retrieve information when needed. For example, they need to remember how to carry out a task such as cleaning and clearing a table, or how to follow safety procedures during science lab. Expressing information includes the tasks of taking tests and writing papers. It also involves tasks such as developing a menu for a fast-food restaurant. Self-advocacy skills help students set realistic school or life goals and develop and carry out a plan to meet those goals. Finally, students need to have the time management skills to organize their time and effort toward meeting their goals.

Although all these skills become more important as students progress through school, independence should be stressed at all levels of instruction. Unfortunately, many students, including those who are at risk or have other special needs, lack basic independent learning skills. Traditionally, when students needed learning-strategy instruction, they were referred to special education classes, remedial reading or math programs, or special study-skills courses. In inclusive classrooms, learning strategies can be taught to students with special needs in several ways. Most often, learning strategies can be covered in class so that all students can benefit. For example, when Mr. Cooper discovered that many of his students in U.S. history were having trouble taking notes, he presented a note-taking strategy to his whole class. Similarly, Ms. Carpenter taught her biology class a strategy for taking multiple-choice tests because her students were scoring low as a group on these kinds of questions.

Occasionally, because of extraordinary student needs, strategy instruction might take place outside the classroom. For example, some students with special needs may need to have a strategy broken down into small steps, view multiple demonstrations of a strategy, and practice the strategy many times before they learn it. If the collaborative support of other education professionals is lacking, this level of instruction may be difficult to deliver within the time and curricular constraints of the general education classroom. Ronald, the student introduced to you at the beginning of this chapter, has just such extraordinary needs. Ronald needed a strategy designed specifically for his organizational problems; a plan for getting to his afternoon job on time would not be relevant for the rest of his classmates. In cases such as these—in which a special educator teaches strategies to individual students—your job is to encourage and monitor student use of the strategy in your class and to provide students with feedback on their performance. However, in most cases, you can teach many of these skills in your class while still covering the required academic content. In fact, teaching learning strategies to students allows you to cover more material because your students become able to learn on their own.

You should do all you can to encourage and teach independent learning strategies to your students. This chapter focuses on three major ways you can build student independence in learning: (1) encouraging student self-awareness and self-advocacy skills; (2) developing and teaching learning strategies directly in class; and (3) teaching students to use specific strategies on their own. Keep in mind that the strategies discussed apply most directly to students with high-incidence or sensory disabilities or to students who are at risk.

How Can You Encourage Student Self-Awareness and Self-Advocacy?

As students move through elementary, middle, and high school and on to postsecondary education or the world of work, the level of independence expected by those around them increases. Teachers expect students to come to class on time, master content through reading and lectures, keep track of assignments, organize study and homework time, set realistic career goals, and participate in curricular and extracurricular activities to meet these career goals. Students also are expected to recognize when they have a problem and to know where to go for help. Clearly, students need to look out for themselves, to become self-advocates.

Adjusting to these changing expectations can be difficult for all students, but especially for students with disabilities. Many students with special needs are not aware of their strengths and weaknesses (Aune, 1991; Brinckerhoff, 1994) and lack self-advocacy skills (Durlak, Rose, & Bursuck, 1994). They need to learn these skills while still in school.

In effective student **self-advocacy** training, students learn their strengths and weaknesses, the potential impact of these strengths and weaknesses on their performance, the support they need to succeed, and the skills required to communicate their needs positively and assertively.

Generally speaking, special educators have much of the responsibility for teaching self-advocacy directly. However, general education teachers are in a good position to teach all students about the opportunities and expectations of the adult world related to self-awareness and self-advocacy. For example, Meredith is a student in Ms. Gay's second-grade class. When Meredith does not understand how to do her seatwork, she is afraid to ask Ms. Gay for help. As a result, she often gets it wrong. Ms. Gay decided to spend 5 minutes with the whole class talking about knowing when and how to ask for help. She felt this discussion would help Meredith and other students in the class be more assertive when they have a problem. Cecil is a student with a vision impairment who is in Mr. Jordan's algebra class. Even though Cecil sits in the front row, he is still unable to see the problems on the board because Mr. Jordan forms his numbers too small. However, Cecil does not feel comfortable asking Mr. Jordan to write larger. With his special education teacher, Cecil practiced asking Mr. Jordan for help. Cecil then asked Mr. Jordan directly, who responded that it would be no problem to write bigger. Mr. Jordan also gave Cecil some additional pointers on how to describe his disability and how to ask his teachers for accommodations.

Cultural Awareness

Self-advocacy relates to social and cultural factors that affect a student's self-concept and self-esteem. Strategies for achieving independence can help students at risk or with special needs overcome learned helplessness and develop a stronger sense of self-efficacy.

Check Your Learning

Why might guiding students in establishing or choosing their own learning goals be an effective approach for introducing self-advocacy skills?

How Can You Effectively Teach Independent Learning Strategies in Class?

Another way you can help your students become more independent is to teach them strategies for learning how to learn (Dickson, Collins, Simmons, & Kameenui, 1998). These methods are collectively referred to as learning strategies. **Learning strategies** are techniques, principles, or rules that enable a student to learn to solve problems and complete tasks independently (Lenz, Ellis, & Scanlon, 1996; Schumaker, Deshler, & Denton, 1984). Learning strategies, which are similar to study skills, not only emphasize the steps needed to perform a strategy (for example, steps to follow in reading a textbook), but they also stress why and when to use that strategy as well as how to monitor its usage. For example, when Ms. Blankenship taught her students a strategy for reading their textbook, she pointed out that the strategy would save them time yet improve their test scores. She also taught them to judge how well they are using the strategy by filling out a simple checklist as they read.

An important component of teaching learning strategies effectively is to present well-designed strategies. As you recall from the discussions of effective materials in Chapters 4 and 9, the better your materials are designed, the greater the chance that they will work for your students with special needs, without requiring you to make major adaptations. Some effective guidelines for designing learning strategies are presented in the Professional Edge.

For students to use learning strategies independently, they must first learn to perform them accurately and fluently. The following teaching steps have proven effective for teaching learning strategies (Schumaker et al., 1984). These steps include many of the effective teaching practices described in Chapters 4 and 9.

Assessing Current Strategy Use

Students often are receptive to instruction when they can clearly see problems they are having and how the strategy you are teaching can help them overcome these problems. Therefore, learning-strategy instruction begins with an assessment of how well your students can currently perform a skill. As you learned in Chapter 8, specific learning strategies can be assessed using direct observation checklists, analyses of student products, and student self-evaluations.

You also need to assess whether your students have the preskills necessary to perform the strategy. For example, students who can discriminate between main ideas and details in a lecture are ideal candidates for learning a note-taking strategy; students who can read all the words on a test and understand the class content will benefit most from a test-taking strategy. On the other hand, students who cannot identify most of the words in their texts would not be logical candidates for learning a textbook-reading strategy; students whose seatwork activities are too hard for them will not benefit from a strategy to help them organize their independent practice activities. As you have learned, students with special needs often lack critical preskills. Before you decide to teach a particular strategy, you should identify its preskills and assess them separately. If most students lack the preskills, they can be taught as part of your everyday instruction. If only a few have problems with preskills, these students need to receive additional instruction in class, with a peer or adult tutor, through co-taught lessons, or in a learning center or special education setting.

Professional Edge

Developing Your Own Learning Strategies

You can use the guidelines here either to create your own learning strategies or to evaluate ones that are commercially produced. By following these suggestions, you will not always need to depend on commercial publishers for your learning materials. Rather, you can develop learning strategies to fit the students in your class.

1. Identify skill areas that are problematic for most of your students, such as taking multiple choice tests or writing lecture notes.

2. For each skill area, specify student outcomes, such as scoring at least 10 percent higher on multiple-choice tests or writing down key main ideas and details from a lecture.

3. List a set of specific steps students need to follow to reach the identified outcomes. You may want to ask other students who have good test-taking and note-taking skills what they do. Presented here is a sample reading comprehension strategy called **RAP:**

   R   *Read* a paragraph.
   A   *Ask* yourself what were the main idea and two details.
   P   *Put* main idea and details in your own words. (Ellis & Lenz, 1987)

4. Your strategy should contain no more than eight steps. Having more steps makes the strategy difficult to remember.

5. Your steps should be brief; each should begin with a verb that directly relates to the strategy.

6. To help students remember the steps, encase the strategy in a mnemonic device (for example, the acronym RAP for the reading strategy just presented).

7. The strategy should cue students to perform behaviors for thinking (remembering), for doing (reading), and for self-evaluation (surveying or checking your work).

8. A textbook-reading strategy that was developed by teachers (Bartelt, Marchio, & Reynolds, 1994) and that meets the guidelines for developing an effective learning strategy follows:

   R   *Review* headings and subheadings.
   E   *Examine* boldface words.
   A   *Ask,* "What do I expect to learn?"
   D   *Do* it—Read!
   S   *Summarize* in your own words.

S O U R C E : Adapted from "Generalization and Adaptation of Learning Strategies to Natural Environments: Part 2. Research into Practice," by E. Ellis, K. Lenz, and E. Sabornie, 1987, *Remedial and Special Education, 8*(2), pp. 6–23. Copyright (c) 1987 by PRO-ED, Inc. Reprinted with permission.

Clarifying Expectations

Learning strategies have the potential of empowering your students because they enable students to learn and succeed in and out of school on their own, without undue help from others. When you introduce learning strategies to students, you need to point out their potential benefits clearly and specifically. Carefully explained expected outcomes can be motivating, particularly as students get older and teacher encouragement alone may no longer be enough to keep them interested. The first step in getting and keeping students motivated to learn is to provide a strong rationale for why learning the strategy is important. This rationale should be directly tied to current student performance as well as to the demands of your class. For example, when introducing a new note-taking strategy, Mr. Washington pointed out

Connections

Applying the INCLUDE strategy is an effective way to identify strategies that students need to succeed in your class.

that the class was able to identify on average only half of the main ideas presented on a note-taking pretest. He also told his class that half of the material on his tests would come from information presented during his lectures. Finally, Mr. Washington explained that taking good notes can help students out of school as well; in many job situations, employers give directions that need to be written down.

The next step in clarifying expectations is to explain specifically what students should be able to accomplish when they have learned the skill. For example, Ms. Thompson told her class that after learning a textbook-reading strategy, they would be able to do their homework faster. Also, give students an idea of how long it will take them to learn the strategy. For example, you could make a chart showing the instructional activities to be covered each day and the approximate number of days it will take to learn the strategy. The advantage of presenting the information on a chart is that steps can be crossed out or checked as completed. The act of checking off completed activities can be very motivating for students. It is also a way of demonstrating self-monitoring, an effective independent learning skill that we discuss later in this chapter.

Demonstrating Strategy Use

In demonstrating strategies, keep in mind three important points. First, remember that the process one goes through in performing a task or solving a problem should be carefully explained. For example, demonstrate both thinking and doing behaviors. Talking aloud to yourself while performing the skill is particularly important for many students with special needs, who often do not develop spontaneously organized thinking patterns. Second, present both examples and nonexamples of appropriate strategy use, carefully explaining why they are examples or nonexamples. This

Demonstrating the use of a learning strategy involves explaining both the thinking and the doing parts of a process, showing examples and nonexamples of effective strategy use, and checking learners' understanding. How do these steps help students with special needs acquire learning strategies?

explanation can help students tell the difference between doing a strategy the right way and doing it incorrectly, a distinction that can be difficult for students with special needs to make without direct instruction. For example, Mr. Washington demonstrated effective and ineffective note-taking strategies using the overhead projector. As a student listened to a short lecture, he took notes systematically, writing down key ideas and details. Next, using the same lecture, he demonstrated ineffective note taking by trying to write down every word. Finally, after you demonstrate, ask frequent questions to test student understanding. Frequent questioning can help you monitor student understanding and determine whether more demonstration is needed. Keep in mind that for many students, including those with disabilities, one demonstration may not be enough. See the Case in Practice for a sample script for demonstrating the **KWL** (*K* = what you already know; *W* = what you want to know; *L* = what you learned) **Plus** textbook-reading strategy (Ogle, 1986).

Encouraging Students to Memorize Strategy Steps

The purpose of having students memorize the steps in the strategy is to make it easier for them to recall the strategy when they need to use it. To help students learn the steps, you can post them prominently in your classroom at first so that you and your students can refer to them throughout the class or day. Students may also need to be drilled on saying the strategy steps. To practice, students could pair off and quiz each other; or you could ask students the strategy steps before and after class. For example, each day during the last several minutes of class, Ms. Henry quizzed four of her social studies students on the steps of the KWL reading strategy.

Even though memorizing a strategy can help students recall it, you may not want to spend too much time on this step, particularly for some of your students with special needs, who may have memory problems. For these students, you might include the steps to all the strategies they are learning in a special section of their assignment notebooks. For strategies used most often, cue cards listing strategy steps can be taped to the inside cover of textbooks or notebooks.

Providing Guided and Independent Practice

As we have already stated, students must learn how to perform strategies accurately and fluently before they can attempt them independently. Such proficiency requires considerable practice. Five ways of providing practice on learning strategies are suggested. One way is to have students practice with controlled materials when they are first learning a strategy. **Controlled materials** are generally at the student's reading level, of high interest, and relatively free of complex vocabulary and concepts. Because controlled materials remove many content demands on the learner, they allow students to focus all their energy on learning the strategy. Controlled materials also allow for initial success, which is important for motivation. For example, Mr. Bernard was teaching his students a strategy for taking essay tests in current events. At first, he had his students practice this strategy on simply worded, one-part essay questions about material familiar to the students, such as people and events in the areas of rock music, movies, television, and sports. As students became better at using the strategy, Mr. Bernard gradually introduced more complex questions on less familiar topics, such as the AIDS epidemic in Africa and the economic conditions in Mexico. Finally, he simply used sample test questions.

Cultural Awareness

Schifini (1994) reports that the KWL strategy is particularly helpful for second-language learners because it gives them the immediate opportunity to relate class discussions and their own thinking to the text and to extend ideas beyond the text. The activities also give students the opportunity to contribute, regardless of their language proficiency, because everyone knows something and has something they want to learn.

Connections

Strategies for memorizing information are also covered in Chapter 11 as part of study strategies.

Connections

Providing support for students when they first learn a skill is discussed in Chapter 4 as part of scaffolding.

C A S E   I N   P R A C T I C E

Teaching Script for Demonstrating KWL Plus

An important component of teaching a learning strategy effectively is to demonstrate its appropriate use. The following script shows how one teacher uses modeling to present a textbook-reading strategy to her eighth-grade class.

Teacher: Let's review the textbook-reading strategy we talked about yesterday. Please take out the cue cards you made in class yesterday.

The teacher has students read each step individually and asks them what each step involves. Questions such as, "What are the steps? What might you do with the information you think of when brainstorming?

What do you do after you read the passage?" are used.

Teacher: Now that we've reviewed each step, we need to learn how to use the whole strategy effectively. Before we move on, though, let's read aloud all of the steps together as a group. When I point to the letter, say the letter, and when I point to the meaning, you read its meaning.

The students read the steps aloud: "*K* means 'what you already know,' *W* means 'what you want to know,' and *L* is 'what you learned.' "

Teacher: Good. Now I'm going to demonstrate how to use the strategy with a story I found about crayons. I'll put the passage on the overhead, as well as give each of you a copy so you can follow along at your desk. I'll work through each step of the strategy orally and write the information obtained at each

step on the board. Use your cue cards to help you see what step of the strategy I'm on.

The teacher then goes through the story, demonstrating correct usage of the steps and asking for feedback. The teacher also goes back over each step asking the students to verify that all of the steps to the strategy were followed and to explain how they were followed.

Teacher: What do we do now that we have a passage assigned to read? First, I brainstorm, which means I try to think of anything I already know about the topic and write it down.

The teacher writes on the board or overhead known qualities of crayons, such as "made of wax," "come in many colors," "can be sharpened," "several different brands."

Connections

Students who are gifted can benefit from learning strategies but, as discussed in Chapter 7, may not need as much practice learning them. An advantage of co-teaching (Chapter 3) is that one teacher can give students more strategy practice while the other works on activities with students who do not need more practice.

A second way to provide students with practice is first to guide them and then to allow them to perform independently. By guided practice, we mean giving students verbal cues when they are first attempting a skill. For example, before and while her students were practicing a strategy, Ms. Waters asked them questions such as, "What will you do first?" "Why did you do that?" "What should you do after you are done with the strategy steps?" "Which key words are you going to look for in the questions?" "How will you know which are the main ideas?" "Was the sentence I just read a main idea? Why?" Once most students seem able to answer your reminder questions, you can gradually stop asking them so that students are eventually performing independently. Some students may need little guided practice or none at all. These students can be allowed to work independently right away.

A third practice technique is to give feedback that is specific and encourages students to evaluate themselves (Lenz et al., 1996). For example, Dominique has just performed the steps of a proofreading strategy in front of the class. Her teacher says, "Good job, Dominique! I knew you could do it." Denise performed the same strategy in front of her class and her teacher asked, "How do you think you did? What do you need to focus on most the next time?" The feedback Dominique received does not clearly tell her what she did right; nor does it encourage self-evaluation. The

mation into a map so I can see the different main points and any supporting points.

At this point, the teacher draws a map on the chalkboard or overhead.

Teacher: Let's talk about the steps I used and what I did before and after I read the passage.

A class discussion follows.

Teacher: Now I'm going to read the passage again, and I want you to evaluate my textbook-reading skills based on the KWL Plus strategy we've learned.

The teacher then proceeds to demonstrate the strategy incorrectly.

Teacher: The passage is about crayons. Well, how much can there really be to know about crayons besides there are hundreds of colors and they always seem to break in the middle? Crayons are for little kids, and I'm in junior high so I don't need to know that much about them. I'll just skim the passage and go ahead and answer the question. Okay, how well did I use the strategy steps?

The class discusses the teacher's inappropriate use of the strategy.

Teacher: We've looked at the correct use of the strategy and we've seen how mistakes can be made. Are there any questions about what we did today? Tomorrow we will begin to memorize the strategy steps so that you won't have to rely on your cue cards.

S O U R C E : From *A Script for How to Teach the KWL Strategy*, by S. Butson, K. Shea, K. Pankratz, and M. Lamb, 1992, unpublished manuscript, DeKalb: Northern Illinois University. Used with permission.

feedback given to Denise encourages self-evaluation, a critical part of independent learning. Of course, if Denise cannot evaluate her own performance at first, the key parts of good performance have to be pointed out to her and practice on self-evaluation provided.

A fourth aspect of practicing learning strategies is to praise students only when they have produced work that is praiseworthy. Praise that is not tied to student performance, or is exaggerated, often for the purpose of enhancing student self-image, may only reinforce student inadequacy. For example, because of a history of failure in learning situations, students with special needs often see little relationship between their efforts and classroom success. When you give nonspecific praise to these students, it is easier for them to attribute your praise to something other than competence, such as sympathy ("I'm so bad at this, she has to pretend I did well").

Finally, encourage students to reinforce themselves and take responsibility for both their successes and failures. For example, after doing well on a note-taking strategy, Alicia was encouraged by her teacher to say, "I did a good job. This time I paid attention and wrote down all the main ideas. I need to do the same the next time." Alicia's teacher was showing her how to attribute her success to factors under her control. This approach can help her become a more active, independent learner.

Administering Posttests

When it appears from your practice sessions that most students have acquired the strategy, give them the pretest again to test their mastery. If according to your posttest, students have not acquired the strategy, identify where the breakdown occurred and then provide additional instruction and/or practice. If more than 20 percent of the students need extra practice or instruction, they can receive additional help in a large or small group. If less than 20 percent of the students require more assistance, those needing more individualized practice can be provided with peer tutors or support staff.

What Are Some Examples of Successful Learning Strategies?

There is a growing research base of learning strategies that work for students who are at risk or who have special needs. These strategies cover many areas, including reading comprehension, written expression, math problem solving, and time and resource management. An array of strategies that incorporate many of these effective practices are summarized in the following sections.

Word Identification Strategies

Students are likely to encounter technical words in their content-area textbooks that have multiple syllables, making them difficult for students to identify. A strategy designed to help students with special needs identify difficult words in their textbook reading is called SCUBA-D (Salembier & Cheng, 1997). **SCUBA-D** has six steps for students to follow when they come across a word they do not know.

1. *Sound* **it out.** In this step students are encouraged to look at the letters and say their sounds.
2. *Check* **the clues in the sentence.** Here, students use the context or clues within the sentence to try to figure out the word.
3. *Use* **the main idea and picture clues.** In this step students decide what the paragraph or reading is mostly about. The chapter title, pictures, and first sentences can provide information helpful in identifying the word.
4. *Break* **the word into parts.** Here students break words into parts (for example, prefixes, suffixes, root words) in a further attempt to figure them out.
5. *Ask* **for help.**
6. *Dive* **into the dictionary.**

The last two steps in the strategy have the students seek outside sources if the first four steps do not lead to identifying the unknown word.

Reading Comprehension Strategies

Reading comprehension strategies are intended to help students meet the independent reading demands of content-area classes successfully, particularly in the middle and upper grades. Although reading primarily involves textbooks, students must be able to read and understand a variety of source books as well.

One example of a reading comprehension strategy is SCROL (Grant, 1993). The **SCROL** strategy teaches students to use text headings to aid their comprehension and help them find and remember important information. The SCROL strategy has five steps. Advise students to follow steps 3–5 every time they encounter a heading in the text they are reading.

1. *Survey* **the headings.** In the assigned text selection, read each heading and subheading. For each heading and subheading, try to answer the following questions: What do I already know about this topic? What information might the writer present?

2. *Connect.* Ask yourself, How do the headings relate to one another? Write down key words from the headings that might provide connections between them.

3. *Read* **the text.** As you read, look for words and phrases that express important information about the headings. Mark the text to point out important ideas and details. Stop to make sure that you understand the major ideas and supporting details. If you do not understand, reread.

4. *Outline.* Using indentations to reflect structure, outline the major ideas and supporting details in the heading segment. Write the heading and then try to outline each heading segment without looking back at the text.

5. *Look* **back.** Now, look back at the text and check the accuracy of the major ideas and details you wrote. Correct any inaccurate information in your outline. If you marked the text as you read, use this information to help you verify the accuracy of your outline.

PARS is a simplified textbook-reading strategy that is good for younger students or students without much experience using textbook-reading strategies (Cheek & Cheek, 1983). The four steps of PARS follow:

1. *Preview* the material by scanning the chapter and surveying the introductory statement, headings, graphic aids, and chapter summary to identify main ideas.

2. *Ask* questions that relate to the main ideas discovered when surveying the chapter.

3. *Read* the chapter to answer the questions developed.

4. *Summarize* the main ideas in the chapter.

CAPS is a self-questioning strategy that can be used to help students find answers to questions about what is important in a story (Leinhardt & Zigmond, 1988). The strategy is composed of the following steps:

    C   Who are the *characters?*
    A   What is the *aim* of the story?
    P   What *problem* happens?
    S   How is the problem *solved?*

Another reading comprehension strategy is **POSSE** (Englert & Mariage, 1991). This strategy includes many reading practices that have been shown to aid reading comprehension, such as graphic organizers, text structures, stimulation of

Connections

Strategies for developing and using graphic organizers were covered in more depth in Chapter 9.

student background knowledge, and self-monitoring. The steps in this strategy are as follows:

P *Predict* ideas.
O *Organize* the ideas.
S *Search* for the structure.
S *Summarize* the main ideas.
E *Evaluate* your understanding.

When students are *predicting*, they can be given a sentence starter such as, *I predict that . . .* For this step, students are taught to use signals from a variety of sources, including title, headings in bold, pictures, key words, and so on. Brainstorming is very important in this step.

A technique used for teaching the POSSE strategy steps is a process called reciprocal teaching. **Reciprocal teaching** is a way to teach students to comprehend reading material by providing them with teacher and peer models of thinking behavior and then allowing them to practice these thinking behaviors with their peers (Palincsar & Brown, 1988). At first, the teacher leads the dialogue, demonstrating how the strategies can be used during reading. As instruction goes on, the teacher gives the students more and more responsibility for maintaining the dialogue. Eventually, students are largely responsible for the dialogue, though the teacher still provides help as necessary. Research shows that the most important part of the technique is the teacher releasing control and turning the dialogue over to the students (Englert & Mariage, 1991).

A sample dialogue for reciprocal teaching is presented in the Case in Practice. After reading the Case in Practice, think of the reasons that reciprocal teaching is such a powerful technique for teaching reading comprehension to students who are at risk or who have special needs. In what other areas could reciprocal teaching be used?

Check Your Learning

What makes reciprocal teaching a powerful technique for teaching reading comprehension to students who are at risk or who have special needs? In what other areas could reciprocal teaching be used?

These students are engaged in a structured dialogue about the newspaper they are reading, a peer-modeled comprehension strategy called reciprocal teaching. What strategies must students be taught before they can practice reciprocal teaching?

C A S E   I N   P R A C T I C E

Teaching Script for Demonstrating POSSE

The students in this class have just read a section of text that focuses on Loch Ness. They are now applying the search, summarize, and evaluate steps of POSSE.

Teacher: What is the main topic the text is talking about?

Peg: The Loch Ness monster.

Teacher: What was this section about? What was the main idea?

Peg: Oh, the lake. I have two questions: "What is a lake?" and "What lives in it?"

Teacher: Do you mean this particular lake or any lake?

Peg: This lake. Joe?

Joe: It's foggy, it's deep, and it's long and narrow.

Peg: Don?

Don: The land beside the lake, you don't know if it is real soft and you could fall through it.

Teacher: So it could be soft and swampy.

Ann: I think the Loch Ness monster lives there.

Teacher: Is Ann answering your question, Peg?

Peg: No.

Teacher: What was your question?

Peg: I had two: "What is a lake?" and "What lives in the lake?"

Joe: But they never answered that. I have a question about the main idea. Aren't we supposed to do a question about the main idea?

Teacher: Just about what we read.

Joe: Yes, but she asked us, "What lives in the lake?" but it doesn't really mention that in the book.

Teacher: That's true. The major idea has to do with Loch Ness and what it looks like. A minor idea that we really inferred rather than directly read in the article was that the Loch Ness monster lives in the lake.

Peg: Are there any clarifications?

Students: [No response.]

Teacher: I have a clarification. You had trouble reading some of these words and I wondered if you knew what some of them mean? What does *ancestors* mean?

[The teacher continues discussing vocabulary.]

S O U R C E : From "Making Students Partners in the Comprehension Process: Organizing the Reading 'POSSE'," by C. S. Englert and T. V. Mariage, 1991, *Learning Disability Quarterly, 14*, pp. 133–134. Used by permission of Council for Learning Disabilities.

Note-Taking Strategies

Because lecturing is a common way for teachers to present information to students, particularly in middle school, junior high, and high school, students need strategies for recording key information in lectures so they can study it later. Suggested note-taking tips are listed in Figure 10.1. These tips help no matter which note-taking strategy is used.

Two research-based strategies for note taking are CALL UP and ANOTES (Czarnecki, Rosko, & Fine, 1998). **CALL UP** is a strategy for taking lecture notes that has the following steps:

C *Copy* from board or transparency.
A *Add* details.
L *Listen* and write the question.
L *Listen* and write the answer.
U *Utilize* the text.
P *Put* in your own words.

Figure 10.1 Tips for Note Taking

1. Take notes using either a two- or three-column system.

2. Take notes on only one side of the paper.

3. Date and label the topic of the notes.

4. Generally use a modified outline format, indenting subordinate ideas and numbering ideas when possible.

5. Skip lines to note changes in ideas.

6. Write ideas or key phrases, not complete sentences.

7. Use pictures and diagrams to relate ideas.

8. Use consistent abbreviations (e.g., w/ = with, & = and).

9. Underline or asterisk information the lecturer stresses as important.

10. Write down information the lecturer writes on the board or transparency.

11. If you miss an idea you want to include, draw a blank line so that you can go back and fill it in.

12. If you cannot automatically remember how to spell a word, spell it the way it sounds or the way you think it looks.

13. If possible, review the previous session's notes right before the lecture.

14. If the lecture is about an assigned reading topic, read the information before listening to the lecture.

15. As soon as possible after the lecture, go over your notes, filling in the key concept column and listing any questions you still have.

16. After going over your notes, try to summarize the major points presented during the lecture.

17. Listen actively! In other words, think about what you already know about the topic being presented and how new information is related to old information.

18. Review your notes before a test.

S O U R C E : From *Strategies for Teaching Students with Learning and Behavior Problems* (3rd ed.), by C. S. Bos and S. Vaughn, 1994, Boston: Allyn and Bacon. Copyright © 1994 by Allyn and Bacon. Reprinted by permission.

When copying from the board or transparency, students listen and look for cue words or phrases that identify main ideas and copy them down next to the margin and underline them. Students also listen for details, writing them 1 inch from the margin with a dash (—) in front of each detail. Students listen for teacher or student questions that they think can inform their understanding and write them, indented, under the appropriate main idea. Students also record answers under the main ideas. The last two steps can be carried out at home or in study hall. Students first read about the main ideas in their textbooks, and then paraphrase the information under each main idea in a space previously left blank. Students record relevant text pages in the margins so they can refer to the text at a later time if needed.

ANOTES is a strategy for revising notes to help students organize their notes for test preparation. Note the following steps:

A   *Ask* yourself if you have a date and topic.
N   *Name* the main ideas and details.
O   *Observe* ideas also in text.
T   *Try* margin noting and use the SAND strategy.
E   *Examine* for omissions or unclear ideas.
S   *Summarize* key points.

In the first step, students skim their notes for a main idea mentioned several times or recall what the teacher said the lesson was about. Students then highlight or underline all the main ideas and supporting details in their notes. Students note main ideas that are also in the text. Next students use the SAND strategy to organize their notes visually. They *star* important ideas, especially those that are also in the text, *arrange* arrows to connect ideas, *number* key points in order, and *devise* abbreviations and write them next to the items. Students then reread the notes to find any missing information and unclear ideas. Finally, students write the overall idea of the lecture in a sentence or two immediately following the notes.

To learn this or other note-taking strategies, students need the preskill of being able to tell the difference between main ideas and details. For example, Inez chose key words that represented main ideas. Some students attempt to write down everything and need to be taught directly how to differentiate main ideas and details. For example, Mr. Abeles discovered that many students in his history class were unable to identify main ideas in his lectures. First, he explained the difference between main ideas and details: main ideas are what a whole section or passage is about; details are what just one part of a section or passage is about. For several weeks he stopped after presenting a section of material and put three pieces of information on the board—one main idea and two details. He asked the students which was the main idea and why. When his students were doing well at these tasks, Mr. Abeles had them write their own main ideas for a section of a lecture, which were shared with the class and corrective feedback was provided as necessary. Students also must be able to summarize material in their own words. One effective strategy for writing summaries involves the following steps: (1) skim the passage (or listen to a section of lecture); (2) list the key points; (3) combine related points into single statements; (4) cross out the least important points; (5) reread the list; (6) combine and cross out to condense points; (7) number the remaining points in logical order; and (8) write out points in paragraph format in numbered order (Sheinker & Sheinker, 1989, p. 135). Finally, students should learn strategies for studying their notes, such as covering up one column and trying to say what is in the column, and then uncovering the column and comparing their responses to the actual information. Although some students can master this study strategy with only a verbal explanation, others may need more support, perhaps in the form of a demonstration and guided practice.

Writing Strategies

Another area that requires student independence is writing and proofreading papers. One strategy that helps students organize all the steps in the writing process is called **POWER** (Englert et al., 1988). The process involves the use of self-questioning, graphic organizers, and peer editing using the following steps:

P *Planning*
O *Organizing*
W *Writing*
E *Editing*
R *Revising*

The POWER strategy teaches students four different organizational structures for writing papers: stories, comparison–contrast, explanations, and problem/solution (Englert et al., 1988). When writing stories, students use key story elements—Who? When? Where? What happened? How did it end?—to organize their papers. A comparison–contrast structure includes information about what is being compared (for example, Native Americans and settlers), on what characteristic they are being compared (views about land), and on how they are alike and/or different (Native Americans shared land; settlers owned land). Explanations involve telling how to do something, such as explaining the steps in changing a tire. Finally, in a problem/solution structure, a problem is identified (for example, it took too long to travel from the east to the west in the early 1800s in the United States), the cause of the problem is explained (the only way to go from the east to the west was by stagecoach), and the solution is stated (the transcontinental railroad was built).

For the *planning* stage, students focus on the audience for the paper, the purpose, and the background knowledge that is necessary to write the paper. In the *organizing* step, students decide which organizational pattern fits their paper (for example, story, comparison–contrast) and then complete a pattern guide to help them organize their ideas. A **pattern guide** is a graphic designed to help students organize their papers. A sample pattern guide for a comparison–contrast paper is shown in Figure 10.2. Notice that the words that are *not* in boxes—*both same, in contrast to, similarly,* and *however*—are key words that are used frequently when making comparisons. These words help students make the transition to writing sentences. For example, in Figure 10.2, two kinds of pizza are being compared and contrasted. The student might write, "The crusts of deep dish and regular pizza are *both the same* in that they both are made of white flour. This is *in contrast to* their thickness; deep dish pizza crust is much thicker."

In the *writing* stage, the teacher demonstrates and thinks aloud to show students how to take the information gathered in the planning and organizing steps and produce a first draft. For example, you can compose an essay comparing two kinds of pizza using an overhead projector, thinking out loud as you write. You can involve students by asking questions such as, What would a good topic sentence be? Is this a good example? How do you think I should end this? Why? You could also have students write the paper along with you.

The *editing* step teaches students to critique their own writing and to identify areas in which they need clarification or assistance, an important self-evaluation skill. Editing is a two-step process involving student self-evaluation and peer editing. For self-evaluation, students reread and evaluate their draft, starring sections of the paper they like best and putting question marks in the margins by passages they think may be unclear. Finally, students think of two questions to ask their peer editors. For example, Jorge asked his peer editor whether he had used capital letters and punctuation correctly. He was also concerned about whether his paper was long enough and asked for suggestions on how to add information.

Figure 10.2 Pattern Guide for Comparison–Contrast

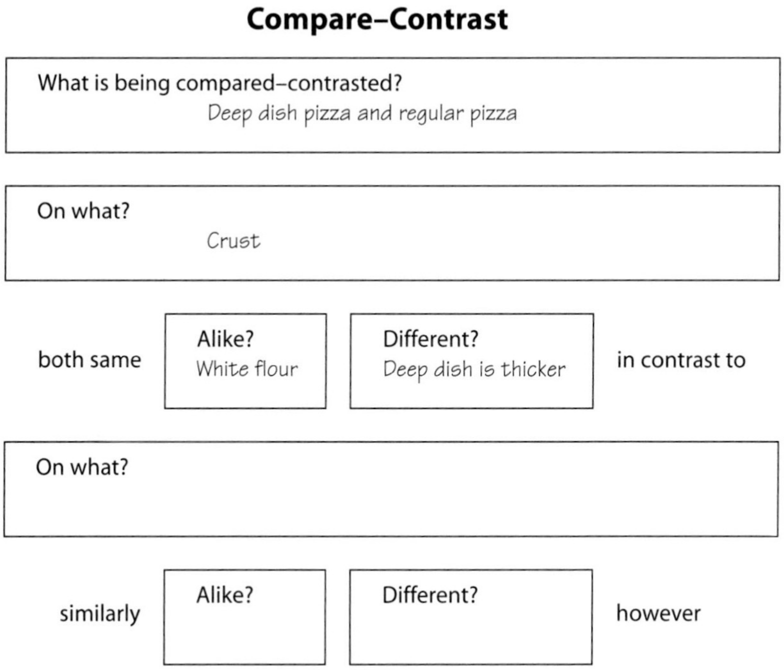

Compare–Contrast

What is being compared–contrasted?
Deep dish pizza and regular pizza

On what?
Crust

both same | Alike? *White flour* | Different? *Deep dish is thicker* | in contrast to

On what?

similarly | Alike? | Different? | however

SOURCE: From "A Case for Writing Intervention: Strategies for Writing Informational Text," by C. S. Englert, T. E. Raphael, L. M. Anderson, H. M. Anthony, K. L. Fear, and S. L. Gregg, 1988, *Learning Disability Quarterly, 3*(2), p. 108.

For **peer editing,** several steps are followed. First, writers read their papers to a peer editor while the editor listens. The peer editors then summarize the paper. Next, the editor evaluates the paper, giving an analysis of salient features of the writing that might guide a revision or lead to improvement. For example, the peer editor might suggest that the writer add key words or reorganize the paper for clarity. These suggestions are shared with the writer. Then the peer editor and the writer brainstorm ways to improve the paper.

A research-based strategy called **TAG** can also help students with the peer editing process (Carlson & Henning, 1993; MacArthur & Stoddard, 1990). The **TAG** strategy involves three simple steps:

T *Tell* what you like.
A *Ask* questions.
G *Give* suggestions.

As discussed previously, students need to be provided with models and guided practice for doing these steps prior to doing them independently.

In the *revise* step, students decide on changes to be made using their self-evaluation sheets and peer feedback. Englert and colleagues (1988) suggest that the teacher model how to insert or change the order of information, all the while providing a rationale for any changes. All modifications are made directly on the first draft. Last, the teacher and

WWW Resources

Inspiration is a program designed to help students plan and organize research projects through outlines and concept maps. For more information on this program, go to http://www.inspiration.com.

student have a conference, and changes in writing mechanics are suggested. Following this conference, a final draft is composed on clean sheets of paper.

When students have to proofread their papers independently, they might use a strategy called COPS (Alley, 1988). In the **COPS** strategy, students question themselves as follows:

C Have I *capitalized* the first word and proper nouns?
O How is the *overall appearance* of my paper? Have I made any handwriting, margin, or messy errors?
P Have I used end *punctuation*, commas, and semicolons carefully?
S Do words look like they are *spelled* right; can I sound them out or use the dictionary?

Although COPS has been shown to be effective, students need preskills to perform this strategy adequately. Before teaching COPS, consider the following questions: Can the students recognize misspelled words? Do the students know rules for using capital letters and punctuation? Can they apply these rules? Can the students use a dictionary? If the answer to any of these questions is no, teach these skills directly before teaching students the COPS strategy.

Several additional strategies can be used to help students with the various aspects of written expression. **SLOW CaPS** (Levy & Rosenberg, 1990, p. 27) is a strategy for writing four kinds of paragraphs: list or describe, show sequence, compare–contrast, and demonstrate cause/effect. The steps for SLOW CaPS follow:

S *Show* the type of paragraph in the first sentence.
L *List* the details you want to write about.
O *Order* the details.
W *Write* details in complete sentences and **CaP** off the paragraph with a **C** (concluding), **P** (passing/transition), or **S** (summary) sentence.

(Notice that the *a* in CaPS is not used and so is lowercased.)

A composition strategy called **DEFENDS** (Ellis & Lenz, 1987) is designed to help students write a paper defending a position.

D *Decide* on an exact position.
E *Examine* the reasons for the positions.
F *Form* a list of points that explain each reason.
E *Expose* the position in the first sentence.
N *Note* each reason and supporting points.
D *Drive* home the position in the last sentence.
S *Search* for errors and correct.

A study strategy can help students learn unknown spelling words (Graham & Freeman, 1986). Students are required to carry out the following five steps:

1. Say the word.
2. Write and say the word.
3. Check the word.
4. Trace and say the word.
5. Write the word from memory and check your spelling.

If students misspell the word in step 5, they need to repeat the five steps.

Check Your Learning

In what ways might the COPS strategy be helpful to Gerald, whom you read about at the beginning of this chapter?

Cultural Awareness

Cohen, and Riel (1989) conducted a study to explore the effects of writing using the Internet for authentic audiences of peers from different cultural backgrounds. They found that essays written for distant peers were superior to essays written to be graded by their teachers; essays for authentic peers were more explicit and detailed.

WWW Resources

The Write Site, at http://www.writesite.org, is designed for language arts students in middle school. The site allows students to take on the role of journalists and editors to research, write, and publish their own newspaper. The site provides unit outlines, handouts, exercises, downloadable teaching material, information about how to write and more.

Computer technology such as word-processing software can also help students with special needs become independent writers. The Technology Notes feature on pages 374–375 describes available computer technology along with comments about its effectiveness in helping students with special needs to write.

Strategies for Using Technology to Improve Student Writing

Using the World Wide Web.   The World Wide Web can enhance the writing process for all your students, including those with special needs. Smith, Boone, and Higgins (1998) have described the different ways the Internet can expand the writing process. (See Figure 10.3 on page 376.) Smith et al. (1998) believe that using the Internet for writing can lead to many positive outcomes in addition to better written products, including the following outcomes:

1. Students are no longer limited to community or school libraries for information and ideas.

2. Students can develop a more highly developed sense of research as they comb the Internet for information.

3. Students can learn how to locate information more efficiently using WWW search engines such as Yahooligans.

4. Students can learn to gather information from many sources and make judgments about its accuracy.

5. Students can learn about important aspects of writing not often covered extensively or clearly in school, such as copyright laws, plagiarism, and publishing restrictions.

6. Students can learn to solve problems and cope with frustration as they experience problems, such as long delays, when using the Internet.

Revising essays.   This strategy uses a word processor for revising essays (Graham & Harris, 1987). Students instruct themselves using the following six steps:

1. Read your essay.

2. Find the sentence that tells you what you believe—is it clear?

3. Add two reasons why you believe it.

4. **SCAN** each sentence:
   S   Does it make *sense*?
   C   Is it *connected* to my belief?
   A   Can I *add* more?
   N   *Note* errors.

5. Make changes on the computer.

6. Reread your essay and make final changes.

Using spell checkers effectively.   Spelling checkers can help students identify misspelled words and spell them correctly. However, one problem with spell checkers is that the correctly spelled version that the student is attempting to write is not

WWW Resources

If you are trying to find information on the Internet, the following sites are useful:

http://www.lib.berkeley. edu/TeachingLib/Guides/ Internet/Findinfo.html

Learn the Net: http:// www.Learnthenet.com/ English/index.html

To make sure your website is accessible, consult Bobby at http://www.cast. org/bobby.

[Technology Notes]

Strategic Readers— Textbooks of the Future

Textbooks are the most common method of delivering subject-matter information to students of all grades, but particularly those who are in middle school or high school. Yet many students with and without special needs experience problems comprehending their textbooks. Whereas some of these problems are due to reading slowly and/or inaccurately, students also lack strategies for locating and retaining important information in their texts.

CAST is an educational, not-for-profit organization that uses technology to expand opportunities for all people, including those with disabilities. In conjunction with a grant from the U.S. Department of Education's Office of Special Education and the publisher Holt, Rinehart, and Winston, CAST developed the Strategic Reader, an enhanced electronic version of a textbook designed to offer support for students in important areas of word identification, comprehension, and study skills. The reader was developed over the course of a three-year project that worked directly with high school history students and their teachers through a process of developing and refining a series of electronic prototypes of chapters from their history book. The Strategic Reader starts with CAST's eReader, which is a computer program that can read any text aloud using Microsoft's latest SAPI 4 text-to-speech operations. The eReader offers students the ability to read text aloud while highlighting each spoken word on the screen. Students can control the speed and other characteristics of the synthetic voice and are able to drag and drop passages of the text into an electronic notepad

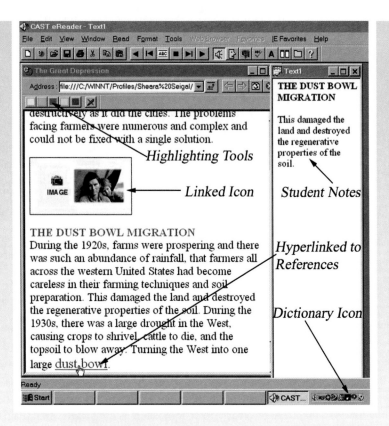

for future reference. The eReader also provides students with a number of options for presentation of content, such as changeable font size and the capacity to change both the foreground and background color of the text. The Strategic Reader also supports student comprehension in three ways: simplification and clarification of content, identification of patterns of organization, and application of study strategies.

Simplification and clarification of content

CAST researchers found that many students preferred to read text without graphics present. For example, students reported that in-text features such as biographies and the lives of the presidents interfered with the basic flow of the text and their ability to un-

always presented as an alternative. This happens when the combination of letters that the student has typed does not approximate closely enough the intended word for the software to offer the needed choices. Because the correct word does not appear on the first attempt, students often click on Go to Next Word or Skip Word without making a change. The result is a paper with many misspelled words. Ashton (1999) describes the CHECK strategy, a sequence of steps designed to help stu-

derstand it. The Strategic Reader hides such features, allowing the reader to access them as needed through the use of icons that can be clicked to reveal the hidden feature. For example, students can view pictures and in-text features after they read the text, when the content of the features may be more meaningful.

Identification of patterns of organization

CAST researchers found that most of the students in their study were unaware of the significance of text features such as boldface print, multicolored headings, and other features intended to help them prioritize and organize the information. To better help students understand and use these supports, the Strategic Reader includes an outline view in which only main headings within the text plus related subheadings and key vocabulary are visible. Clicking on any one of the elements in the outline frame presents the student with the section of the textbook surrounding the selected element so they have more context to get information on any important term or concept.

Use of study strategies

The Strategic Reader also provides support for student use of more strategic approaches to the text. For example, students can use the outline view just described in a number of strategic ways. They can read through the outline view first, prior to actually reading the text, to help activate prior knowledge, an important ingredient in successful comprehension. Students can also read the outline view prior to a quiz or exam to pinpoint important topics and then click to corresponding text when they come across a passage with which they need to become more familiar.

The Strategic Reader has other features that can help students learn more independently. Microsoft's Bookshelf electronic dictionary and reference suite is integrated into the software so that a student who does not understand a word in the text can click on the Bookshelf icon to get a definition and digitized voice that accurately pronounces the word. Students can then drag the definition into a notepad, creating an individualized word list for future reference. Bookshelf also contains the Encarta electronic encyclopedia which makes it possible for students to locate supporting information easily on many topics without leaving the workplace. Text from Encarta can also be dragged into a notepad for future reference. Students often have difficulty using reference materials incorporated into the text itself, such as a glossary or index. The Strategic Reader has what is called a Unified Resource in which all supplementary information on a term or concept is presented together for easy reference. There are also links to the World Wide Web that contain more information and that can be accessed immediately if students are connected to the Internet.

CAST is in the process of adding other enhancements to the Strategic Reader. They are developing monitors large enough to be visible to the entire class. Teachers can use this monitor to highlight important parts of the text or connect to Internet sites that can provide more information on the topic or can view the topic from a different perspective. CAST is also experimenting with the use of graphic organizers to help students learn to organize information they have gathered from other texts and other sources. Using a program called Inspiration, they are designing a range of homework assignments and study strategy templates that students can learn to use. The templates will include varying levels of support, depending on student need.

The creation of the Strategic reader was part of a larger plan to develop research-based guidelines for publishers of content-area textbooks. The guidelines reflected in the readers are being widely disseminated and are available on the CAST website at http://www.cast.org. CAST anticipates that the guidelines will influence the design of textbooks in the future.

dents use any spell checker more effectively. The sequence of steps in the strategy follows.

C *Check the beginning sounds.* Most spell checkers search for similar words beginning with the same letter as the word typed. Therefore, the correctly spelled version of the word is more likely to appear when at least the first letter is correct.

Figure 10.3 The Internet-Expanded Writing Process

Writing Process Phases	Typical Activities	Internet Activities
Prewriting	Brainstorming	Keyword searches
	Outlining	Browsing
	Clustering	Downloading information
	Collecting information	
Writing	Series of drafts	
Revision	Peer response	E-mail drafts to other kids for response
	Teacher response	
	Editing	E-mail drafts to experts for response
	Revision	
Publishing	Final drafts	
	Bound into a book	
	Can be read by others in class	
	Parents can read it	
WWW Revision		Final draft reviewed for possible hypertext links to other WWW sites
		Additional searches made for possible links
		Story is pasted into a WWW creation program
		Hypertext links added
WWW Publishing		Story file is transferred to a classroom WWW site on a networked computer
		URL address is established
		The story WWW page is registered with search page Yahooligans! for international access
		Uncle in Kathmandu can read it

SOURCE: From "Expanding the Writing Process to the Web," by S. Smith, R. Boone, and K. Higgins, 1998, *Teaching Exceptional Children, 30*(5), pp. 22–26.

For this step, students check the beginning sound of the word and ask themselves what other letter could make that beginning sound. For example, if the student is attempting to spell the word *elephant* but has begun the word with *ul*, teach him or her to ask what other letter(s) make that beginning sound (Ashton, 1999).

H *Hunt for the correct consonants.* If trying a new beginning sound does not help, have students change other consonants in the word. Ashton (1999) tells of a boy who was writing about Egypt and wanted to use the word *pyramid*. His first spelling attempt was *perament*, but the only suggested word was *per*. The boy continued to sound out the word and changed the spelling to *peramed*. This still did not produce the word he was looking for, so he changed his spelling again to *peramid*. *Pyramid* then appeared in the suggested word list, and the student recognized it as being the correct spelling (p. 26).

E *Examine the vowels.* Selecting the correct vowel when spelling is especially diffficult because vowels make so many sounds. Spell checkers can help students figure out which sound to use for a particular vowel or vowel combination. For example, a student spelled the place where she ate lunch as *cafitirea*. After substituting other possible vowels in the word she came close enough to the actual spelling to produce the word *cafeteria* on the suggested list (Ashton, 1999).

C *Changes in word lists give hints.* Sometimes students can use words in the suggested word list to find the correct spelling. For example, a student trying to spell the word *favorite* first tried *fovoriute*. When this spelling did not produce the correct alternative, she changed her original spelling from *foariute* to *fovaritue* to *favaritue*. After the last try, the word *favor* was given as a suggested spelling. Using that word, she typed *favoritue*, which brought *favorite* to the list—the correct spelling, which she recognized. (Ashton, 1999).

K *Keep repeating steps 1 through 4.* The most important aspect of using this strategy effectively is to give it repeated chances, trying as many different letter combinations as you can. However, at some point students may want to use another source, such as a dictionary, personalized word list (continually updated list of words students have looked up before), classmate, teacher, or parent.

Research Note

DeLaPaz (1999) reviewed the research on dictation and speech recognition systems and concluded that these systems can allow students with disabilities to circumvent handwriting, spelling, and punctuation problems, freeing them to focus on higher-level concerns, such as planning and generating content. DeLaPaz warns, though, that students need to be taught carefully how to use this technology and that students with disabilities still need to be taught skills for critical planning and content generation that many of them lack.

Strategies for Problem Solving in Math

Increasingly, teachers are focusing on problem solving as a major component of the math curriculum. This concentration is consistent with the math standards developed by the National Council of Teachers of Mathematics (2000), which also stress the importance of teaching problem solving. However, research indicates that if students with special needs are to become good problem solvers, they must be taught *how* to problem solve directly. A common (but by no means the only) way to introduce problem solving to students in a classroom context is through story or word problems. An effective technique for teaching word problems for students with special needs is presented in the Professional Edge on pages 378–379.

DRAW is a strategy for teaching students with special needs to solve multiplication facts that are not yet committed to memory (Harris, Miller, & Mercer, 1995). The DRAW strategy has the following steps:

Connections

The NCTM standards also stress the use of manipulatives, covered in Chapter 4, and performance-based tests, examined in Chapter 11.

D *Discover* the sign. (The student looks at the sign to figure out what operation to perform.)

R *Read* the problem. (The student says the problem aloud or to himself or herself.)

A *Answer*, or draw, and check. (The student thinks of the answer or draws lines to figure out the answer. The student checks his or her drawing and counting.)

W *Write* the answer. (The student writes the answer in the answer space.)

Professional Edge

The Key Word Strategy for Solving Math Story Problems: Is There a Better Way?

The key word strategy is an example of an ineffective strategy that many students with special needs use or are taught to use in solving math story problems (Kelly & Carnine, 1996). In this approach, students associate key words such as *more*, *in all*, *gave away*, and *left over* with certain mathematical operations. The key word strategy is attractive to teachers and students because sometimes it works. For example, the word *more* is commonly associated with subtraction, as in the following problem:

> Jose has 15 cents. Carmen has 10 cents. How much *more* money does Jose have?

Unfortunately, many times the word *more* appears in word problems that call for addition, as in the following problem:

> Charmaine had 15 cents. Her mother gave her 10 *more* cents. How many cents does she have now?

Kelly and Carnine (1996) suggest teaching students with special needs a more effective strategy for solving math word problems using problem maps and math fact families. Their strategy for teaching single operation addition and subtraction problems follows:

> For any addition/subtraction situation, there are two "small" numbers and a "big" number (the sum).
>
> An addition/subtraction number family is mapped this way:

The family above represents the following addition/subtraction facts:

$$7 + 9 = 16 \qquad 16 - 9 = 7$$
$$9 + 7 = 16 \qquad 16 - 7 = 9$$

A missing *big* number implies addition:

$$8 + 22 = \square$$

A missing *small* number implies subtraction:

$$30 - 22 = \square$$

or

$$30 - 8 = \square$$

These maps can then be applied to a variety of addition and subtraction word problems. Kelly and Carnine (1996, p. 6) gave the following example involving comparison problems.

In comparison problems, the difference between two values being compared may be information given in a problem (e.g., Marco sold 57 fewer subscriptions than Lui) or the unknown in a problem (e.g., How much heavier was Mary?). Because of the words *sold fewer* in the following problem, many students with LD will subtract.

> Marco sold 57 fewer magazine subscriptions than Lui. Marco sold 112 subscriptions. How many subscriptions did Lui sell?

You can help students make the transition from pictures to abstract numbers by teaching them the **FASTDRAW** strategy. The FAST part of the strategy has the following steps:

F   *Find* what you're solving for. (Students look for the question in the problem.)

A   *Ask* yourself, "What are the parts of the problem?" (Students identify the number of groups and the number of objects in each group.)

S   *Set* up the numbers. (Students write the two numbers in the problem in a vertical format.)

T   *Tie* down the sign. (Students add the multiplication sign to the problem.) (Harris et al., 1995, p. 6)

Students can use number families to avoid this confusion. The first step is to represent the problem using a number family; students must determine whether each of the two numbers given in the problem is a small number or the big number. The students are shown a simple way to do this:

They find the sentence that tells about the comparison and read it without the difference number. For example, students are taught to read the first sentence without the 57: "Marco sold fewer subscriptions than Lui." Because Marco sold fewer subscriptions, Marco is represented by a small number. By default, Lui is the big number. The students write M for Marco and L for Lui:

$$\xrightarrow{\quad M \quad} L$$

The word problem also gives a number for the difference between Marco and Lui. That number always has to be a small number. Marco sold 57 fewer, so 57 is the other small number:

$$\xrightarrow{\quad 57 \quad M \quad} L$$

Next the students read the rest of the problem. The problem asks about Lui and gives a number for Marco, so the students draw a box around L and replace the M with 112:

$$\xrightarrow{\quad 57 \quad \begin{matrix}112\\ \cancel{M}\end{matrix} \quad} \boxed{L}$$

Because the problem gives both small numbers, the students write an addition problem.

$$\begin{array}{r} 57 \\ +112 \\ \hline \end{array}$$

The answer tells how many magazine subscriptions Lui sold.

See Stein, Silbert, and Carnine (1997) for similar word problem strategies as applied to multiplication, division, and multistep story problems.

FROM THE RESEARCH

Darch, Carnine, and Gersten (1984) compared the effectiveness of the problem-solving strategy described in the Professional Edge with a traditional basal approach that emphasized key words. The subjects were 73 fourth-grade students who were unable to successfully solve math story problems. The results showed that the group receiving the problem-solving strategy outperformed the basal group on a posttest that included 26 math story problems. A student satisfaction survey given at the end of the study showed that more students in the strategy group liked the way the unit was taught and said they were using the strategy to solve problems in their general education classrooms.

SOURCE: Excerpt from "The 'Key Word' Strategy for Solving Math Story Problems," by B. Kelly and D. Carnine, 1996, reprinted by permission of Council for Learning Disabilities.

The **LAMPS** strategy (Reetz & Rasmussen, 1988) can be used as an aid to help remember the steps in regrouping or carrying in addition:

L *Line* up the numbers according to their decimal points.
A *Add* the right column of numbers and ask . . .
M *"More* than 9?" If so, continue to the next step.
P *Put* the 1s below the column.
S *Send* the 10s to the top of the next column.

To help with borrowing in subtraction, teach students to follow the steps in the **SLOBS** strategy (Reetz & Rasmussen, 1988):

S   *Smaller.* Follow steps.
L   *Larger.* Leap to subtract.
O   *Cross* off the number in the next column.
B   *Borrow* by taking one 10 and adding to the next column.
S   *Subtract.*

For the problem

$$\begin{array}{r} 72 \\ -46 \\ \hline \end{array}$$

Connections

More information on how to use self-instruction is included later in this chapter and in Chapter 12.

students would look at the top number on the right to see whether it was smaller or larger than the bottom-right number. If it was smaller, the students would follow the rest of the steps. They would cross off the number in the next column to the left and borrow one unit from that column (reducing that number by one) and add it to the other column. For example, in 72 – 46, borrow 10 from the left column. Then subtract. If the number is larger, students proceed directly to the subtract step. Repeat the steps if more digits are to be subtracted.

The **FOIL** strategy (Crawford, 1980) helps prevent algebra students from missing one of the four products needed to calculate multiplication of a binomial by another binomial. Four steps are followed:

F   Multiply *first* terms.
O   Multiply *outermost* terms.
I   Multiply *innermost* terms.
L   Multiply *last* terms.

For example, apply the FOIL strategy to the following problem:

$$(x + 4)\ (x + 3)$$
$$A\quad B\quad C\quad D$$

In the *F* step, the student multiplies the first two factors in each binomial, $x \times x = x^2$, or using the letters, *AC*. Next, in the *O* step, the student multiplies the first factor in the first binomial and the second factor in the second binomial, $x \times 3 = 3x$, or *AD*. Then in the *I* step, the student multiplies the second factor of the first binomial and the first factor of the second binomial, $4 \times x = 4x$, or *BC*. Finally, in the *L* step, the second factors of both binomials are multiplied: $4 \times 3 = 12$, or *BD*. This strategy applies *only* to the special case of multiplying two binomials. A strategy for solving problems is described in the Special Emphasis On . . . feature on pages 382–383.

Strategies for Managing Time and Resources

In the early 1980s, an informal survey was done on the kinds of problems that lead to a student being referred for special education (Lessen & Bursuck, 1983). Interestingly, the problem behavior mentioned most often was not an academic one, nor was it a discipline problem, such as talking out or fighting. The problem mentioned most often was lack of organization, a common characteristic of students with disabilities (Smith, 1994; Smith, 1980). Ronald, one of the students introduced at the beginning of the chapter, has trouble organizing.

Organizing study materials involves having the appropriate school supplies, making sure these supplies are brought to class when they are needed, and having an organized notebook to ensure easy access to information. First, you can make sure that your students obtain the appropriate school supplies by requiring that they tell their parents what materials they need, because you will not be able to call each of their parents individually each day to remind them what to bring. In many cases, teachers tell their students what to bring and assume that the students will do the rest on their own. However, this method may not be structured enough for some students, who, like Ronald, are likely to forget what you said; are not organized enough to write it down; or even when they write it down, cannot find it when they get home. Second, you can encourage students to write the information down rather than try to remember it. Having the information on the board or overhead helps ensure that their lists are accurate. You may also want to duplicate the list and distribute it to your students. Finally, encourage your students to ask themselves the following, or similar, questions, which can help them remember school supplies as well as assignments throughout the school year:

- What is due tomorrow in school?
- What do I need to do to get it done tonight?
- What materials or other things do I need to get the job done?
- Whom can I ask for help in doing this?

These questions can at first be posted on the board to help students remember them and to prompt their use. You can help motivate students to bring needed materials by providing positive recognition for those who do bring their supplies to school. For example, Mr. Gutierrez gave school pencils to students who had all their supplies in school. Ms. Habner put the names of her students on a "responsible students" list from which she chose people for classroom jobs. You may need to make adaptations for students with special needs. For example, students with physical

Cultural Awareness

Teachers with a multicultural perspective take into account that students from different cultural backgrounds might have different routines as well as different resources for addressing, structuring, and completing projects.

WWW Resources

TimeLiner is a program designed to help students organize information for research projects through a timeline. For more information, go to http://www.teachtsp.com.

Strategies for managing time and organizing materials help provide the structured routines that many students need to succeed in school. What are the three steps in teaching students how to use weekly assignment calendars?

Special Emphasis On . . .

Solving Higher-Level Mathematical Problems

This strategy was developed by Miles and Foircht (1995) for teaching higher-level math to students with learning disabilities or who have other math problems. The strategy is suitable for any students who have reached the abstract level of mathematics, such as algebra, calculus, and trigonometry. The strategy is designed to help you detect and correct errors and guide student problem solving rather than direct it. The strategy begins by giving students a mathematics problem. Students first copy the problem. Students then verbalize and write the mathematical steps. Verbalizing helps students detect and clarify errors without assistance. It also helps in concept formation or understanding the process and allows the teacher to assess the ability of the student. The teacher guides students by questioning their thought process: "How should we approach this?" "What should we do next?" (Miles & Foircht, 1995, p. 94). The teacher also questions and rephrases inappropriate responses. This questioning and rephrasing helps to clarify thought and to correct errors. When the problem is solved, students recall what they verbalized at each step, writing down and numbering in correct sequence the verbalizations on the lower half of the page. Students then place the number of the verbalization at the point within the problem where that step was taken. Students can use the resulting answer for reference, study, and review. An example answer sheet using the strategy to solve algebra problems is shown in Figure 10.4.

Cultural Awareness

African Americans, Hispanic Americans, and Native Americans may have a much more flexible attitude about being punctual (Grossman, 1995). These students can profit from an approach that teaches them the time management skills they need to survive in school and at work, while respecting their cultural differences.

disabilities may need a classmate or parent to bring their supplies into school. Students who live in poverty might be unable to afford supplies other than materials the school or teacher provides.

Besides having to organize their materials, students also need to organize their time, particularly as they get older and the demands made on their time increase. More schools are now teaching their students to use schedule books to help them arrange their time (Bryan & Sullivan-Burstein, 1997; Jenson, Sheridan, Olympia, & Andrews, 1994; Patton, 1994). You can teach your students to use a weekly schedule book in the following ways:

1. Teach students to differentiate between short- and long-term assignments. Short-term assignments are those that can be completed in 1 or 2 days and that take one or two steps to complete, such as reading a chapter in history and answering the questions at the end of the chapter. Long-term assignments take more than 2 days to complete and take more than two steps to get done. Writing a five-page report on a current event is an example of a long-term assignment. The difference between short- and long-term assignments can be taught readily to the whole class at once by giving them the definitions and teaching them to apply these definitions to a series of examples.

2. Teach students to task analyze long-term tasks. Start by modeling the task-analysis process of breaking long-term tasks into component tasks, estimating the amount of time it will take to perform each subtask, and then scheduling time to complete the subtasks in a schedule book. You can model this by distributing an already completed **task analysis** and timeline for your first several long-term assignments. Then, have students begin to develop their own task analyses, first under your guidance and, eventually, independently.

Figure 10.4 **Applying the Problem-Solving Strategy to Algebra**

Given 2X – 7 = 9, Solve for X

2X – 7 = 9

2X – 7 $\overset{①}{+}$ 7 = 9 + 7

2X $\overset{②}{=}$ 16

$\dfrac{2X}{2} \overset{③}{=} \dfrac{16}{2}$

X $\overset{④}{=}$ 8

1. To isolate 2X, – 7 must be removed. Add 7 to both sides of the equation.
2. Simplify what remains and combine like terms.
3. To isolate X, divide both sides by 2.
4. Simplify what remains.

S O U R C E : From "Mathematics Strategies for Secondary Students with Learning Disabilities or Mathematics Deficiencies: A Cognitive Approach," by D. D. Miles, and J. P. Forcht, 1995, *Intervention in School and Clinic, 31*(2), pp. 91–96. Copyright © 1995 by PRO-ED, Inc. Reprinted with permission.

3. Show students how to record information in their schedule books. Have students enter fixed activities or activities you do every week, occasional activities or activities that are different from week to week, and due dates for assignments. Students can also prioritize assignments; schedule time to work on assignments; and monitor assignment completion, including rescheduling or adding time to work on assignments.

Many schools have had success using schoolwide programs with a single system of keeping track of assignments in a schedule book used in every class. The consistency and repetition that are naturally a part of such a system seem to benefit students, including those with disabilities, many of whom are more successful when teachers stick to a daily routine. Students with special needs may require additional adaptations, however, such as having the classroom teacher check and/or initial their schedule book before they leave class. This step is particularly important when students are first learning to use a schedule book.

Connections

The self strategies covered in this chapter apply to academic learning. These same strategies are sometimes referred to as cognitive behavior management, which is discussed in Chapter 12.

How Can Students Learn to Use Strategies Independently?

Some students may have trouble using a learning strategy independently, even after they have learned how to do it. Their problem could be that they do not know when to use a strategy, or how to keep track of how well they are using it and change their behavior if necessary.

Four strategies that can help students perform tasks more independently are self-instruction, self-monitoring, self-questioning, and self-reinforcement. Like all learning strategies, these "self" strategies may need to be carefully taught using the teaching practices described in this chapter.

Self-Instruction

In **self-instruction,** learners are taught to use language to guide their performance. In essence, students are taught to talk themselves through a task. The idea is, if they can talk themselves through a task, they will not need help from anyone else. The first step needed to teach students self-instruction techniques is to explain that self-instruction involves giving yourself instructions on how to do a task. For example, self-instruction can be used to help get seatwork done or to remember to use a strategy for a multiple-choice test. Next, ask students to identify a situation that requires the use of a specific skill, such as getting their seatwork done in reading or taking a 10-minute science quiz on Friday. Demonstrate how to write down the steps needed to perform that task. For example, to get seatwork done, the student first decides how much effort to put into this task. Next, he or she decides what is supposed to be done. Finally, the student decides what the first step in completing the task should be, what the next step should be, and so forth, until the seatwork is done. When students are finished, they praise themselves for a job well done. Ask students to rehearse the steps through self-talk or peer review, going over all the steps involved in completing a seatwork task from beginning to end.

After you have demonstrated how to apply self-instruction, have the students practice in a role-play situation and give them feedback. In the seatwork task, for example, you could put a sample reading task on the screen using the overhead projector and demonstrate the steps by thinking out loud. The students could then practice in pairs and give each other feedback, with you monitoring and also giving feedback. Students could keep a chart or index card listing the task steps, which they should be encouraged to glance at periodically while performing the task.

Self-Monitoring

In **self-monitoring,** students watch and check themselves to make sure they have performed targeted behaviors. Self-monitoring is a critical aspect of independent learning because being independent often requires students to check their performance to see whether it is effective and make a change when a particular strategy is not working (Reid, 1996). Self-monitoring can also be a strong motivator for students by providing them concrete evidence of their progress. In teaching self-monitoring to your students, first explain to them that self-monitoring is a way that they can check their own behavior to make sure they are doing the right thing. Ask the students to identify a behavior or a learning strategy that they need to do in class. For example, students may select a behavior such as being on task or on time for classes, or they may choose a strategy such as the COPS proofreading strategy described earlier in the chapter.

The next step is to select a practical and expedient way for students to measure the behavior. One possibility is to have them count on a card or pocket counter the number of times the behavior occurs. For example, Yashika recorded on an index card the number of her talkouts in reading class. Another possibility is to use a checklist to keep track of behaviors as they occur.

Research Note

McDougall and Brady (1998) taught fourth-grade students with and without disabilities self-monitoring skills in math. Students monitored their attention by asking themselves at regular points during the lecture whether they were paying attention. Students were reminded to check their attention by a prerecorded audio cue. Students monitored their math performance by graphing their scores on daily math fact quizzes. Results showed that students' time on task and math fact performance were greatly improved and that the improvements in math fact performance generalized to a math word problem task.

Teach students to use the measurement system through demonstration, practice, and feedback, and continue to encourage and reinforce the use of self-monitoring in your class. Self-monitoring can be applied to any learning strategy. Two self-monitoring strategies from the research literature are described in the Professional Edge on page 386.

Self-Questioning

Self-questioning is a form of self-instruction in which students guide their performance by asking themselves questions. The idea behind self-questioning is that if students can guide their own behavior by asking themselves questions, then they will not always need a teacher or other adult present to perform. In teaching students self-questioning, have them first identify the behaviors, duties, or tasks that are required in class. For example, students can identify steps needed to proofread a writing paper, such as checking the correct use of capital letters, punctuation, spelling, and appearance. Have students write these tasks in question form, for example, Have I capitalized all words correctly? Have I used the right punctuation marks in the right places? Have I spelled all the words correctly? Is my paper neat?

As in self-monitoring, the next step is to select a practical and expedient way for students to measure the behavior, such as recording behaviors as they occur using a checklist. Students might practice self-questioning in pairs for feedback. Other practical measures include keeping task questions on index cards and putting them in a convenient place. For example, students might put the proofreading questions on an index card and tape it to the inside cover of their notebooks.

Self-Reinforcement

As the term implies, **self-reinforcement** occurs when students reward themselves for behaving appropriately or achieving success in learning tasks. An important part of being an independent learner is recognizing when you have done a good job. As discussed before, students with special needs often attribute their success to factors other than their own efforts, such as luck. Teaching self-reinforcement is an effective way of helping students replace negative attributions with more positive ones. Students need to be coached to use self-reinforcement by praising or rewarding themselves explicitly for doing something right or being successful academically. The first step is to have students set a particular goal for themselves, such as getting all their homework in on time, getting all their seatwork done, being on time for class, taking accurate and complete notes during a lecture, studying for a test, or reading a book. Allow students to decide when and how they can reinforce themselves. For example, younger students might give themselves a star or sticker each time they beat their highest score on a math facts timed test. Older students might give themselves a point for each day they completed their homework. If they have four points by the end of the week, they could go out to lunch with a friend. Self-praise is also a good way of rewarding progress toward personal goals.

Practice setting goals, acknowledging when a goal has been attained, and using different kinds of self-reinforcement. You will want to model for students how self-reinforcement works by demonstrating how you set goals for yourself, knowing when you have reached a goal, and reinforcing yourself for reaching the goal. For example, Mr. Hughes explained to his class that he needs to work on getting his lawn cut on

Cultural Awareness

Family and home supports can play an important role in student management of time and resources, but teachers cannot assume that these supports exist or are understood. Communicating information about independent learning skills and explaining expectations can lead to effective family involvement.

Connections

Reinforcement and related behavioral principles are explored further in Chapter 12.

Check Your Learning

How can students learn to initiate the use of strategies on their own?

Professional Edge

Increasing Student Independence by Having Students Monitor Their Own In-Class and Homework Assignments

Self-monitoring is an important part of being a motivated, independent learner. Here are two research-based self-monitoring strategies that help students with special needs complete assignments either in class or as homework. The first strategy works for any assignment while the second helps students monitor their performance in math.

PACE 1, 2 . . . (Rademacher, 2000) is a self-checking process that can help both students and teachers evaluate finished assignments against a set of precise standards. PACE refers to four standard requirements that can be applied when evaluating the quality of all assignments: "**P**rompt (on time), **A**rranged neatly (no stray marks, even margins, well organized, and pleasing to the reader's eyes); **C**omplete (all directions followed, all questions answered); and **E**dited (mechanics correct, ideas clear, content accurate)" (Rademacher, 2000, p. 153). The "1, 2 . . ." refers to any number of possible additional assignments that go along with a given assignment. For example, teachers may require that students attach all their computations to their answer sheet in math or include the outline they worked from when writing their paper.

When students are using PACE 1, 2 . . . , they write the letters **PACE** along with several numbers, depending on additional requirements, in a designated place on the assignment. Next to each of the numbers, students write down a word or two to indicate the additional requirements specified by the teacher as part of the grading criteria. Under each standard letter and number, students draw two short lines. After students finish the assignment, they place a check mark or zero on the top line to show whether they met the requirements for the assignment. The second line is for the teacher to judge, also with a check mark or a zero, whether the re-

Figure 10.5 The PACE 1, 2 . . . Evaluation Guidelines

How to Use PACE 1, 2 . . . on Completed Assignments

P	A	C	E	1	(7 entries & date)

				2	(3 statements per entry)

				3	(1 good & 1 bad thing)

Note: The student marks the first line below each letter and number. The teacher marks the second line.

SOURCE: "Involving Students in Assignment Evaluation," by J. A. Rademacher, 2000, *Intervention in School and Clinic, 35*(3), pp. 151–156. Copyright © 2000 by PRO-ED, Inc. Reprinted with permission.

time. Each time he cuts the lawn and has to rake up only one bag of grass clippings or less (his measure of lawn length is the longer the lawn, the more grass to rake), he treats himself to a milkshake at the local ice cream shop. Mr. Hughes also praises himself for saving time and effort each time he cuts the lawn and has little grass to rake up.

As students get older, they are expected to learn at home, at school, and in the workplace with less support. They are also expected to set goals for themselves and take independent actions to meet those goals. For some students, being an independent learner does not come naturally. These students need to be taught directly independent learning and self-advocacy skills. They also need to be taught how to apply those skills in school and in real-world settings with minimal support.

quirements for the assignment have been met. Of course, prior to using PACE, you need to provide students with clear definitions of the standards, including a range of positive and negative examples related to quality work. You also need to carefully teach students how to apply the PACE process using the techniques for teaching learning strategies described earlier in this chapter. An example of how the PACE self-monitoring system is used is shown in Figure 10.5.

Rankin and Reid (1995) developed a self-monitoring program for independent work in math. In their program students follow eight steps:

1. Work a problem.
2. Ask myself, Do I think my answer is correct?
3. Check for accuracy.
4. Mark the square on the tally sheet with an *X*.
5. Make corrections, if necessary.
6. Continue until all the problems are worked.
7. Count the number of *Xs* and write the number by the day's barbell.
8. Graph the number.

A sample student self-monitoring sheet is shown in Figure 10.6.

Figure 10.6 HB's Self-Monitoring Record Sheet

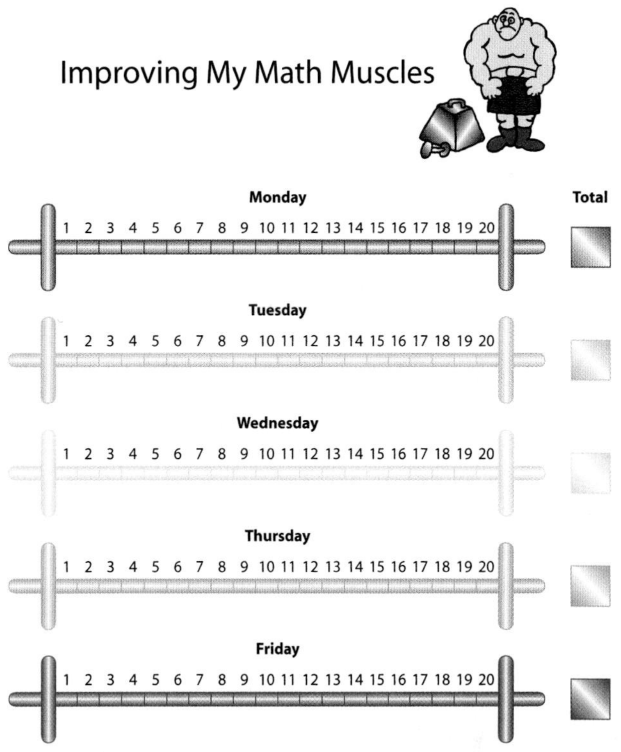

Improving My Math Muscles

Monday
1 2 3 4 5 6 7 8 9 10 11 12 13 14 15 16 17 18 19 20

Tuesday
1 2 3 4 5 6 7 8 9 10 11 12 13 14 15 16 17 18 19 20

Wednesday
1 2 3 4 5 6 7 8 9 10 11 12 13 14 15 16 17 18 19 20

Thursday
1 2 3 4 5 6 7 8 9 10 11 12 13 14 15 16 17 18 19 20

Friday
1 2 3 4 5 6 7 8 9 10 11 12 13 14 15 16 17 18 19 20

Total

SOURCE: "The SM Rap—Or, Here's the Rap on Self-Monitoring," by J. L. Rankin and R. Reid, 1995, *Intervention in School and Clinic, 30*(3), pp. 181–188. Copyright © 1995 by PRO-ED, Inc. Reprinted with permission.

Summary

General education teachers can help all their students, including students with special needs, become independent learners. One way teachers can build student independence is to encourage student self-awareness and self-advocacy.

Another way to help your students become more independent is to design and teach effective learning strategies in class. Effective learning strategies can be developed by identifying skills that are problematic for most of your students, specifying relevant student outcomes, and listing a set of specific steps students need to follow to reach the identified outcomes; these steps should be brief (no more than eight) and encased in a mnemonic device. They should also cue students to perform thinking, doing, and self-evaluating behaviors. Methods of teaching learning strategies to students include assessing current strategy use, clarifying expectations, demonstrating and modeling strategy use, encouraging students to memorize strategy steps, providing guided and independent practice, and administering posttests.

Many strategies that can help students become independent learners are available. Reading strategies include SCUBA-D, SCROL, PARS, CAPS, and POSSE. The reciprocal teaching technique provides teacher and peer models of effective thinking behaviors and then allows students to practice these behaviors with their peers. Some note taking strategies are the five *R*'s of note taking (record, reduce, recite, reflect, and review), CALL UP, ANOTES, and the three *R*'s prelistening strategy (review, read, relate). POWER (planning, organizing, writing, editing, and revising) is a writing strategy that helps students organize themselves to carry out all the steps in the writing process through the use of self-questioning, graphic organizers, and peer editing.

Other strategies for written expression include TAG, COPS, SLOW CaPS, and DEFENDS. Additional strategies for written expression involve the use of technology. These include using the Internet, the SCAN strategy for revising sentences, and CHECK. Strategies for problem solving in math are FASTDRAW, LAMPS, SLOBS, and FOIL. Students also need to learn strategies for managing their time and resources.

Four strategies that can help students learn to use strategies independently are self-instruction, self-monitoring, self-questioning, and self-reinforcement. In self-instruction, students are taught to use language to guide their performance. In self-monitoring, students watch and check themselves to make sure that they have performed targeted behaviors. Self-questioning is a form of instruction in which students guide their performance by asking themselves questions. Self-reinforcement occurs when students reward themselves for behaving appropriately or making progress in learning.

Applications in Teaching Practice

Designing Strategies for Independence

Latasha is a student who has a moderate hearing loss. Although her hearing aid helps, she still has to depend a lot on speech reading to communicate. She also speaks slowly and has trouble saying high-frequency sounds such as *sh* and *t*. Latasha has a poor self-image and is reluctant to interact with her peers and teachers. Design a self-advocacy program for Latasha.

Questions

1. What skills would you teach Latasha to use for self-advocacy?
2. How would you get Latasha to use these skills in your class and in other school and out-of-school situations?

Cal is a student with organizational problems; he is chronically late for class and rarely finishes his homework. Design an organizational strategy for Cal using the guidelines for developing strategies covered in this chapter.

Questions

1. How would you teach the organizational strategy you have designed using the guidelines covered in this chapter for effectively teaching a learning strategy?
2. How would you teach Cal to apply the strategy independently using self-instruction? Self-monitoring? Self-questioning? Self-reinforcement?

Questions

1. Is there anything you would change about the strategy? How would you teach the strategy using the six steps described in this chapter?
2. How would you help students apply the strategy independently using the four "self" strategies discussed in this chapter?

11

Evaluating Student Learning

■ Mr. Stevens is a high school earth science teacher. One of his students, Stan, has a learning disability that causes him to have trouble reading textbooks. Stan also has difficulty figuring out multiple-choice test questions, the kind that Mr. Stevens uses on his exams and quizzes. Stan says that he knows the material but just needs more time to take the tests because he reads slowly. During the past marking period, Mr. Stevens gave four multiple-choice tests, each worth 20 percent of the final grade. Scores on homework assignments counted for the remaining 20 percent. Stan earned a grade of B on his homework, but he had two D's, one C, and one F on the tests. Mr. Stevens assigned him a grade of D for the marking period. Mr. Stevens felt this was a fair grade because most of Stan's peers scored much higher on the tests. Mr. Stevens is also committed to keeping his reputation as a teacher with high standards. When Stan received his grade for the marking period, he asked his parents why he should work so hard when he couldn't seem to get good grades anyway. Stan's parents felt that he had improved during the last marking period but that his grade did not show it. They were afraid that Stan would stop trying and eventually drop out of school. What are the issues here? What could Mr. Stevens do to help Stan?

■ Jennifer is in Ms. Robinson's third-grade class. She has a hearing impairment and has some trouble in reading but is doing well in Ms. Robinson's literature-based reading program. Ms. Robinson is pleased with her progress and has given her an A in reading for the first two grading periods. Recently, Jennifer's parents became very upset when they learned that Jennifer was reading only at the first-grade level according to district standardized tests. They wondered how she could have done so poorly on the standardized tests when she has been bringing home A's on her report card. What would you tell Jennifer's parents if she were in your class? How could you change your grading procedures to prevent communication problems like this from occurring?

■ Lucille is a student with a mild cognitive disability who is in Ms. Henry's fourth-grade math class. On the basis of her current performance in math, which is at the first-grade level, Lucille's IEP team set math goals for her in the areas of basic addition and subtraction. The rest of the class is working on more difficult material based on the fourth-grade math curriculum. Lucille's IEP objective for the second marking period was to compute in writing within 20 minutes 20 two-digit by two-digit addition problems with regrouping with 80 percent accuracy. She received direct instruction on these problems from Mr. Brook, her special education teacher, who was co-teaching with Ms. Henry. As a result, she met her goal for the marking period. How should Ms. Henry grade Lucille? School policy mandates letter grades.

One of a teacher's major jobs is to evaluate the educational progress of students. The information collected during evaluation activities can indicate whether teaching has been effective and can help teachers alter instruction as needed. Classroom evaluations also are helpful in giving students (and their parents) an idea of how well they are performing in school, and they can be used by principals and school boards to evaluate the effectiveness of their schools.

Even though evaluation activities are very important, the ways in which students are evaluated most frequently—testing and grading—can be problematic for students with disabilities, their teachers, and their parents. For example, Stan and his earth science teacher have a problem because Stan's test scores more often reflect his learning disability than his knowledge of earth science. Jennifer's teacher has a problem in communicating the meaning of Jennifer's grades to her parents. She graded Jennifer based on her progress and her effort in class. Jennifer's parents, however, thought she was being graded in comparison with her peers and therefore expected their daughter to be performing at or above grade level, not below. Lucille's teacher needs to give Lucille a grade even though she has different curricular goals than the other students in the class. As you work with students with disabilities or special needs, you will experience these and other challenges in evaluating their learning. In this chapter, you learn a number of ways to solve these problems.

How Can Classroom Tests Be Adapted for Students with Special Needs?

Connections

How do the topics in this chapter fit into the INCLUDE framework presented in Chapter 4?

Although testing has always been a major part of U.S. education, the recent emphasis on school reform, with its dominant theme of raising educational standards, promises to make educators rely even more on tests in the future (Thurlow, Ysseldyke, & Silverstein, 1995). This increasing emphasis on test performance accompanies concerns about the test performance of students with disabilities. As described in the vignette about Stan at the beginning of this chapter, testing can be a very trying experience for many of these students and their families.

Most important in testing students with disabilities is ensuring that test results reflect their knowledge and skills, not their disabilities. Fortunately, classroom tests can be adapted in ways that help you test students with disabilities fairly and with a reasonable amount of accuracy. As shown in Table 11.1, adaptations can be made in three contexts: before the test, during test administration, and after the test during

Table 11.1 Examples of Testing Adaptations

Before the Test	During the Test	After the Test
Study guides	Alternative forms of response	Change letter or number grades
Practice test	Alternative means of response	Change grading criteria
Teaching test-taking skills	Alternative sites	Use alternatives to number and letter grades
Modified test construction	Direct assistance	
Individual tutoring	Extra time	

grading procedures. Many of these adaptations can also benefit students who do not have disabilities.

Adaptations before the Test

You can do a number of things before the test to help students with disabilities. First, you can prepare a study guide that tells students what to study for the test. A study guide can help students avoid wasting valuable time studying everything indiscriminately and instead help them concentrate on the most important information. Study guides can also assist students with memory problems by focusing their efforts on only the most critical material. Second, you can give a practice test. This test can clarify your test expectations and also benefits the class by familiarizing students with the test format. Practice tests are also helpful to students who have trouble following directions or for those who are anxious about taking tests and often fail to cope immediately with an unfamiliar test format. Finally, many students with disabilities also benefit from tutoring before tests. Tutoring can be offered before or after school and carried out by peer tutors or paraprofessionals. Tutors can provide guidelines for what to study or help directly with particularly difficult content.

Teaching test-taking skills. Another option is to teach students **test-taking skills.** Students may need a number of test-taking skills, including ones for studying for tests, for taking objective tests, and for writing essay tests. At first, you might start working with students on test-taking strategies by helping them analyze the kinds of mistakes they usually make on tests. They can then use a test-taking strategy that fits their particular problem. For example, Bill and his teacher looked over his history tests for the last grading period and noticed that most of the questions he missed were taken from class lectures rather than the textbook. Bill begins to check his notes after class with one of his classmates, a "study buddy," to make sure he does not miss any main ideas. He also decides to spend more time studying his notes before the test.

Eric, on the other hand, notices that he tends to choose the first response (a) on multiple-choice tests and that he is not reading the other answer choices carefully. His teacher suggests that he read each choice carefully before responding and put a check next to each answer as a way of making sure he has read each choice.

FYI

Planning your tests and test adaptations at the beginning of instruction helps you clarify what is essential to teach and achieve a good match between your tests and instruction.

Connections

Strategies for developing and using study guides appear in Chapter 9.

Students can help each other prepare effectively for tests using directly taught study strategies. What strategies might these students be using to prepare for an upcoming test?

WWW Resources

Searching for information about testing, grading, or other topics related to inclusion? Just ask Jeeves. Enter a question about the topic you are searching for and Jeeves will direct you to the appropriate sites or ask you questions to help you narrow down your search. Locate Jeeves at http://www.askjeeves.com/.

WWW Resources

The website at http://www.iss.stthomas.edu/studyguides/index.html provides study guides as well as strategies for preparing for and taking tests. The site provides study skills resources including several links to study skills guides and interactive tutorials.

When studying for tests, students often are required to remember a lot of material. This can be difficult for students with learning or cognitive disabilities, who may have memory problems. Students can benefit from strategies that help them remember important content for tests. For example, Greg uses a memorization technique called **chunking.** After he studies a chapter in his text, he tries to recall five to seven key ideas. These key thoughts help trigger his recall of more significant details. After reading a chapter about the life of Harriet Tubman, for example, he remembers information in chunks—her *early years,* her experiences with the *underground railroad,* and so on. These general ideas help him remember details such as when she was born and how many slaves she helped to free.

Mnemonic devices also can help students remember information for tests. **Mnemonics** impose an order on information to be remembered using poems, rhymes, jingles, or images to aid memory. For example, Mr. Charles wants his class to remember the six methods of scientific investigation. He tells the students to think of the word *chrome* (Cermak, 1976). The following six steps make up the **CHROME** strategy:

C *Categorization*
H *Hypothesis*
R *Reasoning*
O *Observation*
M *Measurement*
E *Experimentation*

Another mnemonic device that can help students remember definitions and factual information is called the keyword method (Mastropieri, 1988). The **keyword method** uses visual imagery to make material more meaningful to students and hence easier to remember. First, a vocabulary word or fact is changed into a word that sounds similar and is easy to picture. For example, to help remember that the explorer Hernando de Soto came from Spain, students were shown the picture in Figure 11.1, a bull (to symbolize Spain) at a counter sipping a soda (the keyword for de Soto) (Carney, Levin, & Levin, 1993). When students are asked to name an explorer who came from Spain, they are told to think of the keyword for de Soto. Next, they are told to think back to the picture the keyword was in and remember what was happening in the picture. Finally, they are told to answer the question. (So who was an explorer from Spain?)

Many students do poorly on tests because they do not study for tests systematically. Teach students to organize their materials so that they avoid wasting time searching for such items as notes for a particular class or the answers to textbook exercises. Making random checks of students' notebooks is one way to find out how well organized they are. For example, Ms. Barber stresses note taking in her fifth-grade social studies class. Every Friday afternoon, she checks the notebooks of five students in her class. She gives students bonus points if they have notes for each day and if their notes are legible and include key information. Also, teach students strategies for how to process material when they are studying. For example, Ms. Treacher shows her third graders a verbal **rehearsal strategy** for learning spelling words. She demonstrates how she says the word, spells it out loud three times, covers the word, writes the word, and then compares her spelling to the correct spelling. Mr. Jacobs shows his class how they can summarize text and class material

FYI

The keyword method recommended here for learning vocabulary is not to be confused with the key word strategy for teaching students to solve math story problems referred to in the Professional Edge on pages 378–379 in Chapter 10.

Figure 11.1 **Keyword for De Soto**

SOURCE: From "Mnemonic Strategies: Instructional Techniques Worth Remembering," by R. N. Carney, M. E. Levin, and J.R. Levin, 1993, *Teaching Exceptional Children, 25*(4), p. 27. Reprinted by permission of the Council for Exceptional Children.

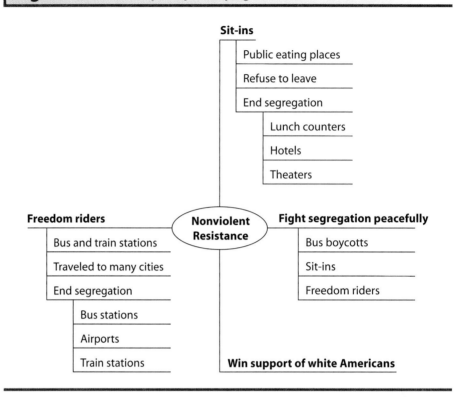

Figure 11.2 Concept Map: Studying for Tests

on the topic of nonviolent resistance using a concept map such as the one shown in Figure 11.2. Another effective rehearsal strategy is for students to ask themselves questions about the most important information to be learned.

Teaching test-taking strategies. Many students, including those with special needs, do not test well because they lack strategies for taking the actual tests. For example, Sal rarely finishes tests in science because he spends too much time on questions that he finds difficult. Laura has trouble with true–false questions because she does not pay attention to key words such as *always, never, usually,* and *sometimes.* Lewis's answers to essay questions contain much irrelevant information and do not focus on what the questions are asking. The Professional Edge on pages 398–399 offers suggestions for teaching students strategies for taking objective tests.

Students also need strategies for taking essay tests. Performing well on essay tests requires that students know the content covered; can follow directions, including identifying and understanding key words; and can organize their ideas. All these areas can be problematic for students with disabilities. The following suggestions might prove helpful to students taking essay tests:

1. Read over the entire exam before you begin. If you have memorized information related to specific questions, jot it down before you write your answer.

2. Look for key instructional words in the questions to help you determine how to structure your answer and determine what information to include. For ex-

Cultural Awareness

Research shows that improving students' test-taking skills, including those of African American, Hispanic, and Native American students, and students who are poor, improves their scores on tests. From 5 to 14 hours of instruction spread over 5 to 7 weeks appears to be the range of time needed to improve students' "test wiseness" (Grossman, 1995). Strategies for teaching "test wiseness" and other independent learning skills are covered later in this chapter.

ample, you would include different information and use a different structure if you were asked to *list* the reasons for the American Revolution versus *discuss* them.

3. Organize your answers. A rule of thumb in answering essay questions is that you should spend at least one-fourth of your time planning what you are going to write.

4. Leave time to proofread your answers for clarity, legibility, spelling, and grammar.

5. When writing an answer, leave margins and do not write on the back of the paper. If your writing is large, write on every other line. Leaving some extra space makes the exam easier for the teacher to grade.

6. If you do not have time to write an answer, write your outline for the answer. Often, teachers give you a substantial amount of credit if they can see that you knew the information and simply did not have time to write the answer.

Adaptations in Test Construction

All students benefit from tests that are written clearly and assess pertinent knowledge or skills. Thus, everything that you have learned about writing good tests in your teacher education program applies here. Still, test items can be well written but constructed in a way that results in problems for students with special needs. For example, Carmen has difficulty reading tests that are visually cluttered. She might benefit from triple spacing between test items and extra space between lines. Juan scores poorly on tests because he is unable to read many of the words used in the items; the items contain complex sentences with many words that are above his reading level and that his teacher did not use while teaching. Consider, for example, the following item taken from a social studies test:

Circle the answer that best fits in the blank.

A country in southern Europe, which is on the Mediterranean Sea, _____ has a capital city by the name of Athens.

a. Greece
b. Italy
c. Poland
d. Croatia

This item could be written much more simply and still test the same information.

Circle the answer that best fits in the blank.

The southern European country whose capital is Athens is _____.

a. Greece
b. Italy
c. Poland
d. Croatia

A student with a reading problem may answer the first question incorrectly because of its awkward wording, not because he or she did not know the answer.

In essay-test construction, several adaptations might benefit students with problems in reading and written expression. For students with reading problems,

Connections

You can design your own test-taking strategies using the guidelines for learning strategies presented in Chapter 10.

Connections

Rewrite or adapt the strategies for taking essay tests as an illustrated handout for younger students who are expected to write one or two complete paragraphs in response to a question. Which key words would you teach younger students to help them answer appropriately?

Cultural Awareness

Strategies to prevent cultural bias on classroom and standardized tests are covered in Chapter 8.

Professional Edge

Teaching Strategies for Taking Objective Tests

Many students flounder when taking tests because they do not approach tests in any organized way. You can help your students approach their objective tests more systematically by teaching them the strategies described here. The following six rules for responding to multiple-choice and true-false items are based on a comprehensive review of the research literature.

1. Respond to the test maker's intention. Answers to test questions should take into account the way material is treated in class. For example, Rob had this item on his social studies test:

> During the occupation of Boston, the British received their most severe losses at Bunker Hill.
> True
> False

Even though Rob learned at a recent trip to the museum that the Battle of Bunker Hill was actually fought on Breed's Hill, his teacher had not brought up this point in class. Therefore, Rob responded by circling *true*.

2. Anticipate the answer. Before students attempt to answer the question, they should fully understand its meaning. Therefore, they should try to figure out the answer before they read the possible answers. For example, Armand was answering the following multiple-choice item:

> What does an astronomer study?
> a. plants
> b. music
> c. history
> d. stars

After he read the question, Armand thought about the word *astronomy* and what his teacher had talked about in class, such as the fact that astronomers use telescopes and that they look at stars and planets. He then read all the possible choices and circled *d, stars*, as the correct answer.

3. Consider all alternatives. Many students with special needs, such as students with learning disabilities, tend to answer too quickly, choosing the first available choice. Students should be encouraged to read all the choices before responding. Students can monitor their behavior by putting a check mark next to each choice after they have read it.

4. Use logical reasoning strategies to eliminate unlikely answers. Even if students do not know the

W W W Resources

For tips on writing tests, go to http://www. gradebook.org/.

highlight key words such as *analyze*, *compare–contrast*, *describe*, and *list*. You can also give students a form to complete to help them organize their responses. For example, this question was used on a science test:

> Compare and contrast plant and animal cells by describing three ways they are alike and three ways they are different.

The following **response format** might aid students in writing an answer:

Ways that plant and animal cells are alike
1.
2.
3.

Ways that plant and animal cells are different
1.
2.
3.

answer to a question, they can improve their chances of getting it right by using what knowledge they do have to eliminate unlikely choices. For example, Dolores read the following item: In which country would it be impossible to use a sled in the winter?

a. Guatemala
b. Canada
c. Zimbabwe
d. Norway

Dolores did not know the geographical locations of Guatemala or Zimbabwe, but she did know that Canada and Norway were countries where it snowed often. She then took a guess between *a* and *c*, and chose *a*, the correct answer. By eliminating two of the items, she improved her chance of getting the question right by 25 percent.

5. Use time wisely. As already mentioned, a frequent test-taking problem is failing to budget time. Some students spend so much time on some items that they have little time left for others. While taking tests, students should check the time periodically to make sure they have enough time left to answer the remaining questions. You can assist students by writing the time remaining on the chalkboard several times during the testing period. Students also can be taught to estimate the amount of time they should spend on each question. For example, if students are taking a 100-item test in a 50-minute period, they should figure on spending no more than one-half minute per question. After 25 minutes, they can then check to see that they have completed at least 50 items. Finally, teach students to spend more time on items on which they have at least partial knowledge and less time on questions for which they have no knowledge.

6. Guess, if all else fails. Most tests do not have a penalty for guessing. On standardized tests especially, tell your students that if they do not answer a question, they have no chance of getting it right, but if they guess, they have a 50 percent chance of getting true-false questions right and a 25 percent chance of getting most multiple-choice questions right.

SOURCE: From "Are Learning Disabled Students 'Test-Wise'? A Review of Recent Research," by T. Scruggs and M. Mastropieri, 1988, *Learning Disabilities Focus, 3*(2), pp. 87–97.

Other practical ways of constructing objective tests that allow you to measure student knowledge more accurately are shown in the Professional Edge on pages 402–403. Note that if changes in test construction are intended for the whole class, they can be incorporated into the original master before duplicating. When changes are intended only for one or two students, you can make them as students take the test. For example, Ms. Minter's co-teacher, Ms. James, blackened two of the four choices on Barry's multiple-choice items and changed a matching question from 12 items to three groups of 4 items each. For another student, she underlined key words in each question and changed several completion questions to true–false items.

Adaptations Involving Test Administration

The ways that tests are given to students with disabilities can also affect the accuracy of the results. Students who, like Stan, have reading comprehension problems might do better on tests if given more time to finish them or if permitted to take them orally. Students with written expression problems might benefit from a dictionary or

FYI

Another consideration in constructing tests is to arrange test items in chronological order to match the sequence of instruction.

Connections

Issues of fairness and other topics concerning student relations are taken up in more detail in Chapter 13.

a handheld spell checker or by dictating their answers. Seating students with attention problems near you when they take a test might help them stay on task longer. The test administration adaptations shown in the Professional Edge on pages 404–405 are grouped according to students' areas of difficulty.

As the Professional Edge shows, students might also benefit from the use of an alternative **test site,** such as a resource room. For example, testing in the resource room might help students with attention problems (by allowing them to take their tests in a setting with fewer distractions) and students with written language problems (by permitting them to answer test questions orally). Changing the test site also protects students who are taking the test in a different way from being embarrassed. However, before sending a student out of class to take a test, you should first try other options.

For example, Ms. Edwards allows her students to choose whether to have a test read to them. Those who do not want the test read aloud can work independently while she reads the test to the rest of the students. She also gives the students to whom she reads the test more help with directions and the meaning of key vocabulary or difficult questions. Mr. Collins and Ms. Klein are co-teaching. Mr. Collins supervises the students taking the test silently while Ms. Klein reads the test to a group of students. If you do find it necessary to send a student out to take a test, be sure to coordinate your plans in advance with the special education teacher to avoid scheduling problems.

Alternative Test-Grading Procedures

You may also need to adapt the ways you grade student tests. For example, because Matt has a learning disability, he has trouble remembering large amounts of information for tests. This memory problem has affected Matt's test scores, which so far include two F's and one D. Matt's teacher, in collaboration with the special education teacher and Matt's parents, identifies the most important information in the chapter and tells Matt to study that for the test. When Matt takes the test, he answers only the 15 questions that his teacher marked with an asterisk, which test the key information he was told to study. The rest of the class answers 30 questions, the 15 that Matt answers plus 15 more covering other material in the chapter. Out of his 15 questions, Matt gets 13 correct. In deciding how to grade Matt, the teacher considers three grading options: changing student grades, changing the grading criteria, and using alternatives to traditional letters and numbers.

You can change student grades with written comments or symbols, or by giving multiple grades. These options can help clarify what a grade means. In Matt's case, his teacher could give him a B on the test, but with an asterisk meaning that the test covered a different amount of content than that of the rest of the class. Giving multiple grades can be helpful on tests that require written responses. For example, on an English test, Jacinto is required to write an essay on the character of Boo Radley in the novel *To Kill a Mockingbird.* When his teacher grades his essay, she assigns him one grade based on the quality of his analysis of the character and another grade for writing mechanics.

A second option is to change the **grading criteria,** or the standard on which the grade is based. For example, Matt's teacher could give him a grade of B by basing his grade on a different standard: 15 questions rather than 30. You may also want to base a student's grade on the percentage correct of the items tried instead of on the total number of questions. This alteration may help students who work accurately but slowly. Giving partial credit is another possible option. For example, when Ms. Jordan grades student answers to math story problems, she gives students points for underlining key words in the question and setting up the equation correctly. These extra points can motivate students who are improving but do not increase their test scores significantly. Students can also be allowed to retake tests. They can then be graded using their score on the retake or averaging their original score with their retake score.

A third grading option you may want to try is using alternatives to letter and number grades, such as pass/fail grades and checklists of skill competencies. For example, Matt could be given a grade of P (pass), because he mastered 7 of 10 key concepts in the chapter, or rated on a **competency checklist** showing which key concepts in the chapter he learned.

WWW Resources

A website index of education-focused discussion groups where you can discuss testing, grading, and many other educational issues is available at http://edweb.gsn.org/lists.html.

How Can Report Card Grades Be Adapted for Students with Special Needs?

Report card grading is perhaps the most prevalent and controversial evaluation option used in schools. The practice of grading by letters and percentages began in the early 20th century, a time of great faith in the ability of educational measures to assess students' current levels of learning accurately and also predict future levels of learning. High grades were seen as a sign of accomplishment, intended to spur students on to greater achievements. Those who received low grades were either placed in basic-level or special classes or were encouraged to join the workforce (Cohen, 1983).

Times certainly have changed. Laws have been passed guaranteeing that our evaluations do not discriminate on the basis of disability, race, or ethnicity. These laws also

Modifications of report card grades for students with disabilities and other students with special needs must be carefully explained to prevent misunderstandings. What grading modifications might these people be discussing?

Professional Edge

Modifications in Test Construction for Students with Disabilities

All of your students will do better on clearly written tests that ask questions pertaining specifically to the material covered in class and in the textbook. But your students with disabilities especially require well-phrased and visually accessible tests if they are to succeed at test taking. The following modifications, although beneficial to all your students, can be crucial for your students with special needs.

1. Tests should be typewritten and photocopied.

2. Make tests visually uncluttered by leaving sufficient space between items (triple space) and between lines of items ($1\frac{1}{2}$ spaces). Do not crowd pages with items; keep wide margins.

3. Use symmetrical spacing. For multiple-choice tests, align possible responses vertically rather than horizontally, and type the question and possible responses on the same page. Permit students to circle the letter of the correct answer rather than write it in front of the item.

4. Provide additional spacing between different types of test questions. Provide separate directions and a sample item for each type of test question.

5. For completion, short-answer, and essay questions, leave sufficient space to write the answer. Students do not do as well when they must continue their answers on the back of the page or on the next page.

6. Leave space for students to answer on the test rather than using machine scoring or answer sheets. Some students have difficulty transferring answers from one page to another.

7. For students who have difficulty with multiple-choice questions, reduce the number of possible answers. Students might choose the correct answer from three, for example, rather than from four or five possible responses.

8. For students who read slowly and for students who have organizational problems, avoid the following constructions in matching items: long matching lists—keep lists to five or six items and group by concepts; lengthy items; and drawing lines to the correct answer, which can be confusing for students with visual–motor problems (Wood, Miederhoff, & Ulschmid, 1989). Lists with 10 to 15 entries in the first column can be

guarantee an appropriate education for all students, not just those who can succeed with minimal intervention. Furthermore, our ability to compete in the emerging global economy depends on better educational outcomes for *all* our citizens, not just a privileged few. These changes have led to new demands that go beyond the relatively simple matter of identifying "good" and "poor" students. For example, how can evaluations be modified to ensure that they do not discriminate against students with disabilities? How can they be used to motivate students to stay in school, to communicate educational competence and progress to parents and students, and to guide our teaching as we strive to meet the needs of an increasingly diverse student body? Although answers to these questions are beginning to emerge, in large part we continue to use a grading system that was intended to fulfill a purpose much more narrow in scope.

The use of traditional letter and number grades has caused problems for teachers, who must communicate with many audiences, including parents, students, administrators, and legislators. These audiences often are looking for information that is not readily communicated using a single number or letter (Munk & Bursuck,

simplified by preselecting three to four choices from the second column for each item in the first column. Record the selected choices beside the item in the first column and have the student select the correct answer from the smaller pool. Consider the following example.

Match the definition on the left with the word on the right by writing the letter for the word in the blank next to the definition.

1. in a sudden way ____	a. brightness
2. not able ____	b. visitor
3. to make bright ____	c. suddenly
4. one who visits ____	d. happiness
5. in a happy way ____	e. rearrange
6. to tell again ____	f. brighten
7. to arrange beforehand ____	g. retell
8. state of being happy ____	h. prearrange
9. to arrange again ____	i. unable
10. state of being bright ____	j. happily

These questions will be less confusing for your students with disabilities if you modify them using the guidelines just described:

1. in a sudden way ____	a. brightness
	b. visitor
	c. suddenly
	d. retell
2. to make bright ____	a. happily
	b. unable
	c. brighten

9. Change fill-in-the-blank items to a multiple-choice format, providing three or four choices for the blank. Students select the correct answer only from the choices given. This modification changes the task from one of recall (memory) to one of recognition.

10. For essay questions, review the questions, key words, and tasks with students individually and help students develop answer outlines. Permit dictated or taped responses when appropriate.

11. Consider color coding, underlining, enlarging, or highlighting key words and mathematical symbols.

SOURCE: Adapted from *Accommodations for Secondary Learning Disabled/Mainstreamed Students on Teacher-Made Tests*, by J. N. Williams, 1986, unpublished manuscript, Wheaton, MD: Wheaton High School.

2001a). For example, students may be interested in how much progress they have made, whereas their parents want to know how their children compare to their classmates as well as to children nationwide. Principals, on the other hand, may need to provide college admissions offices with indicators of student potential to do college work. Teachers also are increasingly left with many conflicting concerns about grading, including upholding the school's standards, maintaining integrity with other teachers, being honest with students, justifying grades with other students, motivating students for better future performance, communicating accurately to the students' next teacher, and avoiding the reputation of being an "easy" teacher (Rojewski, Pollard, & Meers, 1992; Vasa, 1981).

Increased inclusion in schools has put even more burdens on grading systems. As illustrated in the vignettes at the beginning of the chapter, grading can present serious challenges for students with disabilities and their teachers. Stan was not a good test taker, yet 80 percent of his report card grade in earth science was based on his test performance. He was concerned that his grade did not accurately reflect his

Cultural Awareness

What do grades mean in the United States? How are grades used and to what ends? How do values about grades in the national culture affect students with special needs?

Professional Edge

Adaptations in Administering Classroom Tests

Even a well-constructed test can fail to measure the knowledge of students with disabilities accurately if it is inappropriately administered. The adaptations you make in administering tests to students who have special needs depends on the students' area of difficulty. Use the following chart to help you decide which modifications to try with students with disabilities included in your class.

	AREA OF DIFFICULTY				
Adaptation	**Reading**	**Writing**	**Listening**	**Speaking**	**Organizing; Paying Attention**
Oral explanations of directions	X				X
Repetition of directions; student repetition of directions	X		X		X
Oral, taped, or dictated test; oral clarification of written answers by student	X	X			X
Written versus oral test; written versus oral directions			X	X	
Extra time	X	X		X	
Time checks during test					X
Segmented test with separate directions for each section	X		X		X
Peer or other assistance:					
to read directions	X				
to check comprehension	X				
to check spelling		X			

Cultural Awareness

In what ways might grading systems be unfair? Which student groups would be affected the most? What provisions do school districts make for evaluating students who are culturally different or whose first language is not English?

effort or progress in class. Jennifer's parents were surprised to find that their daughter had received A's in reading all year but was reading below grade level on a recent standardized achievement test. Lucille was working on math skills that were more basic than those the rest of the class covered, and her teacher was unsure how to grade her performance.

Despite these problems, a number of reasons support the continued use of grades. First, many parents want to see how their children compare to other students, and they demand grades. In addition, grades are efficient and can make decision making easier, particularly for schools making decisions about promotion to the next grade level and for colleges and universities making admissions decisions (Vasa, 1981). Despite their many limitations, therefore, grades are likely to be used by

	AREA OF DIFFICULTY				
Adaptation	**Reading**	**Writing**	**Listening**	**Speaking**	**Organizing; Paying Attention**
Technological aids:					
placemarks or markers	X				X
word processor		X			
tape recorder	X	X		X	
Visual aids and cues; verbal and visual prompts for word retrieval			X	X	
Use of outlines, diagrams, charts, tables, and webs to organize or answer	X	X			X
Permitted use of noncursive writing		X			
Use of previously prepared notes or rehearsed answers				X	
Alternative sites:					
to minimize noise/distraction			X		X
for alternative testing	X	X			
Seating proximity to teacher			X		X
Teacher paraphrase or summary of student answers in complete thoughts				X	
Checklist for materials needed and preparation					X
Allowing answering directly on test rather than answer sheet		X			

S O U R C E : Adapted from *Accommodations for Secondary Learning Disabled/Mainstreamed Students on Teacher-Made Tests*, by J. N. Williams, 1986, unpublished manuscript, Wheaton, MD: Wheaton High School.

teachers and schools for many years to come. Teachers need to recognize the limitations of certain types of grades, however, and adapt grading systems to ensure they are fair to all students. As summarized in Table 11.2, grades can be adapted by changing grading criteria, making changes to letter and number grades, and using alternatives to letter and number grades.

Changes in Grading Criteria

One way to adapt report card grades is to change the criteria on which they are based. Teachers often consider a number of factors when assigning student grades, including in-class work or seatwork, homework, ability, attendance, class participation,

Table 11.2 Examples of Grading Adaptations

Adaptation	Description	Example
Change Grading Criteria		
A. Vary grading weights.	**A.** Vary how much certain criteria (activities or products) count toward a grade.	**A.** Increase credit for participation in in-class group activities and decrease credit for essay exams.
B. Modify curricular expectations.	**B.** Identify individualized curriculum on which to base grade.	**B.** Write on student's IEP that she will be graded on work on addition while rest of class works on fractions.
C. Use contracts and modified course syllabi.	**C.** Teacher and student agree on quality, quantity, and timelines for specified work.	**C.** Written contract states that student will receive an "A" for completing all assignments at 80% accuracy, attending all classes, and completing one extra-credit report.
D. Grade on the basis of improvement.	**D.** Assign extra points for improvement over previous performance.	**D.** Change a "C" to a "B" if student's total points were significantly higher than previous marking period.
Changes to Letter and Number Grades		
E. Add written comments.	**E.** Add comments to clarify details on criteria used to determine the letter grade.	**E.** Write on report card that student's grade reflects performance on a modified program and not on regular classroom curriculum.
F. Add information from student activity log.	**F.** Keep written anecdotal notes indicating student performance in specific areas over time.	**F.** State on student's report card that while student's grade was the same this quarter, daily records indicate student completed math assignments with less teacher assistance.
G. Add information from portfolios and/or performance-based assessment.	**G.** Collect student work that measures effort, progress, and achievement.	**G.** State on student's report card that student's written language showed an increase in word variety, sentence length, and quality of ideas.
Use Alternatives to Letter and Number Grades		
H. Use pass/fail grades.	**H.** Give student a "pass" if he or she meets the minimum requirements for the class.	**H.** Give student a pass for completing 80% of daily work with at least 65% accuracy, and attending at least 90% of classes.
I. Use competency checklists.	**I.** Construct a list of goals and objectives for the quarter.	**I.** Attach a checklist to report card indicating that during last quarter, student mastered addition facts, 2-digit addition with regrouping, and counting change to $1.00.

S O U R C E : From "Report Card Grading Adaptations for Students with Disabilities: Types and Acceptability," by D. Munk and W. D. Bursuck, 1998, *Intervention in School and Clinic, 33*(5), pp. 306–308. Reprinted by permission of Council for Learning Disabilities.

effort, attitude, reports or papers, extracurricular work, preparedness, organization, notebooks, and progress (Bursuck et al., 1996). One common adaptation is to vary the grading weights of requirements in terms of how much each one counts toward the final grade. In the case of Stan, for example, his teacher counted tests as 80 percent of the grade and homework as 20 percent. Mr. Stevens could help Stan by reducing the percentage he counts for tests from 80 to 60 percent and giving Stan more credit for other accomplishments, such as being prepared, attempting all class activities, and participating in class. Grading students in areas such as effort should be based on the same objective standards that you use to measure the learning of academic content. In Stan's case, Mr. Stevens could define effort as the percentage of school days for which Stan has his materials for class, completes his homework, and asks at least one question in class.

Another way to adapt grading criteria is to base student performance on **modified curricular expectations.** Expectations such as these are reflected in IEP goals and objectives, behavioral contracts, or course syllabi. For example, the vignette at the beginning of this chapter stated that Lucille's IEP contained a modified curriculum in math. Whereas the rest of the class was working on decimals, she was working on two-digit by two-digit addition problems with regrouping. Because her IEP objective was to score 80 percent or better when given 20 of these problems, her fourth-grade teacher and special education teacher agreed to give her an A if she met her objective, a B if she scored between 70 and 80 percent, a C if she scored between 60 and 70 percent, and so forth. To ensure that Lucille's parents had an accurate picture of her standing in relation to her peers, Lucille's teacher included a written comment on Lucille's report card indicating that her grade was based on different curricular expectations.

Grading criteria can also be adapted through the use of **grading contracts** or **modified course syllabi.** Both these adaptations help ensure that grading modifications are clearly defined, based on objective criteria, and explained to the student and his or her parents. A grading contract is an agreement between the classroom teacher and the student about the quality, quantity, and timelines required to obtain a specific grade (Hess, 1987). Hess (1987) provides an example of a grading contract:

- If student comes to class regularly, turns in all the required work that is completed with _____ percent accuracy, and does one extra credit assignment/project, he or she will receive an A.
- If student comes to class regularly and turns in all the required work with _____ percent accuracy, he or she will receive a B.
- If student comes to class regularly and turns in all the required work, he or she will receive a C.
- If student comes to class regularly and turns in 80 percent of the required work, he or she will receive a D.
- If student does not come to class regularly and turns in less than 80 percent of the required work, he or she will receive an F.

In a modified course syllabus, you and the IEP team state the specific course requirements, expectations, grading criteria, and any other changes required because of the student's disability.

Teachers can also base grades on the amount of improvement students make. **Improvement grades** can be incorporated into a traditional grading system by

Connections

How might the strategy of grading on the basis of improvement help Stan and his parents, whom you read about at the beginning of the chapter?

assigning extra points for improvement or by moving students up a grade on the scale if they improve, particularly if they are on the border between grades. A high C, for example, could be changed to a B if the student's test average or total points for the marking period were much higher than those of the previous marking period. Consider the case of Aretha, whose average on spelling tests for the last marking period is 77 percent, an improvement of more than 40 percentage points over the preceding marking period. Although her true grade for spelling is a C, her teacher raises her grade to a B– because she has improved so much. Another student, Roberto, read five trade books this marking period as compared with one book the period before. Although most students in the class have read more books at more difficult levels, Roberto still receives a grade of O (outstanding) in reading because he read so many more books than before. His teacher notes on his report card that the books Roberto read were 1 to 2 years below grade level.

Changes to Letter and Number Grades

Number and letter grades can be clarified by supplementing them with other ways of evaluating and reporting student progress, such as written or verbal comments, logs of student activities, and portfolios. Written or verbal comments can be used to clarify areas such as student ability levels as compared with peers and the extent of student effort. For example, Roberto's teacher gave him an O (outstanding) in reading but commented on his report card that the books he read were below grade level. Such comments about student ability levels can prevent misunderstandings.

FYI

Teacher interviews consistently reveal that graphs documenting student progress are far more understandable to students than are numerical averages of scores over an entire semester (Gersten, Vaughn, & Brengelman, 1996).

In the case of Jennifer in the chapter-opening vignette, Jennifer's mother thought her daughter's high grade in reading meant that she was reading at grade level. An explanation on Jennifer's report card would have put her grade in context. But keep in mind a word of caution as you make report card comments denoting student ability levels. Students sometimes compare report cards with their classmates and might be embarrassed by comments that indicate they are working below grade level. To prevent this situation, you might use an alternative procedure, such as talking to parents or sending them a separate note of clarification. In addition, report card comments should never state that the student is receiving special services; this would be a violation of student confidentiality.

Cultural Awareness

Many metropolitan school districts provide teachers the service of having testing information translated into languages as diverse as Chinese, Korean, Tagalog, or Arabic.

Finally, the basis for arriving at number or letter grades on report cards is often not clear. For example, does the grade represent student performance in comparison with his or her classmates, or is it based on the student's progress toward meeting objectives on his or her IEP? Failure to clarify the bases for grades can lead to communication problems with parents, as shown in the Case in Practice.

Because report card grades are primarily summaries of student performance, they provide little information about student performance over a period of time. You can use **daily activity logs** of student activities and achievement to provide ongoing information for students and their parents. Daily observations of students can be recorded in a notebook or journal, or directly on a calendar. One system uses self-sticking notes to record daily observations of students (Einhorn, Hagen, Johnson, Wujek, & Hoffman, 1991).

WWW Resources

For a listserv that carries messages on a range of topics relevant to inclusive education, go to http://www.jiscmail.ac.uk/lists/inclusive-education.html.

Whatever type of daily activity log used, entries should at least include the date, student's name, classroom activity, and a brief description of the observation. For example, Ms. Parks was concerned about the progress of one of her students, Carrie, in the area of word identification skills. Each day during an hour-long literature class,

C A S E   I N   P R A C T I C E

Explaining Grades

Jose is a student in Ms. Wittrup's fourth-grade class. When Ms. Diaz, Jose's grandmother, received Jose's most recent report card, she had some questions and made an appointment to see Ms. Wittrup and Ms. Talbot, Jose's special education teacher.

Ms. Wittrup: Ms. Diaz and Jose, I'm so glad you came in today. Ms. Diaz, I understand you have some questions about Jose's report card.

Ms. Diaz: Thank you for taking the time to see me. Yes, I do have some questions about Jose's report card. First of all, I noticed that Jose got a B in reading. This is an area where he's getting help in special education. Does this mean he doesn't need any more help?

Ms. Talbot: Jose's IEP objective for the first grading period was to read fluently and comprehend literature books that are at the second-grade reading level. His word-identification skills in that material are good, but he is still having some trouble with comprehension. Sometimes he

has trouble summarizing what he has just read; other times he has a hard time answering questions that I ask him. That is why he received a B rather than an A. I think Jose has a good chance of meeting this objective by the end of this marking period. Still, he is pretty far behind his fourth-grade classmates, so I think he needs to keep getting help from me.

Ms. Diaz: I think I understand better what his reading grade means, but I don't understand how Jose got only a C in math. He has always done better in math than in reading. Has he been fooling around in class and not paying attention?

Ms. Wittrup: No, Jose has been working hard in math. Jose doesn't have any special needs in math so he is in the regular program. As you can see from looking at my grade book, Jose scored an average of 75 percent on his math tests. His average for homework and in-class work was 80 percent. His overall average for the marking period was 78 percent, which is a C.

Ms. Diaz: Is there something I can do to help Jose with his math so that maybe he can get a B next time?

Ms. Wittrup: One thing that hurts Jose on his tests is that he is still making careless mistakes on basic math facts, particularly the multiplication facts. If you could help him with these at home, I think Jose might be able to pull his grade up to a B.

Ms. Talbot: We're very proud of Jose for getting an A in social studies. Remember we had all agreed that because Jose had reading problems we would let him use a taped text and take his tests orally. Well, Ms. Wittrup told me that Jose had an average of 95 percent on the two tests, which is an A. Good for Jose!

R E F L E C T I O N S

Ms. Diaz had a difficult time understanding what Jose's grades meant. What could Jose's teachers have done to prevent this confusion from occurring? Jose received a grade of A in social studies because he was allowed to use a taped textbook and to take the tests orally. How would you explain this adaptation to a concerned student who took the test without any of these supports and received only a C?

Ms. Parks observed how Carrie approached the trade books she was reading. One day she recorded that Carrie spontaneously used the beginning letter sound *r* to sound out the word *rabbit*. Entries can be collected and summarized periodically for evaluations.

Information taken from the logs can be summarized periodically. These summaries can then be shared with parents as often as necessary to clarify student grades. For example, Leroy receives a D in math for the marking period. His parents call Leroy's teacher to set up a conference to discuss the grade and find out how Leroy can improve. Leroy's teacher shares a log summary indicating that Leroy did not follow along while she was demonstrating solutions to math problems on the chalkboard. Leroy's teacher and parents set up a contract for Leroy that encourages him to attend to such demonstrations.

Adding written comments to report card grades also enables you to communicate clearly to your students exactly what they need to do to improve in your class. This is important for students with special needs, who are less likely to be able to evaluate their performance and set goals for themselves based on grades alone (Gersten, Vaughn, & Brengelman, 1996). One large school district in Canada uses computer-generated report card templates and a large database of teacher comments to personalize their report cards by providing more prescriptive information for their students (Bailey & McTighe, 1996). An adaptation of a progress report from this district is shown in Figure 11.3.

Note the presence of two key pieces of information: a clear statement of what the student needs to do to improve his English grade and specification of the important content and/or requirements for each class. Note also that the student's level of effort is evaluated. Although giving students credit for trying can be helpful for students with special needs (Bursuck et al., 1996), effort is much more difficult to assess than academic progress (Gersten et al., 1996). We suggest that great care be taken in assessing measures of effort. For example, Ms. Mosely defined excellent effort in her class as not having any unexcused absences from class, completing all homework and in-class assignments on time, and answering a question in class at least 3 days per week.

Check Your Learning

What are the three options for adapting report card grades for students with special needs? What are some specific strategies for each option? What are the advantages and disadvantages of each strategy?

Alternatives to Letter and Number Grades

The most common alternatives to letter or number grades are pass/fail, credit/no credit grades, and checklists of competencies and skills. In **pass/fail** or **credit/no credit grading systems,** a list of minimum understandings or skills for a class is determined by the general education teacher in consultation with the special education teacher. These minimums may or may not relate specifically to a student's IEP. A grade of pass or credit is assigned if the identified understandings and skills are successfully mastered. No letter grades are given.

The major advantage of this alternative is that it relieves the teacher of the responsibility of grading students based on peer comparisons. Grades based on peer comparisons can be discouraging for students who try hard but do not have the ability to compete on an equal basis. Another advantage of pass/fail and credit/no credit systems is that the student knows what is expected and works toward a goal. A disadvantage of pass/fail grades is that their "all-or-nothing" nature puts a lot of pressure on the teacher, particularly in situations where minimum standards are not well defined. It is important, therefore, to be as specific as possible in setting your minimum standards. Hess (1987) provides an example of pass/fail requirements developed for a U.S. history course that has the necessary specificity:

1. Be in attendance and on time for 90 percent of all class periods each semester.

2. Complete 75 percent of the daily work with at least 60 percent accuracy.

3. Complete a class project (with peer assistance if necessary), earning at least 60 percent of the available points.

4. Participate in class discussions at least once per week and attend all small-group project meetings held in class.

5. Score 60 percent or better on all weekly and semester tests.

Figure 11.3 Personalized Grade Report

In English 10, the class has just completed a unit on poetry that focused on developing an appreciation and understanding of this literary form. Students continue to use exploratory writing to respond to literature read in class. Mander failed to complete two assignments worth 25% collectively this term. This has significantly affected his overall mark. Mander can improve his performance by ensuring assignments are completed and handed in on time.	

Mark to Date	70
Previous Mark	80
Effort	
excellent	
satisfactory	✓
needs improvement	
Periods Absent Since Beginning of Course	4
Periods Late Since Beginning of Course	6

This term Mander has studied the basic skills of algebra. In particular, he has studied units on the operations of polynomials, equation solving, and factoring polynomials. Class time is used wisely. He organizes work effectively. He aims for excellence. Keep up the good work, Mander!	

Mark to Date	90
Previous Mark	75
Effort	
excellent	✓
satisfactory	
needs improvement	
Periods Absent Since Beginning of Course	None
Periods Late Since Beginning of Course	None

SOURCE: Adapted from "Reporting Achievement at the Secondary Level: What and How," by J. Bailey and J. McTighe, in T. Guskey (ed.), *ASCD Year Book: 1996, Communicating Student Learning* (pp. 199–140), Alexandria, Virginia: Association for Supervision and Curriculum Development.

In using competency checklists, the general education teacher lists the goals and objectives of a given course and then checks off the objectives as they are achieved or mastered by the student (Hess, 1987). A key advantage of checklists is that they contain more detailed information about student performance than do grades, which makes them potentially more valuable to students, parents, and future employers. Checklists have several disadvantages, however. They may be time-consuming for teachers to keep up to date; the tasks and objectives may not be

WWW Resources

Find out about testing and grading policies being used around the country by visiting the website of the Council of Chief State School Officers (CCSSO), at http://www.ccsso.org.

Special Emphasis On . . .

A Systematic Way of Adapting Report Card Grades for Middle School Students with Disabilities Using Personalized Grading Plans

Report card grading for students with disabilities in general education classes can be problematic for teachers, students, and parents. Studies show that a majority of included students with high-incidence disabilities receive low or failing grades, a potentially serious barrier to student motivation (Donahue & Zigmond, 1990). Grades also often fail to communicate useful information about student strengths, needs, and progress, in large part because of poor collaboration between parents and teachers in establishing grading purposes, setting grading criteria, and determining grades (Munk & Bursuck, 2001a). In addition, a clear connection between instructional and curricular adaptations and grades is often not established (Schumm & Vaughn, 1995). General education teachers may also feel pressure to pass included students with disabilities, and view adaptations as "watering down" curriculum and teacher expectations (Carpenter, Grantham, & Handister, 1983).

Munk and Bursuck (2001b) have developed a systematic approach to grading included students with disabilities that involves the development of personalized grading plans (PGP). The PGP process stresses collaboration; establishes, in advance, agreed-upon purposes for grading; and links grading adaptations to existing curricular and instructional adaptations. The process involves a number of key steps before, during, and after a meeting at which a student's personalized grading plan is written. These steps, briefly outlined, follow.

Steps in the PGP Process

Before the Collaborative Meeting
1. A facilitator or facilitators for the process is identified.
2. The team (parents and teachers) identifies purposes for grading.
3. Teachers complete worksheet listing all classroom demands and grading criteria for each type of assignment/product.
4. The team describes all curricular and instructional adaptations currently in use.

understood by parents; and they tend to focus on student weaknesses unless care is taken to state objectives in positive terms. The Special Emphasis On . . . features a system for matching students with disabilities to the most appropriate card grading adaptation.

How Can Performance-Based Assessment Benefit Students with Special Needs?

Ms. Johnson has just completed a unit on persuasive writing and has her students write letters to the editor of a local newspaper, trying to persuade readers to support

5. The facilitator summarizes information (may transfer to poster board or sheets).

At the Collaborative Meeting
1. The team proceeds only when all teachers, parents, and student are present.
2. The facilitator presents a visual display of collected information and prepares blank spaces to record ideas for grading adaptations and details to be included in the PGP.
3. The facilitator leads the team through a discussion of the following:
   a. Specific characteristics of student's disability (for example, affects reading, organization)
   b. Description of demands and grading criteria in the class
   c. Pinpointing how disability interacts with classroom demands to cause low performance and potential for low grade
   d. Discussion of how current instructional and curricular adaptations enhance performance and grade
   e. Discussion of whether grading adaptations are warranted and desired
   f. Review of potential grading adaptations

g. Selection of specific adaptation(s) and listing of responsibilities for all team members.

After the Collaborative Meeting
1. Facilitators review sheets from meeting and write PGP that includes the following:
   a. Purpose(s) for grade as determined by team
   b. Description of current curricular and instructional adaptations used in class
   c. Detailed description of grading adaptation(s) to be implemented
   d. Detailed description of each team member's responsibilities in implementation of the PGP
   e. Schedule and method for monitoring effects of the PGP
   f. Signature lines for all team members

Munk and Bursuck (2001b) used the PGP process in a middle school with students with learning disabilities. They found that the process increased parent involvement and that teachers and parents were generally pleased with the PGP process. All the students involved said they tried harder as a result of their PGPs, and were more satisfied with their grades, even though they did not all receive a higher grade as a result of the process.

the building of a new county facility for elderly people. Mr. Repp has been teaching drawing to scale as part of a map-reading unit and has his students make a map of the neighborhood that could be used by visitors from Japan. Ms. Overton's class is working on basic bookkeeping skills and she has her students plan a budget for a fund raiser to earn money to build a new jungle gym for the playground.

All these teachers are checking their students' progress with a method of evaluation called performance-based assessment. **Performance-based assessment** measures what students "can do with knowledge, rather than with the isolated specific bits of knowledge the student possesses" (Poteet, Choate, & Stewart, 1993, p. 5). Performance-based assessments measure learning processes rather than focusing only on learning products. They frequently involve using **authentic learning tasks,** or tasks that are presented within real-world contexts and lead to real-world outcomes. Mr. Repp could have asked his students to compute the mileage between several cities using a mileage key, a more traditional map-reading assignment. Instead, he has them create their own maps, within a real context, because he wants to see how well they can apply what they have learned to an actual problem. Not only does he evaluate their maps, but Mr. Repp also evaluates parts of the learning process, such as how well his students select and implement learning strategies and collaborate with their classmates during problem solving.

Using performance-based assessments can be very helpful for students with disabilities or other special needs who may be included in your classroom. Performance-based assessments can offer students options for demonstrating their knowledge that do not rely exclusively on reading and writing, areas that often impede the successful testing performance of students with disabilities. For example, Calvin, a student with reading problems who is in Mr. Repp's class, completed the map activity successfully but would have had trouble with a traditional paper-and-pencil test of the same material.

Performance-based tests also are not subject to the same time constraints as traditional tests. Time flexibility can benefit students who may need more time, such as students with reading fluency problems, or students who need to work for shorter time periods, such as students with attention deficit–hyperactivity disorder. Again, using the example of Mr. Repp's map-drawing activity, students had some time limits (they had to finish in 1 week) but did not have to do the entire project in one sitting.

Students with disabilities may also have particular difficulty making the connection between school tasks and tasks in the real world. Performance-based assessments can help them understand this connection, particularly if the assessment is followed up with instruction directly geared to skill applications. For example, Ms. Johnson, whose students were required to write letters to the editor, discovered that many of her students were unable to support their arguments directly with specific examples. She therefore spent some class time demonstrating to students how they could support their arguments and guiding them through several practice activities.

Cultural Awareness

Elliott (1998) reviewed the research on the use of performance assessments with students from different ethnic and cultural backgrounds and found mixed results; sometimes these students performed better on performance tests than traditional standardized tests, sometimes they did not. Elliott suggests that although of great potential value, performance tests should continue to be used along with, rather than as a substitute for, traditional standardized assessments.

Developing and Evaluating Tasks for Performance-Based Assessment

Performance-based assessments, like standardized tests and curriculum-based assessments, must be carefully designed and scored so that they can provide information that is helpful for instruction and that is viewed with credibility by parents, students, and administrators. A summary of a number of considerations in designing, administering, and scoring performance-based assessments (Wiggins, 1992) follows.

1. Choose learning outcomes that are not covered by your current classroom and standardized testing program. Traditional standardized and classroom tests are likely to assess student knowledge but to underassess the application of that knowledge. Therefore, choose **learning outcomes** for performance-based tests that stress how well students apply, analyze, or synthesize information. In choosing learning outcomes, try to think of the knowledge you cover as a tool for helping your students perform an important real-world function. For example, reading comprehension can be seen as a tool for reading an auto mechanics manual. Learning the steps in the scientific method can be seen as a tool for designing science experiments to test your own hypotheses. Identifying and using coins can be seen as a tool for making change at a supermarket checkout.

2. Design tasks within contexts that are meaningful for students. The tasks you pick should provoke student thought and interest. Wiggins (1992) suggests that a well-designed task engages students so much that they forget they are being evaluated. Tasks can be made more engaging by embedding them within a meaningful, motivating context. For example, Mr. Barnes wants to see how well his students apply the steps in the scientific method. He has one group of students interested in pop music design and carry out an experiment to see which of the four top radio stations plays the most music by female artists. Mr. Barnes also requires his students to summarize the results of their study and submit them to the editor of the school newspaper.

3. Clarify task expectations by giving students scoring standards and models of excellent performance during teaching. Although coming up with a specific solution to a performance-based task is always the student's responsibility, the goal of the task, as well as the standards on which it is based, should be clearly presented by the teacher. For example, in the music experiment in Mr. Barnes's class, the students were responsible for creating an experiment to see which station played the most music by female artists. However, the students were already familiar with characteristics of effective research design because Mr. Barnes discussed these in class and showed the students model research projects done by previous students.

4. Make testing conditions as authentic as possible. Standardized and traditional classroom tests require many constraints, such as time limits and limited access to references. In real life we have deadlines, but these deadlines rarely involve brief, artificial periods of time, such as having to perform within 45-minute periods. Instead, timelines for performance-based tests should be based on performance of similar tasks in the real world. For example, individuals training to be auto mechanics need to perform tasks based on time limits established by professional mechanics. Access to resources during performance-based tests is also generally not prohibited; in fact, it is encouraged. Imagine denying a lawyer access to case law books while he or she is constructing a defense for an upcoming case! Of course, students must be skillful enough to be able to absorb and apply these resource materials in a timely fashion.

5. Identify standards based on what is most important for doing an effective job. You must take great care in selecting the standards for judging performance-based assessments; a scoring system based on qualities that are widely agreed on can ensure that the results of your performance-based assessments are useful. Identify key areas of performance by consulting the research literature, colleagues, administrators, and parents. These areas can involve both the products of performance-based tests and the processes students perform in constructing these products. For example, effective performance in math problem solving might include (1) understanding the problem, (2) solving the problem, and (3) writing down the solution to the problem (Szetela & Nicol, 1992). Areas of importance in evaluating written expression might be story idea, organization–cohesion, and conventions–mechanics (Tindal & Marston, 1990).

6. Develop an accurate scoring system. For each performance area identified, establish well-defined levels of quality. For example, Step 2, *solving the problem*, in the preceding math problem example could be defined as consisting of the following five levels:

0 No attempt
1 Totally inappropriate plan
2 Partially correct procedure but with major fault
3 Substantially correct procedure with minor omission or procedural error
4 A plan that could lead to a correct solution with no arithmetic errors (Szetela & Nicol, 1992, p. 14)

In written expression, the area of *organization* could be defined as follows:

1 The writer has no paragraph structure. The main points are clearly separated from one another, and they come in a random order, as though the writer had not given any thought to what he or she intended to say before starting to write.
2 Paragraphs are present but lack a topic sentence; sentences within a paragraph are marginally related to each other.
3 Paragraphs are present and have some structure but are not well connected. The organization of this paper is standard and conventional. There is usually a one-paragraph introduction; three main points, each treated in one paragraph; and a conclusion that often seems tacked on or forced.
4 Paragraphs are present, topical structure and supporting detail are well developed, and concluding sentences are used.
5 The writer uses paragraphs that are intact not only in terms of sentences within them, but also in terms of the flow from one paragraph to the next. Structure is well developed; ideas are expressed systematically. This paper starts at a good point, has a sense of movement, gets somewhere, and then stops. (Tindal & Marston, 1990, p. 220)

For each level of quality identified, establish benchmarks or pieces of student work that exemplify each area of quality. For example, Figure 11.4 shows an exam-

---

Figure 11.4 Exemplar for Partially Correct Procedure with Major Fault

Problem
Samantha had $49. She got $20 more from her grandparents for her birthday. Samantha wants to buy a pair of used in-line skates, but she needs to keep $15 to pay for her brother's birthday present. How much can Samantha pay for the in-line skates?

Strategy
To find the answer to the problem, you must first find out how much money she has by adding $49, $20, and $15. That is how much money she can pay for the in-line skates.

$49 ◄— Money Samantha first had
+$20 ◄— Present from grandparents
+$15 ◄— Money set aside for brother's birthday
$84 ◄— Money Samantha can pay for in-line skates

ple of level 2, partially correct procedure but with major fault. In attempting to solve this math problem involving money, the student was partially correct in that she added the $20 present from Samantha's grandparents to the $49 that Samantha originally had. However, a major fault of the student's problem solving is that she misunderstood that the $15 for Samantha's brother's birthday present was not an additional amount of money but a part of the total amount Samantha already had. Therefore, the student's performance was rated as level 2, partially correct procedure but with major fault.

Because the evaluation of performance-based assessments can be quite subjective, try giving another person your level criteria and examples and having him or her score a sample of your products and then check for agreement. Also, prior to testing, make sure students "know the objective of the test (what is to be done), the conditions under which the task is to be performed (use of dictionaries, timed or untimed), and the criteria to evaluate the performance" (Poteet et al., 1993, p. 11).

Adapting Performance-Based Assessments for Students with Disabilities

As we have discussed, using performance-based assessments has many potential benefits for students with special needs. Nonetheless, you may still need to adapt performance-based tests for students with disabilities. For example, Gregory is a student with cerebral palsy in Mr. Repp's social studies class. Gregory has very little control over fine motor movements in his hands. As a result, he is unable to write or draw. Gregory would obviously need to have the drawing-to-scale map task adapted. One possible adaptation would be to have Gregory make an audiotape to accompany the map that would provide the Japanese visitors with a self-guided tour. Or consider Rhonda, a student with a learning disability who has difficulty expressing herself in writing. Rhonda is included in Ms. Johnson's class, which is writing letters to the editor as a way of practicing persuasive writing skills. As an adaptation, Ms. Johnson has Rhonda develop an oral editorial that is sent to the local public radio channel. In some cases, then, adaptations for performance-based tests can be made just as readily as adaptations for traditional tests.

Some students with special needs may have problems with performance-based tests that are more difficult to accommodate. For instance, students might have difficulty making the connection between school tasks and real-world tasks. You need to teach these students directly how to make those connections. For example, Ms. Riley's class is learning to compute subtraction problems. As a performance-based test, Ms. Riley has her class compare prices of various brands of the same products in the grocery store and compute price differences using subtraction. Cleo, a student in the class who has a mild cognitive disability, is unable to perform the task because he has never used subtraction as it applies to money or products in the grocery store. The next day in class, Ms. Riley includes examples of subtracting amounts of money in her daily instruction. She also includes story problems dealing with the subtraction of money, some of which involve grocery store products. This adaptation helps Cleo make the connection between money and the supermarket.

Students with special needs also lack important preskills that are necessary for problem solving. You need either to teach these preskills or to allow them to bypass the preskills altogether to carry out performance-based tasks. For example, Sam has

Cultural Awareness

Because teachers' evaluations of lower-income and non-European students can be prejudiced, performance-based assessments can be subject to bias. However, anecdotal evidence shows that when teachers follow specific scoring procedures, performance-based assessments provide much useful information about non-European students and students with limited English proficiency (Heath, 1993).

Research Note

Johnson (2000) studied whether the accommodation of reading state performance tests in math to students with reading disabilities affected the validity of the test results. She found that reading the test improved the scores of the students with reading disabilities, but not those without. Johnson concluded that reading the math questions to students with reading disabilities is a valid recommendation for performance tests in math.

a learning disability in math; he does not know basic math facts and as a result cannot get Ms. Riley's product comparisons correct. Ms. Riley allows him to perform the task with a calculator. She also requires that he spends 5 minutes per day using a computer-based math fact program until he learns basic math facts. Anna has visual disabilities; another student read to her the prices of the brands and she writes them down.

For students with more severe disabilities, you may need to modify or scale down performance-based tasks by using the guidelines for developing alternative assessments described in Chapter 8 and the environmental inventory process described in Chapter 9. For example, Derek has severe cognitive disabilities and lacks basic math skills other than simple number identification. Ms. Riley has Derek participate in the same task as the other students but has him perform an easier step. She has Derek pick groups of products that students are to compare. This task is more consistent with Derek's IEP goal of being able to classify similar objects, such as three kinds of cola or two types of bread.

Finally, students with special needs may have trouble meeting the problem-solving demands of performance-based tests. For example, Peter has attention deficits and approaches problems impulsively; he rushes to find an answer and fails to consider all the options. For Peter, performance-based tests are important because they give him the opportunity to learn critical problem-solving skills. Nonetheless, for students like Peter to succeed, performance-based tasks need to be modified and problem-solving skills need to be taught directly. For example, Mr. Kelsey's class is applying work they have done in computing areas and perimeters to the task of planning a garden. Before having students design their own gardens, Mr. Kelsey carefully demonstrates how he would design his. This demonstration is very helpful for students in the class, such as Peter, who are not natural problem solvers and need a model to guide them. Mr. Kelsey also scales down Peter's assignment, asking him to design only one section of a smaller garden.

As you can see, the use of performance-based tests with students with disabilities can be helpful, but it can also be problematic. For this reason, use performance-based tests in conjunction with other classroom-based and standardized tests.

As an alternative to pencil-and-paper tests, performance-based assessments allow students to demonstrate their knowledge and skills through application in real-world contexts. What are some ways to adapt performance-based assessments for students with special needs?

Connections

Review Chapters 8 and 9 for information on testing and teaching preskills.

Connections

Scaffolding (see Chapter 4) and learning strategies instruction (see Chapter 10) are good ways to support students as they learn to carry out performance-based tasks.

How Can Portfolio Assessment Benefit Students with Special Needs?

Another promising type of evaluation currently in use is **portfolio assessment.** A portfolio is "a purposeful collection of student work that exhibits the student's efforts, progress, and achievement in one or more areas. The collection must include student participation in selecting contents, the criteria for selection, the criteria for judging merit, and evidence of student self-reflection" (Paulson, Paulson, & Meyer, 1991, p. 60).

A portfolio collection typically contains the observable evidence or products of performance assessment, evidence that may or may not reflect authentic tasks (Poteet et al., 1993). Portfolios include many different sources of information, including anecdotal records, interviews, work samples, and scored samples such as curriculum-

Table 11.3 Examples of Portfolio Contents

Type of Portfolio Sample Contents

Reading	Audiotape of oral reading of selected passages
	Original story grammar map
	Transcript of story telling
	Log of books read with personal reactions, summaries, vocabulary
	Representative assignments; responses to pre- and postreading questions
	Favorite performance
	Journal entries including self-evaluation
Writing	Scrapbook of representative writing samples
	Selected prewriting activities
	Illustrations/diagrams for one piece
	Log or journal of writing ideas, vocabulary, semantic maps, compositions, evaluations
	Conference notes, observation narratives
	Student-selected best performance
	Self-evaluation checklists

based assessment probes. As an example, sources of information for language arts that can be placed into a portfolio are shown in Table 11.3.

Using Portfolios to Maximum Advantage

To use portfolios to maximum advantage, consider the following guidelines:

1. Developing a portfolio offers the student an opportunity to learn about learning. Therefore, the end product must contain information that shows that a student has engaged in self-reflection.
2. The portfolio is something that is done *by* the student, not *to* the student. Portfolio assessment offers a concrete way for students to learn to value their own work and, by extension, to value themselves as learners. Therefore, the student must be involved in selecting the pieces to be included.
3. The portfolio is separate and different from the student's cumulative folder. Scores and other cumulative folder information that are held in central depositories should be included in a portfolio only if they take on new meaning within the context of the other exhibits found there.
4. The portfolio must convey explicitly or implicitly the student's activities, for example, the rationale (purpose for forming the portfolio), intents (its goals), contents (the actual displays), standards (what is good and not-so-good performance), and judgments (what the contents reveal).

Cultural Awareness

Student-centered evaluation, a key component of portfolio assessment, is an important part of effective multicultural education. Student-centered evaluation strategies include self-evaluation questionnaires, interviews, student entries in journals and learning logs, and think alouds (Dean, Salend, & Taylor, 1994.)

Connections

The strategies discussed for scoring performance-based assessments also apply to evaluating student portfolios.

5. The portfolio may serve a different purpose during the year from the purpose it serves at the end of the year. Some material may be kept because it is instructional, such as partially finished work on problem areas. At the end of the year, however, the portfolio should contain only material that the student is willing to make public.

6. A portfolio may have multiple purposes, but these must not conflict. A student's personal goals and interests are reflected in his or her selection of materials, but information included may also reflect the interests of teachers, parents, or the district. One almost universal purpose of student portfolios is to show progress on the goals represented in the instructional program.

7. The portfolio should contain information that illustrates growth. There are many ways to demonstrate growth. The most obvious is by including a series of examples of actual school performance or other real-world performance-based activities that show how the student's skills have improved. Changes observed on interest inventories, on records of outside activities such as reading, or on attitude measures are other ways to illustrate a student's growth.

8. Finally, many of the skills and techniques that are involved in producing effective portfolios do not just happen by themselves. By way of support, students need models of portfolios as well as examples of how others develop and reflect upon portfolios. (Paulson et al., 1991, pp. 61–62)

Using Portfolios with Students with Special Needs

Portfolios can be very helpful for teachers working with students with disabilities. Portfolios can assist teachers in evaluating student progress and guiding instruction. For example, Ms. Pohl is interested in finding out whether the extra math practice sheets she is sending home with Robert are improving his scores on weekly math computation tests. She consults Robert's portfolio and finds that his performance has improved quite a bit over the last 2 months. Ms. Pohl tells Robert's parents of his progress. They agree to continue the extra practice for at least another month.

Portfolios also emphasize student products rather than tests and test scores. This emphasis benefits students with special needs, many of whom are poor test takers. It may also highlight student strengths better than traditional tests, which tend to have a narrow academic focus. For example, Leshonn's teacher uses portfolios to evaluate her social studies students. Leshonn has problems in reading and writing but has good artistic ability and excellent oral language skills. During the last marking period, his class studied the growth of suburban areas after World War II. Leshonn designed a scale model of Levittown, one of the first planned communities. He also developed a tape-recorded explanation to go with the model that explained the key features of the community. His performance on these projects was excellent and enabled him to raise his overall grade for the class because his scores on the two tests given during the marking period were low.

Finally, a key component of portfolio assessments is student self-evaluation. Students with special needs, who are often described as not being involved in their own learning, can benefit greatly from self-evaluations. For example, students might complete a self-assessment after they have finished a unit of instruction. This evaluation can then become a part of the student's portfolio (Einhorn et al., 1991).

The capabilities of portfolio assessment can be greatly expanded through the use of technology. A number of different ways that you can incorporate technology into your portfolio assessment program are shown in the Technology Notes feature.

You may have to make adaptations when using portfolios with students with special needs, particularly in selecting and evaluating portfolio pieces. For example, Jerome was asked to select an example of his "best" work in written expression for his portfolio. However, he was uncertain what "best" work meant: Was it a paper that he tried his hardest on? Was it a paper that was the hardest to write? Or was it one that he or his teacher liked best? Because he did not know, Jerome simply selected one paper at random. Similarly, when LaShonda was asked to evaluate her efforts to solve a word problem in math, all she could come up with was whether she had the correct answer. You need to teach students such as Jerome and LaShonda how to select and evaluate portfolio pieces.

Cole, Struyk, Kinder, Sheehan, and Kish (1997) suggest teaching students the **RICE** strategy to help them become meaningfully involved in the portfolio process.

R—*Rationale*
Why are you keeping this portfolio? What do you want to chronicle? What is the purpose of the portfolio?

I—*Identify goals*
What are the specific things that you want to work on?
Standards: How will you know when you have reached your goal? What will you look for in the samples in your portfolio? Are there any standards that are currently being used that you might apply or adapt?

C—*Contents*
What will you include in your portfolio to show your progress toward your goal (work samples, tests, etc.)? Will you include works in progress or only your best work? Will you include only specific class assignments or will you include "authentic" samples? Will you include self-evaluations of your samples? Will you note conditions in which the sample was collected—cooperative group, independent, paired project, etc.? Will you include evaluations by others—peers, teacher? Will you graph your own progress toward your goal?

E—*Evaluation*
How frequently will you evaluate your portfolio? With whom will you evaluate your portfolio—pair, cooperative group, teacher? How will you show the relationship of the materials in your portfolio? (p. 267).

Finally, although portfolios are potentially valuable evaluation tools, they are also relatively new tools; in many cases, clear guidelines for selecting and scoring portfolio contents have yet to be developed (Salvia & Ysseldyke, 1998). Therefore, if you are using portfolios to evaluate the progress of students with special needs, such as whether they are meeting their IEP objectives, use them as a supplement, not as an alternative, to other assessment and evaluation procedures such as testing, grading, and curriculum-based assessments.

Connections

Portfolios and performance-based tests can also be helpful in making the assessment decisions described in Chapter 8. However, portfolios should supplement, not supplant, standardized achievement, psychological, and curriculum-based measures.

[Technology Notes]

Computer-Based Portfolios

As we have discussed in this chapter, portfolios can be an effective means of evaluating the performance of students. Traditionally, the contents of students' portfolios have been confined mainly to pencil-and-paper products. However, organizing and accessing these products can be overwhelming, even for the most organized teachers. Aurbach has developed a computer-based portfolio program that makes portfolios more efficient and accessible. The program is called the Grady Profile Portfolio Assessment (Aurbach & Associates, 2001). The Grady Profile allows the user to build portfolios using student product media including sound, graphic, video, text, and even other computer programs. The Grady Profile also allows users to tailor their own evaluation criteria and create and print reports.

An example display of a card designed to catalog information is shown in Figure 11.5. Notice that this particular display presents information on student performance in oral reading. Using it, a teacher, parent, or student can listen to an oral reading sample, examine an evaluation of the sample based on a teacher-designed rubric, and then read teacher and/or student

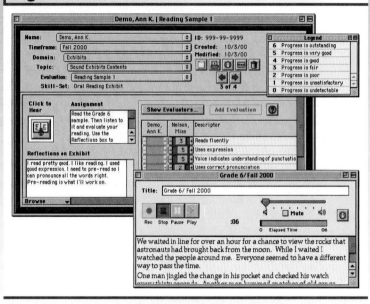

Figure 11.5 Sound Stack

Summary

As a teacher, you have a number of tools at your disposal for evaluating your students' progress, including tests, report card grades, performance-based assessments, and portfolios. Although each of these evaluation methods can also help you measure the progress of students with special needs included in your class, they may need to be adapted to ensure that the evaluation information measures the students' skill levels or content knowledge, not their disabilities or other special needs.

Testing adaptations can be made before testing, during testing, and after testing when tests are graded. Adaptations before the test include study guides, practice tests, tutoring, teaching test-taking skills and strategies, and modifying test construction. During the test, you can allow alternative forms of response, alternative means of response, alternative testing sites, extra time, and direct assistance. Adaptations after the test involve grading tests and include changing letter or number

reflections on the performance. Student progress can be readily appraised by accessing samples of oral reading behavior taken over a period of time.

A display of student writing performance is shown in Figure 11.6. A graphic exhibit of the student's writing was created by scanning a writing sample. As with the oral reading sample, a teacher evaluation of the sample is presented using a writing rubric. Stories written throughout the year can be accessed easily and compared to measure progress.

The Grady Profile is also capable of storing and displaying videotapes of students' work. For example, as part of an ecology unit, students could videorecord an interview with a local recycling company executive and then transfer the video to a video card. Students could record future interviews to see how their interviewing techniques had improved. Finally, electronic portfolios such as the one shown here can facilitate parent–teacher and teacher–student communication. You can show parents multimedia displays of their child's performance in class during parent conferences. In addition, electronic portfolios can motivate students who say they cannot do something by showing them tapes that illustrate how much they have improved.

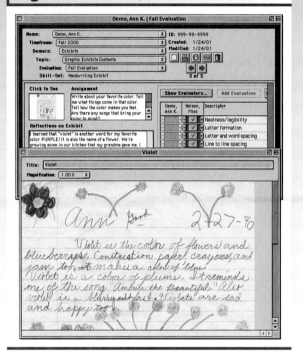

Figure 11.6 Graphic Stack

grades, using alternatives to letter and number grades, and changing the criteria on which grades are based.

Adaptations in report card grades involve changing the grading criteria, making changes to letter and number grades, and using alternatives to letter and number grades. Ways of changing grading criteria include varying grading weights, modifying curricular expectations, using grading contracts and modified course syllabi, and grading on the basis of improvement. Letter and number grades can be changed by supplementing them with other ways of evaluating and reporting student progress, such as written comments, daily activity logs, and recording daily observations. Alternatives to letter and number grades include pass/fail grades, credit/no credit systems, and competency checklists.

Performance-based assessments measure learning processes rather than focusing exclusively on learning products and they frequently involve authentic, or real-world, tasks. They can be helpful in evaluating the performance of students with special needs because they do not rely exclusively on formats that create problems for students with disabilities. These assessments are not subject to the same time constraints as traditional tests, often a problem for students with special needs, and they also help students see the connection between school work and real-world tasks. Performance-based assessments can be developed, administered, and scored according to several guidelines, such as choosing learning outcomes not covered by your current testing programs, designing tasks within meaningful contexts, clarifying task expectations by providing scoring standards and models of excellence, making testing conditions authentic, and designing a scoring system based on what is most important for effective performance. Performance-based tests may need to be adapted for students with special needs by scaling down the task, allowing students to bypass preskills, and teaching problem solving directly using performance-based tasks.

Portfolio assessment can also benefit students with special needs. Portfolios are collections of student work that exhibit student efforts and achievements. Portfolios typically contain the observable evidence or products of performance assessment, such as anecdotal records, interviews, work samples, and scored samples. Necessary features of portfolios include student participation in collecting the contents, criteria for judging merit, and evidence of student self-reflection. Portfolios can benefit students with special needs because they de-emphasize traditional tests and teach students critical self-evaluation skills. However, students with special needs may need to be taught how to select and evaluate their portfolio pieces.

Applications in Teaching Practice

Adapting Evaluations for Students with Special Needs

Eugene, Tara, and Jamie are students in your fourth-grade class. Eugene has been identified as having a specific learning disability. He has good study skills, but his problems in reading and written expression place him at a disadvantage when he takes tests. Failure on tests has increased his test anxiety; he often misses items he knows because when he is anxious during a test he tends to get careless.

Tara has a learning disability and receives intensive reading instruction in the resource room. Her short-term objectives for this marking period include reading a first-grade literature book at a rate of 20 words correct per minute with four or fewer errors per minute and discerning who the main character of the story is, what the main problem in the story is, and how the problem is solved.

Jamie is a student with mild cognitive disabilities. You are about to start a unit on adding and subtracting fractions. The IEP objective for Jamie is to identify the fractions $\frac{1}{4}$, $\frac{1}{3}$, and $\frac{1}{2}$.

Questions

1. What tests will you be giving in this class?
2. For one of these tests, what adaptations might you need to make for Eugene before testing? In constructing the test? In administering the test? In grading the test?

3. At the end of the marking period, should you give Tara a grade in reading? Why or why not? Assuming that Tara met her short-term objectives in reading, what do you think her grade for the marking period should be? Should her grade be adapted in any way?

4. Describe a performance-based test that you could use to measure Jamie's knowledge of her target fractions. How would you score this test? How could you use portfolio assessment to measure Jamie's progress on this unit?

12

Responding to Student Behavior

Learner Objectives

After you read this chapter, you will be able to

1. Outline strategies for promoting positive behavior and preventing misbehavior with groups of students, including students with special needs.

2. Explain simple techniques for responding to individual student misbehavior.

3. Outline systematic approaches for increasing students' positive behaviors and decreasing their negative behaviors.

4. Describe the purpose of a functional behavior assessment and its steps for deciding how to respond to chronic, inappropriate individual student behavior.

5. Identify how to help students manage their own behavior.

Key Terms and Concepts

Behavior contracts (p. 446)

Behavior intervention plan (BIP) (p. 459)

Cognitive behavior management (CBM) (p. 449)

Differential reinforcement of incompatible behaviors (p. 443)

Discipline (p. 428)

Extinction (p. 443)

Functional behavior assessment (p. 450)

Negative reinforcement (p. 440)

Overcorrection (p. 445)

Positive reinforcement (p. 440)

Presentation punishment (p. 445)

Removal punishment (p. 444)

Response cost (p. 444)

Surface behaviors (p. 437)

Time-out (p. 444)

Token economy (p. 433)

■ Joseph, a junior with a learning disability, comes late to his applied algebra class at least twice each week. He seldom participates in class discussions, and he does not ask questions. Unless Mrs. Akers repeatedly asks him not to, Joseph sits with his head down on his desk. When discussing Joseph with the special education teacher, Mrs. Akers describes his demeanor as sullen. Mrs. Akers has been teaching high school math for many years, and she believes that students have the responsibility to be interested in the subject, to attend class, and to participate. She knows that Joseph is heading toward a failing grade for this grading period, even though she thinks he could do the work with a little more effort. What is Joseph's responsibility for his learning? What is Mrs. Akers's responsibility for making instruction appealing to students like Joseph? What strategies could help Joseph meet Mrs. Akers's class expectations for him?

■ Katie has a moderate cognitive disability. Every time she enters the classroom she says loudly, "I'm ba-ack," even if she has only been gone for a moment. Although she is in sixth grade, she frequently sucks her thumb and rocks in her chair. When she needs help, she calls out, "Teacher, Teacher," regardless of what is happening in the classroom at that moment. If assistance is not immediate, she continues to call out—with increasing volume. Katie's language arts teacher, Mr. Lowell, is losing patience with these "babyish" behaviors. He believes that Katie is learning many social skills through the small-group work the class does, and he knows Katie's paraprofessional is ensuring that she is learning basic prereading skills. Mr. Lowell is most concerned about the impact of Katie's behaviors on the class. Despite class discussions about how best to respond to Katie's outbursts, several students continue to snicker when Katie calls out, which often leads to other behavior problems. How could Mr. Lowell address both Katie's inappropriate classroom behaviors and other students' response to them?

■ When Mr. Mosley learned that he would be Buddy's teacher this year, he knew it would be challenging, but he did not realize quite *how* challenging. Buddy receives special education services because he has an emotional disability as well as learning disabilities, and school personnel know that he was abused as a toddler, lived in a series of foster homes, and now his maternal grandparents have custody of him. In fourth grade, he reads at a first-grade level, and he has similar difficulties in other academic areas. When Buddy is given an assignment, he often slaps it off his desk, slouches down, and mutters profanities about doing the work. When it is time for the class to leave for art or music, he often refuses to join the group. During large-group instruction, he is likely to makes jokes out loud about the lesson or other children. When the social worker or psychologist tries to talk to him about his serious behavior outbursts, he repeatedly says, "I know—I'm bad; I know—I'm bad." Buddy's grandmother explains that she is doing the best she can, but that she just can't make him mind.

All teachers spend a portion of their time and energy monitoring student behavior and addressing inappropriate behavior. Whether you teach 5-year-olds in a kindergarten class or 17-year-olds in junior English, how you respond to student behavior significantly affects students' learning. Furthermore, the public has a high degree of interest in and continuing concern about discipline in U.S. classrooms. For example, in the 1998 and 1999 Gallup polls of the public's attitudes toward schools (Rose & Gallup, 1998, 1999), the greatest problems facing public schools were identified as fighting and violence and lack of discipline. In the 2000 Gallup poll (Rose & Gallup, 2000), only the lack of funding was mentioned more often than these issues. The Special Emphasis On . . . feature on pages 430–431 takes a closer look at adolescents and school violence.

To begin our discussion about classroom discipline, we present some basic understandings to provide a context in which you should consider managing student behavior. First, it is essential to recognize that the root word of the word **discipline** is *disciple*, meaning a follower of a teacher. Even though discipline is currently often associated with obedience, discipline is really mostly about learning. It is a means to ensure that students have maximum opportunity to learn from their teachers. Discipline is never an end in and of itself. As you learn about approaches for increasing classroom discipline in this chapter, you will be finding ways to enhance your students' learning.

Second, some professionals and a considerable body of literature characterize discipline and classroom management as negative, implying that these subjects are about teacher control and power (Bloom, Perlmutter, & Burrell, 1999). That view fails to take into account the very real dilemma teachers face in attempting to keep a classroom full of students interested in learning in a way that is safe and respectful of all students. If you are effective in classroom management, you will be providing conditions that enable your students to succeed (Pena & Amerin, 1999). Rather than managing student behavior for your convenience or to command compliance, you will be guiding students in ways that contribute to their own best interests.

Third, teacher beliefs about discipline have a strong cultural basis, and some evidence suggests that teachers are far more likely to refer students for discipline problems when they are from a culture other than the teacher's (Townsend, 2000). In addition, teachers may vary their use of different discipline techniques (for example, talking to the student, punishing the student) depending on the student's culture or

Research Note

The Annual Phi Delta Kappa/Gallup Poll of the Public's Attitudes toward the Public Schools is a snapshot of U.S. perceptions of their schools. The poll often includes information about discipline and violence as well as other issues facing schools.

ethnicity (Ishii-Jordan, 2000). All teachers have an obligation to monitor their behavior to ensure that their responses are not based on racial bias or cultural ignorance.

Teachers also have a responsibility to recognize when their expectations are inconsistent with a student's culture. For example, a teacher described a dilemma his school faced with students from Somalia. The students were spitting, a clear violation of school rules. However, school professionals soon learned that the students were not misbehaving. Part of their religious custom called for complete fasting, including not swallowing their own saliva. Spitting, acceptable in their homeland, was perceived as misbehavior in the U.S. school.

Teachers who actively, carefully, and creatively apply approaches for classroom management and who monitor the success of their strategies, adapting them as needed, can have a positive influence on student learning (Algozzine, Audette, Ellis, Marr, & White, 2000). Many issues are beyond a teacher's control—you do not have the power to increase the financial support available to schools, nor can you remove the public pressures that surround many curriculum, instruction, and school reform initiatives. However, you can affect and are ultimately accountable for the learning of your students. Using effective classroom management strategies increases student learning by creating a positive classroom environment. Furthermore, teachers who use effective management strategies have far less need to change inappropriate student behavior.

The sections that follow present procedures for fostering positive behavior in groups of students, a specific and federally mandated way of problem solving about student behavior called functional behavior assessment, and strategies for responding to individual student behaviors and creating positive behavior supports. Together, these techniques provide a foundation for effective classroom management.

How Can You Prevent Discipline Problems?

Over the past several years, researchers have focused not just on the prevalence of violence in U.S. schools, but on the characteristics of students who are perpetrators and victims. For example, males are most involved in incidents of school violence; bullying behavior is most common among upper-elementary students; African American students are victims of school violence slightly more often than other students; little difference is found in the rate of violence in urban, suburban, and nonmetropolitan schools; and overall student attitude is directly related to participation in violence (Furlong & Morrison, 2000). Information such as this is helpful in addressing discipline and violence, but what it most clearly points out is that the starting point for intervention is prevention.

Thus, strategies for responding to disruptive student behavior and promoting their positive academic and social behavior are discussed later in this chapter, but we begin by outlining ideas for preventing behavior problems (Colvin, Ainge, & Nelson, 1997; Hyman & Snook, 2000). In many cases, you can make the difference between having a classroom in which the stress level is high and "keeping control" is a constant struggle, or having a classroom in which student learning is supported by the environment and behavior problems are rare. You can make this difference by creating a caring instructional environment conducive to learning and using effective communication to foster a positive classroom climate.

Special Emphasis On . . .

Adolescents and Violence

With sad hindsight, some professionals believe that many of the serious school incidents of violence that have occurred in recent years could have been prevented if teachers, administrators, parents, and students had been more alert to warning signs.

If you see the following immediate warning signs in a student, violence is a serious possibility:

- Loss of temper on a daily basis
- Frequent physical fighting
- Increase in risk-taking behavior
- Detailed plans to commit acts of violence

- Significant vandalism or property damage
- Announcing threats or plans for hurting others
- Enjoying hurting animals
- Carrying a weapon
- Increase in the use of drugs or alcohol

If you notice the following signs over a period of time, the potential for violence exists:

- History of violent or aggressive behavior
- Serious drug or alcohol use
- Gang membership or strong desire to be in a gang

Instructional Environments Conducive to Learning

In Chapter 4 you learned that many factors contribute to creating an instructional environment that fosters student learning. Many of these same factors also promote appropriate classroom behavior. For example, you found out that teachers need to set clear expectations in their classroom through rules that students understand and follow (Algozzine et al., 2000). You need only a few rules, but they should use specific and positive wording, be posted and discussed with students early in the school year, be rehearsed while students learn them, and be enforced consistently. Rules also should be monitored and changed as needed. Figure 12.1 contains sample rules and related student and teacher responsibilities that can be adapted for various grade levels.

Another key factor related to the instructional environment and discipline is establishing clear classroom routines. Routines should be established for beginning the school day or class period, for transitioning from one activity to another, for moving about in the classroom, and for ending the school day or class period. Students who have routines are less likely to misbehave because they can meet classroom expectations for behavior.

Effective Classroom Communication

Teachers who treat their students with respect and trust are more successful in creating positive classroom environments in which fewer behavior problems occur (Guetzloe, 2000). Communication between teacher and students is integral to fostering this trust and respect. However, teacher–student communication is a complex matter, and problems often arise. Sometimes, teachers provide students with too much information or information that is not clear. Students become confused when information is not relevant to the instruction being delivered. And sometimes,

- Access to or fascination with weapons, especially guns
- Frequently threatening others
- Trouble controlling feelings such as anger
- Withdrawal from friends and usual activities
- Feeling rejected or alone
- Having been a victim of bullying
- Poor school performance
- History of discipline problems or frequent run-ins with authority
- Feeling constantly disrespected
- Failing to acknowledge the feelings or rights of others

If you are concerned that any of your students has the potential for violence, you should alert your administrator; discuss strategies for immediate intervention with your school social worker, counselor, or psychologist; and act prudently—avoid meeting alone with a student if you have serious concerns about your safety.

S O U R C E : Adapted from "Recognizing Violence Warning Signs in Others," by the American Psychological Association, 1999, in *Warning Signs*, Washington, DC: Author, retrieved December 9, 2000, from the World Wide Web: http://helping.apa.org/warningsigns/recognizing.html.

teachers give one message with words but convey another message with their tone of voice or nonverbal behaviors. The following communication factors affect classroom management (Bauer & Sapona, 1991):

1. The complexity and level of abstraction of the message
2. Students' background knowledge and experience to understand the content of the message
3. Students' understanding of classroom interactions and routines
4. Teacher and student awareness of nonverbal communication
5. Cognitive organization teachers provide before launching into specific content
6. The expectation that teachers and students listen to one another

Teacher–pupil interactions that affect learning and behavior include both formal interactions that are part of instruction and informal interactions in the classroom. One way to gain a sense of students' perceptions of your communication in class is to ask them.

The overall quality of your communication with your students is built in numerous small ways. For example, finding time each week to speak privately with students lets them know that you value them as individuals. Asking older students sincere questions about their friends, out-of-school activities, or part-time jobs also conveys that you care. Taking the time to write positive comments on papers shows students that you appreciate their strengths and are not focusing only on their needs. When you encourage each student to achieve his or her own potential without continually comparing students to one another, you are communicating the idea that each class member has a valuable contribution to make. Teachers who fail to take these small steps toward positive communication with students, or who publicly embarrass a

Cultural Awareness

Students who have limited English proficiency can be inadvertently overlooked in teacher–student communication because of their language difficulties and possible reluctance to interact. Misunderstandings are also more likely. You have the responsibility of fostering positive communication with this group of students.

Figure 12.1 Recommended Rules and Responsibilities for Inclusive Classrooms

Recommended Rules	Student Expectations	Teacher Responsibilities
Enter the classroom quietly.	Walk in and speak softly. Put away belongings. Take assigned seat.	Stand at the door. Wait to share conversations with students. Establish areas for putting away coats, turning in assignments, and so on. Create a permanent seating arrangement. Recognize appropriate behaviors.
Begin work on time.	Listen to/read instructions carefully. Begin to work immediately.	Prepare practice assignments in advance. Expect students to begin work promptly. Monitor student behavior. Recognize appropriate behaviors.
Stay on task.	Ignore distractions from others. Continue to work without interruptions.	Assign developmentally appropriate tasks. Check for student understanding. Provide positive and corrective feedback. Monitor student behavior and assignment completion progress. Prevent/end distracting behaviors. Recognize appropriate behaviors.
Complete work on time.	Check assignment completion requirements. Ask questions to better understand. Set goals for assignment completion.	State complete assignment information, including grading criteria. Provide appropriate models and demonstrations. Teach goal setting. Allow sufficient class time to work. Recognize appropriate behaviors.
Follow directions at all times.	Listen carefully. Ask questions for understanding. Do as all teachers request.	Gain student attention. Give clear directions for particular situations. Check for student understanding Provide examples and/or demonstrations. Monitor student behavior. Recognize appropriate behaviors.
Listen while others speak.	Maintain a positive body posture. Look at the person. Note important information. Signal for more information.	Teach listening skills. Model good listening skills. Encourage verbal elaboration. Encourage "risk free" active participation. Recognize appropriate behaviors.
Use appropriate language.	Avoid angry and foul words. Use kind words to tell how you feel.	Teach appropriate statements for avoiding conflicts. Teach techniques for self-control. Model respect toward students and peers. Recognize appropriate behaviors.
Keep hands, feet, objects to self.	Avoid hitting, kicking, or throwing things.	Teach safety habits and procedures. Teach techniques for self-control. Recognize appropriate behaviors.

S O U R C E : From "How Do Your Classroom Rules Measure Up? Guidelines for Developing an Effective Rule Management Routine," by J. A. Rademacher, K. Callahan, and V. A. Pederson-Seelye, 1998, *Intervention in School and Clinic, 33,* pp. 284–289. Copyright © 1998 by PRO-ED, Inc. Reprinted with permission.

student or punish a group for the behavior of a few, soon create a negative instructional environment that thwarts appropriate behavior and effective learning.

Effective Teaching Methods

One other critical strategy for preventing behavior problems is to provide instruction that is relevant, interesting, and active. Recall from Chapters 9 and 10, for example, how learning is enhanced through the use of clear and systematic instructional approaches and strategies that actively engage students in their learning. We remind you of this information because effective instruction plays a critical role in classroom behavior management. Students who are given boring or outdated materials, who are asked to complete dozens of worksheets with little instructional value, and who have few opportunities to create their own learning through projects or activities are likely to resort to misbehavior.

Not all behavior problems can be prevented. Some will occur despite your best efforts to prevent them. Before you decide that the student is the one who has to change to resolve the behavior problem, remember to examine how your expectations, communication, teaching behavior, and other factors you control might be part of the problem (Daniels, 1998).

> **Cultural Awareness**
>
> Another type of diversity to monitor in your interactions with students is gender. You need to ensure that you interact with boys and girls equitably and that you respond to their behavior needs without bias.

How Can You Promote Positive Group Behavior?

In effective classrooms, teachers and students respect each other and students are busily engaged in learning. Students attend to their work, they interact with each other politely and without verbal or physical fighting, and they ignore the occasional misbehavior of classmates instead of encouraging it. In many classrooms, you can promote positive behaviors such as these by using behavior management strategies that are designed specifically for the whole class (Bloom et al., 1999; Nelson, 1996). For example, all students might participate in discussing classroom discipline issues, in helping each other to monitor their behavior, and in earning privileges or rewards as individuals or as members of cooperative learning groups. The following sections describe effective whole-group strategies, such as token economies, and other peer-mediated approaches to behavior management.

Token Economy

A long-respected group behavior management procedure that might be effective in your classroom is a **token economy** (Kazdin, 1977). This strategy creates a system in which students earn "money" that they exchange for rewards. As in any economy, certain tasks have more or less value than others, and rewards have more or less cost. In one form of token economy students receive imaginary money that they record in checkbooks. When they purchase a privilege, the cost of it is subtracted from the balance. Use the following steps to create a classroom token economy:

1. Identify the behaviors for which students can earn credit. You might select completing and turning in work, keeping hands to oneself, talking in a classroom

What is the responsibility of general education teachers for creating systems to address minor behavior problems in their classrooms? How do such systems benefit all students, both typical learners and those with special needs?

FYI

Group behavior management can foster inclusive education. For example, if a teacher rewards a class for interacting in a way that is age appropriate (not babyish) and socially appropriate (not encouraging disruptive behavior) with a student who has a significant disability, benefits accrue both for the student with the disability and the classmates.

voice, bringing to class all needed (and specified) learning supplies, returning homework, or exhibiting other behavior that can be clearly observed. A number of behaviors can be specified and posted in the classroom. Students can be involved in deciding what behaviors to include.

2. Decide on the classroom "currency." You could use points, punches on a card, X's on a recording sheet, poker chips or other tokens, play money, or any other system. In choosing a currency, keep in mind that you need to award it and monitor its use. In large classrooms, efficiency in issuing and exchanging the currency can become critical.

3. Assign a value to each target behavior. Simple behaviors should have a lower value. More difficult behaviors should have a higher value. In a very simple system, you would assign the same value (for example, one point) for each target behavior on a daily basis.

4. Decide on the privileges or rewards students can earn. Having variety in the possible "purchases" students can make helps maintain interest in the system. For older students, the list of options might include a make-your-own-homework-assignment privilege; for younger students, tokens might be redeemed for lunch with the teacher. It is important to include on the reward list at least one item that costs the minimum amount of currency a student might earn (for example, one point). This ensures that all students have the opportunity to participate in the economy.

5. Assign purchase "prices" to the privileges and rewards. In general, if a reward is readily available and not limited in quantity, its purchase price should be lower. Items that are tangible (and perhaps literally cost more), limited in supply, or time-consuming should have a higher cost. One teacher had access to hundreds of sets of plastic beads; the beads became quite the rage in the classroom, but they were not very costly. However, lunch alone with the teacher was a high-priced privilege.

6. Explain the economy to students. As you have probably discerned, you can make an economy as simple or complex as you have the creativity to develop and your students have the ability to understand. It is often beneficial to demonstrate the economy with several examples to ensure that students understand it. When the economy is new, student participation should be carefully monitored to avoid a problem such as the one that occurred in Mr. Elliott's class when he used poker chips with young students. Mr. Elliott realized that he was running low on chips, and students had not purchased rewards. When he questioned the students, he learned that they thought the poker chips themselves were the reward!

7. Establish a systematic way for students to exchange their currency for privileges or rewards. In most classrooms, it is effective to allow students to use their currency once a week or once every 2 weeks on a particular day. By having a consistent time and a system for the exchange, you avoid a constant stream of student requests for privileges or rewards and the aggravation of the constant monitoring this would require.

WWW Resources

At the website for the Northwest Regional Educational Laboratory, at http://www.nwrel.org/scpd/sirs/5/cu9.html, you can find a number of articles that summarize research on classroom management and discipline.

How you establish your token economy depends partly on the age of your students (Kaplan & Carter, 1995). For younger students, you may need to use tangible currency (for example, tokens, beads, play money). Older students are more capable of using points or other symbolic currencies. Likewise, younger students need more opportunities to exchange their currency, whereas older students are more able to save their currency to earn more expensive privileges or rewards over a longer period of time.

Check Your Learning

What versions of a token economy would be most effective for elementary school students? For middle school or junior high students? For high school students?

Teachers are tremendously creative in adapting token economies to their students' needs and their own teaching styles (Anderson & Katsiyannis, 1997). One teacher held an auction in her classroom every 2 weeks, offering items donated by local businesses or obtained at garage sales. Students bid on items using the currency they had earned. Another teacher wanted to encourage students to learn about real economies. She permitted students to borrow tokens from one another and to purchase items from one another using their currency. One student "sold" his designer pencils to classmates, with tokens as the currency of exchange.

To work effectively, a token economy should be carefully planned with flexibility for adjustment as the need arises. For example, you might need to change the reward list or the amount of currency required to obtain particular rewards. You should also keep in mind that token economies are best used when most or all of a class group need support for appropriate behaviors. Thus, you might use a token economy early in the school year, again right after the holiday break, and not again until the last month of school. During other periods, less comprehensive strategies may be adequate.

Other Peer-Mediated Approaches

Many teachers create their own whole-class approaches for supporting positive behavior and reducing negative behavior. For example, in a school near a Cherokee reservation, students have a weekly council they call Peacekeepers (Bloom et al.,

1999). This classroom meeting is based on written compliments and concerns that students have placed into a specified box; the class applauds those who have received compliments and problem solve about concerns. Approaches such as this one are highly recommended as a strategy for promoting positive behavior for students from racially and culturally diverse backgrounds (Adams & Hamm, 1991; Haynes & Gebreyesus, 1992).

How you group students for instruction can also serve as a group behavior management technique. For example, if you have students work with a learning buddy or peer tutor, you can probably reduce the amount of misbehavior because students become more actively engaged in their learning and have the added responsibility of serving as a "teacher." Similarly, if you have students work in small instructional groups so that no one can earn a reward unless the group completes the work, students have a natural incentive for focusing on their learning activities and are less likely to misbehave. For a student like Buddy, introduced at the beginning of this chapter, peer-mediated instructional approaches can foster appropriate social interactions because they create the need to interact positively within a small-group, structured instructional environment.

Connections

Chapter 13 provides more detailed information on peers teaching each other.

What Are Some Simple and Effective Responses to Individual Behavior?

For some students, including students with special needs, the steps you take to create a positive and productive learning environment may not be sufficient to eliminate behavior problems, nor do group behavior management strategies always work. These students may need much more specialized approaches, and you will find it helpful to follow the steps of the INCLUDE model outlined in Chapter 4. However, before you decide to use that approach, try a number of simpler strategies. Teachers have long relied on the principle of least intervention in addressing student behavior needs. In the following section, the strategies described include minimum interventions, such as Catch 'Em Being Good, and techniques for managing students' surface behaviors.

Minimum Interventions

Research Note

Too often in schools, students with behavior problems are discussed in negative terms. Dr. Michael Epstein (1999) has created a behavior rating scale that emphasizes positives such as apologizing to others when wrong, interacting positively with peers and siblings, and attending school regularly.

Teachers sometimes contribute unintentionally but significantly to student misbehavior. They do this by inadvertently bringing out negative student behaviors and by responding too strongly to minor misbehaviors, actions that sometimes cause the student to misbehave more. For example, when asked directly to begin work, a student might refuse. However, when given choices among which assignment to do first, the student might comply. Similarly, when reprimanded for using profanity in the classroom, some students will use the reprimand as a signal to continue the language to get further attention. Ignoring occasional inappropriate language might lessen the problem.

When working with students with special needs, it is essential to stay alert to how you might be contributing to a student's behaviors, either through your own responses to the behavior or through your classroom structure and lesson format

(Daniels, 1998). Four examples of very simple strategies teachers use to address minor student misbehavior follow.

Catch 'Em Being Good. A versatile and long-recognized strategy for reducing inappropriate student behavior and increasing appropriate behavior is called **Catch 'Em Being Good.** When a student is behaving according to expectations, you acknowledge and reward the behavior. For example, if third-grader Jeff enters the room and immediately begins his work, you might say to him, "I like the way you went right to your desk, Jeff. That's exactly what you're supposed to do!" This comment has the effect of rewarding Jeff's behavior. At the same time, it clearly lets other students know that going directly to one's seat is a behavior they should do, too. In a middle school social studies class, a teacher might privately say to a student who is chronically late, "I noticed you were at your seat with materials ready when the bell rang. Nice going." Although the privacy of the comment eliminates its potential positive impact on other students, it has the benefit of preventing student embarrassment.

Make low-demand requests first. Sprague and Horner (1990) described a successful strategy for helping students with significant cognitive disabilities who have difficulty transitioning between activities, such as coming in from recess or moving from one activity to another within the classroom. With this approach, make several low-demand and unrelated requests of the student prior to expecting the targeted request. For example, if it is time for Angel to put away his crayons to join a group reading a story, first get Angel's attention by saying something like, "Angel, give me five." Follow this with asking Angel to tell you his address (or another appropriate piece of personal information that he is learning). Next ask him to shake hands. Finally, request that Angel leave his coloring and join the reading group. Each of the requests is followed by verbal praise (for example, "Right" or "Good job").

Use grouping strategies. In many schools, students with disruptive behaviors tend to seek out others who misbehave as seatmates or groupmates. One group of researchers documented that a very simple strategy may significantly reduce misbehavior in such situations (Stainback, Stainback, Etscheidt, & Doud, 1986). They arranged for a highly disruptive student to be partnered in science class with students who were not disruptive. When this was done, the student's disruptive behaviors declined dramatically. When the student sat with disruptive peers, disruptive behaviors were far more frequent. The authors argue convincingly that grouping strategies are easily managed and should be part of any plan for addressing disruptive behavior. This strategy also has potential for a student like Buddy, one of the students described at the beginning of the chapter. Because he is extremely quiet, a teacher might decide to place him with a group of students who model positive social skills and who are unlikely to take advantage of his tendency to go along with whatever the group decides.

Managing Students' Surface Behaviors

Another relatively simple strategy for responding to student behaviors is the concept of managing their **surface behaviors.** Long and Newman (1971) long ago proposed that a teacher's initial response to student behavior often determines whether a problem situation develops and how intense it is. If a teacher treats a minor misbehavior

---

Cultural Awareness

For students from diverse backgrounds, especially those with limited English proficiency, a private "catch" on good behavior can be more effective than a public one because you can better gauge the student's understanding of your message.

Check Your Learning

What does it mean to respond to a student's apparent intent? How does this approach differ from traditional responses to student behavior?

Connections

Grouping strategies were introduced in Chapter 4. How to use them to promote student social interactions is described in Chapter 13.

as a major infraction, the result might be a strong negative student response followed by a stronger teacher response until a serious behavior problem comes to exist. For example, if a student mutters under her breath something negative about an assignment and the teacher responds by stating in a stern voice, "What did you say?" the incident is likely to escalate. The student might reply, "Nothing"; the teacher repeats the request, and the student eventually says something that requires a negative consequence. Such interactions can be avoided if teachers are prepared to shift the focus of the interaction. Suggestions for heading off such problems include purposefully ignoring minor incidents and using humor to defuse tense classroom situations. Examples of initial response techniques are outlined in the Professional Edge.

These initial response techniques are most suited to minor misbehaviors and are unlikely to resolve serious discipline issues. Also, responding to students' surface behaviors can have the effect of increasing those behaviors. For example, if you use humor with a student and the student responds by talking back, then your humor may be increasing rather than defusing the inappropriate behavior. If this happens, switch to another approach or work with your colleagues to examine the behavior more carefully and to devise a more individualized response to it, as described in the remainder of this chapter.

What Are Effective Strategies for Responding to Serious, Individual Student Behavior?

Although group techniques and simple, minimal interventions may prevent serious behavior problems for many students, it is likely that these approaches may not be enough for some students. In such cases, you may need a more long-term and systematic response to increase preferred behaviors and decrease undesirable behaviors. The principles for interventions are the same whether you use simple strategies or more intensive interventions, but the latter are usually carried out across time in a consistent and well-documented manner. They may also involve the use of contracts in which the expectations for behavior are specified and rewards and consequences clearly spelled out. In addition, as discussed later in this chapter, responding to more serious student behavior problems often involves a team effort that may include a special education teacher and psychologist or counselor as well as you (Broussard & Northup, 1997; Ervin, DuPaul, Kern, & Friman, 1998; Symons, McDonald, & Wehby, 1998).

Increasing Desirable Behaviors

All students, even the most challenging, have some appropriate behaviors you would like to increase. The primary strategy for increasing appropriate behavior is called **reinforcement.** Reinforcement is any response or consequence that increases a behavior (Jones & Jones, 2000). It is important for you to realize that reinforcement can increase negative as well as positive behaviors. For example, when a teacher puts a sticker on a student chart because the student completed his assignment without calling out for unneeded help, the student is more likely in the future to continue to

Professional Edge

Strategies for Managing Students' Surface Behaviors

Knowing how to manage students' surface behaviors effectively can often head off a potentially tense classroom situation. The following strategies, most suited for responding to minor misbehaviors, can help you deal with problem behaviors as soon as they occur.

1. **Planned ignoring.** If a student's behavior is not likely to harm others or to spread to others, you might decide to ignore it, especially when the behavior signals another problem. For example, a student who repeatedly sighs loudly could be signaling a loss of interest; instead of responding to the sighing, recognize that the student needs to change activities soon.

2. **Signal interference.** Communicate with students about surface behaviors by using nonverbal signals such as eye contact or gestures (for example, finger to lips to request silence).

3. **Proximity control.** Sometimes, simply moving closer to a misbehaving student resolves the problem.

4. **Interest boosting.** If a student appears to be losing interest in a task or activity, refocus attention by asking a specific question about the student's progress or by otherwise paying specific attention to the student's work.

5. **Tension reduction through humor.** For some minor misbehavior, your best response might be humor. For example, a student frustrated with an assignment tossed a textbook into the trashcan. Instead of scolding or lecturing, the teacher exclaimed, "Two points!" and then went to assist the student with the assignment.

6. **Hurdle help.** For some students, beginning an assignment can be overwhelming. As a result, they refuse to start working or they misbehave to avoid starting. You can help them begin and avoid a behavior issue by assisting with the first example, asking questions to facilitate their thinking, or prompting them to follow steps.

7. **Support from routine.** Creating more structure in the classroom can avert discipline problems. For example, having Rhonda begin each day by hanging up her coat, going to her seat, and coloring the picture you have placed on her desk might help her avoid being disruptive.

8. **Removing seductive objects.** When students bring radios, toys, or other distracting items to school, including dangerous objects, teachers should usually hold them for "safe-keeping." Other objects in the classroom environment can also become a focus for misbehavior and should be hidden. For example, if you have costumes at school for the class play, keep them in a closet; if you set up an intriguing science experiment, cover the materials until it is time to use them.

9. **Expressing concern.** If a student appears agitated, the teacher can privately ask the student whether he or she is okay or needs a few minutes alone. This simple act of acknowledging that the student is experiencing difficulty may eliminate a larger behavior issue.

10. **Providing nonpunitive isolation.** When behavior is starting to become an issue, some students benefit from the opportunity to move to a quiet corner of the classroom or to step outside the room to reduce tension. Some students benefit by being sent on a simple errand that takes them out of the classroom and provides them with a purposeful activity.

SOURCE: Adapted from "How to Defuse Confrontations," by G. Colvin, D. Ainge, and R. Nelson, 1997, *Teaching Exceptional Children, 29*(6), pp. 47-51; and "Managing Surface Behavior of Children in School," by N. J. Long and R. G. Newman, 1971, in N. J. Long, W. C. Morse, and R. G. Newman (Eds.), *Conflict in the Classroom: The Education of Children with Problems* (2nd ed., pp. 442-452), Belmont, CA: Wadsworth.

work independently. However, when a teacher says to a student who is wandering around the classroom, "Sit down!" the student is also more likely in the future to wander again. In both instances, reinforcement was applied. In the first case, it rewarded a desirable behavior; in the second, it rewarded an undesirable behavior.

Positive and negative reinforcement.   Any time you respond to a behavior with a consequence that makes it more likely for the behavior to occur again, you are using **positive reinforcement** (Gardner et al., 1994). When you reward a student for appropriate behavior and that behavior increases, it is an example of positive reinforcement. Specifically, if you tell a student that she may use the classroom computer after she completes five math problems and she completes all the problems, you are reinforcing math problem completion through computer rewards.

Negative reinforcement operates somewhat differently. Suppose you set up a system with your freshman English students whereby they must have their homework signed each night by their parents until they have brought it back to school on time at least 9 out of 10 times. Because students see having homework signed by parents as an undesirable consequence, they will increase their promptness in turning in homework to avoid the consequence. Any increase in behavior to avoid a consequence is the result of **negative reinforcement** (Cipani, 1995). Although negative reinforcement can be effective, positive reinforcement should usually be tried first because having students work toward a positive outcome is preferable to having them work under the threat or perception of a negative consequence.

Some professionals object to using positive reinforcement with students because they fear it teaches students that they are entitled to a payoff for appropriate behavior. They contend that students should complete their schoolwork and behave appropriately because these are the right things to do. This discussion is often addressed as one of external versus internal motivation (Cameron & Pierce, 1994). Although learning and behaving appropriately because of internal motivation rather than for external rewards certainly would be preferable, some students who struggle to learn and behave as expected are simply not able or likely to do so. These students may behave and respond appropriately in school because of internal motivation, but only when they are extremely interested in a subject or topic, or when they experience repeated success over an extended period of time.

Types of reinforcers.   For positive reinforcement to be successful for students with special needs, keep in mind that many different types of reinforcers can be used. Four types are described in the following list.

Check Your Learning

What are the four different types of reinforcers? What is an example of each? How should you decide which type of reinforcer to use?

1. **Social reinforcers** are various types of positive interactions that a teacher, parent, or peer can give students for appropriate behavior and to increase the behavior. These reinforcers might include a positive phone call home to parents, a pat on the back or a hug, verbal praise, or selection as Citizen of the Month. Social reinforcers, especially clear and specific verbal praise, should always be tried before other positive reinforcers because they are the most natural type of reward in a school environment. If you find it necessary to employ other types of rewards, you should use them only in conjunction with social reinforcers because your long-term goal should always be to have students respond to rewards that occur naturally in their classroom environment.

2. **Activity reinforcers** involve activities such as playing games, having extra recess, helping a teacher in another class, and participating in other coveted indi-

vidual or group pastimes. Generally, activities that directly relate to a student's educational goals (for example, practicing math skills on the computer) are preferable to those that are solely recreational (for example, playing a noneducational computer game).

3. Tangible reinforcers are prizes or other objects students can earn as symbols of achievement and that students want to obtain. A student who is earning baseball cards for completing assignments is receiving a tangible reinforcer. Stickers on papers is another example of this type of reinforcer. Tangible rewards can often be naturally integrated into classroom activities. For example, a student can earn the rocket pieces and household chemicals needed to create a highly interesting science experiment not offered to other students. However, make sure that the amount of the tangible reinforcer is appropriate for the amount of positive behavior required. Students earning the science materials just mentioned are expected to display appropriate behaviors over a lengthy period of time, not just for an afternoon. Conversely, if the tangible reinforcer is a scented sticker, perhaps an afternoon of appropriate behavior is the right amount for the reward being given.

4. Primary reinforcers are food or other items related to human needs that a student finds rewarding. They are much more basic than secondary reinforcers, which include social reinforcers, activity reinforcers, and tangible reinforcers. Primary reinforcers used in schools often are edible and might include a piece of candy, a soft drink, or a piece of fruit.

Although you might occasionally employ primary reinforcers as a special treat, generally they should be used only if a student is incapable of understanding more natural rewards, or if other types of rewards are not effective. This is important for two reasons. First, the potential negative impact of food reinforcers on student health is a concern. Second, food reinforcers are not a natural part of the school learning process. In school, students are expected to work to learn; to prepare for adulthood; or, more immediately for some, to earn teacher praise or a grade. Candy is not a routine part of the learning environment. If you plan to use primary reinforcers such as food, check with a school administrator to find out about local policies governing their use. Also check with parents, both for permission and about a student's possible food allergies. You should also keep in mind nutritional issues.

Effective use of positive reinforcers. In addition to understanding that there are different types of positive reinforcers, you need to know some principles for using them effectively (McIntyre, 1992). Three principles include the following:

1. Make sure that the positive reinforcers are clear and specific and that students understand the relationship between their behavior and rewards. The rewards students earn need to be specific. For example, rewarding with time on the computer is not precise enough. If it is a reward, the amount of computer time for the specific behavior displayed should be clarified. Clarity and specificity are especially important when you use verbal praise. Saying to a student, "Good job!" is far less effective than saying, "Good job! You asked three other students for help before you asked me." The former praise is vague; the latter praise explicitly states what behavior is being rewarded.

2. Vary how much and how often you reward students. If a student has very little positive behavior, you may reward it heavily at first just to increase it. As the student learns to use the appropriate behavior more readily, you should decrease the amount and intensity of the reward. For example, if at first you were reward-ing a student with free-choice computer time for every two assignments com-pleted, you might gradually change the reward so that the student must complete four assignments—and get at least 90 percent on each—to use the computer to practice math skills. Another way to vary rewards is to enlist parent assistance. For example, Donna's mother might agree to provide a special treat when the teacher sends a note home indicating that Donna completed her independent work within a specified time. The only caution in asking parents for their help is the uncer-tainty of knowing for sure whether the parents are providing the reward agreed upon, and whether they are withholding it when their child has not behaved ac-cording to expectations.

3. Make sure the student desires the rewards selected. If you propose to make a positive phone call home when a student participates in group work but the student does not care what his or her parent thinks, your reward is unlikely to work. Instead, the student may be far more motivated to choose three homework problems *not* to do. You can determine your students' preferences for rewards by asking them what types of incentives they like or having them rank their prefer-ences from a list of rewards you provide.

WWW Resources

Many strategies that foster positive classroom behav-ior for typical students also help students with special needs. You can find some useful behavior manage-ment ideas at http://www.proteacher.com/030001.shtml.

Related to the concept of reward desirability is that of **satiation.** Simply stated, a student who receives the same reward over a period of time may no longer find it rewarding (Schloss & Smith, 1994). If 5 minutes of free time is given repeatedly, after a while the student may come to expect the free time and not work to receive it. When this happens, it is important to change the reward. You can often avoid the problem of satiation by using a **reinforcement menu.** A reinforcement menu is a list of rewards from which students may choose. The menu can be posted in the classroom, or students can keep individual lists. Some rewards might be reserved for extraordinary performance. Many websites provide ideas for rewards and other ways to increase student behavior. Some of these are outlined in the Technology Notes.

Decreasing Undesirable Behaviors

Most teachers find that students with special needs have some inappropriate class-room behaviors that need to be decreased. These might include aggressive behav-iors such as calling classmates names or poking, pinching, or hitting others; verbal outbursts such as calling out answers, swearing, or making nonsense statements dur-ing large-group instruction; or other behaviors such as fleeing the classroom when feeling stressed, copying others' work, or refusing to work. Just as some strategies increase desirable behaviors, other strategies are designed to decrease undesirable behaviors.

Decreasing behavior is generally accomplished through one of these four sets of strategies: (1) differentially reinforcing behaviors that are incompatible with the un-desirable behavior; (2) extinction, or ignoring the behavior until the student stops it; (3) removing something desirable from the student; and (4) presenting a negative or aversive consequence (Jones & Jones, 2000). The latter two sets of strategies, re-moving something desirable and presenting a negative or aversive consequence, are considered **punishment.** Punishment occurs when a consequence applied has the effect of decreasing a behavior. Each of the four sets of strategies is explained in the following sections.

[Technology Notes]

Help on the Web for Responding to Student Behavior

Because student behavior is an ongoing concern for most teachers, you will find that you are always looking for new ideas for responding to it. The following websites can give you a wide range of strategies for creating positive supports for behavior:

- http://www.teachervision.com/tv/resources/tactics/classmngmnt/behave.html
  On the Teacher Vision website, you can find a list of 15 categories of worrisome student behavior ranging from talking out of turn through violence and bullying. When you click on one of the categories, you are given suggestions for responding to the identified behavior.

- http://www.behavioradvisor.com
  At the Behavior Advisor website, you can learn more about students with a wide variety of behavior and emotional problems. The site includes ideas for responding to mischievous as well as serious behavior problems in your classroom, offers opportunities to chat with other teachers, and provides links to other sites.

- http://www.nichcy.org/bib.htm
  At the website for the National Information Center for Children and Youth with Disabilities, you can find a bibliography on positive behavior supports for a wide range of students and situations.

- http://www.nncc.org/Guidance/guide.disc.page.html
  The National Network for Child Care website offers information on many topics related to students with behavior problems. The site focuses on behavior management, social skills, emotions, and self-esteem, with articles containing hints and tips for understanding students and responding to them positively.

- http://www.track0.com/canteach/elementary/classman.html
  At the Can Teach website, teachers can find references and readings about classroom management as well as links to other useful sites. Among the contents included on the website is a list of 49 ways to reward behavior and suggestions for encouraging positive behavior.

Differential reinforcement of incompatible behaviors. Reinforcers can be used to decrease inappropriate behavior by increasing related appropriate behavior. Perhaps you have a student like Patrick in your classroom. Patrick has a severe learning disability. He tends to be very dependent on you for affirmation that he is doing his work correctly; he seems to be constantly at your elbow asking, "Is this right?" To change this behavior, you might want to try praising Patrick when you can catch him working independently at his desk. This technique is called **differential reinforcement of incompatible behaviors.** You are reinforcing a positive behavior—working independently at his desk—that is incompatible with the negative behavior—being at your desk asking for affirmation (Schloss & Smith, 1994). Your goal in this case is to decrease Patrick's tendency to come to your desk (inappropriate behavior) by systematically rewarding him for staying at his desk (appropriate behavior), which prevents him from being at your desk.

Extinction. Another approach to decreasing negative behavior is **extinction.** To extinguish a behavior, you stop reinforcing it; eventually the behavior decreases.

Check Your Learning

What is extinction? What are the risks of using extinction to decrease students' undesirable behavior?

This strategy is often appropriate when a student has a minor but annoying undesirable behavior, such as tapping a pencil or rocking a chair, which, inadvertently, you have been reinforcing by calling attention to it or otherwise responding to it. However, extinction is appropriate only when the behavior is minor and does not threaten student well-being. Also, before an ignored behavior decreases, it is likely to increase; that is, at first the student might tap the pencil more loudly or rock more rapidly before stopping. If you respond to the behavior at this higher level (by telling the student to stop the noise or to keep still), you inadvertently reward the student for the exaggerated behavior through your response. If you think you cannot ignore a behavior while it increases, extinction is not the strategy to use.

Removing reinforcers. In some instances, you can decrease inappropriate behavior by taking away from the student something desired, a strategy called **removal punishment.** One example of removal punishment is **response cost,** which involves taking away a privilege, points, or some other reward (Schloss & Smith, 1994). An informal use of response cost occurs when teachers take away recess or an assembly because of misbehavior. More systematically, a student may lose a certain amount of free time each time he or she swears in class. Similarly, the student may lose the privilege of helping in another classroom because he or she refuses to begin assigned tasks.

If you are considering using response cost, keep in mind that it is effective only if the student currently has reinforcers that you can remove. For example, denying a student access to a special school program will decrease negative behavior only if the student wants to attend the program. Also, response cost sometimes fails because the negative behavior is being reinforced so strongly that the response cost is not effective. In the example just described, if the student receives a lot of peer attention from acting out in class, the response cost of not attending the school program might be too weak to counteract the strong appeal of peer attention. Finally, because response cost teaches a student only what not to do, it is essential that you simultaneously teach the student desired behaviors.

Another widely used removal punishment strategy is **time-out.** Time-out involves removing a student from opportunities for reward (Costenbader & Reading-Brown, 1995). Many elementary school teachers use a simple form of time-out when they require students misbehaving on the playground to spend a few minutes in a "penalty box." The reward from which students are removed is playtime with classmates. Time-out can be used in a number of ways, depending on the age of the student, the nature of the inappropriate behaviors, and the student's response to isolation. For example, it may be sufficient in a kindergarten or first-grade classroom to have a time-out chair in a quiet corner of the classroom. When Heather pushes another child, she is told to sit in time-out where she can observe other students in the reading circle and yet cannot interact with them. If this is not effective, placing a carrel on the student's desk or using a screen (possibly made from a large box) around a chair might be the next step. For older students and for those with more challenging behaviors, time-out may need to be in a location totally removed from the student's class. For example, when Louis swears at his teacher, he is sent to the time-out room, a small, undecorated room with just a desk and chair that adjoins the counselor's office. However, for Cherri, time-out means going to Mrs. Eich's room across the hall, where she doesn't know the students. If you use time-out, keep in mind the following considerations:

Cultural Awareness

Punishments vary from culture to culture. Your students may come from families that use punishments such as shame, ostracizing, or severe physical punishment. Your knowledge of how students are punished at home should help you understand how they respond to punishment in school.

1. The length of the time-out should vary depending on the student's age, the type of challenging behavior, and the amount of time it takes for the time-out to achieve the result of decreasing an undesirable behavior. Younger students and those with limited cognitive ability often require shorter time-out periods than older students with learning and behavior problems.

2. When using time-out, students should be given a warning, should know why they are given a time-out, and should not have access to attractive activities during time-out. The warning provides students an opportunity to correct the behavior; the explanation ensures that students understand the reason for time-out; and the absence of attractions guarantees that time-out does not become a reward for the student.

3. Giving a student attention as part of a time-out process sabotages its effectiveness. Sometimes, teachers who are using time-out accompany a student to the time-out area, explaining the student's behavior on the way, arguing with the student about the time-out procedure, or otherwise providing the student with a great deal of attention. This attention may reinforce the student's behavior and, in effect, negate the purpose of using time-out.

4. If a student refuses to go to a time-out location, you may need to ask for assistance in enforcing your decision. However, you should also keep in mind that if time-out becomes a power struggle between you and a student, it might not be the appropriate strategy to use.

5. Be aware that for some students, isolation is in itself rewarding. For time-out to be effective, the environment from which the student is removed must be rewarding. Some students are happy to be left completely alone for as long as possible. For students who prefer isolation, time-out is clearly not an appropriate strategy for reducing misbehavior.

6. Attend to the safety needs of students in time-out settings. It is highly unethical to send an upset student to an unsupervised time-out location. If time-out is employed, it must include adult supervision, a safe location for the student, and monitoring for student comfort and safety.

Presenting negative consequences.   The final set of strategies for decreasing undesirable student behavior is the least preferable because it involves presenting negative consequences to students (Gardner et al., 1994). It is referred to as **presentation punishment.** For example, when a teacher verbally reprimands a student, the reprimand is a negative consequence intended to decrease student misbehavior. It is a mild punisher, one of the most common used in schools (Johns & Carr, 1995).

Another type of presentation punishment is **overcorrection,** in which a student is directed to restore a situation to its original condition or a better condition than existed before the misbehavior. This strategy is useful when a student has damaged classroom property or otherwise created a mess. For example, a student who scribbles on a chalkboard might be assigned to erase and wash all the boards in the room. A student who writes on a desktop might be required to stay after school to clean all the desktops in the class. A student who throws trash on the floor might be given the task of sweeping the classroom and adjoining hallway. This

WWW **Resources**

You can learn about legal issues related to discipline and students with special needs at the following website: http://www.ecs. org/ecsmain.asp?page=/ html/issues.asp?am=1.

strategy can make clear the undesirable consequences of negative behaviors, but it is not without problems. First, the student must be willing to complete the overcorrection activity; it might be extremely difficult to compel this behavior. If a student refuses to complete the task, a confrontation might occur. In addition, the overcorrection requires close teacher supervision. A student should not be left alone to complete the assigned task, which translates into a significant time commitment from the teacher.

Physical punishment is another traditional presentation punishment. Although corporal punishment, carried out within specific guidelines, is still permitted in schools in some states, most educators strongly oppose its use. Physical and other types of punishment have many potential negative effects, including the following (Morris, 1985):

1. Punishment often suppresses a student's undesirable behavior but does not change it. Once a student realizes or observes that physical punishment no longer follows a behavior, that behavior is likely to recur. Thus, a student who is physically punished for stealing is likely to steal again if he or she is relatively sure that no one can discover the theft.

FYI

School districts that allow corporal punishment usually have clear guidelines, including having advance parent permission, specifying how punishment is administered, and requiring the presence of a witness.

2. Although punishment might reduce or eliminate a particular behavior, other undesirable behaviors might be substituted. For example, a student strongly scolded for talking out might, at the first opportunity, deface a bulletin board as a way of "getting even."

3. Punishment sometimes has an opposite effect on behavior, increasing instead of decreasing it. This is especially true when the student craves adult attention. For example, if you verbally correct a student for using foul language, the student may enjoy your attention and increase the use of foul language to obtain your attention. In this case, the intended punishment clearly has not served its purpose.

4. Through the teacher's modeling, students might learn that they, too, can control people by using punishment. For example, a student might imitate a teacher's scolding when tutoring a younger student. Likewise, the student might hit a classmate perceived as weaker if physical punishment is part of the school's discipline procedures. Similarly, students who are corporally punished at home might use hitting at school with peers.

In general, then, the message for you as a teacher responding to student behaviors in class is this: Increasing positive behaviors through the use of reinforcers, especially when these desirable behaviors can substitute for student undesirable behaviors, is the preferred approach to behavior management. If you find it necessary to decrease undesirable behaviors, the preferred strategies are reinforcing the positive incompatible behaviors and extinction. The use of removal or presentation punishment should be a last resort, only as part of an ongoing behavior intervention plan, and should involve a team decision. If you do use punishment, keep in mind all the potential problems with it and monitor its use closely.

Using Behavior Contracts

One straightforward way to use one of the strategies for increasing or decreasing behavior or combine several is through **behavior contracts.** A behavior contract is an agreement between the teacher and student that clearly specifies the expectations for the student, the rewards for meeting expectations, the consequences of not meeting expectations, and the timeframe for which the agreement is valid (Lassman, Jolivette, & Wehby, 1999). Contracts are best used with students like Joseph and perhaps Donna and Buddy, who are old enough to understand their content and whose disabilities either do not affect their cognitive functioning or affect it only marginally. However, simple contracts can be used with almost any student (Jones & Jones, 2000). As you review the sample contract in Figure 12.2, notice that it has more detail than some student contracts you may have seen. For students with special needs who have behavior challenges, contracts with less detail often are ineffective in changing behavior. The added components of the contract in Figure 12.2 significantly increase its impact on the student.

The original and still most comprehensive information on how to write student behavior contracts comes from Homme (1970). He stresses the following points:

1. The reward that goes with the contract should be immediate, that is, as close in time as possible to the performance of the desired behavior.

2. Initial contracts should call for and reward small amounts of the desired behavior. For example, requiring a student to read an entire book to earn a reward would probably be too frustrating a task for a student with a reading problem. Instead, the student could be rewarded for each chapter (or even each chapter section or page) completed.

3. Rewards should occur frequently in small amounts. This approach has been proven a more effective method than fewer, larger rewards.

4. A contract should call for and reward accomplishments rather than obedience; that is, reward the completion of assigned work or appropriate behavior rather than "teacher-pleasing" behaviors such as staying in one's seat.

5. Reward the performance only after it occurs. This rule seems obvious, but it is often overlooked. Students who are allowed privileges or rewards before or during work performance are far less likely to complete the performance successfully than those rewarded after it.

6. The contract must be fair. The amount of work required of the student and the payoff for completing the work must be balanced.

7. The terms of the contract should be clear to the student. The contract should be put in writing and discussed with the student. Each component of the contract should be expressed in language the student understands. If the student is not able to understand a contract, this strategy is probably not the best one. The student and teacher should sign the contract.

8. The contract must be honest. The teacher should be willing to carry out the contract as written and to do so immediately. In practice, this means that you should be sure you can deliver on the promises you make.

9. The contract should be positive. It should specify student accomplishments and rewards rather than restrictions and punishments.

10. Contracts should be used systematically. If the contract is enforced only occasionally, the result may be worse (or at least very confusing) for the student than not using one at all.

Figure 12.2 **Sample Student Contract**

For _____ Marta _____
(Student name)

I agree to do these things (what, how much, how well, how often, how measured):

In the lunchroom, eat my lunch quietly and without causing a disruption to children
around me for 10 minutes of the 20-minute lunch period. Ms. Longleiter will tell me
whether I'm doing ok.

For doing them I will receive (what, how much, how often, when):

I will leave the lunchroom with Ms. Longleiter for an extra 10 minutes of recess.

Outstanding performance will be if I

Keep my contract 3 days in a row

_____

My bonus for outstanding performance is

15 extra minutes of reading game time with one of my friends (in the afternoon of the
same day the bonus is earned).

If I don't meet the terms of my contract, this is the consequence:

I will have time-out until recess begins and I will not be allowed to choose an activity
during Friday morning "Choices" time.

This contract will be renegotiated on

April 3, 2002

_____Marta_____   _____Ms. Kornick_____
Student signature   **Teacher signature**

_____March 17, 2002_____   _____March 17, 2002_____
Date   **Date**

How Can You Help Students Manage Their Own Behavior?

The strategies just outlined for increasing positive and decreasing negative student behavior rely on the teacher providing rewards or consequences to the student. Another set of strategies, far less teacher directed, involves having students take an active role in regulating their own behavior (Coleman, Wheeler, & Webber, 1993; Jones & Jones, 2000). These strategies are preferred because they promote student independence by giving students skills they can use in many school settings and outside school as well (Johnson & Johnson, 1999). They have been used with very young children, with students who have learning disabilities, emotional disabilities, and cognitive disabilities as well as other special needs, and with a wide range of academic and social behavior (Shapiro, DuPaul, & Bradley-King, 1998).

Cognitive Behavior Management Strategies

In **cognitive behavior management (CBM),** students are taught to monitor their own behavior, to make judgments about its appropriateness, and to change it as needed (for example, see Meichenbaum, 1977). Many elements of CBM have already been introduced in Chapter 10 as a means of increasing student independence in academic learning and organization. In this chapter they are applied to helping students manage their own classroom conduct and social behavior in a variety of situations. For example, Joseph, the student with a learning disability introduced at the beginning of this chapter, might be able to use CBM to manage his own classroom behavior. Two types of CBM are commonly used to teach students how to manage their own behavior (Kaplan & Carter, 1995). These are self-monitoring and self-reinforcement.

Connections

CBM strategies are presented in an instructional context in Chapter 10.

Self-monitoring.   Students learn to monitor and record their own behavior in **self-monitoring.** For example, a student might keep a daily tally of the number of assignments completed or the number of times he or she waited until the teacher was between instructional groups to ask a question. Students with more advanced skills could even wear headphones to listen to an audiotape with prerecorded signals and record whether they were on task at the sound of each tone. Students can also self-record their social behaviors. They can tally the number of times they leave their seat without permission or ask permission before leaving the classroom.

Self-reinforcement.   Another type of CBM, **self-reinforcement,** is often used in conjunction with self-evaluation. In this approach, students self-evaluate and then judge whether they have earned a reward. For example, Eric might award himself three points for a high score, two points for an average score, and no points for a low score. When he accumulates 20 points, he chooses a reward from his personal reinforcement menu. His favorite reward might be working with the kindergartners during their physical education period. The teacher periodically checks the accuracy of Eric's self-evaluation and self-reinforcement. He earns a bonus point for being accurate in his assessment of himself, even if that assessment is occasionally negative. If Eric has to give himself no points for a low score, and his teacher checks his accuracy that day, he will receive a bonus point because he accurately assessed his work.

Teaching CBM Strategies

Generally, teaching CBM strategies to a student with special needs has three main steps:

1. Discuss the strategy with the student and present a rationale for its use.
If you cannot clarify for the student what the strategy is or how it works, the student might not be a good candidate for CBM. To check student understanding,

ask the student to explain the approach back to you. You could even summarize the goal of the strategy and the rewards and consequences in a contract.

2. Model for the student what you expect. For example, you might use an old sample of the student's work and walk through the strategy you plan to use. Alternatively, you might use a brief role-play to demonstrate to the student how to self-monitor behavior and record it.

Connections

How can the steps in the INCLUDE process guide your responses to questions regarding classroom management and student behavior issues?

3. Provide practice and feedback. For this step, the teacher rewards the student for correctly using the approach until the student is confident enough to use the approach without such support. If you are teaching a student to use CBM, use reinforcers with the student until he or she has mastered the strategy. Even after mastery, it is helpful to reward the student periodically for successfully self-managing behavior. This step can be enhanced by helping the student develop a personal reinforcement menu so rewards are meaningful. Parents and colleagues can sometimes assist in implementing this step.

Although CBM is not appropriate for every student behavior problem, it has the advantage of teaching a student to monitor and take responsibility for his or her own behavior. Because of increased student responsibility, cognitive behavior management is a far more effective strategy for some students than are more traditional classroom rewards. Students can transfer self-management strategies to other classrooms and teachers and even into adult life.

How Can Functional Behavior Assessment Help You Respond to Student Behavior?

When students with disabilities have chronic and significant behavior problems, you are not expected to design and use by yourself strategies such as those just outlined. First, you will find that IDEA-97 contains many provisions that guide how teachers and other school personnel should respond to serious student behaviors (Zurkowski, Kelly, & Griswold, 1998). These procedures, addressing everything from contacting parents to limitations on suspension and expulsion, are summarized in Figure 12.3. In addition, you will work with a team of colleagues to complete a more detailed analysis of the behaviors of concern and to plan, carry out, and evaluate systematically the effectiveness of a range of interventions.

This approach, referred to **functional behavior assessment**, is a problem-solving process. Its basis can be found in ongoing conflicts that have arisen between protecting the rights of students with disabilities and respecting education and school administrators' concerns about school violence, maintaining safe schools, and disciplining students with disabilities (Conroy, Clark, Gable, & Fox, 1999). A functional assessment is a detailed and documented set of procedures designed to improve educators' understanding of exactly what a problem behavior looks like, where it occurs, when it occurs, and what function it serves for the student, and it leads to ideas about how to change the behavior and a specific plan for doing so (Sugai, Lewis-Palmer, & Hagan, 1998).

Check Your Learning

What is a functional assessment of behavior? Why is it important to know whether you work in an inclusive school?

Rationale for functional behavior assessment. When a student displays behaviors that are especially aggravating or seem directed at purposely causing a classroom

| **Figure 12.3** IDEA-97 Provisions Related to Student Discipline

1. Parents must be given an opportunity to participate in all meetings with respect to the identification, evaluation, educational placement, and provision of a free appropriate public education.

2. School officials can remove a student to an appropriate interim alternative educational setting or suspend the student for not more than 10 days in the same year (to the extent that such alternatives are applied to students without disabilities).

3. School officials must complete a manifestation determination (to determine whether the behavior is related to the student's disability) and a functional behavioral assessment if a student is to be removed more than 10 consecutive school days or if the removal constitutes a change in placement.

4. Parents have to be notified of all procedural rights under the IDEA, including expanded disciplinary rights, not later than the day on which the decision to take disciplinary action is made.

5. School personnel may remove a student with disabilities to an interim alternative educational setting for up to 45 days if the student has brought a weapon to school or a school function, or knowingly possesses or uses illegal drugs or sells or solicits the sale of a controlled substance while at a school or school function.

6. School personnel have the option of requesting a hearing officer to remove a student with a disability to an interim alternative educational setting for up to 45 days if the student is substantially likely to injure self or others in the current placement.

7. In the case of a student whose behavior impedes his or her learning or that of others, the IEP team must consider, when appropriate, strategies to address that behavior.

8. An agency reporting a crime committed by a student with a disability must ensure that copies of special education records are transmitted for consideration by appropriate authorities, except as limited by the Family Educational Rights and Privacy Act.

S O U R C E : Adapted from "Disciplining Students in Special Education," by E. P. Hartwig, and G. M. Ruesch, 2000, *Journal of Special Education, 33*, pp. 240–247. Copyright © 2000 by PRO-ED, Inc. Reprinted with permission.

disruption, it is tempting to respond by trying to just stop the behavior to get back to the business of educating the student. However, if you do not understand *why* the behavior is occurring and how to address that underlying cause, the behavior is likely to be a chronic concern. In functional behavior assessment, inappropriate behaviors are viewed as serving a function or purpose for the student; understanding this function helps you understand the actual problem the student is experiencing and how to respond to that problem instead of the symptomatic behavior (Bullock & Fitzsimmons-Lovett, 1997). Table 12.1 describes some common functions of student behaviors. Put simply, this conceptualization of student behaviors suggests that before responding you should ask, Why is the student doing this?

The following example might help to clarify the idea of identifying the function of behaviors. Daniel is in the sixth grade. When the sixth-grade teaching team meets to discuss student problems, Mr. Adams expresses concern that Daniel often swears in class. Ms. Jefferson adds that he picks fights with other students several times each week. Dr. Hogue agrees that Daniel is having problems and recounts a recent

Table 12.1 Possible Functions of Student Behavior

Function	Goal	Example of Behavior
Power/control	Control an event or a situation	Acts to stay in the situation and keep control: "You can't make me!"
Protection/escape	Avoid a task or activity; escape a consequence; stop or leave a situation	Has a tantrum at the start of every math lesson; skips social studies class
Attention	Become the center of attention; focus attention on self	Puts self in the forefront of a situation or distinguishes self from others; for example, burps loudly during class instruction
Acceptance/affiliation	Become wanted or chosen by others for mutual benefit	Hangs out with troublemakers; joins a clique or gang
Self-expression	Express feelings, needs, or preoccupations; demonstrate knowledge or skill	Produces drawings, for example, of aerial bombings, body parts, occult symbols
Gratification	Feel good; have a pleasurable experience; reward oneself	Acts to get or maintain a self-determined reward; for example, hoards an object; indulges in self-gratifying behavior at others' expense
Justice/revenge	Settle a score; get or give restitution, apology, or punishment	Destroys another's work; meets after school to fight; commits an act of vandalism

S O U R C E : Adapted from "Behavioral Intent: Instructional Content for Students with Behavior Disorders," by R. S. Neel and K. K. Cessna, 1993, in Colorado Department of Education Special Education Services Unit, *Instructionally Differentiated Programming: A Needs-Based Approach for Students with Behavior Disorders,* Denver, Colorado: Colorado Department of Special Education Services Unit. Used by permission.

Research Note

Broussard and Northup (1997) used functional behavior assessment as a strategy for developing effective peer interventions to reduce disruptive behavior in general education classrooms.

incident in which Daniel was sent to the office. As the teachers talk, they begin to look past Daniel's specific behaviors and focus instead on the function the behavior is serving. They realize that in one class, Daniel was disruptive when a difficult assignment was being given; in another, the problem was occurring as quizzes were being returned; and in the other, the incident was immediately prior to Daniel's turn to give an oral book report. The teachers agree that Daniel's intent has been to escape situations in which he fears he might fail.

Once you identify the function of a problem behavior, you can assist the student in changing the behavior. In Daniel's case, it would be easy for the teachers to decide on a reward system to get Daniel to swear less in Mr. Adams's class. However, this has more to do with the teachers' need to have well-mannered students than it does with Daniel's need to avoid the possibility of failing. An alternative approach would be to permit Daniel to receive his quizzes before the start of class, or perhaps to participate in the after-school homework club that includes a group that studies for the quiz. Another intervention strategy might be to permit Daniel to give oral reports to one peer or to audiotape them beforehand. The question of intervening to address Daniel's behavior has shifted from, How can we get Daniel to be less disruptive in the classroom? to How can we help Daniel use more appropriate strategies to avoid situations in which he fears he will fail?

This approach to understanding student behavior is more complex than looking at the surface behavior the student displays and trying to stop it; it requires looking for patterns in a student's behavior and describing them clearly in concrete terms. It takes more time and effort, but it greatly increases the likelihood that you and your colleagues will be able to design an effective intervention to assist the student. In addition, you should keep in mind that although most students involved in functional assessment and the development of a behavior plan are those with high-incidence disabilities, this method of addressing behavior was first used with individuals with significant cognitive disabilities, primarily for appropriate social and communication behavior. It certainly can also be appropriately used to help students with those disabilities succeed in your classroom. The Case in Practice on page 454 explores using functional assessment for such students.

In the following sections, the process of completing functional behavior assessment is presented in more detail. The procedure includes these specific steps: (1) verifying the seriousness of the problem; (2) defining the problem behavior in concrete terms; (3) collecting data to better understand the behavior; (4) analyzing the data and forming hypotheses about its function; (5) developing a behavior intervention plan (BIP); (6) implementing the plan and gathering data on its impact on the behavior; and (7) assessing intervention effectiveness and proceeding to appropriate next actions (Fitzsimmons, 1998; McConnell, Hilvitz, & Cox, 1998; Quinn, Gable, Rutherford, Nelson, & Howell, 1998).

Verifying the Seriousness of the Problem

As we have noted in this chapter, many classroom behavior problems can be eliminated or significantly reduced through the use of supportive classroom practices, group behavior management techniques, and low-key individual interventions. A first step in functional assessment is to determine whether these standard strategies have already been implemented (Gable, Quinn, Rutherford, & Howell, 1998). For example, if you have a student who is bullying others, a topic addressed in the Professional Edge on page 455, you might be asked to complete a questionnaire about the tactics you have used to address the student's behavior, and a psychologist, special education teacher, or other educator may observe and interview the student. In cases of acting-out classroom behavior, other students may be observed. The latter approach is used to determine whether the student's behavior is typical or significantly different from that of classmates.

Defining the Problem Behavior

The second step of functional behavior assessment is to ensure that the behaviors of concern are described in a specific way. Teachers working with students with serious behavior problems often use a type of verbal shorthand to describe their concerns. They may refer to a student as disruptive, or they may describe the student as being always off task. They may comment that the student is "often up and wandering around the classroom," or express concern that the student is "sullen and unresponsive." Although these general statements may have specific meaning to the teachers making them, they are too vague and tend to be too judgment laden to be useful in addressing the student's behaviors. The alternative is to describe behaviors in concrete terms. It is sometimes helpful to jot down the vague descriptions of behavior and then review them, focusing on the specific incidents and details characterizing the behaviors: "Yesterday during the first 30 minutes of language arts,

CASE IN PRACTICE

Supporting a Student with Autism Using Functional Behavior Assessment

Mary Elizabeth is a student with autism who just moved to the area. At her previous school, she spent most of her day in the general education classroom with the support of an instructional assistant and special educator, and she was nearly at grade level in math and just a year or so behind in reading.

In her first week at John Glenn Elementary School, however, she repeatedly tried to bite and hit staff and students, had several noisy tantrums, and refused to attempt any academic tasks. On 2 different days, it took two adults to remove Mary Elizabeth from the general education classroom to the resource room. Ms. Lieberman, the third-grade teacher, was astonished at this

disastrous beginning especially because she had carefully prepared her other students for their new classmate and done some quick reading about what to expect of a student with autism.

Within the week, she was at her wits' end and even more distraught when the instructional assistant quit. Mr. Poulos, the school psychologist, quickly called together the team, including Ms. Lieberman and himself as well as special education teacher Ms. Daugherty, principal Dr. Cook, and Mary Elizabeth's parents, Mr. and Mrs. O'Toole. Mary Elizabeth refused to be part of the meetings, but Ms. Daugherty spoke with her individually about the problems and ideas to address them.

The first meeting included a brief review of the problems being encountered and a discussion of simple factors that might help to address them, including temporarily shortening the school day. Then

the group looked at the functions of Mary Elizabeth's behavior, and they began to discuss how they could provide positive behavior supports to help her through the difficult transition to her new school.

What function do you think the team decided was relevant for Mary Elizabeth? What was she trying to communicate? What type of data might the team decide to gather to make the best decisions about a behavior intervention plan? What ideas might a review of what you have read about students with autism produce for creating a behavior intervention plan based on student strengths and emphasizing positive supports? If you were Ms. Lieberman, what types of assistance would you request during the transition time as the behavior plan was implemented? What expectations would you have for all the other people at this meeting to participate in implementing an intervention?

Michael left his desk six times"; "When I ask Chenille a direct question, she looks away and does not answer"; or "Juan talks out several times each class period—he does not raise his hand." If several behaviors are identified, it is often most helpful to prioritize the one that should be addressed first instead of trying to design interventions for several behaviors at one time.

Collecting Data to Better Understand the Behavior

The third step in functional behavior assessment requires systematically gathering information about a behavior's occurrence and the situation in which it occurs. By doing this, team members are better able to judge whether the behavior follows a particular pattern, for example, occurring during certain types of activities or at certain times of the day. Patterns assist in understanding the function and the serious-

Professional Edge

Dealing with Bullying

Bullying can be an early sign that a student is developing violent behaviors that may lead to later more serious offenses. Some bullies openly harass their victims, demanding lunch money or insulting them repeatedly. Others are manipulative, deceiving other students into breaking school rules or taking the blame for an act the bully committed. The victims may be singled out because of shyness or anxiety, but some are selected because they are physically small or have a disability.

Students are sometimes reluctant to talk about being bullied. The following suggestions can help:

• Listen to your students. Encourage them to talk about what occurs at lunch, during social events, with other kids in class, and on the walk or ride to and from school so you can identify any problems they may be having.

• Take children's complaints of bullying seriously. Probing a seemingly minor complaint may uncover more severe grievances. Children are often afraid or ashamed to tell anyone that they have been bullied, so listen to their complaints.

• Watch for symptoms that children may be being bullied, such as acting withdrawn, receiving a drop in grades, having torn clothes, or needing extra money or supplies.

• Listen to parents, too. A child may only be comfortable discussing bullying with mom or dad, so you may only hear about incidents secondhand. By being alerted, you can carefully monitor your students' actions and take steps to ensure their safety.

• Help students learn the social skills they need to make friends. A confident, resourceful child who has friends is less likely to be bullied or to bully others.

• Praise students' kindness toward others. Let students know that kindness is valued.

• Teach students ways to resolve arguments without violent words or actions. Teach students self-protection skills—how to walk confidently, how to be aware of what is going on around them, and how to stand up for themselves verbally.

• Provide opportunities for students to talk about bullying, perhaps as part of a unit on resolving conflict or making friends.

• Recognize that bullies may be acting out feelings of insecurity, anger, or loneliness. If you have a student who is a bully, help get to the root of the problem. If you cannot seem to influence the student, seek out the assistance of your colleagues and brainstorm ideas at a team meeting.

S O U R C E : Adapted from "Bullying Is a Problem for Kids," by the National Crime Prevention Council, 2000, retrieved December 9, 2000, from the World Wide Web: http://www.ncpc.org/10adu3.htm#youcan.

---

ness of the behavior in relation to teachers' classroom expectations. At the same time, by accurately measuring the behavior when it becomes a concern and continuing to do so after a plan for addressing it is implemented, team members can decide whether their efforts to change the behavior have been successful. Sometimes you may be able to observe and record student behavior yourself. However, if this is not feasible, a school psychologist, a special education teacher, an administrator, or another professional may complete this task.

Anecdotal recording.   One useful strategy for measuring student behavior is to record specific incidents, including what happened immediately before the behavior (antecedents) and what happened as a result of the behavior (consequences). This approach is called an **antecedents–behaviors–consequences (ABC) analysis.** For example, whenever Ms. Carlisle directs the class to form cooperative groups (antecedent), Carlos gets up from his seat and heads for the pencil sharpener (behavior). Ms. Carlisle then tells Carlos to join his group (consequence). By observing Carlos and keeping an ongoing ABC log of Carlos's behaviors in the classroom, Ms. Carlisle found out that whenever the class is transitioning from one activity to another, Carlos is likely to be off task. A sample ABC analysis is shown in Figure 12.4.

Event recording. One easy way to measure a behavior is to count how many times the behavior occurs in a given period of time. This approach is most useful when the behavior is discrete, that is, has a clear starting and stopping point. For example, it might be appropriate to use **event recording** to count the number of times John is late to class during a week or the number of times David blurts out an answer during a 30-minute large-group social studies lesson. On the other hand, event recording probably would not be helpful in measuring Jane's tantrum or Jesse's delay in starting his assignment, because these behaviors have more to do with how long they last than the number of times they occur.

Event recording is relatively easy. You could keep a tally on an index card taped to your desk or planbook or kept as a bookmark in one of your textbooks. The key to event recording is to have an accurate total of the number of times a behavior occurred.

Permanent product recording. If your concern about student behavior relates to academics, it may be simplest to keep samples of work as a means of measuring behavior, a strategy called **permanent product recording.** For example, if students in a U.S. history class regularly have to respond to 10 discussion questions during a sin-

Figure 12.4 ABC Analysis

Student Name __Denton R.__ Date __2/26__

Location __Science—Mr. B__ Observer __Mr. D__

Start Time __1:02__ Stop Time __1:15__

Antecedents	Behaviors	Consequences
1:03 Students get out books and open to begin class.	Denton pulls out his cap and puts it on.	Students around D. start laughing and saying hey.
1:05 Teacher notices D. and tells him to remove cap.	D. stands, slowly removes cap, and bows.	Students applaud.
1:14 Teacher asks D. a question.	D. says, "Man, I don't know."	Student says, "Yeah, you're stupid." Others laugh.

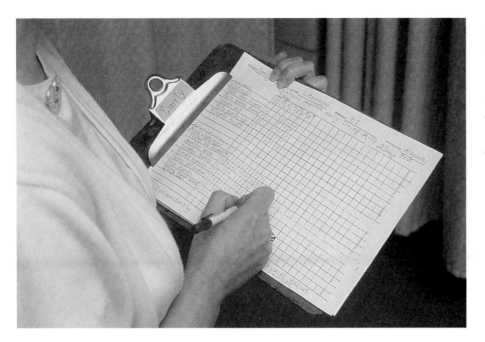

gle class session, you might keep Sam's completed work to document the percentage of questions he is attempting or the percentage of his responses that are correct.

Check Your Learning

For what behaviors besides tantrums might you want to record the duration of a student's behavior?

Duration recording. For some behaviors, your concern is the length of time the behavior lasts. The strategy of **duration recording** might apply to a young student who cries each morning at the start of the school day, a middle school student who takes an extraordinary amount of time to locate all her learning materials, or a high school student who delays beginning assignments. Often, accurately recording duration requires that you have a stopwatch and are able to notice the moment the behavior begins and the moment it ends. However, duration recording can also measure how long students take to complete assignments by asking students to write on their papers the time when they began and finished their work.

Interval recording. Sometimes, you have concerns about a student's behavior not addressed by any of the systems just described. For example, you might be concerned about how well a student is staying on task during an independent assignment or the extent to which a student plays with others during free-choice time. In these cases, **interval recording** may be the best measuring strategy. To use this approach, you specify a length of time for the observation and then divide the time into smaller intervals. For example, you might observe a 10-minute work or play period divided into 30-second intervals. As you observe the student for each 30-second interval, you indicate whether the behavior has been present for that entire interval by marking a + or – on the recording form.

Time sampling. Whereas interval recording requires that you observe a student continually, **time sampling** uses a similar strategy but involves only periodic

Check Your Learning

What is the difference between interval and time sampling as strategies for observing and recording student behavior?

observations of the student. For example, if you wanted to observe whether Patricia played alone or with others during a 30-minute recess, you could divide the time period into ten 3-minute observations. At the end of each 3-minute interval, you would glance *at that moment* to see whether Patricia was playing with others or alone and record your observation accordingly. Time sampling is less demanding than interval recording because you observe only momentarily instead of continuously, but it does include the risk that the behaviors you observe at each sampling are not typical of what has occurred until that moment. This system can also be expedient when your goal is to observe several students at one time; by glancing at three different students and immediately recording the behavior of each one, you can look at the behavior patterns of each student during a single observational period.

Other data sources.   A functional behavior assessment rarely consists of just classroom observations. Most likely, you will be asked questions about your perceptions of how the behavior has developed or changed and about your attempts to contact the parents and otherwise address it. Family members may be interviewed, and an analysis of the structure, length, and characteristics of the student's entire school day may be considered, as may the physical classroom environment and classroom climate. The student is also likely to be interviewed; the student's perspective can add important information to other data gathered (Thorson, 1996). Any factor that might contribute to the behavior may be explored.

Professionals sometimes say that this precise behavior measurement and exhaustive consideration of the causes of the behavior is not realistic. It is certainly true that you may not routinely have the time to use these strategies with many students. However, when you are faced with a student whose behavior is particularly persistent and puzzling, the time you and the team take to analyze it systematically can give you a clearer picture of how to address the problem. Further, by using generic, multipurpose recording forms, and sharing the observation and interviewing tasks, you may find that this step in a functional assessment is not as burdensome as you might imagine.

Analyzing the Data and Creating Hypotheses

At the fourth step in functional behavior assessment, all the pieces come together. For example, Kyle's middle school teachers had expressed concern about his frequent loud and profane outbursts during class. Five 20-minute observation sessions revealed that Kyle spoke loudly using profanity an average of 2.2 times per session (event recording) during large-group instruction (classroom environment). An ABC analysis illustrated that the talking out occurred when the teacher asked the whole class group to read a paragraph in their books, review a chart or graph, or complete some other reading-related task (anecdotal recording). The other students looked at and laughed at Kyle after the talk-outs. The teacher nearly always corrected Kyle, and in just over half the instances he challenged the teacher's reprimand ("I did not," "You're picking on me"). In an interview, Kyle said that he got called on in class only when he did not know an answer, and he said he knew more than teachers gave him credit for.

In analyzing these data, Kyle's teacher and other team members hypothesized that his talking out was serving two functions: First, it was a means of avoiding being called on when the question required a reading task, an area of significant academic difficulty for Kyle. Second, it was a means of getting attention from peers and the teacher.

This step in the process is something like detective work. With the data collected, team members try to identify patterns in the behavior, purposes it might serve for the student, and factors that might make the behavior better or worse. In Kyle's case, the teachers recognize that instead of responding to the profanity and outbursts, they need to address his fear and his need for positive attention.

Developing a Behavior Intervention Plan

Once hypotheses have been generated, team members can develop a **behavior intervention plan (BIP)** based on them. This fifth step in functional behavior assessment may include any number of interventions. For example, the BIP might include modifying the physical or instructional arrangement of the classroom (seating Kyle nearer to where the teacher usually stands, using more cooperative groups); changing antecedents (teacher permitting students to ask each other for help while reading the material being discussed); altering consequences (teacher ignoring at least some occurrences of the talking out); teaching alternative behaviors to the student (having Kyle record his own behaviors and reward himself for raising his hand); or modifying curricular materials (using fewer questions for which reading is required) (Gable et al., 1998).

A behavior intervention plan could include any of the strategies suggested in the preceding sections of this chapter for increasing or decreasing behaviors as well as some of the less intense strategies. These interventions could be captured in a student contract, and if appropriate they could incorporate strategies for helping a student manage his own behavior. Figure 12.5 contains an example of a behavior intervention plan.

Implementing the Plan

Once the BIP is developed, you and the team, often including the student, are faced with the sixth step in functional behavior assessment: the task of implementing your plan. It is important to have a clear plan for implementation because the key to this approach is a systematic response to the behavior. This phase requires several actions: First, teachers and other professionals implementing a BIP should monitor the consistency with which they implement the plan. In addition, if peers or family members have implementation responsibilities, every effort should be made to ensure that their roles are reasonable, that they understand and can carry out their parts of the plan, and that any concerns they may have are addressed. Throughout implementation, data on its impact should be gathered so that monitoring, described next, is facilitated.

Monitoring the Plan

You began the process of functional behavior assessment gathering information about the student's behavior prior to thinking about how to respond to it. If you continue to keep behavior records as you implement the BIP, you can ascertain

> **Cultural Awareness**
>
> Although African American males make up approximately 8.23 percent of the total school population, they receive corporal punishment and are suspended at three times that rate.

Figure 12.5 Sample Behavior Intervention Plan

Student: Tom Clark   School: Middle School

Date Developed: 9/30/97   Date Implemented: 10/3/97

Grade: 7

Baseline Data Results:
Tom destroyed assignments 5 out of 5 observation days.

Hypothesis Statement:
Tom's behavior is related to frustration brought on by a discrepancy between his skill level and the skill level neces-sary to complete the assignments. Much of Tom's destructive behavior is related to his isolated seating from his peers in the classroom. Tom feels singled out because he sits at a table by himself.

Type of Intervention Plan: Educational __X__   Behavioral _____

Person(s) Responsible for Implementing Plan: Science teacher

DESCRIPTION OF THE BEHAVIOR

BEHAVIOR	BEHAVIOR DEFINED
Tom destroys his written assignments.	Tom wads up and tears up his assignment papers.

INTERVENTION GOAL:
To decrease the number of occurrences that Tom destroys his assignments to 0 per week.

INTERVENTION PLAN:

1. Seat Tom with a peer who has good on-task behavior. The peer will review directions with Tom and assist him in getting started with assignments.

2. Provide Tom a daily monitoring assignment checklist to improve the following areas of difficulty:

Assignment Checklist

_____ I understood teacher directions.   _____ I asked for help when I needed it.

_____ I answered all questions.   _____ I understood the assignment.

_____ I need more time.   _____ I turned in my assignment.

3. Provide Tom with academic modifications, including:
   a. Extended time to complete and turn in assignments if needed.
   b. Provide outlines, study guides, and graphic organizers with textbook assignments to assist Tom in identifying important information.
   c. Provide Tom with a word/definition list to use when completing worksheet assignments.
   d. Provide peer assistance with some assignments.
   e. Provide additional instructional modifications as needed.

4. Provide directions to Tom in a variety of ways (verbal, written, direct instruction, and peer assistance).

5. Reinforce Tom's academic productivity and assignment completion.

WHEN AND WHERE THE PLAN WILL BE IMPLEMENTED:

The plan will be implemented in Tom's science class for 3 consecutive weeks beginning 10/3/02.

INTERVENTION DATA COLLECTION SUMMARY:

Week 1.   Decrease in behavior to three occurrences.

Week 2.   Decrease in behavior to two occurrences.

Week 3.   Decrease in behavior to one occurrence.

FOLLOW-UP AND REVIEW DATE(S):

Follow-up and review meeting 10/24/02

COMMENTS:

The intervention plan is successful with Tom.

The team agreed to write the interventions outlined in this plan in Tom's IEP.

The team will meet in 3 weeks for review.

TEAM MEETING PARTICIPANTS:

Name	Position
_____	_____
_____	_____
_____	_____
_____	_____
_____	_____

whether it is working. To proceed with the seventh step, you and the team use the same recording strategies presented in the third step of functional behavior assessment, and you can provide data-recording forms to peers or others who were not initially involved in the process. Remember that behavior does not change rapidly; the team should be committed to following the plan for a specified period of time—perhaps 2 or 3 weeks or even more—before deciding whether it is effective.

As you monitor the plan, you may observe any of a number of effects occurring. First, the inappropriate behavior may cease completely, or the desired behavior may be displayed consistently. If this happens, you may decide to withdraw gradually the rewards and consequences you have implemented. For example, if you are intervening to eliminate a student's profane language in class and no profane language is occurring, you can make it gradually more difficult for the student to earn a reward, and then move to using just verbal praise. This is called **fading out** the reward system.

Second, the plan you are implementing may have value but need modification. Perhaps it requires too much time to implement, or the rewards need adjustment. Such alterations are not unusual; simply modify the plan and continue to monitor its effectiveness. For example, if you created a point system for your sophomore keyboarding student that includes points for being seated when the bell rings, points for turning homework in at the beginning of class, and points for having an assignment notebook and pen in class, you might discover that the system is too difficult to monitor. You might eliminate the points for everything except homework for this student who chronically fails to come to class on time with supplies in hand.

Third, the plan may not be working. As you track the number and duration of tantrums for one of your students, you might learn that they are occurring more often and lasting longer. If a situation like this occurs, the team needs to analyze what is happening and create an alternative plan, following again the steps that have been outlined. If other options do not seem appropriate, a more significant change, such as a change in the student's placement, may be considered.

Finally, it is imperative that you work closely with parents to resolve student behavior problems. Parents can sometimes clarify why a student is behaving in a particular way (for example, a death in the family, a divorce, a weekend trip, a cultural response to a school activity). In addition, they can reinforce school messages at home, and they can help provide tangible or activity rewards at home earned by appropriate behavior during the school day. Parents are likely to be members of the team completing the functional assessment and behavior intervention plan, and their contributions cannot be emphasized enough. By creating partnerships with parents, you increase options for responding to student behavior.

WWW Resources

At the LRE for the Life Project website, at http://web.ce.utk.edu/lre/index.htm, you can find detailed information related to functional behavior assessment, behavior intervention plans, and positive behavior supports.

Summary

Responding to student behavior begins with prevention: By setting clear expectations and fostering respect and communication, teachers can create a classroom learning environment that encourages appropriate behavior and discourages inappropriate behavior. Such basic techniques meet the needs of many students with disabilities. In addition, you can use simple group techniques, such as a token economy, to promote positive student behavior.

Some students, however, need additional behavior supports. By using low-intrusion strategies, such as grouping students and managing surface behaviors, minor behavior problems can be prevented from becoming serious ones. However, when such strategies are inadequate, you may find it necessary to participate in a functional behavior assessment with your team to prepare and follow a behavior intervention plan tailored to the student's needs. Such a plan may be part of the IEP if the need arises for any student with a disability. A behavior intervention plan may include one or many strategies for increasing student behavior (for example, reinforcement) or decreasing student behavior (for example, extinction, overcorrection, punishment); it may also be presented to the student in the form of a behavioral contract. For some students, self-management strategies such as self-monitoring and self-reinforcement also can be employed.

Applications in Teaching Practice

Developing Strategies for Responding to Individual Student Behavior

Ms. Bind teaches eighth-grade English. One of her students is Russell, a student with learning and behavior problems. Russell tends to be a class clown. He makes flippant remarks that border on being disrespectful of other students and Ms. Bind. He is often reprimanded for chatting with other students instead of listening, and then he complains that he doesn't know how to do an assignment that was just explained. The other students generally like Russell, and they sometimes urge him to engage in more classroom antics. Ms. Bind is not alone in her concern about Russell's behavior. His other teachers report a similar pattern. All are concerned about his slipping grades and worry that in high school it will be difficult for him to get the adult supervision that helped him be more successful in middle school. Ms. Bind's tally of classroom incidents from the last week suggests that Russell is reprimanded at least six times per class period. The reprimands tend to occur when the class is transitioning from one activity to another, for example, from a large-group lecture to an individual assignment. Ms. Bind also has noted that Russell brags about his friends in a gang and threatens to "get" other students with these friends.

Ms. Bind, special education teacher Mr. Clark, counselor Ms. Lassaux, and parent Ms. Pinelli have been meeting about Russell. The first step in their functional assessment was to think about whether any simple strategies have been effective and about the intent of Russell's behavior. They decide that the behaviors he has been displaying probably have to do with seeking attention, from both peers and teachers, but conclude that current interventions are inadequate. Using observational data from the classroom and interview information from other teachers, the lunchroom supervisor, and Russell himself, they spend considerable time discussing what sources of appropriate attention are available to Russell, and they weigh the pros and cons of various alternatives for responding to Russell's behavior. They also drift into a conversation about the impact the other students are having on maintaining Russell's behavior when they encourage him. Ms. Bind is convinced that if Russell's audience was not so attentive, many of his problems might take care of themselves.

Questions

1. What strategies could Ms. Bind and the other teachers use to address the group response to Russell's behavior? What cautions would you have for them in trying these strategies?
2. What simple strategies could Ms. Bind use to help Russell behave more appropriately in class? For each strategy, identify potential positive outcomes that could occur but also outline potential problems that could arise.
3. What information do you think the team gathered about Russell? How can this information help them create a behavior intervention plan?
4. What types of reinforcement might work for Russell? How could Ms. Bind ascertain which reinforcers to use if reinforcement is the strategy decided on? Which types of reinforcers would you avoid in this case?
5. How do you think Russell would respond to strategies designed to decrease his negative behavior? For example, how might Russell react if he received a detention each time he disrupted class? What type of negative consequence is detention?
6. Is Russell likely to be able to use cognitive behavior management? Why or why not? If you decided to try a CBM strategy, how would you go about it?

7. Draft a sample behavior plan for Russell. Be prepared to defend the information you create for it and the interventions you plan to implement.
8. How should Russell and his mother be involved in the discussion about his behavior? What contributions could each one make?

13

Approaches for Building Social Relationships

Learner Objectives

After you read this chapter, you will be able to

1. Describe how children with and without disabilities interact with one another and how to promote positive interactions among them.

2. Use a variety of strategies to promote friendship and social support between students with and without disabilities or other special needs.

3. Outline how to establish peer tutoring programs in inclusive schools and describe the characteristics of those programs.

4. Explain how to use cooperative learning strategies as a means of facilitating inclusive education.

5. Describe social-skills needs of students with disabilities and explain how students can learn these skills.

Key Terms and Concepts

Circle of Friends (p. 473)

Cooperative Integrated Reading and Composition (CIRC) (p. 494)

Cooperative learning (p. 489)

Cross-age tutoring (p. 482)

Jigsaw II (p. 492)

Numbered Heads Together (p. 494)

Peer tutoring (p. 480)

Reciprocal tutoring (p. 482)

Same-age tutoring (p. 482)

Simulation (p. 478)

Social skills (p. 495)

■ Errol is a fifth-grade student in Ms. Kim's class at Pleasant Springs Elementary School. He has a moderate cognitive disability. Ms. Kim has been working closely with Mr. Haring, the inclusion facilitator, to ensure that Errol is making friends. The two teachers have worked closely with Errol's parents to enroll Errol in a community recreation program that several other students in class attend, and Errol's mother and father have been very proactive in encouraging him to play with the other children. In school, the teachers have arranged for the social worker to work with the class once per week in group lessons on friendship and diversity, and class members have taken a pledge to make new friends among their classmates. Why is it important for teachers to deliberately address the social interactions of their students with disabilities? What strategies can teachers use to foster friendships between students with and without disabilities? What is the role of parents and families in the development of their children's social skills and relationships?

■ Kathleen's eighth-grade social studies class is studying the impact of civil wars on the citizens and economies of developing countries. Mr. Geib announces at the beginning of class that the students should move into their teams for a cooperative assignment that will take the entire class period. The 32 students shove desks into groups and gather their own materials. After a little reminder that this is not visiting time, the students settle into groups of five or six. Kathleen's group has five members of varying abilities and skills. Behavior stemming from Kathleen's emotional disability is usually not evident in this group. Her peers do not respond to her teasing and inappropriate comments. They assist her to be a constructive group member to help the team get extra points and a possible "free pass" on a future assignment. The two other students in the class who have identified disabilities are in two other groups. Mr. Geib distributes materials to the students and gives directions. When everyone is working, he goes from group to group, answering questions and helping students stay focused on their assignment. What is the impact of this type of grouping arrangement in a diverse classroom? Is it more or less effective than traditional instruction? How can Mr. Geib avoid the problem of some students doing all the work for their groups while other students contribute little? What is the social benefit of this classroom grouping arrangement?

■ Twice each week, Mark is excused from his advisory period to attend a 30-minute FOCUS group. The group, which includes six students and is led by Ms. Kosleski, the school social worker, is designed to enable students to talk about how they respond to other people in different types of situations and how they might improve their social skills. For example, today the group is discussing how to talk to a teacher a student is angry with. They discuss what might have prompted the anger, what they might want to say to the teacher, and what might be best to say. They role-play a situation in which Ms. Kosleski is the teacher. The students provide feedback to each other on their responses, and Ms. Kosleski monitors to make sure the students are following the group rule of no "put-downs." This group has been meeting for 6 weeks. It will end in approximately 3 more. What can the students gain by participating? Why are schools focusing on providing social skills training to students? How might training groups function as support groups for students?

One of the most important reasons given for the trend toward inclusive education for students with special needs is the social benefit (Kennedy, Shukla, & Fryxell, 1997; Krajewski & Hyde, 2000; Salisbury & Palombaro, 1998). Many educators believe that students with disabilities and other exceptional needs learn appropriate social behaviors and develop friendships only when they have opportunities to interact with their nondisabled peers. At the same time, students without special needs learn that individuals with disabilities are people, and they develop sensitivity to people who may not be exactly like themselves and a sense of social responsibility to include individuals with special needs in the classroom community.

How do the social benefits of inclusive education occur? Is it sufficient to integrate students with disabilities into a classroom? Does integration alone help other students become more sensitive and responsive? If not, what does nurture a positive classroom social environment for all students? What if some students continue to have difficulty in their social interactions with peers, teachers, and other adults in school? What if classmates complain that adaptations for students with special needs are not fair? This chapter explores these topics pertaining to approaches for building positive social relationships.

As you begin to think about this aspect of inclusive education, you need to keep in mind a few ideas. First, although the emphasis on teaching and learning in teacher preparation, including the emphasis in this book, concerns academics, your responsibilities as a teacher also include helping all students, whether or not they have special needs, learn social skills. These skills often determine in large part the amount of success any student can achieve in adulthood. Attention to social skills should begin at a very early age and continue throughout students' school years. Second, you do not need to teach students social skills apart from your regular class time. As you read this chapter, you should realize that many skills related to developing positive social relationships can be incorporated into your daily instruction, as Mr. Geib was doing in Kathleen's class. When you think about inclusive educa-

Connections

You can use the INCLUDE strategy presented in Chapter 4 to guide you through a problem-solving process to meet students' social skills needs.

tion, the issue of social relationships becomes part of your classroom expectations; that is, for some students the social component of their education is the primary classroom goal, whereas for others it is just a part. For example, Errol's IEP includes several goals related to peer interactions and the development of friendships; the purpose of him being in fifth grade has as much to do with learning important life social skills, such as talking to peers and participating in group activities, as it does with learning arithmetic skills. Kathleen is learning how to be a member of a group without being disruptive. For Mark, however, academic expectations and social expectations are equally important. One of your responsibilities as a teacher in an inclusive classroom is to clarify these expectations with special educators.

What Is the Teacher's Role in Promoting Positive Social Interactions among Students with and without Disabilities?

A beginning point for creating a classroom in which students understand, appreciate, support, and interact respectfully with each other is studying what we know about children's interactions. This knowledge provides a basis for thinking about how to group students and supervise their interactions to accomplish the social goals of inclusion.

Research on social relationships and interactions among students with and without disabilities has been ongoing almost since special education programs began in public schools (Bennett, 1932). During the 1950s and 1960s, researchers studied the social adjustment and acceptance by peers of students with cognitive disabilities. Sometimes, they found that students in special education classes had better social adjustment than similar students in general education classes (Cassidy & Stanton, 1959). At other times, they found few differences (Blatt, 1958). More consistent were the findings on students' peer acceptance: Researchers found that students with cognitive disabilities were less accepted and more rejected by their peers than students without disabilities (Johnson & Kirk, 1950; Miller, 1956).

> **Connections**
>
> This research is part of the efficacy studies that were mentioned in Chapter 1 in the section on the development of special education services.

When mainstreaming became an important issue during the 1970s, additional studies were completed to help educators understand the social needs of students with disabilities in general education settings. What became clear was that placing students with disabilities, especially those with cognitive disabilities, in classrooms with nondisabled peers did not alone ensure that positive social relationships would develop. In fact, the opposite was true. Students in classes with mainstreamed peers generally disliked peers with disabilities, or did not accept them (Goodman, Gottlieb, & Harrison, 1972; Iano, Ayers, Heller, McGettigan, & Walker, 1974). In attempting to identify why these consistent negative findings occurred, many different characteristics of students with disabilities were examined, including academic potential, label, age, gender, behavior, and physical appearance. Also studied were the ways in which students received special education services, teachers' behaviors, the amount of time students spent in mainstream classrooms, and the types of interactions among students with and without disabilities. The picture that emerged was not clear. Many characteristics and other factors seemed to contribute to student social problems, but none was singularly important.

Special Emphasis On . . .

Understanding the Perspectives of High School Students

The relationships that adolescents have with their teachers are strong predictors of high school completion and academic effort and are an important dimension of their social competence. An obvious, but sometimes overlooked, way of understanding the academic and social experiences of high school students with disabilities is to ask them directly. Lovitt and his colleagues (Lovitt, Plavins, & Cushing, 1999) did just that, surveying more than 200 students and interviewing 54 of them. Among their observations included the following student suggestions for teachers:

- Explain more/better and provide more help.
- Give individual, one-on-one assistance.

- Motivate and make it more fun/interesting.
- Demonstrate how to do it.
- Be more patient.
- Go over it slowly.
- Teach without lectures.
- Keep the student on track.
- Talk to students more.
- Quit trying to treat the student like a 5-year-old.
- Provide a little more freedom.
- Speak the student's language.

When asked how they would improve their high school, students volunteered that they would fire teachers who treated high school like "a prison," and they

WWW Resources

Ability Online, at http://www.ablelink.org/public/about.htm, is a computer friendship network for children with disabilities and their peers. Individuals who wish to participate can interact through e-mail or live chatrooms.

With the trend toward inclusion, attention has focused once again on the interactions between students with and without disabilities. Although some studies continue to confirm earlier research (for example, Conderman, 1995; Sale & Carey, 1995) suggesting that students with disabilities experience difficulty in being socially accepted by peers, other studies suggest a more positive outlook. For example, although Freeman and Alkin (2000) found that the social acceptance ratings for students with cognitive disabilities in general education settings was not as high as those for typical learners, those ratings were higher than for students with cognitive disabilities in separate special education classrooms. Farmer and Farmer (1996) reported that students with disabilities were well integrated into their classroom's social structure and were not "outcasts," and Rosenblum (1998) found that adolescents with visual impairments were successful in establishing and maintaining intimate, best friendships. This complex picture of students' social relationships suggests that simply mixing students with and without disabilities in single classrooms may not result in an integrated social system for them (Hall & McGregor, 2000; Salend, 1999; Siperstein, Leffert, & Widaman, 1996). Especially for adolescents, social interactions in school—with peers as well as teachers—can be challenging. The Special Emphasis On . . . feature takes a look at this important topic.

However, the fact that student social relationships might not occur spontaneously does not mean that inclusion has failed. What it does mean is that teachers have a significant responsibility to ensure that peer relationships grow. Many professionals have been working to develop strategies to help you accomplish this. Generally, these strategies can be grouped into three categories: (1) creating opportunities for students

would require teachers to know multiple ways to reach their students. They expressed a preference for more meaningful instruction and less "busywork." Many of these high school students with disabilities also commented on their peer relationships, noting that they had been "made fun of" by typical peers throughout their school careers.

Recommendations

Based on the results of this study, the researchers recommend the following for teachers and others working with high school students who have disabilities:

1. Assist students to be more independent (for example, self-evaluating and self-scheduling).
2. Make students more aware of what is being done for them (for example, accommodations made and why).

3. Present students with a wider array of postschool options (for example, beyond college and vocational schools).
4. Invest more time in teaching social skills (for example, to help their skills approach the levels of those of their typical peers).
5. Focus effort on a strength (for example, nurturing an area of pride for the student).
6. Continue working on basic skills (for example, not abandoning efforts to help students learn to read, write, and cipher).

SOURCE: Adapted from "What Do Pupils with Disabilities Have to Say about Their Experience in High School?" by T. C. Lovitt, M. Plavins, and S. Cushing, 1999, *Remedial and Special Education, 20,* pp. 67–76, 83. Copyright © 1999 by PRO-ED, Inc. Reprinted with permission.

with and without disabilities to have face-to-face interactions, (2) nurturing support and friendship between students with and without disabilities, and (3) providing positive role models. Figure 13.1 illustrates these strategies.

Creating Opportunities for Social Interactions

The first component for promoting positive interactions among students with and without disabilities is providing opportunities for them to interact. In both elementary and secondary classrooms, this means structuring activities and assigning students to groups so that interactions become part of classroom instruction, as was accomplished in Kathleen's classroom, described at the beginning of this chapter. Eichinger (1990) demonstrated how important heterogeneous grouping is. She reported a study in which pairs of elementary students, one nondisabled and one with a severe disability, were assigned to work on one of two types of activities during a 30-minute, twice-per-week recess period. Some pairs were given a single set of play materials, such as art supplies, and were directed to share them to accomplish a goal. The other pairs were given duplicate sets of materials and directions to work alone on a project or activity. Not surprisingly, in the pairs sharing materials, the students with disabilities interacted with their peers more, engaged in more cooperative play, and showed more positive affect. Turnbull, Pereira, and Blue-Banning (2000) found that if teachers encourage student participation in extracurricular activities that typical peers also enjoy, students with disabilities are likely to develop friendships.

Figure 13.1   **Creating Positive Peer Relationships**

Providing opportunities for social interactions

Nurturing supportive behavior
and friendships

Serving as a role model and providing access to
other positive models

The implications of these and similar studies are clear: Teachers begin the process of developing positive peer interactions by maximizing students' opportunities for interactions, both in school and outside school. In what other ways could you apply this concept to the class setting in which you teach?

Nurturing Support and Friendship

Having students interact is a start, but it is not enough. The second component in building social relationships is to nurture mutual support and friendship between students with and without disabilities. One program that has been demonstrated to be effective in promoting friendships is **Special Friends** (Voeltz et al., 1983). In this program, students without disabilities learn about students with disabilities, including how to play and communicate with them. The basis for the program is friendship, not peer teaching. In one study in which this program was evaluated for its impact on students' interactions (Cole, Vandercook, & Rynders, 1988), it was found that Special Friends students develop reciprocal relationships; that is, the students with disabilities contributed to play, communicated, and expressed positive affect in approximately equal amounts with nondisabled students.

Another strategy for promoting student support is **Circle of Friends** (Forest, Pierpoint, & O'Brien, 1996). When a new student, especially one with many special needs, joins a class group, the students learn to build a circle of friends around that student. As part of this process, they review their own circle of friends by drawing four concentric circles around a figure representing themselves. The first circle contains closest friends, such as family members. The second circle contains others close to the student, such as neighbors and family friends. The third circle contains acquaintances, such as members of the student's soccer team. The outer circle contains people paid to help, such as teachers and camp counselors. The purpose of the activity is to help students understand how many people are part of their lives and to encourage them to become part of the circle of friends for the student with a disability.

The Special Friends and Circle of Friends programs are only two of many strategies for promoting friendship and support. Other strategies include pairing students on the basis of shared interests so that they have a natural basis for becoming friends (Fox, 1989) and making slight changes in activities to encourage participation by students with disabilities (Turnbull et al., 2000). In addition, teachers can nurture supportive interactions by rewarding students when they offer to assist a student with a disability or when they include such students in their games and conversations (Collins, Hall, & Branson, 1997). Teachers of elementary students might also consider incorporating friendship skills into their instruction. By teaching students how to greet one another, how to express friendship, and how to resolve conflicts, teachers can foster positive peer relationships and provide students with a strong basis for lifelong interaction skills (Salend, 1999).

Sometimes you have to address problems related to student support and friendship. Some students (and some teachers, too) express concern about the fairness of making many exceptions for students with special needs, such as changing the consequences for misbehavior, altering the amount or type of work expected, grading on a more generous scale, or using rewards to which other students may not have access. The Professional Edge on page 474 offers advice about responding to issues of fairness.

Cultural Awareness

Students' interactions with others are determined partly by cultural expectations. Be sure to consider this fact as you work to have a positive influence on how your students treat one another.

Parents and friendship.   As you work with students to foster positive social interactions and friendships between students with and without disabilities, keep in mind that parents have a key role to play in this part of their children's lives. For example, parents can provide information about their child's communication strategies and make suggestions about including the student in classroom activities (Clark & Smith, 1999). Parents also can be very effective in exposing their children with special needs to a wide variety of individuals who may become friends (Turnbull, Pereira, & Blue-Banning, 1999). You may also find that parents of students without disabilities may take active steps to foster friendships with classmates with special needs because of the importance they place on helping their children understand the value of each person's *abilities*. Parents may also contribute in small but meaningful ways by providing transportation to recreational activities after school hours, arranging birthday parties and other social functions for students at their homes, and volunteering to lead school activities that bring students together for social interactions (for example, clubs) (Salend, 1999).

Professional Edge

On the Issue of Fairness

Many teachers struggle in deciding how to respond to students who claim that something in class is not fair—whether it is the fact that two students receive the same amount of credit for doing very different types of work or that one student's misbehavior results in a warning whereas another's results in a trip to the office. Although there are no easy answers to this dilemma, Welch (2000) suggests the following strategies:

1. Reflect back the student's feelings, perhaps by asking the student to write you a note about his or her perspective on the issue.

2. Listen for other meanings in students' comments because their complaints may be disguised requests for increased teacher attention.

3. Offer something special to young children for hard work. If one student is receiving stickers, offer them to a complaining student, but only for "extra hard" work.

4. Respond to students' fairness complaints consistently and without explanation. Legally and ethically, you may not discuss a student's work with another student; your response should convey this unambiguously: "You know I won't talk to you about anyone's work but your own. How can I help you to do your work?"

5. Teach students about three types of fairness, including equality (everyone gets the same), equity (reward is based on contribution), and need (reward is greatest to those with the greatest need).

6. Establish a procedure such as class meetings by which students can discuss their concerns about fairness.

7. Develop a caring, cooperative classroom community using strategies suggested throughout this textbook and especially in this chapter.

8. Provide and enforce schoolwide procedures related to fairness so that a consistent approach is used on the playground, cafeteria, gym, and other locations where fairness may become an issue.

9. Clarify within yourself your legal and moral obligation to make accommodations for students with disabilities.

10. Occasionally, a student has a legitimate concern about fairness. It is just as important to know when and how to push a student with a disability to do more as it is to know when to make accommodations.

S O U R C E : Adapted from "Responding to Student Concerns about Fairness," by A. Welch, 2000, *Teaching Exceptional Children, 33*(2), pp. 36–40.

Providing Positive Role Models

FYI

A colleague or community member who has a disability might be a great resource as a positive role model for students.

A third component of promoting positive peer relationships is offering positive role models (Kloomok & Cosden, 1994; Salend, 1999). There are several ways to do this. First, as a teacher in an inclusive school, you might be the most influential model for students learning how to interact with a peer with a disability. If you are positive in your interactions and avoid responding to a student with a disability as a "guest" instead of a full classroom member, students will respond in kind. For example, if you talk to a student with a severe disability as though he or she is a very young child even though you are teaching an eighth-grade class, other students will probably treat the student as a young child. However, if you speak in an age-appropriate voice, so will your students. Similarly, if you expect a student with a learning disability to behave at the same level as other students instead of making exceptions (provided that this expectation is appropriate), peers in the class will have the same expectations. Interacting with students with disabilities in the same way as you interact with anyone else provides the modeling that helps shape all student interactions.

Students without disabilities also need to see that students with disabilities and other special needs have many contributions to make. Pointing out contributions made by a student with a disability, giving students with disabilities standard classroom responsibilities, and recognizing a student's best effort—whether or not it fits within traditional curriculum standards—all these actions lead peers to recognize that the student is a valuable classroom community member (Stainback, Stainback, & Jackson, 1992). Family and community or national support groups also can be resources for providing positive role models. Parents or siblings might gladly talk about a student's abilities as part of school awareness activities (Rothman & Cosden, 1995). The Professional Edge on page 476 presents additional ideas on positive role models for fostering social relationships among students with and without disabilities.

Promoting positive peer relationships needs to be part of your automatic teaching behaviors throughout the course of the school year. Evidence suggests that a long-term approach for fostering peer interactions is most effective and that when teachers stop attending to students' social relationships, these relationships tend to deteriorate (Freeman & Alkin, 2000; Salisbury & Palombaro, 1998).

How Can Teachers Provide Education about Individuals with Disabilities?

Besides promoting positive social interactions between students with and without disabilities, teachers play an important role in educating their students about all types of differences among individuals, including disabilities (Clark & Smith, 1999; Salend, 1999). Even during years in which you have few or no students with disabilities in your class, you can positively affect student understanding and attitude toward individuals with disabilities by incorporating information about them into your curriculum. This section describes the following strategies for doing so: informing students through direct instruction, using video and print media, demonstrating and using adaptive technology, and arranging simulation activities. The Case in Practice on page 477 suggests why there is a strong need for school-based disability awareness and sensitivity training.

Informing through Direct Instruction

One of the most straightforward strategies for teaching students about individuals with disabilities is to provide them with relevant information. For example, you might invite guest speakers to your class to discuss what it is like to have a disability and how people with disabilities lead successful lives. Alternatively, you might arrange to have professionals who provide services to individuals with disabilities talk about their careers. You can also find individuals to speak to your students through local disability advocacy groups or parent groups. A local college or university might also be a valuable resource.

Check Your Learning

Why should your instructional program include information about individuals with disabilities? What strategies can you use to ensure that your instructional program educates your students about people with disabilities?

How do students without disabilities learn about their peers with disabilities? How can teachers promote friendships between students with and without exceptionalities?

Professional Edge

Social Success from Social Support

One of the major goals of current trends toward inclusive practices is to foster in students with disabilities social skills that can help them throughout their lives—in jobs, with family, in recreational settings, in postsecondary school environments, and so on. One way to accomplish this goal is to provide the social support that students need. This support can be established with direct intervention and with efforts to help others in their understanding of and interactions with students with special needs.

Using the Research

The following samples of research results can help you understand your role in establishing social support:

1. How mothers of young children without disabilities speak to their children about children with physical disabilities or Down syndrome significantly affects those children's perceptions of such students (Innes & Diamond, 1999). This suggests that social support needs to be discussed with parents of typical learners.

2. Students with learning disabilities in inclusive settings who are provided with part-time special education assistance experience better social outcomes (that is, increases in peer acceptance and friendship) than do similar students in classrooms where a special education teacher is assigned full time (Vaughn, Elbaum, Schumm, & Hughes, 1998).

3. Students with learning disabilities who perceive themselves to be doing well in their academics base their perceptions largely on feedback they receive in their classroom. Positive teacher feedback is viewed as a critical component of maintaining positive perceptions of student self-worth (Bear & Minke, 1996).

4. Students with cognitive disabilities and other learning problems, when put in a situation in which they have limited resources, seldom initiate sharing with playmates. In contrast, more than half the peers without disabilities share in a similar situation (Siperstein & Leffert, 1999). This study suggests that specific training is needed to teach children a variety of strategies for reaching their goals and strategies for cooperative learning.

These studies suggest that, as a teacher, you can play an active role in fostering student social success. For some students, the social curriculum is primary. For others, it complements the academic curriculum. For all students, you can directly teach them how to create a social network of friends; you can help them understand the nature of their (or their classmates') disabilities; you can provide supportive feedback to them on a frequent basis; and you can teach them to ask friends, adults, and family members for assistance when needed.

You also can educate students about disabilities by incorporating relevant topics into the curriculum. As you teach, you can mention famous individuals with disabilities who contributed to various fields. For example, when studying the presidents, you can raise the fact that Franklin D. Roosevelt had polio and used a wheelchair. In science, you can explain Thomas Edison's hearing loss and Albert Einstein's alleged learning disability. In the fine arts, examples of individuals with disabilities include actress Marlee Matlin, singer Stevie Wonder, and composer Ludwig von Beethoven. Students' understanding and respect for individuals with disabilities are better fostered through an ongoing education program rather than occasional "special events" that highlight this topic. For example, if your school participates in an ongoing program to increase students' understanding of racial, cul-

CASE IN PRACTICE

Intervening to Promote Positive Social Interactions

Mrs. Haynes is in a quandary. This afternoon during her last-period eighth-grade science class, she discovered that four girls who share a lab station had taped a sign to their lab table that said, "Only really cool and cute people are allowed to sit here." The girls had told a less popular student with a mild cognitive disability and mild cerebral palsy that she couldn't join them for the lab because she wasn't cool and certainly wasn't cute. The girl, Shana, had quietly sat at the end of the lab station for the entire period, fighting back tears. The other girls had

been giggling the entire time. With many student questions and an interruption from the office, Mrs. Haynes had not realized what was happening until near the end of the period. She had felt like strangling the four girls, and her heart was broken for Shana. She had decided that Shana needed attention more immediately than the other girls and had spent nearly a half hour after school with her. She would call the girls' parents tonight, as she had told them she would, but she was still extremely disappointed that four of her students could be so cruel. The incident also made her wonder what else went on that she was unaware of. She resolved to spend the evening deciding how to take proactive steps to influence the thinking of these and her other students.

REFLECTIONS

Why might girls in middle school be so insensitive to peers' feelings? How might elementary school students or high school students convey the same message? If you were Mrs. Haynes, what would you have said to Shana after school? Why? How would you talk to the other girls' parents? What consequence would you impose for the girls' cruel prank? How would you go about educating these students about individuals with disabilities and the diversity that exists among all people? What activities could be incorporated into this science class? What similar activities could be used in an elementary school or high school classroom?

---

tural, religious, and other types of diversity, disability awareness is appropriately included as another type of diversity.

A third source of direct information about disabilities is special awareness programs. An example of a program for use in inclusive classrooms in elementary schools is Kids on the Block, a set of puppets and supporting materials and books about disabilities. The puppets "talk" to students about having disabilities and about interacting with classmates and others who have them. This program, typically staffed by volunteers, is available in many communities. Your community might have another similar program with the same purpose. For example, the Mad Hatters, a drama troupe, performs skits about people with and without disabilities and then leads discussions with students about what each character might be feeling (McGookey, 1992). The goal is to promote awareness that people with disabilities are people and to make nondisabled students more comfortable interacting with them. The special educators in your school should know what programs are available in your area and how you can access them.

FYI

In addition to a puppet program, Kids on the Block includes a series of books about many different types of disabilities. The books are available from Twenty-First Century Books in Frederick, Maryland.

Using Video and Print Media

Individuals with disabilities have gained a greater voice in all aspects of our society, and their visibility also has increased in the media (Safran, 1998a). A trip to your local library or video store or a casual reading of television program guides or your newspaper can lead you to a wealth of information. You could identify how the information relates to your instructional goals, find ways to incorporate it into your lessons, and arrange discussions so that your students feel free to ask questions and share their insights.

Your school or district might have educational videos about students with disabilities. Many award-winning movies also address disability and are appropriate for older students. These films include *Amadeus, My Left Foot, Rainman, Gaby—A True Story, Born on the Fourth of July, The Miracle Worker, If You Could See What I Hear, The Other Side of the Mountain, Children of a Lesser God, Forrest Gump*, and *Shine* (McGookey, 1992; Safran, 1998b). Television shows and made-for-TV movies also address disability topics.

Books are written by and for children about virtually every type of disability and other special need (McCarty & Chalmers, 1997; Orr et al., 1997). Reading or assigning an appropriate book to your class can be an excellent strategy for introducing a new student and his or her special needs. A reading assignment can also help open a discussion about interacting and treating a classmate respectfully (McCarty & Chalmers, 1997).

Newspapers carry stories about individuals with disabilities, requirements of the Americans with Disabilities Act, and trends toward inclusive education. National newspapers, such as *USA Today* and the *Wall Street Journal*, are sources of this type of information, but local newspapers also carry stories you can use. For example, when a major league baseball player had a seizure during a ball game, a local newspaper ran a story on what to do when you see someone having a seizure. The high-interest article became a valuable teaching tool for sports-minded middle school students.

Demonstrating and Using Adaptive Technology

Another means of educating students about individuals with disabilities is exploring technology resources (Male, 1997). For example, you can teach students about the powerful tools available to facilitate communication, including touch screens, talking word processors, customized computer keyboards, computer voice input, and word prediction programs. You can demonstrate for students the capabilities of talking computers, calculators, and watches. Some specific ideas for using technology to enhance communication among students with and without disabilities are included in the Technology Notes feature.

Arranging Simulation Activities

In addition to teaching students about disabilities directly, through the use of films, books, other media, and demonstrations of adaptive technology, you can help students understand what it is like to have a disability by arranging simulations (Anderson & Milliren, 1983; Hallenbeck & McMaster, 1991). A **simulation** is an activity in which students experience what it might be like to have a disability as they carry out typical school, home, or community activities. An important component is providing opportunities for students to discuss what they learn from simulation experiences and how they could be more sensitive and respectful to their classmates

Research Note

Obiakor (1999) has studied issues related to minority students and self-concept. He cautions that special education processes have presumptions that can lead to educators labeling students as having poor self-concepts when, in fact, it is a matter of cultural difference.

with disabilities. In one school district, all secondary students attended an assembly at which class members who had participated in simulation activities shared their experiences (Hallenbeck & McMaster, 1991). The following sections describe effective simulations for specific types of disabilities. Keep in mind, however, that students also need to understand that simulating a disability is not like having the disability. Classroom discussions based on simulations should address this fact.

Simulations for physical disabilities. Physical disabilities can be safely simulated in a number of ways using simple materials. For example, to show students what it is like to have limited dexterity, ask them to perform fine motor tasks such as picking up a paper clip, sorting papers, and writing while wearing a bulky glove. Another way of demonstrating limited motor control is to have students keep their dominant hand in their pocket and complete schoolwork or eat lunch using only their nondominant hand. Painting by holding a paintbrush between their teeth sensitizes students to individuals who do not have the use of their arms.

Students might also experience what it is like to use a wheelchair, which you could borrow from your special services office or rent from a health supply store. In one activity, students are paired for a schoolwide scavenger hunt, with one student in a wheelchair and the other as a companion. Students perform simple tasks that they normally take for granted, such as getting a drink from a drinking fountain, using the bathroom, making a phone call from a public phone, and getting to a second-floor classroom or out to a sidewalk.

Simulations for sensory disabilities. Swimmer's earplugs can be used to simulate a hearing loss. Activities that students might try while simulating hearing loss include eating lunch with friends in a noisy cafeteria, watching a television show or video with classmates with the sound unamplified, and talking on the phone. Students could discuss visual clues they used to tell what others were saying and how they felt when they missed important messages. For visual impairment simulation, a blindfold or eye patch can be effective. Partial sight can be simulated by using waxed paper or crumpled plastic wrap inserted into the frames of glasses. Activities while simulating visual impairment might include eating lunch, completing a written assignment, reading from the board, or locating a book on a shelf. Discussion topics might include the difference between not being able to see at all and not being able to see well, and how others were and were not helpful to the student experiencing impaired vision.

Simulations for learning and cognitive disabilities. Students can learn what it is like to have a learning or cognitive disability by experiencing some of the inherent frustrations of these disabilities. For example, students using their nondominant hand to write their names on a card as they hold the card to their foreheads will discover how difficult it can be to make your hand do what you want it to do. Having students write or trace a pattern by watching their hands in a small mirror is also effective. Another simulation is playing the game Simon Says, but in reverse so that students do the opposite of the command given (Anderson & Milliren, 1983). For example, when the leader says, "Jump on your right foot," students must jump on the left foot. They discover the difficulty of reversing operations. One other strategy is giving students a reading assignment far above their reading level and then asking complex questions about it. Discussions based on these simulations can highlight the

[Technology Notes]

Using Technology to Build Positive Peer Relationships

Technology can be a powerful tool for building positive social peer relationships in your classroom. Two examples of how to use technology with students with and without disabilities follow.

Dialogue Journals

Most teachers have learned that computers are important tools for motivating reluctant writers to share their thoughts and ideas. Also, using computers to create dialogue journals can facilitate communication between students with and without disabilities. A dialogue journal is a realistic writing situation in which students are encouraged to share their thoughts and feelings with an agemate while teachers simply manage and monitor the process. Dialogue journals focus on meanings rather than on formality, and they provide a nonthreatening climate for students' writing activities. Students are matched either with a known peer or a "mystery" peer from another class, and they write to each other approximately once each week. Computer disks make transferring journals from class to class a relatively simple task. At

Students with disabilities sometimes communicate with peers and others by using adaptive technology.

some point, teachers should probably arrange for students to meet each other and discuss the journals face to face, but this is not as essential as the writing process itself.

By pairing students with and without disabilities, students can gain greater understanding of each other's perceptions. In a project in which hearing and

frustration of knowing that one is not "dumb" but is not able to complete certain activities successfully, of wanting to give up when tasks are difficult, and of worrying about what others think when one cannot do as well as others can.

Simulation activities can be divided among classroom teams, with each team reporting their experiences to the whole class. Older students might extend their experience by preparing simulation activities for younger students, leading them through the activities, and conducting follow-up discussions.

How Can You Develop and Support Peer Tutoring?

Students also learn about disabilities and other special needs through direct experience and interaction with classmates. **Peer tutoring** is a system of instruction in

deaf students participated (Kluwin, 1996), students responded very positively to the experience. However, teachers commented that some problems occurred when students were mismatched with regard to maturity or developmental levels, or when students in general did not have skills for personal writing. To maximize the effectiveness of dialogue journals, teachers should encourage students to use a conversational style in their journals; students without disabilities should not be overprepared for the experience, or else prejudice may occur; teachers should suggest topics as needed; students should be matched; and teachers should monitor the writing, paying attention to issues of privacy.

Problem-Solving Videos

Teachers can use videotapes of popular television shows, movies, or other instructional video materials to work with students on social skills and problem solving. Using the Improving Social Awareness-Social Problem Solving Project (Elias & Clabby, 1988), teachers can guide students to use the following steps in real-life interactions by applying them as they view a video:

1. Look for signs of different feelings.
2. Tell yourself what the problem is.
3. Decide on your goal.
4. Stop and think of as many solutions to the problem as you can.
5. For each solution, picture all the things that might happen.
6. Choose your best solution.
7. Plan it and make a final check.
8. Try it and rethink it.

This approach to addressing social skills and problem solving appears to have great value because it draws on television as a means of focusing student attention, enables even nonreaders to participate, promotes discussion, and presents opportunities for later role-playing. Younger students and those with attentional problems can be shown shorter videotapes, perhaps 15 minutes or less; older students and those with better attentional skills can view longer tapes. Teachers, of course, play a critical role in guiding student thinking and facilitating student discussion.

S O U R C E : Adapted from "Building Social and Academic Skills via Problem Solving Videos," by M. J. Elias, and M. E. Taylor 1995, *Teaching Exceptional Children*, 27(3), pp. 14–17; and "Getting Hearing and Deaf Students to Write to Each Other through Dialogue Journals," by T. N. Kluwin, *Teaching Exceptional Children*, 28(2), pp. 50–53.

---

which pairs of students with relatively equal standing are given formal roles for promoting each others' achievement (Utley, Mortweet, & Greenwood, 1997). The tutor role is most often held by a peer in the same class, school, or school district. Tutees are the students who receive the instruction from peer tutors. When peer tutoring is used with students with disabilities, the goal is often twofold: (1) fostering social interactions and (2) enhancing academic achievement (Longwill & Kleinert, 1998).

Recent studies of peer tutoring have demonstrated its impact on students' peer interactions. For example, in interviews with elementary students participating in a wide variety of peer interactions, including peer tutoring, they reported that they spent more time interacting with their peers with disabilities, enjoyed their interactions, expressed positive perceptions of the ability of peers with disabilities to learn, and noticed improved social interactions with their classmates (Kamps et al., 1998). In a high school peer tutoring program for students with moderate to severe disabilities, those students accrued benefits in terms of academic achievement and class

WWW Resources

Thousands of websites related to peer tutoring can be found on the Internet. If you type the phrase *peer tutoring* in one of the major search engines (for example, Internet Sleuth, Webcrawler, Yahoo!), you'll find many resources to help you establish a successful program.

Cultural Awareness

According to the U.S. Census Bureau, the overall rate of disability in the United States is 19.4 percent. However, the rate is highest for Native Americans, at 21.9 percent, followed closely by African Americans, at 20 percent. For Asian Americans, the rate of disability is only 9.9 percent. Of what significance is this information when thinking about the social relationships of students with and without disabilities?

participation, but typical tutors also identified benefits. They learned about justice, equality, and choice, and they became familiar with the alternative assessment system used for their peers with disabilities (Longwill & Kleinert, 1998).

In the area of academic achievement, peer tutoring has been demonstrated to improve the achievement of tutees. For example, in a study in which sixth-grade students taught math concepts to younger students with moderate cognitive disabilities, the younger students' knowledge of beginning mathematics improved (Vacc & Cannon, 1991). Similar results have been found when the tutees are students who have high-incidence disabilities or are at risk for school failure and when the subject matter is reading or other school subjects (Fuchs, Fuchs, & Kazdan, 1999; King-Sears, 1997). For example, students at risk for school failure have been found to increase the amount of time they spend on school tasks and their achievement in a peer tutoring program (Greenwood, 1991).

Peer tutoring also has a positive impact on tutors, particularly when older tutors with marginal skills work with younger students. Students who serve as tutors learn their academic content better, and they have more positive attitudes toward school and learning (Utley, Mortweet, & Greenwood, 1997). Not surprisingly, these results are most pronounced when the tutor has not already mastered the academic content used in tutoring (Jenkins, & Jenkins, 1981).

Research on peer tutoring programs has addressed factors such as the age of the tutor and the tutee, the amount of time allocated for tutoring, the content selected for peer tutoring, and the amount of program structure. All these factors influence peer tutoring outcomes.

Developing Peer Tutoring Programs

Developing a **peer tutoring program** can be as simple or complex as you want it to be. You can create your own system within your classroom, partner some or all your students with another group of students, or help coordinate a schoolwide tutoring program. Established and researched programs also exist, such as the Classwide Peer Tutoring program (e.g., Allsopp, 1997; Harper, Maheady, Mallette, & Karnes, 1999; Vadasy, Jenkins, Antil, Phillips, & Pool, 1997) described in Figure 13.2. Steps for setting up a peer tutoring program of your own are described in the following sections.

Selecting tutors. To create a **same-age tutoring** program in your classroom, consider pairing students who are high achievers rather than pairing high achievers with low achievers. Then assign other students whose understanding of the topic is fairly similar. This arrangement reduces the problem of high achievers becoming impatient with other students and the concern about high-achieving students missing their own opportunities for learning. However, same-age tutoring done in this way has two drawbacks: High-achieving students do not learn patience for students with special learning needs, and lower-achieving students lose learning role models. Another approach is to pair students randomly and use a **reciprocal tutoring** approach in which both students alternate between the tutor and tutee roles (King-Sears, 1997).

In a **cross-age tutoring** approach, older students tutor younger ones. For example, if you teach in the primary grades, you might ask the fifth-grade teachers to provide tutors for your students. Teachers could collaborate to partner entire classes and institute regularly scheduled cross-class tutoring. If a middle school, junior high, or high school is located nearby, these students could also serve as tutors. In a

FYI

Give all your students, not just those who are high-achieving, a chance to be tutors. Lower-achieving students can benefit socially and academically from tutoring younger students.

Figure 13.2 Steps in Classwide Peer Tutoring

1. Assign all students to tutoring pairs that are changed weekly.

2. Assign each tutoring pair to one of two classroom teams.

3. Teach all students a specific series of steps for presenting and practicing content.

4. Teach all students specific strategies for correcting tutees and rewarding correct responses.

5. Provide tutoring pairs with daily assignments.

6. Instruct tutors to keep score: When a tutee answers a question correctly, a point is scored for the team.

7. Announce the winning team and post points.

8. Reward the winning team with a privilege or class applause.

9. Reverse the tutor/tutee arrangement each session or have both students take the tutor role within each session.

---

middle school or high school, you might establish a peer tutoring program for the school a level below yours whereby high school students tutor in the middle school and middle school students tutor in the elementary school. At the secondary level, older students might serve as tutors and mentors for younger students. Seniors might be paired with freshmen in this way.

As you decide how to establish a tutoring program, keep in mind students with disabilities and other special needs. Sometimes, students with disabilities can serve as tutors to their classmates. An older student without a disability can be an ideal tutor for a younger student who has a disability. Also, an older student who has a learning or cognitive disability or who is at risk for school failure can be an effective tutor for a younger student with or without a disability. In other words, you can structure a tutoring program in many ways. What is important is making deliberate decisions about how to structure it, basing decisions on the strengths and needs of the students.

Depending on your goals, you might turn to adult tutors. In some school districts, the best available pool of tutors are college students or adult volunteers such as students' parents or grandparents or recently retired teaching staff or local business personnel (Scruggs & Mastropieri, 1992). Adults can make better judgments about the content being taught and learned. Tutees often look up to older tutors, who provide a special type of individual attention. Adults also have the maturity that eliminates potential behavior problems that sometimes occur with peer partners. Of course, if your goals include helping students improve peer relations, some form of *peer* tutoring is your best option.

Deciding how much tutoring should occur. The specific time allocation for peer tutoring depends on the needs of the students and the structure of the program. Although research has not provided clear guidelines, in many cases tutoring in elementary schools occurs two to four times each week for 20 or 30 minutes and up to daily for one class period in high schools (Maheady, Mallette, & Harper, 1991; Mortweet, et al., 1999). This amount of tutoring ensures continuity yet does not detract significantly from the rest of students' educational programs.

WWW Resources

One good source of information on peer tutoring comes from the ERIC Clearinghouse on Educational Management website, at http://www.ed.gov/databases/ERIC_Digests/ed354608.html. This site includes descriptions of peer tutoring and has a list of supplemental resources.

Cultural Awareness

Arrange tutoring groups so that students from differing cultural, racial, ethnic, and socioeconomic backgrounds have opportunities to interact. Giving students a chance to socialize and learn with students from different backgrounds helps reduce stereotyping and prejudice.

Providing time for peer tutoring. Peer tutoring can occur as part of independent work time or as a periodic activity in which an entire class participates. Cross-age tutoring needs to occur on a schedule that accommodates both the tutor and the tutee. Optimal times can include the beginning of the school day as students arrive, the middle of the afternoon when both the tutor and the tutee need a change-of-pace activity, near the end of the school day, or after school. As much as possible, tutoring in a content area should occur within the content-area classes.

Selecting content and format for tutoring. Effective peer tutoring programs provide practice on skills already taught by the teacher and use standard formats that help tutors know how to do their job (Reddy et al.,1999; Vadasy et al., 1997). For example, many studies of peer tutoring have tutors and tutees working on basic math facts, spelling or vocabulary words, or comprehension questions on social studies or science materials already taught in class.

Highly structured formats for tutoring sessions are best. For example, tutors might be instructed to begin the session by reviewing all eight words from last time and then showing each new word, waiting for a response, and marking the response as correct or incorrect. The tutor praises correct responses, corrects errors, and asks the tutee to repeat corrected responses. If the students finish their list, they review it until the end of the tutoring session. This example illustrates the need for a clear set of procedures for tutors to follow, whatever format you use. Clear procedures help keep participants in tutoring sessions on task.

Training tutors. Many authors distinguish between effective and less effective peer tutoring programs on the basis of the preparation tutors receive for their teaching

> **Check Your Learning**
>
> What are the various types of peer tutoring? In what situations might you choose to use each type?

How can peer tutoring programs benefit students in your classroom? What combinations of tutors and tutees might work best for the grade level you plan to teach?

roles. Evidence suggests that intensive tutor training results in better tutoring outcomes (Barron & Foot, 1991). Tutor training should accomplish five main purposes:

1. It should provide tutors with the structures and procedures for tutoring as described above.
2. It should give tutors a systematic way of tracking the tutees' learning.
3. It should help tutors develop positive interaction skills, including ways to praise tutees and ways to correct their errors.
4. Training should prepare tutors in problem-solving skills so that they can generate ideas about how to proceed when the procedures are not working, or when the tutee gets confused or misbehaves.
5. Tutor training adds perceived value and credibility to the program and its participants.

Sample topics for a peer tutor training program are outlined in Figure 13.3.

Supporting Peer Tutoring Programs

Part of a tutor training program includes follow-up and assessment. For example, in a cross-age tutoring program, it is important to bring tutors together periodically to discuss how they are doing and how they have resolved problems and to thank them for their work. When tutoring extends beyond your own class group, it is a nice touch to provide tutor appreciation certificates or other tokens of appreciation.

Several other factors go into the supports needed for a successful peer tutoring program. These factors are discussed in the sections that follow.

Figure 13.3 **Topics for Training Peer Tutors**

1. Sensitivity to others' feelings, needs for acceptance, and fears of rejection
2. Ways to develop positive relationships with tutees, including using respectful language, giving positive reinforcement, showing personal interest, and offering constructive feedback
3. Effective communication and interaction skills: Giving clear directions, making teaching interesting to the tutee, acting interested—and being interested, explaining things in another way, correcting the tutee without criticism, praising correct responses, and admitting mistakes
4. Tutoring procedures and guidelines: Having all needed materials prepared, beginning a session without teacher assistance, breaking big steps into smaller ones, showing how to do something if the tutee does not understand, giving the tutee time to think before responding, helping but not doing the work for the tutee, monitoring time to finish on schedule, and reviewing what has been taught
5. Procedures for gathering data on the tutee's learning, such as using a checklist or helping the tutee chart progress
6. Problem solving about issues that could come up during peer tutoring
7. The tutoring schedule and the need for commitment

Management and supervision. Once your peer tutoring program is established, you should continue to supervise it. This ongoing supervision enables you to praise tutor pairs having constructive work sessions, to identify potential problems when they are small and easily resolved, and to monitor student learning. If you have the assistance of a paraprofessional in your classroom, this person can help with day-to-day supervision responsibilities. As your tutoring program progresses, you might find it necessary to revise the format, regroup students, introduce "graduates," and devise new ways to thank the tutors for their work.

Staff and administrative support. Unless you plan a peer tutoring program that stays within the confines of your classroom, you will need the support of your colleagues and administrators. Other teachers might have ideas on how to pair students and arrange formats and opportunities for tutoring, and the special services staff might have creative ways of including students with special needs in the tutoring program. Administrators can provide support and assistance in arranging schedules, in communicating with parents, and in finding a small budget for the incidental supplies you might need.

Assistance from volunteers. In addition to helping with tutoring, volunteers might also be willing to manage a peer tutoring program, thus relieving you of many of the details of operation. For example, volunteers could establish the procedures for recruiting peer tutors or could offer the tutor training, match tutors with tutees, monitor the tutoring sessions, assess student learning, problem solve with tutors, and arrange a thank-you event for them. Education majors or other teacher trainees in local colleges or universities could assist in these tasks, as could members of a parent or community organization familiar with peer tutoring.

Communication about peer tutoring. Support for peer tutoring programs often depends on communication with parents and other community members. If you plan a peer tutoring program for students, you should alert parents and explain your instructional approach and rationale. If you participate in a tutoring program that includes several classes, you might want to write a letter to parents announcing the availability of the program and providing its rationale. Although most parents will readily agree to permit their children to participate as tutors or tutees, a few might have questions about tutors losing instructional time teaching others and about the effectiveness of tutoring for students who have difficulty learning. Being prepared for questions such as these helps you answer them readily. Also, your administrator can provide support in this area. As your tutoring program progresses, you can keep parents apprised of student activities through periodic notes or class newsletters, or through updates provided by your home–school hotline or district newsletter.

How Can You Use Cooperative Learning Strategies to Facilitate Social Inclusion?

Peer tutoring offers one structured alternative for promoting positive peer relationships. Another option for accomplishing this goal is cooperative learning. Cooperative learning has its roots in the U.S. civil rights and school desegregation movements.

Very soon after the *Brown v. Board of Education* Supreme Court decision established that separate schools cannot be equal, Gordon Allport (1954) wrote that simply putting students of different races in the same schools would not accomplish integration. He went on to clarify that integration would require opportunities for students to interact with one another in situations in which they had equal status. Further, he stated that school administrators would have to endorse the students' interactions strongly. In practice, this meant that students needed opportunities to interact with one another in structured social situations not controlled by teachers but strongly sanctioned by school authorities, situations free of unreasonable academic pressures that might put some students in a lower "status." Cooperative learning was developed as a means of creating these conditions during traditional classroom instruction (Sharan et al., 1984). For nearly 3 decades, cooperative learning has been proposed as a strategy for promoting positive student interactions in diverse classrooms. It has been used as a strategy for achieving racial and cultural integration, for assisting socially isolated learners, for fostering inclusive education for students with disabilities and other special needs, and for accommodating culture-based learning styles.

Understanding the Rationale for Cooperative Learning

As you can see from the history of cooperative learning, its primary purpose was to increase students' ability to interact with each other in appropriate ways. Many studies over the past 20 years have addressed this topic. For example, Gillies and Ashman (2000) found that after 3 school terms, students who had worked in cooperative learning groups were more involved in group activities, and they provided more directions and assistance to other group members than students who participated in loosely structured groups. Students in cooperative classrooms also are more likely to show affection toward other class members, invite others to join a group activity, and thank or praise each other. Although fewer studies on secondary students are available, the same trend exists. For example, in a study of cooperative learning in a tenth-grade biology class, students experienced a higher level of self-esteem than did students in a comparison class; they felt their class was treated more fairly; and they displayed more cohesiveness and less competitiveness as a group (Lazarowitz & Karsenty, 1990).

For students with disabilities, the social benefits of cooperative learning appear to accrue in the same way that they do for other students. In one review of nearly 100 studies of cooperative learning (Johnson, Johnson, & Maruyama, 1983), the positive social impact existed for students with disabilities as well as for students with other special needs, especially when these students were given specific instruction in collaborative skills. In fact, cooperative learning is often recommended as a fundamental component of inclusive classrooms (Cross & Walker-Knight, 1997; King-Sears, 1997). Whereas the value of cooperative learning lies first in its potential for creating positive peer interactions, it also can enhance learning and achievement (Lou et al., 1996; Malmgren, 1998). For students without disabilities, cooperative learning has strongly and repeatedly been demonstrated to be an effective instructional approach for student achievement in reading, math, science, and thinking skills (Lazarowitz & Karsenty, 1990; Slavin, 1994).

The academic outcomes of cooperative learning for students with disabilities vary and cannot always be assumed to be strong (King-Sears, 1997). However, some evidence does suggest that for students with high-incidence disabilities, cooperative learning is at least as effective as other instructional approaches (Mathes, Fuchs, & Fuchs, 1997). Even stronger results have been noted for other students with special

WWW Resources

At http://www.educationplanet.com, you can conduct a search on cooperative learning to find books, websites, and lesson plans on using cooperative learning in your classroom.

Research Note

Gut (2000) has identified several types of social behaviors that students learn by participating in cooperative learning groups, including conversation skills, listening skills, perspective taking, and predicting consequences.

Connections

Chapters 2 and 3 included strategies for parent communication. These strategies could be part of your approach to communicating with parents about peer tutoring.

needs, including students who are gifted and talented (Coleman, Gallagher, & Nelson, 1993) and those at risk for school failure (Cross & Walker-Knight, 1997). For students with severe cognitive disabilities or multiple disabilities, the issue of academic achievement as traditionally measured is not usually a central concern.

Learning the Characteristics of Cooperative Learning Approaches

Cooperative learning generally has four fundamental and essential characteristics (Cross & Walker-Knight, 1997; Malmgren, 1998). First, the students in the groups have positive interdependence. They either reach their goal together, or no one is able to achieve it. For example, in Mr. Reilly's classroom, the students earn points when all the members in their cooperative group get at least 70 percent on their weekly spelling test. Group members work very hard to help all members learn spelling words. Second, cooperative learning requires face-to-face interactions. In Mr. Reilly's class, students have opportunities to work directly with their group members to accomplish their learning goals. Third, members of cooperative groups have individual accountability. On the weekly spelling test, students who have difficulty learning their words are not excused from taking the test, nor are high achievers permitted to answer for all group members. Each member is required to make a contribution. Finally, cooperative learning stresses student interpersonal skills, such as how to ask questions, how to praise classmates, and how to help another student learn.

These four characteristics of cooperative learning distinguish it from other approaches to learning common in schools. For example, much school learning is competitive, that is, based on winners and losers. Spelling matches or other instructional games in which only one student wins are competitive. Another example of school competition is found in many athletic programs. A second type of traditional learning approach is individualistic. In individualistic learning, student achievement is not dependent on how others achieve. For example, a teacher sets up a system in which all students who complete 90 percent of their homework are listed on the class "good work habits" honor roll. If all the students in the class meet the standard of 90 percent, all can be listed. If only one student meets the standard, only that student is listed. All students can be winners; one student's winning does not affect other students' chances of success. An individualistic approach is also the basis for special education and most remedial programs.

All three approaches—cooperative, competitive, and individualistic—have a place in schools. However, the social and interactive components of cooperative learning are not possible in either of the other two approaches, so this approach especially needs to be added to the school curriculum, particularly in inclusive schools striving to foster positive interactions between students with and without disabilities.

Research Note

Gelzheiser, McClane, Meyers, and Pruzek (1998) studied peer interaction needs as reported on the IEPs of students with disabilities. They found that the needs were detailed, but that specific instruction to assist students in developing appropriate social skills was extremely limited.

Developing Cooperative Learning Programs

Given the many positive effects of cooperative learning for all students, you will probably want to use it as an instructional approach in your classroom. You might decide to use cooperative groups three times each week for language arts activities, for instance, or once each week for test review. Regardless of how you incorporate cooperative learning into your classroom, you can achieve the best results by following some basic guidelines.

Form cooperative learning groups.   One of your first considerations in creating a **cooperative learning** program is deciding on the size and makeup of the groups. Regardless of the specific cooperative learning approach you choose, the age, abilities, and needs of your students help determine group size (Cross & Walker-Knight, 1997). For example, if you teach second grade, you will probably use groups of three at the beginning of the school year and consider larger groups after students become accustomed to cooperative learning procedures. If you teach eighth grade, you might be able to begin the year with groups of five. Other factors besides age should be considered, too. In a class with mature students, larger groups are possible; in a class with immature students, groups of three might be best (or even teaming up in pairs). Students with very limited abilities might need a smaller group; more able students can succeed in a larger group. Notice that the range of group size is from two to five or six. Larger groups become difficult for students to participate in and for teachers to manage.

You should assign students to cooperative groups to create heterogeneous groupings; that is, if your class group includes four students with disabilities, you should distribute them among the cooperative groups. Likewise, your students who are high achievers and low achievers should be assigned across groups. The success of cooperative learning is based on students learning to value and respect each person's contributions. Deciding to place students together in groups according to ability undermines the entire purpose of this instructional approach.

Teachers sometimes ask how long cooperative groups should be kept intact. There is no single right answer to that question. If you change groups too frequently, students do not have enough opportunity to learn about each other and to reach a high level of cooperative functioning. However, if you keep the same groups for too long, students do not have the chance to work with other classmates. A general guideline is to keep cooperative groups for at least a 2- or 3-week unit but to change them at least at the end of each grading period.

How can cooperative groups be used to teach both academic content and skills for working with peers? What skills do students need to work successfully?

Prepare students for cooperative learning. A high school English teacher participated in a university class on cooperative learning and decided that she and the special educator could use this strategy in their inclusive class. They carefully planned a series of cooperative activities, assigned students to their groups, and waited for positive results. They quickly learned why *teaching* students to cooperate is such an important component in developing cooperative learning programs! The high school students bickered with each other and were impatient with students who did not immediately answer questions. Some decided to try to complete their work alone, even though it required input from others. Before students work together, it is essential to teach them cooperative skills.

The skills for cooperative group members have been categorized under the headings *forming, functioning, formulating,* and *fermenting* (Johnson, Johnson, Holubec, & Roy, 1984). These skills are summarized in Figure 13.4. Students need forming skills to move into cooperative groups and carry out basic tasks with politeness and respect. Functioning skills are procedural, including monitoring time limits, asking for help, and clarifying other group members' statements. These skills help the group interact constructively and productively. Formulating skills are more advanced procedural skills and include asking other students to elaborate on their comments so that everyone understands them better, devising strategies for remembering important information, and relating new information to information previously learned. Fermenting skills are those students use to participate in their groups as critical thinkers and problem solvers. These skills include integrating members' ideas to form a new idea, questioning others about their ideas to analyze them further, attempting to provide multiple answers, and expressing or testing hypotheses.

Forming and functioning skills are usually introduced to students first and practiced in groups using games or simple instructional activities that have little academic demand. In addition to helping students learn how to get into their groups and how to speak to each other with respect, one clear example of a functioning skill concerns assigning student roles. All cooperative group members should have assigned **group roles** that help the group function effectively. In some classrooms, group-member assignments include the encourager, the monitor, the leader, and the recorder, as shown in Figure 13.5. The *encourager* has the responsibility of making positive comments to other group members. The *monitor* helps keep the group on task and watches the time. The *leader* gets the group started on its task and facilitates its work. The *recorder* writes down any information the group is responsible for producing. Depending on students' ages and skills, additional responsibilities can be added. In some classrooms, group roles rotate so each student has an opportunity to try all roles. If a student with a disability cannot carry out a role (for example, recorder), a classmate might help out, or that student is not assigned that role.

One other functioning skill is especially important: the ability to give feedback. Students can be taught that effective feedback has six key elements:

1. It focuses on the student's behavior, not on the student's personality.
2. It describes what the student did, not what the other person wished the student had done.
3. It is nonjudgmental.
4. It is specific instead of general.
5. It is concise.
6. It occurs immediately after a group activity, not later (Hill & Hill, 1990).

Check Your Learning

Compare the steps for creating a peer tutoring program with those for establishing a cooperative learning program. How are they alike? How do they differ? What accounts for the similarities and differences?

Connections

Additional information on student grouping arrangements can be found in Chapter 4.

Figure 13.4 Student Cooperative Group Skills

Forming Skills

- Move into cooperative learning groups without making undue noise and without bothering others.
- Stay with the group during cooperative lessons; don't move around the room.
- Use quiet voices.
- Encourage everyone to participate.
- Use names.
- Look at the speaker.
- Avoid put-downs.
- Keep one's hands and feet to oneself.

Functioning Skills

- Give direction to the group's work by stating or restating the assignment's purpose, setting or calling attention to time limits, and offering ideas on how to complete the assignment.
- Express support and acceptance verbally and nonverbally (for example, praise, eye contact).
- Ask for help or clarification if you do not understand.
- Offer to explain or clarify if you do understand and someone else does not.
- Paraphrase others' contributions.
- Energize the group by being enthusiastic or suggesting new ideas.
- Describe one's feelings as appropriate.

Formulating Skills

- Summarize out loud what has just been read without referring to notes or other materials.
- Seek accuracy by correcting someone else's summary or adding important information to it.
- Seek elaboration by asking others to relate the information to other lessons and other things they know.
- Seek clever ways to remember important ideas.
- Ask others to explain their reasoning process.
- Ask others to plan out loud how they would teach the information to another student.

Fermenting Skills

- Criticize ideas, not people.
- Identify sources of disagreement within the learning group as the disagreement occurs.
- Integrate a number of different ideas into your point of view.
- Ask others to justify their conclusions or answers.
- Extend others' answers or conclusions by adding other information.
- Probe by asking questions that lead to deeper analysis.
- Go past the first answer to generate other plausible answers.
- Test reality by checking time and instructions.

S O U R C E : Adapted from *Circles of Learning,* by D. W. Johnson, R. T. Johnson, E. J. Holubec, and P. Roy, 1984, Alexandria, VA: Association for Supervision and Curriculum Development. Copyright (C) 1984 by ASCD. Used with permission.

Consider an example of a student providing appropriate feedback to another student: "Cecily, today in the group you told Mel he was dumb because he didn't know the answer. That's against group rules." Notice how this very brief example meets all the characteristics of effective feedback. The student speaking did not tell Cecily that *she* was the dumb one, nor did the student tell Cecily what she should have said.

Figure 13.5   Student Roles in Cooperative Groups

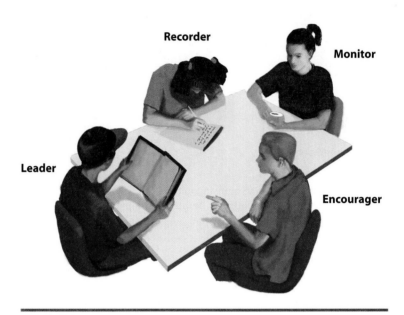

In general, preparing students for cooperative groups includes identifying the skills they need to learn, planning how you will teach them, teaching the skills and allowing students opportunities to practice them, and gradually increasing your expectations for students' cooperative behavior.

Select curricular content.   Almost any subject matter you teach can be adapted for cooperative learning. In elementary schools, cooperative learning is used in language arts for reading and writing activities as well as in math, science, and social studies. In secondary schools, cooperative learning works well in English, but also in math, science, social studies, fine arts, and other coursework. The key to selecting content is to be sure that you have already provided initial instruction to the students so that they are not expected to master new information without your guidance. Further, the content needs to be formatted clearly. It might be a chapter from one of their textbooks, print materials you have duplicated, or a structure for preparing a report on the topic at hand. Students should be able to understand the assignment and how to go about completing it readily.

Choose cooperative learning programs.   The number of approaches to cooperative learning seems to grow each year. For our discussion, three approaches are outlined: Jigsaw II, Numbered Heads Together, and Cooperative Integrated Reading and Composition (CIRC). Other cooperative learning programs are presented in Table 13.1.

In a **Jigsaw II** classroom (Aronson, Blaney, Stephen, Sikes, & Snapp, 1978), students are assigned to heterogeneous work groups. Each member of the work

Table 13.1 Cooperative Learning Approaches

Approach	Source	Description
Group Investigation	Shlomo Sharan and Rachel Hertz-Lazarowitz	Heterogeneous teams of two to six members plan how to complete an assigned project by identifying tasks to do and resources needed and deciding which group members will have which task responsibilities. Once tasks have been completed, group members develop a shared report that is presented to the class. The class provides feedback to the team.
Jigsaw	Elliott Aronson and colleagues	Each of the four members of the heterogeneous work groups is assigned as an expert on a specific part of the assigned materials. Experts from all class work groups meet and learn material on their specific topic as provided by the teacher. Experts then return to their work groups and teach the materials to work-group members. Work-group members have access only to the materials on which they are the expert. Individual quizzes are then given.
Learning Together	David Johnson and Roger Johnson	Heterogeneous groups of two to six members learn specific skills for interacting with one another. They then work together in various formal and informal group structures to learn material.
Student Teams–Achievement Divisions (STAD)	Robert Slavin and colleagues	Heterogeneous four-member teams learn materials together and take quizzes separately. Students earn points based on their own improvement over past quiz scores. These points are contributed to a team score.
Team Assisted Individualization (TAI)	Robert Slavin and colleagues	The four members of heterogeneous teams work at their own pace on individualized math materials. Members help each other and check each other's work, even though they might be on different units. Individual tests are taken to pass out of a unit. Teams earn points each week based on the number of units members have successfully completed.
Teams–Games–Tournaments (TGT)	David DeVries and Keith Edwards	Three-member teams help each other learn material. Team members are then assigned to tournament tables for competition with others from class with similar achievement levels. Quizzes are given or an instructional game based on the material learned is played. Members contribute points to their teams based on their performance at their tournament table.

SOURCE: Based on *Cooperative Learning* (2nd ed.), by R. E. Slavin, 1994, Boston: Allyn and Bacon; *Learning Together and Alone* (4th ed.), by D. W. Johnson and R. T. Johnson, 1994, Boston: Allyn and Bacon; and *Cooperative Learning and Strategies for Inclusion,* by J. W. Putnam, 1993, Baltimore: Brookes.

group is also assigned to an expert group. Work groups meet and decide which member is to be assigned to which expert group. For example, in a unit on the Midwest, experts might be assigned for four topics: geography, economy, culture, and cities. All team members then read the material, with each member focusing on his or her expert topic. After reading, team members join their expert group, composed of all students in the room sharing the same expert topic. The expert groups review their portion of the instructional material, then return to teach it to their work-group members. Group members ask each "expert" questions to help clarify the information being presented. After all group members have taught their segment of the information and the groups have had an opportunity to review their learning, a quiz or other evaluation procedure is used, and each group member is graded individually on this assessment.

FYI

Encourager, monitor, leader, and recorder are group member roles that students might take on during cooperative learning. You can add other roles as needed or eliminate one of these roles for smaller groups.

In **Numbered Heads Together** (Kagan, 1990), students are assigned to cooperative groups and count off by numbers. The teacher then poses a question to the group and students are asked to put their heads together to be sure that all group members know the answer. After a brief time, the teacher brings back the students and calls out a number. All the students with that number stand and one student responds to the question, or they all write the answer on a slate and hold it up for the teacher to see. Students responding correctly score points for their teams.

Cooperative Integrated Reading and Composition (CIRC) is a cooperative learning program designed to help students in upper elementary grades work on reading, writing, and other language arts (Slavin, 1994). If reading groups are used, only two or three groups are formed within the class. In a literature-based language arts program, groups would not be needed. Within one of these structures, students work with one or two other students with similar reading ability, and two such groups form a team. For example, a classroom could have three reading groups, but within those groups, each student is assigned a partner. These partners are parts of teams that cross reading groups; one team might be composed of two students with low reading ability and two students with average reading ability. Teachers introduce stories to the reading groups or the class and distribute story packets to students. Students then read silently and aloud with their partners; work on related writing, spelling, and vocabulary activities; and check each other on completing assigned tasks. At the end of three class periods, students take a comprehension test and complete other assessments of their learning. Other elements of this comprehensive program that require specialized materials include providing direct instruction at least once each week in reading comprehension, using writing activities designed to be integrated into the rest of the language arts program, and reporting about books read independently at home.

Research Note

Some evidence suggests that early intervention pertaining to social skills for students with behavior problems is critical. Kamps, Tankersley, and Ellis (2000) found in a 2-year follow-up on a prevention program for Head Start, kindergarten, and first-grade students that the program increased students' positive interactions with peers compared to a group of children who did not participate in the program.

Monitor program effectiveness. Much of the work in developing a cooperative learning program is deciding which approach to use, preparing materials, and helping students learn cooperative skills. However, once students are established in cooperative groups, your role becomes one of monitoring and managing your class. For example, if you notice that a student is having difficulty in a group, you might decide to join that group briefly to judge whether students can resolve their own problem or need your assistance. If a student seems to be struggling because of the complexity of the lesson content, you can make an on-the-spot adaptation to help the student and the group. If a student is being disruptive, your proximity might be sufficient to settle that student. As you monitor, you can also observe students' use of cooperative skills and check the progress of their learning. For example, you might observe whether students are using the learning strategies described in Chapter 10 to help them succeed in the lesson. By observing, you can plan your next lessons and address any issues concerning cooperative skills.

Many of the teaching strategies presented in this text can be incorporated into cooperative learning experiences. For example, a student in a cooperative group could have adapted materials. The group could use a learning strategy to practice problem solving. You can use an entire array of instructional interventions and strategies for independence as part of your cooperative learning activities. Cooperative groups provide a constructive classroom structure, one that provides opportunities for adapting instruction for individual needs, for building self-esteem and group spirit, for addressing students' own goals, and for promoting positive attitudes toward others. You have an almost limitless number of options for using this structure to accomplish your academic and social goals for students. One example of using assistive technology to facilitate cooperative learning activities for students with learning disabilities is presented in the Technology Notes on page 496.

How Can You Help Students with Disabilities Improve Their Social Skills?

For many students with disabilities and other special needs, your efforts to create a classroom learning environment that fosters positive peer relationships will enable them to be class members who are liked and valued by their peers. For some students, though, you will need to go further. Research has shown that some students with disabilities have persistent problems in their social interactions (Kavale & Forness, 1996; O'Reilly & Glynn, 1995) and that these students benefit from specific instruction to help them learn needed social skills (Leffert, Siperstein, & Millikan, 2000; Prater, Bruhl, & Serna, 1998).

Social skills can be thought of as the behaviors that help students interact successfully with their peers, teachers, and others, and that help students win social acceptance. They include accurately recognizing and responding to emotions expressed by others; identifying and effectively solving social problems, such as disagreements about who can play with a toy or decisions about sneaking out of school with a group of peers; expressing preferences in socially acceptable ways; and initiating kind or helpful acts. Social skills range from very simple to complex. For example, for a young student or a student with a moderate cognitive disability, social skills might include learning how to greet others by saying hi instead of hugging, how to take turns during games or large-group activities, and how to ask to join a group. For adolescents with learning or behavior problems—students like Kathleen and Mark, whom you read about at the beginning of this chapter—social skills might include expressing emotions appropriately, disagreeing with others (especially adults) in acceptable ways, and avoiding situations in which confrontation is likely to occur. Although special educators play an active role in teaching social skills to students with especially strong needs, you can also address them. Ways in which you can bring social skills training to your classroom include informal instruction, behavioral interventions, and formal social skills training.

Using Informal Instruction

As illustrated throughout this chapter by examples of teachers actively nurturing the development of positive peer social relationships in their classrooms, you have many informal opportunities to help students develop social skills needed throughout their lives (McIntosh, Vaughn, & Bennerson, 1995; Yasutake & Bryan, 1995). For example, if you are showing students an instructional video and appropriate student interactions occur as part of it, you might want to point out in a class discussion what made the interactions so positive. Then students could practice the same skills. Similarly, classrooms could include social skills as part of classwide or school themes. For example, in a middle school students illustrated stories that demonstrated how to respond when

[Technology Notes]

Using Assistive Technology to Facilitate Cooperative Learning

Although cooperative learning has long been recognized as an effective education tool, one that enhances academic achievement as well as social interactions, students with disabilities often are at a disadvantage in cooperative learning groups when the groups rely heavily on reading skills or quick communication. Technology is helping students to overcome these barriers. For example, Xin (1999) found that using commercial math software packages with elementary students who worked either in cooperative groups or whole-group arrangements resulted in higher math achievement for the students who learned cooperatively. Furthermore, students with disabilities preferred the cooperative arrangement because they felt accepted and supported. The following table describes many ways to use basic and sophisticated assistive technology to facilitate cooperative learning.

Adaptation	Compensatory Possibility
	display coupled with the auditory feedback provides corrective feedback; the enlarged keys make it easier for younger students to manipulate the symbols.
Electronic spelling devices	Students with spelling problems can use these devices to check and correct misspellings.
Voice recognition	Students with written communication problems and/or fine motor problems can generate printed text.
Alternative input devices	Students with fine motor problems can participate in the process of entering information into the computer.

Adaptation	Compensatory Possibility
Tape recorder	Answers can be recorded.
Talking calculator with enlarged keys	Students with computational difficulties can use the calculator to check their answers; the visual

SOURCE: Adapted from "Using Assistive Technology Adaptations to Include Students with Learning Disabilities in Cooperative Learning Activities," by D. P. Bryant & B. R. Bryant, 1998. *Journal of Learning Disabilities, 31,* pp. 41–54. Copyright © 1998 by PRO-ED, Inc. Reprinted with permission.

peers were pressuring them to make fun of other students. Finally, you can individually instruct students in social skills as appropriate situations occur. When Mr. Calles observed Charles, a sophomore with a moderate cognitive disability, stick his tongue out at another student when the student laughed at him, he made it a point to speak with both boys about other ways to interact.

Even though you may consider your primary responsibility to be teaching academic content to your students, your awareness of the need to develop student social skills and your willingness to incorporate informal social skills instruction into your class instruction can contribute significantly to a sense of classroom community. Forming a positive classroom community is essential for inclusive schools.

Using Behavioral Interventions

Another strategy for teaching social skills to students is to use behavioral interventions such as the ones you learned about in Chapter 12. For example, you can reward your entire class for treating a new class member with respect and friendship. If you have a student whose social problems include teasing class members or talking out of turn, you can reward your class for not responding to the inappropriate behaviors. To use these types of behavioral interventions, you need to identify clearly the behaviors you want to foster and choose an appropriate reward structure, create a simple record-keeping system, explain the intervention to students, and systematically implement your plan. For example, in a first-grade classroom, a student with a mild cognitive disability joined the group. Ashi would periodically leave his seat or group and roam from desk to desk, sometimes leaving the classroom. At the beginning of the school year, the teacher explained to the other first graders that Ashi needed to move about more than other students and that this behavior was acceptable for Ashi but not for the rest of the class. She then asked students not to stop working if Ashi came to their desks and not to make a commotion if he left the room. When she noticed that students were following her directions, she would reward the class with five extra minutes of recess or an extra story in the afternoon. As the school year progressed, she gradually quit this type of reward and transitioned to thanking students for understanding Ashi's needs.

Behavioral interventions can also be used to reinforce appropriate social skills. When teachers see a student with social skills needs interacting appropriately, they should make a positive comment to the student. In secondary schools, these comments are usually offered in private to avoid embarrassing the student. For example, a student advisor overheard a conversation between a chemistry teacher and a student with an explosive temper. The teacher was chiding the student for failing to turn in assignments on time. The student replied, "Yeah, I know I haven't been doing too well on the homework." Later, the advisor congratulated the student for acknowledging the teacher's feedback without becoming defensive or making a comment that might have led to detention.

Using Social Skills Training Programs

If you have several students who need social skills instruction, you might find useful one of the many prepackaged **social skills training programs** available to teachers. For example, Think Aloud (Camp & Bash, 1985) is a social problem–solving package designed for use with elementary school students. Students are taught to ask themselves a series of questions whenever they are faced with a problematic situation. The questions are: What is the problem? What should I do? What is my plan? and Am I following the plan? Teachers rehearse these steps with students and provide opportunities for students to practice the steps in structured situations. Teachers also remind students to look for the steps when they observe students behaving appropriately.

An example of a social skills package for adolescents is Skillstreaming the Adolescent (Goldstein, Sprafkin, Gershaw, & Klein, 1980). This package includes structured procedures for teaching nearly 50 different social skills using modeling, role-playing, and feedback. Teachers can select and use only the skill lessons most pertinent to their class groups. For example, if a high school class is having problems because several students are extremely aggressive, the module on that topic might be helpful.

However you decide to help students develop social skills, keep in mind that several other professionals are available in your school who may have advanced training in teaching social skills and who can assist you in this aspect of your curriculum. For

Connections

Chapter 12 addressed strategies for increasing desirable student behavior. These strategies also can be applied in teaching social skills.

Check Your Learning

How could you apply what you have learned about social skills and student social relationships to the students introduced in the vignettes at the beginning of this chapter? If you were Errol's, Kathleen's, or Mark's teacher, what strategies would you include to foster positive student interactions with each of them?

example, if your school has a teacher for students with emotional disabilities, he or she might be able to co-teach social skills lessons with you. Similarly, a school counselor or social worker could help you build social skills lessons into your instructional program.

With your understanding of strategies and approaches for building student social relationships, you now have the final ingredient for making your classroom a place where students want to come and want to learn. You know about the foundations of special education and the procedures followed for identifying students with disabilities. You have a strategy—INCLUDE—for guiding your decisions about student needs and interventions. You know how important the support and assistance of colleagues and parents are, whether for planning an instructional program for a student, teaching with you in the classroom, or problem solving when concerns arise. You also understand some of the most important characteristics and needs of students with disabilities and other special needs. You have learned many strategies for helping students succeed in your classroom, including creating a positive instructional environment, assessing student needs, making instructional interventions, helping students be independent, and evaluating their learning. You have learned, too, several approaches for responding to students' discipline and behavior needs and for fostering positive social relationships among students.

What is most important, however, is the statement that appeared in the first chapter of this text: Students with disabilities and other special needs are people first. If you keep that in mind and use the knowledge you have gained, you will positively touch the lives and learning of all the students who call you teacher.

Summary

In addition to fostering the academic growth of students in inclusive schools, teachers also work to ensure that their students with and without disabilities and other special needs build positive social relationships. Learning social skills is especially important because research over the past 4 decades has demonstrated that students with disabilities are sometimes more likely than other students to have a negative status in their classrooms.

Teachers can help students develop positive peer relationships in inclusive classrooms by creating ways for students to have face-to-face interactions, nurturing the development of friendship and support among students, and providing positive role models. Another aspect of addressing the social curriculum in general education classrooms is educating students without special needs about individuals who have disabilities or other special needs. Direct presentation of information, the use of print or video media or adaptive technology, and the use of simulation activities are approaches to introducing students to the characteristics and needs of students with disabilities.

One specific instructional approach that helps create positive student relationships is peer tutoring. Peer tutoring has a long history and has recently received renewed attention. It benefits both tutors and tutees, including students with disabilities. Teachers can create tutoring programs that are contained within their classrooms or that use several class groups or even an entire school. A second instructional approach recommended for inclusive classrooms is cooperative learning. In cooperative learning, students accrue both social and academic benefits. To set up a cooperative learning program, teachers need to decide on group issues, prepare students to work cooperatively, identify the instructional content to be used in the groups, and select a cooperative learning approach, such as Jigsaw II, Numbered Heads Together, or Cooperative Integrated Reading and Composition.

Sometimes, students with disabilities need additional intensive instruction to learn social skills. This instruction can involve informal social skills instruction as part of the classroom curriculum, behavioral interventions, and formal social skills training programs, often taught in partnership with special service providers such as special education teachers.

Applications in Teaching Practice

Planning for Promoting Positive Peer Relations

Mr. Barkley is reviewing his class roster and his plans for the upcoming school year. He knows that he will have four students with learning and behavior disabilities—Jay, Doug, Ray, and Jasmine—in his sixth-hour class. He will also have Theodore, a bright young man with cerebral palsy who uses a wheelchair and has a personal attendant. Theodore cannot write or type; he points to symbols on his communication board. Having talked to other teachers, Mr. Barkley is a little worried about this group because several of the other students in the class also have special needs, including Kusi, who has attention deficit–hyperactivity disorder, and Micki, who is gifted/talented. Right now, the following items appear on his planning list:

1. Talk to Ms. M. [special education teacher]. What are reasonable expectations for the students with disabilities? Does Theodore need any extraordinary assistance? What is he going to be like in class? Do I need to know anything special about having the personal attendant in my classroom? Does she know what to do for Theodore? Can she also work with other students if it doesn't negatively affect Theodore? Should Jay, Doug, Ray, or Jasmine sit near each other or be separated? What should they be able to do in class—everything? 80 percent? What are the social goals for these students? Could we review the students' IEPs to clarify what I should stress with them?

2. Talk to counselor. Can she teach some basic social skills lessons with the class during the first 6-week grading period? Twice each week for 20 minutes?

3. Set up cooperative learning groups for first grading period and get all materials ready. Goal: Two cooperative learning activities per week, with first 2 weeks spent on teaching social skills in groups. Group size? Maybe three, given class composition, with a move to four for the second quarter.

4. Check on availability of after-school tutoring program at elementary school this year. Reward for some of the students? Other peer tutoring options?

5. Request more information on Jasmine—see note about her participation in a social work group on Thursdays during advisory period.

Mr. Barkley's planning list goes on along these lines for two more pages.

Questions

1. Why is Mr. Barkley concerned about the social interactions of his students? Why is this part of his responsibility as much as teaching his academic subject matter? How does having students with disabilities in his room increase needs in the social skills area?

2. What could Mr. Barkley do to sensitize his students to Theodore's needs? What might he do if Jay, Doug, Ray, or Jasmine becomes the object of student complaints about fairness during the course of the school year?

3. What approach to peer tutoring is Mr. Barkley considering? What options might he try to arrange? Who in his class might be the best candidates for each of the peer tutoring approaches?

4. What questions might Mr. Barkley have concerning the social needs of Kusi and Micki?

5. Mr. Barkley notes that he needs to spend the first 2 weeks of cooperative learning sessions on social skills. What skills might he teach? How can he teach them? What academic content could be included in the lessons in which social skills are being taught?

6. It appears that Mr. Barkley has one student who will receive social skills instruction in a separate group, and he is requesting that the counselor help him teach social skills during the first grading period. How could a special education teacher also help Mr. Barkley address the social needs of all his students?

Glossary

ABC analysis. Systematic recording of antecedents, behaviors, and consequences as a strategy for analyzing student behavior.

absence seizure. Seizure that is brief and often characterized by momentary lapses of attention. Also called a *petit mal seizure.*

academic learning time. The time students are meaningfully and successfully engaged in school.

academic survival skills. Skills needed to succeed in school, including regular and punctual attendance, organization, task completion, independence, motivation, and appropriate social skills.

acceleration. Approach for educating gifted and talented students based on allowing them to move through all or part of the curriculum at their own, accelerated pace.

accuracy. The extent to which a student's academic performance is without errors.

acquired immune deficiency syndrome (AIDS). Disease resulting from HIV, in which the body becomes unable to fight infection.

activity reinforcer. Positive activity that causes a behavior to increase. An example of an activity reinforcer is a student being rewarded with extra time to work on the computer.

ADA. *See* Americans with Disabilities Act.

adaptive physical educator. Specialist with expertise in assessing students' motor needs and designing and delivering physical education programs that accommodate those needs.

ADD. *See* attention deficit disorder.

ADHD. *See* attention deficit–hyperactive disorder.

administrator. Professional responsible for managing some aspect of schools; includes principals, assistant principals, department chairpersons, team leaders, special services coordinators, district administrators, and others.

advance organizer. Information, often presented as organizational signals, that makes content more understandable by putting it within a more general framework.

advocate. Individual who works to ensure that parents understand their rights and that school professionals provide an appropriate education for parents' children with disabilities.

AIDS. *See* acquired immune deficiency syndrome.

alternative assessment. A form of functional assessment for students with severe disabilities who are unable to participate in the standard state and district-wide assessment programs.

alternative teaching. Co-teaching option in which students are divided into one large and one small group. The large group receives the planned instruction. The small group receives reteaching, preteaching, enrichment, or other special instruction.

American Sign Language (ASL). A sign language not based on the grammmar or structures of English, used by some people with hearing impairments.

Americans with Disabilities Act. Civil rights law passed in 1990 that protects individuals with disabilities from discrimination and requires building and transportation accessibility and reasonable accommodations in the workplace.

anecdotal recording. Strategy for recording behavior in which incidents before and after a behavior are recorded along with a description of the behavior.

annual goal. Broad statement describing estimated yearly outcomes for a student with a disability. Annual goals address areas of identified needs.

annual review. Yearly process of convening a team that includes a parent, teacher, administrator, and others as needed to review and update a student's IEP.

ANOTES. Learning strategy for organizing lecture notes for test preparation. The steps are: ask yourself if you have a date and topic, name the main ideas and details, observe ideas also in text, try margin noting and use SAND strategy, examine for omissions or unclear ideas, and summarize key points.

anticipation guide. Series of statements, some of which may not be true, related to material that is about to be presented during instruction, given to students as a way of activating their knowledge by making predictions about the topic.

anxiety. Condition in which an individual experiences extraordinary worry in some situations or worries excessively about future situations.

articulation. Production of speech sounds.

Asperger's syndrome. Mild form of autism in which an individual develops speech but has gross motor problems, intense interests in a narrow range of topics, and chronic difficulty in forming and sustaining social relationships.

assessment. Process of gathering information to monitor progress and make educational decisions.

assistive technology. Any of a wide variety of technology applications designed to help students with disabilities learn, communicate, and otherwise function more independently by bypassing their disabilities.

asthma. Physical condition in which an individual experiences difficulty breathing, especially during physically or psychologically stressful activities.

at risk. Term used to describe students who have characteristics, live in conditions, or have experiences that make them more likely than others to experience failure in schools.

attention deficit disorder (ADD). Term sometimes used as a synonym for attention deficit–hyperactive disorder.

attention deficit–hyperactive disorder (ADHD). Medical condition in which students have significant inability to attend, excessive motor activity, and/or impulsivity.

attribution retraining. Teaching program that increases student task persistence and performance by convincing them that their failures are due to effort and can therefore be overcome.

augmentative communication. Alternative systems of communication, often using pictures, symbols, and/or words accessed through computer or other technology, sometimes used by students with disabilities.

authentic learning tasks. Tasks used in performance-based assessment that are based on real-world contexts and lead to real-world outcomes.

autism. Condition in which an individual lacks social responsiveness from a very early age, has a high need for structure and routines, and demonstrates significant language impairments. These characteristics interfere with learning.

basal textbook. A book used for instruction in basic-skills areas that contains all key components of the curriculum to be taught for that subject. Often called a *basal.*

basic-skills instruction. Instruction in the tool skills of reading, writing, and math.

behavior contract. Agreement between a teacher (or other adult) and student that clearly specifies student performance expectations, rewards for meeting expectations, consequences of not meeting expectations, and the time frame for which the agreement is valid.

Behavior intervention plan (BIP). A detailed strategy, developed on the basis of a functional behavior assessment, to address significant behavior problems being experienced by a student with a disability. The plan typically includes detailed descriptions of interventions, persons responsible, a timeline, and methods for data collection. This plan is required by federal law when a student with a disability has significant behavior problems.

big ideas. Important principles that help learners understand the connections among facts and concepts they learn.

bilingual education program. Education approach in which students with limited English skills learn core subjects in a separate setting in their native language and spend the remainder of their school day with English-speaking peers.

bilingual special education program. Special education approach in which students with disabilities with limited English skills learn core subjects in a separate setting in their native language.

bilingual special education teacher. Teacher who works with students with disabilities whose native language is not English.

bilingual teacher. Teacher who teaches students whose native language is not English.

blind. Condition in which an individual has little or no vision and relies on auditory and other input for learning.

braille. Writing system, used by individuals who have vision impairments, that uses various combinations of six raised dots punched on paper read with the fingertips.

brainstorming. Strategy for generating solutions to problems in which participants call out ideas, building on one another's responses, deferring all evaluation.

Brown v. Board of Education. Supreme Court decision in 1954 that established that it is unlawful and discriminatory to create separate schools for African American students. This "separate cannot be equal" concept was later applied to students with disabilities.

CALL UP. Learning strategy for taking lecture notes. The steps are: copy from board or transparency, add details, listen and write the question, listen and write the answer, utilize the text, and put in your words.

CAPS. Four-step learning strategy for helping a student decide what is important in a story: ask who the characters are; identify the aim of the story; decide what problem happens; and determine how the problem is solved.

catch 'em being good. Behavior management strategy in which a teacher notices appropriate student behavior and positively comments on it, either privately to the student or publicly to the class.

CBA. *See* curriculum-based assessment.

CBM. *See* cognitive behavior management.

cerebral palsy. Most common type of orthopedic impairment among public school students, caused by brain injury before or during birth and resulting in poor motor coordination and abnormal motor patterns.

CHECK. Learning strategy for using spell checkers more effectively. The steps are: check the beginning sound of the word; hunt for the correct consonants; examine the vowels; check changes in suggested word lists for hints; and keep repeating steps 1–4.

child abuse. Situation in which a parent or other caregiver inflicts or allows others to inflict injury on a child, or permits a substantial risk of injury to exist.

child neglect. Situation in which a parent or other caregiver fails to provide the necessary supports for a child's well-being.

CHROME. Mnemonic for remembering the six methods of scientific investigation: categorization, hypothesis, reasoning, observation, measurement, and experimentation.

chunking. Memorization strategy in which students are taught to remember five to seven key ideas at one time.

CIRC. *See* Cooperative Integrated Reading and Composition.

Circle of Friends. Program designed to help students without disabilities understand how important it is to have friends with disabilities and to encourage them to form friendships with classmates with disabilities.

classroom climate. The overall atmosphere of a classroom, including whether it is friendly and pleasant, based on the expectations of teachers and their interactions with students.

classroom grouping. Various grouping arrangements, such as teaching the whole class at once or in small groups, that modify the classroom environment. Classroom grouping may be teacher centered or peer mediated.

classroom instruction. Strategies through which a teacher presents curriculum content to students.

classroom organization. Strategies through which a teacher establishes and maintains order in a classroom.

cluster programs. Special education service delivery system in which students with similar needs from several schools or an entire district attend a single school to receive special education services.

cognitive behavior management (CBM). Behavior management strategy in which students learn to monitor and change their own behavior.

cognitive disability. *See* mental retardation.

collaboration. A style of interaction professionals use in order to accomplish a goal they share, often stressed in inclusive schools.

community-based education. Approach to instruction in which what is learned in school is related to activities that occur in the community.

competency checklist. Evaluation technique in which student learning is checked against a listing of key concepts or ideas being taught.

comprehension. Reading skill involving understanding the meaning of what has been read.

concept diagram. Specific type of graphic organizer used to present vocabulary words that includes definitions and characteristics.

concept map. Graphic organizer showing relationships among concepts of instruction as well as essential characteristics of the concepts.

constructivistic teaching. Type of teaching based on the belief that students are capable of constructing meaning on their own, in most cases, without explicit instruction.

consultant. Specialist who provides particular expertise to teachers and others when an extraordinary student need arises.

consultation. Specialized problem-solving process in which one professional with particular expertise assists another professional or parent who needs the benefit of that expertise; used as an instructional approach for some students with disabilities.

consulting teacher. Special education teacher who meets with general education teachers to problem solve and monitor student progress but who typically has little or no direct contact with students.

content-area textbook. A book used for instruction in science, social studies, or other content areas.

controlled materials. Instructional materials at the student's reading level, of high interest and free of complex vocabulary and concepts, often used while teaching students a learning strategy.

Cooperative Integrated Reading and Composition (CIRC). Cooperative learning program for teaching reading, writing, and other language arts to students in upper elementary grades.

cooperative learning. Student-centered instructional approach in which students work in small, mixed-ability groups with a shared learning goal.

cooperative learning program. Program in which cooperative learning approaches are integral to instruction.

COPS. Learning strategy for proofreading papers with these steps: Have I capitalized the first word and proper nouns? How is the overall appearance of my paper; have I made any handwriting, margin, or messy errors? Have I used end punctuation, commas, and semicolons carefully? Do words look like they are spelled right; can I sound them out or use a dictionary?

co-teaching. Instructional approach in which two or more teachers or other certified staff share instruction for a single group of students within a single classroom setting.

counselor. Specialist with expertise in meeting students' social and affective needs.

credit/no credit grading system. *See* pass/fail grading system.

cross-age tutoring. Peer tutoring approach in which older students tutor younger ones.

cross-categorical approach. Instructional approach in which the cognitive, learning, affective, and social and emotional needs of students, not their disability labels, form the basis for planning and delivering instruction.

cue words. Words that make patterns of information more conspicuous for students, such as the words "similar" and "different" signalling the presence of a compare/contrast pattern.

curriculum-based assessment (CBA). Method of measuring the level of achievement of students in terms of what they are taught in the classroom.

curriculum placement. Type of assessment decision concerning where to begin instruction for students.

cystic fibrosis. Genetically transmitted disease in which the body produces excessive mucus that eventually damages the lungs and causes heart failure.

daily activity log. Strategy for providing ongoing information for students and their parents about learning by noting daily observations of student work, effort, and outcomes.

deaf. Hearing impairment in which the individual cannot process linguistic information through hearing with or without the use of hearing aids and relies on visual and other input for learning.

deaf–blind. Condition in which an individual has both significant visual and hearing impairments that interfere with learning.

decibel (dB). Unit for measuring the loudness of sounds.

decoding. Reading skill involving accurately identifying words and fluently pronouncing them.

DEFENDS. Learning strategy for writing a defense of a position with these steps: decide on an exact position; examine the reasons for the position; form a list of points to explain each reason; expose the position in the first sentence; note each reason and supporting points; drive home the position in the last sentence; and search for errors and correct.

depression. Condition in which an individual is persistently and seriously unhappy, with a loss of interest or pleasure in all or almost all usual activities. Symptoms of depression include changes in appetite or weight, sleep disturbances, loss of energy, feelings of worthlessness, and thoughts of death or suicide.

developmental disability. A significant, chronic condition, typically physical, cognitive, or a combination of both, that results in the need for special education and related services. IDEA-97 permits the use of this term in lieu of a more specific disability label for children until age 9.

diabetes. Disease in which the body does not produce enough insulin to process the carbohydrates eaten.

diagnosis. Type of assessment decision concerning whether or not a student meets established federal guidelines for being classified as having a disability and, if so, the nature and extent of the disability.

diagnostic teaching. Sample lessons and other instructional activities carried out with students experiencing extreme academic or behavioral difficulty as part of screening.

differential reinforcement of incompatible behaviors. Reinforcing an appropriate behavior that is incompatible with another undesirable behavior in order to increase the positive behavior.

differentiated instruction. A form of instruction that meets students' diverse needs by providing materials and tasks of varied levels of difficulty, with varying degrees of support, through multiple instructional groups, and time variations.

direct instruction. Research-based instructional approach in which the teacher presents subject matter using a review of previously taught information, presentation of new concepts or skills, guided practice, feedback and correction, independent student practice, and frequent review.

disability. Condition characterized by a physical, cognitive, psychological, or social difficulty so severe that it negatively affects student learning. In the Americans with Disabilities Act, a disability is defined as a condition that limits some major life activity.

discipline. Term to describe the set of classroom expectations, including rules for behavior, that serves as a means for facilitating student learning.

discovery learning. *See* inquiry learning.

Down syndrome. Most prevalent type of biologically caused cognitive disability, caused by the failure of one pair of chromosomes to separate at conception.

DRAW. Strategy for teaching multiplication facts that are not yet committed to memory, consisting of these steps: discover the sign; read the problem; answer, or draw and check; and write the answer.

due process. Procedures outlined in IDEA for ensuring that parents' and children's rights are protected and for resolving disputes between parents and school district personnel concerning any aspect of special education.

duration recording. Strategy for recording behavior in which the length of time a behavior occurs is recorded.

echolalic speech. Occurs when an individual communicates by repeating what others have said instead of producing original speech.

ED. *See* emotional disturbance.

educable mentally handicapped (EMH). Somewhat outdated term still used occasionally to refer to persons with mild cognitive disabilities.

Education for the Handicapped Act (EHA). *See* P.L. 94-142.

emotional disturbance (ED). Condition in which an individual has significant difficulty in the social and emotional domain, so much so that it interferes with learning.

enrichment. Approach for educating gifted and talented students based on helping them elaborate on or extend concepts being presented to all students.

environmental inventory. Assessment procedure, often used for students with moderate or severe disabilities, designed to find out what adaptations or supports are needed to increase student participation in classroom and community environments.

epilepsy. Physical condition in which the brain experiences sudden but brief changes in its functioning leading to seizures.

evaluation. Procedures used to determine whether teaching is effective, to provide feedback to students and their parents about student learning, and to inform school boards and communities about school effectiveness.

event recording. Strategy for recording behavior in which each occurrence of the behavior is counted.

example selection. Teacher choice of examples during instruction. Example selection directly affects student understanding of instruction.

example sequence. Order of presentation of examples during instruction. Example sequence directly affects student understanding of instruction.

exemplar. A sample student performance designed to specify a level of achievement in authentic learning evaluation. For example, a writing sample of an "average" seventh grader is an exemplar against which other students' writing can be compared.

expressive language. An individual's ability to communicate meaning clearly through speech.

extinction. Strategy for decreasing negative behavior by no longer reinforcing it; most effective when the undesirable behavior has been inadvertently reinforced by the teacher.

facilitated communication. Method of assisting individuals with autism and other disabilities to communicate by gently supporting the wrist, arm, or shoulder on a typewriter or computer keyboard. This method is controversial.

fading out. Gradual process for decreasing the use of behavioral strategies to support appropriate student behavior.

FAE. *See* fetal alcohol effects.

FAS. *See* fetal alcohol syndrome.

FAST DRAW. Strategy for helping students make the transition from pictures to abstract numbers. The following steps are performed before beginning the DRAW strategy: find what you're solving for; ask yourself, "What are the parts of the problem?"; set up the numbers; and tie down the sign.

fetal alcohol effects (FAE). Mild form of fetal alcohol syndrome (FAS), often without physical characteristics. Students with FAE often experience a variety of learning and behavior problems in school.

fetal alcohol syndrome (FAS). Medical condition caused by prenatal maternal abuse of alcohol, often resulting in slight physical abnormalities and learning, cognitive, or emotional disabilities.

finger spelling. Communication system in which each alphabet letter is assigned a specific hand position. Finger spelling is often used to communicate proper names or technical words for which no other sign language signs exist.

five R's of note-taking. Learning strategy for note-taking with these steps: record the main ideas and important details; reduce to concise phrases; recite key information using your concise phrases as cues; reflect on your notes by adding your own ideas; and review all the key information.

fluency. The rate at which a student performs an academic task such as calculating math problems or reading.

FOIL. Four-step learning strategy for multiplying binomials in algebra: multiply the first terms; multiply the outermost terms; multiply the innermost terms; and multiply the last terms.

Functional behavior assessment. The process of gathering detailed data on a student's behavior and the context in which it occurs for the purpose of determining the reasons for it and creating a behavior intervention plan. This process is required by federal law when a student with a disability has significant behavior problems.

functional curriculum. Instructional approach in which goals and objectives are based on real-life skills needed for adulthood. Examples of skills addressed in a functional curriculum include shopping and making purchases; reading common signs such as exit, stop, and sale; riding public transportation; and interacting with peers and adults.

general education teacher. Elementary, middle school, junior high, or high school teacher whose primary responsibility is teaching one or more class groups.

generalized tonic-clonic seizure. Seizure involving the entire body. Also called a *grand mal seizure*.

gifted or talented. Demonstrated ability far above average in one or several areas including overall intellectual ability, leadership, specific academic subjects, creativity, athletics, or the visual or performing arts.

Good Behavior Game. Strategy for reducing disruptive behavior and promoting positive behavior in the classroom in which students work on teams to earn points for appropriate behavior toward a reward.

grading contract. Agreement between a teacher and student that specifies the quantity, quality, and timeliness of work required to receive a specific grade.

grading criteria. The standard on which a student's academic performance is evaluated and graded.

grand mal seizure. *See* generalized tonic-clonic seizure.

graphic organizer. Visual format that helps students to organize their understanding of information being presented or read and the relationships between various parts of the information.

group-administered standardized achievement test. Standardized achievement test given to large groups of students at one time, usually administered by general education teachers, useful as a screening measure.

group investigation. Cooperative learning program in which teams of two to six members plan and carry out shared projects and develop a report that is presented to the class. Class members provide feedback to each team.

group roles. Assigned roles for students in cooperative groups that help the group function effectively. Roles commonly assigned include encourager, monitor, leader, and recorder.

handicap. Term, generally no longer preferred, to describe disabilities.

hard of hearing. Hearing impairment in which an individual has some hearing through which to process linguistic information, possibly with the assistance of hearing aids or other assistive devices.

hearing impairment. Condition in which an individual has the inability or limited ability to receive information auditorily such that it interferes with learning.

hemophilia. Genetically transmitted disease in which blood does not properly coagulate.

hertz (Hz). Unit for measuring the pitch or tone of sounds.

heterogeneous grouping. *See* mixed-skill grouping.

high-incidence disability. Any of the most common disabilities outlined in P.L. 105-17, including learning disabilities, speech or language impairments, mild mental retardation, and serious emotional disturbance.

HIV. *See* human immunodeficiency virus.

homework. The most common form of student practice.

homogeneous grouping. *See* same-skill grouping.

human immunodeficiency virus (HIV). Viral disease in which the body loses its ability to fight off infection. Individuals with HIV often become infected with AIDS.

hyperactive-impulsive disorder. Type of ADHD characterized by excessive movement and other motor activity including fidgeting, a need to move around a room even when others are seated, and rapid changes in activities.

Individuals with Disabilities Education Act (IDEA). *See* P.L. 101-476.

IEP. *See* individual education program.

IFSP. *See* Individualized Family Service Plan.

improvement grade. Giving credit in evaluation of student performance for progress made, based on the student's level of learning prior to instruction.

impulsivity. The extent to which an individual acts before thinking, often a characteristic of students with high-incidence disabilities or ADHD.

INCLUDE. Strategy for accommodating students with special needs in the general education classroom.

inclusion. Term to describe a professional belief that students with disabilities should be integrated into general education classrooms whether or not they can meet traditional curricular standards and should be full members of those classrooms.

inclusion specialist. Special education teacher responsible for providing a wide variety of supports to students with disabilities and general education teachers who teach them. Inclusion specialists most often work with students with low-incidence disabilities. Sometimes called a *support facilitator.*

independent learning skills. Skills students need to manage their own learning, including note-taking, textbook reading, test-taking, written expression, and time management.

Individualized Education Program (IEP). Document prepared by the multidisciplinary team or annual review team that specifies a student's level of functioning and needs, the instructional goals and objectives for the student and how they will be evaluated, the nature and extent of special education and related services to be received, and the initiation date and duration of the services. Each student's IEP is updated annually.

Individualized Family Service Plan (IFSP). Education plan for children receiving services through P.L. 99-457. Similar to an IEP.

individualized instruction. Instruction designed to meet the specific needs of a student with a disability; a requirement of IDEA.

individually administered diagnostic test. Diagnostic achievement test given to one student at a time, often administered by a special education teacher or school psychologist, useful as a diagnostic measure. These tests provide more specific information than group-administered achievement tests do.

Individuals with Disabilities Education Act Amendments of 1997. Federal education law that updates the 1975 Education of the Handicapped Act and ensures that students with disabilities receive special education and related services through prescribed policies and procedures.

inquiry learning. The most common method of nondirect instruction. *See also* nondirect instruction.

instructional adaptation. Any strategy for adapting curriculum materials, teacher instruction, or student practice activities that increases the likelihood of success for students with special needs.

instructional assistance team. Team of teachers, specialists, and administrators that solves problems about students experiencing academic or behavior difficulty and decides whether students should be individually assessed for possible special education services.

instructional evaluation. Type of assessment decision concerning whether to continue or change instructional procedures that have been initiated with students.

instructional materials. The textbooks, manipulatives, models, and technology used as part of instruction.

integration. The physical, social, and instructional assimilation of students with disabilities in general education settings.

intent. The purpose or goal of a student's behavior, not always clear from the behavior itself. An example of an intent occurs when a student repeatedly calls out in class to gain the teacher's attention; that is, the intent is teacher attention.

interval recording. Strategy for recording behavior in which observation occurs for brief segments of time and any occurrence of the behavior during the segment is noted.

itinerant teacher. Special education teacher who provides services to students with disabilities and teaches in two or more schools.

Jigsaw. Cooperative learning program in which work group team members are assigned to expert groups to master part of the assigned material to which no other group has access. In the work group, each team member has an opportunity to present his or her part of the material. Students are then assessed for mastery individually.

Jigsaw II. Cooperative learning program in which students interact in both work groups and expert groups to learn assigned materials. Students are then assessed separately.

job coach. A special education professional who accompanies students with disabilities to job sites and helps them master the skills needed to perform the job.

keyword method. Mnemonic for remembering definitions and factual information in which visual imagery is used to enhance recall.

KWL Plus. Three-step learning strategy for reading comprehension: what you already know; what you want to know; and what you learned.

LAMPS. Learning strategy for remembering the steps for regrouping in addition with these steps: line up the numbers according to their decimal points; add the right column of numbers; if more than nine continue to the next step; put the 1s below the column; and send the 10s to the top of the next column.

LD. *See* learning disability.

learned helplessness. Characteristic of some students with disabilities in which they see little relationship between their own efforts and school or social success, often resulting in a belief that they cannot perform challenging tasks.

learning and behavior disabilities. Term used to describe collectively learning disabilities, serious emotional disturbance, and mild cognitive disabilities.

learning disability (LED). Condition in which a student has dysfunction in processing information typically found in language-based activities, resulting in interference with learning. Students with learning disabilities have average or above average intelligence but experience significant problems in learning how to read, write, and/or use a computer.

learning outcomes. Specific goals or outcomes students are expected to accomplish as a result of a unit of instruction.

learning strategies. Techniques, principles, or rules that enable a student to solve problems and complete tasks independently.

Learning Together. Cooperative learning program in which groups of two to six members learn specific skills for interacting with one another and then work together in various formal and informal group structures to learn material.

least restrictive environment (LRE). The setting as similar as possible to that for students without disabilities in which a student with a disability can be educated, with appropriate supports provided. For most students, the LRE is a general education classroom.

legal blindness. Visual impairment in which an individual's best eye, with correction, has vision of 20/200 or less, or the visual field is 20 percent or less.

lesson organizer routine. A teaching method that helps teachers convert content into understandable formats that meet the diverse needs of students. The method has three components: the lesson organizer device, linking steps, and cue-do-review sequence.

low demand request. Behavior management strategy in which the teacher helps a student transition from one activity to another by making a series of simple requests of the student that are unrelated to the targeted task.

low-incidence disability. Any of the less common disabilities outlined in P.L. 105-17, including multiple disabilities, hearing impairments, orthopedic impairments, other health impairments, visual impairments, deaf-blindness, autism, and traumatic brain injury.

LRE. *See* least restrictive environment.

mainstreaming. Term for placing students with disabilities in general education settings when they can meet traditional academic expectations with minimal assistance, or when those expectations are not relevant.

maintenance goal. Type of goal teams set that describes what the team wants to accomplish in terms of its own effectiveness.

manipulatives. Concrete objects or representational items used as part of instruction. Examples of commonly used manipulatives include blocks and counters.

MDT. *See* multidisciplinary team.

mediation. Process in which a neutral professional assists parents and school district personnel in resolving disputes concerning any aspect of a student's special education.

mental retardation. Condition in which an individual has significant limitations in cognitive ability and adaptive behaviors that interfere with learning. Also referred to as a *cognitive disability*.

mild cognitive disabilities. Condition in which students have some difficulty meeting the academic and social demands of general education classrooms due in large part to below average intellectual functioning (55–70 on an IQ test).

minimum intervention. Strategy for promoting positive behavior that is nonintrusive and often spontaneous instead of systematic and long term. Examples of minimum interventions include noticing positive student behavior and commenting on it and moving students from one activity to another by making unrelated but easily accomplished requests first.

mixed-skill grouping. Classroom grouping arrangement in which students are clustered for instruction without focusing on specific skill needs. Also referred to as *heterogeneous grouping*.

mnemonic. A device or code used to assist memory by imposing an order on the information to be remembered.

mobility specialist. Specialist who helps students with visual impairments learn to be familiar with their environments and able to travel from place to place independently and safely.

model. Concrete representation that can help students make connections between abstractions and real-life physical objects or processes.

modified course syllabus. A document produced by the IEP team that states the specific course requirements, expectations, grading criteria, and other changes necessary because of a student's disability.

modified curricular expectations. Individualized expectations, different from those of other students, set for students with disabilities on the basis of the goals and objectives summarized in the IEP.

multicultural education. Approaches to education that reflect the diversity of society.

multidisciplinary team (MDT). Team including teachers, specialists, administrators, and parents who assess a student's individual needs, determine eligibility for special education, and develop the IEP.

multimedia software. Computer programs that combine written words, graphics, sound, and animation.

multiple disabilities. Condition in which individuals have two or more of the disabilities outlined in P.L. 101–476, although no one can be determined to be predominant.

multiple intelligences. Concept proposed by Howard Gardner (1993) that suggests there are seven types of intelligence, not just one.

multisensory approach. Instructional approach that emphasizes the use of more than one modality for teaching and learning. For example, having a student read a vocabulary word, spell it out loud, and then write it on paper is a multisensory approach to teaching vocabulary.

muscular dystrophy. Disease that weakens muscles, causing orthopedic impairments. This disease is progressive, often resulting in death during the late teenage years.

negative example. Instructional stimulus that does not illustrate the concept being taught, used with examples to ensure that students understand the instruction. Also called *nonexample*.

negative reinforcement. A potential negative consequence to a behavior that causes the behavior to increase.

nondirect instruction. Instructional approach often used for teaching higher-order thinking skills, including problem solving, in which the teacher guides learning by challenging students' thinking and helping them address problems.

novelty. Approach for educating gifted and talented students based on allowing students to learn traditional content using alternative or unusual strategies that might include working with an adult mentor, creating materials for other students to use, or using a problem-based learning approach.

Numbered Heads Together. Cooperative learning program in which students number off. The teacher poses a question; the students work together to ensure all members know the answer, and then the teacher calls a number. Students with the number stand, and one is called upon to respond to the question, with correct responses scoring points for the team.

nurse. Specialist who has expertise in understanding and responding to students' medical needs and who sometimes serves as a liaison between medical and school professionals.

occupational therapist. Specialist with expertise in meeting students' needs in the area of fine motor skills, including self-help skills such as feeding and dressing.

one-to-one instruction. Classroom grouping arrangement in which individual students work with either a teacher or computer in materials geared to their level and at their own pace.

organizational patterns. Ways in which content area texts are written to reflect main ideas such as compare-contrast, cause-effect, and problem solution.

orthopedic impairments. Physical conditions that seriously impair the ability to move about or to complete motor activities and interfere with learning.

other health impairments. Conditions in which an individual has a disease or disorder so significant that it affects his or her ability to learn. Examples could include sickle-cell anemia and AIDS.

overcorrection. Type of presentation punishment in which a student makes restitution for misbehavior. An example of overcorrection is a student cleaning all the desks in a room as a consequence for writing on one desk.

PACE 1,2. A self-monitoring strategy for evaluating assignments. The steps are: prompt (on time), arranged neatly, complete, and edited.

parallel teaching. Co-teaching option in which students are divided into small groups and each group receives the same instruction from one of the teachers in the room.

paraprofessional. Noncertified staff member employed to assist certified staff in carrying out education programs and otherwise help in the instruction of students with disabilities.

PARS. Learning strategy for reading textbooks with these steps: preview the material, ask questions, read the chapter, and summarize the main ideas.

partially sighted. Condition in which an individual has a significant visual impairment but is able to capitalize on residual sight using magnification devices and other adaptive materials.

pass/fail grading system. Evaluation procedure in which minimum competency levels established by the teacher are identified; students meeting or exceeding these are given a passing evaluation and those not meeting them are given a failing evaluation.

passive learner. Learner who does not believe in his or her own ability, has limited knowledge of problem-solving strategies, and is unable to determine when to use a strategy.

pattern guide. A graphic organizer designed to help students organize their written papers.

peer comparison. A component of curriculum-based assessment in which a student's performance is compared to that of classmates as a means of determining whether a learning problem exists.

peer editing. Component of student writing in which students review, evaluate, and provide feedback to each other about their written work.

peer tutoring. Student-centered instructional approach in which pairs of students help one another and learn by teaching.

peer tutoring program. Program emphasizing the use of peers as teachers.

performance-based assessment. Method of evaluation that measures what students can do with knowledge rather than measuring specific bits of knowledge the student possesses.

permanent product recording. Strategy for recording behavior in which samples of student work and other permanent evidence of student behavior are collected and evaluated.

personal assistant. Paraprofessional specially trained to monitor and assist a particular student with a disability.

personalized grading plans. A systematic approach to grading students with disabilities that stresses collaboration, establishes agreed-upon purpose for grading, and links grading adaptation to existing curricular and instructional adaptations.

personal role. One of the roles individuals bring to a team, consisting of characteristics, knowledge, skills, and perceptions based on life experiences broader than those in the professional area.

petit mal seizure. *See* absence seizure.

physical punishment. Type of presentation punishment, not recommended for use by teachers, that involves a negative physical consequence for misbehavior.

physical therapist. Specialist with expertise in meeting students' needs in the area of gross motor skills.

placement. Location in which education will occur for a student with a disability.

P.L. 94-142. Legislation, also called the *Education for the Handicapped Act (EHA)*, passed in 1975, which set federal guidelines for special education and related services and the procedures for establishing and monitoring them.

P.L. 99-457. Legislation passed in 1986 that extended the provisions of special education to very young children, those birth to 5 years of age.

P.L. 101-476. Individuals with Disabilities Education Act, legislation passed in 1990 that updated and extended P.L. 94-142. P.L. 101-476 is also called *IDEA*.

P.L. 105-17. Individuals with Disabilities Education Act, legislation passed in 1997 that updated and extended P.L. 101-476. P.L. 105-17 is also called *IDEA-97*.

planning think sheet. Set of questions to which students respond as a strategy for assisting them to activate background knowledge in preparation for writing.

portfolio assessment. Method of evaluation in which a purposeful collection of student work is used to determine student effort, progress, and achievement in one or more areas.

positive reinforcement. A consequence to a behavior that causes it to increase. Also called a *reward*.

POSSE. Learning strategy for reading comprehension with these steps: predict ideas, organize the ideas, search for the structure, summarize the main ideas, and evaluate your understanding.

POWER. Learning strategy for writing with these steps: planning, organizing, writing, editing, and revising.

PReP strategy. Strategy for determining how much background information students have about a topic.

prereferral assistance team. *See* instructional assistance team.

present level of functioning. Information about a student's current level of academic achievement, social skills, behavior, communication skills, and other areas that is included on an IEP.

presentation punishment. Presenting negative consequences as a strategy for decreasing behavior.

preskill. Basic skill necessary for performing a more complex skill.

primary reinforcer. Food or other items related to human needs that cause a behavior to increase, used only occasionally in schools. An example of a primary reinforcer is a piece of licorice earned for appropriate behavior.

probe. Quick and easy measure of student performance (accuracy and fluency) in the basic-skill areas of reading, math, and written expression consisting of timed samples of academic behaviors.

probe of basic academic skills. *See* probe.

probe of prerequisite skills. Specific type of probe designed to assess whether a student has the prerequisite skills needed to succeed in the planned instruction.

professional role. One of the roles individuals bring to a team, including knowledge, skills, and perceptions based on professional training and experience.

program evaluation. Type of assessment decision concerning whether a special education program should be terminated, continued as is, or modified.

program placement. Type of assessment decision concerning where a student's special education services will take place.

psychological test. Test designed to measure how efficiently students learn in an instructional situation; often used to assess intelligence and to determine whether learning disabilities exist.

psychologist. *See* school psychologist.

psychometrist. Specialist with expertise in assessment who in some states completes much of the individual assessment required to determine eligibility for special education services.

pullout model. Instructional approach in which students with disabilities leave the general education classroom once or more each day to receive special education services.

punishment. Any response of consequence that has the effect of decreasing a behavior.

rate of introduction. The pace at which new skills are introduced during instruction.

RAP. Reading comprehension strategy consisting of three steps: read the paragraph; ask yourself "What was the main idea and what were two details?"; put the main idea and details in your own words.

READS. Textbook-reading strategy consisting of five steps: review headings and subheadings; examine boldfaced words; ask, "What do I expect to learn?"; do it—read!; summarize in your own words.

reasoning. A range of important learning skills, including comprehension, generalization, induction, and sequencing.

rebound effect. Potential side effect of medication in which as medication wears off the individual displays symptoms worse than those that existed before medication was given. Rebound effects are a particular concern for medications prescribed for students with ADHD.

receptive language. An individual's ability to understand what people mean when they speak.

reciprocal teaching. Teaching students to comprehend reading material by providing them with teacher and peer models of thinking behavior and then allowing them to practice these thinking behaviors with their peers.

reciprocal tutoring. Same-age tutoring approach in which students in the same class are randomly assigned and take turns teaching each other. *See also* reciprocal teaching.

regular class. One placement for students with disabilities. Also referred to as a *general education class.*

rehearsal strategy. Test-taking strategy that involves saying information out loud, repeating it, checking it for accuracy, and repeating it again as part of studying.

reinforcement. Any response or consequence that causes a behavior to increase.

reinforcement menu. List of rewards from which students may choose, often most effective if students participate in its development.

related services. Services students with disabilities need to benefit from their educational experience. Examples of related services include transportation, speech therapy, physical therapy, and counseling.

removal punishment. Taking away from a student something that is desired as a strategy for decreasing inappropriate behavior.

residential facility. Placement for students with disabilities when their needs cannot be met at a school. Students attend school and live at a residential facility.

resource room. Classroom to which students come for less than 50 percent of the school day to receive special education.

resource teacher. Special education teacher who provides direct services to students with disabilities either in a special education or general education classroom and who also meets to solve problems with teachers. Resource teachers most often work with students with high-incidence disabilities.

response cost. Type of removal punishment in which a student loses privileges or other rewards as a consequence of inappropriate behavior.

response format. The way in which a student is expected to respond to test items. Examples of response formats include writing true or false, circling a correct answer from a list of four, drawing a line to match items, or writing an essay.

retention. Ability to remember information after time has passed.

RICE. Strategy for involving students in the portfolio process. Steps include: rationale—why are you keeping a portfolio?; identify goals—what do you want to improve?; contents—what will you include in your portfolio?; evaluation—how, and when, will you assess your portfolio?

Ritalin. Psychostimulant medication commonly prescribed for individuals with ADHD.

same-age tutoring. Peer tutoring approach in which students in the same class or grade level tutor one another, typically with higher-achieving students assisting lower-achieving students.

same-skill grouping. Classroom grouping arrangement in which all students needing instruction on a particular skill are clustered for that instruction. Also referred to as *homogeneous grouping.*

SAND. Learning strategy to visually organize lecture notes. The steps are: state important ideas; arrange arrows to connect ideas; number key points in order; and devise abbreviations.

satiation. Situation in which a positive reinforcer, used repeatedly, loses its effectiveness.

scaffolding. Instructional approach for teaching higher-order thinking skills in which the teacher supports student learning by reviewing the cognitive strategy to be addressed, regulating difficulty during practice, providing varying contexts for student practice, providing feedback, increasing student responsibility for learning, and creating opportunities for independent student practice.

school psychologist. Specialist with expertise to give individual assessments of students in cognitive, academic, social, emotional, and behavioral domains. This professional also designs strategies to address students' academic and social behavior problems.

SCAN. Self-questioning strategy for proofreading sentences. The questions are: Does it make sense?; Is it connected to my belief?; Can I add more?; and Are there any errors to note?

screening. Type of assessment decision concerning whether or not a student's academic or behavior performance is different enough from that of his or her peers to merit further, more in-depth assessment.

SCROL. Learning strategy for teaching students to use text headings to aid their comprehension with these steps: survey the headings, connect, read the text, outline, and look back.

SCUBA-D. Learning strategy for identifying technical, multisyllabic words in content-area texts. The steps are: sound it out, check the clues, use the main ideas and picture clues, break the word into parts, ask for help, and dive into the dictionary.

Section 504. The section of the Vocational Rehabilitation Act of 1973 that prohibits discrimination against all individuals with disabilities in programs that receive federal funds.

self-advocacy. Extent to which a student can identify supports needed to succeed and communicate that information effectively to others, including teachers and employers.

self-awareness. Extent to which a student has an accurate perception of his or her learning strengths, learning needs, and ability to use strategies to learn independently.

self-control training. A strategy in which students who lack self-control are taught to redirect their actions by talking to themselves.

self-image. Individual's perception of his or her own abilities, appearance, and competence.

self-instruction. Strategy in which students are taught to talk themselves through tasks.

self-monitoring. Strategy in which students are taught to check whether they have performed targeted behaviors.

self-questioning. Strategy in which students are taught to guide their performance by asking themselves relevant questions.

self-reinforcement. Strategy in which students reward themselves for behaving appropriately or achieving success in learning tasks.

sensory impairment. Disability related to vision or hearing.

separate class. Classroom in which students with disabilities spend 50 percent or more of the school day.

separate school. School serving only students with disabilities.

shared problem solving. Process used by groups of professionals, sometimes including parents, for identifying problems, generating potential solutions, selecting and implementing solutions, and evaluating the effectiveness of solutions.

short-term objective. Description of a step followed in order to achieve an annual goal.

sickle-cell anemia. Inherited disorder occurring most often in African Americans in which red blood cells are abnormally shaped and weakened.

signed exact English (SEE). A form of sign language in which spoken English is converted word-for-word into signs.

sign language interpreter. Specialist who listens to instruction and other communication and relays it to students with hearing impairments through sign language.

simulation. Activity in which students experience what it might be like to have a disability; in a technology context, simulations are computer programs that teach problem solving, decision making, and risk taking by having students react to real-life and imaginary situations.

SLOBS. Learning strategy to help students with regrouping in subtraction with these steps: if smaller, follow the steps; if larger, leap to subtract; cross off the number in the next column; borrow by taking one 10 and adding to the next column; subtract.

SLOW CaPS. Learning strategy for writing four kinds of paragraphs with these steps: show the type of paragraph in the first sentence; list the details you want to write about, order the details; write details in complete sentences; CAP off the paragraph with a concluding, passing, or summary sentence.

slow learner. Student whose educational progress is below average, but not so severe as to be considered a cognitive disability, and is consistent with the student's abilities.

social cues. Verbal or nonverbal signals people give that communicate a social message.

social reinforcer. Positive interpersonal interaction that causes a behavior to increase. An example of a social reinforcer is a teacher praising a student's appropriate behavior.

social skills. Behaviors that help students interact successfully with their peers, teachers, and others and that help them win social acceptance.

social-skills training program. Systematic instruction designed to help students acquire social skills.

social worker. Specialist with expertise in meeting students' social needs and fostering working relationships with families.

sophistication. Approach for educating gifted and talented students based on helping students learn complex principles about subject matter being presented to the entire class.

special education. Specially designed instruction provided by the school district or other local education agency that meets the unique needs of students identified as disabled.

special education teacher. Teacher whose primary responsibility is delivering and managing the delivery of special education services to students with disabilities.

Special Friends. Program designed to promote friendships between students with disabilities and those without disabilities.

special services coordinator. Administrator responsible for interpreting guidelines related to educating students with disabilities and assisting other school district personnel in carrying out those guidelines.

speech articulation. The ability to produce sounds correctly at the age where they would normally be expected to develop.

speech or language impairment. Condition in which student has extraordinary difficulties in communicating with others due to causes other than maturation and that interferes with learning.

speech reading. Strategy used by individuals with hearing impairments to gain information by watching a person's lips, mouth, and expression. Only a small proportion of a spoken message can typically be discerned through speech reading.

speech/language therapist. Specialist with expertise in meeting students' communication needs, including articulation and language development.

spina bifida. Birth defect in which there is an abnormal opening in the spinal column, often leading to partial paralysis.

spinal cord injury. Condition in which the spinal cord is damaged or severed because of accident or injury, leading to orthopedic impairments.

STAD. *See* Student Teams–Achievement Divisions.

standardized achievement test. Norm-referenced test designed to measure academic progress, or what students have retained in the curriculum.

station teaching. Co-teaching option in which students are divided into small groups and each group receives part of its instruction from each teacher.

stereotypic behavior. An action or motion repeated over and over again. Examples of stereotypic behaviors include spinning an object, rocking the body, and twirling.

story grammar. Description of the typical elements of stories, including theme, setting, character, initiating events, attempts at resolution, resolution, and reactions.

story map. Graphic organizer for narrative material.

strategic reader. An enhanced electronic version of a textbook designed to offer support for students in word identification, comprehension, and study skills.

student evaluation. Determination of the extent to which students have mastered academic skills or other instructional content, frequently communicated through grades.

student self-evaluation. Assessment approach in which students are asked to perform a task, are given a checklist of strategy steps for the task, and then are asked to tell which of these steps they did or did not use.

Student Teams–Achievement Divisions (STAD). Cooperative learning program in which groups of four members learn material together and take quizzes separately. Students earn points based on their own improvement over past quiz scores. These points are contributed to a team score.

study guide. General term for outlines, abstracts, or questions that emphasize important information in texts.

stuttering. Speech impairment in which an individual involuntarily repeats a sound or word, resulting in a loss of speech fluency.

support facilitator. *See* inclusion specialist.

surface behavior. Initial student behaviors that teachers could interpret as misbehavior. Responding appropriately to surface behaviors can prevent them from escalating into more serious discipline problems.

TAG. Learning strategy for peer editing with these steps: tell what you like, ask questions, and give suggestions.

TAI. *See* Team Assisted Individualization.

tangible reinforcer. Prizes or other objects students want and can earn through appropriate behavior and that cause that behavior to increase. An example of a tangible reinforcer is a school pencil earned for appropriate behavior.

task analysis. Six-step strategy for managing time: decide exactly what you must do; decide how many steps are needed to complete the task; decide how much time each step will take; set up a schedule; get started; finish the task.

task goal. Type of goal teams set that describes the business the team was formed to accomplish.

TBI. *See* traumatic brain injury.

teacher-centered instruction. Classroom instructional arrangement in which the pattern of interaction is between teacher and student, with the teacher as the central figure.

team. Formal work group that has clear goals, active and committed members, leaders, clear procedures followed in order to accomplish goals, and strategies for monitoring effectiveness.

Team Assisted Individualization (TAI). Cooperative learning program in which groups of four members work at their own pace on individualized math materials and seek assistance as needed from other team members. Individual tests are taken to pass out of a unit. Teams earn points each week based on the number of units members have successfully completed.

team role. One of the formal or informal roles individuals bring to a team, consisting of contributions made to help ensure effective team functioning. Examples of formal team roles include team facilitator, recorder, and timekeeper. Examples of informal team roles include compromiser, information seeker, and reality checker.

team teaching. Co-teaching option in which students remain in one large group and teachers share leadership in the instructional activity of the classroom.

Teams–Games–Tournaments (TGT). Cooperative learning program in which groups of three members help each other learn assigned material. Team members then compete at tournament tables with classmates at a similar achievement level. Quizzes are given or instructional games played based on the assigned material. Members contribute points to their teams based on their performance at their tournament table.

test administration. The conditions under which a test is given to students.

test construction. The way in which test items are worded, ordered on the test, and formatted.

test site. The location in which a test is given.

test-taking skills. Learning strategies taught to students to help them succeed in studying for and taking tests.

three-year reevaluation. Triannual process of reassessing the needs of a student with a disability, carried out by a multidisciplinary team.

time-out. Type of removal punishment in which a student is removed from opportunities for reward. An example of timeout is a "penalty box" for misbehavior on the playground.

time sampling. Strategy for recording behavior in which a behavior is periodically observed and measured during a specified time period.

token economy. Group behavior management procedure in which students earn a representative or token currency for appropriate behavior that can later be exchanged for rewards.

tracking. Educational practice of grouping students for instruction by their perceived ability level.

transition plan. Document for students with disabilities who are as young as 14 years old that describes strategies for assisting them prepare to leave school for adult life.

transition specialist. Special educator who helps prepare students with disabilities for postschool activities, including employment, vocational training, or higher education.

transition time. The time it takes a group of students to change from one classroom activity to another.

traumatic brain injury (TBI). Condition in which an individual experiences a significant trauma to the head from accident, illness, or injury and that affects learning.

tutorial. Computer program designed to present new material to students in small sequential steps and/or to review concepts.

unison responding. All students responding at once to teacher questions or other instruction.

visual impairment. Condition in which an individual has an inability or limited ability to receive information visually, so much so that it interferes with learning.

wait time. Amount of time a teacher gives a student to respond to a question.

written language difficulties. Problems that students with learning and behavior disabilities have with skills related to handwriting, spelling, and written expression.

References

Aber, M. E., Bachman, B., Campbell, P., & O'Malley, G. (1994). Improving instruction in elementary schools. *Teaching Exceptional Children, 26*(3), 42–50.

Abikoff, H. (1991). Cognitive training in ADHD children: Less to it than meets the eye. *Journal of Learning Disabilities, 24,* 205–209.

Abramowitz, A. J., & O'Leary, S. G. (1991). Attention-deficit hyperactivity disorder: Treatment. *School Psychology Review, 20,* 220–235.

Adams, D., & Hamm, M. (1991). Diversity gives schools infinite learning possibilities: Learning cooperatively proves successful tool to highlight many cultural values. *School Administrator, 4*(48), 20–22.

Adams, G. L., & Engelmann, S. (1996*). Research on direct instruction: 25 years beyond DISTAR.* Seattle: Educational Achievement Systems.

Adams, L. (Ed.). (1994). *Attention deficit disorders: A handbook for Colorado educators.* Denver: Colorado Department of Education.

Adams, L., Carl, C. A., Covino, M. E., Filibin, J., Knapp, J., Rich, J. P., Warfield, M. A., & Yenowine, W. (1991). *Guidelines paper: Traumatic brain injury.* Denver: Colorado Department of Education Special Education Services Unit.

ADHD Owner's Manual. (2000). *Who gets it: Demographics.* Retrieved September 13, 2000, from the World Wide Web: http://www.edutechsbs.com/adhd/00005.htm

Advocacy Incorporated. (2000). *Section 504, students with disabilities, and public schools.* Austin, TX: Author. Retrieved September 12, 2000, from the World Wide Web: http://www.advocacyinc/107.htm

Affleck, J. Q., Lowenbraun, S., & Archer, A. (1980). *Teaching the mildly handicapped in the regular classroom.* Columbus, OH: Merrill.

Algozzine, B., Audette, B., Ellis, E., Marr, M. B., & White, R. (2000). Supporting teachers, principals—and students—through unified discipline. *Teaching Exceptional Children, 33*(2), 42–47.

Algozzine, B., Ysseldyke, J. E., & Campbell, P. (1994). Strategies and tactics for effective instruction. *Teaching Exceptional Children, 26*(3), 34–36.

Alley, G. R. (1988). Effects of generalization instruction on the written language performance of adolescents with learning disabilities in the mainstream classroom. *Reading, Writing, and Learning Disabilities, 4,* 291–309.

Allinder, R. M., Bolling, R. M., Oats, R. G., & Gagnon, W. A. (2000). Effects of teacher self-monitoring on implementation of curriculum-based measurement and mathematics computation achievement of students with disabilities. *Remedial and Special Education, 21*(4), 219–226.

Allport, G. (1954). *The nature of prejudice.* Cambridge, MA: Addison-Wesley.

Allsopp, D. H. (1997). Using classwide peer tutoring to teach beginning algebra problem-solving skills in heterogeneous classrooms. *Remedial and Special Education, 18,* 367–379.

Altwerger, B., & Ivener, B. L. (1996). Self-esteem: Access to literacy in multicultural and multilingual classrooms. In R. Pritchard & Spangenberg-Urbschat K. (Eds.), *Kids come in all languages: Reading instruction for ESL students* (pp. 65–81). Newark, DE: International Reading Association.

Alvarez, L. I. G. (1998). A short course in sensitivity training: Working with Hispanic families of children with disabilities. *Teaching Exceptional Children, 31*(1), 73–77.

American Academy of Pediatrics. (1976). Committee on nutrition: Megavitamin therapy for childhood psychoses and learning disabilities. *Pediatrics, 58,* 910–911.

American Psychiatric Association. (1994). *Diagnostic and statistical manual of mental disorders* (4th ed.). Washington, DC: Author.

Anderson, C., & Katsiyannis, A. (1997). By what token economy?: A classroom learning tool for inclusive settings. *Teaching Exceptional Children, 29*(4), 65–67.

Anderson, K., & Milliren, A. (1983). *Structured experiences for integration of handicapped children.* Rockville, MD: Aspen.

Anholt, K., McNeil, C. B., & Bahl, A. B. (1998). The ADHD classroom kit: A whole-classroom approach for managing disruptive behavior. *Psychology in the Schools, 35,* 67–79.

Archer, A., & Gleason, M. (1997). Direct instruction in content area reading. In D. Carnine, J. Silbert, & E. Kameenui (Eds.), *Direct instruction reading* (3rd ed., pp. 339–393). Columbus, OH: Merrill.

Arends, R. I. (1991). *Learning to teach.* New York: McGraw-Hill.

Armbruster, B. B. (1984). The problem of "inconsiderate text." In G. G. Duffy, L. R. Roehler, & J. Mason (Eds.), *Comprehensive instruction: Perspectives and suggestions* (pp. 202–217). New York: Longman.

Armbruster, B. B., & Anderson, T. H. (1988). On selecting "considerate" content area textbooks. *Remedial and Special Education, 9*(1), 47–52.

Armstrong v. Kline, 476 F. Supp. 583 (E. D. Pa. 1979).

Armstrong, T. (1994). *Multiple intelligences in the classroom* (2nd edition). Alexandria, VA: Associations for Supervision and Curriculum Development.

Aronson, E., Blaney, N., Stephen, C., Sikes, J., & Snapp, M. (1978). *The jigsaw classroom.* Beverly Hills, CA: Sage.

Artiles, A. J., Aguirre-Munoz, Z., & Abedi, J. (1998). Predicting placement in learning disabilities programs: Do predictors vary by ethnic group? *Exceptional Children, 64,* 543–559.

Ashton, T. M. (1999). Spell checking: Making writing meaningful in the inclusive classroom. *Teaching Exceptional Children, 32*(2), 24–27.

Atwood, A. (1993). Movement disorders and autism acquired in review of communication abound. *American Journal of Mental Retardation, 99,* 450–451.

Aune, E. (1991). A transition model for postsecondary-bound students with learning disabilities. *Learning Disabilities Research and Practice, 6,* 177–187.

Aurbach & Associates. (2001). *Grady profile: Portfolio assessment.* St. Louis: Author.

Bahr, M. W., Whitten, E., Dieker, L., Kocarek, C. E., & Manson, D. (1999). A comparison of school-based intervention teams: Implications for educational and legal reform. *Exceptional Children, 66,* 67–84.

Bailey, J., & McTighe, H. (1996). Reporting achievement at the secondary level: What and how. In T. Guskey (Ed.), *ASCD yearbook: 1996 communicating student learning* (pp. 199–240). Alexandria, VA: Association for Supervision and Curriculum Development.

Baker, S., & Baker, K. (1997). Educating children who are deaf or hard of hearing: Bilingual-bicultural education (ERIC Digest No. 553). Reston, VA: ERIC Clearinghouse on disabilities and Gifted Education. (ERIC Documentation Reproduction Service No. ED 416 671)

Banks, J. A. (1993). Multicultural education: Development, dimensions, and challenges. *Phi Delta Kappan, 75,* 22–28.

Barclay, L. (1999). Yo-yo magic or a teacher of the visually impaired learns another lesson in social skills. *RE:view, 31,* 126–128.

Barkley, R. (1995). *Taking charge of ADHD: The complete authoritative guide for parents.* New York: Guilford Press.

Barkley, R. A. (1998). Attention-deficit hyperactivity disorder. *Scientific American, 279*(3), 66–71.

Barnett, C., & Monda-Amaya, L. E. (1998). Principals' knowledge of and attitudes toward inclusion. *Remedial and Special Education, 19,* 181–192.

Baroody, A. J. (1989, October). Manipulatiaves don't come with guarantees. *Arithmetic Teacher,* 4–5.

Barron, A. M., & Foot, H. (1991). Peer tutoring and tutor training. *Educational Research, 33,* 174–185.

Bartlett, L. (2000). Medical services: The disrupted related service. *Journal of Special Education, 33,* 215–223.

Bartelt, L., Marchio, T., & Reynolds, D. (1994). *The READS strategy.* Unpublished manuscript, Northern Illinois University.

Barth, R. S. (1990). *Improving schools from within.* San Francisco: Jossey-Bass.

Battle v. Commonwealth of Pennsylvania, 629 F.2d 269 (3d Cir. 1980).

Bauer, A. M., & Sapona, R. H. (1991). *Managing classrooms to facilitate learning.* Englewood Cliffs, NJ: Prentice-Hall.

Bauwens, J., & Hourcade, J. J. (1995). *Cooperative teaching: Rebuilding the schoolhouse for all students.* Austin, TX: PRO-ED.

Bay, M., & Bryan, T. (1992). Differentiating children who are at risk for referral from others on critical classroom factors. *Remedial and Special Education, 13*(4), 27–33.

Bear, G. G., & Minke, K. M. (1996). Positive bias in maintenance of self-worth among children with LD. *Learning Disability Quarterly, 19,* 23–32.

Bear, T., Schenk, S., & Buckner, L. (1992/1993). Supporting victims of child abuse. *Educational Leadership, 50*(4), 42–47.

Beigel, A.R. (2000). Assistive technology assessment: More than the device. *Intervention in School and Clinic, 35*(4), 237–245.

Beirne-Smith, M., Patton, J. R., & Ittenbach, R. (1994). *Mental retardation* (4th ed.). New York: Merrill.

Bender, B. G. (1999). Learning disorders associated with asthma and allergies. *School Psychology Review, 28,* 204–214.

Benner, S. M. (1998). *Special education issues within the context of American society.* Belmont, CA: Wadsworth.

Bennett, A. (1932). *Subnormal children in elementary grades.* New York: Columbia University, Teacher's College, Bureau of Publications.

Bennett, T., DeLuca, D., & Bruns, D. (1997). Putting inclusion into practice: Perspectives of teachers and parents. *Exceptional Children, 64,* 115–131.

Bergan, J. R., & Tombari, M. L. (1975). The analysis of verbal interactions occurring during consultation. *Journal of School Psychology, 13,* 209–226.

Berger, C. F., Berkheimer, G. D., Lewis, L. E., & Neuberger, H. J. (1979). *Houghton Mifflin Science* (p. 55). Boston: Houghton Mifflin.

Berliner, D. C. (1984). The half-full glass: A review of research on teaching. In P. L. Hosford (Ed.), *Using what we know about teaching (1984 yearbook)* (pp. 69–83). Alexandria, VA: Association for Supervision and Curriculum Development.

Biklen, D. (1993). *Communication unbound.* New York: Teachers College Press.

Blachman, B. A. (2000). Phonological awareness. In M. L. Kamil, P. B. Mosenthal, P. D. Pearson, & R. Barr (Eds.), *Handbook of research: Volume III* (pp. 483–502). Mahwah, NJ: Lawrence Erlbaum.

Blankenship, C., & Lilly, M. S. (1981). *Mainstreaming students with learning and behavior problems: Techniques for the classroom teachers.* New York: Holt, Rinehart, & Winston.

Blatt, B. (1958). The physical, personality, and academic status of children who are mentally retarded attending special classes as compared with children who are mentally retarded attending regular class. *American Journal of Mental Deficiency, 62,* 810–818.

Blatt, B. (1987). *The conquest of mental retardation.* Austin, TX: PRO-ED.

Block, M. E. (1994). *A teacher's guide to including students with disabilities in regular physical education* (p. 187). Baltimore: Paul H. Brookes.

Block, M. E., & Burke, K. (1999). Are children with disabilities receiving appropriate physical education? *Teaching Exceptional Children, 31*(3), 18–23.

Bloom, L. A., Perlmutter, J., & Burrell, L. (1999). The general educator: applying constructivism to inclusive classrooms. *Intervention in School and Clinic, 34,* 132–138.

Bock, R. (1999). Research from NICHD's in learning disabilities. *National Institute of Child Health and Human Development.* Retrieved October 7, 1999, from the World Wide Web: *http://www.nichd.nih.gov/publications/pubs/readbro.htm.*

Bos, C. S., & Vaughn, S. (1994). *Strategies for teaching students with learning and behavior problems* (3rd ed.). Boston: Allyn and Bacon.

Bos, C. S., & Vaughn, S. (1998). *Strategies for teaching students with learning and behavior problems* (4th ed.). Boston: Allyn and Bacon.

Bottge, B. A., & Hasselbring, T. S. (1999). Teaching mathematics to adolescents with disabilities in a multimedia environment. *Intervention in School and Clinic, 35*(2), 113–116.

Bowman, B. T. (1994). The challenge of diversity. *Phi Delta Kappan, 76,* 218–224.

Brandwein, P. F., & Bauer, N. W. (1980). *The United States, living in our world: Research, evaluation, and writing.* Barton R. Clark et al., consulting social scientists. San Francisco and New York: Center for the Study of Instruction/Harcourt Brace Jovanovich.

Brent, R., & Anderson, P. (1993). Developing children's listening strategies. *The Reading Teacher, 47*(2), 122–126.

Brinckerhoff, L. (1994). Developing effective self-advocacy skills in college-bound students with learning disabilities. *Intervention in School and Clinic, 29*(4), 229–237.

Brody-Hasazi, S., Furney, K. S., DeStefano, J., (1999). Implementing the IDEA transition mandates. *Exceptional Children, 65,* 555–566.

Broussard, C., & Northup, J. (1997). The use of functional analysis to develop peer interventions for disruptive classroom behavior. *School Psychology Quarterly, 12,* 65–76.

Brown, G. (1994). Augmentative communication systems: Practical ideas for home and school programs. In F. LaRoy & J. Streng

(Eds.), *A new dawn of awakening: Proceedings of the 1994 conference* (pp. 63–64). Arlington, TX: Future Education.

Brown, G. M., Kerr, M. M., Zigmond, N., & Haus, A. (1984). What's important for student success in high school? Successful and unsuccessful students discuss school survival skills. *High School Journal, 68,* 10–17.

Brown, M. (2000). Access, Instruction, and Barriers. *Remedial and Special Education, 21,* 182–192.

Brownell, M. T., Yeager, E., Rennells, M. S., & Riley, T. (1997). Teachers working together: What teacher educators and researchers should know. *Teacher Education and Special Education, 20,* 340–359.

Bryan, T. (1997). Assessing the personal and social status of students with learning disabilities. *Learning Disabilities Research & Practice, 12*(1), 63–76.

Bryan, T. H., & Bryan, J. H. (1986). *Understanding learning disabilities* (3rd ed.). Palo Alto, CA: Mayfield.

Bryan, T., & Sullivan-Burstein, K. (1997). Homework how-to's. *Teaching Exceptional Children, 29*(6), 32–37.

Bryant, D. P., & Bryant, B. R. (1998). Using assistive technology adaptations to include students with learning disabilities in cooperative learning activities. *Journal of Learning Disabilities, 31*(1), 41–54.

Buck, G. H., Bursuck, W. D., Polloway, E. A., Nelson, J., & Whitehouse, F. A. (1996). Homework-related communication problems: Perspectives of special educators. *Journal of Emotional and Behavioral Disorders, 4*(2), 105–113.

Bulgren, J. A., Schumaker, J. B., & Deshler, D. (1988). Effectiveness of a concept teaching routine in enhancing the performance of LD students in secondary-level mainstream classes. *Learning Disability Quarterly, 11,* 3–17.

Bullara, D. T. (1993). Classroom management strategies to reduce racially-biased treatment of students. *Journal of Educational and Psychological Consultation, 4*(4), 357–368.

Bullock, L. M., & Fitzsimmons-Lovett, A. (1997). Meeting the needs of children and youth with challenging behaviors. *Reaching Today's Youth, 1*(2), 47–53.

Burgess, D. M., & Streissguth, A. P. (1992). Fetal alcohol syndrome and fetal alcohol effects: Principles for educators. *Phi Delta Kappan, 74,* 24–29.

Burns, P. C., Roe, B. D., & Ross, E. P. (1992). *Teaching reading in today's elementary schools.* Boston: Houghton Mifflin.

Bursuck, W. D., & Jayanthi, M. (1993). Programming for independent study skill usage. In S. Vogel & P. Adelman (Eds.), *Programming for success for college students with learning disabilities* (pp. 177–205). New York: Springer-Verlag.

Bursuck, W. D., & Lessen, E. (1987). A classroom-based model for assessing students with learning disabilities. *Learning Disabilities Focus, 3*(1), 17–29.

Bursuck, W. D., Bolas, K., & Miller-Young, R. (2000, April). *Teaching phonemic awareness to at-risk kindergarten children: Curricular and instructional guidelines.* Presented at CEC Annual Convention and Expo, Vancouver, Canada.

Bursuck, W. D., Harniss, M. K., Epstein, M. H., Polloway, E. A., Jayanthi, M., & Wissinger, L. M. (1999). Solving communication problems about homework: Recommendations of special education teachers. *Learning Disabilities Research and Practice, 14*(3), 149–158.

Bursuck, W. D., Munk, D., & Olson, D. (1999). The fairness of report card grading adaptations: What do students with and without learning disabilities think? *Remedial and Special Education, 20*(2), 84–92.

Bursuck, W. D., Polloway, E. A., Plante, L., Epstein, M. H., Jayanthi, M., & McConeghy, J. (1996). Report card grading and adaptations: A national survey of classroom practices. *Exceptional Children, 62*(4), 301–318.

Cameron, J., & Pierce, W. D. (1994). Reinforcement, reward, and intrinsic motivation: A meta-analysis. *Review of Educational Research, 64,* 363–423.

Camp, B. W., & Bash, M. A. (1985). *Think aloud.* Champaign, IL: Research Press.

Canadian Scholars' Press, Inc. (2000). *Percent children living in relative poverty.* Retrieved August 22, 2000, from the World Wide Web: http://www.cspi.org/cjones/messages/278.html

Carlson, C., & Henning, M. (1993). *The TAG peer editing procedure.* Unpublished manuscript, Northern Illinois University.

Carmanico, S. J., Erickson, M. T., Singh, N. N., Best, A. M., Sood, A. A., & Oswald, D. P. (1998). Diagnostic subgroups of depression in adolescents with emotional and behavioral disorders. *Journal of Emotional and Behavior Disorders, 6*(4), 222–232.

Carney, R. N., Levin, M. E., & Levin, J. R. (1993). Mnemonic strategies: Instructional techniques worth remembering. *Teaching Exceptional Children, 25*(4), 24–30.

Carnine, D. W. (1981). High and low implementation of direct instruction teaching techniques. *Education and Treatment of Children, 4,* 42–51.

Carnine, D. W., Caros, J., Crawford, D., Hollenbeck, K., & Harniss, M. K. (1996). Designing effective United States history curricula for all students. In J. Brophy (Ed.), *Advances in research on teaching: Vol. 6. History teaching and learning* (pp. 207–256). Greenwich, CT: JAI Press.

Carnine, D. W., Crawford, D., Harniss, M., & Hollenbeck, K. (1995). *Understanding U.S. history: Volume 1. Through the Civil War.* Eugene, OR: Considerate Publishing.

Carnine, D. W., Silbert, J., & Kameenui, E. (1997). *Direct instruction reading* (3rd ed.). Columbus, OH: Merrill.

Carnine, D. W., Crawford, D., Harniss, M. K. Hollenbeck, K. L., & Miller, S. K. (1998). Effective strategies for teaching social studies. In E. Kameenui & D. Carnine (Eds.), *Effective teaching strategies that accommodate diverse learners* (pp. 139–160). Columbus, OH: Merrill Prentice-Hall.

Carpenter, D., Grantham, L. B., & Hardister, M. P. (1983). Grading mainstreamed handicapped pupils: What are the issues? *Journal of Special Education, 17*(2), 183–188.

Cash, A. B. (1999). A profile of gifted individuals with autism: The twice-exceptional learner. *Roeper Review, 22*(1), 22–27.

Cassidy, V. M., & Stanton, J. E. (1959). *An investigation of factors involved in the educational placement of mentally retarded children: A study of differences between children in special and regular classes in Ohio.* (U.S. Office of Education Cooperative Research Program, Project No. 43) Columbus: Ohio State University. (ERIC Document Reproduction Service No. ED 002 752)

Cawley, J. F., Fitzmaurice, A. M., Shaw, R., Kahn, H., & Bates, A. (1979). LD youth and mathematics: A review of characteristics. *Learning Disability Quarterly, 2*(1), 29–44.

Cawley, J. F., Miller, J., & School, B. (1987). A brief inquiry of arithmetic word problem solving among learning disabled secondary students. *Learning Disabilities Focus, 2*(2), 87–93.

Cawley, J. F., Parmar, R. S., Yan, W., & Miller, J. H. (1998). Arithmetic computation performance of students with learning disabilities: Implications for curriculum. *Learning Disabilities Research 13*(2), 68–74.

Center for the Study of Reading. (1988). *A guide to selecting basal reading programs: Workbooks.* Cambridge, MA: Bolt, Beraneck, and Newman.

Centers for Disease Control and Prevention. (2000). *Attention-deficit/hyperactivity disorder.* Retrieved September 12, 2000, from the World Wide Web http://www.cde.gov/nech/ADHD/adepi.htm

Cermak, L. S. (1976). *Improving your memory.* New York: Norton.

Cesaroni, L., & Garber, M. (1991). Exploring the experience of autism through firsthand accounts. *Journal of Autism and Developmental Disorders, 21,* 303–313.

Chaffin, J. (1975). Will the real "mainstreaming" program please stand up! (Or . . . should Dunn have done it?). In E. L. Meyen, G. A. Vergason, & R. J. Whelan (Eds.), *Alternatives for teaching exceptional children.* Denver: Love.

Chard, D., & Dickson, S. V. (1999). Phonological awareness: Instructional and assessment guidelines. *Intervention in School and Clinic, 5,* 261–270.

Cheek, E. H., Jr., & Cheek, M. C. (1983). *Reading instruction through content teaching.* Columbus, OH: Merrill.

Child abuse characteristics (2000). Retrieved September 13, 2000, from the World Wide Web: http://www.angelfire.com/fl2/ChildAbuse/Characteristics.html

Choate, J. S., Enright, B. E., Miller, L. J., Poteet, J. A., & Rakes, T. A. (1995). *Curriculum-based assessment and programming.* Boston: Allyn and Bacon.

Christenson, S., Ysseldyke, J., & Thurlow, M. (1989). Critical instructional factors for students with mild handicaps: An integrated review. *Remedial and Special Education, 10*(5), 21–31.

Christof, K. J., & Kane, S. R. (1991). Relationship building for students with autism. *Teaching Exceptional Children, 24*(2), 49–51.

Christopolos, F., & Renz, P. (1969). A critical examination of special education programs. *Journal of Special Education, 3,* 371–379.

Cipani, E. C. (1995). Be aware of negative reinforcement. *Teaching Exceptional Children, 27*(4), 36–40.

Clark, B. (1992). *Growing up gifted* (4th ed.). New York: Merrill.

Clark, E. (1996). Children and adolescents with traumatic brain injury: Reintegration challenges in education settings. *Journal of Learning Disabilities, 29,* 549–560.

Clark, E., Russman, S., & Orme, S. F. (1999). Traumatic brain injury: Effects on school functioning and intervention strategies. *School Psychology Review, 28,* 242–250.

Clark, M. D., & Smith, W. S. (1999). Facilitating friendships: Including students with autism in the early elementary classroom. *Intervention in School and Clinic, 34,* 248–250.

Claude, D., & Firestone, P. (1995). The development of ADHD boys: A 12-year follow-up. *Canadian Journal of Behavioural Science, 27,* 226–249.

Clements, D. H., & McMillen, S. (1996). Rethinking concrete manipulatives. *Teaching Children Mathematics, 2*(5), 270–279.

Cline, S., & Schwartz, D. (1999). *Diverse populations of gifted children: Meeting their needs in the regular classrooms and beyond.* New York: Prentice Hall.

Cohen, M., & Riel, M. M. (1989). The effect of distant audiences on students' writing. *American Educational Research Journal, 26,* 143–159.

Cohen, S. B. (1983). Assigning report card grades to the mainstreamed child. *Teaching Exceptional Children, 15,* 186–189.

Cole, C. M., & McLeskey, J. (1997). Secondary inclusion programs for students with mild disabilities. *Focus on Exceptional Children, 28* (6), 1–15.

Cole, D. A., Vandercook, T., & Rynders, J. (1988). Comparison of two peer interaction programs: Children with and without severe disabilities. *American Educational Research Journal, 25,* 415–439.

Cole, K. B., Struyk, L. R., Kinder, D., Sheehan, J. K., & Kish, C. K. (1997). Portfolio assessment: Challenges in secondary education. *The High School Journal, 80*(4), 261–272.

Coleman, M. R., Gallagher, J. J., & Nelson, S. M. (1993). *Cooperative learning and gifted students: Report on five case studies.* Chapel Hill, NC: Gifted Education Policy Studies Program, Frank Porter Graham Child Development Center, University of North Carolina at Chapel Hill.

Coleman, M., Wheeler, L., & Webber, J. (1993). Research on interpersonal problem-solving training: A review. *Remedial and Special Education, 14*(2), 25–37.

Collins, B. C., Hall, M., & Branson, T. A. (1997). Teaching leisure skills to adolescents with moderate disabilities. *Exceptional Children, 63,* 499–512.

Colvin, G., Ainge, D., & Nelson, R. (1997). How to defuse confrontations. *Teaching Exceptional Children, 29*(6), 47–51.

Comer, E., & Fraser, M. (1998). Evaluation of six family-support programs: Are they effective? *Families in Society, 79,* 134–153.

Conderman, G. (1995). Social status of sixth- and seventh-grade students with learning disabilities. *Learning Disability Quarterly, 18,* 13–24.

Connors, C. K., & Blouin, A. G. (1982/1983). Nutritional effects on the behavior of children. *Journal of Psychiatric Research, 17,* 193–201.

Conroy, M., Clark, D., Gable, R. A., & Fox, J. J. (1999). A look at IDEA 1997 discipline provisions: Implications for change in the roles and responsibilities of school personnel. *Preventing School Failure, 43*(2), 64–70.

Cook, B. G., Semmel, M. I., & Gerber, M. M. (1999). Attitudes of principals and special education teachers toward the inclusion of students with mild disabilities. *Remedial and Special Education, 20,* 199–207, 243.

Cook, L., & Friend, M. (1993). Educational leadership for teacher collaboration. In B. Billingsley (Ed.), *Program leadership for serving students with disabilities* (pp. 421–444). Richmond: Virginia Department of Education.

Cook, L., & Friend, M. (1995). Co-Teaching: Guidelines for effective practice. *Focus on Exceptional Children, 28*(2), 1–12.

Cooper, H. (1989). Synthesis of research on homework. *Educational Leadership, 47*(3), 85–91.

Cooper, H., & Nye, B. (1994). Homework for students with learning disabilities: The implications of research for policy and practice. *Journal of Learning Disabilities, 27*(8), 470–480.

Coppola, M. A. (1987). The "perfect" student: Being alert to autism. *Education Digest, 52,* 33–35.

Corman, L. & Gottlieb, J. (1978). Mainstreaming mentally retarded children: A review of research. In M. R. Ellis (Ed.), *International review of research in mental retardation* (Vol. 9, pp. 147–172). New York: Academic Press.

Cortes, C. E. (1978). Chicano culture, experience and learning. In L. Morris, G. Sather, & S. Scull (Eds.), *Extracting learning styles from social/cultural diversity: A study of five American minorities.* Norman, OK: Southwest Teacher Corps Network.

Costenbader, V., & Reading-Brown, M. (1995). Isolation timeout used with students with emotional disturbance. *Exceptional Children, 61,* 353–363.

Cott, A. (1977). *The orthomolecular approach to learning disabilities.* New York: Huxley Institute.

Cott, A. (1985). *Help for your learning disabled child: The orthomolecular treatment.* New York: Time Books.

Council of State Directors of Programs for the Gifted. (1996). *1994 state of the states gifted and talented education report.* Washington, DC: National Center for Education Statistics. Retrieved September 13, 2000, from the World Wide Web: http://nces.ed.gov/pubs/d96/D96T053.html

Cowen, E. L., Pederson, A., Babijian, H., Izzo, L. D., & Trost, M. A. (1973). Long-term follow-up of early detected vulnerable children. *Journal of Consulting and Clinical Psychology, 41,* 438–446.

Crawford, C. G. (1980). *Math without fear.* New York: New Viewpoints/Vision Books.

Cronin, M. E. (1996). Life skills curricula for students with learning disabilities: A review of the literature. *Journal of Learning Disabilities, 29,* 53–68.

Cross, L., & Walker-Knight, D. (1997). Inclusion: Developing collaborative and cooperative school communities. *Educational Forum, 61,* 269–277.

Cullinan, D., & Epstein, M. H. (1994). Behavior disorders. In N. Haring, L. McCormick, & T. Haring (Eds.), *Exceptional children and youth.* Columbus, OH: Merrill.

Cullinan, D., Epstein, M. H., & Lloyd, J. (1983). *Behavior disorders of children and adolescents.* Englewood Cliffs, NJ: Prentice-Hall.

Culross, R. B. (1997). Concepts of inclusion in gifted education. *Teaching Exceptional Children, 29*(3), 24–26.

Cummings, R. E., & Maddux, C. D. (1985). *Parenting the learning disabled: A realistic approach.* Springfield, IL: Charles C. Thomas.

Czarnecki, E., Roskoa, D., & Fine, F. (1998). How to call up note-taking skills. *Teaching Exceptional Children, 30*(6), 14–19.

DaCosta, J. L, Marshall, J. L., & Riordan, G. (1998, April). *Case study of the development of a collaborative teaching culture in an inner city elementary school.* Paper presented at the Annual Meeting of the American Educational Research Association, San Diego. (ERIC Documentation Reproduction Service No. ED 420 630)

D'Amato, R. C., & Rothlisberg, B. A. (1996). How education should respond to students with traumatic brain injury. *Journal of Learning Disabilities, 29,* 670–683.

Daniels, V. I. (1998). How to manage disruptive behavior in inclusive classrooms. *Teaching Exceptional Children, 30*(4), 26–31.

Darch, C., Carnine, D., & Gersten, R. (1984). Explicit instruction in mathematics problem solving. *Journal of Educational Research, 77*(6), 351–358.

Darch, C., & Gersten, R. (1985). The effects of teaching presentation and praise on LD students' oral reading performance. *British Journal of Educational Psychology, 55,* 295–303.

Davis, G. A., & Rimm, S. B. (1994). *Education of the gifted and talented* (3rd ed.). Boston: Allyn and Bacon.

Dean, A. V., Salend, S. J., & Taylor, L. (1994). Multicultural education: A challenge for special educators. *Teaching Exceptional Children, 26*(1), 40–43.

DeBettencourt, L. U. (1999). General educators' attitudes toward students with mild disabilities and their use of instructional strategies: Implications for training. *Remedial and Special Education, 20,* 27–35.

DeBoer, A. (1995). *Working together.* Longmont, CO: Sopris West.

Deitz, D. E. D., & Ormsby, D. (1992). A comparison of verbal social behavior of adolescents with behavioral disorders and regular class peers. *Behavioral Modification, 16*(4), 504–524.

DeLaPaz, S. (1999). Composing via dictation and speech recognition systems: Compensatory technology for students with learning disabilities. *Learning Disabilities Quarterly, 22,* 173–182.

Deluke, S. V., & Knoblock, P. (1987). Teacher behavior as preventive discipline. *Teaching Exceptional Children, 19*(4), 18–24.

Dennis, R. E., & Giangreco, M. F. (1996). Creating conversation: Reflections on cultural sensitivity in family interviewing. *Exceptional Children, 63,* 103–116.

Deno, S. L. (1985). Curriculum-based measurement: The emerging alternative. *Exceptional Children, 52,* 219–232.

Deno, S. L. (1989). Curriculum-based measurement and special education services: A fundamental and direct relationship. In M. Shinn (Ed.), *Curriculum-based measurement: Assessing special children* (pp. 1–17). New York: Guilford Press.

Deno, S., & Fuchs, L. (1987). Developing curriculum-based measurement systems for data-based special education problem solving. *Focus on Exceptional Children, 19*(8), 1–16.

Deshler, D. D., Putnam, M. L., & Bulgren, J. A. (1985). Academic accommodations for adolescents with behavior and learning problems. In S. Braaten, R. B. Rutherford, & W. Evans (Eds.), *Programming for adolescents with behavioral disorders* (Vol. 2, pp. 20–30). Reston, VA: Council for Children with Behavior Disorders.

Díaz-Rico, L. T., & Weed, K. Z. (1995). *The crosscultural, language, and academic development handbook: A complete K-12 reference guide.* Boston: Allyn and Bacon.

Dickson, S. F., & Bursuck, W. D. (1999). Implementing a model for preventing reading failure. *Learning Disabilities Research and Practice, 14*(4), 191–202.

Dickson, S. V., Collins, V., Simmons, D. C., & Kameenui, E. J. (1998). Metacognition: Curricular and instructional implications for diverse learners. In D. C. Simmons & E. J. Kameenui (Eds.), *What reading research tells us about children with diverse learning needs* (pp. 361–380). Hillsdale, NJ: Lawrence Erlbaum.

Dinnocenti, S. T. (1998, Spring). Differentiation: Definition and description for gifted and talented. *National Research Center on the Gifted and Talented Newsletter.* Retrieved September 14, 2000, from the World Wide Web: http://sp.uconn.edu/~nregt/news/spring98/sprng985.html

Dinnocenti, S. T. (1999, Fall). What's in a word? *National Research Center on the Gifted and Talented Newsletter.* Retrieved September 14, 2000, from the World Wide Web: http//sp.uconn.edu/~nregt/news/fall99/fall1992.html

Doman, G., & Delacato, D. (1968). Doman–Delacato philosophy. *Human Potential, 1,* 113–116.

Donnellan, A. M. (1999). Invented knowledge and autism: Highlighting our strengths and expanding the conversation. *Journal of the Association for Persons with Severe Handicaps, 24,* 230–236.

Donahue, K., & Zigmond, N. (1990). Academic grades of ninth-grade students and lower achieving peers. *Exceptionality, 1,* 17–27.

Downing, J. H., & Rebollo, J. (1999). Parents' perceptions of the factors essential for integrated physical education programs. *Remedial and Special Education, 20,* 152–159.

Doyle, W. (1986). Classroom organization and management. In M. Wittrock (Ed.), *Handbook of Research on Teaching* (pp. 392–431). New York: Macmillan.

Doyle, W. (1990). Classroom management techniques. In O. C. Moles (Ed.), *Student discipline strategies* (pp. 83–105). Albany, NY: State University of New York Press.

Drew, C. J., Logan, D. R., & Hardman, M. L. (1992). *Mental retardation: A life cycle approach* (5th ed.). New York: Merrill.

Drugs & Drug Abuse Education. (1994). Prevalence of any illicit drug use 1979–1993. *Drugs & Drug Abuse Education, 25*(8), 56.

Duke, N. K. (2000). 36 minutes per day: The scarcity of informational texts in first grade. *Reading Research Quarterly, 35*(2), 202–224.

Dumas, M. C. (1998). The risk of social interaction problems among adolescents with ADHD. *Education and Treatment of Children, 21,* 447–461.

Dunn, L. M. (1968). Special education for the mildly handicapped—Is much of it justifiable? *Exceptional Children, 35,* 5–22.

DuPaul, G. J., Barkley, R. A., & McMurray, M. B. (1991). Therapeutic effects of medication on ADHD: Implications for school psychologists. *School Psychology Review, 20,* 203–219.

DuPaul, G. J., Ervin, R. A., Hook, C. L., & McGoey, K. E. (1998). Peer tutoring for children with attention deficit hyperactivity disorder: Effects on classroom behavior and academic performance. *Journal of Applied Behavior Analysis, 31,* 579–592.

Dyson, L. L. (1996). The experiences of families of children with learning disabilities: Parental stress, family functioning, and sibling self-concept. *Journal of Learning Disabilities, 29,* 280–286.

Easterbrooks, S. (1999). Improving practices for students with hearing impairments. *Exceptional Children, 65,* 537–554.

Echevarria, J. C. (1998). Preparing text and classroom materials for English-language learners: Curriculum adaptations in secondary school settings. In R. Gersten & R. Jimenez (Eds.), *Promoting learning for culturally and linguistically diverse students: Classroom applications from contemporary research.* Belmont, CA: Wadsworth.

Eichinger, J. (1990). Goal structure effects on social interaction: Nondisabled and disabled elementary students. *Exceptional Children, 56*, 408–416.

Einhorn, R., Hagen, C., Johnson, J., Wujek, C., & Hoffman, L. (1991). *Authentic assessment: A collaborative approach.* Flossmoor, IL: SMA Communication Development Project.

Elbaum, B., Moody, S. W., & Schumm, J. S. (1999). Mixed-ability grouping for reading: What students think. *Learning Disabilities Research & Practice, 14*(1), 61–66.

Elliott, S. N. (1998). Performance assessment of students' achievement. Research and practice. *Learning Disabilities Research and Practice, 13*(4), 233–241.

Ellis, E. (1996). Reading strategy instruction. In D. Deshler, E. Ellis, & K. Lenz (Eds.), *Teaching adolescents with learning disabilities: Strategies and methods* (2nd ed., pp. 61–125). Denver: Love.

Ellis, E. S., & Colvert, G. (1996). Writing strategy instruction. In D. Deshler, E. Ellis, and B. Lenz (Eds). *Teaching adolescents with learning disabilities: Strategies and methods* (2nd ed., pp. 127–207) Denver: Love.

Ellis, E. S., & Sabornie, E. S. (1990). Strategy-based adaptive instruction in content-area classes: Social validity of six options. *Teacher Education and Special Education, 13*(2), 133–144.

Ellis, E., & Lenz, B. K. (1996). Perspectives on instruction in learning strategies. In D. Deshler, E. Ellis, & B. K. Lenz (Eds.), *Teaching adolescents with learning disabilities: Strategies and methods* (2nd ed., pp. 9–60). Denver: Love.

Ellis, E., & Lenz, K. (1987). A component analysis of effective learning strategies for LD students. *Learning Disabilities Focus, 2*, 94–107.

Ellis, E., Lenz, B. K., & Sabornie, E. (1987a). Generalization and adaptation of learning strategies to natural environments: Part 1: Critical agents. *Remedial and Special Education, 8*(2), 6–24.

Ellis, E., Lenz, B. K., & Sabornie, E. (1987b). Generalization and adaptation of learning strategies to natural environments: Part 2: Research into practice. *Remedial and Special Education, 8*(2), 6–23.

Emmer, E. T., Evertson, C. M., Sanford, J. P., Clements, B. S., & Worsham, M. E. (1983). *Organizing and managing the junior high classroom.* Austin: Research and Development Center for Teacher Education, University of Texas.

Engleman, M. D., Griffin, H. C., & Wheeler, L. (1998). Deaf-blindness and communication: Practical knowledge and strategies. *Journal of Visual Impairment and Blindness, 92*, 783–798.

Engleman, D., Griffin, H. C., Griffin, L. W., & Maddox, J. I. (1999). A teacher's guide to communicating with students with deaf-blindness. *Teaching Exceptional Children, 31*(5), 64–71.

Englert, C. S., Raphael, T. E., Anderson, L. M., Anthony, H. M., Fear, K. L., & Gregg, S. L. (1988). A case for writing intervention: Strategies for writing informational text. *Learning Disabilities Focus, 3*(2), 98–113.

Englert, C., & Mariage, T. (1991). Making students partners in the comprehension process: Organizing the reading "POSSE." *Learning Disability Quarterly, 14*, 123–138.

Epilepsy Foundation of America. (1986). *Epilepsy: Questions and answers.* Landover, MD: Author.

Epstein, M. H. (1999). The development and validation of a scale to assess the emotional and behavioral strengths of children and adolescents. *Remedial and Special Education, 20*, 258–262.

Epstein, M. H., Kinder, D., & Bursuck, W. D. (1989). The academic status of adolescents with behavior disorders. *Behavioral Disorders, 4*(3), 157–165.

Epstein, M. H., Patton, J. R., Polloway, E. A., & Foley, R. (1992). Educational services for students with behavior disorders: A re-

view of Individualized Education Programs. *Teacher Education and Special Education, 15*, 41–48.

Epstein, M. H., Polloway, E. A., Buck, G. H., Bursuck, W. D., Wissinger, L., Whitehouse, F., & Jayanthi, M. (1997). Homework-related communication problems: Perspectives of general education teachers. *Learning Disabilities Research and Practices, 12*(4), 221–227.

Epstein, M. H., Rudolph, S., & Epstein, A. (2000). Using strength-based assessment in transition planning. *Teaching Exceptional Children, 32*(6), 50–55.

Epstein, M. H., & Sharma, J. (1997). *Behavioral and emotional rating scale: A strength-based approach to assessment.* Austin, TX: PRO-ED.

Erchul, W. P., & Martens, B. K. (1997). *School consultation: Conceptual and empirical bases of practice.* New York: Plenum.

Erk, R. R. (1997). Multidimensional treatment of attention deficit disorder: A family oriented approach. *Journal of Mental Health Counseling, 19*(3), 3–22.

Ervin, R. A., DuPaul, G. J., Kern, L., & Friman, P. C. (1998). Classroom-based functional and adjunctive assessments: Proactive approaches to intervention selection for adolescents with attention deficit hyperactivity disorder. *Journal of Applied Behavior Analysis, 31*, 65–78.

Etscheidt, S. K., & Bartlett, L. (1999). The IDEA amendment: A four-step approach for determining supplementary aids and services. *Exceptional Children, 65*, 163–174.

Evans, D., & Carnine, D. (1990). Manipulatives—The effective way. *ADI News, 10*(1), 48–55.

Evans, D. W., Harris, D. M., Adeigbola, M., Houston, D., & Argott, L. (1993). Restructuring special education services. *Teacher Education and Special Education, 16*, 137–145.

Evans, S. S., Evans, W. H., & Mercer, C. (1986). *Assessment for instruction.* Boston: Allyn and Bacon.

Everson, J. M., & Zhang, D. (2000). Person-centered planning: Characteristics, inhibitors, and supports. *Education and Training in Mental Retardation and Developmental Disabilities, 35*, 36–43.

Evertson, C. M., Emmer, E. T., Clements, B. S., Sanford, J. P., Worsham, M. E., & Williams, E. L. (1983). *Organizing and managing the elementary school classroom.* Austin Research and Development Center for Teacher Education, University of Texas.

Evertson, C. M., Emmer, E. T., Clements, B. S., Sanford, J. P., Worsham, M. E., & Williams, E. L. (2000). *Classroom management for elementary teachers* (5th ed.). Boston: Allyn and Bacon.

FASWorld. (2000, September 13). *The facts on fetal alcohol syndrome/effects.* Toronto, Canada: Author. Retrieved September 18, 2000, from the World Wide Web: http://www.fasworld.com/facts.ihtml

Feingold, B. F. (1975). *Why your child is hyperactive.* New York: Random House.

Feldhusen, J. F., Van Winkle, L., & Ehle, D. A. (1996). Is it acceleration or simply appropriate instruction for precocious youth? *Teaching Exceptional Children, 28*(3), 48–51.

Felton, R. H. (1993). Effects of instruction on the decoding skills of children with phonological-processing problems. *Journal of Learning Disabilities, 26*(9), 583–589.

Figueroa, R. A. (1989). Psychological testing of linguistic-minority students: Knowledge gaps and regulations. *Exceptional Children, 56*, 145–153.

Filipek, P. A. (1995). Neurobiologic correlates of developmental dyslexia: How do dyslexics' brains differ from those of normal readers? *Journal of Child Neurology, 10* (Suppl. 1), 62–69.

Fischer, T. A., & Tarver, S. G. (1997). Meta-analysis of studies of mathematics curricula designed around big ideas. *Effective School Practice, 16*, 71–79.

Fisher, C. W., Berliner, D., Filby, N., Marliare, R., Cahan, L., & Dishaw, M. (1980). Teaching behavior, academic learning time, and student achievement: An overview. In C. Denham & A. Lieberman (Eds.), *Time to learn* (pp. 7–32). Washington, DC: National Institute of Education, Department of Education.

Fisher, D., Pumpian, I., & Sax, C. (1998). Parent and caregiver impressions of different educational models. *Remedial and Special Education, 19,* 173–180.

Fitzsimmons, M. K. (1998, November). Functional behavior assessment and behavior interventions plans. *ERIC/OSEP Digest* (E571), 3–4.

Fletcher, J., & Martinez, G. (1994). An eye-movement analysis of the effects of scotopic sensitivity correction on parsing and comprehension. *Journal of Learning Disabilities, 27,* 67–70.

Flowers, D. L. (1993). Brain basis for dyslexia: A summary of work in progress. *Journal of Learning Disabilities, 26*(9), 575–582.

Forest, M., & Lusthaus, E. (1990). Everyone belongs with the MAPS action planning system. *Teaching Exceptional Children, 22*(2), 32–35.

Forest, M., Pierpoint, J., & O'Brien, J. (1996). MAPS, Circles of Friends, and PATH: Powerful tools to help build caring communities. In S. Stainback & W. Stainback (Eds.)., *Inclusion: A guide for educators.* Baltimore: Paul H. Brookes.

Forness, S. R., Kavale, K. A., Blum, I. M., & Lloyd, J. W. (1997). Mega-analysis of metaanalyses: What works in special education. *Teaching Exceptional Children, 29*(6), 4–9.

Foster-Johnson, L., & Dunlap, G. (1993). Using functional assessment to develop effective, individualized interventions for challenging behaviors. *Teaching Exceptional Children, 25*(3), 44–50.

Fox, C. L. (1989). Peer acceptance of learning disabled children in the regular classroom. *Exceptional Children, 56,* 50–59.

Fox, N. E., & Ysseldyke, J. E. (1997). Implementing inclusion at the middle school level: Lessons from a negative example. *Exceptional Children, 64,* 81–98.

Frazier, M. R., & Merrell, K. W. (1997). Issues in behavioral treatment of attention deficit/hyperactivity disorder. *Education & Treatment of Children, 20,* 441–461.

Freeman, B. J. (1994). Diagnosis of the syndrome of autism: Where we have been and where we are going. In F. LaRoy & J. Streng (Eds.), *A new dawn of awakening: Proceedings of the 1994 conference* (pp. 1–6). Arlington, TX: Future Education.

Freeman, S. F. N., & Alkin, M. C. (2000). Academic and social attainments of children with mental retardation in general education and special education settings. *Remedial and Special Education, 21,* 3–18.

French, N. (1999a). Paraeducators: Who are they and what do they do? *Teaching Exceptional Children, 32* (1), 65–69.

French, N. (1999b). Paraeducators and teachers: Shifting roles. *Teaching Exceptional Children, 32* (2), 69–73.

Friend, M. (2000). Perspective: Myths and misunderstandings about professional collaboration. *Remedial and Special Education, 21,* 130–132, 160.

Friend, M., & Cook, L. (1997). Student-centered teams in schools: Still in search of an identity. *Journal of Educational and Psychological Consultation, 8,* 3–20.

Friend, M., & Cook, L. (2000). *Interactions: Collaboration skills for school professionals* (3rd ed.). White Plains, NY: Longman.

Fuchs, L. S., Fuchs, D., Hamlett, C. L., & Stecker, P. M. (1991). Effects of curriculum-based measurement and consultation on teacher planning and student achievement in mathematics operations. *American Educational Research Journal, 28,* 617–641.

Fuchs, L. S., Fuchs, D., Hamlett, C., Philips, N., & Bentz, J. (1994). Classwide curriculum-based measurement: Helping general educators meet the challenge of student diversity. *Exceptional Children, 60*(6), 518–537.

Fuchs, L. S., Fuchs, D., & Kazdan, S. (1999). Effects of peer-assisted learning strategies on high school students with serious reading problems. *Remedial and Special Education, 20,* 309–318.

Fuchs, L. S., Fuchs, D., Kazdan, S., Karns, K., Calhoon, M. B., Hamlett, C. L., & Hewlett, S. (2000). Effects of workgroup structure and size on student productivity during collaborative word on complex tasks. *The Elementary School Journal, 100*(3), 201–210.

Fuchs, L. S., Hamlett, D. L., & Fuchs, D. (1990*). Monitoring basic skills progress: Basic reading.* Austin, TX: PRO-ED.

Fujiura, G. T., & Yamaki, K. (2000). Trends in demography of childhood poverty and disability. *Exceptional Children, 66,* 187–199.

Fulton, L., LeRoy, C., Pinckney, M. L., & Weekley, T. (1994). Peer Education Partners: A program for learning and working together. *Teaching Exceptional Children, 26*(4), 6–11.

Furlong, M., & Morrison, G. (2000). The *school* in school violence: Definitions and facts. *Journal of Emotional and Behavioral Disorders, 8,* 71–82.

Gable, R. A., Quinn, M. M., Rutherford, R. B., & Howell, K. (1998). Addressing problem behaviors in schools: Use of functional assessments and behavior intervention plans. *Preventing School Failure, 42*(3), 106–119.

Gallagher, J. J., & Gallagher, S. A. (1994). *Teaching the gifted child* (4th ed.). Boston: Allyn and Bacon.

Garcia, G. E., & Pearson, P. D. (1994). Assessment and diversity. In L. D. Hammond (Ed.), *Review of research in education.* Washington, DC: American Educational Research Association.

Gardner, H. (1993). *Multiple intelligences: The theory in practice.* New York: Basic Books.

Gardner, R., Sainato, D. M., Cooper, J. O., Heron, T. E., Heward, W. L., Eshelman, J. W., & Grossi, T. A. (1994). *Behavior analysis in education: Focus on measurably superior instruction.* Pacific Grove, CA: Brooks/Cole.

Gelzheiser, L. M., McLane, M., Meyers, J., & Pruzek, R. M., (1998). IEP-Specified peer interaction needs: Accurate but ignored. *Exceptional Children, 65,* 51–65.

Gerber, P. J., & Popp, P. A. (1999). Consumer perspectives on the collaborative teaching model. *Remedial and Special Education, 20,* 288–296.

Germinario, V., Cervalli, J., & Ogden, E. H. (1992). *All children successful: Real answers for helping at risk elementary students.* Lancaster, PA: Technomic.

Gersten, R., Baker, S. K., & Marks, S. U. (1998). *Teaching English language learners with learning difficulties.* Eugene, OR: Eugene Research Institute.

Gersten, R., Vaughn, S., & Brengelman, S. U. (1996). Grading and academic feedback for special education students and students with learning difficulties. In T. R. Guskey (Ed.), *ASCD yearbook 1996: Communicating student learning.* Alexandria, VA: Association for Supervision and Curriculum Development.

Getch, Y. Q., & Neuharth-Pritchett, S. (1999). Children with asthma: Strategies for educators. *Teaching Exceptional Children, 31*(3), 30–36.

Giangreco, M. F., Broer, S. M., & Edelman, S. W. (1999). The tip of the iceberg: Determining whether paraprofessional support is needed for students with disabilities in general education settings. *Journal of the Association for Persons with Severe Handicaps, 24,* 281–291.

Giangreco, M. F., Dennis, R., Cloninger, C., Edelman, S. & Schattman, R. (1993). "I've counted Jon": Transformational experiences of teachers educating students with disabilities. *Exceptional Children, 59,* 359–372.

Giangreco, M. F., Edelman, S. W., MacFarland, S., & Luiselli, T. E. (1997). Attitudes about educational and related service provision for students with deaf-blindness and multiple disabilities. *Exceptional Children, 63,* 329–342.

Giangreco, M. F., Prelock, P. A., Reid, R. R., Dennis, R. E., & Edelman, S. W. (2000). Role of related services personnel in inclusive schools (pp. 360–388). In R. A. Villa & J. S. Thousand

(Eds.), *Restructuring for caring and effective education: Piecing the puzzle together.* Baltimore: Paul H. Brookes.

Gibb, G. S., Young, J. R., Allred, K. W., Dyches, T. T., Egan, M. W., & Ingram, C. F. (1997). A team-based junior high inclusion program: Parent participation and feedback. *Remedial and Special Education, 18,* 243–249.

Gillies, R. M., & Ashman, A. F. (2000). The effects of cooperative learning on students with learning difficulties in the lower elementary school. *Journal of Special Education, 34,* 19–27.

Glassberg, L. A., Hoooper, S. R., & Mattison, R. E. (1999). Prevalence of learning disabilities at enrollment in special education students with behavioral disorders. *Behavioral Disorders, 25*(1), 9–21.

Goetz, L., & O'Farrell, N. (1999). Connections: Facilitating social supports for students with deaf-blindness in general education classrooms. *Journal of Visual Impairment and Blindness, 92,* 704–715.

Goldberg, S. S., & Kuriloff, P. J. (1991). Evaluating the fairness of special education hearings. *Exceptional Children, 57,* 546–555.

Goldstein, A. P., Sprafkin, R. P., Gershaw, N. J., & Klein, P. (1980). *Skillstreaming the adolescent.* Champaign, IL: Research Press.

Goldstein, H., Moss, J. W., & Jordan, L. J. (1965). *The efficacy of special class training on the development of mentally retarded children* (U.S. Office of Education Cooperative Research Program Project No. 619). Urbana: University of Illinois Institute for Research on Exceptional Children. (ERIC Document Reproduction Service No. ED 002–907)

Good, T. L., & Brophy, I. E. (1986). School effects. In M. C. Wittrock (Ed.), *Handbook of research on teaching* (3rd ed., pp. 570–602). Upper Saddle River, NJ: Prentice Hall.

Goodman, H., Gottlieb, J., & Harrison, R. H. (1972). Social acceptance of EMR children integrated into a non-graded elementary school. *American Journal of Mental Deficiency, 76,* 412–417.

Graham, S. (1999). Handwriting and spelling instruction for students with learning disabilities: A review. *Learning Disability Quarterly, 22,* 77–98.

Graham, S., & Freeman, S. (1986). Strategy training and teacher- vs. student-controlled study conditions: Effects on LD students' spelling performance. *Learning Disability Quarterly, 9,* 15–22.

Graham, S., & Harris, K. R. (1987). Improving composition skills of inefficient learners with self-instructional strategy training. *Topics in Language Disorders, 7*(4), 66–77.

Graham, S., & Miller, L. (1980). Handwriting research and practice: A unified approach. *Focus on Exceptional Children, 13*(2), 1–16.

Graley, J. (1994). A path to the mainstream of life: Facilitated communication/behavior/inclusion: Three interacting ingredients. In F. LaRoy & J. Streng (Eds.), *A new dawn of awakening: Proceedings of the 1994 conference* (pp. 67–68). Arlington, TX: Future Education.

Grandin, T. (1984). My experiences as an autistic child and review of selected literature. *Journal of Orthomolecular Psychiatry, 13,* 144–174.

Grant, R. (1993). Strategic training for using text headings to improve students' processing of content. *Journal of Reading, 36*(6), 482–488.

Graybill, S. W. (1997). Questions of race and culture: How they relate to the classroom for African American students. *Clearinghouse 70,* 311–319.

Greenwood, C. R. (1991). Longitudinal analysis of time, engagement, and achievement in at-risk versus non-risk students. *Exceptional Children, 57,* 521–535.

Gritzmacher, H. L., & Gritzmacher, S. C. (1995). Referral, assessment, and placement practices used in rural school districts with Native American students in special education. *Rural Special Education Quarterly, 14*(1), 11–19.

Grossman, H. (1995). *Special education in a diverse society.* Boston: Allyn and Bacon.

Grove, K. A., & Fisher, D. (1999). Entrepreneurs of meaning: Parents and the process of inclusive education. *Remedial and Special Education, 20,* 208–215.

Guetzloe, E. (2000). Teacher preparation in the age of violence: What do educators need to know? *Teacher Educator, 35*(3), 19–27.

Guild, P. (1994). The culture/learning style connection. *Educational Leadership, 51*(8), 16–21.

Guptill, A. M. (2000). Using the internet to improve student performance. *Teaching Exceptional Children, 32*(4), 16–21.

Gut, D. M. (2000). We are social beings. Learning how to learn cooperatively. *Teaching Exceptional Children, 32* (5), 46–52.

Hall, L. J., & McGregor, J. A. (2000). A follow-up study of the peer relationships of children with disabilities in an inclusive school. *Journal of Special Education, 34,* 114–126.

Hall, S. J., Halperin, S. T., Schwartz, S. T., & Newcorn, J. H. (1997). Behavioral and executive functions in children with attention-deficit hyperactivity disorder and reading disability. *Journal of Attention Disorders, 1,* 235–247.

Hallahan, D. P. (1998). Sound bytes from special education reform rhetoric. *Remedial and Special Education, 19,* 67–69.

Hallahan, D. P., & Kauffman, J. M. (2000). *Exceptional learners: Introduction to special education* (8th ed.). Boston: Allyn and Bacon.

Hallahan, D. P., Kauffman, J. M., & Lloyd, J. W. (1985). *Introduction to learning disabilities.* Englewood Cliffs, NJ: Prentice-Hall.

Hallahan, D. P., Kauffman, J. M., & Lloyd, J. W. (1999). *Introduction to learning disabilities* (2nd ed.). Boston: Allyn and Bacon.

Hallenbeck, M. J., & McMaster, D. (1991). Disability simulation. *Teaching Exceptional Children, 23*(3), 12–15.

Hamre-Nietupski, S. H., McDonald, J., & Nietupski, J. (1992). Integrating elementary students with multiple disabilities into supported regular classes: Challenges and solutions. *Teaching Exceptional Children, 24*(3), 6–9.

Hansen, C., Weiss, D., & Last, C. G. (1999). ADHD boys in young adulthood: Psychosocial adjustment. *Journal of the American Academy of Child and Adolescent Psychiatry, 38,* 165–172.

Hardman, M. L., Drew, C. J., Egan, M. W., & Winston, M. (1999). *Human exceptionality: Society, school, and family* (6th ed.). Boston: Allyn and Bacon.

Hardman, M. L., McDonnell, J., & Welch, M. (1997). Perspectives on the future of IDEA. *Journal of the Association for Persons with Severe Handicaps, 22,* 61–77.

Harniss, M. K. (1996). *Task requirements of content area textbooks: Effects on the academic achievement and engagement of middle-level students.* Unpublished manuscript, University of Oregon, Eugene.

Harniss, M. K., Epstein, M. H., Bursuck, W. P., Nelson, J. S., Jayanthi, M. (in press). Resolving homework-related communication problems: Recommendations of parents of children with and without disabilities. *Reading and Writing Quarterly.*

Harper, G. F., Maheady, L., Mallette, B., & Karnes, M. (1999). Peer tutoring and the minority child with disabilities. *Preventing School Failure, 43*(2), 45–51.

Harris, C. A., Miller, S. P., & Mercer, C. D. (1995). Teaching initial multiplication skills to students with disabilities in general education classrooms. *Learning Disabilities Research & Practice, 10*(3), 180–195.

Harris, K. C. (1995). School-based bilingual special education teacher assistance teams. *Remedial and Special Education, 16,* 337–343.

Harris, K. R., & Graham, S. (1996). Memo to constructivists: Skills count, too. *Educational Leadership, 53*(5), 26–29.

Harry, B. (1992a). Making sense of disability: Low-income, Puerto Rican parents' theories of the problem. *Exceptional Children, 59,* 27–40.

Harry, B. (1992b). Restructuring the participation of African-American parents in special education. *Exceptional Children, 59,* 123–131.

Harry, B., Torguson, C., Katkavich, J., & Guerrero, M. (1993). Crossing social class and cultural barriers in working with families. *Teaching Exceptional Children, 26*(1), 48–51.

Hartwig, E. P., & Ruesch, G. M. (2000). Disciplining students in special education. *The Journal of Special Education, 33*(4), 240–247.

Hasbrouck, J. E., & Tindal, G. (1992). Curriculum-based oral reading fluency norms for students in grades 2–5. *Teaching Exceptional Children, 24*(3), 41–44.

Haynes, N. M., & Gebreyesus, S. (1992). Cooperative learning: A case for African-American students. *School Psychology Review, 21,* 577–585.

Heath, D. (1993). Using portfolio assessment with secondary LED students yields a cross-cultural advantage for all. *BeOutreach, 4*(1), 27.

Heller, K. W., Fredrick, L. D., Best, S., Dykes, M. K., & Cohen, E. T. (2000). Specialized health care procedures in the school: Training and service delivery. *Exceptional Children 66,* 173–186.

Helmstetter, E., Curry, C. A., Brennan, M., & Sampson-Saul, M. (1998). Comparison of general and special education classrooms of students with severe disabilities. *Education and Training in Mental Retardation and Developmental Disabilities, 33,* 216–227.

Henderson, K., Overview of ADA, IDEA, and Section 504. *KidSource Online.* Retrieved September 12, 2000, from the World Wide Web: http://www.kidsource.com/kidsource/content3/ada.idea.html

Henderson, A. T., Marburger, C. L., & Ooms, T. (1986). *Beyond the bake sale: An educator's guide to working with parents.* Washington, DC: National Committee for Citizens in Education.

Henderson, N., & Milstein, M. M. (1996). *Resiliency in schools: Making it happen for students and educators.* Thousand Oaks, CA: Corwin.

Hendrickson, J. M., Shokoohi-Yekta, M., Hamre-Nietupski, S., & Gable, R. A. (1996). Middle and high school students' perceptions on being friends with peers with severe disabilities. *Exceptional Children, 63,* 19–28.

Henry, B. (1992). Restructuring the participation of African-American parents in special education. *Exceptional Children, 59,* 123–131.

Hess, R. (1987). *Grading-credit-diploma: Accommodation practices for students with mild disabilities.* Des Moines: Iowa State Department of Education.

Hickson, L., Blackman, L. S., & Reis, E. M. (1995). *Mental retardation: Foundations of educational programming* (pp. 121–165). Boston: Allyn and Bacon.

Hill, S., & Hill, T. (1990). *The collaborative classroom: A guide to cooperative learning* (pp. 21–35). Portsmouth, NH: Heinemann.

Hobbs, N. (1975). *The futures of children.* San Francisco: Jossey-Bass.

Hoge, R. D., & Renzulli, J. S. (1993). Exploring the link between giftedness and self-concept. *Review of Educational Research, 63,* 449–465.

Hollowood, T. M., Salisbury, C. L., Rainforth, B., & Palombaro, M. M. (1995). Use of instructional time in classrooms serving students with and without severe disabilities. *Exceptional Children, 61,* 242–253.

Holmes v. Sobol, 1987–88, *EHRL* DEC. 559:463.

Homme, L. (1970). *How to use contingency contracting in the classroom.* Champaign, IL: Research Press.

Hoover, K. H., & Hollingsworth, P. M. (1982). *A handbook for elementary school teachers.* Boston: Allyn and Bacon.

Horton, S. V. (1987). *Study guides: A paper on curriculum modification.* Unpublished manuscript, University of Washington.

Horton, S. V., & Lovitt, T. C., & Christensen, C. (1991). Matching three classifications of secondary students to differential levels of study guides. *Journal of Learning Disabilities, 24,* 518–529.

Howell, K. M., & Morehead, M. K. (1993). *Curriculum-based evaluation for special and remedial education* (2nd ed.). Columbus, OH: Merrill.

Howell, K. W., Evans, D., & Gardner, J. (1997). Medications in the classroom: A hard pill to swallow? *Teaching Exceptional Children, 29*(6), 58–61.

Huberty, T. J., Austin, J. K., Reisinger, M. W., & McNellis, J. (1992). Classroom performance and adaptive skills in children with epilepsy. *Journal of School Psychology, 30,* 331–342.

Hudson, P., & Glomb, N. (1997). If it takes two to tango, then why not teach both partners to dance? Collaboration instruction for all educators. *Journal of Learning Disabilities, 30,* 442–448.

Huefner, D. S. (2000). The risks and opportunities of the IEP requirements under IDEA'97. *Journal of Special Education, 33,* 195–204.

Hunt, P., & Goetz, L. (1997). Research on inclusive educational programs, practices, and outcomes for students with severe disabilities. *Journal of Special Education, 31,* 3–29.

Hutchinson, N. L. (1993). Students with disabilities and mathematics education reform. *Remedial and Special Education, 14*(6), 20–23.

Hux, K., & Hacksley, C. (1996). Mild traumatic brain injury: Facilitating school success. *Intervention in School and Clinic, 31,* 158–165.

Hyman, I. A., & Snook, P. A. (2000). Dangerous schools and what you can do about them. *Phi Delta Kappan, 81,* 489–501.

Hyperstudio [Computer software]. (1996). El Cajon, CA: Roger Wagner Publishing.

Iano, R. P., Ayers, D., Heller, H. B., McGettigan, J. F., & Walker, V. S. (1974). Sociometric status of retarded children in an integrative program. *Exceptional Children, 40,* 267–271.

Idol, L. (1997). Key questions related to building collaborative and inclusive schools. *Journal of Learning Disabilities, 30,* 384–394.

Imber-Black, E. (1988). *Families and larger systems.* New York: Guilford.

Innes, K. F., & Diamond, E. K. (1999). Typically developing children's interactions with peers with disabilities: Relationships between mothers' comments and children's ideas about disabilities. *Topics in Early Childhood Special Education, 19,* 103–111.

Ira, V. B. (2000). Safe and secure on the web: Pointers on determining a web site's credibility. *Exceptional Parent, 30*(1), 148.

Irlen, H. (1991). *Reading by the colors: Overcoming dyslexia and other reading disabilities through the Irlen method.* Garden City Park, NY: Avery.

Isaacson, S. L. (1987). Effective instruction in written language. *Focus on Exceptional Children, 19*(6), 1–12.

Ishii-Jordan, S. R. (2000). Behavioral interventions used with diverse students. *Behavioral Disorders, 25,* 299–309.

Janney, R. E., Snell, M. E., Beers, M. K., & Raynes, M. (1995). Integrating students with moderate and severe disabilities into general education classes. *Exceptional Children, 61,* 425–439.

Jarolimek, J., & Foster, C. D. (1993). *Teaching and learning in the elementary school.* New York: Macmillan.

Jayanthi, M., & Friend, M. (1992). Interpersonal problem solving: A selected literature review to guide practice. *Journal of Educational and Psychological Consultation, 3,* 147–152.

Jenkins, J. R., & Jenkins, L. M. (1981). *Cross age and peer tutoring: Help for children with learning problems.* Reston, VA: Council for Exceptional Children.

Jenkins, J. R., & Jewell, M. (1993). Examining the validity of two measures for formative teaching: Reading aloud and maze. *Exceptional Children, 59,* 421–432.

Jenson, W. R., Sheridan, S. M., Olympia, D., & Andrews, D. (1994). Homework and students with learning disabilities and behavior disorders: A practical, parent-based approach. *Journal of Learning Disabilities, 27*(9), 538–549.

Jitendra, A. K., & Kameenui, E. J. (1993). Dynamic assessment as a compensatory assessment approach: A description and analysis. *Remedial and Special Education, 14*(5), 6–18.

Job Accommodation Network. (2000). *The Americans with Disabilities Act: A brief overview.* Morgantown: West Virginia University. Retrieved June 10, 2000, from the World Wide Web: http://janweb.icdi.wvu. edu/kinder/overview.htm

Johns, B. (1997). Changes in IEP requirements based on the reauthorization of IDEA. *CCBD Newsletter, 11*(2), 1, 4.

Johns, B. H., & Carr, V. G. (1995). *Techniques for managing verbally and physically aggressive students* (pp. 17–22). Denver: Love.

Johnson, D. W., Johnson, R. T., & Maruyama, G. (1983). Interdependence and interpersonal attraction among heterogeneous and homogeneous individuals: A theoretical formulation and a meta-analysis of the research. *Review of Educational Research, 53,* 5–54.

Johnson, D. W., Johnson, R. T., Holubec, E. J., & Roy, P. (1984). *Circles of learning.* Alexandria, VA: Association for Supervision and Curriculum Development.

Johnson, E. S. (2000). The effects of accommodations on performance assessments. *Remedial and Special Education, 21*(5), 261–267.

Johnson, G. O., & Kirk, S. A. (1950). Are mentally handicapped children segregated in the regular grades? *Exceptional Children, 17,* 65–68; 87–88.

Johnson, L. J., & Pugach, M. C. (1996). Role of collaborative dialogue in teachers' conceptions of appropriate practice for students at risk. *Journal of Educational and Psychological Consultation, 7,* 9–24.

Johnson, L. R., & Johnson, C. E. (1999). Teaching students to regulate their own behavior. *Teaching Exceptional Children, 31*(4), 6–10.

Johnson, M. J., & Pajares, F. (1996). When shared decision making works: A 3-year longitudinal study. *American Educational Research Journal, 33,* 599–627.

Johnson, P. (1982). Effects on reading comprehension of building background knowledge. *TESOL Quarterly, 16,* 503–516.

Jones, B. E., Clark, G. M., & Soltz, D. F. (1997). Characteristics and practices of sign language interpreters in inclusive education programs. *Exceptional Children, 63,* 257–268.

Jones, M. M., & Carlier, L. L. (1995). Creating inclusionary opportunities for learners with multiple disabilities: A team-teaching approach. *Teaching Exceptional Children, 27*(3), 23–27.

Jones, V. F., & Jones, L. S. (1990). *Comprehensive classroom management.* Boston: Allyn and Bacon.

Jones, V. F., & Jones, L. S. (2001). *Comprehensive classroom management: Creating communities of support and solving problems.* (6th ed.) Boston: Allyn and Bacon.

Jongsma, E. (1980). *The cloze procedure as a teaching technique.* (pp. 1–33) Washington, DC: United States Department of Health Education and Welfare, Office of Education.

Juel, C. (1988). Learning to read and write: A longitudinal study of 54 children from first through fourth grades. *Journal of Educational Psychology, 80*(4), 437–447.

Kagan, S. (1990). A structural approach to cooperative learning. *Educational Leadership, 47*(4), 12–15.

Kalyanpur, M., & Harry, B. (1999). Legal and epistemological underpinnings of the construction of disability. In *Culture in special education: Building reciprocal family-professional relationships* (pp. 15–46). Baltimore: Paul H. Brookes.

Kameenui, E., Carnine, D., & Diven, R. C. (1998). Introduction. In E. Kameenui & D. Carnine (Eds.), *Effective teaching strategies that accommodate diverse learners* (pp. 1–17). Columbus, OH: Merrill Prentice-Hall.

Kameenui, E., & Simmons, D. (1991). *Designing instructional strategies: The prevention of academic learning problems.* Columbus, OH: Merrill.

Kaminski, R. A., & Good, R. H. (1996). Toward a technology for assessing basic early literacy skills. *School Psychology Review, 25*(2), 215–227.

Kamps, M. D., Tankersley, M., & Ellis, C. (2000). Social skills interventions for young at-risk students: A two-year follow-up study. *Behavioral Disorders, 25,* 310–324.

Kampwirth, T. J. (1999). Collaborative consultation in the schools: Effective practices for students with learning and behavior problems. Upper Saddle River, NJ: Merrill.

Kaplan, J. S., & Carter, J. (1995). *Beyond behavior modification: A cognitive- behavioral approach to behavior management in the school* (3rd ed., pp. 133–183). Austin, TX: PRO-ED.

Katsiyannis, A. (1990). Extended school year policies: An established necessity. *Remedial and Special Education, 12*(1), 24–28.

Katsiyannis, A., & Conderman, G. (1994). Section 504 and procedures: An established necessity. *Remedial and Special Education, 15,* 311–318.

Kauffman, J. M. (1997). *Characteristics of emotional and behavioral disorders of children and youth* (6th ed.). Columbus, OH: Merrill.

Kaufman, M. J., Gottlieb, J., Agard, J., & Kukic, M. (1975). Mainstreaming: Toward an explication of the construct. In E. L. Meyen, G. A. Vergason, & R. J. Whelan (Eds.), *Alternatives for teaching exceptional children* (pp. 35–54). Denver: Love.

Kavale, K. A., & Forness, S. R. (1987). Substance over style: Assessing the efficacy of modality testing and teaching. *Exceptional Children, 54,* 228–239.

Kavale, K. A., & Forness, S. R. (1996). Social skills deficits and learning disabilities: A meta-analysis. *Journal of Learning Disabilities, 29,* 226–237.

Kazdin, A. E. (1977). *The token economy: A review and evaluation.* New York: Plenum.

Kearns, J., Kleinert, H., Clayton, J., Burdge, M., & Williams, R. (1998). Inclusive educational assessments at the elementary school level: Perspectives from Kentucky. *Teaching Exceptional Children, 31*(2), 16–23.

Kearns, J. F., Kleinert, H. L., & Kennedy, S. (1999). We need not exclude anyone. *Educational Leadership, 54*(6), 33–38.

Kehle, T. J., Clark, E., & Jenson, W. R. (1996). Interventions for students with traumatic brain injury: Managing behavioral disturbances. *Journal of Learning Disabilities, 29,* 633–642.

Kelly, B., & Carnine, D. (1996). Teaching problem-solving strategies for word problems to students with learning disabilities. *LD Forum, 21*(3), 5–9.

Kender, J. P., & Kender, M. A. (1998). Education implications relating neuroanatomical research and developmental dyslexia. *Reading Horizons, 38*(3), 217–225.

Kennedy, H. C., Shukla, S., & Fryxell, D. (1997). Comparing the defects of educational placement on the social relationships of intermediate school students with severe disabilities. *Exceptional Children, 64,* 31–47.

Kerschner, J. R. (1990). Self-concept and IQ as predictors of remedial success in children with learning disabilities. *Journal of Learning Disabilities, 23,* 368–374.

Kilcarr, P. J., & Quinn, P. O. (1997). Fatherhood and AD/HD. *LD OnLine.* Washington, DC: WETA. Retrieved June 14, 2000, from the World Wide Web: http://www.ldonline.org/ld_indepth/add_adhd/kilcarr.html

Kinder, D., & Bursuck, W. D. (1991). The search for a unified social studies curriculum: Does history really repeat itself? *Journal of Learning Disabilities, 24,* 270–275.

Kinder, D., & Bursuck, W. D. (1993). History strategy instruction: Problem solution effect analysis, time line, and vocabulary instruction. *Exceptional Children, 59*(4), 324–335.

Kindsvatter, R., Wilen, W., & Ishler, M. (1988). *Dynamics of effective teaching.* New York: Longman.

King-Sears, M. E. (1997). Best academic practices for inclusive classrooms. *Focus on Exceptional Children, 29,* 1–22.

King-Sears, M. E., Burgess, M., & Lawson, T. L. (1999). Applying curriculum-based assessment in inclusive settings. *Teaching Exceptional Children, 32*(1), 30–38.

Kirk, S. A., Gallagher, J. J., & Anastasiow, N. J. (1997). *Educating exceptional children* (8th ed., pp. 512–557). Boston: Houghton Mifflin.

Kirst, M. W. (1991). Improving children's services: Overcoming barriers, creating new opportunities. *Phi Delta Kappan, 72,* 615–618.

Kleinart, H., Kearns, J., & Kennedy, S. (1997). Accountability for all students: Kentucky's alternate portfolio system for students with moderate and severe cognitive disabilities. *Journal of the Association for Persons with Severe Handicaps, 22,* 88–101.

Kleinart, H. L., Kennedy, S., & Kearns, J. F. (1999). The impact of alternate assessments: A statewide teacher survey. *The Journal of Special Education, 33*(2), 93–102.

Kloomok, S., & Cosden, M. (1994). Self-concept in children with learning disabilities: The relationship between global self-concept, academic "discounting," nonacademic self-concept, and perceived social support. *Learning Disability Quarterly, 17,* 140–153.

Kloosterman, V. (1998). Building a bridge: A combined effort between gifted and bilingual education. National Research Center on the Gifted and Talented.

Klorman, R. (1991, September). Cognitive event related potentials in attention deficit disorder. *Journal of Learning Disabilities, 24,* 130–140.

Kluwin, T. N. (1996). Getting hearing and deaf students to write to each other through dialogue journals. *Teaching Exceptional Children, 28* (2), 50–53.

Kovaleski, J. F., Gickling, E. E., Morrow, H., & Swank, P. R. (1999). High versus low implementation of instructional support teams: A case for maintaining program fidelity. *Remedial and Special Education, 20,* 170–183.

Krajewski, J. J. & Hyde, M. S., (2000). Comparison of teen attitudes toward individuals with mental retardation between 1987 and 1998: Has inclusion made a difference? *Education and Training in Mental Retardation and Developmental Disabilities, 35,* 284–293.

Kronick, D. (1977). A parent's thoughts for parents and teachers. In N. G. Haring & B. Bateman, *Teaching the learning disabled child.* Upper Saddle River, NJ: Prentice-Hall.

Ladson-Billings, G. J. (1999). Preparing teachers for diverse student populations: A critical race theory perspective. In Iran-Nejad, A., & P. D. Pearson (Eds.), *Review of Research in Education* (Vol. 24, pp. 211–247). Washington, D.C.: American Educational Research Association.

Lane, K. L. (1999). Young students at risk for antisocial behavior: The utility of academic and social skills interventions. *Journal of Emotional and Behavioral Disorders, 7*(4), 211–223.

Langer, J. (1984). Examining background knowledge and text comprehension. *Reading Research Quarterly, 19,* 468–481.

Lassman, K. A., Jolivette, K., & Wehby, J. H. (1999). "My teacher said I did good work today!" Using collaborative behavioral contracting. *Teaching Exceptional Children, 31* (4), 12–18.

LaVoie, R. (1991). *How difficult can this be? Understanding learning disabilities.* Portland, OR: Educational Productions.

LaVoie, R. D. (1989). *Mainstreaming: A collection of field-tested strategies to help make the mainstreaming classroom more successful for learning disabled children, their classmates . . . and their teachers.* Norwalk, CT: The Connecticut Association for Children with Learning Disabilities.

Lawton, M. (1995, Nov. 8). Students post dismal results on history test. *Education Week, 1,* 12.

Lazarowitz, R., & Karsenty, G. (1990). Cooperative learning and students' academic achievement, process skills, learning environment, and self-esteem in tenth-grade biology classrooms. In S. Sharan (Ed.), *Cooperative learning* (pp. 123–149). New York: Praeger.

Learning and Technology Center, Vanderbilt University (1996). The Adventures of Jasper Woodbury [Videodisc]. Mahwah, NJ: Learning Inc.

Leffert, J. S., Siperstein, G. N., & Milllikan, E. (2000). Understanding social adaptation in children with mental retardation: A social-cognitive perspective. *Exceptional Children, 66,* 530–545.

Leinhardt, G., & Zigmond, N. (1988). The effects of self-questioning and story structure training on the reading comprehension of poor readers. *Learning Disabilities Research, 4*(1), 41–51.

Lenz, B. K. (1983). Using the advance organizer. *Pointer, 27,* 11–13.

Lenz, B. K., & Alley, G. R. (1983). *The effects of advance organizers on the learning and retention of learning disabled adolescents within the context of a cooperative planning model.* Final research report submitted to the U.S. Department of Education, Office of Special Education, Washington, DC.

Lenz, B. K., Alley, G., & Schumaker, J. B. (1987). Activating the inactive learner: Advance organizers in the secondary content classroom. *Learning Disability Quarterly, 10,* 53–67.

Lenz, B. K., Ellis, E. S., & Scanlon, D. (1996). *Teaching learning strategies to adolescents and adults with learning disabilities.* Austin, TX: PRO-ED.

Lenz, B. K., Marrs, R. W., Schumaker, J. B., & Deshler, D. D. (1993). *The lesson organizer routine.* Lawrence, KS: Edge Enterprises, Inc.

Lerner, J. (2000). *Learning disabilities: Theories, diagnosis, and teaching strategies* (8th ed.). Boston: Houghton Mifflin.

Lerner, J. W., Lowenthal, B., & Lerner, S. R. (1995). *Attention deficit disorders: Assessment and teaching* (p. 180). Pacific Grove, CA: Brooks/Cole.

Lessen, E., & Bursuck, W. D. (1983). *A preliminary analysis of special education referral forms for a rural school district.* Unpublished data collection, Northern Illinois University.

Lessen, E., Sommers, M., & Bursuck, W. (1987). *Curriculum-based assessment and instructional design.* DeKalb, IL: DeKalb County Special Education Association.

Levy, N. R., & Rosenberg, M. S. (1990). Strategies for improving the written expression of students with learning disabilities. *LD Forum, 16*(1), 23–30.

Lewis, A. C., & Henderson, A. T. (1997). *Urgent message: Families crucial to school reform.* Washington, DC: Center for Law and Education. (ERIC Document Reproduction Service No. ED418480)

Licht, B. G., Kistner, J. A., Ozkaragoz, T., Shapiro, S., & Clausen, L. (1985). Causal attributions of learning disabled children: Individual difference of their implications for persistence. *Journal of Educational Psychology, 77,* 208–216.

Lilly, M. S. (1971). A training model for special education. *Exceptional Children, 37,* 740–749.

Lilly, M. S. (1979). *Children with exceptional needs.* New York: Holt, Rinehart, & Winston.

Linan-Thompson, S., & Jean, R. E. (1997). Completing the parent participation puzzle: Accepting diversity. *Teaching Exceptional Children, 30*(2), 46–50.

Lindamood, C. H., & Lindamood, P. C. (1984). *Auditory discrimination in depth.* Austin, TX: PRO-ED.

Lindquist, T. (1995). *Seeing the whole through social studies* (pp. 51–78). Portsmouth, NH: Heinemann.

Linehan, M. F. (1992). Children who are homeless: Educational strategies for school personnel. *Phi Delta Kappan, 74,* 61–66.

Liontis, L. B. (1992). *At-risk families and schools: Becoming partners.* Eugene, OR: ERIC Clearinghouse on Educational Management.

Little, J. W. (1993). Teachers' professional development in a climate of educational reform. *Educational Evaluation and Policy Analysis, 15,* 129–151.

Livingston, R. (1999). Cultural issues in diagnosis and treatment of ADHD. *Journal of the American Academy of Child and Adolescent Psychiatry 38,* 1591.

Loechler, K. (1999). Frequently asked questions about ADHD and the answers from the internet. *Teaching Exceptional Children, 31* (6), 28–31.

Logan, K. R., & Malone, D. M. (1998a). Comparing instructional contexts of students with and without severe disabilities in general education classrooms. *Exceptional Children, 64,* 343–358.

Logan, K. R., & Malone, D. M. (1998b). Instructional contexts for students with moderate, severe, and profound intellectual disabilities in general education elementary classrooms. *Education and Training in Mental Retardation and Developmental Disabilities, 33,* 62–75.

Lonergan, G. J. (2000). Some facts and figures about child abuse. *Child Abuse Referral and Education Network.* Bethesda, MD: Uniformed Services University of the Health Sciences. Retrieved September 14, 2000, from the World Wide Web: http://rad.usuhs.mil/rad/home/peds/pedindex.html

Long, N. J., & Newman, R. G. (1971). Managing surface behavior of children in school. In N. J. Long, W. C. Morse, & R. G. Newman (Eds.), *Conflict in the classroom: The education of children with problems* (2nd ed., pp. 442–452). Belmont, CA: Wadsworth.

Longwill, A. W., & Kleinert, H. L. (1998). The unexpected benefits of high school peer tutoring. *Teaching Exceptional Children, 30* (4), 60–65.

Lorenzi, D. G., Horvat, M., & Pellegrini, A. D. (2000). Physical activity of children with and without mental retardation in inclusive recess settings. *Education and Training in Mental Retardation and Developmental Disabilities, 35,* 160–167.

Lortie, D. C. (1975). *Schoolteacher: A sociological study.* Chicago: University of Chicago Press.

Lou, Y., Abrami, P. C., Spence, J. C., Poulsen, C., Chambers, B., & d'Apollonia, S. (1996). Within-class grouping: A meta-analysis. *Review of Educational Research, 66,* 423–258.

Lovitt, T. C., & Horton, S. V. (1987). How to develop study guides. *Journal of Reading, Writing, and Learning Disabilities, 3,* 333–343.

Lovitt, T. C., Plavins, M., & Cushing, S. (1999). What do pupils with disabilities have to say about their experience in high school? *Remedial and Special Education, 20,* 67–77.

Lovitt, T. C., Rudsit, J., Jenkins, J., Pious, C., & Beneditti, D. (1985). Two methods of adapting science materials for learning disabled and regular seventh graders. *Learning Disability Quarterly, 8,* 275–285.

Lowell-York, J., Doyle, M. E., & Kronberg, R. (1995). *Module 3. Curriculum as everything students learn in school: Individualizing learning opportunities.* Baltimore: Brookes.

Lueck, A. H. (1999). Setting curricular priorities for students with visual impairments. *Review, 31,* 54–66.

Lynch, E. W., Lewis, R. B., & Murphy, D. S. (1993a). Educational services for children with chronic illnesses: Perspectives of educators and families. *Exceptional Children, 59,* 210–220.

Lynch, E. W., Lewis, R. B., & Murphy, D. S. (1993b). Improving education for children with chronic illnesses. *Principal, 73*(2), 38–40.

Lyon, G. R. (1998). *Overview of reading and literacy initiatives.* Statement presented to National Institute of Child Health and Human Development. Retrieved October 7, 1999, from the World Wide Web: http://www.nichd.nih.gov/publications/pubs/jeffords.htm

Maag, J. W., & Reid, R. (1994). Attention-deficit hyperactivity disorder: A functional approach to assessment and treatment. *Behavioral Disorders, 20,* 5–23.

MacArthur, C. (1998). From illegible to understandable: How word recognition and speech synthesis can help. *Teaching Exceptional Children, 30*(6), 66–71.

MacArthur, C. A., & Stoddard, B. (1990, April). *Teaching learning disabled students to revise: A peer editor strategy.* Paper presented at the Annual Meeting of the American Education Research Association, Boston.

MacMillan, D. L., Gresham, F. M., Bocian, K. M., & Lambros, K. M. (1998). Current plight of borderline students: Where do they belong? *Education and Training in Mental Retardation and Developmental Disabilities, 33,* 83–94.

Madden, J. A. (2000). Managing asthma at school. *Educational Leadership, 57*(6), 50–52.

Maheady, L., Mallette, B., & Harper, B. F. (1991). Accommodating cultural, linguistic, and academic diversity: Some peer-mediated instructional options. *Preventing School Failure, 36*(1), 28–31.

Mahoney, G., Kaiser, A., Girdametto, G., MacDonald, J., Robinson, C., Safford, P., & Spiker, D. (1999). Parent education in early intervention: A call for a renewed focus. *Topics in Early Childhood Special Education, 19,* 131–146.

Maker, J. C. (1993). Gifted students in the regular classroom: What practices are defensible and feasible? In C. J. Maker (Ed.), *Critical issues in gifted education: Programs for the gifted in regular classrooms* (Vol. III, pp. 413–436). Austin, TX: PRO-ED.

Male, M. (1997). *Technology for inclusion: Meeting the special needs of all students* (3rd ed., pp. 153–168). Boston: Allyn and Bacon.

Malmgren, K. W. (1998). Cooperative learning as an academic intervention for students with mild disabilities. *Focus on Exceptional Children, 31*(4), 1–6.

Mandlebaum, L. H., & Wilson, R. (1989). Teaching listening skills. *LD Forum, 15*(1), 7–9.

Manset, G., & Semmel, M. I. (1997). Are inclusive programs for students with mild disabilities effective? A comparative review of model program. *Journal of Special Education, 31,* 155–180.

Marks, S. U., Schrader, C., & Levine, M. (1999). Paraeducator experiences in inclusive settings: Helping, hovering, or holding their own? *Exceptional Children, 65,* 315–328.

Marsh, L. G., & Cooke, N. L. (1996). The effects of using manipulatives in teaching math problem solving to students with learning disabilities. *Learning Disabilities Research & Practice, 11*(1), 58–65.

Marshall, R. M., Hynd, G. W., Handwerk, M. J., & Hall, J. (1997). Academic underachievement in ADHD subtypes. *Journal of Learning Disabilities, 30,* 635–642.

Marston, D. B. (1989). A curriculum-based measurement approach to asesssing academic performance: What it is and why do it. In M. R. Shinn (Ed.), *Curriculum-based measurement: Assessing special children* (pp. 18–78). New York: Guilford Press.

Marston, D. B. (1996). A comparison of inclusion only, pull-out only, and combined service models for students with mild disabilities. *The Journal of Special Education, 30*(2), 121–132.

Marston, D. B., Tindal, G., & Deno, S. (1984). Eligibility for learning disability services: A direct and repeated measurement approach. *Exceptional Children, 50,* 554–556.

Martin, A. K., Hutchinson, N. L., & Whitehead, L. E. (1999). Gauging field support for a proposed field based teacher education program. *Teacher Education Quarterly, 26* (2), 21–34.

Marzola, E. S. (1987). Using manipulatives in math instruction. *Reading, Writing, and Learning Disabilities, 3,* 9–20.

Mastropieri, M. A. (1988). Using the keyboard method. *Teaching Exceptional Children, 20*(4), 4–8.

Mathes, P. G., Fuchs, D., & Fuchs, L. S. (1997). Cooperative story mapping. *Remedial and Special Education, 18,* 20–27.

McCarty, H. & Chalmers, L. (1997). Therapy intervention and prevention. *Teaching Exceptional Children, 29* (6), 12–13.

McConnell, M. E., Hilvitz, P. B., & Cox, C. J. (1998). Functional assessment: A systematic process for assessment and intervention in general and special education classrooms. *Intervention in School and Clinic, 34* (1), 10–20.

McDonnell, J. (1998). Instruction for students with severe disabilities in general education settings. *Education and Training in Mental Retardation and Developmental Disabilities, 33,* 199–215.

McDougall, D., & Brady, M. P. (1998). Initiating and fading self-management interventions to increase math fluency in general education classes. *Exceptional Children, 64*(2), 151–166.

McGookey, K. (1992). Drama, disability, and your classroom. *Teaching Exceptional Children, 24*(2), 12–14.

McIntosh, R., Vaughn, S., & Bennerson, D. (1995). FAST social skills with a SLAM and a RAP. *Teaching Exceptional Children, 28*(1), 37–41.

McIntyre, T. (1992). *The behavior management handbook: Setting up effective management systems.* Boston: Allyn and Bacon.

McIntyre, T., & Silva, P. (1992). Culturally diverse childrearing practices: Abusive or just different? *Beyond Behavior, 4*(1), 8–12.

McKeown, M. G., & Beck, J. L. (1990). The assessment and characterization of young learners' knowledge of a topic in history. *American Educational Research Journal, 27*(4), 688–726.

McKeown, M. G., Beck, J. L., Sinatra, G. M., & Loxterman, J. A. (1992). The contribution of prior knowledge and coherent text to comprehension. *Reading Research Quarterly, 27,* 78–93.

McLeskey, J., Henry, D., & Axelrod, M. I. (1999). Inclusion of students with learning disabilities: An examination of data from reports to Congress. *Exceptional Children, 66,* 55–66.

Mead, J. F. (1995). Including students with disabilities in parental choice programs: The challenge of meaningful choice. *West's Education Law Quarterly, 4,* 570–603.

Meichenbaum, D. (1977). *Cognitive behavior modification: An integrative approach.* New York: Plenum.

Mercer, C. D. (1997). *Students with learning disabilities* (5th ed.). Columbus, OH: Merrill.

Mercure, C. M. (1993). Project Achievement: An after-school success story. *Principal, 73*(1), 48–50.

Miles, D. D., & Forcht, J. P. (1995). Mathematics strategies for secondary students with learning disabilities on mathematics deficiencies: A cognitive approach. *Intervention in School and Clinic, 31*(2), 91–96.

Miller, R. V. (1956). Social status of socioempathic differences. *Exceptional Children, 23,* 114–119.

Miller-Young, R. (1999). The impact of concrete phonemic representations on phonological awareness acquisition of at-risk kindergartners. Unpublished doctoral dissertation.

Miranda, A., & Guerrero, M. (1986). The funny farola. In *Adventures* (pp. 42–53). Boston: Houghton Mifflin.

Mitchell, A. (1997). Teacher identity: A key to increased collaboration. *Action in Teacher Education, 19* (3), 1–14.

Mittag, K. C., & Van Reusen, A. K. (1999). Learning estimation and other advanced mathematics concepts in an inclusive class. *Teaching Exceptional Children, 31*(6), 66–72.

Moody, J. D., & Gifford, V. D. (1990). *The effect of grouping by formal reasoning ability, formal reasoning ability levels, group size, and gender on achievement in laboratory chemistry.* (ERIC Document Reproduction Service No. ED 326 443)

Moore, D. W., Readance, J. E., & Rickleman, R. (1989). *Prereading activities for content-area reading and learning* (2nd ed.). Newark, DE: International Reading Association.

Morris, R. J. (1985). *Behavior modification with exceptional children: Principles and practices.* Glenview, IL: Scott Foresman.

Morse, W. C. (1987). Introduction to the special issue. *Teaching Exceptional Children, 19*(4), 4–6.

Mortweet, S. L., Utley, C. A., Walker, D., Dawson, H. L., Delquadri, J. C., Reddy, S. S., Greenwood, C. R., Hamilton, S., & Ledford, D. (1999). Classwide peer tutoring: Teaching students with mild mental retardation in inclusive classrooms. *Exceptional Children, 65,* 524–536.

Mosteller, F., Light, R., & Sachs, J. (1996). Sustained inquiry in education: Lessons from skill grouping and class size. *Harvard Educational Review, 66*(4), 797–828.

Mostert, M. P. (1998). Communication in interprofessional collaboration. In *Interprofessional collaboration in schools* (Chapter 6, pp. 91–115). Boston: Allyn and Bacon.

Munk, D. D., & Bursuck, W. D. (in press). The many purposes for report card grades: Perspective of elementary and middle school parents. To appear *in Remedial and Special Education.*

Munk, D. D., & Bursuck, W. D. (2001a). Personalized grading plans: A systematic approach to making the grades of included students more accurate and meaningful. In L. Denti & P. Tefft-Cousin (Eds.), *Looking at learning disabilities in new ways: Connections to classroom practice* (pp. 111–127). Denver, CO: Love.

Munk, D. D., & Bursuck, W. D. (2001b). Preliminary findings on personalized grading plans for middle school students with learning disabilities. *Exceptional Children, 67*(2), 211–234.

Munk, D. D., Bursuck, W. D., Epstein, M. H., Jayanthi, M., Nelson, J. S., & Polloway, E. A. (in press). Homework communication problems: Perspectives of special and general education parents. *Reading and Writing Quarterly.*

Muyskens, P., & Ysseldyke, J. E. (1998). Students academic responding times as a function of classroom ecology and time of day. *The Journal of Special Education, 31*(4), 411–424.

My Words [Computer Software]. (1993). Dimondale, MI: Hartley.

Nation, K., & Hulme, C. (1997). Phonemic segmentation, not onset-rime segmentation, predicts early reading and spelling skills. *Reading Research Quarterly, 32*(2), 154–167.

National Association of State Directors of Special Education. (1997). *Comparison of key issues: Current law and 1997 IDEA amendments.* Alexandria, VA: Author.

National Center for Education Statistics. (1998). *Dropout rates in the United States, 1996: Event, status, and cohort dropout rates.* Washington, D. C.: Author.

National Center for Education Statistics. (2000). *The condition of education 2000: Distribution of public school students.* Washington, DC: U.S. Department of Education. Retrieved September 13, 2000, from the World Wide Web: http://nces.ed.gov/pubs2000/coe2000/section1/s_table4_1.html

National Coalition for the Homeless. (1999, February). *Who is homeless* [NCH Fact Sheet No. 3]. Retrieved September 12, 2000, from the World Wide Web: http://nch.ari.net/who.html.

National Council of Teachers of Mathematics (2000). Principles and standards for school mathematics. Reston, VA: Author.

National Foundation for Gifted and Creative Children. (2000). *Characteristics of gifted and creative children.* Warwick, RI: Author. Retrieved September 14, 2000, from the World Wide Web: http://www.nfgcc.org

National Health and Medical Research Council. (2000, September). *Attention deficit hyperactivity disorder (ADHD): Eight specific issues for preschoolers, adolescents, and adults.* Sydney, Australia: Author. Retrieved September 13, 2000, from the World Wide Web: http://www.health.gov.au/nhmrelpublicat/adhd/part2-4htm.

National Information Center for Children and Youth with Disabilities. (1996, October). The education of children and youth with special needs: What do the laws say? *NICHCY News Digest* (#ND15), 1–17. Retrieved from the World Wide Web: http://www.nichcy.org/pubs/newsdig/nd15txt.htm

National Information Center for Children and Youth with Disabilities. (1998). The IDEA Amendments of 1997 (revised edition). *NICHY News Digest, 25,* 1–41. Retrieved June 9, 2000, from the World Wide Web: http://www.nichy.org/pubs/newsdig/nd26pdf.pdf

National Law Center on Homelessness and Poverty. (1999). *Out-of-sight, Out of mind?: A report on anti-homelessness laws, litigation, and laternative in 50 United States cities.* Washington, D.C.: Author.

National Reading Panel (2000). *Teaching children to read: An evidence-based assessment of the scientific research literature on reading and its implications for reading instruction.* Washington, DC: National Institute of Child Health and Human Development.

Nelson, J. R. (1996). Designing schools to meet the needs of students who exhibit disruptive behavior. *Journal of Emotional and Behavioral Disorders, 4,* 147–161.

Nelson, J. S., Epstein, M. H., Bursuck, W. D., Jayanthi, M., & Sawyer, V. (1998). The preferences of middle school students for homework adaptations made by general education teachers. *Learning Disabilities Research and Practice, 13*(2), 109–117.

Nelson, J. S., Jayanthi, M., Epstein, M. H., & Bursuck, W. D. (2000). Student preferences for adaptations in classroom testing. *Remedial and Special Education, 21*(1), 41–52.

O'Connor, R. (2000). Increasing the intensity of intervention in kindergarten and first grade. *Learning Disabilities Research and Practice, 15*(1), 43–54.

O'Reilly, M. F., & Glynn, D. (1995). Using a process social skills training approach with adolescents with mild intellectual disabilities in a high school setting. *Education and Training in Mental Retardation and Developmental Disabilities, 31,* 187–198.

Oakland, T. (1981). Nonbiased assessment of minority group children. *Exceptional Education Quarterly, 1*(3), 31–46.

Oakland, T., Black, J. L., Standford, G., Nussbaum, N. L., & Balise, R. R. (1998). An evaluation of the dyslexia training program: A multisensory method for promoting reading in students with reading disabilities. *Journal of Learning Disabilities, 31*(2), 140–147.

Obiakor, F. E. (1999). Teacher expectations of minority exceptional learners: Impact of "accuracy" of self-concepts. *Exceptional Children, 66,* 39–53.

Ogle, D. M. (1986). K. W. L.: A teaching model that develops active reading of expository text. *The Reading Teacher, 39,* 565.

Okolo, C. M. (1993). Computers and individuals with mild disabilities. In J. Lindsey (Ed.), *Computers and exceptional individuals* (pp. 111–141). Austin, TX: PRO-ED.

Operation Sickle Cell. (2001). *General information.* Fayetteville, NC: Author. Retrieved January 29, 2001, from the World Wide Web: http://www.uncfsu.edu/osc/

Ornstein, A. C. (1990). *Strategies for effective teaching.* New York: Harper and Row.

Orr, L. E., Craig, G. P., Best, J., Borland, A., Holland, D., Knode, H., Lehman, A., Mathewson, C., Miller, M., & Pequignot, M. (1997). Exploring developmental disabilities through literature: An annotated bibliography. *Teaching Exceptional Children, 29*(6), 14–15.

Osborne, A. G. (1996). *Legal issues in special education.* Boston: Allyn and Bacon.

Overton, T. (1999). *Assessment in special education. An applied approach* (3rd ed). New York: Macmillan.

Paine, S. C., Radicchi, J., Rosellini, L. C., Deutchman, L., & Darch, C. B. (1983). *Structuring your classroom for academic success.* Champaign, IL: Research Press.

Palincsar, A., & Brown, A. (1988). Teaching and practicing thinking skills to promote comprehension in the context of group problem solving. *Remedial and Special Education, 9*(1), 53–59.

Palmer, D. S., Borthwick-Duffy, S. A., & Widaman, K. (1998). Parent perceptions of inclusive practices for their children with significant cognitive disabilities. *Exceptional Children, 64,* 271–282.

Paneri, S., Ferrante, L., Caputo, V., & Impellizzeri, C. (1998). Use of structured teaching for treatment of children with autism and severe and profound mental retardation. *Education and Training in Mental Retardation and Developmental Disabilities, 33,* 367–374.

Pappalardo, R. G. (1999). Curricular issues: The visual arts and students with disabilities. In Nyman, A. L., & Jenkins, A. M. (Eds.), *Issues and approaches to art for students with special needs* (pp. 42–54). Reston, VA: The National Art Education Association.

Patton, J. R. (1994). Practical recommendations for using homework with students with disabilities. *Journal of Learning Disabilities, 27*(9), 570–578.

Patton, J. R., Jayanthi, H., & Polloway, E. A. (in press). Home school communication about homework: What do we know and what should we do? *Reading and Writing Quarterly.*

Patton, J. R., Payne, J. S., & Beirne-Smith, M. (1986). *Mental retardation* (2nd ed.). Columbus, OH: Merrill.

Paulson, F., Paulson, P., & Meyer, C. (1991). What makes a portfolio a portfolio? *Educational Leadership, 48*(5), 60–63.

Pearman, E. L., Huang, A. M., & Melblom, C. I. (1997). The inclusion of all students: concerns and incentives of educators. *Education and Training in Mental Retardation and Developmental Disabilities, 32,* 11–20.

Pearson, P. D. (1996). Reclaiming the center. In M. F. Graves, P. van den Broek, & B. M. Taylor (Eds.), *The first R: Every child's right to read* (pp. 259–274). New York: Teachers College Press.

Pearson, S. (1996). Child abuse among children with disabilities: Implications for special educators. *Teaching Exceptional Children, 29*(1), 14–37.

Peckham, V. C. (1993). Children with cancer in the classroom. *Teaching Exceptional Children, 26*(1), 26–32.

Pedrotty-Bryant, D., Bryant, B. R., & Raskind, M. H. (1998). Using assistive technology to enhance the skills of students with learning disabilities. *Intervention in School and Clinic, 34*(1), 53–58.

Pena, R. A., & Amerin, A. (1999). Classroom management and caring. *Teaching Education, 10,* 169–179.

Pennington, B. F. (1995). Genetics of learning disabilities. *Journal of Child Neurology, 10*(Suppl. 1), 69–77.

Pertsch, C. F. (1936). *A comparative study of the progress of subnormal pupils in the grades and in special classes.* New York: Teacher's College, Columbia University, Bureau of Publications.

Peterson, R. L. & Ishii-Jordan, S. (1994). *Multicultural issues in the education of students with behavior disorders.* Cambridge, MA: Brookline Books.

Phillips, V., & McCullough, L. (1990). Consultation-based programming: Instituting the collaborative ethic in schools. *Exceptional Children, 56,* 291–304.

Pohan, C. A., & Mathison, C. (1999). Dismantling defensiveness and resistance to diversity and social justice issues in teacher preparation. *Action in Teacher Education, 20,* 15–22.

Polloway, E. A., Bursuck, W. D., & Epstein, M. H. (in press). Homework for students with learning disabilities: The challenge of home-school communication. *Reading and Writing Quarterly.*

Polloway, E. A., Bursuck, W. D., Jayanthi, M., Epstein, M. H., & Nelson, J. S. (1996). Treatment acceptability: Determining appropriate interventions within inclusive classrooms. *Intervention in School and Clinic, 31*(3), 133–144.

Polloway, E. A., Epstein, M. H., Bursuck, W. D., Jayanthi, M., & Cumblad, C. (1994). Homework practices of general education teachers. *Journal of Learning Disabilities, 27*(8), 100–109.

Poplin, M. S. (1988). Holistic/constructive principles of the teaching/learning process: Implications for the field of learning disabilities. *Journal of Learning Disabilities, 21,* 401–416.

Poteet, J. A., Choate, J. S., & Stewart, S. C. (1993). Performance assessment and special education: Practices and prospects. *Focus on Exceptional Children, 26*(1), 1–20.

Prater, M. A., Bruhl, S., & Serna, L. A. (1998). Acquiring social skills through cooperative learning and teacher-directed instruction. *Remedial And Special Education, 19,* 160–172.

Pratt, C., & Moreno, S. J. (1994). Including students with autism in typical school settings. In F. LaRoy and J. Streng (Eds.), *A new dawn of awakening: Proceedings of the 1994 conference* (pp. 143–146). Arlington, TX: Future Education.

Prom, M. (1999). Measuring perceptions about inclusion. *Teaching Exceptional Children, 31*(5), 38–42.

Pugach, M. C., & Johnson, L. J. (1995). *Collaborative practitioners, collaborative schools.* Denver: Love.

Purvis, K. L., & Tannock, R. (2000). Phonological processing, not inhibitory control, differentiates ADHD and reading disability. *Journal of the American Academy of Child and Adolescent Psychiatry, 39*, 485.

Putnam, L., & Wesson, C. (1990). The teacher's role in teaching content-area information. *LD Forum, 16*(1), 55–60.

Quinn, M. M., Gable, R. A., Rutherford, R. B., Nelson, C. M., & Howell, K. W. (1998). *Addressing student problem behavior: An IEP team's introduction to functional behavioral assessment and behavior intervention plans.* Washington, D.C.: Center for Effective Collaboration and Practice.

Rademacher, J. A. (2000). Involving students in assignment evaluation. *Intervention in School and Clinic, 35*(3), 151–156.

Ramirez-Smith, C. (1995). Stopping the cycle of failure: The Comer Model. *Educational Leadership, 52*(5), 14–15.

Ramsey, W. L., Gabriel, L. A., McGuirk, J. F., Phillips, C. R., & Watenpaugh, T. R. (1983). *General Science.* New York: Holt, Rinehart, & Winston.

Rankin, J. L., & Aksamit, D. L. (1994). Perceptions of elementary, junior high, and high school student assistant team coordinators, team members, and teachers. *Journal of Educational and Psychological Consultation, 5*, 229–256.

Rankin, J. L., & Reid, R. (1995). The SM rap—Or, here's the rap on self-monitoring. *Intervention in School and Clinic, 30*(3), 181–188.

Raphael, T. E., Kirschner, B. W., & Englert, C. S. (1986). *Text structure instruction within process writing classrooms: A manual for instruction* (Occasional Paper No. 104). East Lansing, MI: Michigan State University, Institute for Research on Teaching.

Rappaport, J. (1982/1983). Effects of dietary substances in children. *Journal of Psychiatric Research, 17*, 187–191.

Raywid, M. A. (1993). Finding time for collaboration. *Educational Leadership, 51*(1), 30–34.

Reddy, S. S., Utley, C. A., Delquadri, J. C., Mortweet, S. L., Greenwood, C. R., & Bowman, V. (1999). Peer tutoring for health and safety. *Teaching Exceptional Children, 31*(3), 44–52.

Reetz, L., & Rasmussen, T. (1988). Arithmetic mind joggers. *Academic Therapy, 24*(1), 79–82.

Reeve, R. E. (1990). ADHD: Facts and fallacies. *Intervention in School and Clinic, 26*(2), 70–78.

Reid, R. (1996). Research in self-monitoring with students with learning disabilities: The present, the prospects, the pitfalls. *Journal of Learning Disabilities, 29*(3), 317–331.

Reid, R., & Maag, J. W. (1997). Attention deficit hyperactivity disorder: Over here and over there. *Educational and Child Psychology, 14*, 10–20.

Reid, R., DuPaul, G. J., Power, T. J., Anastopoulos, A. D., Rogers-Adkinson, D., Noll, M. B., & Riccio, C. (1998). Assessing culturally different students for attention deficit hyperactivity disorder using behavior rating scales. *Journal of Abnormal Child Psychology, 26*, 187–199.

Reid, R., Maag, J. W., & Vasa, S. F. (1994). Attention deficit hyperactivity disorder as a disability category: A critique. *Exceptional Children, 60*, 98–214.

Reimers, T. M., Wacker, D. P., & Koeppl, G. (1987). Acceptability of behavioral interventions: A review of the literature. *School Psychology Review, 16*, 212–227.

Reinhiller, N. (1996). Coteaching: New variations on a not-so-new practice. *Teacher Education and Special Education, 19*, 34–38.

Reis, S. M., Gentry, M., & Park, S. (1996, Winter). Extending the pedagogy of gifted education to all students. *National Research Center on the Gifted and Talented Newsletter.* Retrieved from the World Wide Web: http://www.sp.uconn.edu/~nrcgt/winter96/wintr965.html.

Reyes, M. L., & Molner, L. A. (1991). Instructional strategies for second-language learners in the content areas. *Journal of Reading, 35*(2), 96–103.

Reynolds, M. C., & Heistad, D. (1997). 20/20 analysis: Estimating school effectiveness in serving students at the margin. *Exceptional Children, 63*, 439–449.

Riccio, C. A., Hynd, G. W., Cohen, M. J., & Gonzalez, J. J. (1993). Neurological basis of attention deficit hyperactivity disorder. *Exceptional Children, 60*, 118–124.

Robin, A. L. (1998). *ADHD in adolescents: Diagnosis and treatment.* New York: Guilford Press.

Robinson, S., & Smith, J. (1981). Listening skills: Teaching learning disabled students to be better listeners. *Focus on Exceptional Children, 13*(8), 1–15.

Roblyer, M. D., Edwards, J., & Havriluk, M. A. (1997). *Integrating educational technology into teaching.* Columbus, OH: Merrill.

Rodger, S. (1995). Individual education plans revisited: A review of the literature. *International Journal of Disability, Development, and Education, 42*, 221–239.

Rodgers-Rhyme, A., & Volpiansky, P. (1991). *PARTNERS in problem solving staff development program: Participant guide.* Madison, WI: Wisconsin Department of Public Instruction.

Rojewski, J. W., Pollard, R. R., & Meers, G. D. (1992). Grading secondary vocational students with disabilities. *Exceptional Children, 59*(1), 68–76.

Rose, L. C., & Gallup, A. M. (1998). The 30th annual Phi Delta Kappa/Gallup poll of the public's attitudes toward the public schools. *Phi Delta Kappan, 81*, 41–56.

Rose, L. C., & Gallup, A. M. (1999). The 31st annual Phi Delta Kappa/Gallup poll of the public's attitudes toward the public schools. *Phi Delta Kappan, 81*, 41–56.

Rose, L. C., & Gallup, A. M. (2000). The 32nd annual Phi Delta Kappa/Gallup poll of the public's attitudes toward the public schools. *Phi Delta Kappan, 81*, 41–58.

Rosenblum, P. L. (1998). Best friendships of adolescents with visual impairments: A descriptive study. *Journal of Visual Impairment & Blindness, 92*, 593–608.

Rosenfeld, S. J. (1999). *Section 504 and IDEA: Basic similarities and differences.* Washington, DC: LD Online. Retrieved September 12, 2000, from: http://www.ldonline.org/ld_indepth/legal_legislative/edlaw504.html

Rosenfield, S. A., & Gravois, T. A. (1996). *Instructional consultation teams: Collaborating for change.* New York: Guilford Press.

Rosenshine, B., & Meister, C. (1992). The use of scaffolds for teaching higher-level cognitive strategies. *Educational Leadership, 49*, 26–33.

Rosenshine, B., & Stevens, R. (1986). Teaching functions. In M. C. Wittrock (Ed.)., *Handbook of research on teaching* (pp. 376–391). New York: Macmillan.

Ross, R., & Kurtz, R. (1993). Making manipulatives work: A strategy for success. *Arithmetic Teacher, 40*(5), 254–257.

Rothman, H. R., & Cosden, M. (1995). The relationship between self-perception of a learning disability and achievement, self-concept and social support. *Learning Disability Quarterly, 20*, 203–212.

Rothstein, L. L. F. (1995). *Special education law* (2nd ed.). New York: Longman.

Runge, A., Walker, J., & Shea, T. M. (1975). A passport to positive parent-teacher communication. *Teaching Exceptional Children*, 7(3), 91–92.

Ryan, S., & Paterna, L. (1997). Junior high can be inclusive: Using natural supports and cooperative learning. *Teaching Exceptional Children*, 30(2), 36–41.

Sack, J. L. (1999). Sharp rise seen in identification of autistic pupils. *Education Week*, 19(8), 1.

Sacks, S. Z., Wolffe, K. E., & Tierney, D. (1998). Lifestyles of students with visual impairments: Preliminary studies of social networks. *Exceptional Children, 64*, 463–478.

Sadker, M., Sadker, D., & Klein, S. (1991).The issue of gender in elementary and secondary education. In G. Grant (Ed.), *Review of research in education* (pp. 269–334). Washington, DC: American Educational Research Association.

Safran, S. P. (1998a). Disability portrayal in film: Reflecting the past, directing the future. *Exceptional Children, 64*, 227–238.

Safran, S. P., (1998b). The first century of disability portrayal in film: An analysis of the literature. *Journal of Special Education, 31*, 467–479.

Safran, S. P., & Safran, J. S. (1996). Intervention assistance programs and prereferral teams: Directions for the twentieth-first century. *Remedial and Special Education, 17*, 363–369.

Sale, P., & Carey, D. M. (1995). The sociometric status of students with disabilities in a full-inclusion school. *Exceptional Children, 62*, 6–19.

Salembier, G. G., & Cheng, L. C. (1997). SCUBADive into reading. *Teaching Exceptional Children, 29*(6), 68–71.

Salend, S. J. (1999). Facilitating friendships among diverse students. *Intervention in School and Clinic, 35* (1), 9–15.

Salend, S. J., & Duhaney, L. M. G. (1999). The impact of inclusion on students with and without disabilities and their educators. *Remedial and Special Education, 20*, 114–126.

Salend, S. J., & Taylor, L. (1993). Working with families: A cross-cultural perspective. *Remedial and Special Education, 14*(5), 25–32, 39.

Salend, S. J., Dorney, J. A., & Mazo, M. (1997). The roles of bilingual special educators in creating inclusive classrooms. *Remedial and Special Education, 18*, 54–64.

Salisbury, C. L., & Palombaro, M. M. (1998). Friends and acquaintances. Evolving relationships in an inclusive elementary school. In L. H. Meyer, H. S. Park, M. Grenot-Scheyer, I. S. Schwartz, & B. Harry (Eds.), *Making friends: The influences of culture and development* (pp. 81–104). Baltimore: Paul H. Brookes.

Salvia, J., & Ysseldyke, J. (1998). *Assessment in special and remedial education* (7th ed.). Boston: Houghton Mifflin.

Sánchez, S. Y. (1999). Learning from the sotires of culturally and linguistically diverse families and communities. *Remedial and Special Education, 20*, 351–359.

Sands, S., & Buchholz, E. S. (1997). The underutilization of computers to assist in the remediation of dyslexia. *International Journal of Instructional Media, 24*(2), 153–175.

Savage, R. C., & Wolcott, G. F. (1994). *Educational dimensions of acquired brain injury* (pp. 3–12). Austin, TX: PRO-ED.

Savoie, J. M., & Hughes, A. S. (1994). Problem-based learning as classroom solution. *Educational Leadership, 52*(3), 54–57.

Scarborough, J. S., & Deck, M. D. (1998). The challenges of working for students with disabilities: A view from the front lines. *Professional School Counseling, 2* (1), 10–15.

Schaps, E., & Solomon, D. (1990). Schools and classrooms as caring communities. *Educational Leadership, 48*(3), 38–42.

Scheerenberger, R. C. (1983). *A history of mental retardation*. Baltimore: Paul H. Brookes.

Schifini, A. (1994). Language, literacy, and content instruction: Strategies for teachers. In K. Spangenberg-Unbschat and R. Pritchard (Eds.), *Kids come in all languages: Reading instruction for ESL students* (pp. 158–179). Newark, DE: International Reading Association.

Schloss, P. J., & Smith, M. A. (1994). *Applied behavior analysis in the classroom*. Boston: Allyn and Bacon.

Schuller, C. F. (1982). Using instructional resources and technology. In D. E. Orlosky (Ed.), *Introduction to education* (pp. 400–429). Columbus, OH: Merrill.

Schumaker, J. B., & Deshler, D. D. (1988). Implementing the Regular Education Initiative in secondary schools: A different ball game. *Journal of Learning Disabilities, 21*(1), 36–42.

Schumaker, J. B., Deshler, D. D., & Denton, P. (1984). *The learning strategies curriculum: The paraphrasing strategy*. Lawrence, KS: University of Kansas.

Schumm, J. S., & Vaughn, S. (1995). Getting reading for inclusion: Is the stage set? *Learning Disabilities Research and Practice, 10*, 169–179.

Schunk, D. (1989). Self-efficacy and cognitive achievement. Implications for students with learning disabilities. *Journal of Learning Disabilities, 22*(1), 14–22.

Scott, B. J., Vitale, M. R., & Masten, W. G. (1998). Implementing instructional adaptations for students with disabilities in inclusive classrooms. *Remedial and Special Education, 19*, 106–119.

Scott, P. B., & Raborn, D. T. (1996). Realizing the gifts of diversity among students with learning disabilities. *LD Forum, 21*(2), 10–18.

Scruggs, T. E., & Mastropieri, M. A. (1992). Effective mainstreaming strategies for mildly handicapped students. *Elementary School Journal, 92*, 389–409.

Scruggs, T., & Mastropieri, M. (1994). The construction of scientific knowledge by students with mild disabilities. *Journal of Special Education, 28*, 307–321.

Senesh, L. (1973). *The American way of life* (p. 149). Chicago: Science Research Associates.

Shapiro, E. S., DuPaul, G. J., & Bradley-Klug, K. L. (1998). Self-management as a strategy to improve the classroom behavior of adolescents with ADHD. *Journal of Learning Disabilities, 31*, 545–555.

Sharan, S., Kussell, P., Hertz-Lazarowitz, Bejarano, Y., Raviv, S., & Sharan, Y. (1984). *Cooperative learning in the classroom: Research in desegregated schools*. Hillsdale, NJ: Lawrence Erlbaum.

Shaywitz, S. E., Escobar, M. D., Shaywitz, B. A., Fletcher, J. M., & Makuch, R. (1992). Evidence that dyslexia may represent the lower tail of a normal distribution of reading ability. *New England Journal of Medicine, 326*, 145–150.

Shaywitz, B. A., Pugh, K. R., Jenner, A. R., Fulbright, R. K., Fletcher, J. M., Gore, J. C., & Shaywitz, S. E. (2000). The neurobiology of reading and reading disability (dyslexia). In M. Kamil, P. Mosenthal, P. D. Pearson, & R. Barr (Eds.), *Handbook of reading research: Volume III* (pp. 229–249). Mahwah, NJ: Lawrence Erlbaum Associates.

Shea, T. M., & Bauer, A. M. (1994). *Learners with disabilities: A social systems perspective of special education*. Madison, WI: Brown & Benchmark.

Shinn, M. R., Collins, V. L., & Gallagher, S. (1998). Curriculum-based measurement and problem solving assessment. In M. R. Shinn (Ed.), *Advanced applications of curriculum-based measurement* (pp. 143–174). New York: Guilford Press.

Sigafoos, J., & Littlewood, R. (1999). Communication intervention on the playground: A case study on teaching requesting to a young child with autism. *International Journal of Disability, Development, and Education, 46*, 421–429.

Sileo, T. W., Sileo, A. P., & Prater, M. A. (1996). Parent and professional partnerships in special education: Multicultural considerations. *Intervention in School and Clinic, 31*, 145–153.

Silver, L. (1998). *The misunderstood child: Understanding and coping with your child's learning disabilities* (3rd ed.). New York: Times Books.

Simich-Dudgeon, C., McCreedy, L., & Schleppegrell, M. (1988/1989). *Helping limited English proficient children communicate in the classroom: A handbook for teachers.* Washington, DC: National Clearinghouse for Bilingual Education.

Simpson, R. L. (1995). Children and youth with autism in an age of reform: A perspective on current issues. *Behavioral Disorders, 21,* 7–20.

Siperstein, G. N., Leffert, J. S., & Widaman, K. (1996). Social behavior and the social acceptance and rejection of children with mental retardation. *Education and Training in Mental Retardation and Developmental Disabilities, 31,* 271–281.

Siperstein, G. N., & Leffert, S. J. (1999). Managing limited resources: Do children with learning problems share? *Exceptional Children, 65,* 187–199.

Sirvis, B. (1988). Physical disabilities. In E. L. Meyen & T. M. Skrtic (Eds.), *Exceptional children and youth: An introduction* (3rd ed., pp. 387–411). Denver: Love.

Skinner, D., Bailey, D. B., Correa, V., & Rodriguez, P. (1999). Narrating self and disability: Latino mothers' construction of identities vis-à-vis their child with special needs. *Exceptional Children, 65,* 481–495.

Slavin, R. E. (1994). *Cooperative learning* (2nd ed.). Boston: Allyn and Bacon.

Slavin, R. E., Madden, N. A., Dolan, L. J., Wasik, B. A., Ross, S. M., & Smith, L. J. (1994). "Whenever and wherever we choose": The replication of "Success for All." *Phi Delta Kappan, 75,* 639–647.

Smith, C. R. (1997). *Learning disabilities: The interaction of learners, task, and setting* (4th ed.). Boston: Allyn and Bacon.

Smith, D. D., & Luckasson, R. (1995). *Introduction to special education: Teaching in an age of challenge* (2nd ed.). Boston: Allyn and Bacon.

Smith, J. D. (1998). Histories of special education: Stories from our past, insights for our future. *Remedial and Special Education, 19,* 196–200.

Smith, M. A., & Mirsa, A. (1992). A comprehensive management system for students in regular classrooms. *Elementary School Journal, 92*(3), 354–371.

Smith, S. B., Simmons, D. C., & Kameenui, F. (1995). *Phonological awareness: Curricular and instructional implications for diverse learners.* Technical Report No. 22. Eugene, OR: National Center to Improve the Tools of Educators.

Smith, S. W. (1990). Individualized education programs (IEPs) in special education—from intent to acquiescence. *Exceptional Children, 57,* 6–14.

Smith, S., Boone, R. & Higgins, K. (1998). Expanding the writing process to the web. *Teaching Exceptional Children, 30*(5), 22–26.

Snider, V. E. (1995). A primer on phonemic awareness: What it is, why it's important, and how to teach it. *School Psychology Review, 24*(3), 443–455.

Snider, V. E. (1997). Transfer of decoding skills to a literature basal. *Learning Disabilities Research & Practice, 12*(1), 54–62.

Snow, C. E., Burns, M. S., & Griffin, P. C. (1998). *Preventing reading difficulties in young children.* Washington, DC: National Academy Press.

Sontag, J. C., & Schacht, R. (1994). An ethnic comparison of parent participating and information needs in early intervention. *Exceptional Children, 60,* 422–433.

Soodak, L. C., Podell, D. M., & Lehman, L. R. (1998). Teacher, student, and school attributes as predictors of teachers' responses to inclusion. *Journal of Special Education, 31,* 480–497.

Sparks, S. (2000). Classroom and curriculum accommodations for Native American students. *Intervention in School and Clinic, 35*(5), 259–263.

Speigel, G. L., Cutler, S. K., & Yetter, C. E. (1996). What every teacher should know about epilepsy. *Intervention in School and Clinic, 32*(1), 34–38.

Sprague, J. R., & Horner, R. H. (1990). Easy does it: Preventing challenging behaviors. *Teaching Exceptional Children, 23*(1), 13–15.

Stainback, S., & Stainback, W. (1988). Educating students with severe disabilities in regular classes. *Teaching Exceptional Children, 21*(1), 16–19.

Stainback, S., Stainback, W., & Jackson, H. J. (1992). Toward inclusive classrooms. In S. Stainback & W. Stainback (Eds.), *Curriculum considerations in inclusive classrooms: Facilitating learning for all students* (pp. 3–17). Baltimore: Brookes.

Stainback, W., Stainback, S., & Stefanich, G. (1996). Learning together in inclusive classrooms: What about curriculum? *Teaching Exceptional Children, 28*(3), 14–19.

Stainback, W., Stainback, S., Etscheidt, S., & Doud, J. (1986). A nonintrusive intervention for acting-out behavior. *Teaching Exceptional Children, 19*(1), 38–41.

Stanovich, P. J. (1999). Conversations about inclusion. *Teaching Exceptional Children, 31*(6), 54–58.

Stanovich, K., & Siegel, L. S. (1994). Phenotypic performance profile of children with reading disabilities: A regression-based test of the phonological-core variable-difference model. *Journal of Educational Psychology, 86*(1), 24–53.

Staton, J., Shuy, R. W., Kreeft-Peyton, J. K., & Reed, L. (1988). *Dialogue journal communication: Classroom, linguistic, social, and cognitive views.* Norwood, NJ: Ablex.

Steffensen, M., Joag-Dev, C., & Andersen, R. C. (1979). A cross-cultural perspective on reading comprehension. *Reading Research Quarterly, 15,* 10–29.

Stein, M., Carnine, D., & Dixon, R. (1998). Direct instruction: Integrating curriculum design and effective teaching practice. *Intervention in School and Clinic, 33*(4), 227–234.

Stein, M., Silbert, J., & Carnine, D. (1997). *Designing effective mathematics instruction: A direct instruction approach* (3rd ed., pp. 216–254). Columbus, OH: Merrill.

Stephen, V. P., Varble, M. E., & Taitt, H. (1993). Instructional and organizational change to meet minority and at risk students' needs. *Journal of Staff Development, 14*(4), 40–43.

Strang, J. D., & Rourke, B. P. (1985). Arithmetic disability subtypes: The neuropsychological significance of specific arithmetical impairment in childhood. In B. P. Rourke (Ed.), *Neuropsychology of learning disabilities* (pp. 167–182). New York: Guilford Press.

Strong, K., & Sandoval, J. (1999). Mainstreaming children with a neuromuscular disease: A map of concerns. *Exceptional Children, 65,* 353–366.

Stump, C. S., & Wilson, C. (1996). Collaboration: Making it happen. *Intervention in School and Clinic, 31,* 310–312.

Substance Abuse and Mental Health Services Administration. (1999). *1998 national household survey on drug abuse.* Washington, DC: U.S. Department of Health and Human Service. Retrieved August 18, 1999, from the World Wide Web: http://www.samhsa.gov/NHSDA.htm

Sugai, G., Lewis-Palmer, T., & Hagan, S. (1998). Using functional assessments to develop behavior support plans. *Preventing School Failure, 43* (1), 6–13.

Sutherland, K. S., Wehby, J. H., & Copeland, S. R. (2000). Effect of varying rates of behavior-specific praise on the on-task behavior of students with EBD. *Journal of Emotional and Behavioral Disorders, 8*(1), 2–8.

Swanson, H. L. (2000). What instruction words for students with learning disabilities? Summarizing the results from a meta-analysis of intervention studies. In R. Gersten, E. Schiller, & S.

Vaughn (Eds.), *Contemporary special education research: Syntheses of the knowledge base on critical instructional issues.* Mahwah, NJ: Lawrence Erlbaum Associates.

Swanson, J. M., Cantwell, D., Lerner, M., McBurnett, K., Pfiffner, L., & Kotkin, R. (1992). Treatment of ADHD: Beyond medication. *Beyond Behavior, 4*(1), 13–16, 18–22.

Symons, F. J., McDonald, L. M.,, & Wehby, J. H. (1998). Functional assessment and teacher collected data. *Education and Treatment of Children, 21*, 135–159.

Szetela, W., & Nicol, C. (1992). Evaluating problem solving in mathematics. *Educational Leadership, 49*(8), 42–45.

Taylor, R. L., Richards, S. B., Goldstein, P. A., & Schilit, J. (1997). Teacher perceptions of inclusive settings. *Teaching Exceptional Children, 29*(3), 50–54.

Telzrow, C. F. (1999). IDEA amendments of 1997: Promise or pitfall for special education reform? *Journal of School Psychology, 37*, 7–28.

Terman, L. (1925). *Genetic studies of genius: Vol. I. Mental and physical traits of 1000 gifted children.* Stanford, CA: Stanford University Press.

Thorson, S. (1996). The missing link: Students discuss school discipline. *Focus on Exceptional Children, 29*(3), 1–12.

Thurlow, M. L., Elliott, J. L. & Ysseldyke, J. F. (1998). *Testing students with disabilities: Practical strategies for complying with district and state requirements.* Thousand Oaks, CA: Corwin Press.

Thurlow, M. L., Ysseldyke, J. E., & Silverstein, B. (1995). Testing accommodations for students with disabilities. *Remedial and Special Education, 16*(5), 260–270.

Tindal, G. A., & Marston, D. B. (1990). *Classroom-based assessment: Evaluating instructional outcomes.* Columbus, OH: Merrill.

Tindal, G. A., & Nolet, V. (1995). Curriculum-based measurement in middle and high schools: Critical thinking skills in content areas. *Focus on Exceptional Children, 27*(7), 1–22.

Todd, L. P., & Curti, M. (1982). *Rise of the American nation.* Orlando, FL: Harcourt Brace Jovanovich.

Tomlinson, C. A. (2000). Reconcilable differences? Standards-based teaching and differentiation. *Educational Leadership, 58*(1), 6–11.

Tomlinson, C. A., Callahan, C. M., Tomchin, E. M., Eiss, N., Imbeau, M., & Landrum, M. (1997). Becoming architects of communities of learning: Addressing academic diversity in contemporary classrooms. *Exceptional Children, 63*, 269–282.

Torgesen, J. (1991). Learning disabilities: Historical and conceptual issues. In B. Wong (Ed.), *Learning about learning disabilities* (pp. 3–39). San Diego, CA: Academic Press.

Torgesen, J. K. (2000). Increasing the intensity of interventions in reading: The lingering problem of treatment resisters. *Learning Disabilities Research and Practice, 15*(1), 55–64.

Torrance, E. P., & Sisk, D. (1998). *Gifted and talented children in the regular classroom.* Marion, IL: Pieces of Learning.

Townsend, B. L. (2000). The disproportionate discipline of African American learners: Reducing school suspensions and expulsions. *Exceptional Children, 66*, 381–391.

Trueba, H. T., Moll, L. C., & Diaz, S. (1982). *Improving the functional writing of bilingual secondary school students* (Final Report; NIE 400–81–0023). Washington, DC: National Institute of Education.

Tucker, J. A. (1985). Curriculum-based assessment: An introduction. *Exceptional Children, 52*, 199–204.

Turnbull, A. P., & Turnbull, H. R. (1997). *Families, professionals and exceptionality: A special partnership* (3rd ed.). Upper Saddle River, NJ: Merrill.

Turnbull, A. P., Pereira, L., & Blue-Banning, M. (1999). Parents' facilitation of friendships between their children with a disability and friends without a disability. *Journal of the Association for Persons with Severe Handicaps, 24*, 85–99.

Turnbull, P., Pereira, L., & Blue-Banning, M. (2000). Teachers as friendship facilitators. *Teaching Exceptional Children, 32* (5), 66–70.

U.S. Department of Education. (1999). *To assure the free appropriate public education of all children with disabilities: Twenty-first annual report to Congress on the implementation of the Individual with Disabilities Education Act.* Washington, DC: Author.

U.S. Department of Health and Human Services (2000). *Child abuse and neglect: Statistics.* Washington, DC: U.S Government Printing Office.

United Cerebral Palsy Associations. (n.d.). *Cerebral palsy: Facts and figures.* Washington, DC: Author.

Utley, C. A., Mortweet, S. L., & Greenwood, C. R. (1997). Peer-mediated instruction and interventions. *Focus on Exceptional Children, 29*(1), 1–23.

Vacc, N. N., & Cannon, S. J. (1991). Cross-age tutoring in mathematics: Sixth graders helping students who are moderately handicapped. *Education and Training in Mental Retardation, 26*, 89–97.

Vacca, R. T., & Vacca, J. L. (1986). *Content area reading* (2nd ed.). Boston: Little, Brown.

Vadasy, P. F., Jenkins, J. R., Antil, L. R., Phillips, N. B., & Pool, K. (1997). The research-to-practice ball game: Classwide peer tutoring and teacher interest, implementation, and modifications. *Remedial and Special Education, 18*, 143–156.

Van Tassel-Baska, J., Patton, J. M., & Prillaman, D. (1991). *Gifted youth at risk: A report of a national study.* Reston, VA: Council for Exceptional Children.

Vandercook, T., York, J., & Forest, M. (1989). The McGill Action Planning System (MAPS): A strategy for building the vision. *Journal of the Association for Persons with Severe Handicaps, 14*(3), 205–218.

VanGundy, A. B. (1988). *Techniques of structured problem solving* (2nd ed.). New York: Van Nostrand Reinhold.

Vasa, F. (1981). Alternative procedures for grading handicapped students in the secondary schools. *Education Unlimited,* 16–23.

Vaughn, S., Elbaum, B. E., Schumm, J. S., & Hughes, M. T. (1998). Social outcomes for students with and without learning disabilities in inclusive classrooms. *Journal of Learning Disabilities, 31*, 428–436.

Vaughn, S., Gersten, R., & Chard, D. J. (2000). The underlying message in LD intervention research: Findings from research syntheses. *Exceptional Children, 67*, 99–114.

Vaughn, S., Reiss, M., Rothlein, L., & Hughes, M. T. (1999). Kindergarten teachers' perceptions of instructing students with disabilities. *Remedial and Special Education, 20*, 184–191.

Vaughn, S., Schumm, J. S., Jallad, B., Slusher, J., & Saumell, L. (1996). Teachers' views of inclusion. *Learning disabilities: Research & Practice, 11*, 96–106.

Villa, R. A., Thousand, J. S., Meyers, H., & Nevin, A. (1996). Teacher and administrator perceptions of heterogeneous education. *Exceptional Children, 63*, 29–45.

Voeltz, L. J., Hemphill, N. J., Brown, S., Kishi, G., Klein, R., Fruehling, R., Collie, J., Levy, G., & Kube, C. (1983). *The special friends program: A trainer's manual for integrated school settings.* Honolulu, HI: University of Hawaii, Department of Special Education.

Voix, R. G. (1968). *Evaluating reading and study skills in the secondary classroom: A guide for content teachers* (pp. 46–48). Newark, DE: International Reading Association.

Wade, S. L., Taylor, H. G., Drotar, D., Stancin, T., & Yeates, K. O. (1996). Childhood traumatic brain injury: Initial impact on the family. *Journal of Learning Disabilities, 29*, 652–661.

Wadsworth, D. E., & Knight, D. (1996). Paraprofessionals: The bridge to successful full inclusion. *Intervention in School and Clinic, 31*, 166–171.

Waldron, N. L., & McLeskey, J. (1998). The effects of an inclusive school program on students with mild and severe learning disabilities. *Exceptional Children, 64*, 395–405.

Wallis, S. (1993, September). Multicultural teaching: Meeting the challenges that arise in practice. *Curriculum Update*, 1–8.

Walther-Thomas, C., Korinek, L., McLaughlin, V., & Williams, B. T. (1999). *Collaboration for inclusive education: Developing successful programs*. Boston: Allyn and Bacon.

Wang, M. C., Reynolds, M. C., & Walberg, H. J. (1988). Integrating the children of the second system. *Phi Delta Kappan, 70*, 248–251.

Weaver, R., & Landers, M. F. (1998). The educational implications of ADD/ADHD. *School Business Affairs, 64*(8), 25–28.

WebDoctor. (2000). *Cerebral palsy—General information*. Timmins, Canada: Gretmar Communications. Retrieved September 3, 2000, from the World Wide Web: http://www.gretmar.com/webdoctor/FramesDisease.html

Welch, A. B. (2000). Responding to student concerns about fairness. *Teaching Exceptional Children, 33*(2), 36–40.

Welch, M., Brownell, K., & Sheridan, S. M. (1999). What's the score and game plan on teaming in schools? A review of the literature on team teaching and school based problem solving. *Remedial and Special Education, 20*, 36–49.

Wenz-Gross, M., & Siperstein, G. N. (1998). Students with learning problems at risk in middle school: Stress, social support, and adjustment. *Exceptional Children, 65*, 91–100.

Westberg, K. L., & Archambault, F. X., Jr. (1997). A multi-site case study of successful classroom practices for high ability students. *Gifted Child Quarterly, 41*, 42–51.

Wheelock, A. (1992). The case for untracking. *Educational Leadership, 50*(2), 6–10.

Whitworth, J. (1999). *Seven steps to successful inclusion*. (ERIC Document Reproduction Service No. 436040)

Wiggins, G. (1992). Creating tests worth taking. *Educational Leadership, 49*(8), 26–33.

Williams, W., & Fox, T. J. (1996). Planning for inclusion: A practical process. *Teaching Exceptional Children, 28*(3), 6–13.

Wilson, B. (1996). *Wilson Reading System* (3rd ed.). Milbury, MA: Wilson Language Training.

Wilson, B. A. (1999). Inclusion: Empirical guidelines and unanswered questions. *Education and Training in Mental Retardation and Developmental Disabilities, 34*, 119–133.

Winebrenner, S. (1992). *Teaching gifted kids in the regular classroom: Strategies and techniques every teacher can use to meet the academic needs of the gifted and talented*. Minneapolis, MN: Free Spirit.

Winzer, M. A. (1998). A tale often told: The early progression of special education. *Remedial and Special Education, 19*, 212–218.

Wisniewski, L., & Alper, S. (1994). Including students with severe disabilities in general education settings. *Remedial and Special Education, 15*(1), 4–13.

Witt, J. C., Gresham, F. M., & Noell, G. H. (1996). What's behavioral about behavioral consultation? *Journal of Educational and Psychological Consultation, 7*, 327–344.

Woerz, M., & Maples, W. C. (1997). Test-retest reliability of colored filter testing. *Journal of Learning Disabilities, 30*(2), 214–221.

Wong, B. (1996). *The ABCs of learning disabilities*. San Diego, CA: Academic Press.

Wood, J. W., Miederhoff, J. W., & Ulschmid, B. (1989). Adapting test construction for mainstreamed social studies students. *Social Education, 53*(1), 46–49.

Wood, M. (1998). Whose job is it anyway? Educational roles in inclusion. *Exceptional Children, 64*, 181–196.

Wright, P., & Wright, P. (2000, June). Law library: CaseLaw. *Wrightslaw*. Deltaville, VA: The Special Education Advocate.

Retrieved June 10, 2001 from the World Wide Web: http://www.wrightslaw.com/main_lawlibrary.htm

Wright-Strawderman, C., Lindsey, P., Navarette, L., & Flippo, J. R. (1996). Depression in students with disabilities: Recognition and intervention strategies. *Intervention in School and Clinic, 31*(5), 261–275.

Xin, J. F. (1999). Computer-assisted cooperative learning in integrated classrooms for students with and without disabilities. *Information Technology in Childhood Education*, 61–78.

Yasutake, D., & Bryan, T. (1995). The influence of induced positive affect on middle school children with and without learning disabilities. *Learning Disabilities: Research and Practice, 10*, 22–37.

Yates, G. C. R. (1999). Applying learning style research in the classroom: Some cautions and the way ahead. In R. Riding & S. Rayner (Eds.), *New Directions in Learning and Cognitive Style*. pp. 347–364. Stamford, CT: JAI Press.

Yehle, A. K., & Wambold, C. (1998). An ADHD success story: Strategies for teachers and students. *Teaching Exceptional Children, 30* (6), 8–13.

Yell, M., Clyde, K., & Puyallup, S. K. (1995). School district: The courts, inclusion, and students with behavioral disorders. *Behavioral Disorders, 20*(3), 179–189.

Yell, M. L. (1990). The use of corporal punishment, suspension, expulsion, and timeout with behaviorally disordered students in public schools: Legal considerations. *Behavioral Disorders, 15*(2), 100–109.

Yell, M. L. (1995). The least restrictive environment mandate and the courts: Judicial activism or judicial restraint? *Exceptional Children, 61*, 578–581.

Yell, M. L., & Shriner, J. G. (1997). The IDEA amendments of 1997: Implications for special and general education teachers, administrators, and teacher trainers. *Focus on Exceptional Children, 30*(1), 1–19.

Yell, M. L., Rogers, D., & Rogers, E. L. (1998). The legal history of special education: What a long, strange trip it's been! *Remedial and Special Education, 19*, 219–228.

York, J., Vandercook, T., MacDonald, C., Heise-Neff, C., & Caughey, E. (1992). Feedback about integrating middle-school students with severe disabilities in general education classes. *Exceptional Children, 58*, 244–258.

Ysseldyke, J., & Algozzine, B. (1995). *Special education: A practical approach for teachers* (3rd ed.). Geneva, IL: Houghton Mifflin.

Ysseldyke, J., Algozzine, B., & Thurlow, M. L. (1992). *Critical issues in special education* (2nd ed.). Boston: Houghton Mifflin.

Ysseldyke, J., Algozzine, B., & Thurlow, M. L. (2000). *Critical issues in special education* (3rd ed.). Boston: Houghton Mifflin.

Ysseldyke, J., & Christensen, S. (1987). *TIES: The instructional environment scale*. Austin, TX: PRO-ED.

Ysseldyke, J., & Olsen, K. (1999). Putting alternate assessments into practice: What to measure and possible sources of data. *Exceptional Children, 65*(2), 175–185.

Zentall, S. S. (1993). Research on the educational implications of attention deficit hyperactivity disorder. *Exceptional Children, 60*, 143–153.

Zetlin, A. G., Padron, M., & Wilson, S. (1996). The experience of five Latin American families with the special education system. *Education and Training in Mental Retardation and Developmental Disabilities, 31*(1), 22–28.

Zirkel, P. A. (1994). De jure: Costly lack of accommodations. *Phi Delta Kappan, 75*, 652–653.

Zurkowski, J. K., Kelly, P. S., & Griswold, D. E. (1998). Discipline and IDEA 1997: Instituting a new balance. *Intervention in School and Clinic, 34*(1), 3–9.

Name Index

Subject Index

Photo Credits

Page iii, Bob Daemmrich/Stock Boston; p. iv (top), Will Hart; p. iv (bottom), Robin L. Sachs/Photo Edit; p. v, Bill Aron/Photo Edit; p. vi, vii, viii (top), Will Hart; p. viii (bottom), Will Faller; p. ix, Will Hart; p. x, Brian Smith; p. xi (both), xii, Will Hart; p. xxvi, Bob Daemmrich/Stock Boston; p, 14, Brian Smith; p. 16, Will Hart; p. 22, Billy E. Barnes/Photo Edit; p. 27, 30, 33, Will Hart; p. 34 (top left), Will Faller; p. 34 (all others), Will Hart; p. 42, Corbis Digital Stock; p. 44, Will Hart; p. 52, Laura Dwight/Photo Edit; p. 68, 72, Robin L. Sachs/Photo Edit; p. 79, Will Faller; p. 84, Courtesy of the Northeast and Islands Regional Educational Laboratory (The LAB) at Brown University; p. 87, Will Hart; p. 97, Will Faller; p. 106, Michael Newman/Photo Edit; p. 110, Bill Aron/Photo Edit; p. 117, Shann Kermani/Liaison Agency; p. 122, Will Hart; p. 139, Tony Freeman/Photo Edit; p. 142, Paul Conklin/Photo Edit; p. 146, 152, Will Hart; p. 166 (top), Will Faller; p. 166 (bottom), p. 167 (all), Copyright © Don Johnston Incorporated. Used with permission; p. 172, 182, Will Hart; p. 192, Paul Conklin/Photo Edit; p. 196, 204, Will Hart; p. 221, 223, David Young-Wolff/Photo Edit; p. 230, 248, 253, 256, Will Hart; p. 265, Tony Freeman/Photo Edit; p. 270, Will Faller; p. 273, Will Hart; p. 278, Michael Newman/Photo Edit; p. 282, Paul Conklin/Photo Edit; p. 293, 308, 315, Will Hart; p. 320, Will Faller; p. 335, 347, Will Hart; p. 354, Brian Smith; p. 360, Will Hart; p. 366, Will Faller; p. 381, 390, 394, Will Hart; p. 401, Brian Smith; p. 418, Will Hart; p. 422, 423, Aurbach & Associates, Inc., St. Louis, MO; p. 426, 434, Will Hart; p. 457, Will Faller; p. 462, 466, 472 (top left), Will Hart; p. 472 (top right), Myrleen Ferguson Cate/Photo Edit; p. 472 (bottom), Will Hart; p. 475, Brian Smith; p. 480, 484, Will Faller; p. 489, Will Hart.

Text Credits

List on pp. 145–146 from "The Use of Scaffolds for Teaching Higher-Level Cognitive Strategies" by B. Rosenshine and C. Meister, 1992, *Educational Leadership, 49*(7), pp. 26–33. Copyright © 1985 by ASCD. All rights reserved.

Extract on pp. 324–325 from *Understanding U.S. History, Vol. I,* by Douglas Carnine, Donald Crawford, Mark Harniss, and Keith Hollenbeck, 1995, p. 207, Eugene: Considerate Publishing/University of Oregon. Used by permission of Considerate Publishing.

Extract on p. 416 reprinted with permission of Prentice Hall, Inc. from *Classroom-Based Assessment: Evaluating Instructional Outcomes* by George A. Tindal and Douglas Marston. Copyright © 1990 by Macmillan College Publishing Company.